DUTCH PRIMACY IN WORLD TRADE
1585–1740

Dutch Primacy
in World Trade, 1585–1740

JONATHAN I. ISRAEL

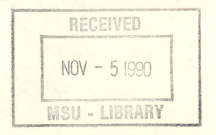
CLARENDON PRESS · OXFORD

Oxford University Press, Walton Street, Oxford OX2 6DP

Oxford New York Toronto
Delhi Bombay Calcutta Madras Karachi
Petaling Jaya Singapore Hong Kong Tokyo
Nairobi Der es Salaam Cape Town
Melbourne Auckland

and associated companies in
Berlin Ibadan

Oxford is a trade mark of Oxford University Press

Published in the United States
by Oxford University Press, New York

© *Jonathan Israel 1989*
First published 1989
First reprinted as paperback 1990

British Library Cataloguing in Publication Data
Israel, Jonathan I. (Jonathan Irvine)
Dutch primacy in world trade 1585–1740.
1. Netherlands. Foreign trade, 1585–1740
I. Title
382'.09492
ISBN 0-19-822729-9
ISBN 0-19-821139-2 (pbk)

Library of Congress Cataloging in Publication Data
Israel, Jonathan Irvine.
Dutch primacy in world trade, 1585–1740 / Jonathan I. Israel.
Bibliography: p.   Includes index.
1. Netherlands—Commerce—History. 2. Netherlands—History—Wars of Independence, 1556–
1648. 3. Netherlands—History—1648–1795.
I. Title.
HF3614 .I87   1989   382'.09492—dc19   88-25356
ISBN 0-19-822729-9
ISBN 0-19-821139-2 (pbk)

Printed in Great Britain by
Butler & Tanner Ltd, Frome and London

For Jenny, my mother, Danny, and Naomi

PREFACE

HISTORICAL research ceaselessly pushes forward the frontiers of knowledge. But it also increases the risk of our gradually losing sight of the wood of historical reality for the trees. Meticulous attention to particular aspects, however worthy in itself, has not infrequently resulted in diminished preoccupation with fundamental phenomena, especially where these are European or world-historical in scope, involving numerous countries and cultures and which can be focused on only by using a great diversity of sources. In consequence, some key developments, even if universally recognized as crucial, can in their full context become largely ignored. The astounding ascendancy exerted by the Dutch maritime provinces—Holland, Zeeland, and Friesland—over world commerce, shipping, and finance from the 1590s for approximately a century and a half is an apt example. Whether we prefer to consider Dutch world-trade hegemony in the seventeenth century as an altogether unparalleled manifestation or, as some maintain, one of a series of global empires of trade which have successively shaped the economic life of the modern age, culminating in British preponderance from the late eighteenth century to the early twentieth and, finally, that of the United States, no one has ever disputed, or is ever likely to, the centrality of Dutch maritime and commercial activity for over a century in the making of the early modern world.

In recent decades a swelling stream of scholarly studies and monographs has increasingly enriched and extended our understanding of many, perhaps most, facets of the subject. Some of these are of superb quality, landmarks in the writing of economic history, works such as those of N. W. Posthumus on the Leiden cloth industry and Dutch prices, of B. H. Slicher van Bath and Jan de Vries on Dutch agriculture and rural society, and of J. A. Faber on the regional economy of Friesland. Then there have been the more fragmented but invariably masterly studies of J. G. van Dillen and Simon Hart on economic activity in seventeenth-century Amsterdam. Also a start has been made, notably by P. W. Klein in his path-breaking work on the Trip family and their business methods, on investigating key Dutch merchants and entrepreneurs of the Golden Age. There has also been a run of first-rate works on aspects of Dutch colonial expansion, such as those of Sinnapah Arasaratnam on Ceylon and southern India under the Dutch, of Om Prakash on Dutch trade with Bengal, of Niels Steensgaard and Femme Gaastra on general problems of Dutch enterprise in Asia, and of Cornelis Goslinga on Dutch activity in the Caribbean.

Yet, despite all these advances and the interest they generate, no one has yet attempted a general history of Dutch primacy in world trade in all its aspects from its origins to its disintegration during the eighteenth century. J. G. van Dillen has thus far come nearest to doing so in his most impressive work of synthesis, *Van Rijkdom en regenten*. But van Dillen was primarily concerned to survey the overall development of the home economy rather than the Dutch overseas trade system as such and its impact on the wider world. This is not to say, though, that there has been any lack of suggestive hypothesis regarding the phenomenon of Dutch world-trade primacy. On the contrary, it is a topic which attracts vibrant debate as is abundantly evident from the proceedings of the international conference which gathered under the auspices of the Fondation de la Maison des Sciences de l'homme at Paris in June 1976. The participants in this remarkable gathering included such well-known historical celebrities as Fernand Braudel, Slicher van Bath, Jan de Vries, Niels Steensgaard, P. W. Klein, Pierre Jeannin, Michel Morineau, and Immanuel Wallerstein. But the results of their collective deliberations, edited by Maurice Aymard under the title *Dutch Capitalism and World Capitalism*, stimulating though they are, represent little more than a preparatory probing of the issues and reveal vast disparities of view.

In these circumstances, the whole subject being shrouded in confusion and scholarly disagreement, an attempt to write a systematic, general account of Dutch primacy in world trade is bound to be a hazardous undertaking. There are pitfalls and scholarly toes to tread on at every turn. But, as any colleague regularly involved in teaching the Dutch Golden Age will surely agree, it is a task which urgently needs to be taken up. If we are to make sense of both Dutch history and world history in the early modern era, the phenomenon of Dutch world-trade primacy has to be tackled systematically. No doubt what follows has many shortcomings. But if it helps to provide a framework for further research and discussion, I shall be more than satisfied.

My essential object is to try to explain the nature of the Dutch world entrepôt, how it functioned and the stages through which it evolved, and to emphasize the fundamental interaction between the different strands of Dutch trade with widely diverse parts of the globe. Where detailed studies exist, my task has been to summarize their findings in such a way as to bring out the essential relationship of the parts to the whole. Where such work is lacking, as in the case of Dutch commerce with Spain and the Mediterranean, I have endeavoured through my own research to erect provisional bridges of sufficient substance to enable us to bring these areas within the scope of the analysis. Our subject-matter, then, is not the Dutch economy as a whole but specifically the Dutch overseas trading system and its impact on the world. This means that the main emphasis is on overseas trade and shipping. Other major aspects of the Dutch economy, such as agriculture, finance, industry and the fisheries, have been brought into the picture only in so far as they bear directly on Dutch performance in overseas markets.

The research on which this work is based was greatly assisted by a grant from the Economic and Social Science Research Council of Great Britain which enabled me to work for periods in the Dutch national archives at The Hague, in the Royal Library at The Hague, and in various Dutch municipal archives. For this I am immensely grateful. I would also like to express my thanks for both scholarly assistance and much stimulating discussion on the subject of Dutch world-trade hegemony to Koen Swart, Patrick Chorley, Edgar Samuel, Franz Binder, Simon Groenveld, J. H. Kluiver, Eco Haitsma Mulier, Henry Roseveare, and Graham Gibbs. Finally, I would like to thank my wife not only for putting up with me but for helping with this work in all manner of ways.

J.I.I.

University College London
September 1987

CONTENTS

LIST OF FIGURES

LIST OF MAPS

LIST OF TABLES

LIST OF ABBREVIATIONS

AAG Bijdragen	*Bijdragen* of the Afdeling Agrarische Geschiedenis of the Landbouwuniversiteit at Wageningen, The Netherlands
ACA CA	Archivo de la Corona de Aragón, Barcelona, section 'Consejo de Aragón'
AGI	Archivo General de Indias, Seville
AGS	Archivo General de Simancas, Valladolid
ARB	Archives Générales du Royaume, Brussels
ARB SEG	Archives Générales du Royaume, Brussels, section 'Sécrétairerie d'Etat et de Guerre'
ARH	Algemeen Rijksarchief, The Hague
ARH SG	Algemeen Rijksarchief, The Hague, archives of the States General
ARH SH	Algemeen Rijksarchief, The Hague, archives of the States of Holland
ARH WIC	Algemeen Rijksarchief, The Hague, archives of the Dutch West India Company
ASV CSM	Archivo di Stato, Venice, archives of the Cinque Savii alla Mercanzia
BGLH	*Bronnen tot de geschiedenis van den Levantschen Handel*, ed. K. Heeringa (2 vols. in 3 parts; The Hague, 1910–17)
BGNO	*Bronnen voor de geschiedenis van de Nederlandse Oostzeehandel in de zeventiende eeuw*, ed. P. H. Winkelman (4 vols. thus far; The Hague, 1971–)
BGOCP	*Bronnen tot de geschiedenis der Oostindische Compagnie in Perzië* (1611–38), ed. H. Dunlop (The Hague, 1930)
BL MS	British Library, London, department of manuscripts

xix

BMGN	*Bijdragen en mededelingen betreffende de geschiedenis der Nederlanden*
BMHG	*Bijdragen en mededelingen van het historisch genootschap gevestigd te Utrecht*
BTLVNI	*Bijdragen tot de taal- land- en volkenkunde van Nederlandsch-Indië*
BVGO	*Bijdragen voor vaderlandsche geschiedenis en oudheidkunde*
EHJ	*Economisch-Historisch Jaarboek*
Cal. St. Papers	*Calendar of State Papers*
GA Amsterdam	Amsterdam City Archive
GA Amsterdam NA	Amsterdam City Archive, notarial archives
GA Amsterdam *vroed.*	Amsterdam City Archive, resolutions of the *vroedschap* (1578–1795)
GA Delft *vroed.*	Delft City Archive, resolutions of the *vroedschap*
GA Haarlem	Haarlem City Archive
GA Haarlem *vroed.*	Haarlem City Archive, resolutions of the *vroedschap*
GA Leiden Sec. Arch.	Leiden City Archive, archives of the sécrétairerie
ISEPA	Istituto Internazionale di Storia Economica 'F. Datini' Prato, Pubblicazioni serie II, Atti delle 'Settimane di Studio'
MGN	*Maritieme geschiedenis der Nederlanden*, ed. G. Asaert *et al.* (4 vols.; Bussum, 1976)
PRO SP	Public Record Office, London, State Papers
RAZ SZ	Rijksarchief in Zeeland, Middelburg, archives of the States of Zeeland
res.	resolution
Res. Holl.	Resolution of the States of Holland
SG	States General
SH	States of Holland
SZ	States of Zeeland
TvG	*Tijdschrift voor Geschiedenis*
VOC	Verenigde Oost-Indische Compagnie (The United Dutch East India Company)

WIC West-Indische Compagnie (The Dutch West India Company)

I
Introduction

WITH the waning of the Middle Ages and the dawn of modern times, western Europe became ever more dominant and assertive in its relations with the rest of the globe. Long before Columbus's first great voyage of discovery, western Europe's expansion and subjection of the wider world was underway. During the course of the fifteenth century Portugal, Castile, and the Genoese extended their spheres of influence in northern Africa and the islands of the Atlantic. The Venetians, even as the Ottoman Turks advanced into the Balkans, consolidated their grip over the commerce of the Near East and, in the 1470s, imposed their rule on Cyprus. Then, from the 1480s, the pace of expansion quickened. The Portuguese circumnavigated Africa and soon began to build their trading empire in Asia and to colonize Brazil. The Castilians traversed the Atlantic, subjugating in rapid succession the Caribbean, Mexico, and Peru, and later, in the 1560s, crossed the Pacific from Mexico, securing a Far Eastern base in the Philippines. The English began to sail to the Levant and opened up the commerce of the Arctic Circle, around the top of Scandinavia, to the White Sea and northern Russia, where the new port of Archangel was founded, as a depot for western ships, in 1584. Under the stimulus of mounting western demand for additional grain and raw materials, the Polish nobility converted vast, previously little used tracts of White Russia and the Ukraine into systematically exploited, export-orientated latifundia.

Western Europe's expansion after 1492 was rapid, relentless, and on a vast scale. In the Americas whole civilizations crumbled in the face of the West's astounding military, technological, and economic superiority, and religious zeal. In Asia and Africa existing kingdoms and empires proved more resilient. But even, as in the case of the Ottoman Empire, where local circumstances precluded the use of force, westerners still increasingly extended their grip over the processes of trade. In this way, for the first

NORTH

SEA

FRISIAN ISLANDS

The Wadden

Emden

GRONIGEN

Leeuwarden

Harlingen   Groningen

TEXEL   FRIESLAND

DRENTHE

Emr

Medemblik

Hoorn   Enkhuizen

Lingen

ZUIDER   Vecht

ZEE

HOLLAND   Zaan

OVERIJSSEL

Haarlem   Deventer

Amsterdam   Zutphen

Leiden   GELDERLAND

The Hague   Gouda   Utrecht   Ijssel

Delft   Rhine   Arnhem

Brielle   Rotterdam

ZEELAND   Nijmegen

Zierikzee   Dordrecht   Maas

Vere

Middelburg   Breda

Flushing   Venlo

Ostend

Antwerp

Dunkirk   BRABANT   Rhine

FLANDERS   Ghent   Cologne

Lys   Scheldt   Maastricht

Brussels

Liège

Maas

⌁⌁⌁⌁ Dutch border (post 1648)

1.1 The North Netherlands maritime zone during the early modern
period.

time, a European 'world economy' came into being[1]. Western Europeans forged a world-trade network which linked all the major zones of the globe, often via intermediary depots, with the great commercial and maritime emporia of the west, channelling wealth and resources from every quarter back to the European heartland. Aside from some sparsely inhabited wastelands, few parts of the globe remained even partially outside western Europe's *Weltwirtschaft*.

The preponderant core to which this burgeoning world economy was subject was comparatively small. Roughly it comprised the western part of Europe from Venice and Lübeck westwards and southwards of England and the Elbe estuary. Such concentration of economic sway in the world was something fundamentally new. Nothing remotely like it was known before the end of the fifteenth century. Even so, compared with the situation later, during the seventeenth and eighteenth centuries, the age of the Renaissance and Reformation was essentially one of dispersal of economic power. It is true that the French *grand maître* Fernand Braudel, who did much to generate interest in the origins of the modern world economy, took a different view, preferring to postulate a long sequence of western world economies, reaching far back into the distant past, each revolving around a single predominant centre.[2] During the later Middle Ages, in Braudel's view, Venice served as the hub of the European world economy. Then about 1500 the centre of gravity shifted to Antwerp, which emerged as the new Venice, exercising a general sway over world commerce and finance. The decline of Antwerp after 1585 then led to the brief pre-eminence of Genoa, which was followed in turn, around 1600, by the rise of Amsterdam.[3] The ascendancy of this dynamic new world entrepôt situated on the Zuider Zee proved more enduring than those of Antwerp and Genoa, lasting for the best part of two centuries until Amsterdam was overtaken by London. London from the late eighteenth century, for a century or so, then functioned as the nerve-centre of the last European world economy. But Braudel's schema implies a greater degree of

---

[1] Braudel, *Civilisation matérielle*, iii. 12, 14, 22; Braudel, *Afterthoughts*, 82–3; Wallerstein, *The Modern World System*, i. 15–16.

[2] Braudel, *Civilisation matérielle*, ii. 22–4; Braudel, *Afterthoughts*, 85; see also de Vries, *European Urbanization*, 159–61.

[3] Braudel, *Civilisation matérielle*, iii. 24.

continuity in the form and functions of these world economic empires than is really warranted by the context. It misses the crucial shift both in scope and degree of concentration of economic power. Given the relatively limited geographical frame of the Venetian trade empire of the later Middle Ages, and subsequently of those of Antwerp and Genoa, it is better to accept that during the fifteenth and early sixteenth centuries western Europe was still in the midst of what has been termed the 'late-medieval poly-nuclear' phase of expansion.[4] The markets and resources of the wider world, that is to say, were subject not to any one but rather to a whole cluster of western empires of commerce and navigation. Portugal, Castile, France, England, the Hanseatic League, the great south German emporia, the Italian trading republics of Venice, Genoa, and Florence, and last but not least the Netherlands, especially the southern provinces of Flanders and Brabant (including Antwerp), were all active arms of the West's expanding apparatus of world-trade dominance. The merchant élites of a dozen western European emporia shared the commerce of the globe.

Of course, Europe's rival empires of commerce were not all of the same type. Several, notably those of Castile and Portugal, concentrated on a ruthless extraction of resources from their conquests and dominions in the Indies. Others were confined by geographical circumstances to a limited set of trade routes. But some were, or developed into, great regional emporia with highly dynamic merchant élites capable of penetrating and subordinating distant markets which they did not control politically. There was thus already a detectable trend towards a hierarchy of exchanges, towards concentration of commercial and financial control, which became more marked during the course of the sixteenth century. Thus while the pattern, around 1500, was still overwhelmingly regional in character, with Genoa presiding over much of the commercial life of south-west Europe, Venice over the eastern Mediterranean and the Balkans, the south German trade centres over central Europe, Lübeck over the Baltic, and Antwerp and London holding sway over the north-western fringes, by the mid-sixteenth century the phenomenon of a general world emporium at the apex of a global hierarchy of markets was clearly emerging

---

[4] Van der Wee, 'Antwoord op een industriële uitdaging', 170; Jeannin, 'Inter-dépendances économiques', 157.

in the shape of Antwerp backed by the industrial resources of Flanders and the shipping of Holland and Zeeland.[5] For several decades the flourishing emporium on the Scheldt presided over the ebb and flow of world commerce, though it possessed only a small merchant fleet of its own and had no direct links with the world outside Europe. Antwerp became the world's storehouse of commodities and centre of distribution. At Antwerp were stockpiled the sugar and spices of the Portuguese colonial empire, the silks and luxury goods of Italy and the Levant, the copper and iron goods of Germany, and the woollen cloth of England.

As a phenomenon in world economic history, Antwerp differed fundamentally from the great trading emporia of the past, but also in significant respects from the great global entrepôts of the future. It was essentially a transitional phenomenon, sandwiched between the characteristically regional emporia of the Middle Ages and the fully fledged world emporium of the seventeenth and eighteenth centuries; for the process of concentration of economic power in Europe began to accelerate shortly after Antwerp's collapse in 1585. Historians often write misleadingly of a vast shift of economic vitality in Europe from the Mediterranean to northern Protestant Europe during the closing stages of that long phase of material expansion—that is of population, food production, and economic activity generally—which Braudel labelled the 'long sixteenth century'.[6] In reality it was by no means only the trade empires of the Mediterranean which withered, or were dislocated, at the end of the sixteenth century and the beginning of the seventeenth. There was no such thing as a general shift to northern or to 'Atlantic' Europe. After 1590 Lübeck and the Hanseatic League were in full decline.[7] The great emporia of south Germany and France were on the wane. After 1572 the economy of the South Netherlands was heavily disrupted. What happened in fact was that economic vitality in Europe was transferred not to a large part of northern Europe in any way comparable with the Mediterranean world but to a mere tiny fringe, the extreme northwestern corner of the continent. By 1600 the commercial primacy

---

[5] Van Houtte, 'Bruges et Anvers', 100–8; Van Houtte, 'Anvers aux xve et xvie siècles', 265–7.
[6] Braudel, *Civilisation matérielle*, ii. 61–3; van der Wee and Peeters, 'Un modèle économique', 112–14; de Vries, *European Urbanization*, 162–3.
[7] Jeannin, 'Commerce de Lübeck', 36–7, 65.

of Venice in the Mediterranean was over.[8] Half a century later, by 1650, Italy, Spain, Portugal, Germany, and the South Netherlands had all ceased to form part of the controlling heartland of the European world economy. These countries had all been reduced to subservience to a tiny number of more developed economies. Even France was, or appeared to be, lapsing into a semi-subordinate role, with some important sectors of her trade subject to the Dutch.[9] Only the previously marginal commercial empire of the North Netherlands maritime provinces, and that of England, continued to expand and grow in vitality during the early and mid-seventeenth century, inexorably gaining ground as the rest receded. But, except in the Mediterranean where the English did conspicuously well from the 1620s onwards,[10] even England failed to capitalize fully on the collapse of the rest, at any rate down to the 1660s. Rather England too entered a phase of difficulty and relative stagnation.[11] The astounding fact is that most of the lost leverage over markets, routes, and commodities was picked up by the Dutch. The Dutch maritime zone moved to the top of the global hierarchy of exchanges, emerging as the hub of what was now definitely a 'mono-nuclear' system, the first and, for most of early modern times, the only true world entrepôt.

But in what precise sense did the Dutch entrepôt achieve hegemony over world commerce? The hallmark of the Dutch trade empire of the sixteenth century was the vast and unprecedented size of its stock of merchant shipping, its incomparably low freight charges, and its unrivalled capacity to transfer bulky goods cheaply and in large quantity. Indeed, the Dutch were already the leading 'carrying' nation of Europe as early as the second half of the fifteenth century. Yet the great regional emporia of the past— Venice, Genoa, Lisbon, Seville, Lyons, Bruges, Nuremberg, and Lübeck—as well as Antwerp, the first general entrepôt, had always focused on the so-called 'rich trades'. These comprised the traffic in high-value merchandise of low bulk, such as spices, textiles, and, latterly, sugar, commodities which did not require an abundant stock of shipping but which did require access to a wide range

---

[8] De Vries, *Economy of Europe*, 26.

[9] Sée, 'Commerce des Hollandais à Nantes', 247–50; Braudel, *Civilisation matérielle*, iii. 217.

[10] Davis, 'Influences de l'Angleterre', 210–19; Rapp, 'Unmaking of Mediterranean Trade Hegemony', 522–3.

[11] Supple, *Commercial Crisis*, 42–50, 259–63.

of textile and finishing industries—such as the North Netherlands during most of the sixteenth century conspicuously lacked.[12] Also, when we speak of a 'general entrepôt', whether one which lacked direct connections with the Indies, such as sixteenth-century Antwerp, or one which possessed them, like the Dutch entrepôt in the seventeenth century, a distinction must be drawn between a passive depot of goods, or general staple, such as Antwerp was especially during the earlier part of its world primacy, and an active entrepôt, with a dominant merchant élite, such as Antwerp was tending to become during the later phase of its world supremacy.[13] Initially, most of the merchants residing at Antwerp had been subsidiaries, or factors, of Lisbon spice exporters, London cloth dealers, and German and Italian exporters, rather than important merchants in their own right.[14] Only after around 1550 did Antwerp progress beyond the status of a general depot for the merchant élites of neighbouring countries and develop into an active entrepôt spreading its tentacles into Germany, Italy, the Iberian Peninsula, and eventually the Baltic. It took time for elements among the native, German, Italian, and Iberian colonies resident in the city to coalesce into a powerful merchant élite able to challenge the older élites for control of regional markets. A crucial difference between the Antwerp entrepôt in its earlier and later phases is that it came to be much more dependent on the industrial resources of its immediate hinterland and especially the textile products of Flanders.[15]

The questions when, how, and in what sense the Dutch entrepôt supplanted Antwerp and the regional emporia of the past to become the first true world entrepôt revolve at bottom around two issues—the relationship between bulk carrying and the rich trades, on the one hand, and, on the other, that between a passive and active entrepôt. Braudel, whose widely acclaimed views we shall employ as landmarks to help plot our course, regarded dominance of bulk carrying as the key to trade hegemony in the circumstances of the late sixteenth century.[16] The bulk trades not only greatly expanded during the course of the sixteenth century

---

[12] Van der Wee, 'Antwoord op een industriële uitdaging', 177.
[13] Van Houtte, 'Anvers aux xve et xvie siècles', 266–7; van Houtte, *Economische en sociale geschiedenis*, 108.
[14] Van Houtte, *Economische en sociale geschiedenis*, 266–7.
[15] Van der Wee, *Growth of the Antwerp Market*, ii. 225–6.
[16] Braudel, *La Méditerranée*, i. 572–5; Braudel, *Civilisation matérielle*, iii. 174.

but became more important than they had been in the past, in relation to the rich trades. Braudel and others argued that bulk carrying, around 1590, became the means to mastery of the rich trades; and, on the whole, economic historians have tended to agree.[17] For Braudel, Dutch preponderance in the shipping of grain, salt, fish, timber, and other high-volume produce led to a general primacy which grew out of profound shifts in Europe's material life. From this standpoint, Dutch primacy in world trade was ultimately a manifestation of European trends in subsistence, consumption, and prices. According to the French *grand maître*, the deteriorating balance of population and food-supply in the Mediterranean undermined the age-old primacy of Italy and the south, giving rise to a growing interplay between southern need and northern ability to supply, which the Dutch, with their unrivalled stock of shipping, were best placed to exploit. Bulk carrying, in Braudel's vision, led directly first to the conquest of the Iberian market, and with it the silver stocks imported from Spanish America, and then, from 1590—the year in which Dutch ships first appeared in large numbers past the Straits of Gibraltar— to dominance of the Mediterranean.[18]

If one accepts this argument, then much of the rest of the history of the Dutch entrepôt falls readily enough within the framework set out by devotees of the Braudelian 'secular trend'. If it is right that Dutch world-trade primacy was essentially a manifestation of the sixteenth-century European *tendance séculaire*, and that Dutch commercial hegemony stemmed from Dutch command of the Baltic bulk trades, then the basic rhythm of development of the Dutch entrepôt must, in essentials, be that of the bulk trades themselves. Since Dutch bulk freightage contracted after 1650, it would follow that the Dutch entrepôt itself declined after that date and that this decline was an inherent feature of what, in the Braudelian terminology, is called the *renversement de la tendance séculaire*. Braudel, stressing the role of material trends, was inclined to dismiss political events which might be thought to have exerted a profound influence on the rise and decline of the Dutch entrepôt—

[17] Verlinden, for instance, speaks of the Dutch attaining hegemony when bulk trade finally came to surpass trade in 'articoli di lusso' in importance ('Amsterdam', 330); see also Faber, 'Decline of the Baltic Grain Trade', 121–31; van der Woude, 'De "Nieuwe Geschiedenis"', 18–24; de Vries, *Economy of Europe*, 117.
[18] Braudel, *La Méditerranée*, i. 572–3; *Civilisation matérielle*, iii. 174; see also Braudel's remarks in Aymard (ed.), *Dutch Capitalism and World Capitalism*, 66–7.

events such as the Spanish recapture of Antwerp in 1585, the closing of the Scheldt to maritime traffic, or the Spanish economic embargoes against the Dutch of 1585–90, 1598–1608, and 1621–47—as of merely marginal significance.[19] The attempts of Louis XIV and Colbert to weaken and supplant the Dutch entrepôt by political means he deemed ineffective and doomed to failure.[20] Braudel was convinced that such events neither did, nor could, influence the basic movements of navigation and commerce.

Yet the view that bulk freightage was the key to general primacy in world commerce has never seemed wholly convincing. Because the Dutch dominated bulk carrying to and from the Baltic throughout the sixteenth century, one tends readily to assume that they therefore dominated Baltic commerce generally. Yet it was pointed out long ago that this is in fact not so. Even in the late sixteenth century, despite the overwhelming supremacy the Dutch by that time exercised over bulk freightage in the Baltic, they not only did not dominate but played only a small part in the distribution of spices, sugar, textiles, and indeed most other commodities in the region.[21] The Baltic rich trades remained securely in the hands of the merchants of Lübeck and, to a lesser extent, of Antwerp and Hamburg. Since bulky goods did not in actual fact loom large in trade with the northern shores of the Baltic and the Gulf of Finland, this means that most international trade with the northern Baltic, even as late as the 1580s, was in Hanseatic and not in Dutch hands. Most of Sweden's foreign trade, including the distribution of her copper, was handled by Lübeck. In 1559 eight times as many Lübeck ships as ships from Amsterdam docked at the Finnish depot of Viborg, to load tar, hides, and timber, and the goods brought by the Lübeckers were worth twenty times as much as the commodities brought by the Dutch.[22] Nor were the Dutch doing much better even by the late 1580s. Until after 1590 practically the only commodity the Dutch shipped to the Gulf of Finland was salt. Many historians insist on emphasizing the dramatic expansion of the European bulk trades during the sixteenth century. But to do so without pointing out the simultaneous

---

[19] See my criticism of Braudel's treatment of the fall of Antwerp in the *Times Literary Supplement*, 15 Oct. 1982.

[20] Braudel, *Civilisation matérielle*, iii. 217–18.

[21] Jeannin, 'Anvers et la Baltique', 99–101; Jeannin, 'Commerce de Lübeck', 99–101; Brünner, 'Excerpt', 191–7.

[22] Brünner, 'Excerpt', 191–2.

and no less dramatic expansion in more valuable products such as spices, sugar, and textiles is potentially seriously misleading.[23]

The early history of the Antwerp staple shows that the rise of a general emporium does not necessarily confer a high degree of control over the strands of international commerce, though Antwerp's development suggests that the one tends to lead to the other. There is a parallel issue with regard to the Dutch entrepôt. It is striking that Braudel, when commenting on Dutch commerce with Spain in the sixteenth century, fails to distinguish between dominance of carrying and control of the trade in the commodities carried. Thus, the French *grand maître* took the appearance of hundreds of Dutch grain ships in Italian ports in the 1590s to mean that the Dutch now dominated the grain trade to Italy.[24] But the documents show that in reality it was not, as yet, Dutch merchants who organized and financed this traffic but the old-established merchant élites of Genoa, Venice, and Tuscany.[25] During the early years of their seaborne commerce with Italy, the Dutch were operating what amounted to little more than a shipping service.[26] This underlines the dangers of attributing Dutch world-trade primacy during the seventeenth century to what were, after all, fundamentally fifteenth-century phenomena—Dutch superiority in shipping and bulk carrying. To explain Dutch primacy in world trade after 1590 down to the early eighteenth century in terms of Dutch supremacy over Baltic bulk freightage is in fact a profound misconception.

In what follows I have tried to explain the formation of the Dutch world entrepôt at the end of the sixteenth century, and its subsequent development, in rather different terms from those of Braudel and others who place the main emphasis on Dutch bulk freightage. In the course of my researches I have come to the conclusion that there has been a persistent tendency to overestimate the importance of the Baltic bulk trades in the making of Dutch world-trade primacy and to underestimate the significance of Dutch participation in the rich trades, including the commerce in high-value products from the Baltic. I have argued that the

[23] Van der Wee and Peeters, 'Un modèle économique', 112.
[24] Braudel, *La Méditerranée*, i. 545, 567–73.
[25] Guarnieri, *Il movimento*, 16; Grendi, 'I Nordici', 30–1; Hart, 'Amsterdamer Italienfahrt', 163–6; Israel, 'Phases of the Dutch *straatvaart*', 3.
[26] Romano, 'Tra XVI e XVII secolo', 489.

post-1590 ascendancy of the Dutch entrepôt over the mechanisms of world trade cannot be explained in terms of anything that happened in the Baltic, or in terms of Dutch Baltic bulk freightage, and that it is also an error to see the Dutch world entrepôt as declining after 1650 in line with Braudel's *renversement de la tendance séculaire*. In place of his rise-and-fall rhythm linked to the ups and downs of the Baltic grain trade, I have urged a more complex pattern, a sequence of seven phases, commencing with the break-through to world primacy during what I have termed Phase One (1590–1609) and ending with the disintegration of the seven-teenth-century Dutch trading system during what I have termed Phase Seven (1713–40). I have concluded by commenting on the subsequent further decline of the Dutch trading system after 1740. These suggested seven phases in the evolution of Dutch world commercial hegemony, some more expansive than others, are still linked in some respects to the ebb and flow of Dutch bulk carrying but are primarily defined by shifts in the Dutch share of the high-value trades, both those in Europe and those in the non-European world.

2
The Origins of Dutch World-trade Hegemony

EXCEPT for Britain after around 1780, no one power in history ever achieved so great a preponderance over the processes of world trade as did the Dutch, for a century and a half, from the end of the sixteenth down to the early eighteenth century. That any one nation, or state, particularly one lacking the early start and past imperial grandeur of the Iberians, Venetians, French, and English, should have achieved so prolonged, and constantly renewed, a capacity to dominate the world economy is, in itself, sufficiently amazing. But what makes it still more astounding is that at the time of its maritime and commercial greatness the Dutch Republic was the smallest of the major European states in territory, population, and natural resources. In all these respects, the United Provinces lagged far behind France, Spain, and England, the obvious and natural great powers of the age.

Furthermore, if for us today it constitutes a historical question of the first order that this tiny entity should, for a century and a half, have functioned as the hub of world commerce, the universal intermediary of trade, possessing, at its height, roughly half of the world's total stock of seagoing ships, this phenomenon struck contemporaries not just as prodigious but also as profoundly disturbing. The meteoric rise of the Dutch Republic to world-trade supremacy at the close of the sixteenth century, and the techniques and strategies by which it was achieved, excited not just universal attention, and eager attempts at emulation, but anxiety, resentment, and a good deal of outright hostility, the latter not infrequently tinged with mockery that so diminutive a state (which a few years before had not even existed and whose territory was so meagre) should cultivate such vast and unprecedented pretensions. 'For it seems a wonder to the world', as the English economic writer Thomas Mun summed it up, that such a small countrey, not fully so big as two of our best shires, having little natural wealth, victuals, timber or other necessary ammunitions, either for war or peace, should notwithstanding possess them all in such extraordinary plenty that besides their own wants (which are very great) they can and do likewise serve and sell to other Princes, ships, ordnance, cordage, corn, powder, shot and what not, which by their industrious trading they gather from all the quarters of the world: in which courses they are not less injurious to supplant others (especially the English) than they are careful to strengthen themselves.[1]

Dutch supremacy in world trade and shipping revolutionized the world economic order and transformed the pattern of Europe's colonial expansion.[2] But what was the function, from an economic standpoint, of this unprecedented hegemony over world commerce? Europe, and to some extent the wider world, had long been familiar with great regional distributive networks, such as those of Venice, Genoa, Lübeck, and Lisbon. Then, in the sixteenth century, Antwerp developed into the first general emporium, at any rate for Europe. But a fully fledged world entrepôt, not just linking, but dominating, the markets of all continents, was something totally outside human experience. The fact is that never before—or perhaps since—has the world witnessed such prodigious concentration of economic power at a single point.

Many scholars have expounded on the uniqueness of Dutch world-trade hegemony during the seventeenth century; relatively few, however, have tried to explain the phenomenon in terms of world economic development. A notable exception was the Dutch economist T. P. van der Kooy, who, as long ago as 1931, put forward a theoretical explanation which has since been frequently discussed and which we shall use here as a point of departure. According to van der Kooy, in early modern times, when an integrated world economy first emerged but before the Industrial Revolution, conditions not only favoured, but in an important sense actually required, the rise of a distributive network based on

---

[1] McCulloch (ed.), *Early English Tracts on Commerce*, 195; as Eli Heckscher expressed it, the 'Netherlands were the most hated, and yet the most admired and envied commercial nation of the seventeenth century' (*Mercantilism*, i. 351).

[2] Wallerstein, 'Dutch Hegemony', 117.

a general world emporium.[3] In an era when transport was highly irregular as well as slow, expensive, and prone to disruption by a variety of factors, the vagaries of supply and demand in any one locality were much greater than was the case later with industrialization, railways, steamships, and motor transport. Indeed, so haphazard and risky was the movement of commodities from one part of the world to another that great advantages attached to the creation of a fixed, stable base, or staple market, where merchandise could be stored prior to final marketing and distribution.[4] By stockpiling commodities, and concentrating storage, transport, and insurance facilities at a single point, it became possible to ensure regular, predictable, and controlled distribution on a long-term basis, reduce marketing costs, and generally hold prices lower and more stable than would otherwise have been the case.[5] For merchants trading with distant, and not so distant, markets, the existence of a central storehouse of commodities and services greatly diminished the uncertainty and risk. Consequently, as van der Kooy saw it, the essential function of the Dutch world entrepôt of the seventeenth and eighteenth centuries was to serve as a central reservoir of goods matching supply with demand, as a regulating mechanism that minimized the disruptive impact of unpredictable delays, stoppages, and bottlenecks.

Van der Kooy's explanation as to why it was the Dutch maritime zone rather than some other region which became the world's general store of commodities was that the location of the Dutch provinces was peculiarly suited for this role.[6] Undeniably, such a geographical explanation does have some force. The Republic was situated at a conjunction of northern waterways, connecting the Atlantic, Baltic, and Rhine, a particularly crucial intersection once the Mediterranean ceased to be the pivot of intercontinental commerce. Some strands of international trade were fundamentally influenced by geography. The major reason why it proved so difficult to furnish French wines direct to the Baltic and northern Russia in early modern times was that France's annual

[3] Van der Kooy, 'Holland als centrale stapelmarkt', 10–12; see also Klein, *De Trippen*, 3–13; Klein, 'De zeventiende eeuw', 101–3; Steensgaard, *Asian Trade Revolution*, 13–14.
[4] Van der Kooy, *Hollands stapelmarkt*, 3–4.
[5] Ibid. 3–4; Jeannin, 'Interdépendences économiques', 166–8.
[6] Van der Kooy, *Hollands stapelmarkt*, 7.

wine production was ready for export too late in the year to be shipped direct to the ice-prone waters of the Baltic and the White Sea until towards the middle of the following year.[7] Only by storing France's wine exports at a convenient, intermediate point, such as Holland or Zeeland, could a steady distribution of French wine in northern parts during spring and summer be assured.

This conception of the early modern world having a particular, structural need of a central reservoir of goods which, in the seventeenth century, could only have been located in the north-western corner of Europe, has long been recognized as a valuable contribution to the discussion. But it is also clear that van der Kooy's idea, in itself, is insufficient as an explanation of Dutch predominance in seventeenth-century world commerce.[8] In the first place, his theory fails to explain why there was just one central emporium and not a whole cluster of interdependent depots strung out around the North Sea, in England, north-west Germany, and elsewhere, as well as in the North Netherlands.[9] Secondly, van der Kooy's approach suppresses the distinction between a passive general staple, a mere clearing-house of goods, such as Antwerp was initially and such as Amsterdam tended to become in the mid-eighteenth century, and an active, controlling entrepôt, such as Antwerp became after 1550 and such as the Dutch entrepôt was during its Golden Age. Van der Kooy's theory, it has been pointed out, ignores the fact that a high concentration of commercial power at a single point will encourage restrictive and monopolistic practices designed to reduce, and even eliminate, competition.[10] After 1590 the Dutch merchant élite was constantly tempted, precisely by the incomparable strength of its position, to seek maximum profit and minimum risk by engrossing commodities and manipulating markets.[11] Up to a point, monopolistic practices and devices of engrossment might help promote stability of supply and prices. Certainly the early modern economic mind was

    [7] Van der Kooy, 'Holland als centrale stapelmarkt', 13.
    [8] De Vries, *Economische achteruitgang*, 3; Klein, *De Trippen*, 2–7; Steensgaard, *Asian Trade Revolution*, 13.
    [9] It was well known in seventeenth-century Holland that England in fact had far more natural advantages than the North Netherlands (La Court, *Interest van Holland*, 23–4, 31).
    [10] Ibid. 6–7; Klein, 'Dutch Capitalism', 90.
    [11] Klein, 'De zeventiende eeuw', 112–14; for some critical comment on Klein's analysis, see Veluwenkamp, *Ondernemersgedrag*, 5–13.

attuned, in a way that we are not, to the idea of what de Malynes called 'commendable engrossing', which serves the public by ironing out the inconvenience of gluts and shortages. But, obviously, if the ascendancy of a single, controlling entrepôt over the processes of international trade becomes too great, it will have the effect of increasing, instead of reducing, prices and costs for consuming countries.

The core of the problem posed by van der Kooy's theory for the historian is that it does not explain why, despite the devices of engrossment and monopolistic practices adopted by the Dutch entrepôt, competition from potential rivals, even English trade rivalry, remained relatively weak, at any rate until the late seventeenth century. As we shall see, the mechanisms by which the Dutch merchant élite and political oligarchy together regulated internal competition within the Dutch entrepôt, in the interests of the entrepôt as a whole, and at the same time thwarted the successive challenges of the rivals of the Dutch in the quest for hegemony over world trade, were various and complex. But the common thread, we shall argue, was a unique and characteristically Dutch blend of political intervention and business efficiency. What it all amounted to was a harnessing of the Dutch entrepôt to the machinery of the Dutch state. The Dutch business world of the seventeenth century was fundamentally shaped by an assortment of companies, national and local, consortia with political links, cartels, and combinations. Locating these Dutch institutions within the wider context of capitalist commercial organization is assuredly no simple task. Commenting on the persistently closer relationship of the Dutch East India Company (VOC) to the Dutch ruling oligarchy, and to Dutch statecraft, than that of its English counterpart to the crown and Parliament of England, Niels Steensgaard held that the Dutch company was not a 'pure' type, since it was strictly neither a business, nor a 'redistributive enterprise' operated by the state, but a complex blend of the two.[12] While agreeing as to the hybrid character of the VOC, in what follows we shall nevertheless classify the VOC as a 'pure' type in the sense that it exactly typified the high degree of interaction of ruling oligarchy with private enterprise which characterized much, if not most, of Dutch overseas commerce.

---

[12] Steensgaard, *Asian Trade Revolution*, 141; see also Schmoller, *The Mercantile System*, 53, 65.

The VOC may have been the single most grandiose exercise in collaboration between the Dutch merchant élite and the Dutch federal state, or elements of the federal state, but, as was pointed out long ago by the nowadays unfashionable nineteenth-century German economic writer Gustav Schmoller in his book *The Mercantile System*, there were numerous others, including the private, long-distance companies, the so-called *voorcompagnieën*, which preceded the VOC down to its establishment in 1602, the Northern Company of 1614, the West India Company (WIC) of 1621, the directorate of Mediterranean trade (1625), the Society of Surinam (1682), the organization of Holland's cloth buyers, and in some respects even the Holland and Zeeland herring fisheries. All of these national and provincial organizations were favoured and promoted, and most were set up, by the state.

The shock administered to their competitors, and all with whom they came in contact, by the rise of the Dutch to world-trade primacy in the 1590s was all the greater in that the process was so sudden. There was nothing gradual about the emergence of the Dutch world-trade entrepôt. As late as the mid-1580s, shortly before it became a fact, there was still little real sign of it other than the traditional Dutch preponderance over northern Europe's bulk-carrying trade, traffic dominated by the Dutch since the fifteenth century. During the 1580s the Dutch provinces in revolt against Spain were caught up in one of the most difficult periods of the long struggle for independence. In the early 1580s Spanish forces reconquered most of Flanders and Brabant, captured Antwerp after an epic siege, in 1585, and then went on to overrun much of the north-east of the embryonic Republic, including Nijmegen, Zutphen, Deventer, and Groningen. Furthermore, in 1585, Philip II imposed a general embargo on Dutch shipping and goods in Spain and Portugal which continued until 1590 and which sharply curtailed the flow of Iberian products, most notably salt, in Dutch bottoms to northern Europe.[13] Thus during the 1580s this shrinking, floundering state with its traditional bulk-carrying trade temporarily contracting, burdened with military costs beyond its means, and surrounded to the south, east, and north-east by Spanish forces, hardly presented a very alluring

---

[13] Kernkamp, *Handel op den vijand*, i. 176, 221; Bang, *Tabeller*, i, tables for Dutch and Hanseatic voyages through the Danish Sound, 1580–90; Hagedorn, *Ostfrieslands Handel*, 228–9; see also Gómez-Centurión Jiménez, 'Relaciones hispano-hanseáticas', 69–76.

spectacle for Europe's great merchant capitalists searching for a secure base for their commercial activity. On the contrary, nothing could have been less likely to inspire confidence than the beleaguered and embargoed Dutch Republic of those years. It required something of an act of faith to believe that the United Provinces had a future at all, let alone one characterized by the most prodigious burst of maritime and commercial expansion ever seen in the world until that time.

It may be true that some of the factors which subsequently made and moulded Dutch world-trade mastery were already in evidence before 1585, in particular Dutch supremacy in the sphere of bulk freightage (see table 2.1) The long-thriving Dutch Baltic bulk traffic, the so-called *moedernegotie* (mother-trade), required many more ships and mariners, and much more in the way of ship-servicing facilities, than did the carrying of high-value merchandise of low volume. For a trading nation to surpass its competitors in bulk carrying what was needed was a prolific mass of shipping, immense stores of timber, masts, sail-canvas, cordage, pitch, and other necessaries, and, consequent on these, competitive freight rates. The Hansa towns lost their age-old struggle with the Hollanders for trade supremacy in the Baltic bulk trade, essentially because they found it more difficult than their Dutch competitors to adapt to the growing scale and complexity of the traffic. Eventual Dutch success in this long-drawn-out contest was partly a matter of geographical location in the sense postulated by van der Kooy. During the Middle Ages the only market outside the Baltic with which Baltic trade was closely linked was that of the Low Countries. The salt supplied to Scandinavia, Russia, and the Baltic came from the salt-mines of north Germany or Poland, and control over the distribution of this commodity was one of the pillars of Hanseatic supremacy. But by the late fifteenth century Baltic bulk traffic was becoming increasingly entwined with other bulk commerce outside the Baltic. It was this which heralded the end of Hanseatic primacy in the north. With the rise of large fleets of full-rigged ships in the later fifteenth century, the Dutch began to fetch cheap and abundant marine salt from the coasts of western France, Portugal, and Spain.[14] They also began to ship large quantities of French wine. The increased speed of the new

[14] Unger, 'Dutch Herring', 256–9; Rau, *Estudos sobre a história do sal português*, 92–4.

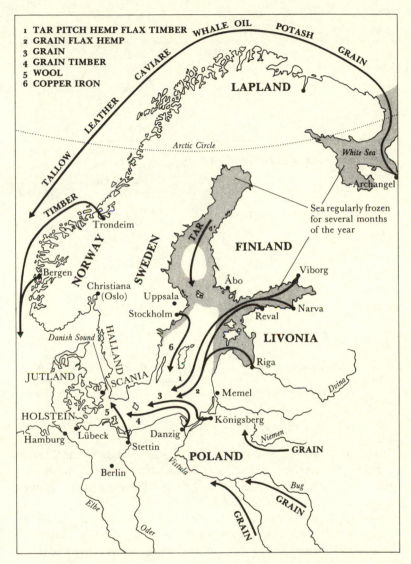

2.1 Scandinavia and the Baltic trade area during the sixteenth century.

TABLE 2.1. *Voyages through the Danish Sound, 1497–1575*

Voyages in both directions

Year	Dutch	North German
1497	567	202
1503	856	295
1528	589	284
1538	945	580
1540	890	413
1546	932	825

Voyages eastwards through the Sound, 1557–1575

Year	Dutch*	North German
1557	622	416
1560	697	562
1562	1,192	480
1564	1,240	340
1566	1,498	268
1568	1,288	321
1569	516	737
1574	1,019	881
1575	832	731

* These ships were overwhelmingly from North Holland, including Amsterdam, and Friesland. It is important to realize that the participation of South Holland and Zeeland in Baltic commerce was always very small (see Bang, *Tabeller*, i. 18, 22); by contrast, the Frisian role was substantial, usually totalling around one-fifth of the total Dutch traffic through the Sound (see Faber, *Drie eeuwen Friesland*, i. 272–3, ii. 602). *Source*: Bang, *Tabeller*, i. 2–63.

full-rigged cargo ships, combined with the fact that the Dutch ports became ice-free earlier in the year than those of the Baltic itself, encouraged the Dutch, from the end of the fifteenth century, to combine voyages to the west and to the Baltic, often first to south-west Europe for salt and then on direct to the Baltic to deliver the salt and load with grain, and then finally back to Holland, all within one season, before the onset of freezing weather. From Baltic ports this simply could not be done.

Furthermore, the very narrowness of the Dutch role in fifteenth- and sixteenth-century commerce boosted Dutch competitiveness in bulk carrying. The Hansa merchants and the English dealt in cloth and costly wares which had to be well protected from the elements, as well as in bulky goods, and were therefore relatively uninterested in specialized craft purpose-built for cheap carriage.[15] English shipping in the late sixteenth century was, generally speaking, multi-purpose and, being often used for voyages to the Mediterranean, tended to be strongly constructed, well manned, and well armed.[16] Dutch shipbuilders, by contrast, concentrated on low-cost hull forms that maximized cargo space, discarded armaments, and used only the simplest rigging. Dutch shipping was designed for minimal crews and maximum economy.

Technical and design innovation was thus crucial to the making of Dutch supremacy in shipping; but it was not the sort of innovation which derived from advanced techniques which others lacked. It was simply that the peculiar circumstances of the Dutch situation favoured a higher degree of rationalization and specialization than prevailed elsewhere. The very lack of major merchants helped the buildup of a vast, broadly based stock of shipping. It meant that new ways of financing ship building and ownership had to be found. At Antwerp or Lübeck during the sixteenth century ownership of ships was often divided, though seldom into more than three or four shares.[17] But, precisely because there were hardly any big merchants in pre-1585 Holland, Zeeland, and Friesland, the practice evolved of dividing shipownership into numerous shares, even though the ships being built were of cheaper kinds. Ownership not just of sixteenth and thirty-second, but also of sixty-fourth shares became commonplace and remained so in the case of the bulk-carrying *fluyts*, or flute-ships (an improved design that began to be built at Hoorn in the mid-1590s) throughout the era of Dutch trade primacy. The same applied also to timber-carrying and fishing ships.[18] During the late seventeenth century, for example, a key difference between the north German and Dutch whaling fleets was that ownership of German whalers was divided into small numbers, and that of Dutch whalers into large numbers of shares, often up to sixty-four.[19] One Amsterdam shipowner, at his death in 1610, left shares

[15] Unger, *Dutch Shipbuilding*, 33–4; Unger, 'Scheepvaart in de Noordelijke Nederlanden', 112.
[16] Davis, 'English Merchant Shipping', 9–10.
[17] Brulez, 'Scheepvaart in de Zuidelijke Nederlanden', 126.
[18] Hart, 'Rederij', 107–8.
[19] Brinner, *Die deutsche Grönlandfahrt*, 122.

in twenty-two ships, consisting of one-sixteenth shares in thirteen vessels, one thirty-second shares in seven, a one-seventeenth share, and a one twenty-eighth share.[20] In this way risk was spread and investment in the Dutch cargo-carrying fleet came to be widely based, both geographically, over the entire coast from Flushing to Friesland, and socially. Typically, the owners of Dutch *fluyts* were timber dealers, shipbuilders, sailmakers, brewers, millers, and so forth. Once again, the early innovative element in the Dutch commercial system lay in a radical extension of commonplace methods and techniques.[21]

Bulky goods from the west played a crucial part in the Dutch conquest of the Baltic bulk trades.[22] In 1580, for instance, 27 per cent of Dutch vessels entering the Baltic carried refined or unrefined salt and we must remember that much of the rest sailed in ballast, carrying no cargo at all.[23] Such purchasing power as the Dutch possessed in the Baltic before 1590 was thus heavily dependent on salt, and this, and the fact that the Dutch herring industry and herring exports were also dependent on Iberian salt, was one of the main reasons why Spanish ministers came to believe that it lay within their power, at least potentially, to break or heavily disrupt the Dutch trading system. Carrying salt from south-western Europe was indispensable to the Dutch Baltic traffic and it also brought the North Netherlands an important processing industry. In the fifteenth century, salt-refining in north-west Europe had been carried on especially in Flanders. But with the steep rise in salt shipments from Spain, Portugal, and France during the sixteenth century, Zeeland emerged as the chief centre for salt-refining, especially the towns of Zierikzee and Goes.[24] As early as 1526 there were seventy-seven salt-boiling kettles in operation at Zierikzee alone, employing several hundred people. This transfer of the salt-refining industry from Flanders to Zeeland may be regarded as a pre-echo of the vast movement of trade-supportive, back-up industries from the South Netherlands to the northern maritime provinces which took place at the close of the sixteenth century.

[20] Hart, 'Rederij', 108.
[21] Klein, 'Dutch Capitalism', 88–9.
[22] Brulez, 'Zoutinvoer in de Nederlanden', 182–4.
[23] Christensen, *Dutch Trade to the Baltic*, 446–7.
[24] *Tegenwoordige Staat van Zeeland*, i. 372; van Houtte, *Economische en sociale geschiedenis*, 113.

Apart from salt, the only commodities which played a significant role in Dutch exports to the Baltic before 1590 were wine and herring. In wine, as with salt, the Dutch far surpassed all rivals long before 1590. Dordrecht had for centuries been the staple for Rhine and Moselle wines shipped down river to the North Sea. Then, with the rise of the Dutch full-rigged fleets sailing to western France during the fifteenth century, the Dutch, especially the Zeelanders, rapidly gained mastery of the carrying of French wines. As early as 1523 the Habsburg government at Brussels recognized the provincial capital of Zeeland, Middelburg, as the official staple for French wine for the entire Netherlands.[25] Antwerp had a local role as a centre for the distribution of wine within the Netherlands; but freightage of wines to northern Europe now rested firmly in Dutch hands. In 1550 a total of 38,000 tuns of wine, of 900 litres each, was imported into the Habsburg Netherlands, 60 per cent of this consisting of French wine shipped to Middelburg.

The third key product on which the Dutch carrying trade to the Baltic rested during the sixteenth century was herring. Here again Dutch supremacy was a direct consequence of the combination of specialized shipbuilding and specially close links with south-west Europe. The key innovation here was the Dutch herring buss, an unprecedentedly large fishing vessel, often carrying fifteen or eighteen crew, more than many of the Baltic grain ships. These vessels were designed to weather storms and stay at sea for long periods, and to carry large stocks of salt, so that the herring could be eviscerated, salted, and packed on board. This new type of specialized fishing vessel, again owned by relatively large numbers of people, arose as far back as around 1400.[26] By the mid-fifteenth century the herring fleets of three Netherlands provinces—Holland, Zeeland, and Flanders—had established a near total ascendancy over the North Sea herring fishery. The Hanseatics, who had once controlled the traffic in herring, and the Danes, Norwegians, Scots, and others interested in the herring grounds, might, in theory, have imitated the Dutch ships and gear. But, in practice, without the salt, barrels (from Norwegian

---

[25] Craeybeckx, *Un grand commerce d'importation*, 29–31; van der Wee, 'Handelsbetrekkingen', 282.
[26] Unger, 'Dutch Herring', 256–9.

timber), methods of non-merchant shipownership, and availability of large numbers of men, it was impossible to do so.

By the 1560s the North Netherlands boasted over 500 herring busses manned by perhaps 7,000 men, divided into a North Holland fleet (based at Enkhuizen), a Maas estuary fleet, and a Zeeland fleet. Holland alone by that time possessed some 1,800 seagoing ships, around 500 of which were based at Amsterdam.[27] The manning needed for this forest of shipping would have been, as near as we can tell, around 30,000 men. And, of course, thousands more men were needed to build the ships, make the rigging and sails, and operate the river craft and barges by which much of the salt, wine, herring, grain and timber was moved from one part of the Dutch entrepôt to another. The Dutch bulk-trading system of the sixteenth century demanded great numbers of men. But there is also another crucial feature of the system that needs to be stressed: most of the bulk-carrying ships and herring busses were based in small ports, especially the West Frisian towns (Hoorn, Enkhuizen, and Medemblik) and the Maas ports, which lacked regular participation in the States of Holland. Participation in maritime activity in the Dutch provinces was not therefore concentrated in a few large centres as was the case in the South Netherlands or north Germany. The great Hansa towns and towns of the South Netherlands neither needed, nor wanted, organizing bodies in which their own hinterlands could participate. But the six so-called 'big towns' of Holland—Amsterdam, Dordrecht, Haarlem, Leiden, Delft, and Gouda (of which only the first was a major seaport)—were compelled by the fact that their economic vitality depended on shipping and fishing fleets based outside their walls to develop a provincial, collectivist outlook which is already quite apparent from the resolutions of the States of Holland by the 1530s and 1540s.[28] This tempering of civic particularism with a much greater measure of provincial collaboration than pertained in any of the South Netherlands provinces was to prove an abiding pillar of strength to the future Dutch world entrepôt. In Holland and Zeeland collective action and policies on the part of the towns

[27] Unger, 'Scheepvaart in de Noordelijke Nederlanden', 112; Venice, at the height of her success, around 1450, had about 300 seagoing ships (Lane, 'Venetian Shipping', 24).

[28] Even inland towns such as Haarlem, Leiden, and Gouda could be prodded by the rest into helping to subsidize the protection of the Holland herring fishery (see, for instance, Res. Holl. 7 Aug. 1548, 7 June 1549).

was the only way. Amsterdam (contrary to what is often supposed) was never to dominate the Dutch entrepôt in anything like the sense that Venice or Genoa dominated policy-making in their respective republics. Braudel's view of the United Provinces as in essence the 'city state of Amsterdam' is fundamentally misleading.

Moreover, while the great cities of the South Netherlands were too self-reliant to show much interest in tightening collective procedures on a provincial level, the great Hanseatic cities lacked administrative and fiscal leverage over their immediate hinterlands. Here too there was simply nothing comparable to the collective dominance of the Holland and Zeeland towns over their immediate surroundings. None of the Hansa towns ruled much territory outside their own walls. Lübeck and Hamburg were, from a territorial point of view, precariously situated practically on the border of Danish territory. They may have been great international trade centres but they had no means of controlling resources, including shipyards, road tolls, and waterways, even short distances from their walls.

The potential impact of all these special characteristics of the North Netherlands on the rest of the world was enhanced by yet another phenomenon which was virtually unique to the Dutch situation: the increasingly highly specialized character of much of Dutch agriculture. Due to rising imports of Baltic grain—annual imports are reckoned to have increased by five times between 1500 and 1560—farmers in the Dutch maritime zone tended to diversify away from traditional patterns of cereal-based agriculture into other, and now more profitable, products especially dairy foods, meat, wool, flax, hops, and fodder crops.[29] To keep the growing herds of cattle alive and fit over the winter, the practice spread of stalling cattle and feeding them on new fodder crops such as clover and parsnips, and on oil-cakes made from pressed rape and coleseed. One major consequence of the agricultural changes in the North Netherlands was a hefty upsurge in cheese and butter exports, which, in turn, tended to strengthen the Dutch carrying trade to France, Germany, and the Baltic. But a still more significant consequence of the shift away from labour-intensive arable farming was the release of a large part of the former rural work-force for employment in non-agricultural sectors.[30] For we can

[29] De Vries, *Dutch Rural Economy*, 138–44.
[30] Ibid.

say with some certainty, given the small population of the North Netherlands in early modern times—around two million at the height of the Dutch Republic's greatness—that there could have been no possibility of manning the large bulk-carrying and fishing fleets, as well as the various supporting industries, had not the level of manpower required by the rural sector been appreciably lower than was the case elsewhere.

Like any economy, the Dutch entrepôt was highly vulnerable to political disruption. It is perhaps a mistake to assume that the North Netherlands possessed permanent advantages over north Germany as a bulk-trading depot. During the first half of the sixteenth century the signs are that the Hanseatics increasingly adopted Dutch designs and methods. Although the Dutch held on to a healthy lead down to the 1560s, north German traffic passing through the Danish Sound tended to increase even faster than the Dutch traffic after 1500. Political factors might well have tipped the balance. After the coming of Alva in 1567, and the intensification of persecution of Protestants with which his regime is associated, appreciable numbers of business people and seamen migrated with their skills, labour, and ships to north Germany. The volume of shipping out of Dutch ports sailing through the Danish Sound fell back, and the volume sailing out of German ports rose, closing the gap between the two. In 1569 and probably in several subsequent years (though there is a gap in the Sound toll data so this is uncertain) the traffic out of north German ports exceeded the volume out of Dutch ports.[31] Had the Dutch Revolt of 1572 never taken place, or taken place and rapidly collapsed, it may be that north Germany would have consolidated its grip over the northern European carrying trade.[32] As it was, it was Spanish power which collapsed, in 1576, with the result that those who had taken refuge in Germany returned to Holland and Friesland with their families, businesses, and ships. From the late 1570s the Dutch grip over the Baltic bulk-carrying trade was again secure.

Yet, despite this, it by no means seemed probable, either in the period before 1572, or for nearly two decades afterwards, that the Dutch provinces were about to develop into a dominant world entrepôt, or were ever likely to. This was not just because of the

---

[31] Bang, *Tabeller*, i. 58–60; Kernkamp, 'Nederlanders op de Oostzee', 82–4.
[32] Snapper, *Oorlogsinvloeden*, 31–2.

deteriorating military situation, but also because of the inherent limitations of the bulk-carrying trades themselves. Whilst no one would wish to claim that cheap freightage and an immense accumulation of shipping were not essential preconditions of Dutch world-trade predominance during the Golden Age, care must be exercised, in view of historians' traditional propensity to insist on the paramountcy of the Baltic in the formation of the Dutch entrepôt, not to exaggerate its role in the making of Dutch world-trade hegemony. It may be true that the bulk trades, of marginal significance in the fifteenth century, played a much greater role during the sixteenth. The fact remains, nevertheless, that Europe's traffic in high-value products of small volume was still paramount when it came to forming a powerful merchant élite, capital accumulation, and the development of banking, insurance, and export-orientated industry. Down to the 1580s Holland and Zeeland played practically no part in the distribution of spices, sugar, textiles, and other valuable commodities even in the Baltic.[33] Nor indeed could the North Netherlands have played a more significant role. For the rich trades demanded large capital resources and a complex network of international connections, as well as appropriately sturdy ships. But trafficking in grain, timber, and salt was, by and large, activity for minor merchants and skippers. It was a sphere which one needed only a modest capital to enter and where profits on individual shiploads were correspondingly small.

Thus, down to the 1580s the Dutch entrepôt was completely unfitted for 'grandes entreprises commerciales'.[34] Holland and Zeeland boasted few if any important merchants and few financial facilities, and such textile industries as there were were lapsing ever more into decay.[35] As far as commerce in high-value commodities was concerned, and industries supportive of trade, banking, and insurance, Holland and Zeeland were until the 1580s, nothing more than a dependency of the South Netherlands and, in particular, Antwerp. The great merchants of the Low Countries, the stocks of textiles and luxury wares, and the money market were all firmly located in Antwerp. The woollen, linen,

---

[33] Bang, *Tabeller*, ii. 76, 80, 122, 126, 130; Jeannin, 'Anvers et la Baltique', 100–1; van Houtte, *Economische en sociale geschiedenis*, 117.

[34] Van Houtte, 'Bruges et Anvers', 100.

[35] Posthumus, *Geschiedenis*, i. 120–9.

silk, and other industries which buttressed Antwerp's far-flung commerce were to be found in Antwerp itself or concentrated in nearby districts of Brabant and Flanders.

The outbreak of the Revolt against Spain in 1572 tended if anything to weaken further the position of the Dutch entrepôt in the short and medium term. Admittedly economic life in the southern provinces of the Netherlands was extensively disrupted during the 1570s. The two principal Flemish industries—linen weaving and manufacture of 'new draperies' such as *says* and fustians—were severely dislocated by the turmoil.[36] Imports of Spanish wool into the South Netherlands practically ceased. Yet, despite all this dislocation, the centre of economic gravity in the Low Countries continued to lie in the south. The damaged, but still resilient, textile industries, with their thousands of skilled workers and sophisticated products, were still concentrated in Flanders. Antwerp, for all the injury it suffered during the Spanish Fury (1576) and internecine religious strife, still housed the merchant élite and what remained of business with Italy, England, and the Iberian Peninsula in the Low Countries. Indubitably, a great deal of commercial activity was displaced from the South Netherlands elsewhere during these years of turmoil. Many wealthy merchants transferred their businesses and families abroad during the 1570s and early 1580s. But few chose the North Netherlands, even as a temporary place of refuge.[37] Antwerp merchant emigrés who left before 1585 migrated to Cologne, Hamburg, Frankfurt, London, and Rouen. What the South Netherlands lost was picked up by north-west Germany and England. It is no accident that a regular English seaborne commerce with Italy and the Levant began specifically in the 1570s; for it was then that the passage of Italian and Persian silks overland from northern Italy, via Augsburg and Frankfurt, to Antwerp was, for the first time, seriously impeded.[38] Meanwhile not only did Amsterdam fail to profit from the displacement of international business from Antwerp in the 1570s, but Holland's foremost city was also par-

[36] Coornaert, *Un centre industriel d'autrefois*, 493–4; Sabbe, *Belgische vlasnijverheid*, 329; Bastin, 'Gentse lijnwaadmarkt', 131–2.

[37] Brulez, 'Diaspora der Vlaamse kooplui', 281–4; Brulez, *De Firma Della Faille*, 83–4, 124–5, 179–81.

[38] ASV CSM 1st ser. 137, fos. 52ᵛ, 57ᵛ–9, 105–6, res. 6 Feb. 1581 and 7 Mar. 1584; the Venetian board of trade now regarded the English as the main threat to Venice's Levant trade.

tially stripped of its own Baltic trade during the years of its political isolation within Holland (1572–8)—years in which Amsterdam adhered stubbornly to the Catholic cause.[39] This trade was temporarily transferred to the West Frisian ports—Hoorn, Enkhuizen, and Medemblik.

Furthermore, many of those who left Antwerp in these years expected to return. By 1580 it looked as if the slide in Antwerp's fortunes might have been halted. Imports of spices and sugar, after the sharp fall of the 1570s, recovered somewhat in the early 1580s.[40] The overland trade between Antwerp and south Germany, and Italy, resumed. The Antwerp silk industry, which at this time employed a work-force of four thousand, actually reached its peak in the early 1580s.[41] The dyeing and dressing of English unfinished cloth outside England continued to be based in and around Antwerp. Business confidence began gradually to revive. During the early 1580s the Antwerp city took vigorous steps to reassert the city's predominance in international commerce. The city fathers welcomed merchants of whatever religious persuasion—Calvinist, Lutheran, or Catholic. Eager to tighten the city's links with Italy and the Levant, not least to check the threatened diversion of the Levant traffic to London, the municipality established contacts with the Jews of Frankfurt with a view to attracting Jewish settlement and, in 1582, invited Greek, Armenian, and Muslim subjects of the Ottoman sultan to reside in the city.[42] In emulation of the English, Antwerp firms began sending ships on a regular basis round to Italy from about 1580.[43] Indeed, during these years Antwerp's trade with Italy and the Near East rapidly expanded, buoyed by a swelling stream of exports of linen, *says*, and English finished cloth, wares manufactured (or in the latter case, partly manufactured) in the towns of Flanders and Brabant.[44]

What finally blighted Antwerp's revival, and permanently dashed the city's prospects of re-emerging as the principal trade emporium of northern Europe, was, as historians have always recognized, the epic siege of 1584–5 and the Spanish recapture of

[39] Snapper, *Oorlogsinvloeden*, 31–2.
[40] Van der Wee, *Growth of the Antwerp Market*, i. 310, 324; Pohl, *Portugiesen in Antwerpen*, 154–8.
[41] Thijs, *Zijdennijverheid te Antwerpen*, 4, 96–7.
[42] Prins, 'Orange and the Jews', 96–101; Voet, *Antwerp: The Golden Age*, 219, 251.
[43] Brulez, 'Navigation flamande vers la Méditerranée', 1211–13.
[44] Van der Wee, *Growth of the Antwerp Market*, ii. 181, 190.

the city.[45] With Antwerp in Spanish hands but the estuary of the Scheldt, the city's sole outlet to the sea, remaining firmly in the grip of 'rebel' Dutch garrisons and naval power, Antwerp's hitherto flourishing seaborne commerce came to an abrupt end. It was to remain permanently paralysed. From 1585 onwards seagoing vessels were not permitted to sail direct through the estuary and up to Antwerp. Henceforth, goods marked for Antwerp arriving at the mouth of the Scheldt had to be unloaded in the Zeeland ports, which now replaced Antwerp as the primary terminal on the Scheldt, and sent on in lighters.[46]

The fall of Antwerp in 1585 was undeniably a crucial event in economic as well as in political and religious history. But the fall of Antwerp, and the closing of the Scheldt to maritime traffic, do not, as is so often assumed, in themselves explain the subsequent transference of Antwerp's entrepôt role to Holland and Zeeland. Control over Europe's rich trades did not simply migrate from the South to the North Netherlands in this straightforward way, however alluring such a notion might be. What actually transpired was much more complex. Certainly there was an immediate and huge exodus of refugees from the southern provinces to the north. Most of the merchants and industrial work-force in Flanders and Brabant had lapsed from Catholicism, especially after 1576. With the Spanish reconquest, and the suppression of Protestant worship, great numbers—fearful of Spanish reprisals and the catastrophic economic situation as well as moved by Protestant allegiance—packed their bags and streamed out of the South Netherlands. Over 100,000 refugees joined the trek, most, at any rate of the poorer *émigrés*, migrating directly to Holland and Zeeland.[47]

In the long run this vast infusion of manpower and skills accrued very much to the advantage of the infant republic in the north. But it cannot be argued that the migration as such brought about the shift of trade primacy to the North Netherlands. For as yet there was no such transfer of primacy, at any rate not to the North Netherlands. Nor are the reasons for this hard to discern. After the recapture of Antwerp, the Spanish troops went on to retake much of the east and north-east of the 'rebel' republic, cutting all the rivers and other waterways linking Holland with Germany

---

[45] Van Houtte, *Economische en sociale geschiedenis*, 137–8.
[46] Ibid.; Baetens, *Nazomer van Antwerpens welvaart*, i. 40–1.
[47] Briels, *Zuidnederlandse immigratie*, 15, 21–2.

and the overland routes to Italy. Thus what remained of the United Provinces was also plunged into economic recession during the late 1580s, albeit a recession less severe than that gripping the south.[48] Moreover, in 1585 Philip II imposed his general embargo on Dutch ships and goods in Spain and Portugal. It may be, as has often been claimed, that Philip II's embargo of 1585–9 was only haphazardly enforced.[49] This may be so. But its effectiveness was enhanced by the retaliatory prohibition on trade with Spain and Portugal as well as the Spanish Netherlands imposed by the Earl of Leicester, Elizabeth I's governor-general of the United Provinces, in April 1586.[50] In any case, there can be no doubt that there was a sharp falling off in the flow of Iberian products, especially Portuguese salt, in Dutch bottoms to northern Europe, the direct traffic from the Iberian Peninsula to the Baltic in Dutch ships being cut to a trickle in the years 1587–9 despite the lifting of Leicester's ban in 1587 (see table 2.2). In some ways the recession of the late 1580s may have actually helped the Revolt. By impeding

TABLE 2.2. *Dutch voyages direct from the Iberian Peninsula to the Baltic, 1580–1591*

Year	Dutch	North German
1580	86	26
1581	92	68
1582	76	63
1583	78	48
1584	93	51
1584	71	66
1586	22	53
1587	12	85
1588	4	87
1589	3	85
1590	101	133
1591	169	92

Source: Bang, *Tabeller*, i. 86–110.

[48] Baasch, *Holländische Wirtschaftsgeschichte*, 256–7.
[49] Braudel, *La Méditerranée*, i. 574–5; Gómez-Centurión Jiménez, 'Relaciones hispano-hanseáticas', 70–2.
[50] Kernkamp, *Handel op den vijand*, i. 185–8.

the export of butter, cheese, and other farm produce by river it depressed the price of food in Holland and Zeeland.[51] But it was all the same a time of contraction and difficulty for Dutch overseas trade and shipping.

As a consequence of the depression of the late 1580s, the tendency was for commerce and shipping to be diverted away from rather than to the United Provinces between 1585 and 1590. Although there was less diversion of business to Emden in these years than there had been in the years 1569–77, Leicester's trade ban certainly caused some diversion to north-west Germany as well as to England, Scotland, and France.[52] The Spanish embargo of the late 1580s clearly diverted much of the previous Dutch traffic between the Iberian Peninsula and northern Europe into the hands of the Hansa towns, especially Lübeck, which enjoyed a spectacular boom during the late 1580s.[53] Once again Dutch merchants and seamen began to migrate from the West Frisian ports to the towns of northern Germany.[54]

A trade entrepôt as severely boxed in as the Dutch emporium during the years 1585–9,[55] and which was losing its grip even over some strands of its traditional sphere of dominance, that of bulk freightage, was scarcely likely to exert much appeal on élite merchant *émigrés*, handling expensive commodities, who required viable routes across Germany, and safe navigation past Flanders and Gibraltar, to conduct their business. And so it was, during the late 1580s, that north-western Germany proved more attractive than the beleaguered North Netherlands to commercially minded refugees from the South Netherlands. North-west Germany was by no means the only focus of migration. A number of *émigré* merchants from Antwerp, perhaps especially younger sons, settled in Venice, where there were at least twenty-one 'Flemish' firms active by the early 1590s.[56] Others settled in other great southern emporia, especially Genoa, Lisbon, and Seville. The emergence of this Mediterranean diaspora of Antwerp *émigré*

[51] Velius, *Chronyk van Hoorn*, 470; Baasch, *Holländische Wirtschaftsgeschichte*, 256–7.

[52] Bang, *Tabeller*, i. 86–107; Hagedorn, *Ostfrieslands Handel*, 173; Snapper, *Oorlogsinvloeden*, 36.

[53] Bang, *Tabeller*, i. 86–107; Hagedorn, *Ostfrieslands Handel*, 228–9.

[54] Velius, *Chronyk van Hoorn*, 470.

[55] Baasch, *Holländische Wirtschaftsgeschichte*, 256–7.

[56] Brulez, 'Diaspora der Vlaamse kooplui', 288–90; Gramulla, *Handelsbeziehungen*, 208–9.

businessmen was indeed one of the striking features of these years. The hub, Antwerp, was now paralysed; but paradoxically its *malaise* further enhanced the European trade network it had created. But the 'Flemish' merchant colonies in the Mediterranean were, and remained, part of a distributive network. In the circumstances of the time, only an emporium located on the North Sea had any real prospect of inheriting Antwerp's mantle as Europe's general emporium; and, at this stage, north-western Germany seemed the most likely candidate. Requiring good maritime connections with the Iberian Peninsula, some key merchants, including a number who were later to establish some of the foremost merchant houses of Amsterdam, gravitated towards Hamburg and the Elbe estuary, which enjoyed an explosive boom during the second half of the 1580s.[57] Prominent among these were Balthasar Coymans, Guillielmo Bartholotti, Jan van der Straeten, and Hans de Schot. Other notable figures such as Samuel Godijn (Godin), who settled at Emden, or Andries van der Meulen, who established himself at Bremen, chose other ports along the German North Sea coast. The well-known Antwerp–Italian merchant dynasty of Calandrini, which later became prominent at Amsterdam, after moving there in the 1590s, chose Stade.[58] Stade was also the choice of the English Merchant Adventurers, who moved their continental staple away from the Netherlands in 1587.

But it was not just the north-west German coast which attracted *émigrés* from Antwerp. The key firms were eager to retain their hold on the overland trade to Italy as well as the seaborne traffic to the Peninsula. Relatives of the Antwerp *émigrés* domiciled on the north-west German coast and in the Mediterranean, settled in appreciable numbers at Cologne and Frankfurt. In the years 1585–90 there were some forty South Netherlands expatriates trading overland with Italy from Cologne alone.[59] Both routes to the south were vital. The wealthy van der Straeten family, closely linked with Genoa, traded in part by sea, from Hamburg, but also overland via their branch at Frankfurt.[60] Another notable Antwerp *émigré*, Samuel Godijn, at Emden, imported large quantities of sugar and Brazil-wood from Lisbon, where his

[57] Kellenbenz, *Unternehmerkräfte*, 184, 197, 222.
[58] Van Dillen, *Het oudste aandeelhoudersregister*, 64, 85, 126.
[59] Gramulla, *Handelsbeziehungen*, 205.
[60] Ibid. 250.

brother, Louis Godijn resided; but he also handled Italian silks and had other brothers, the firm of 'Giacomo e Felippo Godin di Francfort', positioned on the overland route.[61] Most of the Portuguese New Christian merchants who abandoned Antwerp in 1583–5 were drawn to Cologne.[62]

For a time north-western Germany also seemed preferable to the North Netherlands as a refuge for the more specialized industries which took flight from Flanders and Brabant, for industry and the rich trades were inextricably linked. This is well illustrated by the experience of Antwerp's *émigré* sugar-refiners. Until 1585 Antwerp functioned as the unchallenged sugar depot of northern Europe. But in that year many sugar dealers and refiners joined the swelling exodus from the South Netherlands. Some gave Holland a try. One prominent sugar-refining family, the van der Broecke, settled briefly at Alkmaar, others at Amsterdam. But during the late 1580s the Dutch entrepôt had practically no share in the international sugar trade and little prospect of getting any.[63] The van der Broecke, Pels, and other sugar-refining families soon packed up and transferred to Hamburg, which, from 1585, for about a decade, served as northern Europe's sugar depot as well as the principal northern emporium for pepper, spices, and Mediterranean products.[64]

North-west Germany, however, was fragmented politically, a major disadvantage. Also the emporia for the overland trade with Italy—Cologne and Frankfurt—were relatively distant from Hamburg and Lübeck. North-west Germany was the first true successor to Antwerp as the hub of the European trade system in the immediate aftermath of the events of 1585. But the question was could north-western Germany consolidate its newly acquired hold over Europe's rich trades? Those industries which required large quantities of cheap but skilled labour could not migrate to Germany, only to nearby Holland. Flemish 'new draperies', especially the *says* of Hondschoote, were a major ingredient in the overland traffic to Italy, and Holland was best placed to acquire what Flanders now lost. The sudden upsurge in *say*-production at

[61] Gramulla, *Handelsbeziehungen*, 366–7.
[62] Pohl, *Portugiesen in Antwerpen*, 80, 83.
[63] Roosbroeck, *Emigranten*, 315, 344; Ratelband (ed.), *Reizen naar West-Afrika*, pp. xxiii–xxvi.
[64] Bang, *Tabeller*, ii. 126, 130, 138, 184; Kellenbenz, 'Der Pfeffermarkt um 1600', 33–6.

Leiden in the years 1584–5 in fact marked Holland's début in Europe's rich trades. As a result a few Antwerp *émigré* merchants trafficking with Italy, such as Jean Pellicorne and Daniel van der Meulen, settled at Leiden in or soon after 1585.[65] But for the time being Leiden *says* and Haarlem linen were Holland's only fingers in the pie of Europe's rich trades.

It is clear, then, that in itself the mass exodus from the South Netherlands to Holland and Zeeland in the years 1584–5 did not impart the decisive impetus which raised the Dutch entrepôt to global primacy. What it did do was add a vital ingredient to the mix without which there could have been no subsequent dramatic breakthrough to world supremacy in the 1590s. No matter how successful in carrying bulky goods of low value, the Dutch entrepôt would never have achieved anything remotely like its post-1590 hegemony in world trade without some such massive infusion of manufacturing capacity and skills. For mastery of the rich trades, as the examples of Venice and Antwerp abundantly show, was impossible without acquiring the means to furnish great quantities of textiles and the potential to process a vast range of other high-value products.

A high proportion of the thousands of textile workers who joined the exodus from Flanders and Brabant in 1584–5 settled in Leiden and Haarlem, though several other towns, such as Delft, Gouda, and Middelburg, where much smaller numbers of refugee artisans settled, also acquired new textile skills at this time.[66] By the early 1580s almost all the Dutch inland towns were in a state of deepening decay. Then, in the mid-1580s, the picture was instantly transformed.[67] Leiden and Haarlem in particular grew with tremendous speed over the next few years. Leiden's population rising from 12,016 in 1581 to 26,197 by 1600.[68] Output of *says* was already up to 34,000 cloths by 1585 and rose steadily thereafter through the late 1580s and 1590s.[69] However Leiden's second most important product in the early period, fustians, modelled on the fustians of Bruges, grew much more slowly, output by 1587 amounting to only 2,000 pieces.[70] Meanwhile at Haarlem groups

---

[65] Van Dillen, *Het oudste aandeelhoudersregister*, 210–11.
[66] Gezelschap, 'Lakennijverheid', 136–7, 147.
[67] Eggen, *Invloed*, 178–81.
[68] Van Maanen, 'Vermogensopbouw', 11, 24–7.
[69] Posthumus, *Geschiedenis*, i. 128–9.
[70] Ibid.

of Flemish linen-bleachers, attracted by the qualities of the water along the coastal dunes to the west of the town, began to settle in the suburbs of Brederode and Overveen, and started to bleach linen to the highest standard of whiteness then known in Europe.[71] This was to prove a crucially important development for the Dutch entrepôt. For, in an age which lacked artificial fibres, linen was a fundamental item in international trade, being especially in demand in southern European and colonial markets.

The late 1580s were a time of political gloom and economic recession for the infant republic, but also of fundamental restructuring which furnished the Dutch entrepôt with the potential to play an altogether more broadly based and dominant role in overseas commerce than it had in the past. But there was still one essential factor lacking. Economic assets on their own were not enough. Despite its temporary gains, north-western Germany was basically unsuited to function as the hub of Europe's rich trades owing to its political fragmentation. In a world of relentless economic rivalry stamped by an increasingly mercantilist attitude, there was little likelihood that Germany, the United Provinces, or any other place could secure and consolidate a position of world-trade hegemony without the protection and active support of a powerful state.

But on this score too by the end of the 1580s there were signs of major new potential. After the defeat of the Armada, in 1588, it began to look as if the infant republic might, after all, survive its life and death struggle with Spain. At all events Dutch naval strength was increasing. The Dutch blockade of the Flemish coast was becoming tighter. With the failure of Spanish arms to clear the Dutch from the Scheldt estuary, it was beginning to look as if the Dutch stranglehold on Antwerp was becoming an enduring fact. Moreover, the Dutch state was beginning to deploy its naval power further afield. Earlier, in the years 1569–76, much of the carrying traffic which the Dutch lost had been diverted to Emden. During the period of Leicester's trade ban of 1586–7, however, while there was some diversion of traffic to England, Scotland, and Calais, the States General at The Hague prevented any serious seepage to Emden by the simple expedient of sending warships to

[71] GA Haarlem MS E11/2178, 'Rekest van de bleker Pieter van Halle', fo. 2; Regtdoorzee Greup-Roldanus, *Geschiedenis*, 24–7.

block the Ems estuary.[72] By the end of the 1580s it was beginning to look as if the Dutch Republic might be capable of developing into a state geared to intervene systematically and effectively to protect and advance Dutch trade, shipping, and industry.

[72] Bang, *Tabeller*, i. 106–4; Hagedorn; *Ostfrieslands Handel und Schiffahrt*, 171–6.

3
The Breakthrough to World Primacy, 1590–1609

Is it helpful to draw a clear dividing line at 1590? Is there an important sense in which anything so complex as the world-trade hegemony of a particular entrepôt can be said to have commenced in a single year? In fact there is. The year 1590 was a decisive turning-point for the hitherto floundering United Provinces. After two decades of implacable, often seemingly hopeless struggle against tremendous odds, the Republic emerged from the gloom of its desperate political, military, and economic predicament of the late 1580s almost overnight. The deadening pressure of the 1580s suddenly lifted with Philip II's decision of 1590 to switch his priorities, go over to the defensive in the Netherlands, and intervene in the civil war in progress in France. By 1590 the Spanish monarch had come to fear the consequences of France becoming united under the Huguenot Henri of Navarre more than he dreaded the implications of halting Spain's creeping reconquest of the North Netherlands. In 1590 the famed Spanish army of Flanders, under its great commander, Farnese, marched into France leaving only skeleton forces to face the Dutch. The infant Dutch state was granted life, prospects, and the strategic initiative on a plate. Within a matter of months the Dutch leadership, Johan van Oldenbarnevelt, Advocate of the States of Holland, and the Stadholder, Prince Maurice, had begun to grasp the extent of their good fortune and the vast implications of Philip II's decision to concentrate against France. In the United Provinces preparations began for a general offensive.

At the same time, Philip II, dissatisfied with his attempts to form close maritime and commercial links with the Hansa towns, and urgently requiring Baltic grain and naval stores not least for his war fleets and the trans-atlantic convoys, lifted his general embargo against the Dutch whilst leaving the embargo against his other maritime enemy, England, in force. The result was a sudden

Map labels:

NORTH

SEA

ZUIDER
ZEE

HOLLAND

FRIESLAND

OVERIJSSEL

UTRECHT

ZEELAND

FLANDERS

BRABANT

LUXEMBURG

Delfzijl (1591)
Emden
Groningen (1594)
Steenwijk (1592)
Coevorden (1592)
Lingen (1597)
Deventer (1591)
Amsterdam
Zutphen (1591)
Grol (1597)
The Hague
Rhine
Geertruidenberg (1593)
Nijmegen (1591)
Grave (1602)
Breda (1590)
Bishopric of Liège
Antwerp
Bruges
Cologne
Brussels
Luxemburg

Ems
IJssel
Rhine
Maas
Lys
Schelde
Maas

Legend:

☐ Dutch territory

▨ Spanish Netherlands

▨ Regions cleared of Spanish Garrisons, 1590–1602

3.1 The clearing of the Spaniards from the Dutch inland waterways and routes to Germany, 1590–1602.

resurgence of Dutch shipping to the Iberian Peninsula (see table 2.2) and the diversion of much of England's formerly flourishing commerce with Spain and Portugal to the Dutch entrepôt.[1] It was during the early 1590s that Holland and Zeeland emerged for the first time as a general entrepôt for Iberian, Ibero-American, and Portuguese East India commodities, distributing to a wide range of markets in northern Europe. It was in the early 1590s that the bitter tension over commerce between London and the Dutch entrepôt which from this point on was to be a constant feature of Dutch world-trade primacy first began.

Having expanded their army and navy to take advantage of the opportunity, the Dutch launched their first full-scale offensive in 1591. Prince Maurice retook Deventer and Zutphen, drove the Spaniards from the Ijssel, and reopened several of the routes between Holland and Germany. With these gains and the general rapid economic growth of these years, it was possible now further to strengthen both the army and the navy. In a series of offensives in the years 1592–7, the Dutch recaptured Nijmegen and Groningen, cleared the Spaniards from the eastern borders of the Republic, won back the Ems estuary, and restored their leverage over Emden, as well as pushing the Spaniards back in the south and reopening all the Republic's river and overland routes to Germany and Italy. In seven years the United Provinces had not only been made secure and effectively doubled its territory but had emerged as a European great power in terms of its military and naval strength.

These gains, combined with the lifting of Philip II's embargo against Dutch shipping and goods in the Iberian Peninsula, and the mounting cloth and linen output of Leiden and Haarlem, made the Dutch entrepôt seem much more attractive to Europe's leading merchants as a potential base for long-distance, high-value commerce than it had in the years 1585–9. Moreover, this sudden, dramatic amelioration of prospects was further enhanced by the tightening blockade of the Flemish sea-coast. This was important for two reasons. Firstly, the blockade, together with scarcity of resources on the Spanish side, checked the growth of the Flemish privateering effort, based especially at Dunkirk;[2] during the 1590s

---

[1] Bang, *Tabeller*, i. 90–107; Rau, *Estudos sobre a história do sal português*, 155–6, 175; Gómez-Centurión Jiménez, *Felipe II*, 279–81.

[2] Pollentier, *Admiraliteit*, 67–72; Kernkamp, *Handel op den vijand*, ii. 153–6.

Dutch shipping losses to the Dunkirkers, though worrying, were kept sufficiently down to keep Dutch freight and insurance rates from rising to such an extent as to cut seriously into Dutch competitiveness in the bulk-carrying traffic and shipping generally. Secondly, it was only by maintaining a strict blockade of the Flemish sea-coast that Holland and Zeeland could profit fully from their blocking of the Scheldt estuary. Historians have long insisted on the great significance of the Dutch grip on the mouth of the Scheldt. It is important to realize, therefore, that the Dutch blocking of the Scheldt on its own could not have prevented the South Netherlands in general, and Antwerp in particular, from recovering a significant part of their former role in Europe's rich trades now that the worst of the disruption in Flanders and Brabant was over. In fact, blocking the Scheldt estuary in itself did little more than impede the movement of bulky goods such as salt and timber to and from Antwerp and, in this sphere, Antwerp had, in any case, never been able to compete with Holland and Zeeland. But the traffic in high-value commodities was not so dependent on movement by water, which meant that the Dutch grip on the Scheldt estuary was only to a very limited degree an obstacle to Antwerp's traffic in spices, sugar, textiles, Spanish American dyestuffs, and Mediterranean products. These could still be imported and exported via the Flemish seaports. Had Flanders' access to the sea remained intact, then Antwerp would certainly have captured back a good part of the traffic in high-value commodities lost since 1585 to Hamburg and Lübeck.[3] The Dutch blockade of the Flemish coast, however, rendered the seaborne trade to and from the South Netherlands increasingly difficult, risky, and inconvenient;[4] and it is this which prevented any great degree of economic recovery in the South Netherlands. Imports of Brazilian sugar to Antwerp from Lisbon, for example, stagnated at a low level from the early 1590s down to 1609, by which time it was too late to recover what had been lost.[5] The crucial point, then, is that the long-term economic subjection of the South Netherlands to the North was not the result of the closure of the Scheldt alone but of a more complex mechanism imposed by the

[3] Pohl, *Portugiesen in Antwerpen*, 154; Voeten, 'Antwerpens handel', 69–71; Voeten, 'Antwerpse reacties', 202–14.
[4] Kernkamp, *Handel op den vijand*, ii. 153–6, 212.
[5] Pohl, *Portugiesen in Antwerpen*, 154.

Dutch state: it was the blocking of the Scheldt combined with the blockade of the Flemish coast which ensured Dutch mastery of the economic life of the Low Countries for the next two centuries and this combination became effective only in the 1590s.

The sudden amelioration in the Republic's fortunes after 1590 attracted a new wave of immigration, this time including many merchants. The largest and most important group to arrive were exiles from Antwerp who had spent the intervening years since 1585 in north-western Germany. It was during the 1590s that key figures such as Balthasar Coymans, Jan van der Straeten, Hans de Schot, and the Calandrini moved from Hamburg and Stade to Amsterdam.[6] There was also a considerable influx from Bremen, Emden, Frankfurt, and Cologne.[7] But by no means all the merchants who arrived in Holland from abroad in the 1590s migrated from Germany. The disruption of Rouen's recently flourishing commerce by the civil strife in the Rouen area during the early 1590s undermined Rouen's chances of inheriting part of Antwerp's mantle and precipitated a flight of businessmen abroad, some of whom moved to the North Netherlands.[8] Also, now that Amsterdam was beginning to rival Antwerp and Hamburg as a sugar depot, some of the New Christian merchants fleeing from the Inquisition began to move to Holland from Lisbon and Oporto as well as from Antwerp and Hamburg.[9] This mixed influx of foreign entrepreneurs continued unabated after 1600. Among the notable new arrivals in the opening years of the seventeenth century were the Walloon merchant prince Samuel Godijn, from Emden, and two other key Antwerp exiles, Gaspar van Collen, who moved to Amsterdam from Venice, and Guillielmo Bartholotti, who migrated from Hamburg to Emden, then to Haarlem around 1602, and finally, in 1608, to Amsterdam.[10] Later more former exiles from Antwerp moved to Amsterdam from Hamburg, men such as Samuel Blommaert and Gabriel Marcellis, bringing with them great wealth and vast international connections.

---

[6] Van Dillen, *Het oudste aandeelhoudersregister*, 68; Kellenbenz, *Unternehmerkräfte*, 192, 222–5.
[7] Gramulla, *Handelsbeziehungen*, 251–2.
[8] Benedict, 'Rouen's Trade', 62–5.
[9] Israel, 'Economic Contribution', 506–9.
[10] Schneeloch, 'Das Kapitalengagement', 172.

THE DUTCH CONQUEST OF THE RUSSIA TRADE

With so many factors now running in favour of the Dutch entrepôt, it needed only the arrival of a corpus of élite merchants from abroad, bringing with them their capital and connections, to enable the Dutch not just massively to penetrate the rich trades but also rapidly to outstrip the three other main rivals for Antwerp's legacy—Hamburg, Rouen, and London. In the early and mid-1590s, as the Dutch entrepôt blossomed, Rouen sank back and Hamburg's recently flourishing rich trades with Spain and Portugal rapidly shrank.[11] In these years the old mould of Dutch commerce, largely confined to cheap carriage and bulky goods, was suddenly and spectacularly transformed. The first phase of Dutch world-trade primacy had begun.

One major market in which a striking change took place in just a few years was Russia. Since the Swedish occupation of Narva in 1581, which had cut Muscovy off from direct access to the Baltic, the policy of the Czars had been to channel the larger part of Russia's traffic with the west northwards out via the new White Sea port of Archangel. For more than a century, until the establishment of St Petersburg by Peter the Great at the beginning of the eighteenth century, the route along the Northern Dvina River to Cholmogory and Archangel remained Moscow's chief link with the west, though there also persisted a lively subsidiary commerce through the Swedish-controlled Baltic littoral, especially Narva. Initially, the shift of the main Russia traffic northwards worked in favour of the English Muscovy Company, which had been using the White Sea route to Russia around the top of Scandinavia since 1553. The Dutch had had a sporadic trade with Lapland before 1580 and during the 1580s began a regular commerce with Archangel.[12] But their traffic was a marginal one in bulky commodities such as salt and herring shipped in small quantities. The trade in cloth, spices, copper, and other valuable commodities remained firmly in English hands. In the years around 1590 the London Muscovy Company was at the height of its fortunes, freighting fourteen or fifteen 'tall marchaunts shippes yearlie' to northern Russia.[13]

---

[11] Kellenbenz, *Unternehmerkräfte*, 47; Benedict, 'Rouen's Trade', 62–5.
[12] Bushkovitch, *Merchants of Moscow*, 26, 43.
[13] Willan, 'Trade', 315.

The entry of the Dutch into the valuable commerce with northern Russia took place during the 1590s.[14] Their progress was so rapid that by 1600 the Dutch had replaced the English as the leading western nation trading with Muscovy, though the English still held on to some strands of the valuable traffic.[15] In 1600 thirteen Dutch ships docked at Archangel as against twelve English and in 1604 seventeen Dutch as against nine English. By 1604 70 per cent of the pepper and much of the cloth entering Muscovy from the west was being dispatched from Holland; but the English still handled the copper and some of the cloth. It was not until after 1609 that the Dutch can be said to have been overwhelmingly dominant in the Russia trade and their supremacy in this sector (as indeed in most others) was not to reach its fullest extent until the decades after 1650.[16]

From the initial entry of the newly settled élite merchants of Amsterdam in the Russia trade, to the ousting of the English from first place in the traffic took only five or six years. How is this remarkable shift to be explained? Fundamentally, it was a case of England's basic weakness at that time as a depot for the rich trades and the inherent superiority by the 1590s of the Dutch entrepôt as a link between southern and northern Europe. For, while England's Muscovy trade, like all English overseas commerce in this period, was based on the export of cloth, the Russian market required from the west not only cloth but a wide range of costly commodities, including silks, pepper, fine spices, Mediterranean fruit, sugar, paper, and then, on top of this, also small quantities of bulky and semi-bulky goods, in particular wine, herring, and salt.[17] Furthermore, like the Narva trade to Novgorod and Moscow, the Archangel traffic was a deficit trade which required appreciable quantities of Spanish silver, amounting to 20 or 30 per cent of the value of the Russian wares purchased, for the settling of balances.[18] For a time, whilst the Low Countries were engulfed in disruptive strife, it made sense for London to ship a wide range of goods imported from the continent to Archangel—

[14] Hart, *Geschrift en getal*, 301–3.

[15] Ibid.; de Buck, 'Rusland en Polen', 226–7; Bushkovitch, *Merchants of Moscow*, 45, 61; Lubimenko, 'Struggle of the Dutch', 48.

[16] Bushkovitch, *Merchants of Moscow*, 45–6.

[17] Willan, 'Trade', 309–10, 316.

[18] De Buck, 'Rusland en Polen', 213, 225; Attman, *Dutch Enterprise*, 69; Kellenbenz, 'Economic Significance', 551.

even indeed Dutch herring and refined salt. But as soon as the Dutch Republic achieved stability, cleared the routes to Germany by river, and acquired an élite of wealthy immigrant merchants with vast connections in southern and central Europe and the capital to fit out large, strongly built ships to sail to the White Sea, the English traffic was bound to collapse. By the early 1590s not only did the Dutch have better access to silver, spices, sugar, and silks than their English competitors but they were beginning to dye and finish English woollen cloth to a higher standard than could then be attained in England itself. The Dutch conquest of the Muscovy trade in the 1590s, in other words, was based not on the traditional Dutch predominance in bulk carriage but on two factors which took effect only as from 1590: a large injection of capital and mercantile expertise from Hamburg, Cologne, and other rival depots and readier access to the costly wares of Germany, Italy, Spain and Portugal. The Dutch forged a Russia trade which was based on valuable commodities from central and southern Europe and the Indies, and the dyeing of English unfinished cloth with dyestuffs from southern Europe and Spanish America, but in which bulky goods nevertheless continued to play a role. Here, too, of course, the Dutch, with their vast salt traffic and their dominance of the herring fisheries, had the advantage, and it is probable that London ceased exporting such products to Russia fairly soon after 1595. Some of the Dutch ships freighted to Archangel in the 1590s were sent first to Setúbal for salt, or to Enkhuizen for herring.

The élite immigrant merchants who forged Dutch primacy in the Russia trade in the 1590s formed small consortia, in twos and threes. The first major company trading from Amsterdam with northern Russia was that of Isaac le Maire, Dirk van Os, and Pieter van Pulle.[19] All three were immigrants from the South Netherlands. This firm alone organized at least twenty voyages to Archangel in the years 1594–1600. Still more important, however, was the consortium which began trading with Muscovy in the late 1590s headed by Marcus de Vogelaer, another Antwerp exile and one of the greatest Amsterdam merchants of the early seventeenth century.[20] Two other major consortia were that of Hans van

---

[19] GA Amsterdam NA 65, fos. 47ᵛ, 180ᵛ, freight contracts of 18 June 1594, 25 Feb. 1595; ibid. NA 71, fo. 130ᵛ, NA 79, fo. 177; Hart, *Geschrift en getal*, 301–2.
[20] Hart, *Geschrift en getal*, 301–2; GA Amsterdam NA 71, fo. 130ᵛ, NA 197, fo. 747ᵛ.

Uffelen and Herman Heesters, and a group of five or six investors headed by Pompeus Occo and Abraham Verbeeck, all of these men being recent immigrants, mostly having been exiled from Antwerp in 1585.[21]

The Muscovy trade around the top of Scandinavia was essentially a traffic in high-value goods, even though traditional Dutch bulky commodities such as salt and herring also played a part.[22] It follows that the small clique of Amsterdam merchants who captured this traffic possessed large resources and a wide experience of rich trades elsewhere. The fact that practically all of those involved in this particular instance happened to be recent immigrants originally from Antwerp is less significant in itself than the fact that they had wide-ranging southern European and colonial connections. Isaac le Maire, for example, was extremely active in commerce with Portugal, Spain, Italy, France, and the East Indies,[23] as well as with Russia, and, to a somewhat lesser extent, the same can be said for the others, especially Dirk van Os and Marcus de Vogelaer. Furthermore, these merchants were used to dispensing with local commission agents and, as far as possible, to relying on their own establishments, partners, and factors. They soon saw that to gain a firm grip over the Russia trade they needed to establish their own warehouses in Moscow.[24] For Moscow was the crossroads of Russia, the pivot linking the Caspian and Volga with the rivers of the north and the routes to Siberia. At Moscow were stockpiled the furs, leather, caviare, and other valuable goods exported from Russia to the west. Accordingly, during the 1590s there arose a sizeable Dutch merchant colony in Moscow and soon there were also satellite Dutch colonies at Vologda, the main transit depot on the route between Moscow and the White Sea, and at Yaroslavl and Cholmogory as well as at Kola.[25] The most remarkable of the 'Dutch' merchants residing in Moscow in the early seventeenth century—he was really a German—was Georg Everhard Klenck, factor of the brothers de Vogelaer. He arrived at the end of the 1590s. Years later he himself became a key Russia merchant at Amsterdam.

[21] GA Amsterdam NA 45, fo. 2^v, NA 196, fos. 195^v–96.

[22] Attman, *Swedish Aspirations*, 14; Willan, *Early History*, 186, 252–3.

[23] Van Dillen, *Het oudste aandeelhoudersregister*, 111–12.

[24] Le Maire and van Os had a resident factor at Moscow at least as early as 1594 (see GA Amsterdam NA 70, fo. 112^v).

[25] Raptschinsky, 'Uit de geschiedenis', 64, 79.

Most of the Dutch ships freighted to northern Russia sailed direct to Archangel. But, especially in the early period, some voyages included lengthy visits to Kola, Petsjenga, and other estuaries along the Lapland coast where they could procure salt salmon, hides, and whale oil. A ship chartered by de Vogelaer in February 1598, for example, was engaged to cruise for three months along the Lapland coast as well as subsequently to sail to 'St Nicholas or Archangel'.[26] All of the ships freighted to the White Sea area were under instructions, in the time-honoured manner of the rich trades, to load with a wide mix of commodities so as not to plunge the rival firms too deep in any one commodity and even out the risk. When chartering a ship to sail to Archangel in May 1595, for example, Abraham Verbeeck specified that the return cargo was to consist of 100 vats of tallow, 12,000 lb. of wax, 15 lasts of whale oil, 300 hides, and 'all available caviare'.[27] All the firms clamoured for caviare and the rivalry for the limited stocks percolating through from the Caspian was intense. Few obtained the quantities they would have liked, though Klenck seems to have had a special knack for doing so: 'thanks to the caviare trade', noted a rival years later, 'Klenck has become almost as rich as his former bosses, the brothers de Vogelaer'.[28] Most of the caviare the Dutch procured in Russia was shipped on eventually to Italy. De Vogelaer, indeed, regularly freighted ships to sail from Amsterdam to Archangel and then on direct, with caviare and Russian leather (which also sold well in Italy), to Genoa and Livorno. The Italian market continued to dominate the caviare trade throughout the seventeenth century. In 1667 an English diplomat at Florence noted that 'Italy consumes thirty-nine parts of forty of that commodity'.[29]

The upsurge of Dutch trade with the White Sea in the 1590s was widely noticed in Holland and Zeeland and greatly added to the sense of exhilaration and burgeoning opportunity which permeated the Dutch maritime zone at that time. In particular, the excitement fuelled speculation as to what lay beyond Nova Zemblaya and whether there existed a viable north-east passage to the East Indies. In 1593 Balthasar de Moucheron at Middelburg,

[26] GA Amsterdam NA 53, fo. 37ᵛ.
[27] GA Amsterdam NA 70, fo. 71ᵛ.
[28] Raptschinsky, 'Uit de geschiedenis', 66.
[29] PRO SP 98/8, Finch to Arlington, Livorno, 7 Mar. 1667.

perhaps the most daring of all the Republic's merchant princes at that time, approached the States of Zeeland and the Stadholder, Prince Maurice, with proposals for state backing for his schemes to find a shorter route to the Far East around the top of Siberia.[30] The three attempts to find a north-east passage, in the years 1594–6, proved fruitless. De Moucheron and his backers failed. But the joint involvement of the States of Holland and Zeeland, and in particular the burgomasters of Amsterdam, Middelburg, and Enkhuizen, in de Moucheron's Siberian voyages, and the large sums of public money spent on them, were an early and highly significant indication of the Dutch merchant élite's capacity to harness the resources of the Dutch state, and to commit the burgomasters of leading mercantile towns, to long-distance, high-risk enterprise of this sort.

THE BALTIC

In terms of volume of shipping, and of goods shipped, the Dutch had, by 1590, been preponderant in Baltic commerce for over a century. This, in itself rather crude, criterion has sufficed to convince most historians that Dutch hegemony in Baltic trade was complete in all essentials by the middle decades of the sixteenth century. The prevailing assumption is that Dutch Baltic commerce was performing essentially the same buttressing function for the Dutch economy as a whole after 1590 as it had before. The best-known study on Dutch Baltic commerce in the late sixteenth century briefly remarks that the Dutch shipped hardly any textiles or other valuable wares to the Baltic in this period and left it at that.[31] It has seemed quite sufficient to stress that the Dutch concentrated overwhelmingly on the transportation of bulky goods of low value and to assume that this was the basis of Dutch world-trade hegemony.

At first glance the statistics showing many hundreds of Dutch vessels sailing through the Danish Sound each year, bound, in most cases, for Danzig, Königsberg, or Riga, do look impressive. Closer scrutiny, however, reveals that Dutch enterprise in the

---

[30] Stoppelaer, *Balthasar de Moucheron*, 94–9; L'Honoré Naber, *Reizen*, p. lxiv.
[31] Christensen, *Dutch Trade to the Baltic*, 365–6.

Baltic before 1590 was, in reality, a much flimsier traffic than one would suppose from the large number of Dutch voyages involved. Many of the vessels were very small, of only thirty or forty lasts, often manned by crews smaller than those of the North Sea herring busses. Furthermore, so deficient was the Dutch entrepôt in products which sold in the Baltic down to the 1590s that some two-thirds of the Dutch vessels which sailed to the Baltic passed through the Danish Sound in ballast, without cargo. Most of the rest carried salt, a bulky commodity of low value. The only other saleable products of any significance were wine and herring. But the fact that the Dutch were not selling a wide range of commodities, or any valuable commodities, or manufactures, in the Baltic does not mean that the Baltic was not, like the rest of Europe, a rapidly expanding market for a wide range of manufactures and new wares or that the area played only a minor role in the circulation of high-value merchandise. By the late sixteenth century the land-owning nobility of Poland, Lithuania, and the Ukraine were at the height of their prosperity and absorbing large quantities of spices, manufactures, jewellery, and other luxury goods from distant parts of Europe and beyond. The simple fact is that the Dutch down to 1590 were playing hardly any role in large sectors of Baltic commerce. Textiles were distributed mainly by the English and the Hanseatics.[32] Spices, sugar, and other colonial products were, in the late 1580s, mainly distributed from Hamburg and Lübeck to Danzig, Königsberg, Riga, Reval, Narva, Viborg and Stockholm.[33] Where Dutch ships did carry some pepper it was usually for the account of Hanseatic merchants.

Because the Dutch disposed of only a modest level of purchasing power, what they shipped back to the Dutch entrepôt from the Baltic down to the 1590s consisted almost entirely of the Baltic's low-price goods, that is grain and timber purchased with modest sums of cash. The valuable commodities of the Baltic were bought up by the merchants of Lübeck, Hamburg, and London. These included yarns, leather, furs, tallow, tar, and also Swedish copper, which in this period was exported almost entirely through Lübeck.[34] Trade with Sweden, Finland, and Reval, and the

---

[32] Ibid.; Jeannin, 'Sea-borne and Overland Trade', 45, 59.
[33] Jeannin, 'Sea-borne and Overland Trade', 48; Brünner, 'Excerpt', 191–3.
[34] Klein, *De Trippen*, 328–9; Attman, *Dutch Enterprise*, 65, 68.

subsidiary Russia traffic through Narva to Novgorod, were at this time also mainly in the hands of Lübeck merchants.[35]

The failure of the Dutch to make any impact on the Baltic rich trades before 1590 means, in the first place, that during the sixteenth century the Dutch not only did not dominate, but played only a minor role, in the more northerly strands of Baltic commerce—with Reval, Narva, Viborg, and Stockholm—where grain was not a factor. Secondly, it means that the Dutch possessed little purchasing power and played no real part in exchange transactions or the financing of trade in the region. Thirdly, with the exception of timber for the Dutch shipbuilding industry, it means that the Baltic region exerted hardly any stimulating influence on Dutch manufacturing activity.

During the 1590s, however, a fundamental change came about which led to a marked strengthening of the Dutch position. The process by which the Dutch conquered most of the rich trades of the Baltic now began. During the 1590s there was little sign of any progress in textiles. The burgeoning exports of Leiden *says* and fustians, and Haarlem linens, from Holland were destined almost entirely for southern Europe. But it was precisely the rapid strides that the Dutch were now making in the southern rich trades which acted as a lever of commercial penetration in the Baltic, opening up that market to the Dutch entrepôt. In the early 1590s, for the first time, we find substantial numbers of Dutch ships arriving in the Baltic carrying highly varied cargoes of 'southern' and colonial goods, in particular pepper, sugar, figs, raisins, almonds, currants, olive oil, and fine spices.[36] These 'southern' wares were the key to what we might term the second Dutch conquest of the Baltic.

One major Baltic port for which detailed trade statistics are available for these years is what was then the great Prussian grain and timber depot of Königsberg. In the 1590s, as we see from table 3.1, the majority of the Dutch vessels arriving at Königsberg came either with cargoes of little value or (still more common) with no cargo at all. These ships returned to Holland loaded with modest quantities of grain and timber. Few of the Dutch salt ships reaching Königsberg exceeded eighty lasts.[37] The quantities of

---

[35] Attman, *Dutch Enterprise*, 68; Brünner, 'Excerpt', 191–3.

[36] *BGNO*, i. 175–275; Jeannin, 'Sea-borne and Overland Trade', 48; Brünner, 'Excerpt', 196–7.

[37] *BGNO* i. 225, 229–30.

TABLE 3.1 *Cargoes of Dutch ships arriving at Königsberg, 1593*

Cargo	Ships
No cargo	225
Salt	130
Herring	31
Herring plus spices and 'southern goods'	8
Spices, sugar, and 'southern goods'	23
Wine	5
TOTAL	422

Source: BGNO i. 175–275.

herring and wine shipped in remained relatively modest. But there was now the substantial number of thirty-one Dutch vessels arriving with most of their cargoes consisting of spices, sugar, and 'southern commodities', and it was these, as we see from the lists, which then returned to the Netherlands with the more valuable cargoes.

It is possible, from the published Sound Toll data, to identify the point at which the Dutch captured control of the Baltic pepper and spice traffic with some precision. Hamburg's supremacy in this sector lasted for about a decade until 1595. In 1591, for example, 2,587 bales of pepper and fine spices were shipped to the Baltic in Hanseatic vessels as against only 110 bales shipped from the North Netherlands.[38] The corresponding figures for the years 1593–5 were 497 to 158, 290 to 93, and 236 to 196.[39] The Hanseatics were still just ahead in 1596. But in 1597 the Dutch broke through to clear superiority. In 1598 the Dutch dispatched 320 bales of spices to the Baltic, as against 110 for Hamburg–Lübeck, and, in 1599, 363 as against 111;[40] and from this point on the Dutch lead only increased, though the Hanseatics continued to play a subsidiary role for a few years more.

The expansion and growing diversification of Dutch commerce in the Baltic after 1590 led to a growing integration of this traffic within the wider framework of Dutch trade with western and southern Europe, with which, in the past, the Dutch Baltic trade

[38] Bang, *Tabeller*, ii. 138.
[39] Ibid. 146, 150, 161.
[40] Ibid. 184, 188, 192.

had been closely linked only through salt. If, as an adviser to the Spanish crown put it in 1605, salt was the *la madre* (mother) of Dutch commerce in general,[41] salt together with a whole range of other southern and colonial goods were certainly 'the mother' of the expanded, more dynamic Dutch Baltic trade of the post-1590 era. Even so, despite the increasing Dutch involvement in the rich trades of the Baltic after 1590, the Baltic area was never to be one of the main areas of activity of the élite merchants of Holland and Zeeland. Few of the newly arrived immigrant merchants took any interest in the Baltic, and those that did, did so only in connection with their southern trade. Isaac le Maire, for instance, did sometimes freight ships to Danzig, but only because he needed grain and timber for the Lisbon market.[42] Gaspar van Collen did not normally trade with the Baltic, but in 1605-7, a time of grain shortage in Italy, he chartered a few ships to sail there with orders to load with grain and sail on direct to Venice.[43] Furthermore, even those native North Netherlanders who joined the ranks of the merchant élite of Holland and Zeeland during this opening, phase one of Dutch world-trade supremacy (1590–1609)—men such as Jan Corver, Jan Munter, Pieter Bas, and the Lutheran Lambert van Tweenhuysen—seem to have done so by entering the rich trades of western and southern Europe, just like the Antwerp *émigrés*, rather than by concentrating on the Baltic, though Corver and Tweenhuysen did charter some ships to sail to Portugal with orders to load salt and sail on direct to the Baltic.[44]

By 1609 the Dutch still had a long way to go before attaining their fullest sway over the commerce of the Baltic. They were still exporting remarkably few manufactures to the area and what they did export were often *kerseys* and other fabrics woven and finished in England. Swedish trade was still firmly in the hands of Lübeck merchants. Most of the Dutch processed goods which figured prominently in Baltic trade in the later seventeenth century, goods such as fine cloth, tobacco, and gin, had, as yet, hardly even appeared on the scene. But the process by which the Dutch were eventually to dominate nearly all sectors of Baltic trade was now, since 1590, under way.

---

[41] Brulez, 'Zoutinvoer in de Nederlanden', 185.
[42] *BGNO* ii. 287, 289, 395, 356-8, 442.
[43] Ibid. iv. 351, 365, 368, 374.
[44] *BGNO* ii. 40, 234, 405, 256, 396, 409.

THE RISE OF DUTCH MEDITERRANEAN TRADE
(THE STRAATVAART)

The commercial ascendancy of north Europeans in the Mediterranean, according to Braudel, began with the massive influx of Dutch and Hanseatic grain ships which commenced in 1590.[45] Baltic grain, in his opinion, was the key to trade supremacy in the Mediterranean at the end of the sixteenth century until the middle of the seventeenth. For Baltic grain, so Braudel argued, enabled the Dutch to obtain more Spanish silver than their rivals, and together Baltic grain and Spanish silver placed the Dutch in an impregnable position throughout the Mediterranean for more than half a century. These were the twin instruments of commercial control which in his view enabled the Dutch to outstrip the English, even though the English had established a regular seaborne trade with Italy and the Levant earlier than the Dutch, back in the 1570s.[46]

But the notion that Baltic grain played any such role in the Mediterranean is very much open to question, as is Braudel's opinion that the Dutch did outstrip the English in the 1590s. In fact, the Dutch shipped Baltic grain to Italy—neither they nor anyone else shipped grain in any quantity to the eastern Mediterranean—only at certain times, in comparatively short bursts such as the early 1590s and the years 1605–8, interspersed with longer intervals, such as the periods 1595–1601, 1614–17, and the entire 1620s, when Italian harvests were mostly adequate and consignments of grain from the Dutch entrepôt lapsed to low, even negligible levels.[47] Moreover, even when the Dutch were shipping massive quantities of grain to Italy, as in the early 1590s when as many as two to three hundred Dutch vessels sailed to Italy each year, the limited impact achieved by the Dutch in other sectors of Mediterranean commerce at this early stage suggests that the grain traffic was not after all particularly important in the struggle for trade supremacy. On the contrary, all the signs are that Dutch grain shipments had very little bearing on the age-old contest for mastery of the traffic in spices, silks, and cloth, which remained,

---

[45] Braudel and Romano, *Navires et marchandises*, 51; Braudel, *La Méditerranée*, i. 545, 567–9, 572–3.

[46] Braudel, *La Méditerranée*, i. 572–4; Braudel, *Civilisation matérielle*, iii. 174–7.

[47] Grendi, 'I Nordici', 67; Hart, 'Amsterdamer Italienfahrt', 147–9.

as in the past at the heart of international trade rivalry in the region.[48]

But, if the importance of Dutch grain shipments to Italy, which in the 1590s were, in any case, usually for the account of Genoese or Tuscan merchants, has been greatly overrated, this is not to say that the Dutch did not make major progress in the Mediterranean rich trades during the period 1590–1609. It was indeed in the years around 1590 that the Dutch first became a significant force in the Mediterranean rich trades, but essentially because of their burgeoning sales of Leiden *says* and other 'new draperies' to Italy and the Iberian Peninsula and the growing role of the Dutch entrepôt as a central reservoir for valuable commodities not produced in the Mediterranean. Dutch progress in the rich trades elsewhere fed Dutch progress in the Mediterranean. A clear early instance of this, in the second half of the 1590s, was the acquisition by the Dutch of control over the supply of Russian products, particularly leather, wax, furs, and caviare, to Italy.[49] This latter, it is worth noting, was achieved by prominent Antwerp *émigrés* such as Marcus de Vogelaer, Isaac le Maire, Dirk van Os, and Guillielmo Bartholotti, none of whom showed much interest in the Baltic. The Dutch did become a force in the Mediterranean rich trades during the 1590s, but, just as in the Baltic, it is vital not to overstate the extent of their progress during this early phase down to 1609.[50] The Dutch were only just beginning to challenge the older established trading powers of the region. Until 1599, for instance, there was no direct contact between the Dutch entrepôt and the commercial centres of the Levant. Cotton from Cyprus, Turkish mohair yarn, Ionian currants, and Near Eastern raw silk did reach Amsterdam in Dutch vessels during the 1590s, but the ships were loaded at Venice and the goods were consigned by Venetian merchants.[51] It is true that by the 1590s the Venetian Board of Trade was already deeply worried by signs that Venice's age-old grip on the traffic of the Adriatic and the Levant was being undermined by 'northerners'. But the 'northerners' who so profoundly troubled the Venetians at this time were not the Dutch but the English.[52]

[48] Israel, 'Phases of the Dutch *straatvaart*', 1, 7–8.
[49] Hart, *Geschrift en getal*, 288–91.   [50] Israel, 'Phases of the Dutch *straatvaart*', 7–8.
[51] Tenenti, *Naufrages*, 184–5, 219, 233, 275 *et seq.*
[52] ASV CSM 1st ser. 140, fos. 98–101ᵛ, res. 26 Aug. 1600, fo. 122ᵛ, res. 19 Feb. 1601; 141, fos. 44ᵛ–47, res. 22 Mar. 1603.

The first Dutch vessel to participate in the trade of the Ottoman Near East in a significant way arrived off the Syrian coast in 1595 carrying 100,000 ducats in silver with which to buy spices and silks at Aleppo. The stir this created among the resident Venetian, French, and English merchant colonies is well attested.[53] In 1600 the English envoy at Constantinople reported home that the 'Flemings merchants doe beginne to trade into these countryes which will cleane subvert ours, although it be now but little worth', an indication of the apprehension with which the English now regarded the Dutch threat but also confirmation that Dutch commercial penetration of the Levant had at this date only just begun.[54] The statistics on the trade of Aleppo, the pre-eminent depot of the Levant at this time, provided by the Portuguese traveller Pedro Teixeira show that even a few years later the Dutch role was still considerably less important than that of the English (see table 3.2).

TABLE 3.2 *Western remittances in cash and goods to Aleppo, 1604 (Venetian ducats)*

Trading nation	Value	Trading nation	Value
Venice	1,250,000	England	300,000
France	800,000	United Provinces	150,000

Source: *Relaciones de Pedro Teixeira*, 181–3.

How is the historian to account for the comparatively slow progress the Dutch achieved in Mediterranean commerce, except for the grain trade, in the period 1590–1609? Attention needs to be drawn to two major factors. Firstly, while the Dutch entrepôt was now making significant advances into the rich trades of Europe both in the south and the north, it was still at an early stage in its industrial development and produced very few manufactured goods which sold either in the Baltic or the Mediterranean. In particular, the Dutch produced no fine or medium-quality woollen cloth, the items most in demand from the west in the Ottoman Empire. It was with their woollen cloth, made from Spanish wool,

[53] Berchet (ed.), *Relazioni dei consoli veneti nella Siria*, 102–3.
[54] *BGLH* i. 169.

that the Venetians still held on to first place in the Levant trade. It was with their cheaper woollen cloth that the English were beginning to undermine Venice's trading position. The Dutch, on the other hand, possessed no textile product which sold in the Levant and were forced to effect their purchases at Aleppo and elsewhere with Spanish silver supplemented with small quantities of Venetian cloth which they bought for this purpose.[55] Another crucial gap in the Dutch armoury in this early period, as far as southern Europe was concerned, was in spices. For centuries spices had been pivotal in determining the balance of commercial power in the Mediterranean. In northern Europe the Dutch emerged as major purveyors of spices in the early 1590s, using spices procured from Lisbon. But in the Mediterranean, for the time being, it was still the Genoese, buying at Lisbon, and the Venetians, buying at Aleppo, who dominated the scene.[56]

Deficiencies in the stockpiles of the Dutch entrepôt were one major reason for the limited progress the Dutch achieved in the Mediterranean down to 1609. But there was another which is also of great significance: the impact of Spain's first sustained economic war against the Dutch. Braudel insisted that the Spanish embargoes against the Dutch were ineffective and that, in any case, mere political 'events' could not substantially influence the basic patterns and realities of European trade. But Braudel's opinions on this have been shown not only to be wrong but a serious impediment to a proper understanding of what was happening to Mediterranean commerce at this time.[57] In reality, the impact of Philip III's measures against Dutch trade from 1598 onwards was very great. If we tabulate the yearly totals of voyages by Dutch ships from Amsterdam to Spain and Portugal in the years around 1600, as recorded in the surviving freight contracts, we see (table 3.3) that the general embargo of 1598 banning Dutch ships and goods from all Iberian ports (Portugal was then under Spanish rule) had overall a devastating effect.

In 1597 Dutch voyages to Spain were already well down on some previous years since 1590 owing to the many specific arrests

[55] ASV CSM 1st ser. 143, fo. 48; Berchet (ed.), *Relazioni dei consoli veneti nella Siria*, 158–9; van Dillen, *Van rijkdom en regenten*, 76.

[56] Sella, *Commerci e industrie*, 73–4; Bicci, 'Olandesi', 52, 57, 59.

[57] Braudel, *La Méditerranée*, i. 567–73; Braudel, *Civilisation matérielle*, iii. 175; Alcalá-Zamora, *España*, 182–4; Israel, 'Phases of the Dutch *straatvaart*', 5–6, 13–16.

TABLE 3.3 *Voyages from Amsterdam to the Iberian Peninsula, 1597–1602*

Year	Total	In Hanseatic ships	To Portugal	To Castile	To Valencia and Mallorca
1597	192	1	117	65 .	10
1598	201	4	149	44	8
1599	15	8	12	1	2
1600	57	10	49	4	4
1601	62	10	52	8	2
1602	34	9	25	5	4

Source: IJzerman, 'Amsterdamsche bevrachtingscontracten'.

TABLE 3.4 *Voyages direct from the Iberian Peninsula to the Baltic, 1595–1609*

Year	Total	Dutch	Hanseatic and East Frisian	Danish and Norwegian
1595	256	194	56	5
1596	173	133	28	11
1597	90	30	53	6
1598	167	107	54	6
1599	166	12	130	20
1600	213	26	153	31
1601	171	42	103	25
1602	97	10	80	7
1603	115	28	73	14
1604	128	27	84	17
1605	101	1	80	16
1606	96	0	79	14
1607	123	0	98	24
1608	151	19	105	18
1609	131	68	50	11
1610	141	98	40	2

Source: Bang, *Tabeller*, i. 146–206.

of Dutch ships in Castilian ports that year.[58] But the subsequent collapse over the years 1598–1608 was altogether more serious. In 1597 there were still more than one hundred Dutch voyages direct

[58] Velius, *Chronyk van Hoorn*, 497; Gómez-Centurión, *Felipe II*, 326–9.

from the Iberian Peninsula to the Baltic, carrying a large part of the salt and 'southern' products which formed the bulk of Dutch exports to northern Europe. In 1599 the equivalent figure was only twelve (see table 3.4). In the years 1606–7 this direct navigation in Dutch ships between the Peninsula and the Baltic was not just paralysed but totally eliminated. The gap was filled by Hanseatic and some Danish–Norwegian and English ships.

Spanish advisers to Philip III were convinced, so crucial were Iberian and Ibero-American products to the functioning of the Dutch entrepôt by the 1590s, that if the Dutch could be cut out of Iberian trade completely all Dutch overseas commerce would be disrupted, in northern as well as southern Europe.[59] This was perhaps over optimistic even had the general embargo of 1598 been fully enforced. As it was, the embargo was not strictly enforced in Portugal[60] or the eastern realms of the Spanish monarchy, such as Valencia, though even in the cases of Portugal and Valencia over half the previous Dutch traffic was cut out (see table 3.3). In Castile, the larger part of Spain, however, the impact was overwhelming. In several years between 1599 and 1608 so few Dutch ships sailed from Amsterdam to the ports of Castile, including Bilbao, Corunna, and Seville, that they could be counted on one hand. The shock waves from such a blow, inevitably, were felt in every part of the Dutch world-trade system. In the north, Dutch merchants could limit the damage by using Hanseatic ships to import some of the salt they needed from Portugal and by increasing their shipments of French salt.[61] But the first expedient was inconvenient and costly and was used only to a small extent (table 3.3), while French salt was less suitable for preserving fish than the Portuguese salt and so could not fully replace it, particularly not for the Dutch herring industry and the Scandinavian market. Of course, the ratio of French to Portuguese salt in total Dutch salt exports to the Baltic rose sharply at the end of the 1590s owing to the sharp drop in the quantity of Iberian salt available on the Dutch entrepôt (see table 3.5). But there was not much increase in the actual quantity of French salt shipped. Overall, the Dutch, as a result of the Spanish action, lost some of their leverage over the commerce of northern Europe.

[59] Brulez, 'Zoutinvoer in de Nederlanden', 184–5.
[60] RAZ SZ 2102, 'Deductie' 24 Jan. 1622, fos. 1ᵛ–3.
[61] Snapper, *Oorlogsinvloeden*, 53; Kellenbenz, 'Spanien', 307–8.

TABLE 3.5 *Percentages of French and Portuguese salt among total Dutch salt exports to the Baltic, 1580–1646*

Dates	French	Portuguese
1580–9	30.74	39.59
1590–8	28.13	41.44
1599–1609	45.21	25.96
1610–18	45.40	40.70
1619	39.60	39.26
1621	58.67	13.89
1622	48.14	8.69
1623–27, 1629	66.61	7.15
1631, 1633, 1635–40	55.07	13.78
1641–6	54.60	23.50

Source: Collins, 'Role of Atlantic France', 505–6.

In the Mediterranean, too, the Spanish embargoes were a serious blow to Dutch enterprise. Diminished access to Spanish silver had the effect of impeding Dutch purchasing in the Ottoman Levant, where silver was, for the Dutch, the only practicable means of exchange. The embargoes also cut the Dutch out of the carrying trade between Spain and Italy, the foremost carrying traffic of the Mediterranean, which was based on the shipping of Spanish wool and salt to Genoa, Livorno, and Venice.[62] In these ways, the Spanish embargoes had a vitiating effect on Dutch commercial activity throughout the Mediterranean region, an effect aggravated by the impact of Spanish sea power which subjected Dutch shipping to a degree of risk from which neutral shipping was exempt. Nevertheless, it is possible that the generally adverse effect of the Spanish measures on Dutch seaborne trade in the Mediterranean was partly offset precisely by the diminished flow of Iberian products to the Dutch entrepôt. For, just as Philip III's general embargo forced the Dutch to look elsewhere for their salt and colonial products, so it compelled Dutch merchants to seek alternative sources of the Mediterranean fruit which was now a vital ingredient of their Baltic and Russian trade. It is noticeable at any rate that the Amsterdam élite merchants who opened up the Dutch Levant trade in the years 1600–9—Jan Corver, Jan

[62] Israel, 'Phases of the Dutch *straatvaart*', 7, 11.

Munter, Gerard Reynst, and Pieter Bas—chartered large, heavily armed ships to sail not only to Venice, Cyprus, and Syria for raw materials such as cottons, silks, and mohair but also to Zante, Crete, and other Greek islands for currants, figs, and other fruit.[63]

By 1609 the Dutch had successfully extended their seaborne commerce to all parts of the Mediterranean and were buying a wide range of commodities. Nevertheless, they were playing a smaller role in the region's rich trades than the English and it is clear that they had a long way to go before they achieved anything like a position of commercial hegemony in the area. It was only in the shipping in of Baltic grain and other northern bulky products that the Dutch were overwhelmingly dominant; but, Braudel's strictures notwithstanding, this was a marginal activity which had little influence on the real balance of commercial power.

THE GUINEA TRADE

A regular Dutch seaborne commerce with West Africa begins, like so much else connected with Dutch world-trade primacy, in the early 1590s.[64] The Guinea traffic was a capital-intensive business in which bulky products played little part. The businessmen who opened up the Dutch commerce with West Africa were élite merchants such as Balthasar de Moucheron, Jacques de Velaer, the brothers van der Meulen, and Pieter van der Haegen, another recent immigrant who had settled at Rotterdam.[65] They were men with little or no interest in the Baltic but with a vast range of commercial connections in western and southern Europe. As in the case of the Russia trade, the key figures were Antwerp *émigrés* and, again as in the Russia trade, they operated in consortia in order to pool resources and spread the risk. There was, however, also some participation, and increasingly so after 1600, by the new category of Dutch élite merchants native to Holland. From the late 1590s, for example, Gerrit and Laurens Bicker, sons of a wealthy Amsterdam brewer who had risen to the ranks of the

[63] *BGNO* iv. 57, 59, 107, 210, 266, 303.
[64] Velius, *Chronyk van Hoorn*, 493.
[65] Unger, 'Nieuwe gegevens', 195–201.

Amsterdam regent class in the 1580s, began to invest heavily in the traffic to Guinea as well as to the West and East Indies.[66]

During this early period, Dutch firms trading with West Africa did not try to engage in the slave trade.[67] Their interest was confined to the region's gold, ivory, and gum, and, especially at first, to buying sugar from the Portuguese West African plantation island of São Thomé. Initially, until 1599, whilst only three or four Dutch ships arrived each year, relations with the Portuguese remained reasonably amicable. From 1599, however, impelled by Philip III's general embargo of 1598 which barred the Dutch from obtaining African as well as all other goods in Portugal, Dutch vessels began to arrive in much greater numbers, swamping Portuguese enterprise in the area. Some two hundred Dutch ships sailed to West Africa in the decade 1599–1608, an average of twenty per year.[68] By 1600 the Dutch already dominated the scene and no longer needed the Portuguese as intermediaries. The Portuguese were left with the sugar of São Thomé, the slave trade, and a little of the gold.

The Dutch Guinea trade was based in Zeeland and at Rotterdam as well as at Amsterdam. Competition was stiff and there was heavy investment in the traffic at Delft, Dordrecht, and Flushing as well as at the three main depots. The rival consortia sent out whole fleets, such as the five ships (four from Rotterdam) dispatched in 1599 by Pieter van der Haegen and the brothers van der Meulen.[69] Before long the merchants became worried that unrestricted rivalry was cutting profits to the disadvantage of all. As a result negotiations began, with the encouragement of the States of Holland, to find some way of federating the trade and achieving collaboration in place of competition. In 1599 the eight Guinea companies in Holland agreed to form a cartel to impose order on the traffic.[70] But the programme of cartelization succeeded only partially. The Zeeland companies remained outside; and soon new companies were formed in Holland which competed with the old. A curious mixture of collusion and rivalry continued to characterize the Dutch Guinea trade down to the formation of

---

[66] Ibid.

[67] Van den Boogaart, 'Nederlandse expansie', 222.

[68] *Kroniek*, xxvii (1871), 262; Unger, 'Nieuwe gegevens', 208; Pontanus, *Historische beschrijvinghe*, 267–8.

[69] GA Amsterdam NA 83, fo. 137ᵛ.

[70] Unger, 'Nieuwe gegevens', 208.

the West-Indische Compagnie (WIC)—the Dutch West India
Company—with a monopoly of the traffic, in 1621.

THE CARIBBEAN

As in the cases of northern Russia and the Mediterranean, the
Dutch were conspicuously slower than the English to penetrate
the commerce of the New World. A regular Dutch traffic to the
Caribbean began only in the years 1593–4. However, to an even
greater extent than in the Russia trade, it took only a few years
before the Dutch displaced the English and vastly outstripped
them. Once again, a handful of élite merchant immigrants, notably
de Moucheron, at Middelburg, and van der Haegen, at Rotterdam, led the way, and, as with the other new, long-distance trades,
the States of Holland and Zeeland were eager to encourage their
efforts.[71] In 1596 de Moucheron sent two ships to the Caribbean,
in collaboration with Burgomaster Adriaen Hendriks ten Haeff of
Middelburg, one of the very few native Zeelanders to join the
ranks of the country's élite merchants.

By 1596 several consortia were active, sending ships to cruise
along the Venezuela coast and among the islands. A favourite
haunt of the Dutch in this early period was the coast of north-west
Española. At Española, and probably elsewhere, the Dutch forged
links with Portuguese New Christians (i.e. descendants of Jews),
an appreciable number of whom migrated to Spanish America in
the late sixteenth century and who specialized in devising new
methods of trade, circumventing the official Spanish monopoly
traffic, via Seville.[72]

During the years 1593–7 there was a slow but perceptible
increase in Dutch activity in the Caribbean. But, as with the
Dutch Guinea trade, Dutch Caribbean commerce involved only a
handful of ships each year until after the imposing of the Spanish
general embargo of the autumn of 1598.[73] It was this, or rather
the chronic shortage of good salt and Ibero-American products in
the Dutch entrepôt which resulted from the Spanish measures,

---

[71] *Notulen Zeeland* (1595), 53, res. Mar. 1959; Netscher, *Geschiedenis*, 32; Unger, *Oudste reizen van de Zeeuwen*, p. xxv.
[72] Sluiter, 'Dutch–Spanish Rivalry', 173; Israel, *European Jewry*, 59.
[73] Pontanus, *Historische Beschryvinghe*, 181; Velius, *Chronyk van Hoorn*, 506.

which was the decisive factor behind the massive escalation of Dutch activity in tropical America at the end of the 1590s. The seventeenth-century chronicler, Velius, tells us that Spanish inter-ference had already prompted the salt merchants of Hoorn to look for new sources of high-grade salt outside the Iberian Peninsula before 1598.[74] A dozen ships from Hoorn sailed to fetch salt from the Cape Verde Islands, off West Africa, as early as 1596. But it was not until the year 1599 that the first Dutch salt-fleet sailed to the Caribbean for salt. The next year a larger fleet of twenty-five vessels was sent out to the salt-lagune of Punta de Araya, on the coast of Venezuela.[75] Altogether, in the six and a half years from the summer of 1599 until December 1605 a total of 768 Dutch vessels sailed to the coast of Venezuela.[76] Some 10 per cent of these were sent crammed with goods, for the account of élite merchants, to trade off Maracaibo, Río de la Hacha, and Caracas; the rest, sent by modest salt merchants, especially those of Hoorn, came empty in order to load salt.

But, while Venezuela remained the chief focus of activity during this initial phase of expansion, four subsidiary focuses of activity were of considerable and growing significance. These were, firstly, the main Spanish Caribbean islands—Española, Cuba, and Puerto Rico; secondly, the Guyana coast from Wiapoco to the Orinoco, a steamy, inhospitable region where there were no resid-ent Spaniards or Portuguese but where the Indians were friendly and keen to trade; thirdly, further south, the still more torrid stretches around the Amazon estuary where Portuguese rule was still purely nominal; and, finally, still further south, the sparsely populated northern fringe of the Portuguese sugar plantations of Brazil, the zone around Paraíba and Ceará which was sufficiently isolated from the main centres of Portuguese authority for Dutch interlopers to be able to procure some sugar. Dutch commercial strategy in tropical America during Phase One was, to a great extent, shaped by the overriding need to keep clear of the focuses of Iberian power. For not only was it out of the question to conduct any regular trade in districts firmly controlled by the Iberians but to attempt to do so was extremely dangerous. Dutch seamen

---

[74] Velius, *Chronyk van Hoorn*, 495.
[75] Ibid. 505.
[76] Sluiter, 'Dutch–Spanish Rivalry', 178.

caught by the Spaniards in the New World could expect little mercy. An appreciable number were executed on the spot.

The Dutch frequented the Caribbean to trade and to fetch salt. But the merchants of Middelburg, Amsterdam, and Rotterdam who handled the trade quickly came to appreciate that the short-term visitor who has crossed the ocean in a ship which is also his shop, and who lacks local bases, is at a disadvantage when it comes to doing business. Lacking a depot where he can stockpile his merchandise, such a trader can neither bide his time nor play his potential customers off against each other. Thus the need to establish permanent trading bases, and forts to defend them, was felt from the outset. A sizeable fort, Fort ter Hooge, built in 1596 on a small island at the mouth of the River Essequebo, in Guyana, was destroyed by a Spanish expedition a few months later. But other, mostly Zeelandian forts soon appeared both along the Guyana coast and around the mouth of the Amazon, an area much frequented by the Dutch during these years. Eager to place their commerce with the Caribbean and northernmost fringe of Brazil on a firm footing, the merchants petitioned the States of Holland, and Zeeland, not just for exemption from customs duties, which was regularly conceded for such hazardous enterprises, but also for help in the form of canon, munitions, building supplies, and even, in some instances, the loan of soldiers.[77]

The salt traffic was bulk trade dominated in particular by the town of Hoorn. But otherwise Caribbean commerce was one of the rich trades. Commerce, as distinct from digging salt, may have occupied only 10–20 per cent of the Dutch shipping which sailed to the Caribbean area in the period down to 1609, but it accounted for a much higher proportion of the investment in, and profits from, Dutch enterprise in the region. Once again, the traffic was opened up by small consortia or major merchants unconnected with bulk trade. De Moucheron joined forces with Burgomaster ten Haeff to form one grouping in Zeeland. Another was formed by the Flushing merchants Abraham and Jan van Pere, Pieter van Rhee, Jan de Moor, and Adriaen and Cornelis Lampsins, refugees from Ostend who had made a fortune out of privateering.[78] At Amsterdam, Gerrit Jacob Witsen, a regent and former Baltic trader, and Jan Commelin headed a group which formed the

---

[77] *Notulen Zeeland* (1597), 350, res. 22 Oct. 1597; ibid. (1599), 349, res. 20 Nov. 1599.
[78] Goslinga, *Dutch in the Caribbean* (1971), 33.

Guyana and Wiapoco Company and sent out a series of factors to reside on the Guyana coast.[79] This company stockpiled axes, knives, and also coral beads obtained from the western Mediterranean at its Guyana trading posts to sell to the Indians, in particular for tobacco.[80] The Indians also supplied the company's employees with food in return for western goods.

One of the main firms trading with Española, Cuba, and Puerto Rico was that of Balthasar and Gaspar Coymans, a name which was later to resound through the length and breadth of the hispanic world. Balthasar's father, Hieronymus Coymans, had been a prosperous merchant at Antwerp down to 1585, at which time the family had moved to Hamburg. In 1592 the family had transferred its operations to Amsterdam but also developed close links with Haarlem, where the house of Coymans ranked high among the early backers of the city's linen industry.[81] Buying up Haarlem linens for export to the Iberian Peninsula, Italy, and the Caribbean was, and was to remain, the Coymans's speciality. Balthasar Coymans (1555–1634) was a pre-eminent and in many ways archetypal example of Amsterdam's new merchant élite. He deployed a large capital, had close links with the textile industry, and traded with numerous countries; but he had no interest in the Baltic. He was also, in a social sense, an outsider, being neither a member of the Holland regent class nor part of the traditional stratum of Holland traders and shippers dealing with bulky commodities.

According to a Dutch statement of 1608, the 'hide trade' to Española, Cuba, and Puerto Rico was, by that date, employing around twenty Dutch ships of 100 lasts per year.[82] These ships carried linen, woollens, metal goods, paper, and wine.[83] They anchored for weeks in small groups in remote bays well away from the Spanish garrisons at Havana, Santo Domingo, and San Juan. In January 1605 there were at least seven Dutch ships anchored together in the Bay of Gonaïves in north-west Española, which was perhaps the most favoured haunt,[84] although many others

---

[79] GA Amsterdam NA 102, fos. 4, 13.

[80] GA Amsterdam NA 195, fo. 497.

[81] GA Haarlem *vroed.* xxi, fo. 201ᵛ.

[82] Sluiter, 'Dutch–Spanish Rivalry', 184.

[83] Coymans's exports to the Caribbean islands certainly consisted chiefly of linen (GA Amsterdam NA 57, fo. 516ᵛ, NA 195, fo. 214ᵛ).

[84] Sluiter, 'Dutch–Spanish Rivalry', 184.

were used. Along the south coast of Cuba, to the west of Cabo de Cruz, there were half a dozen bays which were regularly visited by Dutch ships during these years.[85] Besides hides, the Dutch visiting the islands procured pearls, bullion, and some tobacco. Most of the tobacco the Dutch obtained, however, came from Venezuela or the Guyanas. Tobacco smoking was not yet a widespread habit in Europe; but in the United Provinces it was beginning to catch on. At this early stage 'Cracostabak' (i.e. Caracas tobacco) was the variety most frequently in evidence on the Dutch market.

The massive influx of Dutch shipping to the Caribbean area in the aftermath of 1598 inevitably provoked a powerful reaction from Spain.[86] During the opening years of the new century the royal councils at Madrid became increasingly concerned at the scale of Dutch activity in the Caribbean, Amazonia, and off Brazil, and especially the Dutch frequenting of the coasts of Española and Venezuela. In 1603 Philip III of Spain decreed the complete depopulation of the cattle-ranching zone of north-western Española in the hope of choking off the thriving traffic with the Dutch. Eventually, 150 soldiers were dispatched from Puerto Rico to the area, sparking off a short revolt. The soldiers burnt the ranches and scattered the cattle, driving away the Spanish settlers. The crown also took action in Venezuela. In September 1605 eighteen galleons sent from Spain attacked the Dutch ships anchored at Punta de Araya and other places along the coast, seizing a dozen vessels and scattering the rest. A large number of Dutch seamen were summarily executed. Then, in 1606, the authorities enforced a ten-year ban on the growing of tobacco in Venezuela. The signs are that Dutch activity in the area during the last few years before the signing of the Twelve Years' Truce, in 1609, was drastically cut back.[87]

[85] GA Amsterdam NA 57, fo. 155ᵛ, 102, fo. 91.
[86] Gomes Solis, *Discursos*, 88; Sluiter, 'Dutch–Spanish Rivalry', 188–90.
[87] Sluiter, 'Dutch–Spanish Rivalry', 192–3.

THE EAST INDIES

Of all the world's rich trades massively invaded by the Dutch during the 1590s, that with the East Indies was to be the most consistently important from then on. This strand of Dutch enterprise commenced just as de Moucheron and his backers launched their attempt to discover a north-east passage to China, in 1594. It started with the setting up of the Compagnie van Verre ('long-distance' Company) at Amsterdam by a consortium of nine businessmen, most of whom, it is worth noting, were native Hollanders.[88] The most prominent figure was Reinier Pauw (1564–1636), son of an Amsterdam burgomaster who had made his fortune in the Baltic trade, but who himself combined participation in city government with a zealous interest in long-distance, capital-intensive commerce, to the Caribbean and Brazil as well as to the East Indies. Other participants were Hendrik Hudde, another regent, Pieter Hasselaer (1554–1616), who, like Pauw, was also a participant in the trade to the Caribbean, and Arent ten Grootenhuis (1570–1615). The only Antwerper among the group was that veteran of the Russia trade, Dirk van Os. The group pooled a capital of 290,000 guilders, enough at that time to buy sixty or seventy large houses in Amsterdam. Armed with political influence as well as capital, the group applied for, and obtained, not just exemption from customs on their East India traffic but a hundred canon, small arms, gunpowder, and other munitions supplied free of charge from the arsenals of the States of Holland.[89] From the outset, Dutch enterprise in southern Asia was state-backed and heavily armed. When the Zeeland merchant élite entered the field, forming two companies for the East India traffic, in 1597, one based in Vere and the other in Middelburg, the States of Zeeland readily agreed to follow Holland's example, furnishing free arms and munitions, as well as agreeing to customs exemption.[90]

Of the early Dutch expeditions to the East Indies, only one returned to the Republic before 1598—in 1597—and (at least partly because spices were still being imported from Lisbon) the

---

[88] Van Dillen, 'Nieuwe gegevens', 346–50.
[89] *Notulen Zeeland* (1597), 333, app. v; van Dillen, *Het oudste aandeelhoudersregister*, 5–6.
[90] *Notulen Zeeland* (1598), 21, res. 12 Jan. 1598.

profits were but modest.[91] The vast enhancement of profitability which fuelled the sudden proliferation of Dutch enterprise in the East Indies was a phenomenon of the years 1598–9 and was largely due to the exclusion of the Dutch from the Lisbon spice market.[92] In 1598 two more East India companies were set up, at Rotterdam, one consisting almost entirely of Brabanters, headed by Pieter van der Haegen, who was also the pre-eminent figure at Rotterdam trading with the Caribbean and Guinea. In 1599 a second Amsterdam company was set up by Isaac le Maire, called the New Brabant Company.[93] As the name implies, most of the participants in this venture were also Brabanters, though one important member, Gerard Reynst, a son of an Amsterdam soap manufacturer, who later became governor-general of the Dutch East Indies, was a Hollander whose sons became prominent in trade with Venice.[94]

By the end of 1601 no less than fourteen fleets totalling sixty-five ships had sailed from the United Provinces to the East Indies. Only six years on from the founding of the Compagnie van Verre, Dutch trade with Asia already far outstripped that of the Portuguese. The profits, especially at first, were high. Companies proliferated at Amsterdam, Rotterdam, in Zeeland, and in the North Quarter, based at Hoorn and Enkhuizen; in addition investment was drawn in, especially to the Rotterdam companies, from inland towns such as Delft and Dordrecht. But the competition between the rival companies was such that, by 1601, it seemed (not only to many merchants but also to the burgomasters of the towns) to be getting out of hand. According to contemporary Dutch reports, the competition for pepper supplies in the East Indies was so intense that the price of the pepper the Dutch purchased in Indonesia rose in the six years to 1601 by 100 per cent.[95] Meanwhile, with the accumulation of pepper and fine spices in the United Provinces, the prices being charged to the consumer inexorably fell.

The merchants convinced Oldenbarnevelt and the States of Holland that the trade would soon be ruined—and, worse, that

---

[91] Van Dillen, 'Nieuwe gegevens', 350.
[92] Pontanus, *Historische beschryvinghe*, 181, 267; van Dam, *Beschryvinge*, i. 8.
[93] Van Dillen, *Het oudste aandeelhoudersregister*, 10.
[94] Logan, *The 'Cabinet' of the Brothers Gerard and Jan Reynst*, 15, 19.
[95] *Gedenkstukken van Johan van Oldenbarnevelt*, ii. 311, iii. 27, 47.

the Portuguese would get it back—unless the state intervened to curb this ruinous rivalry and rescue the investors from their predicament.[96] But how was this to be done? Never before had a joint-stock company been created which organized investment, and balanced the interests, of different towns and regions, on the basis of a federal concept of management. Nor, clearly, could this have been attempted had the United Provinces not been a federal republic, organized to prevent the concentration of power at any one centre. As it was the setting up of the Dutch Republic's most original commercial institution, the Verenigde Oost-Indische Compagnie (VOC)—the United Dutch East India Company—in 1602, took many months of intricate negotiation.

The States General, guided by the States of Holland, began by convening a conference of directors of the various Holland and Zeeland companies on federal premises, at The Hague, in December 1601, so that they might 'together draw up a good and reasonable order and regime for the said traffic'.[97] Each company drew up its own proposals and these were eventually hammered into a single set of proposals from the side of the merchants. But, of course, it was not the merchants, but the States of Holland and Zeeland which finally determined the form of the new company. As the merchants saw it, Amsterdam, with roughly half the capital invested in the traffic, should have half the voting power, eight out of sixteen seats, on the future company's board of directors. Most of the merchants wanted the North Quarter and South Holland chambers to carry equal weight; but the North Quarter representatives argued that they should have more voting power than South Holland since the North Quarter's investments were higher (see table 3.6). But Oldenbarnevelt, whose power-base lay outside Amsterdam, and especially in South Holland, was unwilling either to accord Amsterdam fully half the influence in the running of the VOC or to accord the North Quarter more weight than South Holland. Needless to say, neither was he willing to increase Zeeland's voting power at the expense of Holland. The Advocate's solution to this conundrum was the famous board of seventeen (the Heren XVII), on which eight, or slightly under half, of the directorships were allocated to Amsterdam, four to Zeeland, and two each to the North Quarter and South Holland;

---

[96] Ibid. ii. 300, 311.
[97] Ibid. ii. 300.

TABLE 3.6 *The starting capital of the VOC, as lodged in its constituent chambers* (*guilders*)

Amsterdam	3,674,915
South Holland	
Delft	469,400
Rotterdam	173,000
West Friesland	
Hoorn	266,868
Enkhuizen	540,000
Zeeland	1,300,405
TOTAL	6,424,588

Source: Van Dillen, *Het oudste aandeelhoudersregister*, 35.

the seventeenth and last member of the board was to be nominated by Zeeland, the North Quarter, and South Holland in rotation.[98] Special arrangements were made to safeguard the interests of individual towns, such as Delft or Enkhuizen, whose citizens had exceptionally large investments in the traffic.

Oldenbarnevelt and his political colleagues not only determined the final form of the VOC; they also encouraged the merchants to assert Dutch naval and military power in the East Indies and establish fortified bases there. It was Oldenbarnevelt who chiefly insisted on the need to fortify 'two or three strong places' in Asia to be garrisoned with the help of the state and who stressed the need to base Dutch warships permanently in eastern seas.[99] As far as the States of Holland and Zeeland were concerned, the VOC was an arm of the state empowered to deploy armies and navies in Asia in the name of the States General and to conduct diplomacy under the States General's flag and seal.[1]

The finishing touches were put to the VOC's charter after a final meeting of directors of the *voorcompagnieën*, at The Hague, with Oldenbarnevelt presiding, in January 1602. Two months later the States General formally established the new Company with a monopoly of all Dutch trade east of the Cape of Good Hope. The VOC was accorded vast commercial, military and political

---

[98] Van Dillen, *Het oudste aandeelhoudersregister*, 17.
[99] *Gedenkstukken van Johan van Oldenbarnevelt*, ii. 311–13.
[1] Steensgaard, *Asian Trade Revolution*, 128–32.

powers, but was subject to supervision and periodic renewal of its charter by the States General. The charter stressed that the VOC's purpose was not just to enable all subjects of 'these United Provinces' to invest in the East India traffic, but also to attack the power, prestige, and revenues of Spain and Portugal in Asia.

Whilst there was some investment from outside Holland and Zeeland, the VOC's starting capital derived overwhelmingly from those two provinces. The Amsterdam Chamber alone accounted for over half the starting capital, the bulk being invested from within the city. At Amsterdam there were 184 individual investments of more than 5,000 guilders, or the cost of a large house, and in Zeeland 69 of above that level.[2] Altogether 785 native Hollanders and 301 immigrants from the South Netherlands placed money in the Amsterdam Chamber. Native Hollanders also surpassed the South Netherlanders in the total size of their investment, accounting for 55 per cent of the total. Foremost among the native Hollanders who were active merchants were the now well-defined native Amsterdam merchant élite headed by Reinier Pauw, who invested 30,000 guilders, Gerrit Bicker (f21,000), Jonas Witsen (f12,000), Gerard Reynst (f12,000), Jan Huydecoper (f12,000), and Pieter Hasselaer (f12,000). But, whilst the South Netherlanders living in Amsterdam, or, in some cases, elsewhere in Holland, accounted for only 38 per cent of the Amsterdam Chamber's total starting capital, it is nevertheless true that most of the really large individual investments, notably those of Isaac le Maire (f85,000), Jan van der Straeten (f57,000), Dirk van Os (f47,000), Jaspar Quingetti, one of Amsterdam's principal handlers in trade with Italy (f45,000), Marcus de Vogelaer (f18,000), Balthasar Coymans (f18,000), Gaspar Coymans (f18,000) and Jacques de Velaer (f57,000), were made by *émigrés* from Antwerp.[3]

The VOC was a unique politico-commercial institution, and one that could be imitated nowhere else in the world, because the United Provinces were the world's only federal republic in which a collectivity of town governments, committed to the advancement of trade, industry, and navigation, also wielded great military and naval power. Given that the VOC was the creation of the Dutch state, as much as of the merchants who had actually opened up the East India traffic, it was inevitable that some who invested in it, or contemplated doing so, had strong reservations about its style of management and general strategy and objectives—and the rigidity of the Company's monopoly. In the first years of the Company's expansion in Asia there was constant muttering among the investors at how much money was being spent on arms, munitions, troops, and fortifications.[4] It was alleged that profit was being sacrificed to the political objectives of the Dutch state. Discontent was particularly strong in Friesland, the Republic's third maritime province, which had been accorded no say in the setting up or running of the Company despite the fact that 700,000 guilders of Frisian money, lodged in the North Quarter and Amsterdam chambers, figured in the VOC's starting capital.[5] In 1604 a group of Frisian merchants enlisted the support of the States of Friesland for their scheme of setting up a rival Frisian East India Company. In theory Friesland, as a sovereign province under the terms of the Union of Utrecht, could do this. But, of course, in practice Friesland was blocked by Holland and Zeeland. Other Dutch merchants, dissatisfied with the VOC, proposed to Henri IV of France the setting up of a rival Franco-Dutch East India Company which would attract investment from both France and the United Provinces. Henri IV, who saw himself as the Republic's chief protector as well as principal ally, saw no reason why the Dutch, Portuguese and English should reap all the profits of the East India trade and took up the project with avid interest. The States of Holland became extremely alarmed. Oldenbarnevelt knew that if there was one power that the Republic at that time (1604–9) could not afford to antagonize, it was France. But such was the determination to keep all Dutch investment in the East India trade within the confines of the VOC that it was decided to risk an outright rejection of the king's request. Henri was told that Dutch merchants would not be permitted to participate in another East India Company, nor would any ships, naval stores, or facilities be made available to such a company.[6]

The incorporation of all Dutch enterprise in Asia within the VOC was, thus, essentially the work of the Dutch state. And, as an arm of the state, as well as a trading operation, the VOC was

---

[4] *Gedenkstukken van Johan van Oldenbarnevelt*, iii. 49.
[5] Hallema, 'Friesland en de voormalige compagnieën', 84–5.
[6] *Gedenkstukken van Johan van Oldenbarnevelt*, iii. 49–50.

to prove astoundingly successful within a short space of time. Within three years the pre-1602 'trade only' policy of the old companies had been transformed into a full-scale strategic offensive, involving dozens of warships and many hundreds of troops. In 1605 the Dutch achieved a major breakthrough in the East Indies, conquering Amboina, Tidore, and Ternate, the legendary 'Spice Islands', from the Portuguese. Fortified bases, manned by fixed garrisons, were established on the islands. The Dutch now had a near monopoly of the world's supply of nutmeg, mace, and cloves. The Dutch literally conquered their supremacy in the spice trade.

FINANCE AND BANKING

Besides being a world reservoir of commodities, the seventeenth-century Dutch entrepôt was also a general depot of financial and insurance services. For, just as tenuous, irregular communications created the conditions for a central store of commodities, so the same slowness and unpredictability of communication favoured the concentration of financial services at a single point.[7] In the sixteenth century world trade had been in the hands of several trading empires. A network of great regional exchanges where goods were stockpiled and where commodity prices were fixed and speculated in, had arisen. But by the 1590s what van der Kooy termed a 'hierarchy of exchanges' was emerging, with the Dutch entrepôt taking a presiding role. By the century's end Holland was the world's central store of commodities and, at the same time, the hub of its system of commercial finance and exchange. In the main, the latter was a consequence of the rise of the Dutch staple market. A central reservoir of goods requires a comprehensive set of mechanisms of exchange, remittance, commodity classification, insurance, and credit and, at the same time, inevitably foments speculative dealing. But there was also an element of cause. Certain innovative features of the Dutch financial system, not least its exceptionally low interest rates,[8] helped reinforce and prolong Dutch world-trade supremacy.

---

[7] Van der Kooy, *Hollands stapelmarkt*, 5–6.

[8] Child, *A New Discourse*, 3–4, 8–10; according to Child, writing in 1672, low Dutch interest rates 'hath robbed us totally of all trade not inseparably annexed to this Kingdom (England)' (ibid. 12A).

No great commercial centre can function without a bourse of some kind, a waterfront meeting-place for merchants where shipping and commodity news is gathered and circulated, deals negotiated, and financial backing secured. During the sixteenth century Venice, Genoa, Lyons, Lisbon, Seville, and Lübeck all had flourishing exchanges. The more sophisticated, closely regulated, bourse established—on ᴧ the initiative of the merchants—at Antwerp in 1485, which brought commodity dealing, money-changing, and commercial insurance together under one roof, served as the model for the later exchanges of London and Amsterdam.[9] Amsterdam was, in fact, rather late, compared with London, in acquiring a purpose-built bourse. For it was not until 1608 that the city council decided to build one, and it was not until 1611 that the building (which its architect, Hendrik de Keyser, modelled on the London Exchange, itself architecturally an imitation of the Antwerp bourse) was completed. Nevertheless, by the late 1590s Amsterdam already far outstripped London, or Antwerp, in the range of its commodity dealings and had become a world rather than a regional exchange. Furthermore, greater range and volume quickly led on to innovation in the sense of specialization. In the 1590s and the first decade of the new century there was an unprecedented proliferation of licensed brokers and brokerage services. Since 1581 Amsterdam's brokers had not been permitted to deal themselves in the wares and services for which they mediated. The necessity for specialized knowledge led the brokers' guild to admit outsiders, including Jews, where they possessed expertise others lacked. By 1612 there were three hundred licensed brokers at Amsterdam, ten of whom were Sephardi Jews specializing in Levant silks and Ibero-American colonial products, especially sugars.[10] Weekly commodity price-lists were printed at Amsterdam from the late 1580s onwards and, from 1613, were closely regulated by the sworn brokers' guild.[11]

But, despite the advent of a purpose-built exchange and of an army of licensed brokers, the old-style informal gatherings in smoke-filled taverns and, later, in the coffee-houses around the Exchange, continued to flourish. Power and influence at the Amsterdam Exchange was often exerted in back-rooms. The

[9] Denucé, 'Beurs van Antwerpen', 81–2; Verlinden, 'Amsterdam', 333.
[10] Bloom, *Economic Activities of the Jews*, 183.
[11] Posthumus, *Nederlandsche prijsgeschiedenis* i, introduction.

Amsterdam Exchange may have developed into the world's first true stock exchange but, throughout the era of Holland's primacy in world commerce, the dealing which counted often went on in informal surroundings. Joseph Penso de la Vega, whose *Confusión de Confusiones* (1688) is the world's first account of a stock exchange, describes how the dealers in VOC and WIC shares in the 1680s generally met in coffee-shops, where they could lounge interminably over their tobacco and cups of coffee and tea, contemplating trends and the latest news and doing deals.[12]

But innovation at the Amsterdam Exchange involved more than just greater specialization in commodity dealings. It was a matter also of new techniques. The traditional emphasis on grain dealings—for which a separate exchange was built in 1617—and other bulky goods encouraged the practice of buying ahead, on deposit, under a variety of terms. For, as Gerard de Malynes noted, these commodities were especially prone to sharp, short-term oscillations in price. Amsterdam merchants became skilled at dealing in grain that had not yet arrived and the 'buying of herrings before they be catched'.[13] Later the Amsterdam Exchange was to specialize in purchases of German and Spanish wools, and Italian silks, twelve, fifteen, eighteen, and even twenty-four months ahead of delivery.[14] Buying ahead, the vast and unprecedented range of commodities stockpiled, the unparalleled sophistication of Dutch methods of shared ownership of ships and cargoes, and then, from 1602, dealing in VOC shares (actions) all helped stimulate new forms of speculative trading. In this way, the Amsterdam bourse developed from a conventional commodity exchange of the established European type into something new: a world exchange which itself became an instrument of trade control.[15] The Amsterdam commodity price-lists were more detailed, exerted more influence, and appeared more regularly than any others printed in the seventeenth century. Although stocks and shares were traded sporadically, and on a small scale, in other European financial centres, notably at Hamburg and Antwerp, there was to be no real rival to Amsterdam as a world centre for speculative commodity and

---

[12] Penso de la Vega, *Confusión de confusiones*, 157.
[13] De Malynes, *Lex mercatoria*, 203–4.
[14] Savary des Bruslons, *Dictionnaire universel*, ii. 1251.
[15] Ibid. i. 451: 'La Bourse d'Amsterdam est regardée par tous les négocians comme la plus considérable de toutes.'

share dealings until London emerged as an international stock exchange in the 1690s.[16]

The potential of VOC shares as a focus of speculative trading was first revealed in 1605 with the Company's breakthrough in Amboina and the Moluccas. These conquests implied new terms of trade in spices throughout the globe, and faster accumulation of profits at the Dutch entrepôt. When the news broke, shares in the Amsterdam Chamber of the VOC rose to 140 per cent of their face value.[17] By 1607 further successes in Asia, and expectation of more, had pushed the value of the shares to 158. Some believed that the rise would continue.[18]

Brokers were needed to determine quality and classification of commodities, deal in present and future stocks, handle shares, organize shipping and storage space, and arrange insurance. Dutch marine insurance had begun to develop around 1590, when the Dutch first progressed beyond the old bulk trades. The first printed forms, used in the early 1590s, expressly follow the practices of Antwerp and London. Then, in 1598, the Amsterdam city council set up a civic chamber of insurance to increase confidence all round by ensuring the proper registration and processing of policies and facilitating the resolution of disputes. On completion of the new bourse, several prime locations were reserved for insurers.

One of the brokers' major functions was to help arrange financial backing for trade. Until the setting up of the Amsterdam Loan Bank in 1614, commercial credit in Holland was generally furnished by wealthy merchants. Even after that date loans carrying high risk and high interest tended to be confined to the private sphere. One of the pillars of the Dutch system of trade credit were bottomry loans.[19] These were loans for financing voyages to distant destinations which carried high rates of interest to be paid on the return of the vessel on which the loan was raised, or, if the ship were lost, not at all. Bottomry loans were a form of credit combined with insurance which enabled businessmen of modest means (in the years 1599–1608 often part-owners of salt-carrying ships) to risk their vessels and cargoes in remote parts of the globe. The

[16] Barbour, *Capitalism in Amsterdam*, 76–9.
[17] Van Dillen, 'Isaac le Maire', 15.
[18] *Kroniek*, xxviii (1872), 236.
[19] Penso de la Vega, *Confusión de confusiones*, 93; Hart, 'Rederij', 122–3.

riskier the voyage, and the more remote the destination, the higher the interest. The going rate for bottomry loans on voyages to northern Russia in the 1590s oscillated at around 15 per cent.[20] The interest on loans for voyages to West Africa and the Caribbean was usually at least 30 per cent and often higher. A loan arranged in 1598 on a vessel owned in twelfth and sixteenth shares was to be repaid with interest at 44 per cent.[21] But, as the loan was only repaid with the accruing interest if the vessel returned safely, the owners could still manage a good profit. Various members of Amsterdam's newly formed merchant élite, including Gerard Reynst and Jan Poppen (*c.* 1545–1616, one of the richest men in the city, an immigrant from Holstein, who invested 30,000 guilders in the VOC in 1602), risked considerable sums, often more than 1,000 guilders per time, in the shape of bottomry loans on voyages to Africa and the Caribbean.

One of Holland's most important financial institutions was the Amsterdam Wisselbank (Exchange Bank), founded, on the model of the Giro Bank in Venice, in 1609. The Wisselbank was the first major public bank in Europe outside Italy and, for over a century, much the greatest. For most of the seventeenth century, until the founding of the Bank of England, the only northern counterpart to the Wisselbank was the Hamburg Bank founded in 1619. The setting up of the Wisselbank was preceded by several years of active discussion and planning on the part of the Amsterdam city fathers and mintmasters.[22] The principal reason for setting it up was the growing anxiety over the rapid and uncontrolled escalation in money-changing and settling of bills of exchange. By 1606 the vast scale and complexity of the money-changing business in Amsterdam was creating a chaotic situation with wide discrepancies in rates of exchange and excessive discounting.[23] Thus the Bank's purpose was not to provide credit but to prevent unscrupulous money-changers 'ruling the course of exchanges for all places' and to provide fast, efficient, and reliable exchange facilities. It developed into a vast pool of controlled capital organized for the speedy remission, transfer, and settlement of bills. The Bank's most vital feature was that it was a civic and not a privately

[20] Hart, *Geschrift en getal*, 299–300.
[21] GA Amsterdam NA 80, fos. 134ᵛ–5.
[22] *Bronnen tot de geschiedenis der Wisselbanken*, i. 6–8.
[23] Ibid. i. 7, 13–14.

owned or managed institution. Its accounts and deposits, in contrast to those of modern financial institutions, remained secret: confidence in its operations rested entirely on the fact that it was controlled by the burgomasters, guaranteed by the city, and protected by the power of the Dutch state to ensure the stability of the civic regime. Estimates of the bank's holdings varied wildly, but all were agreed that it represented the most prodigious accretion of treasure on the face of this earth. One informed estimate of the early eighteenth century put the Bank's holdings in specie at around 300 million guilders.[24]

The Bank's statutes guaranteed immediate access, rapid changing, prompt settlement of bills, and also low bank charges. All this was provided by the municipality as a service to the business community. The Bank's doors had to be open to the public for at least six hours each working day. The institution was managed by three governors, two of whom had to be members of the city council, the *vroedschap*. Since money lodged in the Wisselbank was safer and more readily transferred or changed than other money and paid out only in good coin, Amsterdam 'bank money' soon acquired a premium or *agio* over cash which, after 1650, rose to around 5 per cent.[25] This indeed was eloquent testimony to the value of the Bank's services to the Dutch trading system.

Amsterdam's financial institutions undeniably helped bolster Dutch world-trade primacy in several crucial respects. If the Dutch entrepôt as a whole furnished goods more efficiently and cheaply than any rival, Amsterdam provided an unrivalled array of mechanisms for settling bills and balances, financing trade, and investing in commodities expected or already stockpiled. But no feature of the Dutch entrepôt in the seventeenth century was more universally admired and envied abroad than the perenially low interest rates at which one could borrow. If Dutch merchants constantly outdid their rivals in the buying up of stocks of key commodities around Europe, this was due in no small measure to the fact that they could borrow in Holland at 2.5, 3, or 4 per cent whereas in England rates were double and in France or Germany higher still.[26] As early as the 1590s we encounter Dutch factors in

---

[24] Savary des Bruslons, *Dictionnaire universel*, i. 236.

[25] *Bronnen tot de geschiedenis der Wisselbanken*, i. 166.

[26] Child, *A New Discourse*, B3–4, 8–10; Schröder, *Schatz und Rent-Kammer*, 228; *Correspondance administrative*, iii. 410.

Germany buying up Silesian linens and Pomeranian wool ahead and on advantageous terms.[27] The buying up of French wines and brandy and, after 1648, of Spanish wool, *en bloc*, well in advance, and at a hefty discount, was to be one of the most characteristic features of the Dutch trading system.[28] The merchant élite of Holland and Zeeland had at their disposal financial institutions and resources, and a degree of specialization in financial, brokerage, and insurance techniques, such as none of their rivals possessed and which together afforded an immense and continuous advantage in the international arena.

[27] Baasch, *Holländische Wirtschaftsgeschichte*, 313; Zimmermann, 'Schlesische Garn- und Leinenhandel', 204.
[28] De La Court, *Interest von Holland*, 13.

4

The Twelve Years' Truce, 1609–1621

IT may appear strange, even bizarre, at first glance to date a fundamental reshaping of the structure of the Dutch trading system, the onset of Phase Two (which corresponds to the duration of the Twelve Years' Truce), to a single year, even such a politically resonant year as that in which the Truce was signed, but there is an abundance of hard evidence to justify our doing so. In 1609 the Spanish embargoes against the Republic were lifted. Dutch shipping costs for all European destinations fell dramatically. The Dutch resumed their former massive traffic with the Iberian Peninsula. The obstacles to a flourishing Dutch commerce with the Mediterranean were removed.

The spectacular advances achieved by the Dutch since 1590 had inevitably generated a vast and growing tension with other trading powers in Europe, the Caribbean, the East Indies, and West Africa. During Phase One the Dutch trading system had expanded in the face of mounting resentment. In particular the dual monarchy of Spain and Portugal (joined during the sixty years 1580–1640), England, and the Hansa towns had suffered grave setbacks at Dutch hands. However, at that stage only the Spanish Monarchy wielded the economic, administrative, and colonial power to try to curtail the process of Dutch maritime expansion; and if Spain met with only limited success, she nevertheless exerted a very heavy pressure over a long span of years. Then, quite suddenly, the pressure was lifted. During Phase Two the resistance to the process of Dutch commercial expansion was cut right back. Dutch penetration of overseas markets therefore accelerated. Thus, on reflection, we see that it is not after all surprising, in an age rife with mercantilist calculation, when access to markets and security of sea lanes were highly susceptible to manipulation and disruption by Europe's more powerful regimes, that a key political watershed, such as the onset of the Twelve

Years' Truce, should have had immense implications for the whole of the world economy.

The political leaders of Spain and the United Provinces, locked in difficult negotiations through the years 1606–9, undoubtedly expected that a halt to the age-old Dutch–Spanish war would, at that stage, profoundly affect both European trade and Europe's relations with the Indies 'east and west'.[1] Indeed, the main reason why Philip III and his favourite, the duke of Lerma, decided to enter into negotiations with their 'rebels' was their need to find some immediate expedient to check the Dutch breakthrough, since 1605, in the Indies. Aghast at the scale of Dutch activity in the Caribbean since 1599, in West Africa, and the East Indies, and lacking the naval power to reverse the tide of Dutch maritime expansion, Spanish ministers had come to recognize by 1606 that they faced an awesome dilemma. The Hollanders and Zeelanders could not be allowed to go on seizing Iberian possessions, shipping, and trade in the Indies indefinitely. But neither, experience showed, could they be removed by force or by economic pressure. The only solution, it appeared to the duke of Lerma, was to concede the Dutch the independence they had been demanding for so long in exchange for their evacuating all the places in Asia and the Americas which they had occupied and agreeing to cease their navigation to the Indies. What Lerma offered Olden-barnevelt in 1606–7 was *de jure* recognition by Spain, and therefore also by the rest of the community of states, of Dutch 'freedom' from the Spanish crown, complete independence, provided the Dutch dissolved the VOC, aborted the plans which were now current in the States of Holland and Zeeland for the setting up of a Dutch West India Company, and accepted the exclusive dominion of Spain and Portugal in all the Indies, east and west. In terms of commerce, the Dutch would give up all they had gained since 1599 outside of Europe in return for Spain removing all the obstacles to Dutch hegemony over European trade.[2]

From the moment Oldenbarnevelt and his colleagues began to consult more widely among the regents and nobles of the provinces, a deep split opened up both among the ruling élites and the Dutch business community. There was a good deal of support for

[1] Israel, *Dutch Republic and the Hispanic World*, 44–50, 53–9.
[2] Ibid.; Rodríguez Villa, *Ambrosio Spínola*, 156–7; Gómez-Centurión Jiménez, *Felipe II*, 370–1.

Oldenbarnevelt's view that it was time to seek a settlement with Spain. He and his supporters acknowledged that any settlement would involve the Republic's merchants giving up at least some of their traffic with the Indies.[3] But they argued that it was well worth making concessions outside Europe in return for peace and *de jure* recognition as well as the lifting of the Spanish embargoes. As against this, there was a substantial and highly vocal party of regents and élite merchants who opposed negotiations with Spain in present circumstances. Both sides to the argument accepted that the Spanish embargoes in force since November 1598 had seriously hampered Dutch commerce in Europe.[4] Since the Anglo-Spanish peace treaty of 1604—a key section of which was devoted to England's agreeing to co-operate with the Spanish embargoes against the Dutch, and accept the confiscation of all English cargoes sent to Spain and Portugal not authentically certified as being non-Dutch[5]—the English as well as the Hanseatics had been prospering hugely at Dutch expense. Circumstances were now precisely the reverse of those which had given the Dutch the impetus for their initial breakthrough to world-trade primacy: it was now the Dutch who were embargoed, and encumbered by Spanish raiding activity and high insurance charges, and the English who were unobstructed in their traffic to the Peninsula, Italy, and the Levant. It was obvious that the Dutch could not win a leading role in the trade of any part of southern Europe unless and until the Spanish embargoes were lifted.[6] Yet many powerful figures in Dutch politics insisted that the concessions demanded by Spain for peace, or a long truce, were too high a price to pay.

Not all the opposition to Oldenbarnevelt's stance in the Dutch–Spanish negotiations of 1606–9 was motivated by economic considerations. But a good deal of it was. The Amsterdam city council, dominated by a hard-line faction headed by one of the most prominent of the regent-merchants involved in long-distance trade, Renier Pauw, emerged as the most obdurate adversary of

[3] *Gedenkstukken van Johan van Oldenbarnevelt*, iii. 311.
[4] Ibid. iii. 69, 145, 311; *Kroniek*, xxvii (1871), 270; Kaper, *Pamfletten over oorlog of vrede*, 16–19.
[5] Abreu y Bertodano, *Colección*, reynado de Phelipe III, i. 256–8.
[6] Israel, *Dutch Republic and the Hispanic World*, 20–1, 44–7.

the proposals for a settlement.[7] Amsterdam was determined to protect the interests of the now burgeoning Dutch East India traffic, to maintain the now flourishing Dutch Guinea traffic, and to press on with the scheme to set up a Dutch West India Company.[8] This seemed all the more urgent in that Dutch enterprise in the Caribbean had now lost much of the impetus it had achieved in the years 1599–1606 as a result of Spanish counterpressure. Without pooling the resources of the small private companies which had opened up the Dutch Caribbean trade and building up a powerful armed force with the aid of the States General, there was clearly little prospect of restoring the traffic to its previously flourishing condition.

Outside Amsterdam, the most obstinate resistance to a settlement with Spain emanated from Zeeland. The Zeelanders too were now heavily committed to the new long-distance trades to the East Indies, Guinea, and the Caribbean. Middelburg and especially Flushing also had the largest stake in the privateering activity which had been carried on successfully against Portuguese shipping in the southern Atlantic since the 1590s. But what chiefly motivated the Zeelanders' vociferous opposition was their anxiety for the future of their transit trade with the Spanish Netherlands. For even if the Dutch managed to reach an agreement with Spain in which they avoided lifting their ban on the passage of maritime traffic through the Scheldt estuary, there was bound to be a diversion of traffic through the Flemish seaports.[9] The argument over the pros and cons of a full peace, or a truce, with Spain continued ceaselessly in the years 1607–9 in the provincial assemblies, municipal councils, inns and taverns, and a host of political pamphlets. The debate pervaded Dutch national life. The most forceful Dutch economic writer of the period, Willem Usselinx, devoted much energy trying to persuade the public of what, according to him, would be the disastrous consequences of halting the conflict with Spain.[10] First and foremost, he trumpeted the merits of the projected West India Company. He was convinced

---

[7] GA Amsterdam *vroed.* ix. 264, 300–1, 311, res. 22 Mar., 29 and 30 Oct., and 22 Nov. 1607; GA Delft *vroed.* 23 Aug. and 9 Dec, 1608; *Kroniek,* xxviii (1872), 252–61.

[8] *Kroniek,* xxviii (1872), 261.

[9] Israel, *Dutch Republic and the Hispanic World,* 41–2.

[10] Jameson, *Willem Usselinx,* 28–44.

that, in a world of despots and Popish superstition, unarmed, unprotected European trade would never suffice to ensure the economic well-being of the Republic. The Spanish embargoes of 1598, and the losses of Dutch shipping to the Dunkirkers, demonstrated for all to see that Dutch European trade would always be vulnerable to political interference. Only expansion across the oceans and in the Indies, and above all the planting of colonies, would place the country's trade and industry on a sound basis. But Usselinx was more than just a propagandist for the West India interest. His central proposition was that the rise of the Dutch entrepôt to supremacy was the fruit of a constellation of war-related circumstances, especially the Dutch blockade of the Scheldt and the Flemish seaports. Lift that blockade, he warned, and the South Netherlands, which excelled the North Netherlands in location, experience, and in the size and industriousness of its population, would revive from its present stagnation and resume its former primacy.[11] House rents, the cost of living, and wage levels, he pointed out, were all much lower in Flanders and Brabant than in Holland, so that, once the Dutch pressure was removed, Holland would stand little chance of competing successfully.[12] Nor, he admonished, should the Dutch public believe that their present Protestant sympathies would be enough to keep the textile workers who had fled from the South Netherlands in 1584–5 in Holland, once the textile industries of Flanders and Brabant revived.[13]

Hopes for a full peace proved short-lived. Oldenbarnevelt did briefly raise the spectre of Dutch withdrawal from the East as well as from the West Indies but quickly retracted on perceiving the intensity of the opposition.[14] Nevertheless, he and those who backed him did end up making some substantial concessions to Spain. The West India Company project was aborted and removed from the agenda of the States of Holland and (for a few years) of Zeeland. This step was bitterly denounced by Oldenbarnevelt's opponents and, indeed, it was no small concession, for, had the Company been launched as originally intended in 1607,

[11] Usselinx, *Grondich discours*, fos. 1–4; Usselinx, *Naerder bedenckingen*, fos. 3–4; Laspeyres, *Geschichte*, 169–70.
[12] Usselinx, *Grondich discours*, fos. 1–4.
[13] Ibid.
[14] *Reden van dat de West-Indische Compagnie*, 7.

instead of being shelved until 1621, there is every reason to suppose that it would have achieved greater success at Spanish and Portuguese expense than later was the case. Also the States General agreed that the Dutch in Africa and the VOC in Asia would, for the duration of the Truce, keep to the places they now occupied and cease their attacks on Iberian strongholds, shipping, and trade. This was much less than Lerma had originally demanded in return for Spanish recognition of the 'freedom' of the Dutch provinces. But it was enough to persuade Philip III and Lerma, albeit only after much soul-searching and years of acute financial difficulty, to agree to an interim settlement—the Twelve Years' Truce, acknowledging the United Provinces for the time being 'as if' they were a sovereign, independent state.

The international community regarded the Truce as decidedly more prestigious for the Dutch than for Spain. Yet the strong vested interests which opposed Oldenbarnevelt's policy continued to resist the Truce almost to the moment it was signed. The Zeelanders complained that as soon as the Dutch naval blockade of the Flemish seaports was lifted their transit trade to the South Netherlands would be diverted to Dunkirk, Ostend, and Nieuwpoort.[15] Amsterdam admonished that long-distance trade in general and the East India traffic in particular would suffer severe damage.[16] The directors of the various Guinea companies based at Amsterdam, Rotterdam, Delft, Dordrecht, and Middelburg pleaded that the Republic's annual gold, gum, and ivory imports were being jeopardized.[17] Similarly, the VOC directors argued that Dutch commerce with the East Indies had begun to flourish only since the year 1598, when the Spanish embargoes had been imposed, and that signing a truce with Spain would mean sacrificing key Dutch interests. No sooner would Portuguese East India carracks be safe from Dutch attack, prognosticated the Heren XVII, and Dutch traders be allowed to return to the Lisbon spice market, than the Portuguese East India trade would begin to recover.[18] In addition, complained the directors, the Company would lose its opportunity to gain control of the China silk traffic

---

[15] *Discours op den swermenden Treves*, fo. 7; Gielens, 'Onderhandelingen met Zeeland', 206–14.

[16] *Kroniek*, xxviii (1872), 252–3; 255–60.

[17] *Kroniek*, xxvii (1871), 263.

[18] Ibid. 271–2.

which was then still in Iberian hands at Macao and Manila. Winning preponderance in the China trade, they urged, the Republic would acquire the means to break Italy's age-old hold on the European silk market and would thereby divert immense profit and employment to herself. Finally, the Heren XVII pointed out that they had built a network of alliances with the potentates of Bantam, Johore, Tidore, Ternate, Borneo, Amboina, Banda, and Calicut against the Iberians, so that, were they to be compelled to cease hostilities, their prestige and entire diplomacy would be gravely compromised.

In 1609 it seemed unquestionable that the new circumstances would appreciably weaken Dutch enterprise outside Europe and the Near East. Like the directors of the companies, investors in VOC shares also reacted with great coolness to the prospect of an end to hostilities with Spain and Portugal. Since the breakthrough in the Moluccas in 1605, the value of the Company's shares had gained steadily, hovering at between 180 and 200 by 1607–8.[19] But once it became clear that the Truce with Spain would be signed, early in 1609, VOC share quotations on the Amsterdam Exchange began to slide, wiping out the gains of recent years and dipping by the summer to 132.[20] Many folk of modest means as well as big investors lost heavily. In August 1610 the VOC share price was still languishing at a dismal 153. This was the first big slide in the history of the Amsterdam share market and, like those which were to follow, it was precipitated essentially by international political circumstances. From the outset Dutch investors had a shrewd grasp of the fact that international power politics was the single most important influence on the terms and context of colonial trade.

THE BULK TRADES

The Truce was finally signed at Antwerp in April 1609. Dutch–Iberian hostilities ceased. Dutch shipping and goods returned to Spain and Portugal. The Dutch blockade of the Flemish coast was lifted. Both sides ceased hindering the commerce of the other

---

[19] Van Dillen, 'Isaac le Maire', 42–3.
[20] Ibid. 64, 81, 105; Penso de la Vega, *Confusión de confusiones,* 21–2.

except where, in Africa and the Indies, territories possessed by one side were penetrated by the other.

TABLE 4.1. *Dutch freight charges for voyages to fetch salt from Portugal, 1595–1609*

Month	Ship (lasts)	Rate (guilders/last)
July 1595	*Jonas* (80)	22.00
Aug. 1597	*De Griffoen* (100)	27.00
Aug. 1597	*De Melckmeijt* (70)	27.50
Mar. 1599	*'t Fortuijn* (40)	38.00
May 1599	(Danish vessel) (75)	45.00
June 1599	(Hamburg vessel) (25)	36.00
July 1599	*De Veldmuijs* (70)	60.00
Apr. 1600	*De Sloep* (70)	37.00
July 1601	*De Moeriaan* (50)	29.00
Oct. 1604	*'t Paradijs* (60)	29.50
May 1609	*De Boschieter* (80)	12.75

Source: GA Amsterdam card index to Notarial Archive, 'Soutvaart'.

A key element in the restructuring of the bulk trades within Europe which resulted from the signing of the Truce was the sudden drastic fall in Dutch shipping and marine insurance charges relative to those of the English—who since the signing of the Anglo-Spanish peace of 1604 had been the Republic's foremost rivals—the Hanseatics, and the Danes. Almost overnight the competitive position of Dutch shipping with respect to English Hanseatic and Danish–Norwegian shipping was fundamentally transformed (see tables 4.1, 4.2, and 4.3). The dramatic fall in Dutch freight charges which took place in 1609 proved to be 'structural' in the sense that Dutch shipping charges remained at the new, much lower levels attained in 1609 for the whole of the duration of the Truce, the period which we have termed Phase Two in the evolution of Dutch world-trade primacy. The fall was a result partly of the lifting of the embargoes and partly of the cessation of hostilities at sea. It is true that, in the period down to 1609, the Dunkirk privateers had been largely kept in check and that Dutch losses in the North Sea had been relatively light. But besides these losses there had been a continuous stream of interceptions around the coasts of Spain and Portugal and in the

TABLE 4.2. *Dutch freight charges for voyages to fetch salt from Portugal, 1610–1620*

Month	Ship (lasts)	Rate (guilders/last)
July 1610	*De Pellicaen* (114)	9.5
June 1611	*De Waterhont* (105)	9.5
Apr. 1612	*De Witte Valck* (90)	11.0
July 1613	*De Rode Leeuw*	11.0
Oct. 1616	*De Bruijnvis* (100)*	13.0
Apr. 1618	*De Swarte Raven* (150)	9.5
May 1619	*De Coninck Davidt* (105)*	10.0
Sept. 1620	*De Schuijr* (120)	9.0

* To Dunkirk.
Source: GA Amsterdam card index to Notarial Archive, 'Soutvaart'.

TABLE 4.3. *Dutch freight charges for voyages to fetch salt from Portugal and then on direct to the Baltic, 1600–1618*

Month	Ship (lasts)	Destination	Rate (guilders/last)
Jan. 1600	(Danish vessel) (50)	Danzig	49.00
May 1601	*De Witte Valck* (72)	Danzig	40.00
Mar. 1603	*'t Land van Beloften* (115)	Riga	41.00
July 1608	*De Hollandschen Tuin* (80)	Danzig	27.00
July 1608	*De Witte Windhont* (96)	Riga	33.00
July 1608	*De Waterhont* (90)	Danzig	27.00
May 1609	*De Bonte Leeuw* (150)	Riga	24.75
Aug. 1609	*De Waterhont* (90)	Danzig	19.00
Aug. 1609	*St Pieter* (120)	Danzig	18.00
July 1610	*De Pellicaen* (114)	Danzig	11.50
June 1611	*De Waterhont* (105)	Danzig	11.50
April 1612	*De Witte Valck* (90)	Riga	15.00
Aug. 1612	*'t Rode Meer* (100)	Riga	20.00
July 1616	*De lange Berck* (120)	Danzig	18.00
July 1618	*De Fortuijn* (110)	Danzig	16.00

Source: GA Amsterdam card index to Notarial Archive, 'Soutvaart'.

Mediterranean. In 1591, for instance, the Dutch lost a total of twenty-six ships to the Spaniards, mainly around the coasts of Spain and Italy.[21] In the year 1602 the West Frisian town of Hoorn

[21] Hart, 'Amsterdamer Italienfahrt', 146.

alone lost fourteen ships to the Spaniards in all theatres, including two salt-ships intercepted in the Caribbean.[22] But it seems that other factors also contributed to the general fall in Dutch shipping

TABLE 4.4. *Dutch freight charges for voyages to fetch salt from France and then on direct to the Baltic, 1598–1619*

Month	Ship (lasts)	Destination	Rate (guilders/last)
July 1598	*St Joris*	Riga	22.00
Feb. 1599	*De Witte Winthont* (65)	Riga	22.00
Mar. 1599	*De Pellicaen* (80)	Danzig	20.00
Mar. 1603	*De Leeckerkerck* (75)	Königsberg	19.25
Mar. 1603	*Jonas* (95)	Königsberg	19.00
June 1605	*De Zwarte Arent* (110)	Riga	25.50
Dec. 1607	*De Dwerspijp* (120)	Danzig	22.00
Aug. 1609	*De Metselaer* (110)	Danzig	14.00
Aug. 1609	*De Witte Leeuw* (70)	Danzig	15.00
May 1612	*De Groene Leeuw* (100)	Danzig	15.00
Apr. 1615	*De Rode Leeuw* (130)	Danzig	15.50
Mar. 1618	*De Hennepclopper* (130)	Danzig	14.25
Mar. 1619	*St Pieter* (100)	Riga	14.75
May 1619	*Jonas* (120)	Danzig	12.50

Source: GA Amsterdam card index to Notarial Archive, 'Soutvaart'.

costs as from 1609. The suspension of Zeeland privateering and the rapid run down of the Dutch navy, for instance, released large numbers of extra seamen on to the market, exerting a downward impact on seamen's wages as well as on prices for naval stores.

The combined impact of readmission to the ports of Spain and Portugal, and cheaper freightage, led to the general restructuring of the Dutch bulk trades in 1609. The fall in freight charges was less steep in the case of bulk-carrying trade not linked to the Iberian Peninsula or Spanish Italy.[23] But it was substantial, as we see from tables 4.4 and 4.5, showing the fall in the cost of shipping salt and wine from western France to northern Europe in Dutch

---

[22] Velius, *Chronyk van Hoorn*, 506.
[23] On the restructuring of Dutch trade with Naples in 1609, see Coniglio, *Viceregno di Napoli*, 104.

ships in the early seventeenth century. Once again, the decisive shift takes place specifically in 1609.

The restructuring of 1609 extended also to the Baltic. The Baltic trade had long been, and remained, the most vital and largest component of the Dutch carrying traffic. The Dutch over-whelmingly dominated this commerce both before and after 1609. But during the Twelve Years' Truce there were major changes in both the form and the extent of Dutch domination of the traffic. For the Baltic trade by no means consisted just of an exchange of commodities between the Baltic and the Netherlands. Apart from herring, the principal Dutch exports to the Baltic—salt, wine, spices, and cloth—came from south-west Europe or further afield. Furthermore, apart from the Low Countries themselves, Portugal, Spain, and Italy were the principal markets in the west for Baltic grains, for there was little or no demand for Polish rye and wheat in France or England. Spain and Portugal were also two of the major markets for timber, masts, Swedish copper, pitch, and hemp.

TABLE 4.5. *Dutch freight charges for voyages to fetch wine from Bordeaux to Amsterdam 1594–1620*

Month	Ship (lasts)	Rate (guilders/last)*
Aug. 1594	*St Pieter* (60)	29.0
May 1595	*De Blauwe Leeuw* (95)	24.0
Sept. 1595	*St Pieter* (100)	29.0
Sept. 1600	*St Pieter* (75)	24.0
Aug. 1603	*'t Fortuijn* (65)	22.0
Apr. 1605	*De Witte Winthond* (40)	22.0
July 1606	*De Pellicaen* (50)	18.0
Dec. 1607	*'t Jonge Calf* (50)	20.0
Sept. 1608	*De Rode Molen* (48)	19.3
Aug. 1609	*De Nachtegael* (90)	15.0
Aug. 1609	*De Snoeck* (60)	13.0
Sept. 1610	*De bernende kers* (50)	14.0
Sept. 1617	*'t Rode Meer* (50)	14.0
Sept. 1618	*De Vredewaten* (60)	14.0
Nov. 1619	*De Fortuijn* (75)	14.0
Oct. 1620	*De Roos* (80)	13.0

* 1 last = 2 vats of wine.
Source: GA Amsterdam card index to Notarial Archive, 'De vaart op Bordeaux'.

With the fall in Dutch freight charges, the cost of shipping Baltic grain, timber, and naval stores to the Iberian Peninsula and the Mediterranean in Dutch ships fell markedly, while the shipping costs of the Hanseatics and other rivals of the Dutch remained fixed. Thus, for example, the cost of shipping grain from Danzig to Genoa or Livorno in Dutch vessels in the years 1600–1608 ranged from 11 to 14 ducats per last.[24] During the twelve years from 1609, the level stood at between 7 and 10 ducats.[25] No wonder that Dutch merchants in the 1620s recalled that 'during the Truce we, through our skill and good management, swept all nations from the seas, took over nearly all the trade of other lands and served the whole of Europe with our ships'.[26]

By widening the gap between Dutch freightage costs and those of their rivals, the Truce boosted the proportion of Baltic trade in Dutch hands. The Danish Sound toll data show that the Dutch share of the traffic rose in the second decade of the seventeenth century to the highest peak that it was ever to reach, rising from 60 per cent to over 70 per cent of the total (see fig. 4.1).[27] Correspondingly, the shares of the Hanseatics, English, and Danes contracted.[28]

From 1609 Dutch Baltic trade grew and became more competitive. But the restructuring amounted to more than this. Dutch Baltic trade now came to be organized on a different basis. Restored access to Iberian markets, lower shipping costs, and less risk tightened the links between the Dutch Baltic traffic and Dutch commerce with southern Europe. In the years 1609–20 many more Dutch ships sailed direct from the Baltic to the Mediterranean, or vice versa, than was the case before or after the Truce.[29] Indeed it was by no means uncommon during the Truce years for Dutch ships to ply back and forth between the Baltic and the Mediterranean several times before returning to the Netherlands. During the Truce, around three hundred Dutch ships sailed each year with Baltic grain to Portugal alone.[30] Of these, the Danish

---

[24] *BGNO* iv. 60, 80, 96, 301, 465.
[25] Ibid. v. 251, 335, 348; vi. 181, 188, 292.
[26] Blok (ed.), 'Koopmansadviezen', 47.
[27] Kernkamp, 'Nederlanders op de Oostzee', 75; Christensen, *Dutch Trade to the Baltic*, graph 2; Olechnowitz, *Schiffbau*, 37.
[28] Vogel, 'Beiträge', 135; Kellenbenz, *Unternehmerkräfte*, 101–2.
[29] Bogucka, 'Amsterdam and the Baltic', 436–9.
[30] Nykerke, *Klaer-Bericht*, B.

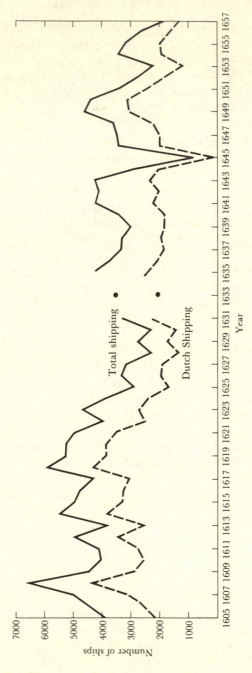

FIG. 4.1 Total shipping and Dutch shipping entering the Baltic, 1605–1657.

Sound toll data show that, something like half sailed direct, usually from Danzig or Königsberg, to Portugal. In the same way, from 1609 considerable numbers, in some years well over one hundred Dutch ships, sailed direct from Spain and Portugal to the Baltic (see table 4.6). This represents a dramatic change from the pre-1609 position. In the years 1599–1608 the direct traffic between the Baltic and the Iberian Peninsula was dominated by the Hanseatics and Danes (see table 3.4), the Dutch, in 1608, accounting for scarcely one-eighth of the volume. From 1609 onwards the Dutch did indeed sweep their rivals from the scene, each year handling over three-quarters of the traffic down to—but not one year beyond—the last full year of the Truce.

T A B L E 4.6. *Voyages direct from the Iberian Peninsula to the Baltic, 1607–1621*

Year	Total of all nations	Dutch	Hanseatic	Danish and Norwegian
1607	123	0	98	24
1608	151	19	105	18
1609	131	68	50	11
1610	141	98	40	2
1611	189	135	52	2
1612	76	53	20	0
1613	188	158	27	2
1614	187	145	37	4
1615	132	105	27	0
1616	165	139	23	2
1617	240	225	15	0
1618	181	168	11	2
1619	135	119	15	0
1620	105	91	10	4
1621	61	36	22	2

Sources: Bang, *Tabeller*, i. 194–250; Rau, *Estudos sobre a história do sal portugues*, 208–9; see also Vogel, 'Beiträge', 135.

The Truce led to a restructuring of the Baltic trade. But it also proved the need for constant vigilance on the part of the Dutch state in the Baltic if Dutch supremacy over the Baltic carrying traffic was to endure. Oldenbarnevelt had always recognized that disengagement from the long struggle with Spain would free the Republic to intervene more forcefully than hitherto elsewhere, thereby enhancing the Republic's capacity to protect and promote Dutch trade. In the Baltic area, Dutch commerce was especially at risk at and around the Danish Sound, a narrow passage, the only route by water in and out of the Baltic, commanded on both sides by the Danish monarch's Sound castles; and it was now precisely from Denmark that the United Provinces faced a mounting challenge. Under its ambitious, mercantilist-minded king, Christian IV (1596–1648), Denmark embarked on a restless pursuit of political and military hegemony in the north which was bound to collide with Dutch interests sooner rather than later.[31] In the past Sweden could be relied on to check Danish ambitions; but in the War of Kalmar (1611–13), the Danes inflicted a crushing defeat on Sweden which brought Christian to the verge of the supremacy which he sought. During the War of Kalmar, Christian banned Dutch shipping from sailing to Sweden and Finland, arrested a number of Dutch vessels for violating his ban, and imposed a hefty additional toll on Dutch and other shipping passing through the Sound. After the war, the Danish king brusquely refused to cancel this new toll. Christian had long resented Dutch supremacy in the carrying traffic to, and from, his dominions and was displeased by Dutch progress in the Spitsbergen whale fishery, over which he claimed sovereignty.[32]

Danish actions in the years 1611–13 caused a shipping slump in North Holland and Friesland and syphoned off large sums of Dutch cash into Danish coffers. At Amsterdam the merchants were furious though the city council insisted on blaming Oldenbarnevelt and the Truce as well as the Danes.[33] But what the War of Kalmar demonstrated in no uncertain terms was the utter dependence of the Dutch Baltic trade on the ability of the Dutch state to impose favourable conditions in the Baltic. If the Dutch Republic could not intervene successfully to ensure that the Danish Sound remained open to Dutch shipping and that the Sound tolls (whatever the Danish monarch might want) remained low, then the Dutch Baltic carrying traffic simply could not thrive. In this sense the Baltic crisis of 1611–14 was a test not just of Oldenbarnevelt's statecraft but of the capacity of the Dutch state to

[31] Kernkamp, Sleutels van de Sont, 16–18.

[32] Ibid.; Kolkert, Nederland en het zweedsche imperialisme, 9–11; Brinner, Die deutsche Grönlandfahrt, 130–1.

[33] Usselinx, Waerschouwinghe, 20; van Dillen, 'West-Indische Compagnie', 147.

protect and promote the vital interests of the first world-trade
entrepôt.

Denmark firmly rejected the States General's initial demands
that the new toll at the Sound be removed 'in accordance with
former treaties, usage and precedent'.[34] The Dutch were facing
an outright challenge to their vital interests.[35] Oldenbarnevelt's
response was to negotiate first his alliance of 1613 with Lübeck,
subsequently widened to encompass the rest of the Hanseatic
League, and then the alliance of 1614 with Sweden. The Dutch–
Hanseatic accord makes no direct reference to Denmark but bound
both parties to contribute men, money, and ships, in stipulate
quotas, to ensure 'free navigation, commerce and traffic in the
Baltic and North Sea as well as the estuaries, rivers, and waterways
feeding into the Baltic and North Sea'.[36] The Dutch–Swedish
alliance, which has been described as 'designed to safeguard
mutual commercial interests and assure reciprocal military assistance in case of war',[37] was an equally blunt declaration that force
would be used unless Denmark backed down. Christian IV was
forced to give way, and cancel his additional Sound toll of April
1611.

The Dutch Republic, with its treaties of 1613–14, imposed
something like a *Pax Neerlandica* on the waters of the Baltic and
the north. The rules were that no one state would be permitted
to obstruct the trade and shipping of the rest and that the
Dutch were the guarantors of freedom of the seas, of the Sound
staying open, and the Sound tolls remaining low. The principle
of *mare liberum* upheld by the Republic in the north stood in
stark inconsistency with its policy regarding the Scheldt; but
it was none the less profitable for that. The years 1615–20
witnessed the most spectacular boom in the history of Dutch
Baltic commerce.[38]

[34] *Resolutiën der Staten Generaal, 1613–1616*, 67, res. 25 May 1613.
[35] Hill, *The Danish Sound Dues*, 83–4.
[36] Beutin and Entholt, *Bremen und die Niederlande*, 8, 31–2.
[37] Lindblad, *Sweden's Trade*, 12.
[38] Bang, *Tabeller*, i. 194–250; den Haan, *Moedernegotie*, 141.

THE RICH TRADES OF EUROPE AND THE LEVANT

Meanwhile the truce lent added momentum to Dutch progress in the rich trades, in the north as well as in the south and not only by reducing shipping charges.[39] The most dramatic gain in northern parts was the capture of control of the traffic in Swedish copper, then Sweden's most valuable export. Copper in the seventeenth century was big business, requiring large capital resources and also good political connections, since the Swedish crown closely regulated the country's copper exports. Control over this trade had little to do with the usual Baltic factors of shipping and freight rates. Indeed, until the War of Kalmar, Lübeck retained its grip over the copper business intact. Europe's copper mills were consequently located principally in northern Germany and at Aachen, in proximity to the iron and coal of Liège. But this central pillar of the continuing Hanseatic role in the Baltic commerce in high-value goods was broken in the aftermath of 1609. In 1613 the States General commenced purchasing massive consignments of Swedish copper as part of a wider package designed to assist Sweden pay off the crushing indemnity imposed by Denmark. From 1613 onwards there were regular large annual shipments of copper from Sweden to Amsterdam and Amsterdam replaced Lübeck as Europe's copper staple.[40] Control of the copper traffic coupled with the burgeoning investment of Dutch firms, notably that of Louis de Geer (1587–1652) in Swedish mines and foundries, and a variety of technical assistance, led in turn to Dutch stimulation of, and dominance over, Sweden's soon rapidly growing exports of cannon, shot, and other war *matériel*. Within a few years de Geer's dynamic brother-in-law, Elias Trip (*c.*1570–1636), whose original business had been the importing of cannon and ammunition from Liège by river to Dordrecht, emerged as the foremost purveyor of munitions in Europe. Trip's pre-eminence in the Dutch munitions trade through the Thirty Years' War period was based on contracts from the state and his politico-commercial links with Sweden. The Dutch capture of the Swedish copper and arms trades are both clear instances of the pivotal role of Dutch

[39] See, for instance, the freight contracts in GA Amsterdam NA 123, fos. 190ᵛ, NA 125, fo. 98.
[40] Bang, *Tabeller*, ii. 165, 294, 311, 315; Klein, *De Trippen*, 328–9.

state intervention, cartels, and monopolistic practices in the advancement of the Dutch seventeenth-century trade system.

After 1609, as a result of increased Dutch state intervention in the Baltic, lower freight rates, and improved linkage with southern Europe, the Dutch made massive new strides in their engrossment of the northern rich trades.[41] They extended their grip over the White Sea traffic, achieving a more decisive superiority over their English competitors than they had had before 1609; they made notable advances in the Baltic cloth traffic, again at English expense (see table 4.9); they generated a flourishing Finnish tar trade which came to employ ten to fifteen ships per year sailing to Viborg; they now eliminated the Hanseatics from the Baltic spice trade, and they captured the Swedish copper and munitions trades. This was impressive, but Dutch progress in the Mediterranean after 1609 was still more dramatic. Part of this consisted of new bulk carrying and provision of shipping services for others, notably Genoa and Venice. During Phase Two the Dutch were the main carriers of Valencian salt to Italy and of Puglian and Sicilian grain to eastern Spain.[42] But the most crucial changes were in the commerce in fine goods. Lower freight charges and access to Spain and Spanish silver transformed the entire situation. An added factor was the sudden influx of Dutch East India spices into the region. Dutch pepper and fine spices began to arrive in quantity at Genoa and Livorno from 1609 precisely.[43] Within a few years spices distributed from Aleppo, by the Venetians, and from Lisbon, by the Genoese, had vanished from the scene. By the middle years of the Truce the Dutch (and to a lesser extent the English) were the undisputed masters of the Mediterranean spice traffic.

On top of the boost from Spanish fine goods and silver, East India spices, and cheap freightage, the efforts of the Dutch merchant élite in the Mediterranean were now also powerfully backed by the state. The first big Dutch convoy to the Levant, ten heavily armed and manned ships, crammed with bullion, cloth, and spices, which sailed to 'Cyprus, Syria, Palestine and Egypt' in 1609, was

[41] Bang, *Tabeller*, ii. 252, 256, 320; Bushkovitch, *Merchants of Moscow*, 46–8; Federowicz, 'Anglo-Polish Commercial Relations', 368; Aström, 'Commercial and Industrial Development', 443, 450.

[42] Castillo Pintado, *Tráfico marítimo*, 78, 168–77; Grendi, 'I Nordici', 32–5.

[43] *BGLH* i. 15–16, 98, 105; Sella, *Commerci e industrie*, 73–4.

furnished with guns, munitions, and additional men, free of charge, by the States General.[44] In 1612 the States General established diplomatic relations with the Ottoman sultan, obtaining—despite Anglo-French efforts to prevent this—a charter of privileges which placed Dutch factors in the Levant on the same legal footing as their older established rivals. Then, after 1612, the States General built up a network of resident representatives and consuls all around the Mediterranean—except for Spain and territories subject to Spain from which official representatives of the Dutch state were barred. The main postings were those of a resident ambassador at Constantinople (1612) and the consulates at Livorno (1612), Aleppo (1613), Larnaca (1613), Venice (1614), Genoa (1615), Algiers (1616), and Zante (1618).[45]

The impact of the quickening Dutch penetration of the Levant from 1609 proved quite a shock to their Venetian, French, and English rivals. At Aleppo, which remained the pre-eminent emporium of the Middle East throughout the first half of the seventeenth century, the change since 1609 was strikingly evident. In July 1611 the Venetian consul at Aleppo reported home that the Dutch had become much more formidable rivals 'seguito la tregua col re cattolico'— that is since their truce with the King of Spain—and that in the last two years 'many houses' of Dutch merchants had suddenly sprung up at Aleppo.[46] Moreover, the statistics we have fully confirm the Venetian consul's impressions. Whereas in 1604 Dutch commerce at Aleppo was running at only half the level of that of their English rivals, by 1613 the position had been exactly reversed, the Dutch now accounting for twice as much business as the English (see table 4.7).

Appraising the position in a petition to the States General in 1611, the Amsterdam Levant merchants claimed with some justification that the Levant trade had latterly emerged as one of the most vital plied by the Dutch in any part of the globe.[47] They argued that their commerce with Turkey, Cyprus, Egypt, and the Aegean now compared with that of the VOC with the East Indies in value and was potentially even more important for the future

[44] *Relazioni veneziane*, 37.
[45] *BGLH* i. 51–4; Israel, 'Dutch Merchant Colonies', 93–4.
[46] Berchet (ed.), *Relazioni dei consoli veneti nella Siria*, 151.
[47] *BGLH* i. 429–31.

TABLE 4.7. *Western remittances in cash and goods to Aleppo, 1604 and 1613* (Venetian ducats)

Trading nation	1604 (Teixeira)	1613 (Morosini)
Venice	1,250,000	850,000
France	800,000	1,750,000
England	300,000	250,000
United Provinces	150,000	500,000

Sources: *Relaciones de Pedro Teixeira*, 181–3; for Morosini, Berchet (ed.), *Relazioni dei consoli veneti nella Siria*, 180–1.

'well-being of the fatherland' than the East India traffic.[48] They maintained that the Levant furnished an abundance of valuable raw materials, in particular silks, cottons, and mohair, which were indispensable to the manufacture of a wide range of luxury and middle quality textiles in the west. Should the Dutch succeed in achieving, and consolidating, a degree of trade mastery in the eastern Mediterranean comparable with what they had already achieved in the Baltic, Russia, and the East Indies, then a glowing future for Holland's textile towns—Leiden and Haarlem—would be assured and the manufacturing towns of southern Germany, which hitherto had procured their cottons and silk from Venice, would be made dependent on the Dutch entrepôt for their supplies.

Our evidence shows that the Dutch did best during their brief period of success in the Levant, from 1609 to 1621, in the cotton trade.[49] In commerce with Cyprus, which then exported 6,000 sacks of cotton (around three million lbs.) per year and where the Venetians and English had reigned supreme before 1609, the Dutch quickly gained an overwhelming ascendancy, ousting their rivals from the scene. Much the same is true of the trade with Egypt. The Dutch made rather less impressive progress, however, in the Aleppo trade, where the main item was Persian raw silk.[50] The Amsterdam Levant merchants were acutely aware that the Aleppo silk trade was still predominantly in Venetian and French

[48] Ibid. i. 429; in 1611 when the Dutch Levant trade was valued at around 4 million guilders yearly, it may have come slightly ahead of the Dutch East India traffic in value.

[49] Ibid. i. 429–30; *Relazioni veneziane*, 37; Sella, *Commerci e industrie*, 28; *Relaciones de Pedro Teixeira*, 198.

[50] ASV CSM 1st ser. 153, fo. 48, res. 4 Aug. 1611; *Relazioni veneziane*, 37.

hands. Indeed they expressly state that, until they had wrested what they recognized as the most valuable strand of the Levant commerce from the Venetians and French, overall mastery of the commerce of the eastern Mediterranean would elude them. The difficulty was that France and Italy, with their more developed silk industries, had the advantage of a much larger home demand for raw silks than the Dutch.

During the first phase of Dutch world-trade primacy, from 1590 to 1609, the Dutch role in the rich trades of the Mediterranean had been largely confined to supplying *says*, linen, and Russian fine goods, especially furs, caviare, and leather, to Italy. In the Levant proper Dutch enterprise had been marginal and considerably less significant than that of the English. The Dutch had lacked the textiles and spices needed for a wider role and had been greatly impeded by the Spanish embargoes and high freight costs. After 1609—though Braudel completely missed this—Dutch enterprise in the Mediterranean was thoroughly restructured.[51] The Dutch returned to Spain in large numbers, began servicing the carrying traffic between Spain and Italy, deployed more silver, and shipped in a much wider range of fine goods, including for the first time large quantities of pepper, spices, Ibero-American dyestuffs, Swedish copper, and munitions. Consequently, the carrying of Baltic grain and timber to the Mediterranean ceased to be the driving force behind Dutch enterprise in the region. Down to 1609 Baltic grain had been the basis of Dutch Mediterranean trade. When Italian harvests had been plentiful and Baltic grain superfluous, as was the case during the late 1590s, Dutch Mediterranean trade had shrivelled almost to insignificance. But after 1609 the situation was quite different. In the years 1614–16, for example, Italian harvests were again plentiful and there was no call for Baltic grain. But this time there was no collapse, or even any slackening in the momentum of Dutch commercial expansion in the Mediterranean. One piece of evidence which illustrates this is the list of eighty-five Dutch ships which reached Venice during the sixteen-month period from September 1615 to December 1616.[52] The new Dutch consul at Venice itemized the cargoes of the first forty-three of these arrivals down to April 1616. It is

---

[51] Israel, 'Phases of the Dutch *straatvaart*', 5–10.
[52] ASV CSM new Ser. 24, 'Nota delli vascelli dei paesi et stati bassi venuti a Venetia'; *BGLH* i. 61–2.

remarkable that not a single one of these forty-three ships carried any Baltic grain. Seven had sailed in convoy from Seville with a massively valuable cargo of Castilian wool for the Venetian cloth industry. Five more had sailed in convoy from Alicante, bearing wool and salt. Another five had sailed from Crete, Zante, and other Venetian islands with wine and currants and two from Cyprus with cottons. Six had sailed from Sicily and Puglia with grain, two from Constantinople with Turkish wools and yarns, two from Tunisia with hides, wool, and amber, one from Lisbon with sugar, one from the Aegean with raw silk, and the rest from Holland with pepper, fine spices, fish, metals, and naval stores— especially tar. Remarkably, no less than nineteen of these forty-three Dutch vessels arrived at Venice sailing from ports under Spanish rule.

In the years 1609–21 the Dutch displaced the English as the dynamic, up-and-coming force, undermining the age-old commercial predominance of the Italians and French in the Mediterranean. After making continual and impressive gains ever since the 1570s, the English share of the Levant trade suddenly slumped, under the impact of the Dutch. In the circumstances of Phase Two of the evolution of Dutch world-trade primacy, the English simply could not compete with Dutch shipping, their freight rates, their access to Spanish silver, their range of commodities offered, or their primacy in the distribution of pepper and spices. But England's eclipse in the Mediterranean was to be brief. It ended in 1621 no less abruptly than it had begun.

THE EAST INDIA TRADE

If the Twelve Years' Truce precipitated a major expansion of Dutch commerce in the Mediterranean, in the East Indies it led to a certain loss of dynamism and momentum. Certainly, the setback was less severe than Oldenbarnevelt's critics had predicted.[53] Yet, there was, undeniably, some deterioration in the Dutch position. As we have seen, VOC share price quotations on the Amsterdam Exchange fell back sharply in 1609 and remained at a low level down to the 1620s. Down to 1608 the Dutch captured,

---

[53] *Kroniek*, xxviii (1872), 255–60.

or destroyed, some thirty Portuguese East India carracks.[54] Now the obstruction of this shipping ceased. As predicted, this led to a revival in Portuguese pepper and spice shipments to Lisbon which then competed with Dutch spices on the European market.[55] At the same time, whilst there was now a rapid growth in the volume of English trade with the East Indies, there was actually a slight falling off in the number of Dutch ships returning from Asia to the United Provinces in the decade 1610–19 compared with the first decade of the century. Indeed, this was the only decade of the century in which there was a fall in the volume of Dutch shipping returning from the East Indies (see table 4.8).

In theory, the Truce involved the complete disengagement of

TABLE 4.8. *VOC ships returning to the Dutch entrepôt from the East Indies, 1600–1699*

1600–9	59	1650–9	103
1610–19	50	1660–9	127
1620–9	71	1670–9	133
1630–9	75	1680–9	141
1640–9	93	1690–9	156

Sources: Steensgaard, *Asian Trade Revolution*, 170; Gaastra, 'Geld tegen goederen', 250.

Dutch and Iberians in Asia. This, to the Portuguese and Spaniards, meant that the Dutch must stay out of such sectors of Asian commerce as the Iberians still dominated. But, as the duke of Lerma urged Oldenbarnevelt (in his secret peace feelers to The Hague during 1611–12), a renewal of strife could hardly be avoided whilst the two sides continued in such close proximity in the East Indies.[56] Nevertheless, governors-general Gerard Reynst (1613–15) and Laurens Reael (1616–19) did try to keep the friction to a minimum. For the moment, the Dutch held back, accepting their exclusion from the China silk trade, from the cinnamon trade of Ceylon, and from the Portuguese-dominated Malabar coast of south-west India.[57] But they were not willing to observe the same

[54] *Kroniek*, xxviii (1872), 255.
[55] This Portuguese revival was especially noticeable in the years 1610–13 (see Steensgaard, *Asian Trade Revolution*, 170; Disney, *Twilight*, 51, 162).
[56] AGS Estado 2026, consulta 20 Feb. 1612; Israel, *Dutch Republic and the Hispanic World*, 16–17.
[57] Reael, 'Verslag', 202, 205.

restraint on the Coromandel coast of south-east India, where the Portuguese also had forts and claimed hegemony. For it was clear that the VOC could not consolidate its control over the spice trade of the Indonesian archipelago without also taking over the traffic in cotton cloth from south-east India, this being the commodity most in demand in the spice-producing areas.[58] If the Portuguese were left undisturbed on the Coromandel coast, this would only encourage the revival of their spice trade in the islands. The Dutch had had a trading lodge at Masulipatam, at the northern end of the coast, since 1605; but, after 1609, they began to penetrate further south, establishing their main factory, in 1612, at Pulicat. When the Portuguese responded by sacking this factory, the VOC returned in force and erected a large stone fortress at Pulicat which they named Fort Geldria. This fortified base then quickly developed into the principal European factory in south-east India. Within a few years, to the dismay of ministers at Madrid, the Dutch assumed effective control over the flow of Indian cotton cloth to the Indonesian Archipelago.[59]

Before long, fighting flared up also among the islands. The Dutch seized the Portuguese fort commanding the island of Solor, the source of sandalwood, a red, scented dyewood, which sold well in Java, China, and India. The most serious strife, though, took place in the Moluccas, where several Dutch and Spanish forts were located in close proximity. In 1614 the States General blamed the fighting on the Iberians and proclaimed the Truce in the East Indies to be at an end. The VOC was encouraged to increase its forces in the Archipelago. The States General's annual subsidy to the Company was increased to 200,000 guilders and an additional five navy warships were handed over 'to be used in the Indies'.[60]

Throughout the Truce years the Dutch remained much the strongest European power in Asia. By 1617 the Dutch possessed around twenty well-garrisoned fortresses strung out from Pulicat to the Moluccas and around forty fighting ships. Nevertheless, except on the Coromandel coast and on Solor, the Portuguese, Spaniards, and English were all steadily consolidating their hold in their respective zones of influence. The Portuguese tightened

[58] Gomes Solis, *Discursos*, 82–3.
[59] ARB SEG 183, fos. 161–3, Pedro Alvares Pereira on the East India trade; Reael, 'Verslag', 198, 203; Raychaudhuri, *Jan Company in Coromandel*, 20–3.
[60] Res. Holl. 6 Sept. 1614.

their grip on Goa, Malacca, and Ceylon and expanded their trade in the Archipelago, especially with Macassar.[61] The Spaniards strengthened their bases in the Moluccas and the Philippines, inflicted a stinging naval defeat on the Dutch in Manila Bay, in April 1617, and continued to ply a lucrative traffic with China from their base at Manila.[62] But it was the English who now increasingly posed the most serious threat to Dutch supremacy over the commerce of the East Indies. The English East India Company established trading factories at Bantam, Macassar, and on Sumatra and began to penetrate the Banda Islands, the source of the world's supply of nutmeg and mace. To counter the threat, the VOC erected a large stone fortress (Fort Nassau) on Banda Neira, the largest of the Bandas, in 1609. The English replied by switching to the smaller islands, including Pulo Run, and instigating an anti-Dutch rising among the islanders. It was also during these years that the English emerged as formidable competitors to the Dutch in north-west India and the Arabian sea.

In Oldenbarnevelt's view, it was definitely not in the Dutch interest to antagonize England, of whose aid, against Spain, the Republic might well soon again be in need. But neither were the States of Holland willing to see Dutch primacy in the Spice Islands progressively eroded. Within a few years of the Truce English competition in the Archipelago had reached a level which, in the view of the Heren XVII, was seriously prejudicing the profitability of Dutch spice sales in Europe.[63] The Dutch were not blind to the fact that the English too were now selling appreciable quantities of pepper and spices in the Mediterranean. The first Dutch attempt to deflect English enterprise from the Archipelago consisted of a States General deputation to London. This delegation included the renowned Dutch scholar–politician, Hugo Grotius, who tried to overwhelm the English with a flood of Latin erudition. It apparently caused Grotius—whose celebrated *Mare liberum* (1609) employed every conceivable argument to prove (in opposition to Portuguese claims) that the seas were open to all—no trouble to reverse his own arguments and insist in London that the English had no right to participate in a traffic which the Dutch had

[61] Reael, 'Verslag', 199.
[62] Ibid. 188–9.
[63] Van Dam, *Beschryvinge*, i, pt. 2, 152.

'conquered' from the Portuguese at great cost in blood and treasure.[64]

Predictably, negotiations on this basis, led nowhere. Yet, in the Dutch view, something had to be done to abate both the tension and the competition. A second London conference, in 1615, discussed possibilities for a merger of the two East India Companies but without result. Meanwhile, in Asia the position steadily worsened. In January 1616 a Dutch force ejected the English from their factory on the Banda Island of Ay. By 1618 the scene was set for an Anglo-Dutch mini-war for control of the trade of Java and the Bandas.[65] 'These butterboxes are groanne soe insolent', complained one English factor, 'that yf they be suffred but a whit longer, they will make claime to the whole Indies, so that no man shall trade but themselves or by their leave; but I hoope to see their pride take a falle.'[66] The friction spread. Both sides vied for the support of the local sultans. At length fighting broke out at Bantam, where the English concentrated a considerable force, in the Bandas, and at Jacarta, where the Dutch had recently erected a fortress. In the siege which now ensued the English helped the sultan blockade the base which the Dutch now renamed 'Batavia'.

The new governor-general of the Dutch East Indies, Jan Pietersz. Coen (1587–1629), was of much more aggressive disposition than his predecessors, and had strongly criticized Reael for his caution. Coen struck out, relieving Batavia and capturing half a dozen English ships along the north coast of Java. But the English held on at Bantam, precariously in the Bandas, and at several places on Sumatra. The Heren XVII were extremely alarmed at the news of the escalating conflict in the Archipelago. The Truce was nearing its end, and they viewed with horror the possibility of the VOC becoming locked in conflict with both the Iberians and the English. Again the directors concluded that they must have a merger or at least an agreement with the English to share the spice trade which would obviate the ruinous competition which was driving down profits for both companies. The VOC's idea of an equitable compromise was that the English should receive 20 per cent of the traffic and the Dutch be assigned 80 per cent. This was rejected out of hand. In the end, the VOC settled

[64] Knight, *Life and Works of Hugo Grotius*, 140–2.
[65] Furber, *Rival Empires of Trade*, 42.
[66] Foster, *English Factories . . . 1618–21*, 49.

for a loose treaty of collaboration and an English promise to help pay the defence costs of the Dutch bases. Under this accord, the English were assigned one-third of the traffic in fine spices, as against two-thirds for the Dutch, and a free hand in pepper.[67]

The Twelve Years' Truce was thus a period of relative decline for the Dutch in Asia, which ended with the VOC voluntarily abandoning its ambition to monopolize the spice trade in the Archipelago for the sake of ending the conflict with the English. For the moment, caution was the keynote of Dutch policy in Asia. Coen, a hard-liner, was furious when he learned the news of the Anglo-Dutch pact signed in London. With undisguised sarcasm he assured his superiors that the English owed them a great debt: for, having been practically ejected from the Archipelago, the English were being put back in by the Heren XVII. Even so, Coen lost no time in reinforcing the Dutch military position in the Bandas and other parts of the Archipelago. Under the terms of the agreement, the English now established trade lodges at Batavia, Amboina, and in the Bandas and began to contribute to the costs of confronting the Iberians.

THE CARIBBEAN AND BRAZIL

If the restructuring of 1609 led to a dramatic expansion of the Dutch rich trades in Europe and the Near East but a certain loss of momentum in the East Indies, the setback in American waters was altogether more serious. In 1607 the Dutch merchant élite had expected to be on the verge of a massive breakthrough in tropical America. Then the Truce had dashed these hopes. The salt-fleets from West Friesland ceased plying to Punta de Araya or any other American salt deposits for the duration of the Truce.[68] The ban on tobacco growing in Venezuela proved largely effective in paralysing Dutch enterprise along the mainland coast of Spanish South America. The traffic to Santo Domingo, Puerto Rico, and Cuba persisted but very probably at a reduced level. Furthermore, all along the coastline of the Guyanas and in the Paraíba–Ceará

---

[67] Van Dam, *Beschryvinge*, i, pt. 2, 157, ii, pt. 3, 117; Elias, *Het voorspel*, ii. 38; Furber, *Rival Empires of Trade*, 44.

[68] Goslinga, *Dutch in the Caribbean* (1971), 124–6.

area the Dutch position deteriorated, for the Truce enabled the Spaniards to regain the initiative at sea in the Caribbean and to render the Dutch footholds more precarious. The Spaniards launched several successful raids, in 1613 liquidating the Zeelandian fort at the mouth of the Cormantine. At the same time, the Portuguese began their offensive to eliminate the Dutch forts from around the estuary of the Amazon, an objective which they finally achieved in 1622–3.[69] As against these setbacks, the only solid Dutch success was the establishment of Fort Kijkoveral, erected in 1616 by colonists from Flushing at a strong position, 20 miles up the River Essequebo.

A striking feature of the Dutch commerce in American commodities during the Truce is that the vigorous revival of Dutch importing of Brazil sugar and dyewood to the Dutch entrepôt (which began in 1609) was almost exclusively an indirect traffic via Lisbon and the ports of northern Portugal.[70] Every year from 1609 to 1621 dozens of Dutch vessels sailed from Portugal to Holland laden with the produce of Brazil. After 1609 Dutch endeavours to establish a direct commerce with Brazil, which before 1609 had met with some success, at any rate with respect to the northernmost Brazilian captaincies, were now almost completely thwarted. Like the Spaniards in Venezuela, the Portuguese authorities in Brazil proved largely effective at putting a stop to the interloping. The Amsterdam notarial records show that voyages from Holland to Brazil direct became very infrequent. A number of Dutch merchants, including two factors who had lived in Brazil for long periods, testified before Amsterdam notaries that attempts to trade direct with Recife and Paraíba generally failed, consignments of illegally imported linens having been seized.[71] Dutch ships sailing from Portugal were allowed into Brazilian ports provided their cargoes had been registered and taxed in Portugal. On departing Brazil, skippers had to leave caution money to ensure that they delivered their cargoes only in Portugal.[72] Moreover, whereas English or French ships encoun-

[69] Netscher, *Geschiedenis*, 55; Edmundson, 'The Dutch on the Amazon', 652–3, 658.
[70] RAZ SZ 2102, 'Deductie' (1622), fos. 1–2; Israel, 'Economic Contribution', 509–11; Kellenbenz has noted in the case of Hamburg that the direct traffic with Brazil ceased around 1600 (see *As relacões*, 16–17).
[71] GA Amsterdam NA 196, fo. 299, deed 30 June 1609.
[72] GA Amsterdam NA 197, fo. 173, deed. 30 Jan. 1612.

tered in tropical American waters would often draw up alongside Dutch vessels for purposes of trade, the Portuguese prevented their ships from doing so.[73] The Portuguese crown, by political means, retained control over the flow of goods into Brazil, and of Brazil products being shipped to northern Europe, syphoning off much of the profit and minimizing the economic influence of North Europeans in its Brazilian colony. Amsterdam merchants who handled imports of Brazil wood to the Dutch entrepôt in these years—Samuel Godijn and Nicholas du Gardin—were really just factors of the Lisbon *asentistas* who held the dyewood monopoly.[74]

Dutch enterprise in the Caribbean and Brazil in these years was trapped in a vice of Iberian power, bureaucracy, and trade restrictions. What was needed if the mould was to be broken, the merchants realized, was for the companies to pool their resources and advance Dutch interests in tropical America by deploying overwhelming force. Plans for setting up a Dutch West India Company were continually being revived during the Truce period, especially at Amsterdam, in Zeeland, and at Hoorn.[75] With the downfall of Oldenbarnevelt, in 1618, and emergence of the Stadholder, Prince Maurice, at the helm of the Dutch state, hopes rose that the political obstacles to the setting up of the West India Company had been removed. But Prince Maurice was not so set on resuming the war with Spain as historians used to think.[76] The Prince knew that, if he allowed the Company to be established before the Truce expired, this would make the resumption of war inevitable; he preferred to keep his options open. Consequently, while the Amsterdam city council instructed its deputies to the States of Holland to do their utmost to advance the formation of the Company,[77] the Prince saw to it that the project remained shelved until after the expiry of the Truce.

---

[73] GA Amsterdam NA 196, fo. 325, deed 14 Aug. 1609.

[74] GA Amsterdam *vroed.* ix. 460, res. 20 Apr. 1610.

[75] Ibid. x. res. 8 Sept. 1614; *Notulen Zeeland* (1614), res. 16 and 18 Nov. 1614.

[76] PRO SP 84/101, fos. 170ᵛ, 175, Carleton to Calvert, 22 June/2 July 1621; Israel, *Dutch Republic and the Hispanic World*, 81–2.

[77] GA Amsterdam *vroed.* xi. 153, 186, res. 10 and 13 June, 15 and 16 Sept. 1619.

NEW MONOPOLIES AND TRADING COMPANIES

But, if the merchants trading to the Caribbean and Brazil could not prevent the delay in setting up the West India Company, the Truce period was a time of intense interest in setting up new companies, several of which obtained temporary monopolies from the States General. What recent events taught the Dutch merchant élite was that, if they were to achieve trade supremacy outside Europe, they had to combine commercial dexterity, and cost competitiveness, with monopolistic structures designed to restrict competition among the Dutch and block foreign rivals.

Some of these monopolistic devices were justified on the grounds that a particularly remote, difficult, or dangerous area was being opened up, involving an exceptional degree of risk to the entrepreneur. In 1616, for example, Elias Trip, king of the munitions business, petitioned the States General for a twelve-year monopoly for trade to south-western Africa from the Congo to the Cape of Good Hope, principally to obtain saltpetre for his gunpowder works.[78] The States General granted him sole rights only for an initial four voyages. But even where there was no question of a formal monopoly forming new companies still offered the advantage of pooling resources and capital. In May 1614 a new Middelburg Guinea company was set up involving a large number of participants, several of them, such as Balthasar van de Voorde, mintmaster of Zeeland, passive investors with close links with ruling circles.[79]

Two important state-chartered monopoly companies were set up during the Truce—the New Netherland Company and the Northern Company, both of 1614. The New Netherland Company is a classic instance of cartel formation to eliminate competition and boost profitability. Dutch commerce with North America was a late starter, having begun on a regular basis only in the years 1611–12. The first private company to purchase beaver furs from the Indians at, and around, Manhattan, and the mouth of the Hudson River, comprised a group of Amsterdam Lutheran merchants, headed by Lambrecht van Tweenhuysen (son of an Overijssel regent family) and the fur-dealer, Arnout Vogels (an

---

[78] *Resolutiën der Staten-Generaal (1613–1616)*, 613, res. 30 Apr. 1616.
[79] ARH SH 2687, fo. 113, petition of Middelburg participants, 8 May 1614.

immigrant from Antwerp).[80] To begin with profits were good. But soon a second company appeared on the scene and the price in axes, knives, and other metal goods obtained by the Indians for their furs began to rise.[81] The rival companies tried to reach an agreement, through the good offices of Prince Maurice among others; but van Tweenhuysen refused to accept that his rivals should have an equal share of the trade, offering participation only on a two-to-one basis. Negotiations broke down. Then in 1614 a third Amsterdam company, this time headed by influential members of the city council, Gerrit and Jonas Witsen, entered on the scene. With this, it became clear to all parties that there was no alternative, if the traffic was to thrive, but to form a cartel. A monopoly company was set up and chartered by the States General. Besides the participants of the original companies, other leading merchants invested in the New Netherland Company, notably Samuel Godijn, the importer of Brazil wood from Lisbon and former member of the Walloon Church at Emden and Middelburg who had moved to Amsterdam in 1604. He was one of the largest account-holders with the Amsterdam Wisselbank and subsequently a director also of the Northern Company and the Amsterdam Chamber of the West India Company.[82]

When the New Netherland Company's charter expired in the autumn of 1618, van Tweenhuysen and his colleagues tried to have it renewed. But by this time Oldenbarnevelt had fallen—and hopes of the imminent setting up of a West India Company were rising—so that Amsterdam and the States of Holland preferred to allow the New Netherland monopoly to lapse. Van Tweenhuysen seems to have been the dominant personality in the fur trade with New Netherland from 1618 down to the absorption of the traffic into the West India Company's monopoly, in the early 1620s.

Van Tweenhuysen was also a leading figure among the founders of the Northern Company. This remarkable merchant had been the treasurer of the Lutheran congregation at Amsterdam since 1595, and was involved in overland trade with Germany, as well as in trade with Danzig, Königsberg, south-west France, and the Setúbal salt trade. He also participated in the Archangel trade,

[80] Hart, *Prehistory of the New Netherland Company*, 20, 39–40.
[81] Ibid. 22–3.
[82] Ibid. 67.

which gave him his initial expertise in furs and whale products. Whales had been hunted off the north of Norway by Spanish Basque whalers, sailing from San Sebastián, for over a century. Then, in the 1590s, the English Muscovy Company began hunting whales in the seas around Nova Zemblaya and Beren Island, as well as walrus on land. Around 1609 the first Dutch whaling ships went out to Nova Zemblaya. Then, in 1611 the English began to exploit the richer whaling grounds around Spitsbergen, the Muscovy Company claiming that territory as a sovereign possession of the English crown. It was a claim hotly disputed by the Dutch, Danes, French, and Spaniards. The very next year, 1612, French, Spanish, and Dutch firms began to follow the English example. The competition around Spitsbergen became fast and furious. In 1613 the London Muscovy Company sent seven vessels, which were joined by four other English whaling ships. But seventeen French, Flemish, Spanish, and Dutch whalers also reached Spitsbergen that year, two of the three Dutch vessels fitted out by van Tweenhuysen and his associates.[83] The Muscovy Company ships seized several non-English vessels, including one from Hoorn, and drove the rest off with warnings not to return.[84]

It was as a result of this episode that van Tweenhuysen and other merchants interested in the whale fishery appealed to the States General, with the backing of several town councils, including Amsterdam, for protection and a monopoly. The States General granted the Company a monopoly of exploiting the whale and walrus grounds around Nova Zemblaya, Spitsbergen, and Greenland from the United Provinces—though the States of Zeeland did not consent to it—in the first instance for ten years. Investment in the Company was open to all subjects of the Republic and there was a good deal of investment from Rotterdam, Delft, Zaandam, Hoorn, and Enkhuizen, as well as from Amsterdam.[85] The Company's annual Spitsbergen fleet was given a naval escort, consisting in 1614 of three warships, which was paid for in part by a 1.5 per cent levy on the Company's whale-product imports.

Compared with the Dutch East and West India Companies, the Northern Company was a relatively short-lived operation, its

[83] Hart, *Geschrift en getal*, 231.
[84] Gerritsz, *Histoire*, 96, 102; Lootsma, *Bijdrage*, 2–4.
[85] *Resolutiën der Staten-Generaal (1613–1616)*, 232, res. 4 Apr. 1614.

monopoly being allowed to lapse in the year 1642.[86] But it should not go unnoticed that, for a time—the second and third decades of the seventeenth century—this company played a key role in widening the hegemony of the Dutch world entrepôt. Whale oil in early modern times was an important commodity, being the basis of many soap products and lighting fuels. At the time this organization was formed, in 1614, the Dutch were not playing a leading part in the whale fishery, or in the processing of whale and walrus products, or in the marketing of the soaps and fuels manufactured from them. All this changed with the setting up of the Northern Company. Though the Company's charter does not expressly say so, its essential purpose was to create a sufficiently powerful organization to oust the English and other rivals from the scene.[87] In the next clash, in 1615, the Muscovy Company was definitely worsted. Amid a stream of complaints from London, the Dutch extended their grip over the whaling grounds. While the English traffic fell back to a low level, the Dutch whale fishery flourished. By 1619, when the Dutch whale-processing village of Smeerenburg was founded on the north-west corner of Spitsbergen, on what was known as Amsterdam Island, the Dutch already enjoyed an overwhelming superiority over the rest. Smeerenburg, with its blubber-boiling works, stores, and warehouses, developed into a vast industrial summer-camp which came alive each year with hundreds of Dutch seamen, workmen, and whale and walrus hunters.

ZEELAND DURING THE TRUCE

The reorganization of the Dutch trading system during the Twelve Years' Truce in some respects strengthened the Dutch entrepôt and enhanced Dutch primacy in world commerce. But the new conditions of trade brought contraction and decay in other sectors in particular the direct trade with tropical America and the Zeeland entrepôt. Usselinx's view of the likely negative effects of the Truce on the Dutch economy proved exaggerated but was by no means unfounded. The Truce did provide scope for commercial

---

[86] Van Brakel, *Hollandsche handelscompagniën*, 28–30.
[87] Elias, *Het voorspel*, i. 29–31; de Jong, 'Walvisvaart', 310.

and industrial revival in the South Netherlands and this worked
to the disadvantage especially of Zeeland and the Dutch textile
industry.

In 1609 both the merchants and the regents of Zeeland were
convinced that the Truce would depress the economy of their
province; and they were right. The other provinces had given an
undertaking to Zeeland that the Scheldt restrictions would be
neither lifted, nor modified, during the Truce.[88] But the value of
the Scheldt restrictions to the Zeeland entrepôt was diluted by the
lifting of the Dutch naval blockade of the Flemish seaports. The
Truce meant that Zeeland's stranglehold over the maritime trade
of the South Netherlands was, for the moment, broken.[89] To
encourage the growth of trade through Ostend and Dunkirk, the
regime in Brussels declined to reduce the wartime tolls on its side
on river traffic entering from Dutch territory, while simultaneously
offering low tariffs in the Flemish seaports.[90] Efforts were made to
improve the canals linking the Flemish ports with Bruges, Ghent,
and Antwerp, the main centres of commerce and industry. Consequently, the South Netherlands' imports and exports by sea were
diverted, as from 1609, from Zeeland to the Flemish coast. This
applied both to high-value goods shipped from Spain and Portugal
and also to Baltic timber and naval stores and other bulky goods.[91]
The States of Zeeland noted, in October 1614, that imports of salt
into the South Netherlands, for refining at Ghent, had now been
diverted completely from the Scheldt to Ostend.[92]

The slump in Zeeland's trade and shipping as a result of the
Truce was too obvious to be denied. When the States of Zeeland
requested a reduction in the province's tax quota under the federal
budget in 1612, the Amsterdam city council agreed that this was
only just, in view of the 'decadence' into which the province of
Zeeland had now fallen.[93] Acknowledging the point meant that
Holland had to furnish a higher proportion of the federal budget
than previously.

[88] *Gedenkstukken van Johan van Oldenbarnevelt*, iii. 237.
[89] Gielens, 'Onderhandelingen met Zeeland', 194–7.
[90] Kernkamp, *Handel op den vijand*, ii. 343–4; Voeten, 'Antwerpens handel', 70–1;
Voeten, 'Antwerpse reacties', 214.
[91] *Notulen Zeeland* (1614), 241, 'Advys' of the Gecommitteerde Raden, Middelburg,
17 Oct. 1614.
[92] Ibid.
[93] GA Amsterdam *vroed.* x. 124. res. 8 May 1612.

INDUSTRY

Had Dutch primacy in world commerce during the seventeenth century been based primarily on bulk carrying, it would be right to treat the Dutch trading system as if it functioned more or less independently of any industrial base. Even then, industries would enter the picture. Much of the timber imported to Holland from Norway, the Baltic, from Luxemburg and up the Rhine was destined for the shipyards of Zaandam, Hoorn, Amsterdam, and the Maas estuary. Much of the salt carried by the Dutch to Scandinavia, Russia, and Poland was refined and blended in the salt-refineries of Zierikzee, Goes, and Dordrecht. Even timber which was re-exported was frequently sawn into planks, beams, or barrel-staves at Amsterdam or on the Zaan. In 1630 fifty-three of the 128 industrial mills of diverse kinds on the Zaan were engaged in timber-sawing.[94] Another four were engaged in hemp processing. But a large part of the bulk-carrying trade consisted of shipping grain, wine, fish, dairy products, and unprocessed timber and salt, activity which neither needed, nor benefited, home industry. With the rich trades, however, the relationship to industry was rather different. Supremacy over the trade in textiles, dyestuffs, copper goods, sugar, jewellery, and whale products was out of the question without the right finishing techniques to process and prepare these products for the market. Consequently, if the crucial difference between the Dutch trading system of the sixteenth century, and that of the post-1590 period, lies in the acquisition of the rich trades, then it follows that Holland's industries, contributing fundamentally to the transformation of the Dutch entrepôt into the first world entrepôt, must have gained greatly in variety and importance from the end of the sixteenth century. Indeed, we may expect to find a close linkage between the subsequent history of Dutch industry and the changing fortunes of the Dutch trading system itself.

But was there any sense in which Holland was a leading industrial producer or that, as has been suggested, the United Provinces became 'the leading producer of industrial products' of the seventeenth century?[95] Expressed like this the claim is certainly too crude. With its meagre territory and resources, the Dutch Republic

[94] Hart, *Geschrift en getal*, 17.
[95] Wallerstein, 'Dutch Hegemony', 98–9.

was never in a position to achieve the sort of general preponderance in the industrial sphere that Britain attained during the later eighteenth century. Overall, Dutch textile output never matched the levels reached in seventeenth-century England or France, or indeed India or China. Nevertheless, there were certain key sectors of textile production which had a particular significance for international trade and where the Dutch did eventually surpass, or come close to surpassing, their rivals. In addition, there were numerous highly specialized industries, where success depended chiefly on technical sophistication and access to rare raw materials, or raw materials over which the Dutch entrepôt exerted a high degree of control, in which the Dutch not only outstripped all their rivals but, in some cases, surpassed all other contemporary trading powers put together. Among these were the processing of dyes and glazes, tobacco spinning and blending, diamond cutting and polishing, lens grinding, whale-oil refining for the soap and lighting fuel industries, and, for a time, sugar-refining. Dutch 'industrial capacity', in other words, was not simply a matter of high output in certain sectors. To a large extent it was also a matter of specialized techniques, which for a variety of reasons others found it difficult to emulate, and the attainment of high quality. Specialized techniques and superior quality were often in fact as important as high output in progressively strengthening the Dutch grip over the international traffic in manufactured and processed goods. If the Dutch provinces never produced as much linen as France, Germany, or the South Netherlands, the linen-bleaching industry at Haarlem finished linen to a higher standard than could be achieved elsewhere. In the same way, the dyeing and finishing of English broadcloth was carried on in Holland to a higher standard than could be attained in England itself at least down to the middle of the seventeenth century.[96]

The expansion of the Dutch world-trading system to its first peak during Phase Two was characterized by both the growth of existing Dutch industry and a proliferation of new industries. Dutch mastery of the Arctic whaling grounds after 1614 encouraged the setting up of dozens of whale-oil refineries and soap factories, especially on the Zaan and around Rotterdam. One of van Tweenhuysen's establishments was a soap factory at

---

[96] Posthumus (ed.), *Nationale organisatie*, pp. xxv–xxvi; Supple, *Commercial Crisis*, 261–2.

Haarlem.[97] The Dutch conquest of the Swedish copper trade in the years 1613–14 soon led to the setting up of copper mills at Amsterdam, Dordrecht, Utrecht, and Amersfoort, frequently with skills and equipment imported from Germany, especially Aachen.[98] By 1612 Amsterdam brokers were assuring buyers that Dutch copper pots and kettles were as serviceable as the German products on which they were modelled. Within a few years, Dutch copperware was rivalling the German product everywhere from the Baltic to West Africa. In the same way, the taking over by the Dutch, after 1609, of the carrying of Portugal's sugar re-exports to northern Europe led to a spectacular revival of the Dutch sugar-refining industry, which had, owing to the Spanish embargoes, been in a somewhat depressed state since the late 1590s. From only three or four in the 1590s, the number of sugar-refineries just at Amsterdam soared to twenty-five by 1620 and there were two more at Middelburg, another at Delft, and another on the Zaan.[99]

Meanwhile, at Leiden, output of 'new draperies', especially *says*, fustians, bays, and rashes, grew even faster after 1609 than it had before. Where output rose from 53,570 pieces to 71,205 in the twelve years from 1595 to 1608, during Phase Two output reached almost the 100,000 mark.[1] Moreover, this accelerating growth of the 'new drapery' industry in Holland coincided with the revival of the industry in the South Netherlands which Willem Usselinx had forecast. Production of *says* at Hondschoote rose by over a third during the Truce, that is even faster than output at Leiden.[2] This meant stiffer competition for the Dutch textile towns, though up to a point this development worked to the advantage of Dutch exporters. Usselinx notes that after 1609 Dutch merchants took to playing the two rival centres of production off against each other so as to depress prices and swell their stockpiles.[3] What made it possible for the Dutch cloth industry to expand rapidly in these harshly competitive circumstances was the opening up of the Iberian market to Dutch products after 1609 and the growing

[97] Hart, *Geschrift en getal,* 17, 107–8.
[98] *Bronnen ... bedrijfsleven,* ii. 17, 26, 359–60; Klein, *De Trippen,* 324–7.
[99] IJzerman (ed.), 'Deductie', 103.
[1] Posthumus, *Geschiedenis,* ii. 9, 128–9, 136.
[2] Coornaert, *Un centre industriel d'autrefois,* 493–5.
[3] Usselinx, *Waerschouwinghe,* 20.

success of the Dutch in undermining England's position as the dominant cloth supplier to the Baltic.[4]

The increasing competitiveness of the Dutch in the textile sphere, and in manufacturing generally, is especially remarkable in that the Dutch were hampered throughout the period of their primacy in world trade by much higher wage costs than prevailed at that time in England, Flanders, or Germany. Dutch manufacturers claimed that their wage costs were vastly higher, in some cases as much as twice as high, and such evidence as we have suggests that they were right.[5] Yet so great was the advantage afforded by the Dutch entrepôt, as a central storehouse of raw materials and semi-manufactured goods, to the Dutch manufacturer, and such were the technical skills available to him, that the obstacle of high wage costs was more than offset. While the Dutch could not hope to match England's total output of woollen cloth, or produce cloth as cheaply, they had the advantage when it came to dyeing and 'dressing' the cloth. Whilst the Spanish embargoes continued in effect, the full impact of this was not felt. But the lowering of Dutch tariffs and shipping costs in 1609, and the resumption of the flow of Ibero-American dyestuffs such as indigo, cochineal, and Brazil wood to Amsterdam, lent added impetus to the Dutch dyeing and finishing industries.[6] It was in the years around 1609 that Dutch cloth exports to the Baltic and other markets began to pose a serious challenge to England's position as northern Europe's prime cloth supplier (see table 4.9). After 1609 Dutch superiority in dyeing and 'dressing' was thus not only a means of syphoning off a large part of the profits from England's own output (for most of the benefit accrued to those who handled the finishing processes and distribution) but also a means of undermining English trade with the Baltic generally. After 1609 a progressively lower proportion of English cloth was exported dyed and finished to northern Europe and a gradually rising proportion dispatched undyed and unfinished to the Dutch entrepôt.[7]

This marked shift to England's detriment around 1609 added

---

[4] Federowicz, *England's Baltic Trade,* 92–3, 96.

[5] Usselinx, *Gronich discours,* fos. 2, 6; Wilson, 'Cloth Production', 219; Slicher van Bath, 'Economic Situation', 34.

[6] ARH SG 4981/i, Merchant Adventurers to SG, Middelburg, 16 May 1609; Israel, *Dutch Republic and the Hispanic World,* 58.

[7] Friis, *Alderman Cockayne's Project,* 231; Supple, *Commercial Crisis,* 261–3.

TABLE 4.9. *Dutch and English cloth exports to the Baltic, 1600–1620*

Year	Dutch cloths	English cloths
1600	5,390	40,579
1601	3,503	37,203
1602	1,417	30,062
1603	3,060	28,820
1604	4,178	29,950
1605	4,241	28,402
1606	6,264	34,184
1607	9,472	25,580
1608	11,266	38,970
1609	12,381	39,063
1610	9,895	27,136
1611	9,418	27,136
1612	13,505	29,956
1613	6,943	26,813
1614	8,121	37,448
1615	5,326	33,341
1616	5,665	27,266
1617	6,069	20,697
1618	26,835	37,113
1619	34,820	42,743
1620	22,545	26,009

Source: Bang, *Tabeller*, ii. 196–325.

to the tension which grew up in these years, in the immediate aftermath of 1609, arising from the increasing rivalry in the East Indies and the Levant and the encounters in the whaling grounds around Spitsbergen. By 1612 England and the United Provinces were locked in confrontation over a whole range of economic issues. It was a confrontation which in other circumstances might well have led eventually to war. But, in contrast to what happened the next time the Dutch benefited from peace with Spain at England's expense (after 1648), this time the English government preferred to confine the argument to the economic sphere, which is perhaps what ensured that it was the Dutch who came off best.

England's answer to the rapid strides made by the Dutch in northern cloth markets after 1609 was the Cockayne Project. This was designed to break the hold of the Dutch entrepôt over a rising proportion of English cloth exports by means of a radical solution imposed by the crown. The plan was to ban the export from England of undyed cloth, thereby compelling the producers to complete manufacture at home. English cloth exporters would then reap the whole benefit of selling the cloth abroad and distribution of English cloth from the Dutch entrepôt would be curbed. Up to a point the Cockayne Project worked. English cloth exports direct to the Baltic shot up. Dutch cloth exports were depressed. But the Project, it soon became clear, had an essential flaw. It failed to take account of the capacity of the Dutch Republic to retaliate and of the likely impact of Dutch measures on the English economy. The Amsterdam city council,[8] as well as the Holland textile towns, reacted with great anger, and on 16 October 1614 the States General imposed a general ban on the importing of dyed and dressed cloth, and for good measure also kerseys, into the Republic.[9]

Drafted by Oldenbarnevelt himself, the Dutch ban astutely avoided any mention of England, English cloth, or retaliation. It simply banned the importing of all foreign dyed and dressed cloth into the United Provinces on the grounds of the inferior quality of foreign dyeing and finishing. But no one was taken in by the disguise, or was unaware that it was practically only English cloth exports which were hit. The effect was devastating. The collapse of English cloth exports to the Dutch provinces, and a large part of their German hinterland, could only be partially compensated for by increased sales of finished cloth in the Baltic. The inevitable result was a paralysing slump, and widespread distress at home.[10] By 1616, with the recession deepening, James I's ministers were ready to give in.

But the States of Holland were in no hurry to revert to the *status quo ante*. They were determined to press home their advantage, and so were the merchants and clothiers. The cloth buyers of Holland, some thirty or forty of them, formed a national cartel, or, as the English ambassador described it, a 'society absolutely to exclude our cloths', which extended its organization to all the

---

[8] GA Amsterdam *vroed.* x. 136, res. 6 Oct. 1614.

[9] *Groot Placaet-Boeck*, i. 1170–1.

[10] Friis, *Alderman Cockayne's Project*, 267, 343–5; Grayson, 'From Protectorate to Partnership', 195–7.

main towns.[11] Indeed, the merchants were reportedly even more 'eager and earnest' to go on with the contest than Oldenbarnevelt and his colleagues. It was beginning to be seen what a formidable economic power in the world the Holland merchant élite working hand in hand with the Dutch federal state represented. Finally, in 1617 the English government threw in its hand and allowed exports of undyed and unfinished cloth to the United Provinces to resume without having persuaded the States General to withdraw their ban on English finished cloth. Thus, the Dutch ban, introduced as retaliation, remained permanently in force and was regarded as a cornerstone of Dutch economic policy over subsequent decades.[12] From 1618, with the defeat of the Cockayne Project, there was a dramatic jump in Dutch cloth exports to the Baltic (see table 4.9). The process of the Dutch conquest of the Baltic rich trades was accelerating.

By 1620 the Dutch world-trade system had reached its first zenith. Rapid expansion had been in progress since 1609, an expansion in which Dutch industries played an increasingly vital role. But the question of how much further the Dutch commercial empire could expand within the limits set by the country's industrial capacity was not yet to be answered. For in 1621 the process of expansion was suddenly halted, because of a new politico-economic offensive launched by Spain. Phase Three (1621–47), except in the Indies, was to be one of stagnation.

---

[11] *Letters from and to Sir Dudley Carleton*, 59–61; Posthumus (ed.), *Nationale organisatie*, 167–9.

[12] Van Dillen, 'Leiden als industriestad', 35–6; Wilson, 'Cloth Production', 214–16.

5

The Dutch and the Crisis of the World Economy, 1621–1647

THE RESUMPTION OF THE DUTCH–SPANISH CONFLICT

Historians of early modern Europe broadly agree that the European and world economy entered an age of general crisis around 1620. The major manifestations of this world economic general crisis were the depression in the Mediterranean (which set in in 1621 and continued down to the eighteenth century), the slump of the 1620s in the Baltic, the disruption of the economies of Germany and central Europe during the Thirty Years' War, and, beginning in the years 1622–3, the onset of a long-term decline in Spain's transatlantic trade with the New World.[1] This contraction in international trade went hand in hand with a reversal of activity in other spheres, including industrial output, which was particularly severe in Italy, Germany, and Flanders, though in France and England also this was a period of difficulty and instability.[2] Around 1620 the long, sustained expansion of the world economy since the late fifteenth century came to a definitive end.[3]

For the Dutch economy, the period 1621–47, Phase Three in the evolution of Dutch world-trade primacy, was one of relative stagnation and profound restructuring. But, if we are to grasp the nature and significance of this restructuring process, it is essential that we analyse it against the background of changes in the world economy, just as Phases One and Two of Dutch world-trade hegemony have to be grasped in the light of the major world economic shifts of the time. Historians have produced a variety of explanations for the decades-long world economic crisis which began around 1620. Some of these are of a purely economic nature.

[1] Chaunu, *Séville et l'Atlantique*, viii. pt. 2, 1519–21.
[2] De Vries, *Economy of Europe*, 16–21.
[3] Ibid.; van der Wee and Peeters, 'Un modèle économique', 114; Romano, 'Tra XVI e XVII secolo', 487–8.

The historian of Spain's transatlantic commerce, Pierre Chaunu, for instance, argued that the falling off of silver shipments from Spanish America to Europe caused a shortage of precious metals which acted as a brake on international commerce, reducing investment in commodities, industry, and shipping. But subsequent research has shown that the drop in silver output in the Americas, and its impact on bullion circulation in the Old World, was less drastic than was formerly believed, and few would now accept that this was anything more than a subsidiary factor to the general crisis.

But perhaps the most influential approach to the general crisis has been that of Braudel. According to Braudel, the 'secular trend' in Europe's material existence, after several minor, temporary reversals, was finally and decisively reversed in the decades 1620–50. What Braudel called the 'decline of material existence' was most marked, and began first, in the Mediterranean. This led to a displacement of economic leadership and vitality from the Mediterranean to north-western Europe. The 'slow but powerful upsurge' of all forms of economic activity, in progress since the mid-fifteenth century, was ended by the failure of food and industrial output, especially in southern Europe, to keep up with the expansion in population and consumption. Fixing an exact date, or set of dates, for his *renversement de la tendance séculaire* proved something of a problem, because the turning-point in northern Europe could hardly be dated before 1650, when the Baltic bulk trade began to decline.[4] This is why, in the first edition of his acclaimed work on the Mediterranean, Braudel dated the decisive turning-point as 1600 'or 1620', but later decided, in view of the data for northern Europe, that '1650 was a likelier date'.[5]

The view that the *renversement* took place in the north around 1650 has had considerable appeal for scholars working on Dutch economic trends. Indeed, if one approaches the rise and decline of the Dutch entrepôt from the perspective of the bulk trades, there is something to be said for claims that the long expansion of the North Netherlands economy since the fifteenth century was finally reversed around 1650; and that the subsequent waning of the Dutch entrepôt was rooted in shifts in patterns of consumption

---

[4] Jeannin, 'Les Comptes du Sund', 322–4.
[5] Braudel, *The Mediterranean*, ii. 1240–2.

elsewhere.[6] Adopting the Braudelian approach, some Dutch scholars have come to see the *renversement* of bulk-trade trends around 1650 as the most fundamental turning-point in the history of the Dutch entrepôt and its role in Europe's material existence.[7]

Emphasizing trends in material existence, Braudel denied that there was any short, sharp shock in the sphere of international power politics which precipitated the economic general crisis of the seventeenth century. Some scholars have tended to follow him in this. However, most general economic historians have come to accept that no purely economic explanation offers an adequate basis of interpretation, though there is still a marked unwillingness to accept that the world economic crisis was, after all, primarily the result of non-economic and non-demographic factors. Jan de Vries, for example, has argued that, whilst warfare must be taken into account as a significant factor,

we must ... discount warfare as a general cause of the economic crisis. Aside from the fact that the timing of military destruction and economic stagnation does not lend unqualified support to this view, the major weakness of the argument is that the destruction and dislocation of warfare was local and that a compensating economic stimulus of orders for equipment and payments for services very likely made up for these losses. Thus, the incessant wars stimulated some sectors of the European economy while they wrought havoc with other sectors; the taxes imposed by the wars overburdened some regions and acted as a leaven in the economic life of others.[8]

This is perfectly true provided one defines 'local' as used here in a wide enough sense. For it was not only Germany, Bohemia, Hungary, Italy, Denmark, and the South Netherlands where economic life was dislocated by the struggles of the Thirty Years' War (1618–48). It should not be forgotten that the conflicts of these decades, and those that followed, also disrupted material life in regions far removed from the main theatre of war, either from a spilling over of the fighting, as in Brazil, Ceylon, the Philippines, and the Caribbean, or through fiscal and other forms of war-related pressure, as in Spain, Portugal, southern Italy, and France. But, in any case, since most general economic historians, including

[6] Faber, 'Decline of the Baltic Grain Trade', 126–31.
[7] See, in particular, van der Woude, 'De "Nieuwe Geschiedenis"', 22–4.
[8] De Vries, *Economy of Europe*, 22.

de Vries himself, accept that the economic crisis itself was 'local' in as far as some pockets of Europe and the wider world were untouched by, or profited from, the general *malaise*, it is hardly convincing to argue that war was not the major factor on the grounds that its impact was unevenly spread.

But was the warfare of the 1620–50 period, and subsequent decades, significantly more destructive than earlier warfare? There is little doubt that it was. In the first place, the armies employed after 1618 were very much larger than those in use during the fifteenth and sixteenth centuries. To sustain these large armies for decades on end, the tax burden and pressure on manpower and resources, especially food stocks, horses, cattle, wagons, and building materials, rose to unprecedentedly high levels. Moreover, this pressure extended to many regions which were not directly involved in the fighting, such as Switzerland, Norway, southern Italy, and Spanish America.[9] Then, in addition, one must take into account (Braudel notwithstanding) the impact of the blockades, embargoes, and maritime offensives of the era. The wars caused unprecedented destruction on land but also disrupted Europe's shipping and shipping-routes to a greater extent than had ever been seen previously. Thus, while there is a persistent reluctance to accept that the political context of international rivalry and war was the major factor in the world economic crisis of the seventeenth century, there has, as yet, been no convincing reply to the proposition that it was. Furthermore, if we examine the pressures and setbacks which caused the restructuring of the Dutch trading system, beginning in 1621, and the shifts and adaptations which resulted from it, it is hard to avoid the conclusion that escalating warfare was in reality the root cause of those pressures, setbacks, and shifts

The decisive political 'event' of this period for the Dutch, Spanish, and Portuguese economies and dependencies, and indeed for the entire Mediterranean and much else besides, was the resurgence of economic conflict between Spain and the Dutch in 1621.[10] This marks the onset of Phase Three. In April 1621 the new king of Spain, Philip IV (1621–65) reimposed the sweeping embargoes on Dutch ships, goods, and assets throughout the Iberian Peninsula which his father had introduced in 1598. The

[9] Israel, *Dutch Republic and the Hispanic World*, 68–9, 293–6.
[10] Ibid. 86, 134–43.

ban was also extended to Spanish southern Italy.[11] The Spanish navy and Flemish privateers resumed their raiding against Dutch shipping and fisheries; the Dutch recommenced their naval blockade of the Flemish coast, blocking commercial freightage by sea to the South Netherlands, and reverted to the war tariff of 1603, which put up a protective barrier against the textiles of Flanders.

The impact of the Spanish embargoes of 1621 on the European world economy—despite Braudel's claims to the contrary[12]—and in particular on Dutch carrying to and from the Iberian Peninsula and between the Peninsula and Italy and therefore on Dutch salt, sugar, and dyestuff stocks, on freightage and insurance, on the herring fishery and the Amsterdam sugar-refineries, was—and could not be otherwise than—immense. All Dutch ships left the ports of Spain and Portugal in April 1621 and, except where deception could be used, were forced to keep away from then on.[13] Dutch trade with the Iberian Peninsula was severely curtailed. In Portugal and the realms of eastern Spain, the embargoes were less rigorously enforced than in Castile. But there too the ban unquestionably had a major impact.[14] From between four hundred and five hundred Dutch ships visiting Iberian ports yearly during the Truce, the annual total after 1621 was cut to a tiny fraction, at most about 5 per cent of the previous level. From 1630 onwards, admittedly, the Spanish crown issued passes for Dutch vessels to bring grain and timber and collect salt at Setúbal, Aveiro, and Cadiz. But the quantity of shipping admitted remained small and the traffic was tightly regulated to exclude Dutch-owned, or produced, manufactures and spices.[15] It was only when Portugal broke free of Spain and regained her independence in December 1640 that Dutch ships returned to Portuguese ports in large numbers. But in Spain the embargo remained in force down to 1647 and Dutch shipping continued to be shut out.[16] Clear examples of the continuing effectiveness of the Spanish embargoes

[11] AGS Estado 1883, Philip III to the Italian viceroys of Spain, Madrid, 27 Mar. 1621.

[12] Braudel, *La Méditerranée*, i. 572–3; Braudel, *Civilisation matérielle*, iii. 175.

[13] Israel, *Dutch Republic and the Hispanic World*, 93–4, 134–42.

[14] Ibid.; Rau, 'Subsidios', 219–27; Rau, *Estudos sobre a história do sal português*, 209.

[15] AGS Estado 2239, 'Condiciones ... para venir por sal a España; GA Amsterdam *vroed.* xv, fo. 149ᵛ, res. 29 May 1630.

[16] AGS Estado 2067, consulta 5 Aug. 1647; *Correspondencia diplomática de los plenipotenciarios españoles*, i. 492–3.

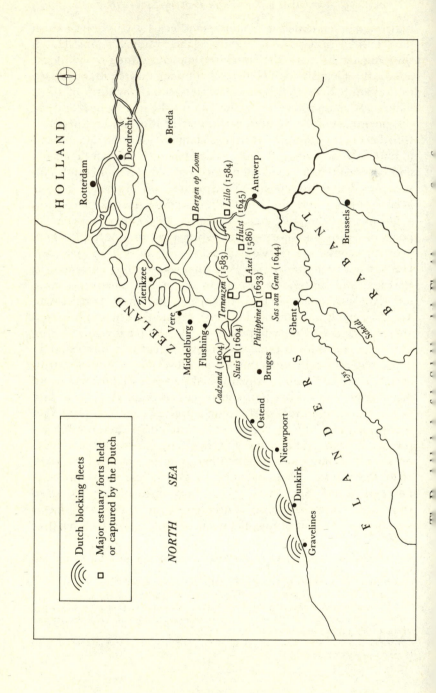

NORTH SEA

HOLLAND

ZEELAND

BRABANT

FLANDERS

Rotterdam

Dordrecht

Breda

Bergen op Zoom

Lillo (1584)

Hulst (1645)

Antwerp

Zierikzee

Vere

Middelburg

Flushing

Termeuzen (1583)

Axel (1586)

Philippine (1633)

Sas van Gent (1644)

Ghent

Brussels

Cadzand (1604)

Sluis (1604)

Bruges

Ostend

Nieuwpoort

Dunkirk

Gravelines

Schelde

L⁹⁵

Dutch blocking fleets

Major estuary forts held
or captured by the Dutch

even in the very last year that they remained in force, after more than a quarter of a century, can be given. In 1646 most Spanish goods percolating through to the Dutch entrepôt were still being freighted in Hanseatic ships. Thus, of fourteen ships which returned from the Mediterranean to Amsterdam in the year down to April 1647 and which called at Spanish ports to collect Spanish commodities *en route*, no less than twelve, six-sevenths of the total, were listed in Amsterdam as being north German.[17]

It is true that, to begin with, much of the commerce the Dutch had had with the Peninsula before 1621 was merely re-routed through Hamburg and other north German ports, and freighted in a mixture of Hanseatic ships and Dutch vessels purporting to be Hanseatic, carrying false papers and flags. 'The Hansa towns', reported the Dutch resident at Hamburg in 1622, are now 'flourishing owing to their free and uninterrupted commerce with Spain which has much increased since your High Mightinesses [the States General] resumed the war.'[18] But even this involved a reduction in the scale of the commerce, as well as greater risk, cost, and inconvenience for Dutch merchants; for the Hanseatics simply did not possess enough large ships to carry all the traffic of which the Dutch had been stripped. Thus, if we look at the figures for ships sailing direct from the Iberian Peninsula to the Baltic in the years 1620–40 (table 5.1 and fig. 5.1), we see that, while the Dutch share almost completely collapsed in the 1620s, and recovered to only a modest extent in the 1630s, the Hanseatics and Danes were unable to fill the whole of the gap left by the departure of the Dutch. From 1613 to 1619 substantially more than one hundred Dutch vessels had sailed each year direct from the Iberian Peninsula to the Baltic carrying salt, olive oil, figs, almonds, raisins, and other southern European products (see table 4.6). After 1621 the highest total of Hanseatic and Danish–Norwegian vessels which sailed from the Peninsula to the Baltic direct in any one year never exceeded ninety-three and usually the equivalent total was vastly less. The Hanseatics and (except in the years 1625–30) the English were able to take over most of the functions the Dutch had fulfilled in the carrying traffic between the Peninsula and northern Europe but they lacked the ships to

---

[17] ARH Levantse Handel 264, fos. 21, 88, 194ᵛ; Wätjen, *Niederländer im Mittelmeergebiet,* 221–6.

[18] Wurm, *Über den Lebensschicksale,* 32.

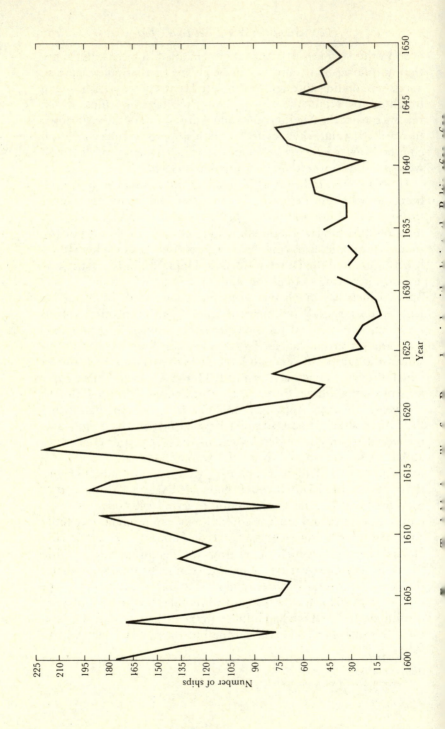

TABLE 5.1. *Voyages direct from the Iberian Peninsula to the Baltic, 1620–1641*

Year	Total of all nations	Dutch	Hanseatic	Danish and Norwegian
1620	105	91	10	4
1621	61	36	22	2
1622	56	2	41	12
1623	99	3	62	31
1624	86	2	65	16
1625	40	0	31	8
1626	36	0	35	1
1627	22	1	21	0
1628	9	0	7	2
1629	14	0	11	3
1630	28	3	22	3
1631	64	10	42	9
1632	30	6	20	3
1634	55	25	28	1
1636	43	18	22	2
1637	39	10	28	1
1638	66	27	35	4
1639	64	41	20	2
1640	30	14	15	1
1641	56	34	17	4

Source: Bang, *Tabeller*, i. 218–340.

carry as much Iberian salt as the Dutch had previously with the result that acute shortages developed in the United Provinces and the Baltic and the price of high-grade salt in northern Europe rose, and remained, substantially higher than it had been in the years 1609–21 until after the secession of Portugal from Spain in December 1640.[19] The carrying of salt from the eastern Spanish salt-pans of La Mata and Ibiza to Italy was still harder hit by the lack of ships resulting, as a Spanish official put it, from the 'wars of Flanders'.[20] The shipping of other Spanish products to Italy, notably high-quality Castilian wool for the cloth industry of Venice, was also seriously hampered at least down to the mid-

[19] Israel, *Dutch Republic and the Hispanic World*, 214–15.
[20] ACA CA 603, doc. 6, Pedro Martínez de Vera to Nicolas Mensa, Valencia, 9 Mar. 1623.

1620s. It was not that the Hanseatics and English were slow to see, or to seize, their opportunity in the carrying traffic between Spain and Italy.[21] Braudel, misled by his belief that political pressures could not determine shipping patterns, assumed that the previous disappearance of Hanseatic vessels from the Mediterranean after 1609 was part of some long-term shift: 'au début du XVIIe siècle', he wrote, 'les Hanséates étaient éliminés et leurs navires ne dépassaient plus guère l'escale de Málaga'.[22] In this, once again, he was fundamentally mistaken. There was a marked revival of the Hanseatic role in the western Mediterranean after 1621. But it took time for Hamburg and Lübeck to acquire or build the additional ships.

Trade in Iberian and Ibero-American products had been vital to the functioning of the Dutch world entrepôt from the outset. As in 1598, the imposing of the Spanish embargoes had, and were bound to have, serious implications for every sector of the Dutch trading system. If the commerce in Mediterranean fruit, wine, and olive oil could be abandoned to the English and Hanseatics without excessive loss, and if there was initially the expectation that Iberian salt would be replaced with high-grade salt from the Caribbean, there was no alternative to Spain as the main source of silver. The percolation of Mexican and Peruvian silver, via Spain, to the Dutch entrepôt did not, of course, cease. But after 1621 the flow had to be re-routed, usually through Calais, Antwerp, Hamburg, and (after 1630) London, and was now dealt in and shipped by other trading powers. The transfer of Spanish American bullion to the Dutch entrepôt, consequently, became slower, costlier, and more difficult, with the result that the price of silver on the Amsterdam Exchange inexorably rose.[23] The whole of Dutch commerce suffered from this scarcity of specie. But the VOC, which required an immense regular input of bullion to settle its balances in the East Indies, faced a particular problem, especially as the natives of Indonesia had acquired a well-known

---

[21] ASV CSM 1st ser. 146, fo. 158, res. 2 Mar. 1625; Israel, 'Spanish Wool Exports', 199–202.

[22] Braudel, *La Méditerranée*, i. 568–9; Beutin, *Der deutsche Seehandel*, 29–45; Baetens, *Nazomer van Antwerpens welvaart*, i. 50, 70.

[23] Van Dam, *Beschryvinge*, i. 1, 633; van Dillen, 'Amsterdam als wereldmarkt', 545.

preference for Spanish pieces-of-eight, and less of the bullion still reaching Holland was arriving in the shape of Spanish coins.[24]

Dutch merchants adopted various subterfuges in their efforts to continue with their Iberian commerce. One method used by Balthasar Coymans and other Dutch élite merchants down to 1635 was to employ French agents and shipping, based at Calais. Using French ships and papers was expensive, as well as indirect, and risky, but to some extent this ploy did succeed.[25] A still more thriving route, at any rate until the Franco-Spanish frontier was closed to commerce in 1635, was via Bayonne and St Jean de Luz, overland across the Pyrenees, via the viceroyalty of Navarre, and through the 'dry ports' of Castile, to Madrid. This traffic was even more tortuous and costly than using French ships based at Calais and was only worthwhile for spices and other high-value wares. But it served as the main method for supplying northern Castile and Aragon with Dutch spices and textiles, and bringing out silver and wool to the Dutch entrepôt down to 1635.[26] This traffic was chiefly in the hands of Amsterdam Sephardi Jews working hand in hand with the Portuguese New Christian community at Bayonne and their fellow Portuguese New Christians at Madrid.[27] But others also used this subsidiary depot for fine goods at Bayonne, and, owing to the sudden interest in this back-door route to Spain from 1621, 'various merchants of Amsterdam', backed by the Amsterdam city council, petitioned the States General in August 1624 to establish a Dutch consul at Bayonne to gather information from Spain and assist the overland traffic across the Pyrenees to Pamplona and Madrid, 'for as long as the war with Spain shall continue'.[28]

Enquiries made by Spanish officials revealed that around thirty Dutch ships delivered spices, and other fine goods for Castile and Aragon, at Bayonne, during the two opening years of the war.[29] The Bayonne route, Philip's ministers quickly realized, was a serious loophole. But there were others. In particular it was

[24] Van Dam, *Beschryvinge*, i. pt. 1.

[25] ARH SG 5492/ii, exhibitum 15 May 1626; ARH SG 3185, fo. 82, res. SG 12 Mar. 1626 on request of Balthasar Coymans.

[26] AGS Hacienda 592, consulta 31 Oct. 1622; AGS Estado 2645, Viceroy of Navarre to Philip IV, Pamplona, 24 Jan. 1624.

[27] Israel, *European Jewry*, 108, 116.

[28] ARH SG 3183, fos. 445ᵛ–446, res. 17 Aug. 1624.

[29] AGS Hacienda, 592, consulta 31 Oct. 1622.

well known in Holland and Zeeland that the small, remote ports of Viana and Aveiro in northern Portugal had been exceptionally resistant to the enforcement of the embargoes of 1598–1609 and continued to be so in the 1620s.[30] There is evidence that Dutch ships continued to enter these ports even in the late 1620s.

To a modest extent, then, the Spanish general embargo of 1621–47 was evaded, especially in the early 1620s. But this does not mean that the Spanish embargo of 1621–47, any more than that of 1598–1609, failed to exert an immense impact. On the contrary, it is certain that it did. The very lengths to which Dutch entrepreneurs were forced to go in their efforts to evade the Spanish ban—the use of mule tracks across the Pyrenees and Navarre, the hiring of French, Scottish, and Hanseatic shipping at exorbitant rates, the suddenly disproportionate role of the Jews in what remained of Dutch trade with the Peninsula—confirm that the setback to the Dutch world entrepôt was a massive one. Moreover, Olivares and his colleagues strove unremittingly to tighten up their programme of economic warfare against the Dutch during the 1620s.[31] Spanish ministers soon realized that it was impossible to achieve the systematic enforcement they were aiming for relying on the existing judicial and administrative machinery of the Spanish realms and Portugal. Consequently, in 1624 the king set up the Almirantazgo, initially only in Andalusia, an institution conceived as a counterpart to the Casa de Contratación (House of Trade), at Seville, designed to serve as a commercial inspectorate, court, and supervisory body in the same way that the Casa supervised Spanish trade with the Americas. The Almirantazgo was assigned 'jurisdiction civil and criminal' over all Andalusia's commerce with northern Europe and was granted sweeping powers. Investigation of irregularities and prosecution of offenders was removed from the sphere of the ordinary courts. By 1626 the Almirantazgo had a staff of sixty-six inspectors in Andalusia's ports.[32] To ensure zeal in the checking of ships, cargoes, and warehouses, the Almirantazgo borrowed an important operating principle from the Inquisition: the salaries of its inspectors were paid out of the proceeds from confiscations. As the new organ-

---

[30] RAZ SZ 2102, 'Deductie' (1622), fos. 1ᵛ–2; AGS Estado 2646, consultas 13 Jan. 1627, 24 May 1628.
[31] See, for instance, AGS Estado 2037, consulta 14 June 1623, *voto* of Olivares.
[32] Dominguez Ortiz, 'Guerra económica', 105.

ization expanded, Philip extended its jurisdiction first to northern Castile, then to Portugal, and eventually to the eastern realms of Spain. This enlarged, national organization was regulated from Madrid by a newly set up royal council and tribunal known as the *Junta de Almirantazgo* which was now made responsible for all aspects of Spanish administration in the sphere of ports, shipping, and commerce.

The Almirantazgo was a heavy-handed organization which confiscated large numbers of neutral ships and cargoes in Iberian ports on suspicion that these were of Dutch origin or Dutch-owned, and it rapidly acquired a reputation for draconian severity abroad. Its bite derived from the fact that its officers and courts did not have to prove that confiscated goods were Dutch; it was enough if the accompanying certificates were unsatisfactory. The Almirantazgo's ability to operate on this basis rested on an elaborate framework of diplomacy which represents one of the most striking features of Spanish foreign policy at this time. Particularly notable in this respect were the Anglo-Spanish peace treaty of 1630 and Spain's various agreements with Denmark. Under the Anglo-Spanish treaty, Charles I conceded, as had his father under the treaty of 1604, that English, Scottish and Irish merchants were forbidden to export Dutch products and wares belonging to Dutch merchants to Spain and its dominions, that all English, Scottish, and Irish vessels and cargoes entering Iberian ports must be accompanied by certificates drawn up in an approved form, signed and countersigned by authorities in the places where the goods originated, and that ships and cargoes which lacked such certificates were subject to outright confiscation by the Almirantazgo without any recourse to the English crown.[33]

In collaboration with Denmark, the Spanish crown posted an 'Agent' at Glückstadt, on the lower Elbe and, after 1630, insisted that all German cargoes shipped to the Peninsula on Hanseatic, Danish, or other 'neutral' shipping must henceforth be accompanied by special certificates issued at Glückstadt. Consignments of German goods which lacked these special certificates were subject to outright confiscation. According to the Hansa agent at Madrid, the Almirantazgo 'caused commerce to cease and many fleets which had been prepared for trade [with Spain

---

[33] Abreu y Bertodano, *Colección*, reynado de Phelipe IV, ii. 218–21.

and Portugal in the Hansa ports] not to be sent lest their cargoes be confiscated'.[34] According to Danish merchants, the Almirantazgo was so heavy-handed that it sometimes even seized cargoes that were covered by certificates issued by the Spanish agent at Glückstadt.[35]

The pressure Spain exerted on the Dutch trading system from 1621 down to 1647 consisted of two main elements—the embargoes and an ambitious raiding campaign. The main weapons for harassing Dutch shipping at sea were the new royal armada based at Dunkirk and the Flemish privateers whom the crown now spared no effort to encourage. At first the results were fairly meagre.[36] But from 1625 onwards raiding out of Dunkirk, Ostend, and Nieuwpoort rapidly grew in scale and effectiveness and was supplemented by a subsidiary raiding campaign out of Spanish ports. In 1627 the Dunkirkers alone captured or sank 150 Dutch and English vessels (Spain and England were at war in the years 1625–30) and in 1628 no less than 245. It was this powerful upsurge in Flemish privateering against Dutch merchant shipping in the late 1620s—and not the Swedish–Polish war then in progress—which was the principal reason for the sudden huge rise in Dutch freight and maritime insurance rates during the late 1620s (see table 5.2). This is shown particularly clearly by the evidence of the freight charges for shipping bulky goods from western France only as far as Holland and Zeeland. During the Truce the cost of shipping salt from western France to Amsterdam in Dutch ships was in most years as low as 8 or 9 guilders per last. In the years 1629–30 the charges for this route rose as high as 26 and 28 guilders per last before falling back to 17 and 18 guilders, about twice as high as the Truce-time level by the late 1630s.[37] As additional evidence, we may cite the similar, if less steep, pattern of rises in charges for shipping wine in Dutch ships from Bordeaux to Holland (see table 5.3). Here there was no rise before 1626, but, again, particularly steep rises in the late 1620s and in the late 1630s.

The revolution in Dutch freight rates of the 1620s affected all the Dutch sea lanes in European waters and had a serious impact

[34] Alcalá-Zamora, *España*, 281; Israel, 'Politics of International Trade Rivalry', 542–7.

[35] Johnsen, 'Relations commerciales', 80–1.

[36] Israel, *Dutch Republic and the Hispanic World*, 114–6.

[37] GA Amsterdam NA 239, fos. 5, 7, 10, 12ᵛ, 26.

TABLE 5.2. *Dutch freight charges for voyages to fetch salt from western France and then on direct to the Baltic, 1619–1640*

Month	Ship (lasts)	Destination	Rate (guilders/last)
Jan. 1619	*St Pieter* (100)	Riga	14.75
May 1619	*Jonas* (120)	Danzig	12.50
Aug. 1622	*Ouden Tobias*(135)	Danzig	18.00
June 1623	*Graef Maurits* (130)	Danzig	17.00
May 1624	*De Zon* (120)	Danzig	17.5
Mar. 1626	*St Jacob*(116)	Danzig	17.00
July 1626	*'t Fortuijn* (120)	Danzig	18.30
June 1627	*Tonjin* (140)	Danzig	21.50
Jan. 1629	*De Haes* (95)	Königsberg	49.00
Mar. 1629	*De Waterhont* (100)	Danzig	40.00
July 1630	*De Witte Duif* (125)	Danzig	30.00
Mar. 1635	*'t Zeepaard* 75)	Königsberg	33.00
Jan. 1640	— (150)	Danzig	29.50

Source: GA Amsterdam card index to Notarial Archive, 'Soutvaart'.

TABLE 5.3. *Dutch freight charges for voyages to fetch wine from Bordeaux to Amsterdam, 1619–1643*

Month	Ship (lasts)	Rate(guilders/last)
Nov. 1619	*De Fortuijn* (75)	14.00
Oct. 1620	*De Roos* (80)	13.00
Sept. 1622	*De Ploeger* (75)	13.00
Sept. 1625	*'t Schaekboort* (90)	13.00
Sept. 1625	*De Metselaer* (110)	12.00
Oct. 1627	*De Swarte* (65)	18.00
Sept. 1629	*de Krab* (100)	27.50
Sept. 1629	*'t Fortuijn* (120)	24.50
Sept. 1630	*t' Swarte Calf* (120)	18.00
Sept. 1635	*Gideon* (100)	17.75
Oct. 1636	*De Soutpan* (120)	18.00
Oct. 1638	*De Blauwe Duif* (100)	22.00
Sept. 1639	*St Jan* (80)	26.00
Aug. 1640	*De Fortuijn* (90)	33.00
June 1641	*'t Lam* (120)	28.00
Aug. 1641	*De Schout* (120)	27.50
Aug. 1643	*De Karseboom* (140)	24.00
Sept. 1643	*De Gecroonde Korf* (120)	22.00

Source: GA Amsterdam card index to the Notarial Archive, 'De vaart op Bordeaux'.

on trade to Russia and Norway as well as on the traffic to France and the Mediterranean. The cost of shipping timber from Norway to the Republic in Dutch vessels rose from under 10 guilders per last in 1620, to a peak of 24 guilders in 1640–1;[38] and, although charges fell back slightly in the next few years, they remained very high until after the fall of Dunkirk to the French in 1646. After reaching a peak in 1640–1, losses of Dutch shipping to the Dunkirkers continued to be substantial in the years 1642–4 (see table 5.4). In 1642 royal ships from Dunkirk captured eight richly laden Dutch merchantmen returning in convoy from Archangel.[39] This was a blow which cost Amsterdam's merchant élite hundreds of thousands of guilders.

As one would expect, the most sensational rises were in Dutch freight charges for voyages to the Iberian Peninsula. After 1630, down to 1640, Dutch ships which sailed to Portugal for salt carried passes which were obtained from the Spanish authorities in Brussels.[40] But even with these, freightage to Portugal was never less than three times as expensive as during the Twelve Years' Truce (see table 5.5). Also severely affected were Dutch freight rates for voyages to Italy. In 1621 these doubled within three months of the expiry of the Truce.[41]

The combined impact of the Spanish embargoes, Almirantazgo, and Dunkirkers engineered the second major restructuring of the Dutch trading system since 1590. Dutch trade with Spain was all but eliminated; Dutch trade with Portugal drastically reduced; and Dutch competitiveness in shipping seriously damaged by the steep rise in freight and insurance costs. The momentum of the Truce period was lost; contraction set in. Some strands of the Dutch trading system were paralysed, even decimated. One of these was the direct traffic in Dutch ships between the Baltic and the Mediterranean. In the seven years 1614–20 no less than 1,005 Dutch vessels had sailed direct from the Mediterranean, Spain, and Portugal through the Danish sound to the Baltic. The comparable total for the next seven years, 1621–27, was a mere fifty-two. An astounding nineteen-twentieths of this traffic was

[38] Schreiner, *Nederland og Norge*, 49; Schreiner, 'Die Niederländer und die norwegische Holzausfuhr', 324.
[39] ARB Admirauté 581, doc. 33.
[40] GA Amsterdam NA 670 c, 16; NA 762, fo. 58.
[41] *BGNO* vi. 81, 191, 197, 281, 440, 446, 449–50.

TABLE 5.4. *Dutch shipping losses to the Dunkirkers, 1642–1644*

Dutch ships seized or sunk	1642	1643	1644
Warships	1	1	1
Heavily armed merchant vessels	12	1	1
Large *fluyts* (over 100 lasts)	37	33	20
Small *fluyts* (under 100 lasts)	12	4	1
Smacks and boats under 50 lasts	18	12	37
Fishing vessels	38	47	78
TOTAL	118	98	138

Source: ARB Admirauté 581, doc. 33.

TABLE 5.5 *Dutch freight charges for voyages to fetch salt from Portugal to Amsterdam, 1618–1636*

Month	Ship (lasts)	Rate (guilders/last)
June 1618	(to Rotterdam)	9.25
Apr. 1619	*De Swarte Raven* (150)	9.50
Sept. 1620	*De Schuijr* (120)	9.00
Sept. 1622	*De Makreel* (170)	21.50
Oct. 1622	*De Landman* (160)	20.00
Apr. 1623	(French ship)	60.00
Apr. 1624	(Hanseatic ship)	34.00
Apr. 1630	*De vergulde snoeck* (120)*	30.00
May 1630	*De geele Pynas* (150)*	32.00
Mar. 1635	*De Nooteboom* (90)*	28.75
Mar. 1636	*De Hoope* (140)*	42.00

* Ships with passes issued by the Spanish authorities.
Sources: GA Amsterdam NA 241, fo. 85; NA 670, fo. 16; NA 1041, fo. 22; card index to the Notarial Archive, 'Soutvaart'.

eliminated. Dutch handling of Portuguese salt was reduced to a tiny fraction of previous levels. It is true that there was, in consequence, a rise in the proportion of French salt among total Dutch salt exports to the Baltic (see table 3.5). But it was not a compensating shift. In fact, the figures for numbers of Dutch ships sailing direct from western France to the Baltic after 1621 show no increase over the figures for previous years. For French salt, with its high magnesium content, was unsuited for preserving fish and therefore in little demand in Scandinavia or the Dutch herring ports.[42]

Initially, the salt dealers were confident that the gap could be filled, as in the years between 1598 and 1607, with Caribbean salt. The expectation was that the newly set up West India Company would now become the chief supplier of high-grade salt to the Dutch entrepôt. But Philip IV's ministers were also aware of the now crucial significance of the great salt-lagune at Punta de Araya and determined to prevent a recurrence of what had happened after the imposition of the 1598 embargoes. The Dutch salt-fleet, consisting mainly of ships from the West Frisian ports, especially Hoorn, did fetch salt from Punta de Araya in 1621 but, on returning the following year, found that the Spaniards had built a large fort at the entrance to the lagune. Part of the fleet, fitted out by pacifist Mennonites, had sailed unarmed and determined to avoid any combat. The rest attacked several times but were driven off. The fleet then partially dispersed in search of salt in other parts of the Caribbean. But a core of seventy ships was forced to return to Hoorn in the spring of 1623, their holds totally empty.[43] The dismay caused by this spectacle long lingered in the local collective memory. Punta de Araya had to be given up. Worse still, the exploitation of alternative salt-pans at Tortuga and St Martin succeeded only to a limited extent owing to Spanish raids.[44] In 1633, directed by an Italian military engineer, the Spaniards succeeded in flooding the salt-pan at Tortuga rendering it permanently useless. The same year, the Spaniards drove the Dutch from St Martin and established a strong garrison there.

The Dutch lost the battle for Caribbean salt and this, in turn, inevitably had major adverse consequences for both the Baltic carrying trade and the herring fishery. The contraction of the Dutch herring fishery was indeed one of the most serious setbacks suffered by the Dutch world-trade system during Phase Three. The shrinkage of the Dutch herring fleet, of the catch, and therefore also of Dutch herring exports, was partly a result of salt shortage and the high price of suitable salt on the Dutch entrepôt.[45] But there

---

[42] ARH SG 5501/ii, Amsterdam *vroedschap* to SG, 9 Apr. 1630; Blommaert, 'Brieven', 114.

[43] Velius, *Chronyk van Hoorn*, 606.

[44] Wright, *Nederlandsche Zeevaarders*, i. 136–40; Goslinga, *Dutch in the Caribbean* (1971), 127–39.

[45] Israel, *Dutch Republic and the Hispanic World*, 214.

TABLE 5.6. *Dutch voyages direct from western France to the Baltic, 1618–1639*

1618	199	1628	35
1619	131	1629	197
1620	174	1630	42
1621	178	1631	72
1622	168	1633	100
1623	402	1635	119
1624	297	1636	124
1625	177	1637	97
1626	241	1638	154
1627	165	1639	144

Source: Bang, *Tabeller*, i. 240–70.

was also another factor resulting from Spanish action: the attacks on the herring fleet itself.[46] The first large-scale raid on the herring busses by the Dunkirkers took place in 1625: eighty busses were burned and the men taken captive. Subsequent attacks in 1627, 1635, and 1637 also caused severe losses, over one hundred herring busses from the Maas ports and Enkhuizen being destroyed by the royal ships based at Dunkirk in 1635.[47] And then, on top of the main raids, there was also a continual harassment from smaller packs of privateers.

All of the Dutch fishing ports felt the weight of the Dunkirk offensive, the haemorrhage continuing down to 1646. For some of the Maas fleets we have statistics which indicate the scale of the losses. The Schiedam herring fleet caught one third less herring in the 1620s than in the previous decade, and in the 1630s registered the lowest catch over a decade in the town's history from the early sixteenth century down to 1720.[48] For Zeeland and the West Frisian ports we lack comparable data, but it is safe to infer that over the quarter century 1621–46 the overall drop in Dutch herring output compared with the previous quarter of a century was considerable, and probably as much as a third or more. The chronicler of Enkhuizen contented himself with remarking that,

[46] Ibid. 116–17, 192, 264–5; Centen, *Vervolg*, 48–9.
[47] ARH SG 5515/ii, Enkhuizen *vroedschap* to SG, 22 Sept. 1635; Centen, *Vervolg*, 76–7.
[48] Feijst, *Geschiedenis*, 104–6.

as a result of the Dunkirk offensive, the Enkhuizen herring fleet was 'notably diminished'.[49]

The knock-on effect of the blows to the herring fishery on Dutch Baltic trade is clearly evident. Dutch herring exports to Danzig, for example, were down by $12\frac{1}{2}$ per cent in the decades 1621–40 compared with the first two decades of the century.[50] It might be objected that this could have been caused by falling demand in Poland rather than problems on the supply side. But prices for herring at Danzig rose substantially during this period, which indicates that there was no lack of buoyancy on the demand side. Had their rivals been able to take advantage of the difficulties the Dutch were facing in supplying the Baltic with herring after 1621, they might well have succeeded in wresting part of the market away from the Dutch entrepôt. Indeed the English did send a trial consignment of herring in 1627. But it was no easy matter sufficiently to master the techniques of curing and packing in a short space of time so as to afford a product of acceptable taste and texture. The English herring reportedly found few buyers owing to its poor flavour.[51] The Dutch may have shipped appreciably less herring to Germany and the Baltic in the quarter century 1621–46 than they had before; but they nevertheless continued to supply practically all the herring these markets absorbed.[52]

THE BALTIC

The rise in Dutch freightage costs, together with the salt shortage, lower herring catch, and the collapse of the traffic direct between the Baltic and the Iberian lands except in Hanseatic and Danish vessels, reduced and weakened the Dutch Baltic carrying trade and placed it on a somewhat changed basis. The Dutch still heavily dominated the bulk-carrying traffic to Poland, East Prussia, and Riga, as well as to Sweden and Finland, but their Baltic commerce was now at a reduced level, contracting rather than expanding, and no longer directly linked, as it had been before, to the markets

---

[49] Centen, *Vervolg*, 95.
[50] Unger, 'Dutch Herring', fig. 1; van der Woude, *Het Noorderkwartier*, ii. 406.
[51] Abbing, *Geschiedenis*, 18.
[52] Baasch, 'Zur Geschichte', 70.

of southern Europe. As a result of the erosion of Dutch competitiveness with respect to freight rates, the overall share handled by the Dutch of the total traffic fell back, if only marginally, and there was a corresponding revival in the bulk carrying of the English, Hanseatics, and Danes. The freight rates offered by the competitors of the Dutch were now better value than before, so that their ships came into greater use.[53] In stark contrast to Phase Two, English vessels now carried appreciable quantities of grain to western markets, albeit mainly to those under Spanish control. When the threat of the Dunkirkers was at its height, in the years around 1640, even Dutch merchants began hiring English vessels to carry bulky goods to and from the Baltic.[54]

Initially the most damaging development for the Dutch entrepôt, however, was the diversion of the main carrying traffic between the Baltic and the Iberian kingdoms from Dutch hands to those of the Hanseatics (see table 5.7). Every year from 1621 down to the end of Phase Three large convoys, consisting of between fifty and seventy ships sailing together, plied to the Iberian kingdoms and back from Hamburg while smaller convoys sailed from Lübeck and sometimes also from Danzig.[55] It was these Hanseatic convoys which carried the masts, tar, and other naval munitions which enabled Spain's armadas and transatlantic *flotas* to keep functioning. Since the Dutch States General prohibited the movement of these supplies to the Peninsula, and its navy removed naval stores from the holds of westward-bound neutral vessels in the North Sea and Channel, the main Hanseatic convoys sailed 'northabout' round Scotland and Ireland to their Iberian destinations. On their return voyages, these convoys carried a wide range of fine goods, including Spanish American dyestuffs and considerable quantities of bullion. From 1621 right down to 1647, Hamburg not Amsterdam was the pivot at which the world of Baltic commerce linked up with the Hispanic world and the mechanism of Spain's transatlantic *flotas*.

The initial very high level of traffic between Hamburg and the Iberian lands of the early 1620s fell back markedly as from 1625

---

[53] Hinton, *The Eastland Trade*, 46–7; Israel, *Dutch Republic and the Hispanic World*, 51, 213.
[54] Hinton, *The Eastland Trade*, 47.
[55] Baasch, 'Hamburgs Seeschiffahrt und Warenhandel', 316, 324; Vogel, 'Beiträge', 135–41; Kellenbenz, *Unternehmerkräfte*, 61–3.

TABLE 5.7. *Return voyages from the Iberian Peninsula to Hamburg, 1623–1633*

| Year | Ports of departure | | | Total |
	Cadiz and San Lúcar	Other Spanish ports	Lisbon,Setúbal, and Oporto	
1623	38	16	102	156
1624	32	27	79	138
1625	20	7	24	51
1628	37	28	26	91
1629	46	28	25	99
1631	19	12	28	59
1633	12	7	28	47

Source: Baasch, 'Hamburgs Seeschiffahrt und Warenhandel', 331.

(see table 5.7). It is likely that this can be explained by the intensification of efforts in Spain and Portugal in 1624 to eradicate from the traffic Dutch vessels masquerading as Hanseatic. This is suggested by the fact that the main decline was in the number of ships used to fetch salt from Setúbal, for it was in this sector that it was hardest to find suitable genuine Hanseatic vessels to replace the Dutch ships which had formerly handled the traffic. Indeed, the number of ships sailing direct from Spanish ports alone to Hamburg was higher in the late 1620s than in the years 1621–3. However, the level of Hanseatic traffic with Spain was boosted in the late 1620s by the fact that England as well as the United Provinces was at war with Spain in the years 1625–30. During the 1630s the Hanseatics gradually lost ground in the Spanish trade to the English.

The Dutch share of the total Baltic traffic in the decades 1621–40 fell by roughly one-eighth compared with Phase Two (1609–21).[56] A large, and after 1630 increasing, proportion of the gains was achieved by England. Nevertheless, the Hanseatic gains continued to exert a stimulating effect on the entire north German maritime area down to the end of Phase Three. Even in 1625, a bad year, ninety-eight vessels sailed from Hamburg alone for Spain and Portugal. This represented only 4 per cent of the shipping

[56] Christensen, *Dutch Trade to the Baltic,* diagram ii; den Haan, *Moedernegotie,* 199; Israel, *Dutch Republic and the Hispanic World,* 51, 213.

clearing the Elbe port that year but around 20 per cent of the total tonnage, for the *Spanienfahrt* required large, sturdy ships, the construction of which flourished along the north German coast throughout the greater part of the Thirty Years' War.[57]

During Phase Three the Dutch lost an eighth of the Baltic traffic which they had handled during the Truce. Their exports of salt, herring, and Iberian products to the Baltic region all suffered. Nevertheless, despite these setbacks, Phase Three in some respects marked a further extension of the Dutch grip over the economic life of the Baltic, because the loss in volume was in some degree compensated for by a further jump in Dutch consignments of non-Iberian fine goods and manufactures.[58] Until 1590 the Dutch had shipped practically only bulky products such as salt, herring, and wine to the Baltic. During Phases One (1590–1609) and Two (1609–21) they had begun to ship large quantities of spices, sugar, Mediterranean fruit, and textiles to the region and, as a result, had won hegemony over the rich trades of the northern Baltic and of Poland and East Prussia. Then, after 1621, there was a further marked jump in Dutch consignments of spices and manufactures. Baltic demand for spices was increasing and the Dutch succeeded in supplying virtually the whole of the market, the English role being so small as to be negligible by comparison. At the same time, the Dutch increasingly gained ground in their contest with the English for control of the Baltic cloth market (see table 5.8). By the late 1620s the Dutch had overtaken the English in the quantity of cloth they shipped to Poland and East Prussia. No doubt the value of the English exports was still greater for the time being, since a larger proportion of the Dutch consignments consisted of cheap 'new draperies', which were now shut out of the Iberian market. But the Dutch were also extending their grip over the traffic in more expensive cloth. During the 1620s this was mainly reflected in the upsurge of English broadcloth dyed and 'dressed' in Holland. After 1635, however, Dutch fine cloth made from Spanish wool also began to cut into English sales. By the 1640s the Dutch had effectively replaced the English as the leading suppliers of textiles to the Baltic, supplying the best cloth as well as the greater quantity. The evolution of Dutch Baltic commerce

---

[57] Olechnowitz, *Schiffbau*, 37–9.
[58] Bang, *Tabeller*, ii. 320, 353, 396; Christensen, *Dutch Trade to the Baltic*, 465–6; Federowicz, *England's Baltic Trade*, 92, 96, 164–5.

TABLE 5.8. *Dutch and English cloth exports to the Baltic, 1580–1649*

Decade	English cloths	% of total imported into the Baltic	Dutch cloths	% of total imported into the Baltic
1580–9	176,385	91	8,663	4
1590–9	246,811	84	23,426	8
1600–9	332,713	82	61,172	15
1610–19	308,974	69	126,597	28
1620–9	317,149	49	295,532	46
1630–9*	262,667	42	314,303	50
1640–9	189,998	32	318,023	54

* The totals for this decade omit the figures for 1632 and 1634, which are lacking.
Sources: Bang, *Tabeller*, ii. 76–536; Federowicz, *England's Baltic Trade*, 92.

in the 1621–47 period thus marked a new stage in the long-term shift away from bulk freightage which characterizes the entire development of the Dutch world entrepôt from the 1590s down to the early eighteenth century.

   The resumption of the conflict with Spain significantly depressed the Dutch share of the total volume of Baltic trade. But it also weakened the Dutch position in the area in other respects. For it was now harder for the Republic to deploy sea power in support of its commerce in Baltic waters, as the Dutch navy had its hands tied coping with Spain and the Dunkirkers. Initially, with Sweden quiescent and Denmark allied with the Dutch against the Habsburgs, this did not matter. But circumstances soon changed. When, in the late 1620s, the Swedish king, Gustavus Adolphus, embarked on an expansionist policy along the Polish coast, captured Pillau and Elbing, and imposed a naval blockade on Danzig, Dutch trade with Poland collapsed.[59] In other circumstances the Republic would not have stood by and watched its Baltic interests being trampled on by Sweden, but, at this time, there was no alternative. After defeating Denmark in 1626, Habsburg armies had overrun much of north Germany and Jutland, threatening to bring the entire Baltic area under the joint hegemony of Spain, Austria, and Catholic Poland. In the years 1628–30 Spain in collusion with Austria and Poland began build-

[59] Roberts, *Gustavus Adolphus*, ii. 323–6.

ing a powerful armada on the German coast, at Wismar. It was plain enough that one of the main purposes of this armada would be to disrupt Dutch Baltic trade.[60] In this potentially dire situation it was clear to the Dutch regents that Sweden was the only available counterweight to Habsburg ambitions. The Dutch merchants were left to absorb their losses as best they could.

With grain prices on the Amsterdam Exchange soaring, it became attractive for the Dutch merchant élite to dispatch large ships around Scandinavia to the White Sea to load grain at Archangel.[61] One consortium which organized this traffic was headed by Elias Trip and Guillielmo Bartholotti, while a rival grouping was led by de Vogelaer and Klenck.[62] Dutch imports of grain from the White Sea reached their peak in the years 1629–30. In 1630 roughly one hundred Dutch vessels sailed to Archangel. Since the normal Dutch traffic in years when the Holland entrepôt was not procuring Russian grain amounted to around thirty ships, it would seem that something like seventy ships were sent for grain.[63]

The Dutch Baltic grain traffic began to recover in 1631, the year after Gustavus Adolphus withdrew from Poland and invaded Germany to tackle the Habsburg threat head-on. During the early 1630s the diversionary Dutch grain trade to Archangel faded away as suddenly as it had arisen. By the mid-1630s Dutch grain ports from Poland were back up to fairly high levels. At the same time the growing size of the Protestant armies operating in a now partly devastated Germany generated a strong, rising demand for provisions of all kinds, which the Dutch were uniquely well placed to meet. From 1630 onwards, masses of mostly small Dutch vessels, mainly from the West Frisian ports and Friesland, ferried great quantities of meat, fish, grain, and dairy produce, as well as wine and tobacco, to Hamburg, Bremen, Stettin, and other ports, from where the victuals were shipped up the rivers Elbe, Weser, and Oder to the armies.[64] But scarcely was the problem of Swedish obstruction removed than Denmark, having signed peace treaties

[60] Günter, *Die Habsburger-Liga*, 28–31; Israel, 'Politics of International Trade Rivalry', 529–35; Häpke (ed.), *Niederländische Akten*, ii. 408–11.
[61] Hart, *Geschrift en getal*, 310–11.
[62] Raptschinsky, 'Uit de geschiedenis', 80–2; Klein, *De Trippen*, 152–5.
[63] Nykerke, *Klaer-Bericht*, B3; Öhberg, 'Russia and the World Market', 142.
[64] Staatsarchiv Hamburg, Admiralitätskollegium, lists of Dutch vessels and cargoes arriving at Hamburg in the 1630s, Cl VII Lit Ea, pars 1.

with Spain and Austria, shifted course and adopted an attitude of increasing hostility to both Sweden and the Dutch. After 1630 there was a trend towards growing mercantilist collaboration between Denmark–Norway and Spain. Denmark agreed, under the Spanish–Danish commercial treaty of 1632, to co-operate with the Spanish Almirantazgo in its efforts to eradicate Dutch contraband trade with the Iberian lands.[65] In return Denmark and Norway were granted special terms in the carrying traffic to Spain and Portugal, which led to a noticeable increase in the Danish traffic[66] and a programme of building large ships for the *Spanienfahrt* in the ports of Norway.[67]

There was a long history of friction between the Danish crown and the Dutch over Sound toll policy and Baltic maritime affairs generally, which Christian IV's post-1630 alignment with the Habsburgs and collaboration with the Almirantazgo could only intensify. Relations were further aggravated by Christian's insistent claims to sovereignty over the whaling grounds around Spitsbergen.[68] Then, in March 1638, the Danish monarch reverted to his provocative Sound toll policy of 1613–14.[69] Danish mercantilist policy, including a new toll imposed at Glückstadt on the now burgeoning Elbe traffic, amounted to an open challenge to Dutch trade hegemony throughout the north. By raising the Sound dues, Christian began to cream off large sums at Dutch expense and discriminated in favour of Danish and Norwegian shipping, which was exempt. Furthermore, in 1639, emboldened by the lack of Dutch response thus far, he also changed the units of measure for accounting the Sound dues on grain, flax, and herring, proclaiming that a last of herring was henceforth to be counted as twelve and not thirteen barrels. In practice, this amounted to a further raising of the tolls.

Dutch payments to the Danish crown in Sound dues consequently rose steeply from 1638, without there being any corresponding increase in the traffic (see table 5.9). The inevitable response among the public in North Holland and Friesland was

[65] Laursen, *Danmark-Norges traktater*, iv. 87–91; Israel, 'Politics of International Trade Rivalry', 541–7.

[66] Johnsen, 'Relations commerciales', 79–81; Köhn, 'Ostfriesen und Niederländer', 82–3.

[67] Johnsen, 'Relations commerciales', 79–81.

[68] Brinner, *Die deutsche Grönlandfahrt*, 131–4.

[69] Kernkamp, *Sleutels van de Sont*, 19–20; Hill, *The Danish Sound Dues*, 114–15.

TABLE 5.9. *The Danish Crown's revenue from the Sound dues, 1627–1642*

Year	Ships passing the Sound	Yield (Danish rigsdalers)
1627	3,187	108,706
1628	2,324	77,258
1629	2,747	255,719
1630	2,323	121,593
1631	3,365	293,789
1636	3,764	226,000
1637	3,384	229,000
1638	3,327	482,000
1639	3,020	616,000
1640	3,454	450,000
1641	4,236	505,000
1642	4,127	405,000

Sources: Pringsheim, *Beiträge*, 20; Fridericia, *Danmarks ydre politiske historie*, ii. 212–88.

one of outrage and anger. The States General sent an embassy to Denmark to demand the reduction of the Sound dues to their pre-1638 level as well as the cancellation of the new toll at Glückstadt and a satisfactory resolution of the Spitsbergen dispute.[70] Christian, calculating that he had the advantage for as long as the Dutch were unable to use their fleet, brusquely rejected the demands. The tension rose further, but still the Republic took no action. Locked in conflict with Spain in the Low Countries, it was no easy matter for the Dutch to divert forces to deal with Denmark, especially as the Dunkirk offensive was now at its height. A second Spanish–Danish maritime treaty was signed at Madrid in March 1641 and this time the collaboration between Spain and its Protestant ally was openly directed against the Dutch. In fact, the treaty contained nothing else except joint measures against Dutch interests. The agreement was a prime example of the growing sophistication of mercantilist techniques.[71] The two powers agreed to work together to eradicate disguised Dutch participation in the carrying trade between north Germany and the Iberian kingdoms, checking ships, cargoes, warehouses, and commercial certificates at both ends and sharing the proceeds of confiscations.

[70] Kernkamp, *Sleutels van de Sont*, 19–20.
[71] Laursen, *Danmark-Norges traktater*, iv. 280–311; Israel, 'Politics of International Trade Rivalry', 546–7.

But Christian overplayed his hand. His calculations, with respect to Sweden at least, proved over optimistic. In 1643, tired of Danish scheming, the Swedes suspended their war in Germany and invaded Jutland. This *coup de main* was warmly applauded by the Dutch public. Yet Amsterdam and the West Frisian towns failed in their efforts to have a Dutch fleet sent to join the Swedes.[72] Rotterdam, the other South Holland towns, and Zeeland had never shown much interest in the Baltic, as their commerce was largely directed towards the west and south. The entire southern half of the Dutch maritime zone supported the Stadholder's view that the Republic should not divert forces away from the struggle against Spain and the Dunkirkers. Instead of intervening, the States General sent only a double embassy to Denmark and Sweden in the hope that this would suffice to establish Dutch mediation and secure the required lowering of the Sound tolls. For the moment all that the Amsterdam city council could do was to encourage Louis de Geer in his fitting out of ships, and hiring of men, for the Swedish navy. But the anxieties of the North Holland ports at the lack of Dutch intervention proved amply justified. For, when Danish–Swedish peace negotiations commenced, late in 1644, it emerged that the Swedes saw no reason why they should extract lower Sound tolls for the benefit of the Dutch when the Republic had failed to provide anything more than words in support of its Swedish ally.[73]

This time Amsterdam pulled out all the stops. The political temperature in the States of Holland reached boiling point. The South Holland towns, Zeeland, and the Stadholder still insisted that Baltic affairs must take second place; but this time they were forced into a compromise.[74] The main Dutch fleet would stay in the west, but money would be found to send a makeshift second fleet to the Sound. A force of forty-eight vessels, including six specially hired VOC ships and some converted merchantmen, was scraped together and sent off to escort three hundred merchantmen through the Sound.[75] Their instructions were to pay no tolls at all, serving notice on Denmark that nothing more would be paid until Dutch demands were met. Should the Danes attempt

[72] Aitzema, *Historie*, v. 637–41.
[73] Kolkert, *Nederland en het zweedsche imperialisme*, 19–20.
[74] Aitzema, *Historie*, vi. 237.
[75] Centen, *Vervolg*, 107–8; Kernkamp, *Sleutels van de Sont*, 193–4.

to interfere, they were to be repelled by force. The Dutch admiral Withe de With—later known to the English as 'Double-Witt'—sailed through the Sound on a mid-July day, in 1645, commanding a force mounting 4,300 men and 1,400 guns, escorting a dense mass of merchantmen, including forty Enkhuizen vessels loaded with herring. It was an imposing spectacle which the Danish monarch watched in person from the parapets of Helseneur castle. The Dutch fired their guns in salute, the admiral raising his hat to the king as he passed. Christian offered no response.

The episode was a humiliating one for Denmark and, as the Dutch fleet was in no hurry to leave Danish waters, Christian had little choice but to give in. He was well aware of how vulnerable Copenhagen was to Dutch naval power. Under the treaty signed at Christianopel a few months later, the Dutch extracted a large number of concessions which formed the basis of their maritime primacy in the Baltic for the rest of the century.[76] The Sound tolls were lowered in accordance with Dutch wishes. Dutch shipping sailing through the Sound was formally exempted from 'visitation' or boarding by Danish officials. The Dutch were exempted from the Elbe toll at Glückstadt. In the eyes of Europe, the Dutch had slapped the Danes down in no uncertain terms and resentment against the Dutch for the events of 1645 was to linger on at Copenhagen for many a decade. Even so, the merchants trading with the Baltic in Holland were far from fully content. There was a widespread feeling that intervention had come too late and that, if proper pressure had been applied earlier, better results could have been achieved. There was a certain amount of grumbling at the way the Dutch interests in the Baltic had been subordinated to other priorities.

THE MEDITERRANEAN

The restructuring of Dutch overseas trade as from 1621 extended to every part of the Dutch trading system. Second to Iberian commerce, it was the trade with Italy and the Levant which suffered most. During Phase Two the Dutch had rapidly expanded their commerce with the entire Mediterranean world from the

[76] Hill, *The Danish Sound Dues*, 149–50.

Straits to Aleppo. Lower shipping charges, access to Iberian fine goods and silver, and mastery of the spice trade had given the Dutch the means to gain ground rapidly at the expense of the Venetians, French, and English alike.[77] In some sectors of Mediterranean commerce, most notably the carrying traffic between Spain and Italy, and the trade with Cyprus and Egypt, the Dutch had by 1620 achieved an overwhelming ascendancy. All the evidence confirms that in these years the Dutch were playing both a more important and a more dynamic role than the English.

This flourishing phase of Dutch activity in the Mediterranean came to an abrupt end in April 1621. In the Baltic the impact of 1621 depressed Dutch commerce somewhat and led to a certain amount of reorganization of the Dutch carrying traffic. But it certainly did not overthrow Dutch trade primacy in northern waters as such. But in the Mediterranean the impact was far more drastic. The loss of access to the Iberian Peninsula, the doubling of Dutch freight charges for voyages to Italy within a matter of months, and the policy of Genoa, adopted under Spanish pressure, of discouraging contact with the Dutch after 1621,[78] severely depressed all sections of Dutch Mediterranean commerce for the next quarter of a century. The Dutch carrying traffic between Spain and Italy came to an abrupt end, leaving the salt-pans of Ibiza and La Mata deserted. Dutch trade with Algeria simply collapsed.[79] The shipping of bulky goods to and from Italy was sharply curtailed as a result of the huge jump in freight and insurance charges,[80] opening up a gap into which the Hanseatics and especially the English now stepped. Even high-value wares from the central Mediteranean, including Italian silks, were now either left to the English or else diverted overland (despite the Thirty Years' War) across Germany to the Netherlands.[81] What was left of Dutch maritime trade with Italy consisted of shipping spices, naval stores, and Russian products, together with modest quantities of grain, usually to Livorno or Venice.

In the Levant the impact was still greater. Here the effects took the form both of a catastrophic slump in volume and a disastrous

---

[77] Israel, 'Phases of the Dutch *straatvaart*, 12–16.
[78] AGS Estado 1884, Philip IV to viceroy of Naples, 22 Jan. 1622; Haitsma Mulier, 'Genova e l'Olanda nel seicento', 435–6.
[79] Romano, 'Tra XVI e XVII secolo', 489.
[80] Blok (ed.), 'Koopmansadviezen', 64, 67.
[81] Ibid.; Blendinger, 'Augsburger Handel', 304, 308.

narrowing in the scope of Dutch commerce. So swift was the collapse that by 1623 the Dutch ambassador at Constantinople could report to The Hague that all of the subsidiary branches of the Dutch Levant trade had now withered away, Dutch commerce with 'Alexandria, Cairo, Smyrna, and Constantinople being completely ruined'.[82] Dutch voyages to Egypt and Palestine ceased. Before long the Dutch merchant colony which had arisen at Smyrna during Phase Two simply disappeared.[83] In their deepening predicament, the Amsterdam merchant élite, headed by Elias Trip, Guillielmo Bartholotti, Philippo Calandrini, Gerrit Hudde, Jan Bicker, Gerard Reynst, and Marcus de Vogelaer, appealed in 1625 to the States of Holland for help. 'In the last few years,' they petitioned, 'partly owing to the wars this country wages against the King of Spain and partly owing to the charters granted to the East and West India Companies,' Holland's merchants had been 'stripped and denuded of all their commerce and traffic [with the Ottoman Empire] except for a few places and islands in the Mediterranean' and that 'as a result the traffic to Italy has also become very bad.'[84]

In response the States General, in June 1625, set up the so-called 'college' of *Directeuren van den Levantschen Handel en Navigatie in de Midellandsche Zee* (Directors of the Levant Trade and of Navigation to the Mediterranean) at Amsterdam, which, from 1625 onwards, acted as the representative body of Dutch commerce in the Mediterranean. The Dutch Levant directorate was not itself a trading company like the English Levant Company, or the VOC.[85] It conducted no trade on its own behalf. Its function was to act as a political and administrative platform for the élite merchants who dominated Dutch Mediterranean trade and who took it in turns to serve as 'directors' of the college. The directorate served as a bridge between government and merchants, dealt with the Dutch admiralty colleges over convoy discipline and escorts, and kept up the network of Dutch consulates in the Mediterranean, which, owing to the shrinkage of Dutch traffic, was on the point of collapse.

The plight of the Dutch trading system in the Mediterranean

---

[82] *BGLH*, i. 497–8.
[83] Samberg, *Hollandsche gereformeerde gemeente te Smirna*, 26.
[84] *BGLH*, i. 505–6.
[85] De Groot, 'Organization', 234–5.

became still worse in the late 1620s owing to the effects of the Spanish river blockade around the United Provinces imposed in the years 1625–9. Before 1625 a significant proportion of the Levant goods imported to the Dutch entrepôt, especially cotton from Cyprus and Egypt, had been re-exported up the Rhine to Frankfurt, Ulm, and other German textile towns. But in the years 1625–9 Dutch re-exports of cotton, like other Dutch re-exports to the Rhineland and southern Germany, were caught, as one Amsterdam businessman put it, 'as if in a sack'.[86] As a result, the flow of cottons to Germany reverted to its pre-1609 route, being shipped to Venice and then overland to Germany. Nor was this the only sector which the Venetians wrested back from the Dutch during the 1620s. By 1626 the Venetians were once again supreme in the Cyprus trade and were also recovering ground in Egypt, Syria, Turkey, and the Holy Land.[87] In the years 1621–45 the Venetians shared commercial supremacy in the Levant with the English.

Yet not all of what the Dutch lost in the Mediterranean after 1621 was lost to the Dutch trading system as a whole. The steep rise in Dutch freight and insurance charges to the Mediterranean improved the competitive position of the Dutch merchants operating in, and through, Russia, so that before long quantities of Persian raw silk, which in the past had been transported overland from Persia to Aleppo, were shipped across the Caspian Sea and by river to Moscow. From there they were sent on, together with caviare and Russian products, to Archangel, for shipment on the Muscovy convoys to Amsterdam. A small group of élite merchants, notably Elias Trip, Pieter Ranst, Marcus and Johan de Vogelaer, and Marcus and Pieter Pels, organized this shift.[88] Simultaneously, the collapse of the Dutch Levant trade inspired the VOC to launch its ambitious attempt to capture control of the traffic in Persian silks by re-routing the flow out, on its own ships from the Persian Gulf, and round Africa to Holland. By the late 1620s the VOC was already having some success with this initiative. Together, the VOC and the Dutch merchants in Russia may well have been

---

[86] Blok (ed.), 'Koopmansadviezen', 65.

[87] Ibid. 13, 64–5, 85; Roberts, *Marchants Mapp of Commerce*, 128–9, 139, 141; Sella, *Commerci e industrie*, 53–4; *BGLH* i. 533, 559–60; Israel, 'Phases of the Dutch *straatvaart*', 16.

[88] Scheltema, *Rusland en de Nederlanden*, i. 116–18.

shipping more Persian raw silk to the United Provinces than had the Dutch Levant ships down to 1621. But their success served to depress the Dutch Levant trade itself still further. As proof of how marginal Dutch trade with the Levant and Italy now was in supplying the Dutch entrepôt with raw silks, we may cite the statistics supplied to the Amsterdam admiralty college in 1630 by the Sephardi silk broker, Sebastian Pimentel (see table 5.10). According to his figures, a mere 20 per cent of total Dutch silk imports were then being shipped from the Mediterranean, a remarkably low proportion. The bulk of the raw silk reaching the Dutch entrepôt—and the total was equivalent to the entire annual production of Persia—was arriving either around Africa or from the north of Russia. Then, in the mid-1630s, the VOC directors stepped up their efforts to corner the trade in Persian silk. The VOC's factors in Persia bought up all the raw silk they could—in 1636, 1,000 bales out of an estimated total output of 1,473—in the hope of completely halting the flow of silks across the Near East to Aleppo, thereby ruining the English and Venetian Levant trades and making Europe dependent for its silk supply on the VOC.[89] But this was too ambitious. The VOC buyers in Persia were unable to corner enough silk. At least a third of the total continued to seep out overland to Aleppo. Even so, from the mid-1630s down to the early 1640s the VOC bought up so much Persian silk at source as to remove all incentive for Dutch merchants to go on importing silk from the Levant. Nor was Persian silk the only commodity diverted away from the Mediterranean by the VOC in this way. The same happened with a number of drugs, including rhubarb, then prized for its supposed medicinal properties and obtainable only from Tibet and other regions of central Asia. Rhubarb was also re-routed through the Persian Gulf and round Africa.[90]

The Dutch Levant trade reached its nadir in the late 1630s and early 1640s. There was simply no incentive to participate in it. In his *Marchants Mapp of Commerce*, published in 1638, Lewes Roberts could assert that the English, French, and Venetians were the 'onely three Christian nations that have any trade of moment', at Aleppo, 'the trade driven here by the Dutch [being] not worthy

[89] *BGOCP* i. 598–9, 612; Steensgaard, *Asian Trade Revolution*, 374–6, 390–6.
[90] *BGOCP* i. 587, 656.

TABLE 5.10. *Estimated annual imports of raw silk to the Dutch entrepôt, 1630* (280–lb. bales)

Persian and Armenian silk via Moscow and Archangel	400
From Surat in VOC ships	400
From the Persian Gulf in VOC ships	400
From the Levant and Italy	300
TOTAL (equivalent to 420,000 lb.)	1,500

Sources: ARH Admiraliteiten 5501/i, Sebastian Pimentel, 'Memorij van den rau zijde dij jaerlicks indese Landen comt'; Israel, 'Dutch Merchant Colonies', 95.

of consideration'.[91] In 1644 Amsterdam merchants were still saying that the Dutch Levant trade was ruined 'so that in many years we have had no ships sailing to or returning from there, the English having wholly taken over that commerce'.[92] Indeed, the English were the principal beneficiaries of the Dutch collapse. The English East India Company made no attempt to emulate the VOC in making massive purchases of raw silk in Persia. Instead, the Levant Company stepped up its purchases of silk at Aleppo, relying on rising sales of cloth to settle its balances.[93] Before 1621 little English cloth—other than modest quantities of kerseys—had sold in the Levant. In the 1620s this changed radically. By the mid-1630s the Levant Company was selling some 6,000 long- and short-cloths yearly at Aleppo alone, a significant proportion of England's total exports of 'old draperies'.[94] At the same time, English shipping replaced that of the Dutch in the carrying of grain, salt, and olive oil from Sicily and Puglia, and of wool and salt from eastern Spain, to northern Italy.[95] The English also now came to dominate overwhelmingly—except briefly during the Anglo-Spanish War of 1625–30—the traffic in wool and colonial dyestuffs from Spain to Northern Europe.[96] Not the least of the ironies which arose from

[91] Roberts, *Marchants Mapp of Commerce*, 139; he refers to the English as 'the most eminent in the trade of Aleppo' and the Venetians as the 'next merchants of consequence here resident'.

[92] *BGLH* i. 1075.

[93] Davis, 'English Imports', 202.

[94] Roberts, *Marchants Mapp of Commerce*, 139; in exchange chiefly for silks and drugs.

[95] Blok (ed.), 'Koopmansadviezen', 51, 65; Israel, 'Phases of the Dutch *straatvaart*', 23.

[96] See the lists of ships loading wool in the Spanish north coast ports in AGS Tribunal Mayor de Cuentas 815; Israel, 'Spanish Wool Exports', 205–10.

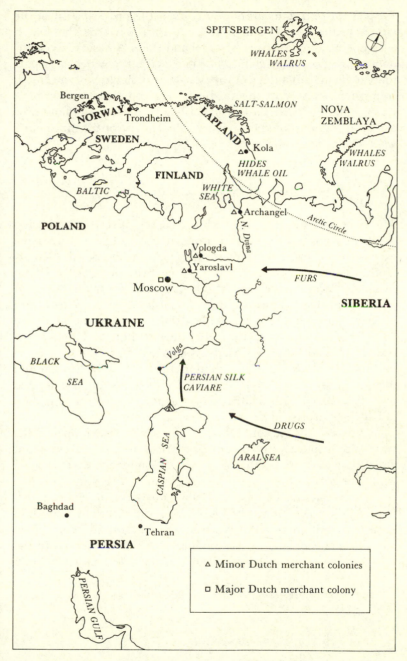

5.2 The trade route from Persia via Moscow to the White Sea during the seventeenth century.

the general restructuring of 1621, given the pro-war zeal of the Dutch textile towns, was that from 1621 onwards the Dutch entrepôt could obtain Spanish wool and Ibero-American dyestuffs only indirectly, via England.[97] If the English succeeded only partially in taking advantage of the post-1621 difficulties of the Dutch commercial system in the north, in the commerce of southern Europe and the Near East, from Lisbon to Aleppo, England now achieved an undisputed hegemony. The Dutch, for the time being, were wholly eclipsed.

THE WEST INDIA COMPANY

The general restructuring of 1621 had the effect of weakening the Dutch position in most European trade. There were some exceptions to this. Zeeland's transit traffic to the South Netherlands unquestionably benefited from the resumption of the Dutch blockade of the Flemish coast.[98] The Dutch textile towns acquired their protective barrier against Flemish 'new draperies' and linen.[99] The Dutch Russia trade drew some benefit from the collapse of Dutch enterprise in the Levant. But, on balance, the restructuring of 1621 decidedly weakened the Dutch grip on the main mechanisms of international commerce in Europe and the Near East. The major compensation for this, or so it seemed until the débâcle in Brazil in 1645, was the general revitalization of Dutch enterprise in the Indies east and west.

The renewal of the conflict with the Spanish crown opened the way to fresh endeavours to capture more of the Indies from Spain and Portugal. Initially there was much confidence that progress would be rapid. But, in the Americas and Africa at least, the process of renewed Dutch expansion proved in the event much harder and slower than the public and the merchant élite had expected, or than would have been the case, in all probability, had the WIC been set up, as originally intended, in 1607. In the years 1618–21 the Stadholder, Prince Maurice, purposely held up

[97] Taylor, 'Trade, Neutrality, and the "English Road" ', 250; Kepler, *Exchange of Christendom*, 162.

[98] ARH SG 4853, 'Tot justificatie . . . vande Heeren Staten van Zeelandt'; Snapper, *Oorlogsinvloeden*, 71.

[99] Israel, *Dutch Republic and the Hispanic World*, 88–9.

the establishment of the new company in the States of Holland and States General so as not to rule out all prospect of renewing the Truce with Spain. Then, in the years 1621–3 more frustrating delay ensued due to the opposition of the three West Frisian towns to the inclusion of the Caribbean salt traffic in the WIC's official monopoly.[1] These towns, and especially Hoorn, had hitherto dominated the trade and, while their salt fleets would still have to be extensively used, they had no wish to see supervision of the traffic transferred to the Company. It was not until 1623–4 that the WIC materialized as a formidable organization ready for action.

The Company was also held back by the fact that it was set up by the Dutch state just when the country's commerce was facing its first prolonged setback since 1590 as a result of the Spanish general embargo of April 1621, the war situation, and the onset of a general European slump. In their publicity campaign to attract investors, the Company's directors sought to exploit the general *malaise* of Dutch trade in European waters, trumpeting the allegedly superior allurements of investment in colonial commerce, dismissing Mediterranean commerce in their brochures as now 'very dangerous and virtually fruitless'.[2] In the long run, urged the WIC's publicity machine, the only way to place the Dutch trading system on a permanently viable and prosperous footing was to acquire colonies and captive markets, guarded by garrisons and naval might, in the Indies. But the investing public was not exactly overwhelmed by such arguments. On the contrary, it was to prove a slow and laborious business amassing the necessary starting capital.[3] A few of the merchant élite who had figured prominently in the original expansion of Dutch enterprise in the Caribbean, Brazil, and Guinea did invest heavily. Guillielmo Bartholotti invested 100,000 guilders and Balthasar Coymans 20,000, while Laurens Reael, Samuel Blommaert, Samuel Godijn, and Cornelis Bicker, all of whom were directors of the Amsterdam Chamber of the Company during the 1620s, also put in substantial sums.[4] In Zeeland, Jan de Moor, the powerful Flushing burgomaster and merchant, Cornelis Lampsins, and other prominent

---

[1] Res. Holl. 30 Sept., 13 Oct. 1621, 10 Jan., 19 Apr. 1622.
[2] Israel, *Dutch Republic and the Hispanic World*, 125–6.
[3] Ibid. 127; van Winter, *Westindische Compagnie*, 8, 12–13, 18.
[4] ARH WIC 18, 'Kapitaalboek vande kamer Amsterdam', fos. 1–40.

merchants responded enthusiastically. But by and large, at any rate in Holland, the response was disappointing. Very many key merchants invested only modest sums or not at all.

Nor did the Company do better among the middling and lower strata of society in the commercial and shipping towns. Surprisingly little capital was afforded by ports such as Rotterdam, Enkhuizen, and Hoorn. A number of highly placed office-holders did invest handsome sums. These included the diplomat François van Aerssen, now a leading member of the States of Holland, who invested 25,000 guilders, and Adriaen Pauw, son of Renier, who, unlike his father, was not actively engaged in trade but devoted his full energies to politics. But the crucial factor which eventually made it possible for the WIC to accumulate a substantial starting capital of seven million guilders was its success in the inland towns among a public who had little or no first-hand knowledge of the sea, ships, and matters maritime let alone of the Indies (see table 5.11). Here the town councils took up the cause of the new Company with a zeal which was political and religious as well as commercial. At Leiden, for instance, now in the hands of a resolutely hard-line Calvinist town council, the burgomasters set aside an ample room in the town hall where a specially appointed investment-raising committee—which included the Company's future historian, Johannes de Laet—expatiated every Wednesday afternoon on the wonders the new organization would achieve, the vast profits investors would reap, and the godliness of the task of undermining the rule of Catholic Spain in the Americas.[5] It was owing to this zealous fund-raising drive that Leiden invested 269,800 guilders, almost 10 per cent of the total invested in the Amsterdam Chamber of the new Company; and in the same way remarkably large sums were raised in Utrecht, Dordrecht, Haarlem, Deventer, Arnhem, and, most impressive of all, Groningen.[6] Thus we see that the WIC's special contribution to the machinery of Dutch world-trade hegemony during the seventeenth century was its unparalleled success in tapping inland, non-mercantile investment on a sustained basis for what, especially at first, was highly speculative long-distance maritime expansion.

---

[5] GA Leiden Sec. Arch. Gerechtsdagboek 186, fo. 33, res. 22 July 1621; Luzac, *Hollands rijkdom*, i. 318.

[6] Luzac, *Hollands rijkdom*, i. 318; Centen, *Vervolg*, 39; van Winter, *Westindische Compagnie*, 8, 12.

TABLE 5.11. *The starting capital of the WIC as lodged in its constituent chambers* (guilders)

Chamber	Total capital	Lodged		Source	
Amsterdam	2,846,520	Amsterdam		Leiden	269,800
				Utrecht	214,775
				Gelderland	170,000
				Deventer	110,000
				France	121,200
				Haarlem	134,150
				Germany and Denmark	80,000
				Amsterdam	(under 1,700,000)
Zeeland	1,379,775	Middelburg		Middelburg	897,475
				Flushing	199,600
				Veere	132,700
				Tholen	100,000
Maas	1,039,202	Rotterdam	250,660	Arnhem	35,000
		Delft	336,165	Deventer	10,000
		Dordrecht	468,377	Zwolle	10,000
				Gelderland	80,000
Groningen	836,975	Groningen		City of Groningen	c.400,000
				Drenthe	50,000
North Quarter	505,627	Hoorn and Enkhuizen		Enkhuizen	123,235
TOTAL	6,608,099				

Source: Israel, *Dutch Republic and the Hispanic World*, 128.

Although over 40 per cent of the Company's starting capital was lodged in the Amsterdam Chamber, it is evident that Amsterdam's own contribution was remarkably modest, constituting at most only around 20 per cent of the total. Like the VOC, the WIC was a federal, joint-stock concern, built out of a federation of regional chambers set up, supervised, and guaranteed by the States General, which also provided a regular annual subsidy. Each chamber kept its own books, capital, and accounts and had its own fixed quota of trading operations and voting power. The

Amsterdam Chamber, in which roughly half the investment came from outside Amsterdam, was allocated four-ninths of the total weighting, Zeeland half that influence at two-ninths, and the other three chambers—Groningen, Maas, and North Quarter (Hoorn and Enkhuizen)—one-ninth each. On the federal governing board of the Company, the so-called Heren XIX, Amsterdam possessed eight out of nineteen votes, Zeeland four, and the other three chambers two each, the nineteenth director being nominated by the States General.[7] While the directors of the Amsterdam and Zeeland chambers tended to be a mixture of town regents and élite merchants (the latter, men such as Guillielmo Bartholotti, Samuel Godijn, Samuel Blommaert, and Marcus de Vogelaer, the younger, often of South Netherlands extraction), it is striking that the directors of the Groningen, Maas, and North Quarter chambers were almost always burgomasters, other regents, or provincial office-holders.[8] In any case, at all levels the new company was intimately entwined with the ruling Dutch regent oligarchy.

The Company's opening offensive was a colossal fiasco. Bahia, the chief town of Brazil, was captured in May 1624 but lost again the following year to a massive joint Spanish–Portuguese armada organized by Olivares. The fact that the Spanish crown was put to enormous expense and inconvenience to recover Bahia was small comfort for most of the WIC's investors. In 1625 WIC forces were repulsed from Puerto Rico in the Caribbean and from Elmina, the main Portuguese base on the Guinea coast. Also in 1625, the Dutch lost their remaining forts around the Amazon estuary.

This unremitting catalogue of failure consumed much of the Company's starting capital and disheartened the investors. Nevertheless, there were signs in this early period that the Company might after all develop into a major pillar of the Dutch world-trading system. If the New Netherland fur traffic, mainly in beaver and otter, was worth at most 50,000 guilders per annum in the 1620s, a mere flea-bite by comparison with the Company's naval

---

[7] Schneeloch, *Aktionäre*, 21.

[8] De Laet, *Iaerlyck verhael*, i. 32–7; van Winter, *Westindische Compagnie*, 9, 75; a considerable proportion of directors of the Gronigen chamber were in fact Groningen *jonkers* (nobles).

and military expenditure,[9] the Company did have one major asset in the shape of the Guinea gold trade. Moreover, the inclusion of the Guinea trade in the WIC monopoly significantly improved the profitability of this asset. In 1620 there were about half a dozen Dutch companies trafficking with the Gold Coast, competing so fiercely that the price in copper goods and linen that the Dutch were paying for the gold and ivory they obtained from the Africans had risen steadily. According to Samuel Blommaert (a correspondent of the Swedish chancellor, and expert in the marketing of Swedish copper, as well as a director of the WIC), the private Guinea companies had, by 1620, been exchanging seventy to eighty pounds of copperware for every two ounces of Guinea gold. By contrast, the WIC, on taking charge of Dutch enterprise in West Africa, ended both the competition and the high prices the Africans were obtaining. The Company, noted Blommaert, 'has brought that commerce on so far that they have been exchanging only thirty five pounds of copper goods for every two ounces of gold'.[10] The Company, in other words, extracted twice as much gold from the Africans for the commodities it supplied as had the private companies. From 1623 to 1636 the WIC imported to the United Provinces the great bulk of the gold reaching Europe from West Africa, 40,461 marks, valued at nearly twelve million guilders, or a good deal more than the Company's own starting capital, without counting the value of the hides and the many hundreds of elephant tusks the Company shipped back from West Africa each year.[11]

Besides the Guinea gold trade, the Company had little else of major value except for its raiding against Spanish and Portuguese shipping. The Dutch colonies in western Guyana, particularly that at Essequebo, developed steadily but proved to be of little value to the Zeeland chamber which supervised them, as Essequebo was, in effect, farmed out to the private company of Jan de Moor, a prominent figure of the Zeeland merchant élite, the founder of Fort Kijkoveral, and a director of the Zeeland chamber of the Northern Company.[12] The raiding campaign proved fairly

[9] De Laet, *Iaerlyck verhael*, iv. 297; RAZ SZ 2099, WIC directors to SG, 23 Oct. 1629, fo. 3.

[10] Blommaert, 'Brieven', 72–3.

[11] De Laet, *Iaerlyck verhael*, iv. 295–6.

[12] RAZ SZ 2099, WIC directors to SG, 23 Oct. 1629, fo. 3ᵛ; Edmundson, 'The Dutch in Western Guyana', 668–71.

successful especially in the late 1620s, culminating in Piet Heyn's capture of the Mexican treasure fleet off the Cuban coast in 1628, a coup which netted the Company over eleven million guilders, or almost as much as its first thirteen years' involvement in the Guinea gold trade. In those same thirteen years the WIC captured a total of 547 Spanish and Portuguese vessels.[13] Foremost among the booty, apart from the bullion seized by Piet Heyn, were some forty thousand chests of Brazil sugar, valued at eight million guilders.[14]

But Guinea gold and raiding, except in such exceptionally propitious circumstances as those of 1628, were insufficient to render so vast a concern as the WIC commercially viable, or to make a major contribution to strengthening the Dutch world entrepôt. In its first thirteen years the Company built, or bought, a total of 220 ships of larger than ninety lasts, amassed a vast store of guns and munitions, and spent over eighteen million guilders on wages and salaries alone. This latter sum was enough to maintain the entire Dutch army on a war footing for a year and a half. The Company received an annual, albeit modest, subsidy from the States General. But by 1630 it was obvious that only a dramatic breakthrough to greater profitability could secure the Company's future. In that year the WIC succeeded in conquering a foothold in north-eastern Brazil at Recife (Pernambuco) and Olinda. But for several years thereafter the forces which the Company poured in were hemmed in by the Portuguese, the sugar plantations of the region being devastated in the fighting. During the early 1630s, with the Company's expenditure still far outstripping its income, WIC shares on the Amsterdam exchange lurched as low as 60 per cent of their starting value (see table 5.12).

Only in 1634 did the outlook begin to improve. In Brazil, the Portuguese were pushed back. A large part of the country was subjugated and garrisoned. Sugar production in the area under Dutch control resumed. In the years 1634–6 sugar, tobacco, and Brazil wood exports from Netherlands Brazil built up to the point that the Company finally appeared to have succeeded in gaining its essential objectives. In spite of past failures, it seemed that the Company was now assured of a profitable future and a central role in underpinning Dutch world-trade supremacy. As a result of

[13] De Laet, *Iaerlyck verhael*, iv. 282–5.
[14] Ibid. 286.

TABLE 5.12. *WIC share prices on the Amsterdam Exchange, 1628–1650*

15 Nov.	−1628	115	June	1641	117
Jan.	1629	206	13 June	1642	102
11 Sept.	1630	120	3 June	1643	92
2 Feb.	1633	61	14 Mar.	1644	68
6 May	1634	93	8 Aug.	1645	46
16 Aug.	1635	120	9 June	1646	37
6 Mar.	1637	94	15 June	1648	34
4 May	1640	134	8 Feb.	1649	26
Apr./May	1641	128/114	21 Mar.	1650	14

Sources: Van Dillen, 'Effectenkoersen', 9–10; Goslinga, *Dutch in the Caribbean* (1971), 509.

the WIC's endeavours, the Dutch now controlled the international sugar trade for the first time and, as a direct consequence, also the Atlantic slave trade. Plantations and slaves went together. The more Dutch Brazil prospered, the more the flow of slaves from West Africa on WIC ships increased. In the decade 1636–45 the Company auctioned no less than 23,163 African slaves in its Brazilian territory.[15] As the WIC's prospects brightened, so the price of its shares rallied. As confidence revived, it became feasible to recruit more troops and seamen, and launch new military ventures. The number of employees of the Company rose from six thousand in 1633, to over ten thousand by 1644.[16] In 1637 WIC forces finally captured Elmina, which now replaced Fort Nassau, at Mouré, as the headquarters of the Company's 'directeur-général' on the Gold Coast. In 1642 WIC forces overran Angola, Axim, and the sugar island of São Thomé, for the time being virtually eliminating the Portuguese from western Africa.

Under the first and last 'governor-general' of Dutch Brazil, Count Johan Maurits of Nassau-Siegen, in the years 1637–44, the fortunes of the WIC in Brazil reached their zenith. In these years the territory under Dutch control was extended and a sustained effort made to develop the country's economic potential. The major issue which the Company faced in determining its trade strategy was whether to retain all the colony's trade in its own

[15] Wätjen, *Das holländische Kolonialreich in Brasilien*, 311.
[16] *BMHG* 21 (1900), 367; *Aenwysinge datmen van de Oost en West-Indische Compagniën . . .*, 6.

hands, maintaining a strict monopoly, or to operate a partial monopoly, reserving some strands while opening up the rest to private merchants in the United Provinces.[17] For years the directors of the various chambers argued over this question. Advocates of the former view urged that the Company's investors had paid for its conquests and garrisons and had a right to monopolize the profits. The main argument for throwing the trade open was that this would enlarge the traffic, expand the area under cultivation in Brazil, and stimulate emigration from the Republic, all of which would help build up the colony and guarantee the Company a rising revenue in taxes and recognition fees.[18]

But there was also another dimension to the argument. Since those Dutch subjects who knew Portuguese, had experience of the sugar trade, and showed an interest in acquiring sugar plantations in Brazil were primarily Amsterdam Sephardi Jews, opening up the Brazil sugar trade was expected to be a means of sucking in the bulk of the Brazil trade, and therefore also of the sugar-refining business, to Amsterdam. Not surprisingly, it was a policy favoured mainly by the Amsterdam chamber, though there was some support from the North Quarter. In the other chambers, especially Zeeland and Groningen, there was strong opposition; but, eventually, this was overruled. Johan Maurits, impressed above all by the need to find more colonists, threw his weight behind the open-trade policy.

Under the arrangements finalized in April 1638—over the vehement objections of Zeeland—the Company reserved the traffic in slaves, dyewoods, and munitions to itself, throwing open the trade in sugar and tobacco under payment of taxes, fees, and dues. As a result, the already emerging trend towards collaboration between the WIC and the Amsterdam Sephardi community was greatly strengthened. Most of the private trade came into the hands of Sephardi Jews at Amsterdam, and their relatives and factors, who now migrated in their hundreds to Brazil.[19] Even much of the private trade carried in ships chartered by the Groningen, Maas, and North Quarter chambers came to be for the account of Amsterdam Sephardi Jews.[20] Only in Zeeland was there

[17] Boxer, *Dutch in Brazil*, 75–82.
[18] Ibid.; Laspeyres, *Geschichte*, 80–2.
[19] Bloom, *Economic Activities of the Jews*, 132–4.
[20] Van Winter, *Westindische Compagnie*, 154.

a substantial non-Jewish private traffic in Brazil products. The Company allowed more liberal terms for Jewish religious practice and community organization in Brazil than were then in force in Holland itself. The Sephardi community both at Recife and in its hinterland rapidly increased, amounting by 1644 to some 1,450 souls, or between one-third and one-half of the total white civilian population of Netherlands Brazil.[21] As most of the other white civilians, including a majority of the sugar planters, were Portuguese Catholics, there were in fact considerably more Jewish than Dutch Protestant colonists in the territory.

The Jews thus became central to the WIC's commercial and colonizing strategy in Brazil, and the Company became central in the life of Dutch Sephardi Jewry. Since the loss of most of their pre-1621 trade with Portugal and the re-imposition of the Spanish embargoes, Dutch Sephardi Jewry had lacked a secure role in the Dutch trading system.[22] The commercial policy adopted by the WIC in the 1630s once again made Amsterdam Sephardi Jewry and its offshoots an integral part of the mechanism of Dutch world-trade supremacy.

The achievement of supremacy in the world sugar market and slave trade did much to vindicate the earlier pretensions of the WIC—or so it seemed during the triumphant decade 1635–44. But ominous clouds were gathering on the horizon. If the Company appeared to be succeeding in Brazil and West Africa, it continued to fail in the Caribbean. In 1634 WIC forces captured Curaçao with its excellent harbour, two neighbouring islands, and location close to the Spanish American mainland. If ever there was a perfect depot from which to infiltrate the commerce of Venezuela and New Granada, this was it. But the Company's officials found that, with the war continuing, opportunities for trade with the Spanish colonies were practically non-existent.[23] The grip of the Spanish crown on its colonists was simply too strong. A decade after its capture, the Curaçao islands were yielding no profit and some WIC directors were proposing abandoning the islands to save the cost of garrisoning them.[24] But the Heren XIX refused to

[21] Wiznitzer, *Jews in Colonial Brazil*, 120–38.

[22] Israel, 'Economic Contribution', 514–17.

[23] Van Brakel, 'Bescheiden over den slavenhandel', 49–50; Menkman, *Nederlanders in het Caraïbische zeegebied*, 44–5.

[24] Van Brakel, 'Bescheiden over den slavenhandel', 49–50; Menkman, *Nederlanders in het Caraïbische zeegebiet*, 44–5.

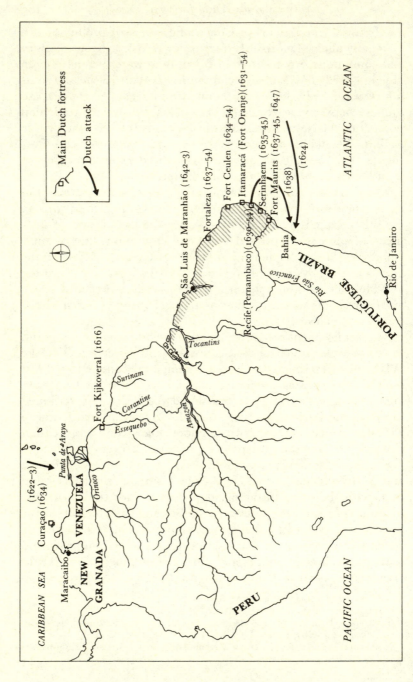

5.3 Netherlands Brazil at its greatest extent, c. 1640.

give up their ambition to break open a lucrative trade with Spanish America. The Company diverted forces from Brazil to the Caribbean, unleashing a new wave of raids on Spanish bases and shipping and, in 1643, sending an expedition round the southern tip of South America to southern Chile. In 1644 the governor of Curaçao, Pieter Stuyvesant, attacked the Spanish-held island of St Martin with a thousand men but was repulsed after a four-week battle. After a promising start, the expedition to Chile proved fruitless.

Paring down the Dutch forces in Brazil for the sake of high-risk schemes in the Caribbean and Spanish America proved to be a major strategic blunder. Matters began to go wrong in Netherlands Brazil as early as 1641. In December 1640 Portugal revolted against Spanish rule and broke free. This event was of great strategic and commercial advantage to the Dutch in Europe, so that, when the new Portuguese king, John IV, appealed for a long truce to end the Dutch–Portuguese conflict early in 1641, Holland, most of the other provinces—though not Zeeland—and the Stadholder were happy to agree. The WIC directors, however, opposed this truce, because it would halt Dutch territorial expansion in Brazil and put a stop to the Company's raiding campaign against Portuguese shipping in the South Atlantic. Investors did not like the truce either.[25] WIC shares, having shot up from 105 to 128 on the news of the Portuguese secession (which, it was supposed, initially, would strengthen the WIC in Brazil and Africa), then fell back, as the truce negotiations progressed during May, from 128 to 114 per cent.

The most serious consequence of the Dutch–Portuguese truce of 1641 for Netherlands Brazil was that it ended the Company's campaign against the Portuguese sugar traffic from southern Brazil to Europe. The Company ceased maintaining its war fleet and rapidly declined as a naval power in the South Atlantic.[26] The result was a strong revival of the sugar economy of southern (Portuguese) Brazil, mounting competition between Dutch and Portuguese sugar on the European market, and a fall in sugar prices on the Amsterdam Exchange (see table 5.13). By 1643 these trends, combined with the failure in the Caribbean, had driven WIC share prices down to 92 and, by March 1644, to a mere

---

[25] Aitzema, *Historie*, v. 198–9; Boxer, *Dutch in Brazil*, 103.
[26] Van Hoboken, 'West-Indische Compagnie en de vrede van Munster', 361–3.

68. By this date directors and investors alike were filled with apprehension for the future.[27] An acute sense of unease permeated Netherlands Brazil.

But worse was to come. The revival of Portuguese fortunes in southern Brazil, together with the inspiration the Portuguese colonists drew from the restoration of Portuguese independence, led to mounting restlessness and an increasingly conspiratorial atmosphere among the Portuguese Catholic planters in Dutch Brazil. They disliked Dutch rule and passionately hated the Jews, both on religious grounds and because of the dominance of the latter in the sugar and import trades. As they mostly bought their supplies and textiles from the Jews, often on credit, against future sugar output, many of the Catholic Portuguese were heavily indebted to Jews living at Recife and in Amsterdam.

The revolt when it came was devastating in its impact. Armed and encouraged from southern Brazil, the rebels swept the hinterland of Recife burning plantations and sugar-mills as they went.[28] The Dutch troops withdrew to their forts, and to Recife, along with the Jews. Sugar production was paralysed. The Company had sufficient stockpiles of Brazil wood,[29] as well as sugar, to keep up the flow of its own traffic until the end of 1646, when it collapsed (see table 5.14). Exports of private sugar collapsed in 1646 (see table 5.15). Within months Netherlands Brazil had been reduced from an immense asset furnishing the Dutch entrepôt with many millions of guilders worth of sugar, dyewood, and tobacco per year into a costly liability saddled with vast military expenses. The revolt of the Portuguese Catholics in Netherlands Brazil was a shattering blow from which the Company never really recovered. Reinforcements were rushed to Brazil, but the military situation continued to deteriorate throughout the late 1640s. The setback was keenly felt in many parts of the Republic, especially Zeeland and Groningen. But at Amsterdam, since it was the Jews who incurred the losses, reaction was more muted. For years relations between the Amsterdam city council and the WIC had been rather cool. At this juncture the city fathers by no means agreed with Zeeland, Groningen, and the Sephardi community that the Dutch state should go all out to rescue the

---

[27] *Correspondência diplomática de Francisco de Sousa Coutinho*, i. 139, 162, 181.
[28] Cabral de Mello, *Olinda restaurada*, 43–4, 273–5, 301.
[29] Wätjen, *Das holländische Kolonialreich in Brasilien*, 327

TABLE 5.13. *Sugar prices on the Amsterdam Exchange, 1624–1669* (guilders/lb.)

1624	0.43	1646	0.65
1625	0.47	1648	0.60
1626	0.51	1649	0.66
1628	0.57	1650	0.67
1630	0.67	1651	0.73
1632	0.70	1652	0.69
1640	0.55	1653	0.66
1641	0.51	1655	0.69
1642	0.46	1664	0.39
1643	0.44	1665	0.40
1645	0.46	1669	0.35

Source: Posthumus, *Inquiry*, i. 122, 131.

TABLE 5.14. *WIC sugar imports from Netherlands Brazil to the Dutch entrepôt, 1638–1650* (chests)

1638	2,043	1645	1,086
1639	3,874	1646	2,045
1640	1,848	1647	—
1641	3,450	1648	—
1642	3,483	1649	—
1643	1,213	1650	—
1644	797		

Source: Wätjen, *Das holländische kolonialreich in Brasilien*, 322–3.

TABLE 5.15. *Private sugar imports from Netherlands Brazil to the Dutch entrepôt, 1638–1650* (chests)

1638	3,644	1645	6,193
1639	4,414	1646	659
1640	7,126	1647	812
1641	11,092	1648	714
1642	7,256	1649	963
1643	9,559	1650	538
1644	7,790		

Source: Wätjen, *Das holländische kolonialreich in Brasilien*, 322–3.

WIC in Brazil. The Sephardi community at Amsterdam was so incensed against Portugal that the Portuguese ambassador at The Hague feared unruly scenes and even that he might be physically attacked in the streets.[30] In deference to the Amsterdam city council, the heads of the Portuguese synagogue warned congregants, on pain of fines, not to cause 'scandal' when discussing Brazilian affairs and not to insult the Portuguese ambassador.[31]

Shaken by the débâcle in Brazil, the WIC directors were compelled to rethink their entire commercial and political strategy. Down to 1644 the Heren XIX had opposed all moves towards peace with Spain, seeing the war against Spanish interests in the Americas as fundamental to the Company's *raison d'être* and prospects.[32] But by the summer of 1646 the Company cut a very different figure on the Dutch political scene. The Company was so weakened at sea that, when the States General, in 1646, authorized a limited privateering war against Portuguese shipping in the Atlantic, the WIC was unable to participate, leaving the privateering offensive of 1646–7 to a conglomeration of Zeeland firms with financial backing from the Sephardi community in Amsterdam.[33] By June 1646 the Company's shares on the Amsterdam Exchange were selling at a disastrous 37 per cent of their nominal value (see table 5.12). The directors ceased opposing Amsterdam's wishes to make peace with Spain and instead drew up plans to penetrate the commerce of Spanish America by peaceful means, rightly identifying the slave trade as one possible lever of entry.[34] Thus the year 1646 stands out as a turning-point in the WIC's assessment of its role in the Dutch world-trading system. It was then that the directors accepted the transformation of the Company from a trading war-machine into a non-belligerent commercial organization content to supply the colonies of other powers and relying for protection of its own modest assortment of territories on the States General.[35] The grandiose and aggressive spirit of the old WIC had vanished for ever.

[30] *Correspondência diplomática de Francisco de Sousa Coutinho*, i. 308.
[31] GA Amsterdam, archive of the Portuguese Jewish Community, xix. 281, res. Mahamad, 22 elul 2405.
[32] ARH SG 4854, 'Consideratien vande Westindische Comp.', 18 June 1644; *Kroniek*, xxv (1869), 397–9.
[33] Van Hoboken, 'West-Indische Compagnie en de vrede van Munster', 361–2; Boxer, *Dutch in Brazil*, 280–90.
[34] ARH SG 4856, Heren XIX to SG, 14 Nov. 1646.
[35] *Kroniek*, xxv (1869), 446–50; Israel, *Dutch Republic and the Hispanic World*, 334.

DUTCH EXPANSION IN ASIA

An important part of the restructuring process which began in 1621 with the resumption of the Dutch–Spanish conflict was the new phase which now began in VOC expansion in Asia. The resumption of war with the Iberians signalled the onset of a general offensive to undermine the position of the Portuguese and Spaniards and encompass more of the commerce of Asia within Dutch control. The offensive had a considerable effect, first in the Far East and later also in India and Ceylon. At the same time, the collapse of Dutch trade in the Mediterranean and the Near East opened up new trade possibilities for the VOC in western Asian waters. Phase Three was the period of the Company's greatest impetus in north-west India and the Persian Gulf.

But the resumption of war with the Iberian powers also raised new difficulties. Silver was the VOC's principal means of effecting its purchases and buying its supplies in Asia, and the war reduced the flow of Spanish bullion to the Dutch entrepôt. The shortage of specie at Amsterdam, and the rise in its price, just at the moment when VOC military and naval expenditure had to be sharply increased, threatened to paralyse the Company's efforts.[36] It was chiefly for this reason that Governor-General Coen concentrated his efforts during the opening years of the renewed struggle on the Far East–Japan, China, and the Philippines. Here was a network of trade links which, in the Company's hands, would immeasurably improve its strategic and commercial position throughout Asia. Japan was the principal alternative source of silver to the Spanish imperium and a country with which the Dutch had had tenuous relations since 1609. But until the early 1620s the Dutch wielded no control over the main category of commodities imported into Japan—Chinese silks. Down to 1622 a half to two-thirds of the trade was in Chinese and Japanese hands, and the rest in those of the Portuguese. Consequently, very little Japanese silver reached Batavia (see table 5.16). But Dutch ambitions to wrest the traffic from their rivals received encouragement from the difficulties the English encountered from Japanese officials and the increasing dislike of the Japanese court for the missionary activities of the Portuguese and Spaniards.[37] The Dutch studiously

---

[36] Van Dam, *Beschryvinge*, i, pt. 2, 167.
[37] Goodman, *Dutch Impact on Japan*, 10–14.

avoided advancing the cause of Christianity, which their enemies denounced as shameful subservience to Japanese superstition and arrogance.[38] Subservient or not, VOC diplomacy in Japan certainly paid off. The English closed down their factory in Japan in 1623. The Spaniards were expelled in 1624. The Portuguese were placed under progressively tighter restrictions, until they too were banished from the scene in 1638. From 1640 the Dutch were the only European nation permitted to enter and do business in Japan. Meanwhile, in 1635 the Shogunate forbade Japanese to leave Japan, putting an end to their participation in the China trade. It was neither superior commercial technique, nor force, which gave the VOC its eventual pre-eminence in commerce with Japan, but diplomacy and the exclusion policy of the Shogunate. Dutch access was tightly restricted. The VOC was allowed just one trading factory, on a secluded island at Nagasaki. The Dutch personnel living there, who usually totalled less than twenty, were confined to their small island and kept under stifling restrictions. They were supplied with food and prostitutes but otherwise permitted no contact with the Japanese populace. To preclude any need for the Dutch to learn Japanese, a small corps of local scribes were made to learn to speak, read, and write Dutch.

The Dutch were left with a unique advantage in having access to Japan. But, if they were to exploit their opportunity, they had to supply what the Japanese market required, namely Chinese commodities, in particular silks; and it was precisely here that the VOC faced a serious difficulty. Angered by the way the Dutch interfered with Chinese traders attempting to buy pepper and spices in Java and Sumatra, the Chinese court preferred to deal with the Portuguese and Spaniards.[39] Before and during the Twelve Years' Truce, China's silk exports almost completely bypassed the Dutch *comptoirs* in the Archipelago, the bulk flowing, in part via Macao, to Japan and much of the rest to Manila, from where the goods were shipped on the Spanish trans-Pacific galleons to Acapulco in Mexico, and from there also to Peru. Dutch requests for access to the Chinese market having failed, and the Truce having expired, the VOC directors in the Republic, egged on by their bellicose governor-general at Batavia, decided to break into the Chinese market and wrest control over China's export trade by

[38] Kato, 'Unification and Adaptation', 226, 229.
[39] Dermigny, *La Chine et l'Occident*, i. 112–13.

TABLE 5.16. *Silver shipped from Japan by the VOC, 1622–1669* (guilders)

1622	410,000	1636	3,012,450
1623	252,000	1637	4,024,200
1625	338,500	1638	4,753,800
1626	236,000	1639	7,495,600
1627	851,000	1640	2,500,000
1632	643,270	1640–49	1,518,870*
1633	194,803	1650–59	1,315,120*
1634	849,570	1660–69	1,048,000*
1635	1,403,100		

* Annual average.
Sources: Kato, 'Unification and Adaptation', 224; for the post-1640 annual averages, see Nachod, *Beziehungen*, table E; Glamann, *Dutch–Asiatic Trade*, 58.

force. The first step was the sending of a joint Anglo-Dutch naval expedition to blockade the Spaniards at Manila. There was little fighting but, in Coen's words, 'many junks trading from China to Manila were captured and reasonably valuable prizes taken'.[40] Next, in 1622, Coen dispatched an all-Dutch expedition of sixteen ships and 1,300 men to capture the Portuguese base at Macao. After a promising start, the Dutch attack was flung back, leaving the VOC with nothing and the Chinese emperor even more angry than before. Coen now resorted to the tactic of ravaging Chinese shipping right along the southern China coast. China's overseas trade was paralysed. The Chinese court was being given to understand that either the Dutch were to be permitted to supplant the Iberians as the main carriers of China's foreign commerce or else there would no longer be any.[41] Eventually, the emperor gave in. In 1624 the Dutch, who had in the meantime established a fort in the P'êng-hu Islands between Taiwan and the Chinese mainland, were granted permission to establish a permanent, fortified trade factory on Taiwan, provided that they withdrew from the P'êng-hu Islands.

By the time they ceased their action against Chinese shipping, in 1624, the Dutch had captured or destroyed hundreds of defenceless junks. But the merchants of Canton showed no inhibitions about

[40] *Kroniek*, ix (1853), 113–14.
[41] *Journalen Bontekoe*, 59, 63–5, 69; Groenevelt, *Nederlanders in China*, 90–106; Dermigny, *La Chine et l'Occident*, i. 115–16.

trading with the new fortified trade factory, Fort Zeelandia, which the VOC now established on Taiwan. By the late 1620s Fort Zeelandia was one of the most flourishing Dutch depots in Asia. There the Dutch stockpiled the silks, porcelain, and drugs which they supplied to Japan and, in lesser quantity, to India and Persia. There too, during the 1630s when the Brazilian sugar plantations were devastated and there was a shortage of sugar in Europe, the Dutch accumulated large stocks of Chinese sugar, most of which was shipped to Holland. During the 1630s the VOC shipped over one million pounds of Chinese sugar from Taiwan to Europe.[42] When the Dutch first established themselves on Taiwan, the Spaniards attempted to block their progress, establishing several forts in the north of Taiwan. But Dutch sea power countered the threat and in 1641 the Dutch forced the surrender of the Spanish forts, completing their temporary domination of the island.[43]

The other arm of the VOC offensive of the early 1620s was designed to stifle the Portuguese empire of trade further west. Coen was determined to cut off the flow of pepper, cinnamon, diamonds, and pearls reaching Lisbon. With English support, fleets were sent from Batavia to blockade Goa and Malacca. 'Great damage was done to the enemy', as Coen observed,[44] and we can rest assured that the 20 per cent share of the European pepper market which the Portuguese had consolidated during the Twelve Years' Truce was substantially cut back.[45] These were tangible gains. But the costs of Coen's overall strategy were so heavy that by April 1623 he had no choice but to suspend operations, especially as the English now refused to collaborate further.

But during the brief period of the offensive, 1621–3, a decisive shift had taken place.[46] All the trends were now running strongly in the VOC's favour. There was a sharp rise in the quantity of silver reaching Batavia from Japan. The Chinese market had been broken into and control of the China silk trade wrested from the Iberians. Portuguese trade on the west coast of India and at Malacca was disrupted. And meanwhile, the position of the English was steadily deteriorating. The English were coming more

[42] Glamann, *Dutch–Asiatic Trade*, 156–7.
[43] MacLeod, *De Oost-Indische Compagnie als zeemogendheid*, ii. 309–10.
[44] *Kroniek*, ix (1853), 118.
[45] Van Dam, *Beschryvinge*, i. pt. 2, 167; Disney, *Twilight*, 51, 162.
[46] Israel, *Dutch Republic and the Hispanic World*, 117–20.

and more to rue the arrangement that they had entered into with the Dutch: 'we thought to enter into their conquests without disbursements of any former charges, but their sinister proceedings in their false and dissimuled promyses, with their insolent comportements in the places of command, doe daylie teach us that our masters had better have bought further lyberty with more expense.'[47] The weakening of the English position in Asia was partly due to this burden of costs, the English East India Company having agreed, in return for a third of the spice trade, to shoulder a third of the costs of the Dutch forts and garrisons where English lodges were established in the Archipelago, and half of the costs of Fort Geldria, at Pulicat, as well as to contribute to the fleets blockading Goa, Malacca, and Manila.[48] But the main reason for England's lack of success in the East India spice trade in this period was that the new English lodges were placed in Dutch strongholds, surrounded by Dutch garrisons. The English had their agreed quotas, but the Dutch had the power. It was easy for Coen to manipulate sales and purchases, and the movement of commodities, to the advantage of the Dutch. The English factors found themselves obstructed and delayed at every turn. This was the reality behind the incessant complaints of the English in India and the East Indies in these years over the 'insufferable insolencies' of the Dutch, whom the English were accustomed to look down on as a new and small nation. The reports of the English officials at Batavia to the directors in London grew steadily more pessimistic: 'in all places where wee are under the Hollanders', wrote the factors in March 1622 'you purchasse nothinge but excessive charges and a slavishe subjectione to their insolent wills.'[49]

A bad situation was made worse by lack of ready cash to make spice purchases and delayed contributions to the Dutch garrisons which were steadily growing. By 1623 the Dutch had ninety ships in the East Indies and two thousand regular troops posted in their twenty forts, the largest of which were at Batavia, in the Bandas (Fort Nassau), Amboina, and Ternate.[50] It was this combination of Dutch military and financial power which rendered the English

[47] Foster, *English Factories . . . 1622–3*, 47, factors at Masulipatnam to Surat, 26 Feb. 1622.
[48] Ibid., p. xxxv.
[49] Ibid. 63.
[50] *Kroniek,* ix (1853), 114.

position in the East Indies hopelessly uncompetitive. The Company was forced to cut back its operations substantially during the early 1620s, closing its factories at Pulicat, Hirado (Japan), and in Siam. The elimination of the English presence from Amboina with the so-called 'Amboina massacre' of February 1623 was isolated in its extremity, the local Dutch leadership having suspected their English guests of plotting to take over the fort, but was nevertheless a symptom of the overwhelming distrust which now characterized Anglo-Dutch relations throughout the East. The 'massacre' put paid to all further military collaboration and made the 1619 agreement unworkable. The English Company ceased trading at its Banda Island base of Pulo Run, although it continued to claim sovereignty over the island. By 1628, when the English factory at Batavia was shut down, the East India Company retained footholds in the Archipelago only at Bantam, Macassar, and on Sumatra.[51]

Superior cash resources were a major factor in the Dutch success in squeezing the English out of the fine spice traffic during the 1620s. Yet, with the falling off of silver remittances from the United Provinces, the VOC still faced major problems in financing its East India trade, despite the growing influx of bullion to Batavia from Japan.[52] Dutch success from 1621 in trade with China and Japan saved the VOC from disaster and made it possible to resume the process of expansion. Nevertheless, even when the flow of Japanese bullion was at its height, in the 1630s, when the VOC procured more silver from Japan than from Holland,[53] the VOC's bullion stocks in Asia were simply inadequate to finance both the war and the new commercial initiatives on which the Company was eager to embark (see table 5.17).

During the phase 1621–47 the VOC in Asia thus found itself in a position of rapidly growing superiority over all rivals, and widening commercial opportunity, but also of inadequate injections of purchasing power from the Dutch entrepôt. In this predicament, the only way the Dutch could sustain their expansion, political and economic, in Asia was by generating vast new profits through the mechanisms of local, inter-Asian trade. The Company became an Asian trader on a large scale and, by doing so, generated the

[51] Elias, *Het voorspel*, ii. 39–42.
[52] Prakash, *Dutch East India Company*, 16–17.
[53] Glamann, *Dutch–Asiatic Trade*, 58.

TABLE 5.17. *Silver shipped from the Dutch entrepôt to the East Indies by the VOC, 1602–1700* (guilders)

1602–09	5,179,000	1650–60	8,400,000
1610–19	9,658,000	1660–70	11,900,000
1620–29	12,479,000	1670–80	10,980,000
1630–39	8,900,000	1680–90	19,720,000
1640–49	8,800,000	1690–1700	29,005,000

Source: Gaastra, 'Geld tegen goederen', 253.

additional purchasing power, in coin and commodities, which it needed to settle its mounting balances.[54]

The resumed Dutch–Spanish conflict engineered vast shifts in commodity prices in Europe and created new shortages. Using profits from the carrying of Asian products from one part of Asia to another, the VOC generated the means to exploit these shortages with commodities needed in Europe and bought in Asia. On this basis, the Company launched its ambitious attempt to corner the traffic in Persian raw silk, to exploit the devastation of Brazil with Chinese sugar, to manipulate the European market for indigo with indigo bought in India, and to try to wrest control of the cinnamon trade from the Portuguese. To an extent, the VOC succeeded. Shipping fine spices, Chinese silks and porcelain, and Japanese copper to India, the Company purchased cotton textiles in Gujarat and Coromandel which it then sold in the Archipelago for pepper and fine spices. In the same way, spices, Chinese silks, Japanese copper, and also coffee from Mocha helped pay for the VOC's purchases of silk and drugs in Persia.[55] Pepper and spices also supplemented silver in the Company's purchases of Chinese wares, on Taiwan.

The rise of the VOC's triangular carrying trade between Gujarat (Surat), the Persian Gulf, and the Red Sea typified the post-1621 restructuring of the Dutch trade empire in Asia. In the early 1620s the VOC was at its most preoccupied with the problem of how to finance its escalating military offensive and at the same time sustain its commercial operations on an inadequate infusion

[54] Prakash, *Dutch East India Company*, 19–20; see also Gomes Solis, *Discursos*, 53–4, 82–3.
[55] Gomes Solis, *Discursos*, 127; van Dam, *Beschryvinge*, ii. pt. 3, 347.

of silver from the United Provinces.[56] The original motive for launching the VOC's trade initiative in north-west India, in the early 1620s, was to supplement the supply of cotton textiles from Coromandel to be sold in Indonesia for spices.[57] The essence of the VOC's post-1621 strategy was to seek to maximize purchasing power in Indonesia with a minimum of silver by selling more Indian textiles, and to maximize purchasing power in India with a minimum of silver by shipping in spices, supplemented with Chinese and Japanese commodities. For example, in 1623 Batavia instructed the Company's factors in India to procure 400,000 guilders' worth of textiles in Coromandel, and 250,000 guilders' worth at Surat, over the next year;[58] the attraction of Gujarat was that there a higher proportion of the Company's cloth purchases could be paid for from spice sales. Batavia calculated that 40 per cent of its cloth purchases on the Coromandel coast could be paid for in spices; most of the rest would then have to be bought with silver specie. But at Surat 60 per cent of the cloth could be purchased from spice sales, especially cloves, while much of the rest could be bought from the proceeds of selling spices at Mocha.

But if cotton cloth was the original motive, the VOC, like the English, soon woke up to the availability of good quality indigo in Gujarat and the implications of this for the European dyestuffs market. The Spanish embargoes were impeding the flow of Spanish American indigo to the Dutch entrepôt and substantially raising its price.[59] As the price of Guatemalan indigo on the Amsterdam Exchange soared, the VOC responded by buying up large quantities of indigo at both Surat and Coromandel.[60] It was this post-1621 demand for indigo, and need for Gujarat textiles, which explains the sudden emergence of Surat from playing practically no role in the pre-1621 Dutch world-trading system to its functioning as a major depot for the duration of the 1621–47 phase. As a source of textiles for Indonesia, and of indigo and saltpetre for the Dutch market, Surat became the hub of the Dutch carrying

[56] Prakash, *Dutch Factories in India*, 249, 257, 261.
[57] Bos Radwan, *Dutch in Western India*, 53, 66.
[58] Prakash, *Dutch Factories in India*, 261–2.
[59] Israel, *Dutch Republic and the Hispanic World*, 296, 432.
[60] Raychaudhuri, *Jan Company in Coromandel*, 163–4; van Santen, *Verenigde Oost-Indische Compagnie in Gujarat*, 30, 32; in 1625, the English factor at Surat accused the Dutch of buying indigo frantically 'without fear or wit' (Bos Radwan, *Dutch in Western India*, 66–7).

traffic in western Asian seas (see table 5.18). The value of Dutch exports from Surat climbed steadily from the early 1620s, reaching its peak in the late 1630s and then falling away in the 1650s as Dutch demand for Indian indigo ceased and the Dutch carrying trade to Persia lapsed.[61] From the early 1620s until the middle of the seventeenth century the Dutch dominated the market for indigo throughout northern Europe except for England. Meanwhile the English, with their post-1621 supremacy in the Mediterranean, marketed their Gujarati indigo in Italy and the Levant. For the years 1626–7 it has been shown that no less than three-quarters of all re-exports of indigo from England were shipped to the Mediterranean, virtually none being marketed in France, Germany, or the Baltic.[62]

In north-west India, the Dutch encountered fierce Portuguese, English, and Gujarati competition. The Portuguese could be dealt with by force and until 1623 with the help of the English. A series of naval clashes in the early 1620s weakened the Portuguese position, while the fall of the Portuguese stronghold of Hormuz to a combined English and Persian attack in 1622 ended Portuguese control of the mouth of the Persian Gulf. Dutch action along the Malabar coast in the 1620s disrupted not only Portuguese but also Gujarati commerce up the western coast of India.[63] But, despite such setbacks, the Gujarati merchant community remained a formidable competitor to Dutch enterprise in the area, as did the English. Under the jurisdiction of the Mughal authorities, the Dutch lacked any long-term political or military advantage over either set of rivals. Furthermore, the Gujaratis showed great resilience both in their overland trade to Persia and in their seaborne traffic to Persia and the Red Sea, proving resourceful, shrewd, and sophisticated in their forming of partnerships and methods of credit.[64] On this basis there seems little justification for categorizing Gujarati enterprise as a 'pedlar traffic' which was in some way innately backward compared with Dutch or English commercial practices. What then did Dutch primacy amount to in an area such as Gujarat where they possessed no greater political leverage

---

[61] Van Santen, *Verenigde Oost-Indische Companie in Gujarat*, 32.

[62] Steensgaard, *Asian Trade Revolution*, 174.

[63] Prakash, *Dutch Factories in India*, 259.

[64] Bentley Duncan, 'Niels Steensgaard', 513; van Santen, *Verenigde Oost-Indische Companie in Gujarat*, 197–8, 208.

TABLE 5.18. *Dutch ships arriving at Surat, 1614–1646*

Date	Total	From Batavia	From Persia	Date	Total	From Batavia	From Persia
1614/15	0	—	—	1630/1	0	—	—
1615/16	0	—	—	1631/2	15	9	6
1616/17	1	—	—	1632/3	10	5	2
1617/18	2	—	—	1633/4	15	5	3
1618/19	0	—	—	1634/5	16	10	4
1619/20	0	—	—	1635/6	16	—	—
1620/1	2	1	—	1636/7	—	—	—
1621/2	4	2	—	1637/8	11	7	4
1622/3	7	6	—	1638/9	8	1	4
1623/4	7	2	2	1639/40	—	—	—
1624/5	8	3	4	1640/1	9	3	2
1625/6	15	6	6	1641/2	13	6	—
1626/7	12	2	4	1642/3	12	5	4
1627/8	15	8	7	1643/4	9	4	3
1628/9	13	5	6	1644/5	11	5	3
1629/30	11	6	5	1645/6	14	6	6

Sources: Van Santen, *Verenigde Oost-Indische Companie in Gujarat*, 214; on the virtual absence of Dutch ships at Surat during the Truce years, see Bos Radwan, *Dutch in Western India*, 25, 33.

than their competitors? Only this: the Dutch trade network in Asia, which, like that in the world more generally, relied on a mixture of force and trade advantages, furnished a much wider range of commodities than did that of any actual or potential rival. Only the Dutch were in a position to ship in cloves—the fastest-selling spice in Gujarat— Japanese copper, and Chinese goods to Surat, Persia, and Arabia.[65] As in Europe, the entrepôt system was the key to their strength.

The process of Dutch expansion in Asia slowed in the late 1620s. Then, in the mid-1630s, revitalized by several favourable shifts, the process of expansion accelerated once more. In the mid-1620s, Coen's offensive having exhausted itself and funds being stretched to the limit, the Company was forced back on a defensive footing. Naturally, the VOC's opponents endeavoured to take advantage

[65] In the 1620s only a minority of Dutch purchasing power in Persia derived from silver (van Dam, *Beschryvinge*, ii, pt. 3, 347).

of the respite. Backed by the Portuguese at Malacca, the ruler of the strongest of the Islamic states of Java, Sultan Agung of Mataram (1613–45), launched a war to cut the Dutch down to size, culminating in his two attacks on Batavia, in 1627 and 1629, which the Dutch beat off only with difficulty with the help of their Ambonese and Chinese auxiliaries.[66] At the same time the Portuguese mobilized the trading sultanates around the Straits of Malacca, such as Johore and Atjeh at the northern tip of Sumatra, against the web of diplomacy with which the VOC had sought to underpin its influence in the region.[67]

Then, in the mid-1630s, the trends swung back in favour of the Dutch. There was a further steep rise in the amount of silver the Dutch were obtaining from Japan (see table 5.16). This was due partly to the 1635 ban by the Shogunate on Japanese subjects undertaking trading voyages overseas;[68] and partly to the falling off in exports of Chinese silk from Macao to Manila, following the Spanish decree of November 1634 forbidding the shipping of Peruvian silver, via Acapulco, on the Spanish Pacific galleons to Manila for the purchase of Chinese silks—a decree which had a considerable impact on trans-Pacific trade between Spanish America and the Far East.[69] The combined effect of these actions by the Japanese and Spanish governments was to strengthen the Dutch grip over China's silk exports and the provision of Chinese silks to Japan. The extra bullion from Japan provided the means for both the new Dutch military ventures of the late 1630s and the tremendous buying offensive which the VOC now launched in Persia. Finally, in their energetic new governor-general, Antonio van Diemen (1636–45), the VOC found a strategist, politician, and promoter of trade of quite exceptional ability and astuteness.

Van Diemen believed above all in the efficacy of sea power.[70] He lost no time in resuming the blockades of Malacca, Malabar, Goa, and Macao with an eye to paralysing Portuguese seaborne communications and trade and undermining Portuguese influence in the sultanates. Before long he had managed to turn the tables on both Malacca and the Muslim sultanates. A vast engine of

---

[66] Pigeaud and de Graaf, *Islamic States in Java*, 42–3.
[67] Lombard, *Le Sultanat d'Atjeh*, 27, 97.
[68] Kato, 'Unification and Adaptation', 226–8.
[69] Israel, *Race, Class and Politics in Colonial Mexico*, 101–2, 196–7.
[70] Boxer, *Jan compagnie*, 17.

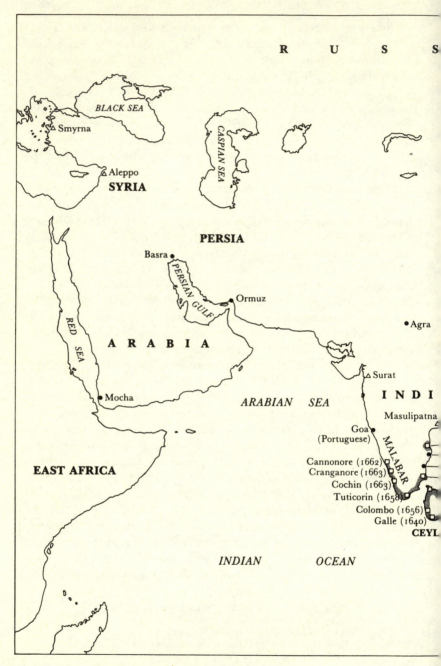

5.4 The Dutch empire in Asia at its height, c.1670.

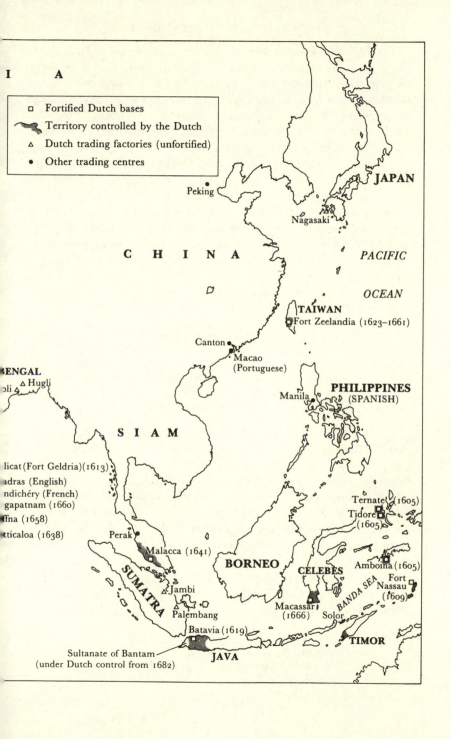

I   A

▫	Fortified Dutch bases
∿	Territory controlled by the Dutch
△	Dutch trading factories (unfortified)
●	Other trading centres

Peking

JAPAN

Nagasaki

C H I N A

PACIFIC

◻

OCEAN

TAIWAN
◻Fort Zeelandia (1623–1661)

Canton ●

● Macao
(Portuguese)

ꞮENGAL

ɔli ᴬ△Hugli

PHILIPPINES
(SPANISH)

Manila ●

S I A M

licat (Fort Geldria) (1613)
adras (English)
ndichéry (French)
gapatnam (1660)
ꞽna (1658)
tticaloa (1638)

Ternate ◻ (1605)

Tidore ◻
(1605)

Perak ●

Malacca (1641) ◻

BORNEO

CELEBES

Amboina (1605) ◻

Fort
Nassau
(1609) ◻

△Jambi

Macassar ▦
(1666)

Solor

BANDA SEA

● Palembang

Batavia (1619) ◻

Sultanate of Bantam
(under Dutch control from 1682)

JAVA

TIMOR

sea power, diplomacy, and commerce was set in motion. 'Our blockade', reported van Diemen in December 1636, 'causes very slack trade at Malacca and, as a result, we find commerce here at Batavia grows greater each day.'[71] Persistent efforts were made to break into the Malabar pepper trade.[72] In January 1639 the English factors at Surat reported to London that the 'Hollanders ... have allready two yeares together blockt upp Goa and domineered alongst the whole coast'.[73] Meanwhile, in May 1638 van Diemen launched his invasion of Ceylon, sending an expedition from Batavia, at the invitation of the king of Kandy, to capture Batticaloa, one of the six main fortresses the Portuguese had constructed around the coastal plain of the island. In 1639 VOC forces captured Trincomalee and, the next year, yet another of the fortresses, Galle, dominating the island's southern coast. Nor was it only the Portuguese and Spaniards who were aghast at the extent of the Dutch gains. In January 1640 the English factors at Surat reported to London that the Portuguese

are undoubtedly in a most miserable predicament: Mallaca and Ceylon besieged and (the Dutch say) as good as seized; theire galleons fired; theire souldiers decayed; themselves disheartened; and all precipitating them (except suddaine and ample succors from Europe reinforce them) even to utter ruine; whilst the insolent Dutch domineere in all places, styling themselves already kings of the Indian seas.[74]

Having blockaded Malacca for several years, in August 1640 van Diemen, undaunted by the town's massive bastions and notoriously malaria-ridden environs, set siege to the town also from the landward side, deploying two thousand Dutch troops and seamen and one thousand Johorese auxiliaries to help with the digging. The full siege lasted five months and became legendary in the East for the appalling suffering it caused both sides. It was said to have cost a thousand Hollanders their lives. What was left of the besieging army finally stormed the bastions on 14 January 1641. A vital trade artery through which the Portuguese had been syphoning off part of the spice traffic from the Archipelago had been cut. Dutch power was now supreme amid the cluster of

[71] Colenbrander, *Koloniale Geschiedenis*, i. 149.
[72] Meilink-Roelofsz, *De vestiging*, 68, 83, 95–6.
[73] Foster, *English Factories ... 1637–1641*, 93.
[74] Ibid. 230.

sultanates and trade emporia at the point where the routes of the Indian and China seas meet.

This acceleration in the VOC's expansion in the late 1630s thoroughly alarmed the English, who began now to help the Portuguese by carrying their supplies and goods.[75] But at home the investors were delighted. The late 1630s saw the most spectacular rise in VOC share values on the Amsterdam Exchange of the century. After a long, laborious climb from 1615 to 1630, the shares doubled in value between 1630 and 1639, and then rose a further 20 per cent in 1640. What burst the bubble was the news of the Dutch–Portuguese Truce, which in April–May 1641 brought the shares crashing down from 500 per cent to 440 and then to 386 by November.[76] But news of the fall of Malacca and continued Dutch advances in Ceylon, despite the onset of the Truce, put new heart into the investors. By 1642 VOC shares had regained most of the lost ground (see table 5.19). In Ceylon, the fighting continued until 1645, by which time the Dutch had taken a fourth great fortress, Negombo, and controlled much of the cinnamon-producing zone. After this van Diemen's successor turned his attention to the Philippines. Fleets were sent against Manila in 1645, 1646, and 1647, the last a very powerful expedition, but all with little effect, the Spaniards showing plenty of determination to resist. The cost was largely offset, however, by the disruption of the Chinese junk traffic to Manila during these years to the advantage of the Dutch entrepôt at Taiwan and the Dutch trade to Japan.[77] The very last battle between Dutch and Spaniards of the Eighty Years' War, fought anywhere on the globe, took place in the wooded interior of the island of Ternate in July 1649, over a year since the ratification of the peace of Münster in Europe but before the news had filtered through to the remoter corners of the Far East.

Despite the spectacular successes, the offensives of the 1630s and 1640s proved that there were limits to what the Dutch could achieve in Asia by force and diplomacy. In the Philippines the Spaniards held firm. The Portuguese still held major bases in Ceylon and India and were determined to retain what they still had of the cinnamon, pepper, and diamond trades. The English

[75] Furber, *Rival Empires of Trade*, 53.
[76] Aitzema, *Historie*, v. 198–9.
[77] MacLeod, *De Oost-Indische Compagnie*, ii. 360, 363.

TABLE 5.19. *VOC share prices on the Amsterdam Exchange, 1625–1649*

Nov.	1625	152	Nov.	1641	386
Dec.	1629	189	June	1642	412
Apr.	1630	192	Sept.	1642	453
Sept.	1630	194	Nov.	1642	473
Nov.	1635	235	Jan.	1643	445
Mar.	1636	229	June	1643	460
July	1639	397	Mar.	1644	453
Aug.	1639	412	Apr.	1644	462
Early	1641	500	Sept.	1644	405
Mar.	1641	481	Apr.	1648	539
May	1641	440	Dec.	1649	410

Sources: Van Dillen, 'Effectenkoersen', 10–11; the data for early 1641 are taken from Aitzema, *Historie*, v. 198–9.

in India and Indonesia were thoroughly alienated. There was also a plethora of powerful Asian states which were by no means willing simply to acquiesce in Dutch trade supremacy. The policy of the Japanese court happened to suit Dutch interests. But the Chinese court harboured deep resentments, as the Dutch were to learn to their cost. The Mughal emperors in India were not to be trifled with, as they showed by preventing the Dutch from extending their control over the indigo producers in Gujarat in the 1630s and adopting the role of intermediary between the producers and the Dutch.[78] In Persia, during the 1640s, the VOC was frustrated in its efforts to corner the silk trade by the power of the Shah and the ingenuity of Gujarati, Armenian, and Jewish merchants. Another example of the limits of Dutch commercial power in Asia was the failure of the VOC, after the capture of Malacca, to control the valuable tin trade of Malaya.[79] Malacca in fact rapidly decayed as a commercial entrepôt after 1641, the tin traffic being diverted to other ports by Gujarati and other Indian merchants operating in collusion with the sultans of Perak and Atjeh.[80]

Yet, when all due qualification is made, there can be no doubt that the way the VOC harnessed political and military power to its

[78] Van Santen, *Verenigde Oost-Indische Companie in Gujarat*, 162–9.
[79] Arasaratnam, 'Some Notes on the Dutch in Malacca', 481–6; Irwin, 'Dutch and the Tin Trade of Malaya', 278–80.
[80] Irwin, 'Dutch and the Tin Trade of Malaya', 278–80.

commercial operations was both highly innovative and effective. It made possible an inter-Asian trade network extending from the Red Sea to Japan such as had never existed before and was unique in its day. This rendered the VOC's role in Asia quite different in kind from that of the English East India Company.[81] The English company was also a powerful force in commerce between Europe and Asia but not in inter-Asian trade in anything like the same sense as the VOC. The Dutch Company connected the various trade zones of Asia, systematically exchanging commodities between the Near East, India, Indonesia, and the Far East in ways that the English Company could not do and never did. This, in turn, during the seventeenth century at least, assured the VOC not just a larger but a much more broadly based role in the interaction between Europe and Asia than its English rival could aspire to. The VOC indeed ruled the seas in the East.

HOLLAND'S TEXTILE TOWNS

Each of the grand sequence of European world economies, according to Braudel, revolved around a single 'pole or centre', a great trading and shipping metropolis which for a period presided over the commercial and financial life of the rest of the globe.[82] In this context, the French *grand maître* classified Amsterdam as typologically the successor to Venice, Antwerp, and Genoa, and as essentially the same kind of phenomenon, exercising an overwhelming political and economic sway over its own immediate hinterland as well as commercial hegemony wider afield. This is what led him to classify the Dutch Republic, whatever its formal political structure, as being in essentials the 'city state' of Amsterdam.[83]

But Amsterdam was not a new Venice, Antwerp, or Genoa. To view the United Provinces as essentially an extension of the needs and interests of Amsterdam is to miss totally the special character of the Dutch state and the precise nature of its contribution to the making of Dutch world-trade hegemony. In reality, it was not

[81] Prakash, *Dutch East India Company*, 19.
[82] Braudel, *Civilisation matérielle*, iii. 22; Braudel, *Afterthoughts*, 81.
[83] Braudel, *Civilisation matérielle*, iii. 24; Braudel, *Afterthoughts*, 95.

Amsterdam but the province of Holland which dominated the political life of the Republic and determined its economic policy; and the States of Holland represented a mass of towns, ten of which were of some size (see table 5.20). Amsterdam rarely had the rest of the States of Holland at its beck and call. Indeed Amsterdam frequently, and before 1650 usually, failed to get her way.[84] For long periods Amsterdam was held in check by powerful combinations of other towns, usually centring round Leiden and Haarlem, respectively the second and third largest towns of the province. This relatively restricted influence enjoyed by Amsterdam reflected the fundamentally decentralized, federal character of the Dutch entrepôt itself.

One might imagine that a radically decentralized state such as the Dutch Republic would be less, rather than better, able to mobilize resources and investment for overseas expansion than a centralized state.[85] But, in reality, in early modern Europe, republics inspired more confidence among businessmen and investors than absolute monarchies, while centralized republics, such as those of Italy, were less well equipped to mobilize resources than a federal republic such as the United Provinces. In the Italian republics the subordination of the territory of the state to the ruling city and its interests tended to limit participation in international commerce and finance to that ruling city, be it Venice, Genoa, or, until the 1530s, Florence. Antwerp, meanwhile, may have drawn extensively on shipping and industrial resources outside of the city but exerted no political control over those resources. Only in a decentralized but cohesive republic such as the Dutch state was a process of systematic federation of resources feasible. Dutch world-trade primacy was built on an unprecedentedly broad foundation of shipping, fishing, and industrial resources, the bulk of which were based outside Amsterdam and which were dispersed right across the country, albeit weighted towards the maritime zone. In this unique situation, so different from the past hegemonies of Venice, Antwerp, and Genoa, Amsterdam was merely the hub of a large clustering of thriving towns, all of which directly participated in the process of Dutch penetration of foreign markets. The federal machinery of the Dutch state, by linking the many towns, waterways and outports which collectively constituted the

---

[84] Israel, *Dutch Republic and the Hispanic World,* 262, 300, 323.
[85] Klein, 'Dutch Capitalism', 85–6.

TABLE 5.20. *Estimated population and numbers of houses of the ten largest towns of Holland, 1622 and 1632*

Town	Population (1622)	Houses (1632)	Town	Population (1622)	Houses (1632)
Amsterdam	104,932	14,840	Rotterdam	19,532	4,860
Leiden	44,475	8,358	Dordrecht	18,270	3,278
Haarlem	39,455	5,377	The Hague*	15,825	3,262
Delft	22,769	4,323	Gouda	14,627	2,314
Enkhuizen	20,967	3,615	Hoorn	14,139	2,556

* The Hague possessed no vote in the States of Holland.
Source: Van Dillen, 'Summiere staat', 184, 188.

Dutch entrepôt, provided a context of continuous political and economic collaboration.

It was a system which encouraged investment in overseas trade in all parts of the country and which enabled the various secondary centres to participate in the framing of maritime, foreign, and colonial policy. The Dutch federal machinery prevented Amsterdam from controlling Dutch foreign policy, limited Amsterdam's influence over the supervision of shipping, trade, and fisheries, and precluded Amsterdam from dominating the VOC and WIC to anything like the extent that would have been the case had investment in the colonial companies not been federated into regional chambers.

The major disadvantage of the system was that it encouraged disparities of view as to how best to advance the economic interests of the Republic, leading at times to protracted divisions. One of the most damaging of these persisted through nearly the whole of Phase Three, beginning shortly after the resumption of war with Spain, in 1621, when the pro-war grouping at Amsterdam, led by Reinier Pauw, lost power and was replaced by a new grouping less closely linked to the colonial interest and more responsive to the needs of merchants involved in European commerce.[86] It was obvious from the outset that the resumed conflict was damaging most strands of Dutch trade in Europe, so that from this point on the Amsterdam city council vigorously supported moves towards a new truce, or peace, with Spain.[87] But, while, in pursuing this

[86] Elias, *Vroedschap van Amsterdam*, i, pp. lxxiv–lxxvii.
[87] Israel, *Dutch Republic and the Hispanic World*, 167, 180, 201, 300–1.

policy, Amsterdam received the backing of several other towns, such as Rotterdam and Dordrecht, pro-war elements continued to dominate the Dutch political scene down to the mid-1640s. Amsterdam, far from being the tail that wagged the dog, continually failed to get her way, just as had been the case in the time of Oldenbarnevelt. After 1633 the Stadholder, Frederick Henry, pursued a policy of prolonging the struggle in alliance with France. In this he was backed by elements of the States of Holland as well as the provinces of Friesland, Groningen, Zeeland, and Utrecht and the two colonial companies. In the States of Holland it was the regents of Leiden and Haarlem who were the most forthright backers of this policy. Indeed, Leiden persisted with it until the very end, even refusing to participate in the public rejoicings which the rest of Holland put on to celebrate the end of the Eighty Years' War in 1648.[88]

One reason for the pro-war attitude of Leiden and Haarlem was the inland towns' relatively large investment in the WIC, which, until 1646, stridently opposed all talk of peace with Spain. But the major factor was the textile interest: for the struggle was perceived as working to the advantage of the textile towns of Holland and to the disadvantage of those of Flanders, which continued to be regarded as the main rival down at least to the 1640s. For where, except in the case of English broadcloth dyed and 'dressed' in Holland, England and the Republic produced quite distinct ranges of textiles, the 'new draperies' and linens of Holland were in many cases practically identical to the Flemish products on which they had been modelled. It was the fact that they produced substantially the same products which gave such an edge to the rivalry of the textile towns of the two regions. The main concern of Spanish ministers was how officialdom in the Iberian kingdoms was to tell the two sets of fabrics apart: until the setting up of the Almirantazgo, in 1624, it was relatively easy to camouflage Dutch textiles as 'Flemish'.[89] What worried the Dutch was that the costs of production, especially wages and rents but also taxes, were vastly lower in Flanders than Holland.

The Dutch textile towns were locked in rivalry with Flanders. Despite the major clash with England over the dyeing and 'dressing' of English broadcloth in the years 1614–17, England was not

---

[88] GA Leiden Sec. Arch. 963, fo. 237, *vroed.* res. 4 June 1648.
[89] AGS estado 2847, 'Manuel Lopez Pereira dize', Mar. 1624.

perceived as being a threat at this time in anything like the same sense. For, while England did also produce some of the 'coarser sorts', there was little likelihood that England could compete in this sphere. For the cheap wools used for the manufacture of 'new draperies', such as *says* and rashes, imported from northern Germany, especially Pomerania, sold for lower prices in the Low Countries than did English wool in England. Thus 'the Dutch undersell us in our coarser sorts', as one English observer noted;[90] but, on the other hand, they did not try to compete with the better quality serges and *bays*, in which the English 'new drapery' industry specialized. The Dutch in 1614 banned the importing of English finished woollen cloth into the Republic, which left practically only serges, *bays*, and perpetuans among finished textiles imported to the Dutch entrepôt from England (see table 5.21).

The Dutch dominated the traffic in Pomeranian and other low-price Baltic wools. But this, their one tangible advantage in the 'new drapery' sector, was of little use to the Dutch textile industry as an instrument against the Flemish textile towns during the Twelve Years' Truce, when Dutch vessels could carry Baltic wool to the Flemish seaports almost as cheaply and easily as to Holland.[91] Dutch dominance of the traffic in Baltic wool was only of any use to the Dutch textile interest as a weapon against Flanders in a situation in which wool and other raw material imports to the South Netherlands could be hindered. But it was precisely this possibility which the return to war with Spain afforded.[92] In April 1621 (and not, as most of the secondary literature states, in 1625), the States General reintroduced the war-tariff list of 1603, a list designed to function hand in hand with the Dutch naval blockade of the Flemish seaports which was reimposed at the same time.[93] The Dutch war-list involved hefty increases in tariffs on Baltic wool and other materials transported via the Scheldt or other waterways through the Dutch entrepôt and represented a serious blow to the Flemish textile industry. For there were no Dutch ships carrying goods to the Flemish seaports between 1621 and 1647; and the only way that Baltic wool could now reach Flanders was either via Calais and overland across the

---

[90] Supple, *Commercial Crisis*, 46.
[91] Usselinx, *Grondich discours*, fos. 2–4; Usselinx, *Naerder bedenckingen*, fo. 4.
[92] Israel, *Dutch Republic and the Hispanic World*, 88–9.
[93] Ibid.; *Notulen Zeeland* (1621), 89.

TABLE 5.21. *Imports of English cloth to the Dutch entrepôt, 1618*

Category	Pieces	Cost per piece (guilders)	Value (guilders)
Undyed and unfinished broadcloth	72,000	200	14,400,000
Serges	71,502	40	2,860,080
Bays	38,676	40	1,546,040
Perpetuans	50,196	30	1,505,880
Says	11,784	30	353,520
Kerseys	15,008	25	375,200
Other	—	—	1,778,552
TOTAL			22,819,272

Source: Diferee, *Geschiedenis*, 297.

border between France and the South Netherlands, paying French duties, or else via the Dutch entrepôt. At the same time, the Dutch war-list erected a protective barrier against imports of Flemish *says* and linens into the United Provinces (see table 5.22). Then in 1623 the States of Holland at the instigation of Leiden, took the further step of banning altogether the export of Frisian and other home-produced Dutch wools.[94]

But was this type of intricate protectionist strategy, designed originally to prop up the Dutch *say* and linen industries, an effective way of safeguarding the future of the Dutch textile industry and of maximizing its contribution to sustaining Dutch trade? *Says* were a cheap fabric manufactured from coarse wools, but the Dutch were now increasingly penetrating the markets of northern Europe as purveyors of fine goods as well as of low-price products. Moreover, the inherent logic of the Dutch situation dictated that they should, from now on, concentrate on producing more expensive fabrics, for an industrial trading power saddled with higher labour costs than those of its competitors is most likely, in the long run, to compete successfully by manufacturing high-quality products, where the expensiveness of the raw materials, and the refined techniques required, minimize the proportion of the final cost constituted by labour.[95]

[94] GA Amsterdam *vroed.* xxii, fos. 195ᵛ–7ʳ; *Groot Placaet-Boeck*, i. 1172–3.
[95] Wilson, 'Cloth Production', 218–19.

TABLE 5.22. *Dutch tariffs on re-exports of raw materials and imported materials and manufactures under the lists of 1609 and 1621* (guilders)

Commodity	Incoming or outgoing	1609	1621
To and from the Spanish Netherlands			
Baltic wool (100 lb.)	out	0.3	2.6
Baltic flax (100 lb.)	out	0.3	2.5
Peat (per 'hundred')	out	2.5	(forbidden)
weaving yarn (100 lb.)	out	3.0	21.0
Spanish wool (100 lb.)	out	0.3	2.60
Flemish *says*	in	0.4	1.55
Lille *says*	in	0.3	0.68
Brabant *lakens*	in	2.5	5.6
Flemish linen	in	0.25	1.13
To and from neutral markets			
Baltic wool (100 lb.)	out	0.3	1.10
indigo (100 lb.)	out	1.0	2.5
indigo (100 lb.)	in	3.0	6.0
gallnuts (100 lb.)	in	0.5	1.25
English *bays*	in	0.5	1.13
English unfinished broadcloth	in	(free)	(free)

Source: *Groot Placaet-Boeck*, i, cols. 2388–485.

Dutch textile strategy in the 1620s was chiefly motivated by the interests of the *say* and linen industries. But the strategy adopted turned out to be effective also as a means of facilitating the shift that was now set in motion from production of low-value to high-price textile products. For, just as the Dutch war-list of 1621, combined with the blockade of the Flemish seaports, starved the Spanish Netherlands of Baltic wool and flax and impeded Flemish exports of *says* and linens, the Dutch measures obstructed the entry of high-quality Spanish wool and Spanish American dyestuffs and the export of Brabant *lakens*.[96] Admittedly at first the impact of this was negligible. Spanish wool continued to reach the Brabant textile towns via Calais, and Brabant *lakens* remained the best quality fine cloth of northern Europe. In the early 1630s Leiden's

[96] Pringsheim, *Beiträge*, 86.

production of fine cloth made from Spanish wool was still insignificant compared with her production of *says* and fustians (see
table 5.23 and fig. 5.2).

During the mid–1630s, however, there occurred a sudden,
massive jump in Dutch fine-cloth output. It seems likely that this
was in part due to the important technical innovations which were
soon to make Leiden fine cloth famous throughout the globe and
which gave it its characteristic smoothness of texture.[97] Unfor-
tunately the precise nature and timing of these technical innovations remain unclear. What is evident is that the upsurge as
from 1635 was also closely linked to the sudden re-routing of the
Spanish wool traffic which took place that year owing to the
outbreak of the long war of 1635–59 between France and Spain.[98]
The great bulk of Spain's wool exports to northern Europe had
been shipped during the early 1630s, almost invariably in English
vessels, to northern France, especially Calais, from where the
wool was transported overland to Spanish Brabant. The Dutch
themselves played no role in the shipping of Spanish wool between
1621 and 1647 owing to the Spanish embargoes. But when France
went to war with Spain in 1635, closing her border with the
Spanish Netherlands, Calais ceased to be the open door through
which the Brabant cloth industry received its supplies of Spanish
wool. This depressed the price of Spanish wool and led to its being
stockpiled at Dover. This gave Dutch merchants the opportunity
to buy up the supply cheaply and to encourage the manufacture
of fine cloth in Holland.

The changes of 1635 revolutionized the entire Dutch cloth
industry. Fine-cloth manufacture was much more labour-intensive
than that of 'new draperies', so that, from the moment Holland
began to produce *lakens* in quantity, labour was inexorably drawn
off from the cheaper lines where it was being less profitably
employed. This is the reason that the upsurge in Leiden fine-cloth
production precisely coincided with a decisive and irreversible
downturn in output of the coarser sorts, that is of all the other
major branches except for camlets, which were made from expensive Turkish mohair yarn and which were produced only in small
quantities in Holland until after the general restructuring of the
Dutch overseas trade system at the end of Phase Three.

[97] Marperger, *Beschreibung*, 107–8; Pringsheim, *Beiträge*, 86.
[98] Israel, 'Spanish Wool Exports', 205, 208.

TABLE 5.23. *Value of annual textile output at Leiden, 1630–1654* (guilders)

Branch	1630	1642	1654
Says	1,630,000	1,380,000	960,000
Fustians	570,000	310,000	150,000
Rashes	300,000	340,000	140,000
Camlets	110,000	330,000	3,000,000
Lakens (fine cloth)	110,000	3,000,000	4,000,000

Source: Posthumus, *Geschiedenis*, ii. 941

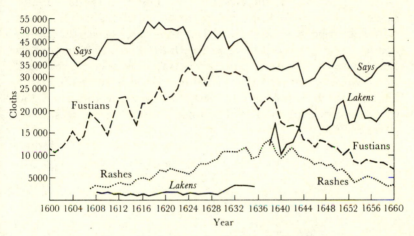

Source: Posthumus, *Geschiedenis*, ii. 883–6.
FIG. 5.2. The rise of the Leiden *laken* industry and the decline of the 'new draperies'.

By 1638 output of Leiden fine cloth had climbed to six times the highest point achieved before 1630.[99] By 1640 *lakens* had definitively replaced *says* as Holland's most important woollen textile product. The fact that the cheaper branches were all in decline after 1635, and that the total number of cloths manufactured at Leiden began to fall after the middle of the century, has sometimes led historians to suppose that the Leiden cloth industry had now entered a phase of stagnation. But it is quite incorrect to draw this inference. In reality, the expansion of the *laken* industry,

[99] Posthumus, *Geschiedenis*, i. 128, ii. 932.

followed in the late 1640s by the upsurge of the camlet industry, implied not only an increasing shift over to high-quality products but also a continuing overall expansion of the Leiden cloth industry. Nor was it only the value of Leiden's cloth output which climbed steeply after 1635; the size of the work-force increased also. A considerable wave of new immigrant textile workers settled at Leiden during the 1630s and 1640s, coming not just from the South Netherlands but also from France, England, and Germany.[1] At the same time additional textile workers were sucked in from Delft and Gouda. At the end of Phase Three, in the late 1640s, Leiden was just at the beginning of the period of its greatest impact on the European textile scene. During Phase Three the Dutch textile industry evolved in ways which significantly enhanced its capacity to contribute to Dutch penetration of overseas markets. Meanwhile, by the mid-1640s the long period of stagnation since 1621 in Dutch European commerce was drawing to a close and the process of expansion of the Dutch trading system was about to resume.

[1] Posthumus, *Geschiedenis*, ii. 883–6.

6

The Zenith, 1647–1672

THE treaty of Münster of 1647–8 represents a decisive watershed in Dutch, Spanish, and in all economic history and marks the onset of what we shall term Phase Four (1647–72) in the evolution of Dutch world-trade primacy. The ending of the Dutch–Spanish conflict was assuredly not the only factor which imparted fresh momentum to Dutch maritime and commercial expansion—except in the Baltic—for a quarter of a century after 1647. There were several notable contributory causes which will enter into the discussion, such as the effects on English overseas trade of the English Civil War and the gruelling Venetian–Turkish struggle of 1645–69 which paralysed Venetian enterprise in the Levant. But the conclusion of the Dutch–Spanish conflict was the most important factor in determining the conditions in which the Dutch world-trade system reached its zenith, the peak of its sway over the markets of the globe, during the quarter of a century down to 1672.

In 1647–8 Spain finally abandoned her long struggle to cut back Dutch maritime and commercial power and in so doing lifted the sustained pressure to which Dutch overseas commerce had been subjected since 1621. It is true that the combined impact of the Spanish embargoes and the privateering campaign had not sufficed to inflict major, lasting damage on the Dutch world entrepôt. But this was due to the fact that the setbacks which the Dutch had suffered, some of which were very serious, had in part been compensated for by Dutch gains in the Indies, the Russia trade, and in manufacturing, which were also in large measure the direct results of the war situation which had prevailed through Phase Three (1621–47). In other words, even though the Dutch world-trade system as a whole had not been heavily disrupted, some strands of it unquestionably had been, and the Spanish pressure had been the pre-eminent factor determining the shifts and responses of the Dutch trading system since 1621. This being the case, the lifting of that pressure, finally, in 1647–8 was bound to precipitate an immediate and fundamental restructuring of the Dutch world-trade system no less decisive than the restructuring processes of 1609 and 1621. In the first place there was, as in 1609, a general fall in Dutch freight and marine insurance charges.[1] Predictably, charges for voyages to the Iberian Peninsula and the Mediterranean fell most dramatically, but the fall in charges for North Sea, White Sea, Baltic, and whaling voyages was also significant. For some northern, as well as southern routes, the lowering of shipping costs was very substantial: rates for freightage of timber from Norway to Holland, for instance, fell between early 1646 and April 1648, the month in which the treaty of Münster was finalized, by as much as half.[2] Moreover, the 1647–8 revolution in Dutch freight charges was 'structural' in the sense that the new lower levels were sustained, except for the relatively short interruptions of the First and Second Anglo-Dutch Wars (1652–4; 1665–7), down to 1672.

Then, in addition to the fall in Dutch freight rates, there was the return of large numbers of Dutch vessels for the first time since 1621 to Spanish, southern Italian, and Flemish ports, and the re-entry of the Dutch into the carrying traffic between Spain and the rest of the Mediterranean.[3] Moreover, not only were Dutch vessels readmitted to European ports under the Spanish crown as from the summer of 1647, but Philip IV's ministers made every effort to ensure that the Almirantazgo, local magistrates, and the Inquisition gave their crews an untroubled reception.[4] Even more favourable treatment for Dutch ships and seamen in Spanish harbours was arranged subsequently under the Dutch–Spanish maritime treaty of 1650.[5]

Under the peace package hammered out by Dutch and Spanish diplomats at Münster, the Dutch were assured commercial access to European markets under the Spanish crown on favourable terms, while Spain's harassment of Dutch shipping, already much reduced since the fall of Dunkirk to the French in 1646, totally ceased. In addition, Spain handed over North Brabant including

[1] Schreiner, *Nederland og Norge*, 49–50; Hart, *Geschrift en getal*, 282; Bruijn and Davids, 'Jonas vrij', 155–7.

[2] Schreiner, *Nederland og Norge*, 49–50.

[3] Israel, *Dutch Republic and the Hispanic World*, 345–7.

[4] AGS Estado 2067, consulta 5 Aug. 1647; *Correspondencia diplomática de los plenipotenciarios españoles*, i. 492–3.

[5] AGS Estado, consulta 3 July 1650.

the textile-weaving district of Helmond, Eindhoven, and Tilburg to the States General, recognized all the Dutch conquests in the Americas, Asia, and Africa, including Netherlands Brazil at its furthest extent, as it had been in 1644, guaranteed low tariffs and tolls in the Spanish Netherlands, and, of crucial significance in the eyes of the regents of Holland and Zeeland, accepted the permanent possession by the Dutch of the south bank of the Scheldt estuary and the permanent closure of the Scheldt to maritime traffic.[6] The Dutch were also granted the right to participate, via Seville and Cadiz, in the Spanish America trade on the same basis as the English and Hanseatics.[7]

The overall effect of the restructuring of 1647–8 was to lend new impetus to the Dutch world-trade system while simultaneously depressing the commerce of the rivals of the Dutch. Not that contemporaries saw anything surprising in this. For years pro-peace pamphleteers in the United Provinces had urged that the way to curb the gains which the English and Hanseatics had been making at Dutch expense in European waters was to make peace with Spain. In England the probable consequences for trade of an end to the long struggle between Spain and the Dutch had been pointed out by Sir Thomas Roe in Parliament in 1641 at a time when the re-entry of the Dutch into the Portugal trade afforded a foretaste of what was to come. England's commercial success since 1630 rested essentially on the reverses the Dutch trading system had suffered since 1621 under Spanish pressure. Remove that pressure and it was inevitable that the foundations of England's prosperity should crumble. 'Now it is true', declared Roe, 'that our great trade depends upon the troubles of our neighbours and we enjoy almost the trade of Christendom; but if a peace happen betwixt France, Spain, and the United Provinces, all these will share what we now possess alone, and therefore we must provide for that day; for nothing stands secure but upon its own foundation.'[8] It was a prophetic warning except that after 1647 France and Spain gleaned precious little of what England now lost. No sooner did Spain and the Dutch make peace than the bubble of England's prosperity burst. English freight rates became less competitive. England no longer carried essential Baltic

---

[6] Aitzema, *Nederlantsche Vreedehandeling*, ii. 80–90.
[7] AGS Estado 4126, consulta 3 May 1649.
[8] Taylor, 'Trade, Neutrality and the "English Road" ', 239.

stores to Spain and Flanders. The Dover entrepôt, still flourishing in the early 1640s, not only ceased to represent a serious challenge to the Dutch emporium; it collapsed completely.[9] The transmission of Spanish silver for Flanders through England simply stopped dead as the Madrid bankers switched over to Amsterdam.[10]

For the English, Hanseatics, and Danes, it was the Dutch recapture of the Spanish traffic which hurt most. Since 1630 Spain had become England's most important market. Down to 1646 English ascendancy over the Spanish trade was overwhelming and great quantities of English textiles were sold there. Then suddenly it all fell apart. Between 1641 and 1646 around three-quarters of all foreign vessels entering the port of Bilbao were English.[11] Within a year or two the English share had been cut by half. But in the most valuable commodities the setback was still more disastrous. The great bulk of Spain's wool exports, for example, were handled until June 1647 by the English.[12] So complete was the English collapse that by 1650 Dutch merchants handled around 80 per cent of the trade.[13] Where, down to 1646, English cloth dominated the Spanish market, in the late 1640s there was a sudden ruinous drop in English cloth sales as Dutch *lakens* and camlets took over a major slice of the market.[14] It took only a year or two for Holland to supplant England as the central staple for Ibero-American dyestuffs. Prices of American dyestuffs on the Amsterdam market came tumbling down in the years 1648–52, prices for Mexican cochineal, for instance, being cut by over a third (see table 6.1).

The rapid gains made by the Dutch at English and Hanseatic expense in the years 1647–52 were a direct consequence of the Dutch–Spanish peace. But the economic factors which powered the rapid Dutch conquest of the Spanish market were not simply a matter of renewed access on favourable terms and reduced shipping costs. In the Dutch capture of the traffic in Spain's high-value commodities what mattered most were certain other strengths of the Dutch trading system which could be brought to bear in the aftermath of peace. Dutch interest rates were funda-

---

[9] Kepler, *Exchange of Christendom*, 98–100.
[10] Ibid. 90, 98; van Dillen, 'Amsterdam als wereldmarkt', 546–50.
[11] Taylor, 'Trade, Neutrality and the "English Road"', 258.
[12] Israel, 'Spanish Wool Exports', 205–11.
[13] BL Tracts on Trade 816 M 11/57; *Brief Narration*, 1–3; Thurloe, *State Papers*, i. 200–1; De la Court, *Interest van Holland*, 162; Worsley, *The Advocate*, 2, 5, 7.
[14] Thurloe, *State Papers*, i. 200–1; *Brief Narration*, 1–3; Farnell, 'Navigation Act', 450.

TABLE 6.1. *Prices for Mexican cochineal on the Amsterdam Exchange, 1640–1654 (guilders)*

1640	27.15	1649	15.92
1641	24.98	1650	15.60
1642	33.90	1651	13.95
1645	22.53	1652	13.20
1646	20.91	1653	16.50
1648	14.63	1654	16.50

Source: Posthumus, *Nederlandsche prijsgeschiedenis*, i. 420–1.

mental:[15] as they were only half the level of those of the English, Dutch merchants could buy up Spanish commodities ahead more cheaply than their rivals. Just as important were the high productivity and profitability of the Dutch fine-cloth industry since the mid-1630s, resulting from technical innovations.[16] The combined consequence of low Dutch interest rates and better techniques was that the Dutch could offer the wool exporters of Madrid higher prices than could the English for their wools and effect wool and dyestuff purchases up to two years ahead of delivery.[17]

But the strengthening of the Dutch entrepôt at English and Hanseatic expense which flowed from the restructuring of 1647–8 affected a great deal more than just the traffic with Spain and the Spanish dependencies. The shift in freight rates, and the ousting of the rivals of the Dutch from carrying Baltic stores to Flanders and Spain,[18] seriously damaged England's Baltic trade, as did the boost to Dutch fine-cloth production which followed from the Dutch capture of the Spanish wool and dyestuffs traffic (see table 6.18). The restructuring imparted fresh impetus to Dutch fine-cloth sales in the Baltic, which, in turn, now cut more sharply than before into English cloth exports to the region.[19] English cloth exports to the Baltic, having recovered quite well

---

[15] Child, *A New Discourse*, preface; Schröder, *Schatz und Rent-Kammer*, 227.

[16] Marperger, *Beschreibung*, 107; Pringsheim, *Beiträge*, 86; Boissonade, 'Colbert, son système', 11–12.

[17] BL *Tracts on Trade* 816 M 11/57; *Brief Narration*, 1–2, 9; Thurloe, *State Papers*, i. 200.

[18] Johnsen, 'Relations Commerciales', 82; Baetens, *Nazomer van Antwerpens welvaart*, i. 44.

[19] Thurloe, *State Papers*, i. 200–1.

from the effects of the Civil War, slumped to disastrously low levels after 1648.[20] The years 1649 and 1651, when English cloth sales to the Baltic fell to 6,784 and 7,689 cloths respectively, were especially bad. As the Dutch share of total shipping entering the Baltic rose, that of their rivals correspondingly fell. Every year from 1647 to 1651 registered a further drop in English voyages through the Danish Sound (see table 6.2).

TABLE 6.2 *English and Scottish voyages eastwards through the Danish Sound, 1645–1654*

Year	English	Scottish	Year	English	Scottish
1645	58	40	1650	48	19
1646	92	89	1651	20	5
1647	129	21	1652	44	11
1648	92	21	1653	0	0
1649	66	26	1654	58	12

Source: Bang, *Tabeller*, i. 338–74.

More alarming still for the merchants of London was the post-1647 erosion of their trade with Italy and the Levant. This threatened the very vitals of England's commercial prosperity. Since the restructuring of 1621 English merchants had become accustomed to dominate the commerce of the Mediterranean, which had become the main market for their spices and one of the most important for their cloth. They soon forgot that there had once been a time when the Dutch had been the more dynamic trading power in the region. Nor, down to the mid-1640s, was there the least indication that the seemingly impregnable position achieved by England in the Mediterranean since 1621 might in reality be extremely fragile. As late as 1644 Amsterdam merchants wrote off the trade to Italy and the Levant as completely lost.[21] Apart from Venetian fine cloth, English woollens were, until the late 1640s, the only western textiles that mattered in Ottoman markets. England consumed most of the olive oil of Puglia and Gallipoli exported outside the Mediterranean and overwhelmingly dominated the traffic in Zante currants, which, reportedly, were in great demand

[20] Bang, *Tabeller*, ii. 528, 532, 536, 544.
[21] *BGLH* i. 1075.

among England's 'women's and children' for their 'cakes and mincepyes'.[22] But the very completeness of England's success in the Mediterranean during Phase Three rendered the shock of the restructuring of 1647–8 all the greater. Almost immediately the Dutch resumed their former dominance of the carrying traffic between Spain and Italy. The Genoese Senate, having avoided the Dutch in deference to Spain untl 1647, now switched back to the Dutch entrepôt for making its major purchases in the north. Genoa, as from 1647, employed Dutch ships 'in a very considerable number for the transportation of corn, salt and other provisions for the state'.[23] But what caused most anxiety in London was the suddenness and huge impetus of the Dutch revival in the Levant. The Levant Company directors in London ascribed the rapid strides achieved by the Dutch chiefly to the lowness of Dutch freight rates.[24] This, indeed, was a factor. Dutch élite merchants were able to ship mixed cargoes, and large quantities of grain, to Italy in these years at rates as low as 9 to 10 ducats per last, almost as cheaply as during the Twelve Years' Truce.[25] But two other factors were also of major importance: renewed access to Spanish silver *en route* to the Mediterranean and the recent rise of the Dutch fine-cloth industry. From the late 1640s onwards the shipping of large quantities of bullion from Cadiz to Livorno and Venice, for the settling of Dutch balances in the Balkans, North Africa, and the Levant, became a permanent and typical feature of the Dutch world-trade system.[26] It also became usual for large quantities of silver to be shipped from Cadiz back to Holland, minted into special coins called *leeuwendaalders*, and then re-exported to the Levant. Analysing Dutch bullion exports in the 1679–81 period, the Dutch mintmasters later calculated that just this part of Dutch silver remittances to the Levant—about two million guilders a year—was equivalent to the annual bullion remittances of the VOC to the East Indies or to those of private merchants to Russia.[27]

A crucial factor in the sudden strengthening of the Dutch position in the Ottoman Near East was Dutch progress in fine-cloth

[22] Child, *A New Discourse*, preface; Israel, 'Phases of the Dutch *straatvaart*', 25.
[23] Thurloe, *State Papers*, ii. 144–5.
[24] *Cal. St. Papers Domestic, 1649–50*, 12.
[25] GA Amsterdam NA card index, 'Livorno'.
[26] ARH SG 7045, J. van den Hove to SG, Cadiz, 17 Aug. 1653; Barbour, *Capitalism in Amsterdam*, 51.
[27] *Bronnen ... wisselbanken*, i. 216; Attman, *Dutch Enterprise*, 37–8.

production. The outbreak of the Venetian–Turkish war of 1645–
69 turned out to be of great significance in the evolution of
Mediterranean commerce. The Cretan war opened up a yawning
gap in the textile market of the eastern Mediterranean: the 'usual
[Venetian] traffic to Constantinople, Smyrna, Syria and Alexandria', the Venetian board of trade later explained, 'was halted;
whereas these before were major outlets for our cloth, now this
rich commerce is extinct and sales of [Venetian] cloth weakened'.[28]
The English too might have hoped to capture some of what Venice
now lost in the Near East. But the English had already squeezed
the Venetian trade by 1645 to the point that it was only the high-
quality cloth, made from Spanish wool, that Venice still supplied
and here it was the Dutch who were now best placed to step in
and fill the gap.

As a result of the restructuring of 1647–8 the English were
thrown back on to the defensive in trade with Italy and the Levant
and lost ground rapidly. The fact is that very suddenly, almost
from one year to the next, the English were unable to compete.
Once again the Dutch were outstripping the English and, as a
result, large quantities of Italian and Levantine raw silk, olive oil,
and Zante currants began pouring into England from Amsterdam.[29] Quite suddenly, massive quantities of fine goods began to be
loaded on to Dutch vessels at Livorno for the English as well as
for the Dutch market. Much the same happened with the wine of
the Canary Islands, which, at that time, accounted for a large part
of English wine consumption. Benjamin Worsley, in his pamphlet
The Advocate written at this time, was not in fact exaggerating
when he complained that 'at Spain, Canaries, Zante, with several
other places in the Streights where they formerly rarely laded
hither one ship of goods; they now lately laded hither more than
wee'.[30]

Of course, there was little prospect that the Dutch could push
the English right back to the rather weak position in overseas trade
in which they had been in 1621. England had acquired too much
in the way of shipping, market leverage, stockpiles of spices, and
textile capacity in the meantime for that. The English held on to
their position as the main suppliers of middle-quality cloth in the

[28] BL MS. Add. 10130, fo. 79ᵛ; Rapp, *Industry and Economic Decline*, 153.
[29] *Cal. St. Papers, Domestic, 1649–50*, 12.
[30] Worsley, *The Advocate*, 7; Hinton, *The Eastland Trade*, 205.

Levant, Spain, and Portugal and as a major alternative supplier
of spices to the Dutch. In the Portugal trade, where the Dutch
revival had begun earlier than in Spain and the Mediterranean
proper, in 1641, the English were rolled back; but they nevertheless
retained a large share of the traffic, except in salt, from which they
were completely ousted. Until 1598, and again from 1609 to 1621,
Dutch commerce with Portugal had by far surpassed that of
England. But those days were now gone for ever. In the years
1621–5 and again in the 1630s it had been the turn of the English
to dominate overwhelmingly. But in the 1640s the two trading
powers found themselves dividing the Portuguese market (see table
6.3), jostling with each other at every turn.

TABLE 6.3. *Foreign ships entering the ports of Lisbon and Faro, 1642–1648*

Year	Lisbon				Faro		
	Total	English	Dutch	Hanseatic	Total	English	Dutch
1642	72	19	22	13	12	7	1
1643	98	22	54	16	15	4	3
1644	64	19	32	8	8	2	2
1645	42	13	22	7	11	4	4
1646	46	15	19	6	12	2	3
1647	107	34	49	19	16	6	5
1648	77	21	38	13	14	3	5

Source: Rau, 'Subsidios', 241 and Table A.

The restructuring of the late 1640s and its adverse consequences
for English trade extended also to the Caribbean area. Here the
Dutch had been unable to ply any appreciable entrepôt trade
during the war with Spain, being shut out of both the Spanish
and the English colonies.[31] Lack of opportunity, and the high risk
to small groups of Dutch merchantmen, had confined the Dutch
presence in the area during Phase Three to that of the Zeeland
privateers and WIC war fleets. In the late 1640s however, the
pattern of Dutch activity in tropical America was totally transformed. Under the Dutch–Spanish peace treaty, Spain not only

---

[31] Van Brakel, 'Bescheiden over den slavenhandel', 49–50; Menkman, *Nederlanders
in het Caraïbische zeegebied*, 44–5.

recognized the Dutch colonies but accepted Dutch navigation throughout the area except for ports and coastlines directly controlled by Spain. The Dutch transit trade with the Spanish American mainland in fact remained difficult, sporadic, and meagre down to the end of the 1650s. But we know that a regular Dutch traffic to the Spanish Caribbean islands, especially those old haunts of the Dutch—Española and Puerto Rico—commenced immediately.[32] At the same time, the Dutch were now better placed than before to penetrate the commerce of the English colonies, particularly Barbados and Surinam; for these were mainly royalist in sentiment and, with Parliament's victory at home, were effectively cut off from England for some years. The royalist governor of Barbados 'ordered a mannage of trade to be onely with the Hollanders'.[33] During the late 1640s and early 1650s the Dutch engineered vast changes, a full-scale revolution in the English and French Caribbean colonies. The devastation of Dutch Brazil with the planters' insurrection of 1645 caused an enormous surge in European sugar prices (see table 5.13), which acted as a lever extending sugar cultivation from Brazil through the Caribbean. Before 1645 sugar cultivation was hardly known in the English and French colonies. The sudden prolific spread of sugar plantations in the decade 1645–54, most of all on Barbados, was essentially due to Dutch (and Dutch Jewish) demonstration, investment, loans, and provision of sugar-crushing and boiling equipment. 'The more industrious and prudent planters became storehousekeepers for the Dutch', who provided them with their slaves and the European commodities they wanted in exchange for their sugar.[34] The Dutch transformed the islands by 'their great credit they gave the planters'.

Thus in American as well as in European waters the general restructuring of the late 1640s vastly strengthened the Dutch trading system. Dutch trade primacy now became, or threatened to become, a fact in many major markets—the Caribbean, Ottoman Empire, Italy, Spain, Flanders, and Portugal—where there had been little or no hint of it during Phase Three. Quant-

---

[32] AGS Estado 2076, consultas 7 July and 7 Oct. 1651; AGI Audiencia de Santo Domingo 2, ramo 1, consultas 17 Sept. and 23 Nov. 1658.

[33] BL MS Sloane 3662, fo. 58.

[34] Ibid. fos. 59–60; du Tertre, *Histoire générale*, i. 460–4; Harlow, *History of Barbados*, 65–70; Deerr, *History of Sugar*, i. 163.

ative evidence which reflects this can be found in the States General's customs returns, the so-called *convoyen* and *licenten*, which reached their peak in the years 1647-51 (see tables 6.21 and 6.22). Every rival trading power—England, the Hanseatics, Denmark, Venice, Genoa—was hard hit by this sudden strengthening of the Dutch world-trade system. But England's losses were the most extensive and the most resented. In England a menacing backlash of anti-Dutch feeling, reminiscent of the mood of the Twelve Years' Truce period, soon became evident. If Spain had once aspired to the 'Universal Monarchie of Christendom', the Dutch were now perceived, as Worsley put it, as laying a 'foundation to themselves for ingrossing the universal trade not only of Christendom, but indeed, of the greater part of the knowne world'.[35]

THE FIRST ANGLO-DUTCH WAR

In the aftermath of the Dutch–Spanish peace, the Dutch world entrepôt was simply too successful for its own good. England lost too much too quickly for the government just to stand idly by. If Denmark and the Hanseatic League were too weak to react, England had emerged from the Civil War militarily and politically strengthened. But it did not follow from this that there had to be a war. For a variety of political and religious reasons, many of the leadership of the new regime, including Cromwell, had little appetite for conflict with their fellow Protestants across the North Sea. By 1651 the English mood was grim and implacable but not necessarily set on halting Dutch economic expansion by war. Initially, there was a preference for the idea of a political union in which England would be the dominant partner, an arrangement of the sort recently imposed, albeit by force, on Scotland. In March 1651 a high-level mission was dispatched to The Hague to demand a 'more strict and intimate alliance and union' between England and the United Provinces.[36] The States General endeavoured to show their lack of interest in any such arrangement as tactfully as they could while attempting to steer the English delegates into

---

[35] Hinton, *The Eastland Trade*, 205.
[36] ARH SG 5899/i, English ambassadors to SG, The Hague, 30 Mar. 1651; Wilson, *Profit and Power*, 49.

discussing ways to ease the growing tension in Anglo-Dutch relations. The English mission departed in June 1651 angry and frustrated.

A more aggressive English initiative was bound to follow. Bowing to the complaints of the merchants, Parliament now passed the bill known as the first Navigation Act. This was essentially a response to the post-1647 English shipping slump and the merchants' demand that the regime step in to halt the burgeoning influx into England of commodities from the Baltic, Spain, the Canaries, Italy, Turkey, and the Caribbean via the Dutch entrepôt. Under the act it was permissible to import commodities into England only from the country of origin, or the port whence normally first shipped, and only in English bottoms or those of that country or first port.[37] Furthermore, henceforth all fish products and goods originating from outside Europe could be shipped to England only in English vessels. The Dutch were not expressly mentioned but obviously this was a measure designed specifically to cut out their intermediary trade. The tension increased further. At the moment the act was passed a richly laden Dutch vessel, the *Prophet Jonas*, sailed from Livorno for home, carrying three hundred bales of raw silk worth £700,000, of which £200,000 worth was earmarked for the English market.[38] The Amsterdam merchant élite was aghast. The States of Holland debated whether to demand the abrogation of the act.

Yet in itself the Navigation Act was not so devastating a blow to Dutch interests that the maritime provinces would have contemplated going to war with England on that ground alone.[39] The English market had become much more important to the Dutch since 1647 than it had been before, but it was still not one of the most vital markets for the Dutch entrepôt. It could be written off, as it had been before 1647, without too much regret. What made a full-scale war between the Dutch Republic and England inevitable was the increasingly aggressive attitude of the English towards Dutch shipping on the high seas. During 1650 English-commissioned privateers and Parliament's navy had begun seizing Dutch vessels in some numbers on a variety of pretexts, including

---

[37] Harper, *English Navigation Laws*, 39–40, 54–6; van Winter, 'Acte van Navigatie', 35–7.
[38] ARH SG 5899/i, SG to Dutch envoys in London, 8 Jan. 1652.
[39] Wilson, *Profit and Power*, 58.

the carrying of munitions to enemies of the English Com-
monwealth in Scotland and Ireland. In 1651 this pressure rapidly
escalated, a total of 140 Dutch ships being intercepted in the North
Sea, Channel, Irish Sea, Atlantic, and Caribbean and brought
into English ports.[40] The Dutch sent ambassadors to London to
try to stop the harassment, but without success. The States General
filled all Europe with complaints over English 'tyranny' and viol-
ence on the high seas. But this had no effect either. Another thirty
Dutch vessels were seized in January 1652 alone.[41] The fact of
the matter was that either the Dutch state possessed the power to
put a stop to such massive interference or Dutch world-trade
hegemony was at an end. The Dutch regents were well aware of
how formidable Parliament's navy now was. In May 1652 there
occurred a major clash between the two navies in the Channel.
Another Dutch embassy was sent to London in a last effort to
avoid war but was treated so brusquely as to provoke an angry
backlash in the Republic. There was now nothing left but to fight
it out.

In the struggle that followed the balance of advantage lay
heavily on the side of England. Neutral onlookers, such as the
Venetian ambassador in London, considered that it was the Dutch
who had just cause and the English who were in the wrong.[42] But
it was equally obvious that England was considerably superior in
fire-power, thanks to her naval build-up over preceding years.[43]
Her navy had many more of the larger warships, of over forty
guns, than that of the Republic and her 'first-rates' also mounted
heavier guns than their counterparts. On top of this Britain's long
southern and eastern coasts lay astride all of the Republic's sea-
routes, while the winds mostly blew from the west—that is to say
against the Dutch. Finally the Dutch were forced to disperse their
strength to a greater extent so as to cover their fisheries and major
merchant convoys. The greater experience and possibly flair of
the Dutch admirals could hardly offset so many disadvantages.

The Dutch strategy of seeking out the main English battle fleet
while at the same time protecting their merchant fleets led to
disaster. There was no answer to England's greater weight of

---

[40] Groenveld, 'English Civil Wars', 561.
[41] ARH SG 5899/i, Dutch ambassadors to Parliament, London, 19 Jan. 1652.
[42] *Cal. St. Papers, Venetian*, xxviii. *1647–52*, 256.
[43] Berchet, *Cromwell e la Repubblica di Venezia*, 73; Wilson, *Profit and Power*, 65.

guns. In the huge, confused mêlées which ensued the Dutch were continually holed and dismasted, and lost men, at a faster rate than their opponents. In home waters the contest reached its climax in the summer of 1653 with two great English victories, off Harwich in June and off Scheveningen in August. In the latter battle the Dutch lost eleven warships and four thousand men, including their commanding admiral, Tromp.

The war severely depressed Dutch trade, industry, and the fisheries. The navy succeeded in escorting some massive convoys in and out, but this did not suffice to prevent acute shortages, redundancy, and distress. Worse still, the English captured vast quantities of Dutch shipping, which represented a double blow in that this was now promptly absorbed into England's merchant fleet.[44] Contemporary reports put the total number of Dutch ships seized variously at between 1,000 and 1,700. The most reliable estimate is probably that of the Amsterdam burgomasters, who reckoned the total loss in ships captured or burnt at 1,200.[45] This was unquestionably the greatest single maritime disaster suffered by the Dutch world entrepôt during its great age.

Given the North Sea victories and the Dutch losses, it is understandable that it is usual to account the First Anglo-Dutch War as a triumph of sorts for England. But it is questionable whether this is correct. After all, the war sprang from commercial and maritime conflict. Yet Parliament in the end, to obtain peace, was forced to abandon every single one of its economic, maritime and colonial demands on the Dutch. Despite English naval superiority in the North Sea, what the conflict really proves, if one looks closely, is the underlying strength of the Dutch world-trade system at this time and the potency of the strategic props which buttressed it. It is certain that Dutch world-trade primacy could not have continued, and that the Dutch could not have retained their recent commercial gains at English expense, had the United Provinces lacked the power and means to neutralize England's capacity to harass and obstruct Dutch shipping and trade. The ability to neutralize England's maritime power was in fact an absolute precondition of the continued survival of the Dutch world entrepôt in anything like the form which it had now attained. And it is here that the true significance of the First Anglo-Dutch War lies.

[44] Aitzema, Historie, vii. 768, 872, 900; Davis, 'English Merchant Shipping', 32.
[45] Berchet, Cromwell e la Repubblica di Venezia, 73.

Outside the North Sea the Dutch enjoyed an overall strategic advantage and they made remarkably effective use of it to pile tremendous pressure on England. The Republic succeeded in bringing Denmark over to her side, preventing England from procuring naval stores in the Baltic. The hemp, pitch, and masts loaded on the twenty-two English ships seized at the Sound in 1652 were sold by the Danish crown to Gabriel Marcellis, who, in turn, sold them to the States General.[46] After Denmark officially entered the war on the Dutch side in February 1653, the Danish Sound was closed to English shipping and England's Baltic navigation was brought to a complete halt. A Dutch fleet was stationed at the Sound and Copenhagen to cover the Danes, who themselves had only some twenty warships. Not only did the Dutch prevent English shipping from entering or leaving the Baltic; they also now halted Hanseatic and Swedish vessels attempting to sail westwards through the Sound carrying naval munitions.[47] The Hanseatics protested vociferously that the Dutch, having filled the entire world with complaints about English 'tyranny' and misbehaviour, were now behaving just as tyrannically themselves.[48]

The Dutch strategy of dispersing their naval strength also paid handsome dividends in the Mediterranean. The richly laden returning English Levant convoy of 1652 was trapped by a Dutch force at Livorno. For the moment England was largely ousted from Mediterranean commerce, the 'Dutch by giving protection to their merchants', as the London Levant Company directors ruefully noted in January 1653, 'having now totally gained the same to the dishonour and losse of this nation'.[49] The attempt to retrieve the trapped Smyrna ships was crushed by the Dutch admiral van Galen, in a battle off Livorno (March 1653) in which the English lost six warships. After that, the English gave up in the Mediterranean. Through the summer of 1653, whilst one Dutch war fleet cruised in Italian waters, another, of eighteen ships, was stationed at the Straits of Gibraltar to 'examine all manner of ships that come in, or go out'.[50] England was excluded from the Turkey trade for the interim, the gap being filled by the

---

[46] Aitzema, *Historie*, vii. 742–5.
[47] Ibid. 783, 807, 818–23.
[48] Ibid. 1025.
[49] PRO SP 105/151, p. 183.
[50] Thurloe, *State Papers*, i. 437, 458.

Dutch and French.[51] Nor was the cost only in lost trade and ships. The English agent at Livorno reported, in January 1654, that, while he did not doubt the correctness of concentrating England's naval strength at home, 'yet our losses here have been so visible to all Europe, Asia, and Africa that they will not believe but our condition is as bad at home'.[52]

In Asian waters too the Dutch swept the English from the seas.[53] From the Persian Gulf, where they captured four English ships, the Dutch shut out both the English and the Portuguese and displayed, the English factors reported, an imperiousness 'almost past beliefe'. If the Dutch suffered great losses in shipping around the coasts of Britain, away from British shores it was the English who took the brunt of the losses. The English captured some 1,200 Dutch vessels of which a high proportion were low-value *fluyts*, herring busses, and the like, though there were some valuable cargoes also, most notably a returning Dutch Levant convoy, intercepted off Boulogne in September 1652, and carrying supplies of Turkish mohairs and cottons for Leiden and Haarlem, as well as two thousand bales of Italian rice.[54] The Dutch for their part brought in some 350 English prizes to their home admiralty colleges.[55] But to this we must add at least another thirty valuable prizes sold off in Spain and the Mediterranean,[56] the twenty-two ships seized in Denmark in 1652, an unknown number of English prizes sold off by Dutch privateers in Danish–Norwegian ports during 1653–4, and some very valuable ships captured by the VOC. From the data for captured English vessels brought into Dutch ports it does not appear that many of them were fishing-craft or colliers or the like. The fact is that English merchants trading with the Baltic, Mediterranean, Asia, and the Americas suffered very substantial losses.

There can be no doubt that the disruption or closure of England's sea lanes and the loss of over four hundred mostly valuable ships and cargoes put heavy pressure on England and that this helped bolster Dutch morale. According to Venetian

---

[51] Thurloe, *State Papers*, i. 458, 595.
[52] Ibid. i. 656.
[53] Van Dam, *Beschryvinge*, ii. pt. 3, 315.
[54] *Hollandsche Mercurius* (1652), 93.
[55] I have assembled this figure from the monthly totals in *Hollandsche Mercurius* (1653), 23, 38, 46, 53, 62 *et seq.*, and Centen, *Vervolg*, 168, 172, 179.
[56] Thurloe, *State Papers*, i. 656.

reports from London, the impact of the Dutch successes over the winter of 1652–3 already largely undermined support for the war in England.[57] If England's merchants had been unhappy before, they were now even more unhappy. By the spring of 1653 Parliament was reportedly not just ready but positively eager to make peace as soon as this could be done without loss of face.[58] One by one all the main English demands on the Dutch were discarded, leaving only the political demand that the House of Orange should be excluded from the stadholderate, to which the Holland regents were known to be basically sympathetic. The English negotiators tried to get some economic and maritime concessions. But the Dutch would yield no ground. The negotiations dragged on for nearly a year. Each time they broke down the gloom in London deepened.[59] That a war which cost so much in men, ships, and trade should have ended without any tangible gains is the measure of England's failure.

THE DECLINE OF DUTCH BALTIC TRADE

A key feature of Phase Four was the contraction of the 'mother-trade'—Dutch commerce with the Baltic. As the Dutch entrepôt became increasingly orientated towards trafficking in costly, low-volume commodities, Baltic bulk carriage, while always remaining important, nevertheless gradually receded as an element of the whole. After the European famine of 1647–51 was over, as the Mediterranean and the Indies loomed ever larger in Dutch commercial life, the Baltic tended to lose its former centrality. No doubt this did involve some decline in the number of lightly manned, bulk-carrying Dutch *fluyt* ships. But, as we shall see, it is quite fallacious to infer from this that Dutch seaborne commerce as a whole was now contracting.

The waning of the Baltic carrying trade after 1650 was, in part, due to the impact of war. The great Cossack rebellion of 1648–51 devastated vast stretches of the Ukraine, White Russia, and south Poland. Then there was the Swedish–Polish war of 1655–60, which

---

[57] *Cal. St. Papers, Venetian*, xxix. *1653–4*, 67–8, 144.
[58] Ibid. 51, 102, 106–7.
[59] Ibid. 172, 174, 178; see also Farnell, 'Navigation Act', 451.

ravaged much of northern and central Poland and disrupted the country's seaborne exports. But war was not the sole factor. After 1660 the Dutch Baltic grain traffic continued at a notably low

TABLE 6.4. *Voyages eastwards through the Danish Sound, 1661–1672*

Year	Total*	Dutch	English/Scottish	French	Swedish
1661	1,023	607	89/19	5	100
1662	1,199	740	85/18	12	110
1663	1,227	725	87/20	6	78
1664	1,225	692	105/21	9	86
1665	711	181	23/ 4	20	79
1666	958	460	0/ 0	12	191
1667	1,045	496	5/ 1	6	230
1668	1,909	991	72/28	2	295
1669	1,945	1,005	93/34	9	300
1670	1,714	917	103/30	11	269
1671	1,629	872	106/34	18	248
1672	862	163	6/ 7	3	274

* Includes Hanseatic traffic.
Source: Bang and Korst, *Tabeller over skibsfart og varetransport*, i. 1–12.

level compared with those of the pre-1650 period (see table 6.4). The long-term trend in Poland from the middle of the century onwards was one of falling grain-yield ratios. Polish grain was becoming less abundant and less cheap than it had been formerly.[60] In the year 1664, for instance, the Dutch shipped only 29,000 lasts of grain from the Baltic using around 280 ships.[61] This is no more than half the number required to shift France's annual wine exports.

Taking the second half of the seventeenth century as a whole, the Dutch shipped approximately 18 per cent less grain from the Baltic than during the first half, an average yearly reduction of around 12,700 lasts, representing employment for around 140 *fluyts* and a little over 2,000 seamen. At first sight this might appear to support the view (that has been so often reiterated in recent years) that the decisive downturn in the Dutch Golden Age economy took place around 1650, coinciding with the Braudelian *renversement de*

[60] Faber, 'Decline of the Baltic Grain Trade', 114.
[61] Ibid. 118.

la tendance séculaire in northern Europe generally.[62] One historian has written: 'The prosperity of colonial trade and shipping, of certain industries and of the specie-trade cannot have been an adequate compensation for the decrease in employment caused by the decline of the voluminous grain trade.'[63]

Yet, however entrenched, such views are mistaken. We need only consider the much greater size of the 'great ships, used in the newly revived traffic to Spain, Italy, and the Levant (which were heavily armed and manned by up to twenty times as many men as a Baltic *fluyt*), the post-1650 growth of the Caribbean and East Indies trades, and the enormous expansion of the whaling fleet (which increased from around thirty-five ships in the early 1640s to 148 ships by 1670),[64] to see that in reality there was an overall expansion in Dutch maritime activity and employment after 1650.

Furthermore, part of the reduction in the Baltic grain traffic was compensated for, especially during the Baltic War of 1655–60 and its immediate aftermath, by shipping Russian grain from Archangel. In the year 1656, for example, with Danzig blockaded by the Swedes, seventy-four large Dutch vessels sailed to Archangel, thirty-seven of which, we are told, were sent to load three thousand lasts of rye, roughly a quarter of the average annual reduction in Dutch Baltic grain shipments during the second half of the century.[65] In 1659 seventy-two Dutch ships sailed to northern Russia, half again for grain.[66] This traffic in Russian grain shipped around the top of Scandinavia continued to flourish in the early 1660s whilst Poland recovered from the effects of the recent war.[67]

Besides loss of volume there was also some erosion of Dutch predominance over Baltic carrying. One should not exaggerate the extent of this for the period down to 1672. The Dutch still dominated the traffic. Only, whereas before 1650 Dutch shipping had accounted for around 70 per cent of total volume, after 1650 the Dutch share oscillated between 50 per cent and 60 per cent.[68]

---

[62] Jeannin, 'Les Comptes du Sund', 322–4; van der Woude, 'De "Nieuwe Geschiedenis" ', 21–3.

[63] Faber, 'Decline of the Baltic Grain Trade', 119.

[64] De Jong, 'Walvisvaart', 313–14.

[65] *Hollandsche Mercurius* (1656), 104.

[66] Ibid. (1659), 159.

[67] Van Dillen, *Van rijkdom en regenten*, 344–5.

[68] Unger, 'Publikatie', 150.

The tough mercantilist stance adopted by Sweden in the 1650s, and again after 1667, eventually broke the Dutch grip on carrying to and from Sweden itself, but had much less impact on carrying to other Baltic lands, including Finland and Livonia, which were under Swedish rule (see table 6.5).

TABLE 6.5. *Dutch and Swedish ships sailing westwards from Sweden, Finland, and Riga out of the Baltic, 1661–1674*

Year	From Sweden		From Finland		From Riga	
	Dutch	Swedish	Dutch	Swedish	Dutch	Swedish
1661	76	82	20	0	57	2
1662	77	76	16	0	45	2
1663	70	90	18	0	62	1
1664	64	77	27	0	58	8
1665	8	61	0	0	16	2
1666	42	143	1	0	59	9
1667	74	133	23	0	41	8
1668	51	191	12	0	92	10
1669	36	206	30	1	152	15
1670	32	179	20	0	113	15
1671	77	170	6	2	151	13
1672	16	158	2	0	21	25
1673	15	151	1	2	51	38
1674	43	153	19	0	156	17

Source: Bang and Korst, *Tabeller over skibsfart og varetransport*, i. 2–15.

But here, as elsewhere, it is crucial to distinguish between freightage, on the one hand, and control exerted by the Dutch entrepôt, on the other. The Swedish crown may have succeeded in forcing the carrying trade to Stockholm into Swedish bottoms; but this, in itself, did not free the Swedish market from dependence on the Dutch entrepôt. Despite loss of primacy in the carrying of goods to and from Sweden, the sway of the Dutch over the country's economic life remained much more extensive than it had been in the sixteenth century, when the Dutch had overwhelmingly dominated the carrying traffic. It is striking, for example, how few of the Swedish ships that passed westwards through the Sound in the 1660s sailed to France, Spain, or Portugal for wine, salt, or colonial goods. The vast majority of Swedish ships which sailed westwards through the Sound, down to 1672, were either *en route*, for Göteborg, on Sweden's west coast, or else for Holland, where, most commodities for Sweden were still loaded (see table 6.6).[69] Dutch storage facilities were still decisive in the complex business of transporting French wines and brandy to Sweden, and Dutch salt-refining was needed in the preparation of salt for the Swedish

TABLE 6.6. *Dutch and Swedish ships sailing from France and Portugal into the Baltic, 1661–1670.*

Year	From France		From Portugal	
	Dutch	Swedish	Dutch	Swedish
1661	124	2	21	4
1662	147	4	33	12
1663	109	2	45	6
1664	80	4	39	13
1665*	11	14	0	8
1666*	15	13	13	13
1667*	20	30	10	24
1668	111	20	29	28
1669	120	11	31	23
1670	112	13	30	26

* Second Anglo-Dutch War.
Source: Bang and Korst, *Tabeller over skibsfart og varetransport*, i. 2–15.

market. Whereas in 1559 only 12 per cent of Sweden's imports (in value) consisted of spices, in 1661 the equivalent figure was 21 per cent;[70] most of this was supplied from Holland, as was the bulk of the sugar, textiles, and processed tobacco which Sweden imported from the west. Similarly, most Swedish copper and iron exports continued to be shipped to, stored at, and distributed from, the Dutch entrepôt.[71]

The Baltic continued to be an area of vital concern to the Dutch, at any rate in the view of North Holland and Friesland. The rest of the Dutch maritime zone, South Holland and Zeeland, orientated towards the west and south, had never taken much

[69] Bang and Korst, *Tabeller over skibsfart og varetransport*, i. 2–15.
[70] Heckscher and Boëthius, *Svensk handelsstatistik*, L.
[71] Heckscher and Boëthius, *Svensk handelsstatistik*, 748; Lind, *Göteborgs handel och sjöfart*, 132–3.

interest in the Baltic and now showed a distinct reluctance to be dragged into the affairs of a region where politico-economic tension was becoming ever more acute.[72] The Swedes had been annoyed by the Dutch–Danish toll treaty of 1649, which, in effect, discriminated against Swedish and Hanseatic shipping in favour of Dutch, and were still more annoyed by Dutch–Danish collusion during the First Anglo-Dutch War (1652–4), when the Dutch guard fleet at the Sound prevented the Swedes shipping naval stores and canon to the west.[73] In the Republic there was, for a time, still some lingering sentiment in favour of the old Swedish alliance, but this was soon greatly outweighed by the need to link arms with Denmark, mistress of the Sound, in an age of struggle with England.

Swedish coolness towards the United Provinces increased with the accession of Charles X (1654–60) to the Swedish throne. He was one of the most ambitious and expansionist of Swedish kings. When he went to war with Poland in 1655, imposing a naval blockade on Danzig and obstructing the Dutch grain traffic, there was an outcry in the Republic. Dutch demands that the Swedes cease their blockade were ignored. The Swedish resident in Holland protested that Sweden had not opposed the Dutch blockade of the Flemish coast from 1621 to 1647 and saw no basis for Dutch complaints over Sweden's 'siege' of Danzig.[74] Amsterdam and the North Holland towns pressed for immediate armed intervention. But the new Pensionary of Holland, the skilful Johan de Witt, had to balance North Holland's preoccupation with the Baltic against South Holland's unconcern for the Baltic and the decided preference of Zeeland, Utrecht, and Groningen for action against Portugal to recover the lost Dutch territory in Brazil and Africa. As usual, de Witt forged an elaborate compromise. The States of Holland agreed that much was at stake in both Brazil and the Baltic and that the Republic should lean on both Portugal and Sweden.

Just as it was the Dutch state which stepped in, in 1652, to stop the English disruption of Dutch shipping on the high seas, and therefore to enable the Dutch entrepôt to function, so it was the Dutch state which stepped in in the years 1656–61 to force Portugal

[72] Van der Hoeven, *Bijdrage*, 98–102, 106.
[73] Aitzema, *Historie*, vii. 743, 807.
[74] Kolkert, *Nederland en het zweedsche imperialisme*, 78–80, 115.

to make at least partial amends and Sweden to desist from obstructing Dutch navigation in the Baltic. Once again it was shown that
the success of the Dutch world-trade system depended on the
ability of the Dutch state to prop up Dutch trade primacy, by
force, in a wide variety of theatres. In July 1656 a fleet of forty-
two ships, under Obdam, was dispatched to Danzig. The Swedes
were forced to lift their blockade and troops were landed to stiffen
the Polish garrison.[75] The next year Obdam was sent to Portugal
with the fleet to demand the restitution of Dutch Brazil and the
African territories the Portuguese had recovered in 1648, Angola
and São Thomé. The Portuguese crown rejected the Dutch ulti-
matum. War was declared. Obdam blockaded Lisbon for some
months. The Zeeland privateers launched a relatively unsuccessful
onslaught on Portuguese shipping in the Atlantic, netting twenty-
five vessels during 1657.[76] The VOC resumed its offensive against
the Portuguese in Ceylon.

Meanwhile, the Danes declared war on Sweden, eager to strike
whilst the Swedes were embroiled in Poland and calculating that
the Dutch would have to back them. Charles X, however, suspended operations in Poland and turned, with lightning speed,
against Denmark. Early in 1658, to the amazement of all Europe,
Swedish forces overran the main Danish islands and closed in on
the Sound. The States General at The Hague became extremely
alarmed. But, despite the evident danger to the Sound, Zeeland
and the South Holland towns did not share North Holland's zeal
for an immediate strike against Sweden. It was only when repeated
Dutch demands that the Swedes pull back from the Sound were
ignored and when Charles X set siege to Copenhagen itself, in
June 1658, that the States General agreed to act. Obdam returned
to the Baltic, braving the cross-fire from the batteries both sides
of the Sound—all now in Swedish hands—to attack the Swedish
fleet. The Swedes were beaten and pulled back. Obdam landed
six thousand troops and relieved Copenhagen.

The Dutch had two central objectives during the great Baltic
crisis of 1658–60. On the one hand, their concern was to prevent
Sweden from controlling both sides of the Sound and to preserve
Copenhagen. But equally important was the long-standing Dutch
desire to bind Sweden not to penalize Dutch shipping in Swedish

[75] *Hollandsche Mercurius* (1655), 66–7.
[76] Binder, 'Zeeländische Kaperfahrt', 68.

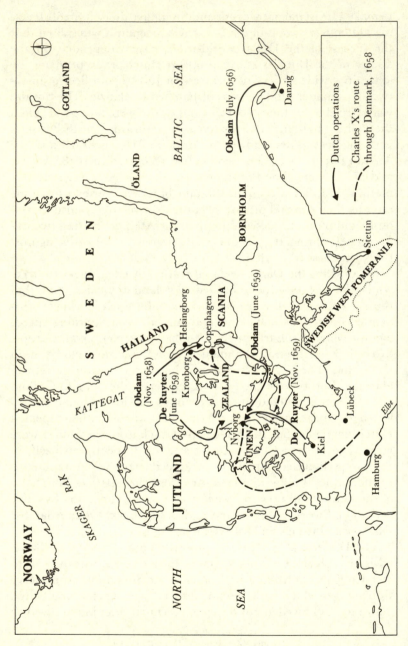

6.1 Dutch intervention in the Baltic, 1656–1659

ports.[77] The States General was quite happy to see Denmark pay for Swedish concessions to Dutch interests by ceding territory, provided it was all on the Swedish side of the Sound, to Sweden. But Charles wanted more and, backed by England, was determined to prevent the imposition of a *Pax Neerlandica* on the region.

A powerful English fleet of fifty ships was sent to the Sound early in 1659 to help Sweden prevent the Dutch from consolidating their naval supremacy around the Sound and in Scandinavian waters generally. What followed was one of the great maritime dramas of early modern history. The States of Holland did not relish risking another gruelling war with England. But so much was at stake that it was decided to escalate the war of nerves. To reinforce Obdam, a second Dutch fleet was dispatched under de Ruyter. During the summer of 1659 the Dutch concentrated seventy-eight warships and seventeen thousand men in the narrow passage between the Danish islands of Fuenen and Zealand, anchored close to the combined naval might of England and Sweden.[78] The English eventually withdrew. In November 1659 de Ruyter ejected the Swedes from Nyborg, breaking the Swedish line of communications across Denmark and forcing Charles X to come to terms.[79] In the negotiations which followed, the Swedes agreed to evacuate all the Danish territory they occupied on the western side of the Sound and to accept curbs on tolls and regulations in Swedish ports which prevented any effective discrimination against Dutch shipping in favour of Swedish.[80]

By 1660 the Dutch had established a general *imperium maris* throughout the north which was resented in different degrees by Danes, Norwegians, and Swedes, as well as the English, and was beginning to attract the disapproval of Louis XIV. By 1664 both England and France were at work in Copenhagen and Stockholm fomenting all manner of politico-commercial schemes directed against Dutch economic supremacy. The English envoy, Sir Gilbert Talbot, sent by Charles II during the run-up to the Second Anglo-Dutch War to detach Denmark from its troublesome Dutch alliance, detected plentiful ill-feeling on which to build. The Danish court, he found, was rife with recollection of the humili-

---

[77] Res. Holl. 21 Sept. 1656; Aitzema, *Historie*, ix. 544–60.
[78] Bowman, 'Dutch Diplomacy', 347; Blok, *Michiel Adriaanszoon de Ruyter*, 161–3.
[79] Blok, *Michiel Adriaanszoon de Ruyter*, 170–2.
[80] Aitzema, *Historie*, ix. 556–8.

ation heaped upon Denmark by the Dutch in 1645. Alignment with England, he assured his hosts, was the way to 'restore Denmark to the same condicion and freedom of imposing customes in Norway and the Sound as they had before Holland and Sweden joyned to restrayne them by the Articles enforced upon Denmark in the year '45'.[81]

An English alliance, he urged, was the only practicable means of breaking the Dutch hold. He poured scorn on French efforts to mobilize the Danes and Norwegians against Dutch trade hegemony. He was sure that the French would not be able to persuade the Norwegians to dispense with Dutch refined salt and turn to France, dismissing this as 'altogether impracticable in regard that the French salt is not good for the salting of herrings in Norway where they make use of Portugal salt for that purpose. The French resident hath a long time laboured to gain the whole salt trade in Norway but cannot compass it for the reasons I have given.'[82] The Danish court seemed responsive and definite plans took shape. In the event of a new Anglo-Dutch war, Denmark–Norway would this time side with England. Charles II would provide a subsidy and at least twelve warships for the defence of Copenhagen. The Sound would be closed to all Dutch shipping, halting their Baltic commerce completely, and the many Danes and Norwegians serving in the Dutch navy would be recalled. The latter, Talbot prognosticated, would cause a 'greate weakening, nay an utter disabling of the Holland fleete'.

Yet it all turned out very differently. In reality, Danish ministers were, as seventeenth-century diplomats liked to say, merely 'entertaining' him with illusions. Disappointed, Talbot rebuked the Danes for lacking true resolve to break free from the Dutch grip, comparing Denmark's attitude unfavourably with that of Sweden. The reply was that

Swede lyeth remote and out of danger, but he [the Danish king] is exposed soe much to the mercy of the Hollanders that if they appear with twenty fregates in the Sound, they may block up all provisions for this towne [Copenhagen]. To this they addith that all his subjects are ruined if theyr commerce be obstructed with Holland, for in that case noe part of his dominions can afford him anything; his woods and other

[81] PRO SP 75/17, fo. 314, Talbot to Arlington, Copenhagen, 15 Apr. 1665.
[82] PRO SP 75/17, fo. 190ᵛ, Talbot to Bennet, Copenhagen, 11 Oct. 1664.

commodityes of Norway and corn and cattle in Zealand, Funen, and Holstein will all lye dead upon his hands, which is not the case of Swede, theyr commodityes being such as Holland can have from none but themselves.[83]

After the outbreak of war it became clear that Denmark would not, after all, align with England. Talbot reassured Charles II, however, that 'all the promises of Holland shall never be able to make them act against you'. Again, Talbot's prognostications proved lamentably wrong. Denmark did enter the war on the side of the Dutch and, again, the Sound was closed against England.

After 1667 it was the turn of France to orchestrate Scandinavian resentment against the Republic's commercial hegemony. Colbert planned to establish a general staple for French wine, brandy, and salt in south-west Sweden, at Göteborg, as the pivot of a direct Franco-Swedish commerce, bypassing the Dutch entrepôt. In principle, the Swedish crown, which now broke the 1660 agreement with the Dutch on shipping tolls in Swedish ports not to discriminate against Dutch shipping, was eager to collaborate. Sweden was keen to break the Dutch hold. But in practice there were all sorts of difficulties. For one thing, the Swedish public proved no keener than the Norwegians on salt shipped direct from France, owing to its high magnesium content, which imparted an unattractive, blackish colour. The French ambassador at Stockholm reported, in March 1668, that, unless better ways of purifying French salt were found, he could see little prospect of much progress: 'le limon qui se trouve dans le sel de Brouage qui le rend noir, et qui gaste les salaisons, empeschera tousjours que ces paysans s'y accoustument.'[84] Nor was he much encouraged by Swedish drinking habits. He found that even those few Swedes who drank wine in preference to beer preferred Rhenish to French wine; and over Rhenish wine the Dutch exerted an unshakeable grip.

Colbert pressed on, however, with the setting up of his Compagnie du Nord to handle the new direct carrying traffic between France and the Baltic. This ambitious venture, based at La Rochelle, near the salt deposits at Brouage, commenced operations in 1669. Both the French and Swedish crowns took steps to pro-

[83] PRO SP 75/17, fo. 314, Talbot to Arlington, Copenhagen, 15 Apr. 1665.
[84] *Correspondance administrative*, iii. 410.

mote the enterprise, Louis paying export premiums on wine and salt shipped in French bottoms directed to Sweden–Finland, its subject territories, and Poland. But, from the first, this French northern company ran into insuperable problems. French salt sold better in the Baltic provinces, Prussia, and Poland than in Scandinavia, for further east it was used mainly for preserving meat not fish. But the Compagnie found it impossible to offer competitive freight rates. The Bordeaux wine exporters proved distinctly reluctant to dispense with Dutch freightage, storage, and other facilities in favour of the Compagnie, or do without Dutch payments in advance of delivery.[85] The Compagnie was never able to sell enough French products in Sweden–Finland to balance its purchases of masts, tar, and copper. In this contest, the Dutch held all the cards; for their *coup de grâce* they dumped cut-price timber and naval stores in La Rochelle, Nantes, and Bordeaux, to undercut the Compagnie also in the sale of such Swedish products as it did ship back.[86] A dismal failure, staggering from one setback to the next, Colbert's Compagnie du Nord was finally wound up in 1675.

THE MEDITERRANEAN AND SPAIN

In the Mediterranean, the revival of Dutch commerce in the late 1640s was, in part, a repeat of the hectic upsurge in traffic which followed the conclusion of the Twelve Years' Truce. Once again Dutch shipping sailed with much less risk to and through the Straits of Gibraltar. Dutch freight and insurance charges for the Mediterranean tumbled. Dutch shipping crowded into Spanish ports as it had in the years 1609–21. Each year from 1648 the Dutch shipped millions of pesos of Spanish American bullion, dyestuffs, and tobacco back to the Dutch entrepôt and more silver and fine goods on to Italy and the Levant. Spanish silver again played an important role in the settling of Dutch balances in Italy and the Ottoman Empire. From 1648 onwards, just as during the Truce, the Dutch dominated the carrying both of salt and other

[85] Boissonade and Charliat, *Colbert et la Compagnie du Nord*, 71, 83, 88.
[86] Ibid. 98–9; *Lettres, instructions et mémoires de Colbert*, ii. 488–9.

bulky goods, and of fine goods, between Spain and Italy.[87] Nevertheless, there were also major differences between the vigorous Dutch Mediterranean traffic of the Twelve Years' Truce and the new Dutch *straatvaart* which flourished during the 1647–72 period. Dutch Mediterranean trade during the Truce had shown great dynamism but also serious limitations. It had outstripped the trade of the English but not that of the Venetians and French. The main reasons for this had been the failure of the Dutch to export manufactures of their own making to southern Europe in any quantity, except in the case of Leiden *says* to Italy, and, as a consequence of this, their relatively limited purchasing power. During the Truce the Dutch had had to rely on specie, spices, and Russian products to settle their balances.[88]

After 1647 the position was very different. The Republic was now a much more formidable producer and purveyor of manufactures than it had been during the early seventeenth century; and, whilst this profound shift in the Dutch economy exerted its influence in all markets, nowhere was its impact greater than in the Mediterranean. In the late 1640s, following the outbreak of the Venetian–Turkish war, the Republic emerged as the main European producer of camlets and the main consumer of Turkish mohair yarn.[89] After the end of the war with Spain, the Republic finished and exported more high-grade Flemish linen than before.[90] Most crucial of all, in the late 1640s the Dutch captured control of the trade in Spanish wool and increased their output of fine cloth just at the moment when the Cretan war excluded Venetian fine cloth from the Ottoman market. The Dutch stepped into the gap. The essence of the revived Dutch Levant trade of the post-1647 period was the exchange of Dutch fine cloth made from Spanish wool, as well as silver and spices, for raw silk, gallnuts, and, in particular, Turkey's output of mohair yarn. At first, the reviving Dutch traffic focused on Aleppo and Constantinople. But, after the re-establishment of the Dutch merchant colony at Smyrna in 1651, Smyrna, which was closer to the

---

[87] Brugmans, 'Notulen', 307–10; Israel, 'Phases of the Dutch *straatvaart*', 17–19.
[88] ASV CSM 1st ser. 143, fo. 143; Berchet (ed.), *Relazioni dei consoli veneti nella Siria*, 102–3.
[89] Posthumus, *Geschiedenis*, iii. 272–9.
[90] Wätjen, *Niederländer im Mittelmeergebiet*, 355–9; Sneller, 'Stapel', 180–5; Blendinger, 'Augsburger Handel', 304–8.

mohair-weaving districts, rapidly emerged as the main Dutch trading base in the eastern Mediterranean.[91]

During the 1620s and 1630s the English had ousted the French and Venetians from most sectors of the Levant trade and, excepting only Venice's traffic in camlets and fine cloth, enjoyed almost undisputed hegemony over maritime trade from Spain to Syria. Inevitably, the sudden, vigorous revival of Dutch Mediterranean trade in the late 1640s led to a head-on clash with the English for mastery of the commerce. After 1648 the Dutch had the edge in freight rates as well as fine cloth, linens, spices, and caviare. But the English were now too powerful in southern European commerce just to be thrust aside. England's Navigation Act of 1651 blocked the importing of Mediterranean goods into England from Holland. As England was the main market for Zante currants and the oils of Gallipoli and Puglia, this in itself paralysed Dutch enterprise in those trades. Also the English too profited from the collapse of the Venetian Levant trade after 1645. English cloth exports to the Ottoman Empire rose from 6,000 long- and short-cloths yearly in the 1620s to around 12,000 yearly by the early 1660s.[92] In terms of quantity this was no less impressive than the rise in Dutch woollen cloth exports to Turkey, which rose from practically nothing in 1640 to around 6,000 *lakens* yearly in the 1650s and 1660s.[93] Dutch profits rose faster, however, as Dutch fine cloth was a more highly finished and a costlier product than English woollen cloth.[94] By 1650 Dutch fine cloth was the western product most highly esteemed by the Turks.[95]

The Dutch and English, therefore, found the trade of the Mediterranean divided between them and something like a division of labour set in.[96] The Dutch sold the fine cloth, linens, camlets, and most of the spices; the English sold the lower-grade cloth. Both nations bought raw silks in Italy and Turkey. But, after the Navigation Act, the English largely monopolized the buying up of southern Italian olive oil and Zante currants, whilst the Dutch monopolized the traffic in Idrian quicksilver and Po valley rice

[91] *BGLH* ii. 306.

[92] BL MS 36785, fos. 6, 33; Roberts, *Marchants Mapp of Commerce*, 139.

[93] *BGLH* ii. 97–8, 303; Masson, *Histoire*, 126; the main Dutch Smyrna convoy of 1669 carried 4,589 *lakens* (see PRO SP 98/10, fo. 26).

[94] Posthumus, *Geschiedenis*, ii. 940–1.

[95] Sella, *Commerci e industrie*, 64.

[96] Israel, 'Phases of the Dutch *straatvaart*', 21–2.

and bought the bulk of the cottons and mohair yarn.[97] On balance, the English seem to have continued to purchase more raw silk in Italy and the Levant than the Dutch: the shipping of raw silk from the Mediterranean remained a marginal activity for the Dutch entrepôt, designed to supplement the supplies shipped direct from Persia and India by the VOC and via Russia and the Dutch Muscovy convoys.

Structurally, Dutch Mediterranean trade differed from that of the English during Phase Four also in other respects. England tended to export much less to Italy than she imported from that market, owing to the policy of Venice, Tuscany, and other Italian states of shutting out foreign woollen cloth. The Dutch, on the other hand, enjoyed a favourable balance of trade with Italy in this period, as they were able to balance their purchases with large sales of spices, linen, dyestuffs, and Leiden *says*.[98] It was only in southern Italy, where England dominated the olive-oil traffic, that the old pre-1647 English ascendancy survived.[99] In balancing their trade with Italy and North Africa, the Dutch also had an advantage over the English in being the chief supplier of masts, ropes, pitch, and other naval stores. In the distribution of spices in the Mediterranean, Dutch superiority over the English tended to increase after 1650 with the growing success of the VOC's efforts to monopolize the Asian spice traffic[1]. During the 1647–72 period, Amsterdam's élite merchants—such as the Coymans, van Colen, Godijn, Sautijn, van Goor, van der Straeten, and Bartholotti—shipped immense quantities of pepper to Genoa, Livorno, and Venice, the main depots from where Dutch products were distributed all over Italy, North Africa, and the Balkans.[2] The Dutch Smyrna convoy of six 'great ships' and two men-of-war which docked at Livorno in September 1670 *en route* to the Levant carried 600,000 lb. of pepper in 1,700 bales,[3] an amount equivalent to over 10 per cent of Europe's total annual pepper consumption.

As the Dutch dominated Mediterranean trade in fine goods after 1647, the directors of the Dutch Levant trade were much

---

[97] *BGLH* ii. 305–6; Posthumus, *Geschiedenis*, ii. 937–9, 941.
[98] BL MS Add. 36785, fos. 21, 38ᵛ; PRO SP 98/9, fos. 73, 181, 241–2, 330; Israel, 'Phases of the Dutch *straatvaart*', 25–6.
[99] Pagano de Divitiis, 'Mediterraneo nel XVII secolo', 129, 146.
[1] See pp. 250–2.
[2] Wätjen, *Niederländer im Mittelmeergebiet*, 355; Paci, '*Scala' di Spalato*, 117–18.
[3] PRO SP 98/11, Dethick to Williamson, Livorno, 8 Sept. 1670.

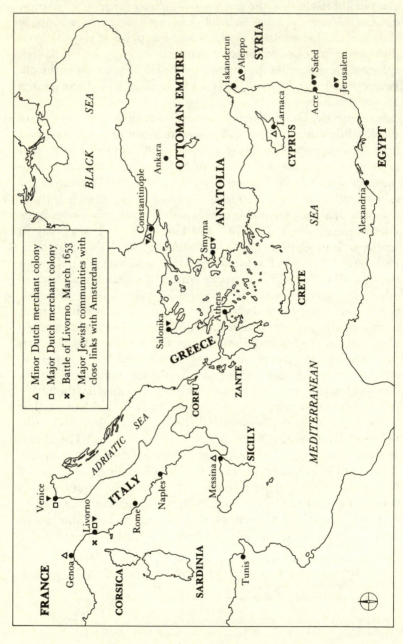

6.2 The Dutch merchant colonies in Italy and the Levant during Phase Four, 1647–1672.

Minor Dutch merchant colony

Major Dutch merchant colony

Battle of Livorno, March 1653

Major Jewish communities with close links with Amsterdam

preoccupied with ensuring the security of their traffic. The Republic was now at peace with Spain; but there were always difficulties
with the Algerian corsairs and Anglo-Dutch tension ran high
throughout these years. Security thus became a major issue. Pieter
de la Court, indeed, went so far as to attribute what he regarded
as Dutch primacy in Mediterranean trade specifically to the naval
escorts and the great size of the ships the Dutch now employed in
this traffic.[4] It was the heavily armed convoys, which carried the
most valuable part of the Dutch traffic which, according to de La
Court, drew the custom of the Italian, Armenian, and Jewish
middlemen who handled the distribution of spices and western
textiles to the secondary commercial emporia of the Mediterranean. Until 1647 the English, as neutrals in the Spanish–Dutch
conflict, had been the principal carriers.[5] After 1648 the Dutch
quickly supplanted the English in this as in so many sectors: 'The
reason is', commented the English envoy in Tuscany,

the Dutch, observing that all forreigners gave greater freights to our ships
than theirs, by reason of the goodnesse of our vessels, they, partly for their
own security, against the Barbary Coast, partly to invite forraigners to
load on their vessels, send out a yearly convoy to protect theyr ships
which takes up all the Spanish money and fine goods from Spayn for
Italy, from Italy for the Levant and agayn from the Levant for Italy and
from Italy for Spayne and in this trade they employ theyr men of warr.[6]

There were, in fact, usually two of these convoys each year
during Phase Four, a small spring convoy, and a larger autumn
fleet which sailed after the return of the VOC and Muscovy ships so
that the Amsterdam Exchange would know what supplementary
stocks of raw silk might be needed.[7] Both were escorted in peacetime by two men-of-war. Thus, for example, in 1662, the smaller
convoy—two 'great ships' and two warships—docked at Smyrna
on 12 June and the larger—five 'great ships' and two warships—
on 10 November. But this was just the core of the traffic. Ten other
Dutch ships arrived at Smyrna singly that year, usually from
Livorno or Venice.[8] The convoys provided security but had the

---

[4] De La Court, *Interest van Holland*, 62.
[5] Blok (ed.), 'Koopmansadviezen', 51, 65.
[6] PRO SP 98/8, Finch to Arlington, Florence, 13 June 1667.
[7] ARH Levantse Handel vi, res. 11 Sept. 1686; Israel, 'Phases of the Dutch *straatvaart*', 22.
[8] ARH Levantse Handel 122, 'Notitie van schepen in Smirna gearriveert' (1662).

disadvantage of being excessively rigid and slow. They visited Cadiz, Malaga, Alicante, Genoa, and Livorno on both the way out and the way back. Consequently, a large part of the Dutch traffic, even in fine goods, went on outside the convoy framework, which meant occasional heavy losses. Most Dutch vessels captured by Muslim corsairs were carrying grain, salt, or other cargoes of low value; but by no means all. A Dutch ship captured *en route* from Cadiz to Genoa in 1662 was carrying 140 bales of Castilian wool, 50,000 pieces-of-eight, and other costly goods, the whole cargo being valued at 195,000 guilders.[9]

During Phase Four England was the main challenger to the Dutch position in the central and eastern Mediterranean. In the Spanish trade, however, the principal challenger, after 1648, was not England but France. Indeed, some scholars have been so impressed by the French role in this crucial market that it has been claimed that there was no real rival to French supremacy. One historian has even written that 'from the early seventeenth to the late eighteenth century, French economic domination of the (Iberian) Peninsula was unquestionable'.[10] Leaving aside the undoubted fact of Anglo-Dutch domination of the Portugal trade, this resounding assertion needs to be seriously qualified also with regard to Spain. For one thing, during the great Franco-Spanish war of 1635–59 French ships and goods were officially excluded from Spain and the Almirantazgo was put to work to seek out French-owned merchandise. A reduced quantity of French products still seeped into Spain despite the embargo, but these goods often belonged to other, and after 1648 especially to Dutch merchants.[11] To speak of French economic preponderance in Spain in the 1635–59 period thus makes little sense. In the late 1650s, when England as well as France was at war with Spain, Dutch predominance was almost total. The Dutch consul at Seville reported in January 1658 that apart from a few Hamburg vessels the only foreign ships to be seen in the ports of Andalusia were Dutch.[12]

---

[9] Brugmans, 'Notulen', 308.

[10] Kamen, 'Decline of Spain', 44; Kamen, *Spain*, 119, 121.

[11] ARH SG 7047/2, Gamarra to SG, The Hague, 17 Nov. 1655 and 6 May 1656, and Dutch consul at San Sebastian to SG, 4 Mar. 1656; Girard, *Commerce français*, 77, 349.

[12] ARH SG 7052/i, Dutch Consul at Seville to SG, 20 Jan. 1658.

Nevertheless, after the treaty of the Pyrenees (1659) France did indeed acquire a very strong position in the Spanish trade. This was principally due to the fact that linen, most of which then came from France, was the single most important commodity imported from outside Spain for the Castilian and Spanish American markets.[13] France also rivalled Italy as a supplier of finished silks. The taste for French fashions and haberdashery thus gave French merchants from 1659 onwards an enviable advantage over their competitors. Where the Dutch had enjoyed an unchallenged primacy in the Spanish trade from 1648 to 1659, after 1659, at least in those periods when France was at peace with Spain, Holland was forced to share its dominance of the markets of the Hispanic world with the French. In many years, especially between 1659 and 1672, the French did supply the largest share of manufactures exported via Cadiz to Spanish America and consequently received the chief share of the private silver shipped back on Spain's trans-atlantic convoys (see table 6.8)—hence Sir William Godolphin's remark, ''tis certain that of all others the French are the greatest gainers by the Spanish trade, especially through their manufacture of linnen'.[14]

But the French lead during these years was much smaller in reality than appears from data such as those compiled by the French consul Pierre Catalan in 1670 (see table 6.7). The consul's list masks the fact that much of what sold in Spain and originated from Flanders, Germany, and France was finished, packed, and shipped from Holland and for the account of Dutch merchants, this being especially true of a large proportion of the Flemish and Silesian linen. Also some of the bullion shipped from Cadiz to destinations other than Holland (see table 6.8) nevertheless belonged to Dutch merchants, this being especially true of much of the specie exported to Italy.[15] Furthermore, as Girard realized but subsequent scholars have lamentably failed to mention, no sooner were France and Spain locked again in war, as in the years 1673–8, than the Spanish king again prohibited trade between France and Spain and imposed a general embargo on French

---

[13] Girard, *Commerce français*, 341–2, 361.

[14] Godolphin, *Hispania illustrata*, 237.

[15] ARB SEG 222, fos. 160–1; PRO SP 98/8, Finch to Arlington, Florence, 13 June 1667.

TABLE 6.7. *Goods shipped to Cadiz from northern Europe and Italy according to the French consul, Pierre Catalan, 1670* (valued in livres tournois)

Country of origin	Value	% of total
France	12,000,000	29.9
Italy		22.4
via Genoa	7,500,000 ⎫	
via Venice	1,500,000 ⎭	
United Provinces	6,000,000	14.9
England	4,500,000	11.2
Flanders	4,500,000	11.2
Germany (through Hamburg)	4,200,000	10.4

Source: Everaert, *Internationale en koloniale handel*, 453.

TABLE 6.8. *Silver remittances from Cadiz, 1670* (pesos)

Destination	Value
France	4,000,000
Italy	2,500,000
United Provinces	2,000,000
Flanders	1,000,000
England	1,000,000

Source: Girard, *Commerce français*, 445.

goods in his dominions, drastically curtailing French trade with Spain.[16]

In any case, French penetration of the Spanish and Spanish American markets was limited to linens, silks, and haberdashery shipped on the official Spanish transatlantic *flotas*. For at this time France played no part in the direct transit trade to the Spanish American colonies via the Caribbean, which was almost entirely in Dutch hands, and played little part in the sale of woollen cloth, a sector hotly disputed between the Dutch and English, or in the supply of spices, naval stores, or candles, which were imported for the churches of Spain and Spanish America from northern Europe in immense quantities. After textiles, spices were in fact the second most valuable category of foreign imports into Spain and Spanish

[16] Abreu y Bertodano, *Colección*, Reynado de Carlos II, ii. 216–28; Girard, *Commerce français*, 448; Morineau, *Incroyables gazettes*, 302.

America and here there was no basis on which France could compete with the Dutch.[17]

The Dutch, furthermore, possessed some additional mechanisms of commercial control in Spain which the French were in no position to challenge. The most important strand in the Spanish trade apart from the traffic through Cadiz was the handling of Spain's wool exports, and in this sector the Dutch exercised an overwhelming supremacy during Phase Four. Dutch fine-cloth techniques and low interest rates put Amsterdam in a uniquely

TABLE 6.9. *Wool imports to Amsterdam, 1 Oct. 1667–30 Sept. 1668* (lbs.)

High-quality Castilian	2,167,560
Aragonese and Basque	283,860
English and Scottish	105,300
German and Baltic	1,036,620

Source: Brugmans, 'Statistiek', 181.

strong position. After 1648 Spanish wool was regularly imported to the Dutch entrepôt in much larger quantities than the Baltic wools which had once formed the staple raw material of the Dutch cloth industry (see table 6.9). The Dutch capture of the Spanish wool trade was indeed one of the main factors in what an English observer called the 'overswelling greatness of the Dutch', the lever by which the Dutch in Spain 'have almost eaten us out and greatly swelled their trade'.[18] The traffic was tightly controlled by a small clique of Amsterdam élite merchants, namely Jan and Balthasar Coymans, Everhard Scott, Adriaen Temminck, Jean Deutz, Francesco Ferroni, and the Sephardi firm of Joseph and Abraham Felix.[19] No doubt the special strengths of the Dutch woollen industry also contributed to Dutch dominance of the trade in Spanish American dyestuffs. It is striking, for example, that the Dutch textile industry itself consumed practically one-third of Europe's total consumption of Campeche wood in the 1660s, 30,000 out of 100,000 quintales, which was considerably more than was used in France.[20]

[17] *Correspondance administrative*, iii. 437; Savary des Bruslons, *Dictionnaire universel*, i. 930.
[18] PRO SP 94/46, fos. 196–7.
[19] Becher, *Politische Discurs*, 742.
[20] Biblioteca Nacional, Madrid MS 899, fo. 79ᵛ, Manuel de Belmonte's 'propuesta' on the Campeche wood trade.

To speak of French domination of the Spanish trade when the Dutch handled four or five times as much as did the French of Spain's most valuable commodity export, her wool, is clearly absurd (see table 6.10). Not only was France not dominant in the export of spices, woollen cloth, naval stores, and candles to Spain and Spanish America, but she played little part in these sectors. France, moreover, never challenged the Dutch entrepôt as Europe's staple for Spanish American dyestuffs, at least not in the seventeenth century.[21] The fact is that the Dutch and French shared dominance of the Spanish trade, each controlling different strands of the traffic.[22]

In Portugal, by contrast, it was again the English who were the chief rivals and here the Dutch did less well, after the late 1640s,

TABLE 6.10. *The destinations of Spain's wool exports, 1668 and 1671* (180 lb. bales)

Destination	1668	1671
Holland	22,000	16,000
Spanish Netherlands	—	2,500
France	6,000	3,000
England	2,000–7,000	3,000
Italy	3,000	—

Sources: 1668: Godolphin, *Hispania illustrata*, 108; 1671: Becher, *Politische Discurs*, 740.

than in perhaps any other continental European market. In Spain, crown policy, hostile to France and suspicious of England, was a key factor in Dutch success from 1648 down to the end of the Habsburg era, in 1700.[23] In Portugal, the crown, at loggerheads with the Dutch in Africa and the East Indies as well as Brazil, was the crucial factor in Dutch failure.[24] In their home market, as well as in India and Brazil, the Portuguese, from the late 1640s onwards, leaned towards England for backing against the Dutch. In 1654, seizing the opportunity of the First Anglo-Dutch War, the Portuguese completed their reconquest of Dutch Brazil, an

---

[21] De Pinto, *Traité de la circulation*, 251.
[22] Savary, *Le Parfait Négociant*, ii. 67.
[23] Savary des Bruslons, *Dictionnaire universel*, i. 930.
[24] Lúcio de Azevedo, *Épocas de Portugal económico*, 403–5; Sideri, *Trade and Power*, 20–3.

outcome the Dutch, for the moment, refused to accept. Subsequent
Dutch–Portuguese tension deteriorated into open war in the years
1657–61. In theory, under the Dutch–Portuguese peace of 1661,
Dutch merchants obtained privileges for their trade in Portugal
as favourable as those enjoyed by the English. But in practice
relations remained cool and the Dutch merchant élite never succeeded in making as much progress as they had expected.[25] The
English continued to dominate the export of cloth to Portugal and
her colonies and to buy up her wines.[26] Portugal also excluded
Dutch spices.

It would be untrue to say that the Dutch were wholly excluded
from the rich trades with Portugal and, via Portugal, with Brazil.
The Dutch did sell linen, *says*, and some other manufactures in
some quantity in Portugal. Nevertheless, in the high-value, low-
volume traffic to Lisbon it was the English who had the upper
hand from the 1650s onwards. Nevertheless, as the Portuguese
historian Virginia Rau has pointed out,[27] for the period from 1661
down to the beginning of the eighteenth century it is best to speak
of joint Anglo-Dutch domination of the Portuguese market rather
than to insist on English primacy solely. For, besides the rich
trades, in which the Dutch did have a share, there was also the
not inconsiderable bulk traffic; and here it was the Dutch who
had the upper hand. This was partly a result of the superiority of
the Dutch entrepôt in supplying Baltic grain and naval stores
which Portugal continued to import in substantial quantities. The
indispensability of Dutch shipping for Portugal's salt exports is
shown by the Portuguese decision after the outbreak of the 1657–
61 war to issue passes through the 'agent of Portugal in the United
Provinces', the Jewish merchant Jeronimo Nunes da Costa, for
Dutch vessels to continue coming to obtain salt at Setúbal (see
table 6.11).[28] Under the subsequent Dutch–Portuguese peace
treaty (1661), Portugal agreed partially to compensate the WIC
for its losses in Brazil and Africa with four million cruzados worth
of salt, to be shipped duty-free from Setúbal.[29] Though this agreement was initially for sixteen years only, the time limit was later

[25] Luzac, *Hollands rijkdom* iii. 373–4; Israel, 'Diplomatic Career', 181–4.
[26] Sideri, *Trade and Power*, 20–3; Bentley Duncan, *Atlantic Islands*, 54, 73–6.
[27] Rau, *Estudos sobre a história do sal português*, 238–41.
[28] GA Amsterdam NA 1540, p. 154; Israel, 'Diplomatic Career', 184–5.
[29] Israel, 'Diplomatic Career', 185.

TABLE 6.11. *Dutch voyages to Setúbal to fetch salt, 1659–1675*

Year	Ships	Quantity (Portuguese moios)	Year	Ships	Quantity (Portuguese moios)
1659	69	33,640	1667	42	22,738
1660	68	27,953	1668	108	60,852
1661	98	60,079	1670	38	—
1662	145	85,876	1671	110	82,132
1663	135	76,669	1672	37	—
1664	114	62,323	1673	1	
1665	12	7,168	1674	36	74,257
1666	42	22,433	1675	45	

Sources: Rau, *Estudos Sobre a história do sal português*, 287; ARH 7013/2, Barlaeus, 'Lijste vande schepen en mooijen sout'.

extended; indeed, the Dutch continued to obtain salt at Setúbal on special terms down to the end of the century and beyond.

THE CARIBBEAN AND WEST AFRICA

After the débâcle of 1645 in Brazil, it seemed that the once triumphant WIC was a spent force, close to collapse. Its territories in the Americas were devastated or of little value. The planters' insurrection had paralysed the sugar economy of Netherlands Brazil while saddling the WIC with huge military expenditures for which, without the colony's sugar and dyewood, it lacked the resources to pay. The peace treaty with Spain brought Spanish recognition of the Dutch colonies in the Americas, including Netherlands Brazil at its greatest extent, but expressly excluded Dutch commercial access to the Spanish American colonies.[30] Nor, initially, did the rise of a flourishing private Dutch commerce with the English and French Caribbean colonies from the late 1640s seem in itself to contribute greatly to prospects for a revival of the Dutch empire in the New World and of the WIC.

Anxious to bolster the ailing WIC, the regents of Holland and Zeeland repeatedly urged the Spanish crown, in the immediate

---

[30] Aitzema, *Nederlantsche Vreedehandeling*, ii. 188.

aftermath of the 1648 peace treaty, to reconsider and permit some limited WIC access to Spanish America. The Amsterdam burgomasters urged Madrid to allow the WIC to ship slaves from West Africa to those parts of Spanish America where there was now, since the Portuguese secession from Spain in 1640 and the subsequent Spanish ban on Portuguese slave shipments, an acute shortage of slave labour.[31] It was also proposed that the *status quo ante* be restored at Punta de Araya, meaning that Spain should allow the Dutch to obtain salt there as they had until the erection of the Spanish fort in 1622, only now under the auspices of the WIC.[32] All such suggestions were firmly rejected in Madrid.

In the meantime Dutch private commerce in the Caribbean area, and especially with the English and French islands initially, flourished under the stimulus of the devastation of the plantations of Brazil: 'upon the unhappie Civill War that brake out in England', noted an English contemporary, 'they managed the whole trade of our western colonies and furnished the islands [of Barbados] with negroes, coppers, stills, and all other things appertaining to the Ingenious [i.e. *engenhos*] for making of sugar.'[33] But, while the real breakthrough for the moment was in the traffic to the English islands and Martinique, Amsterdam merchants also achieved some success in the Spanish Caribbean islands well away from the main centres of Spanish colonial authority. It was later reported to Madrid, in 1658, in answer to enquiries emanating from the royal Council of the Indies, that at least twenty-two Dutch vessels had delivered cargoes to Española between 1648 and 1657, bringing slaves, spices, linen, and brandy to exchange for hides, silver, and tobacco.[34] There was also, the signs are, a regular Dutch commerce through the 1650s with Puerto Rico and Cuba.

Penetration of the Spanish American mainland, however, proved more difficult. Both Dutch and Spanish sources agree that there was no established, regular Dutch access before the late 1650s when the Anglo-Spanish War of 1655–60 seriously impeded

---

[31] AGS Estado 2070, 'Papal que dieron los de Amsterdam', 9 Oct. 1649; Menkman, 'Van de verovering van Curaçao', 166.
[32] AGS Estado 2070, consultas of the Consejo de Indias, Madrid, 1 Nov. 1648 and 1 Feb. 1649.
[33] BL Sloane MS 3662, fo. 59; *engenho* is the Portuguese for sugar-mill.
[34] AGI Santo Domingo 2, ramo 1, consulta of the Consejo de Indias, Madrid, 28 Aug. 1658.

the official commerce with Spain.[35] There were undoubtedly determined attempts to trade before 1655. One recorded instance is of
two well-stocked Dutch vessels which lay at anchor at Río de la
Hacha for an entire month in 1652 but totally without success.[36]
Nevertheless, this and similar attempts are significant in that they
show that Spanish America was no longer sealed off from Dutch
commercial contact in the same way as during the 1621–47 period.
The Spanish authorities made no attempt to interfere with the
Dutch ships. Local Spaniards were simply warned, under threat
of severe penalty, not to trade. In January 1654 the Council of the
Indies, at Madrid, confirmed, in answer to enquiries from Spanish
governors in the Caribbean, that Dutch vessels attempting to trade
along the coasts of Spanish America were not to be attacked or
fired on.[37]

Given that the Spanish guard-ships would no longer fire even
on the most persistent Dutch interlopers frequenting the coasts of
Maracaibo, Río de la Hacha, and so forth, it was perhaps only a
matter of time before a regular illicit traffic started up. It was
reasonable to assume, moreover, that even a modest trickle of such
commerce would directly benefit the WIC and the Dutch colonies
both in the Caribbean and West Africa. Dutch shipping in the
Caribbean required local bases, warehouses, supplies, and repair
facilities. The WIC, in addition, could expect to dominate the
supply of African slaves to the region and this, in turn, would
enhance the value of the Company's establishment along the
Guinea Coast, where, despite the loss of São Thomé and Angola
to the Portuguese in 1648, Dutch trade predominance was now at
its height. Down to 1660 the Dutch continued to ship the bulk of
the slaves being transported across the Atlantic and they remained
by far the most important exporters of gold from the Gold Coast
until long after, shipping a total of 31,000 marks, worth eight and
a half million guilders, during the decades 1655–75.[38]

Unless the Dutch could establish flourishing sugar colonies of
their own or a major transit trade to the Spanish American mainland, there was unlikely to be any real recovery in the fortunes of

[35] Van Brakel, 'Bescheiden over den slavenhandel', 49–50; Hartog, *Geschiedenis*, iii.
pt. 1, 360–1.
[36] AGI Santa Fé 215, consulta of the Junta de Guerra de Indias, Madrid, 31 Jan.
1654.
[37] AGI Santa Fé 215, consulta of the Consejo de Indias, Madrid, 31 Jan. 1654.
[38] Binder, 'Goldeinfuhr', 142–3.

the WIC. The Company had more than enough potential to play a major part in Caribbean commerce alongside Dutch private trade. It had the slaves, the power to keep intruders away from large stretches of the Guinea coast, an assortment of Caribbean islands and enclaves in the Guyanas, and the resources to colonize further. A significant potential further asset were the Dutch Jewish refugees from Brazil, many of whom, with their knowledge of Spanish and Portuguese, sugar cultivation, and the sugar trade, had migrated since 1645 to the Caribbean.[39] Yet, for the moment the Company's hands were tied. In the 1650s it could obtain no part in the Spanish American traffic while its existing colonies were either too barren or too small in area to serve as equivalents to Barbados or Martinique.

Barbados was the most prolific of the new sugar colonies, and for some years Dutch private traders sustained a burgeoning trade with the island, giving 'great credit to the most sober inhabitants'. Plied with slaves by the Dutch, the island's black population rose from 5,680, in 1645, to no less than 82,023 by 1667.[40] But Parliament in England was hardly likely to leave the English Caribbean colonies in the hands of the royalists, or in tranquil contact with the Dutch, for long. The parliamentary expedition sent to conquer Barbados in 1651 seized twenty-four Dutch vessels found trading there, five of them Zeelanders.[41] The weakness of English sea power away from British shores during the First Anglo-Dutch War (1652–4) enabled the Dutch to regain the traffic for a time. The English fleet sent out under Venables, in 1655, surprised another twenty Dutch ships at anchor at Barbados and caught eighteen of them.[42] But still the *Barbados-vaerders*, as they were known in Holland and Zeeland, returned. Another six were seized in 1658. But, eventually, during the early 1660s, this direct Dutch trade was finally suppressed and the furnishing of European goods taken over by London merchants and of slaves by the newly set up Royal Africa Company.

By the time that happened, however, the Dutch had greatly expanded their traffic with both the French and the Spanish colonies. Soon Martinique was almost as prolific as Barbados. By

---

[39] Emmanuel, *History*, i. 38–45; Israel, *European Jewry*, 107, 155.
[40] Harlow, *History of Barbados*, 44.
[41] Gardiner, and Atkinson (eds.), *Letters and Papers*, ii. 76.
[42] Res. Holl. 3 June 1655; *Hollandsche Mercurius* (1655), 39.

the early 1660s, it was alleged in Paris, around one hundred Dutch ships were visiting France's Caribbean islands each year.[43] This figure was doubtless an exaggeration, but there is no doubting the large scale of the commerce. Furthermore, it is likely that Dutch direct trade with the lesser English islands and Surinam persisted rather longer than in the case of Barbados. Finally, even when the direct contact was broken off, there remained an appreciable indirect Dutch commerce through the Jewish community on Barbados which had been established at the end of the 1640s and early 1650s, as one of the island's governors put it, by 'thirty Jew families of Dutch extraction from Brazil' who were closely linked with Amsterdam through London as well as with the other Sephardi Jewish communities in the Caribbean.[44]

But it was the rise of the Dutch transit traffic with the Spanish American mainland which laid the foundations for a WIC revival and for a renewal of Dutch colonial expansion in the New World. In the immediate aftermath of 1645 the collapse of confidence in the Company had been almost total. By the spring of 1650 the WIC share price on the Amsterdam Exchange had sunk to 14 guilders and by 1654, the year in which Dutch Brazil was finally liquidated with the loss of Recife, to practically nothing. A tentative revival in the share price then began in the late 1650s, a trend subsequently strengthened by the Dutch–Portuguese peace treaty of 1661 which partially compensated the WIC for its territorial losses with 4 million cruzados worth of Setúbal salt. By November 1664 the WIC share price on the Amsterdam Exchange had revived to 40 guilders.[45]

The rise of Curaçao to become the jewel of the Company's territorial assets arose from the growing need for a regional Dutch trading depot in the Caribbean, a secure base for the Dutch carrying traffic in the area. Curaçao, the largest of the WIC's Caribbean islands, was barren and unsuited to plantation agriculture. But it possessed a superb deep-water harbour and its location close to the Spanish American mainland made it the ideal haven for barques and long-boats engaged in semi-clandestine commerce with the coasts of nearby Venezuela and New Granada,

[43] Du Tertre, *Histoire générale*, i. 460–4, ii. 462; Bondois, 'Colbert', 12–20, 46; Cole, *Colbert*, ii. 9–10.

[44] Harlow, *History of Barbados*, 93–4; Samuel, 'Review', 13.

[45] *Hollandsche Mercurius* (1664), 181.

which were mostly lacking in anchorages adequate for larger vessels. Dutch and Dutch Jewish merchants began stockpiling valuable commodities on Curaçao towards the end of the 1650s. The island's subsequent progress was rapid. In March 1661 the Spanish ambassador at The Hague warned his king that the Dutch had now 'established large stores with every kind of merchandise there which they deliver during the night, using long boats, taking back silver bars and other goods'.[46]

It is possible that the decision taken in Madrid soon after this to legalize the transportation of slaves to the Spanish colonies from Curaçao sprang from the realization that the Dutch direct-transit traffic to the Spanish American mainland, especially in slaves, had now taken too firm a hold to be easily eradicated and that to ignore it would be to lose a large potential revenue for the crown. Philip IV in any case the next year signed a general asiento for slaves with the Genoese contractors, Grillo and Lomelín, whereby a large number of slaves were to be purchased for Spain's American colonies from sources other than Portuguese, Spain still being at war with Portugal until 1668.[47] The asiento made no stipulation as to where the slaves should be procured; but the only immediately available alternative was the WIC. Soon after the signing of the asiento in Madrid, factors of the asiento in Amsterdam signed a series of sub-contracts with the WIC, arranging for the slaves to be delivered to Curaçao, from where they were to be distributed around the Spanish Caribbean.[48] The Spanish crown sanctioned the use of Dutch ships for this purpose. By the mid-1660s Dutch vessels were also being used to transport slaves legally to Buenos Aires.[49]

The WIC supplied most of the slaves shipped by the Dutch to the Spanish Indies from the late 1650s but by no means all. Dutch interlopers, especially Zeelanders, procured a substantial number from the Guinea coast avoiding the WIC's forts and guardships.[50] There was also, in the early 1660s, a consortium of Amsterdam merchants which specialized in obtaining slaves from Angola with the co-operation of the factors of the asiento in flat contradiction

---

[46] AGS Libros de la Haya 43, fo. 94.
[47] Scelle, *Traite négrière*, i. 484–5.
[48] Unger, 'Bijdragen', 148–51.
[49] Van Brakel, 'Bescheiden over den slavenhandel', 61–6.
[50] Goslinga, *The Dutch in the Caribbean* (1985), 156–7, 176.

to the terms of that arrangement. This group included Francesco Ferroni, the Italian agent of the asiento in Amsterdam and a prominent merchant in the Spanish trade, and also the Sephardi 'Agent' of Portugal, Jeronimo Nunes da Costa, who provided the passes. In 1664 a vessel chartered by this consortium delivered 350 Angolans to Grillo's factors on Curaçao and returned to Amsterdam loaded with Venezuela tobacco and 45,000 pesos in bullion.[51] In April 1666 a Dutch vessel reached Curaçao loaded with another 350 Angolans and a large quantity of spices, including 15,000 lb of cinnamon consigned by Nunes da Costa.[52]

Much of the transit traffic to the Spanish and French colonies was carried on via Curaçao, using the fleet of barques and long boats which thronged the island's harbour, Willemstad, from the late 1650s onwards. This benefited Curaçao, which developed into a thriving colony during the 1660s, and the WIC, which collected commissions and recognition fees and shipped back a proportion of the returns from Curaçao to Amsterdam in its own ships. But by no means all the Dutch transit traffic to the Spanish Indies was based on Curaçao or other WIC enclaves. There was also a substantial traffic bypassing the Dutch colonies. The merchants involved in this long-distance commerce, we learn from contemporary reports from Amsterdam, included Philips van Hulten, Francesco Ferroni, Henrique Mathias, Jan Broers, Leonard van Ceulen, Guillaume du Bellin, and Jeronimo Nunes da Costa.[53] These were the regulars, so to speak; but some of the most respectable élite merchants, such as Everhard Scott and Cornelis Gijsberts van Goor, were also sporadically involved. Van Hulten and his associates operated through the Canary Islands, where they had accomplices who sent ships on furnished with fraudulent passes.[54] The rest specialized in long-haul voyages mounted from Amsterdam, which generally took in a variety of Caribbean destinations. A Dutch vessel chartered by Mathias and his associates in 1664, for instance, sailed to La Guaira, Río de la Hacha, Maracaibo, and Cuba before sailing back to Amsterdam around Scotland (to escape the English) in September 1665, carrying 300 canasters of

[51] AGS Libros de la Haya 53, fo. 266.
[52] Ibid. fo. 268.
[53] See the series of reports by Andrés de Belmonte in AGS Libros de la Haya 47–53.
[54] Ibid. 50, fos. 19, 61, 64, 262.

tobacco, 4,000 hides and 30,000 silver pesos.[55] Du Bellin, the 'seigneur de la Guarde', was essentially an agent for French interests: he chartered ships to the Caribbean loaded with both French and Dutch wares, a large part of the returns being destined for Le Havre.[56]

The Dutch emerged during Phase Four as the principal carriers of the Caribbean. This new Dutch breakthrough was rooted in the later 1640s and was based on the fact that the Dutch were now the region's neutrals, able to supply the slaves and equipment essential to the sugar 'revolution' which they set in motion and to offer the best prices for sugar,[57] but also on the fact that the Spanish crown now preferred to deal with the Dutch in so far as it had to have dealings with outsiders in the Americas, rather than the English, Portuguese, or French, with each of whom it was at war for part of the period. The feeling in Madrid was that it was best to deal with the Dutch, because, unlike the English and French, they now posed no political threat to Spanish hegemony in South and Central America.[58]

Dutch trade in the Caribbean from the later 1640s onwards does indeed present a striking contrast to the position during the previous period, after 1621, when the Dutch had had practically no commerce with the Spanish colonies, and Curaçao, after its conquest in 1634, had seemed an almost useless liability. During Phase Three the WIC had controlled larger resources and posed an intrinsically greater threat to Spain's monopoly of the trade of its American empire. But it had failed. From the late 1640s private Dutch and Dutch Jewish merchants, working hand in hand with the now weakened WIC up to a point, had finally succeeded in adding a major new strand to the growing batch of rich trades which collectively constituted the core of Dutch world-trade primacy. There can be little doubt that political factors, such as the English Civil War, the Dutch–Spanish peace, and the weakness of France's grip over her Caribbean colonies down to the late 1660s, greatly contributed to this development. But at the root of it, interacting with these political factors, was the basic economic

[55] Ibid. 51/2, fo. 204.
[56] Ibid. 47, fo. 193; GA Amsterdam NA 1536, p. 239.
[57] BL Sloane MS 3662, fo. 59ᵛ.
[58] AGS Estado 2081, 'Parecer del Conde de Peñaranda sobre union con holandeses' (1653).

fact that in this period the Dutch could buy and furnish in the Caribbean more efficiently than all their rivals. The English colonists, just as much as the French and Spaniards, saw trade with the Dutch as a way of emancipating themselves from the oppressive economic grip of their home merchants and governments, which, after all, was in every case designed to reduce them to the role of passive dependents of the mother country. The plain fact was that one had a better deal trading with the Dutch. 'The islanders here', it was reported from Barbados in 1655, 'much desire commerce with strangers [i.e. the Dutch and Jews] our English merchants trafficquing to those parts being generally great extortioners.'[59]

THE EAST INDIES

A seasoned observer of the world-trade scene appraising Dutch prospects after the Dutch–Spanish peace of 1648 would certainly have been inclined to predict major shifts in international commerce liable to strengthen the Dutch at the expense of their rivals— always assuming that no new major conflict broke out of a sort apt to disrupt Dutch overseas enterprise. Any habitué of the Amsterdam Exchange would know that Dutch freight and insurance charges would fall, that Dutch goods would now re-enter Spain and Spanish America on a massive scale, and that Dutch seaborne trade with Italy and the Levant would revive. He would appreciate that the WIC was now in poor shape following the débâcle in Brazil but would realize that the end of the Dutch–Spanish struggle would open up new possibilities for Dutch navigation and the Dutch colonies in the Caribbean. He would also know that the cumulative effect of these shifts would be to tighten the grip of the Dutch entrepôt over high-value raw materials and dyes and that this would strengthen the Dutch textile industry, which, in turn, would further reinforce Dutch progress within the rich trades of Europe and Spanish America. Needless to say all this would happen irrespective of any changes in Baltic bulk freightage.

On turning to the East Indies, however, the discerning mercantile eye would undoubtedly have arrived at very different

---

[59] Thurloe, *State Papers*, iii. 142.

perceptions. Here there was less reason to postulate a new phase of Dutch expansion. The impact of the Spanish peace seemed likely to be more diffuse east of Africa than in Europe and the Americas and in some respects detrimental rather than beneficial to Dutch interests. The Dutch blockade of the Philippines would now be lifted. This would mean that Manila would recover as a major Far Eastern emporium and draw off some of the junk traffic from Fort Zeelandia and Batavia. The revival of the Dutch Levant trade would be bound to prejudice VOC silk purchases in the Persian Gulf and generally depress VOC activity in western Asian seas, especially as the pending influx of indigo to Amsterdam from Central America would remove the incentive to ship large quantities of indigo to Holland from Surat and Coromandel.[60]

Admittedly the Spanish peace did offer some definite advantages to the Dutch in Asia. The price of silver on the Amsterdam Exchange would now fall, enabling the VOC to increase its bullion shipments to the East Indies. In 1648 the Company also had an unprecedented opportunity to recruit seasoned troops released from the Dutch army for service in the East, enabling it to reinforce its strategic position throughout Asia. Indeed, the Heren XVII were not slow to take advantage of this. They recruited and sent out a total of 10,500 troops in the years 1648–52, greatly strengthening the Dutch garrisons in the Archipelago and Ceylon.[61] As tension with England increased, the Company also took the opportunity to occupy and establish a permanent fort at the Cape of Good Hope.

But increased military expenditure did not necessarily mean more trade and profits; all the signs are that in the years around 1650 neither the VOC leadership, nor the investors, were inclined to view the prospects for Dutch trade in Asia in a particularly optimistic light. Indeed, surveying the position in 1655, Ryckloff van Goens, one of the three great VOC leaders in Asia during the third quarter of the century, took a distinctly pessimistic view. He stressed that all the main Dutch trade centres in Asia—Batavia, Fort Zeelandia, Malacca, Surat, Amboina, and the Bandas—were now in decline.[62] It was clear that the steep fall in the amounts of

[60] Posthumus, *Inquiry*, ii. 266–8; van Santen, *Verenigde Oost-Indische Compagnie in Gujarat*, 32–3.

[61] Aalbers, *Ryckloff van Goens*, 47–8.

[62] Van Goens, 'Vertooch', 141–2.

silver the VOC was obtaining in Japan in the 1650s was exerting a generally depressive effect on the Company's operations,[63] as was the general deterioration of life (under the pressure of the Dutch monopoly system) in Amboina and the Bandas. Fort Zeelandia was lapsing into decay as a result of the increasingly successful efforts of the Chinese to prise the silk trade to Japan out of Dutch hands. In addition, the English were now not only more hostile but increasingly successful in syphoning off pepper and spices through Macassar, Bantam, and other loopholes in the Dutch system.[64] Meanwhile repeated VOC attempts to revive the once flourishing entrepôt of Malacca met with scant success.[65] Heavy pressure was brought to bear on the neighbouring Malay sultans. The sultan of Perak was made to accept a permanent Dutch *comptoir* on his coast, north of Malacca, and to sign an agreement excluding the rivals of the Dutch from trading with his subjects. But the VOC was never able to concentrate enough troops and ships along the Malay coast to render such tactics effective. Malacca continued to stagnate and Malay tin and pepper exports continued to be diverted through lesser ports and shipped to India largely by Gujaratis.

Unease about the future gripped the experts and the investing public alike. The VOC share price on the Amsterdam Exchange remained depressed throughout the decade 1648–57 (see table 6.13). The Company was perceived to have arrived at a general crisis in its fortunes which required a thorough rethinking of basic strategy. But, as always, it was easier to discern the difficulties than the right solutions. Van Goens, true to the traditions of his mentor, van Diemen, advocated even more aggressive and rigidly monopolistic policies than had been applied in the past. But not everyone was swayed by such traditional, no nonsense attitudes to Dutch trade problems in Asia. Pieter van Dam, secretary of the Amsterdam Chamber of the VOC and future author of the colossal *Beschryvinge van de Oostindische Compagnie*, arguably the most impressive of all economic writings of the Dutch Golden Age, submitted a report on the Company's trade problems in 1662 urging a much more flexible and liberal approach. Van Dam was

---

[63] Nachod, *Beziehungen*, 360–1; Wills, *Pepper, Guns and Parleys*, 32.

[64] Van Goens, 'Vertooch', 150.

[65] Arasaratnam, 'Some Notes on the Dutch in Malacca', 487–9; Irwin, 'Dutch and the Tin Trade of Malaya', 282–7.

deeply troubled that the Company was expanding steadily in terms of employees, forts, factories, and ships while simultaneously losing its hold on commerce and becoming less profitable.[66] He criticized the VOC's rising wage bill and administrative costs and the diversion of shipping space from trade to transporting provisions, materials, and wages for Dutch garrisons.[67] His recipe was one of cost cutting and new commercial strategies to restore profitability. He proposed in particular that the Dutch inter-Asian traffic, as distinct from procurement of spices and other fine goods for Europe, be thrown open to private Dutch colonists, who should be encouraged to settle in the Company's territories.[68] Free burghers, using their own small craft, would, in his view, be able to handle the carrying traffic between the Archipelago, India, and the Malay coast at a fraction of the cost the Company incurred employing its large, heavily armed ships. This, he urged, was the way to revive the Dutch inter-Asian trade and the emporia of Batavia, Malacca, and Amboina.

There was a good deal of debate about the future of the VOC during the 1650s;[69] but it was perhaps inevitable that in the end the directors should decide to resume the expansionism of Coen and van Diemen rather than to adopt a policy of economic innovation. The Company opted to bludgeon its way out of difficulty by building up its forces and extending its political grip. Despite the loss of the large amounts of bullion the VOC had been procuring in Japan during Phase Three, the sort of massive infusion of new resources needed to increase Dutch military power in Asia was still feasible in view of the peace with Spain. The resumed flow of Spanish silver direct to Amsterdam after 1647 made it possible to reverse the decline in VOC bullion remittances to the East Indies which had been in progress since 1621 and, indeed, after 1660, increase them far beyond any levels known before (see table 5.17). In effect, the restructuring of the Dutch trade system in the years 1647–8 meant that the VOC was now able to finance its continued expansion in Asia without the China silk trade and the bullion of Japan.

The VOC's military build-up finally began to pay commercial

---

[66] Van Dam, 'Concept', 270–1.

[67] Ibid.

[68] Ibid. 279, 286–7; Arasaratnam, 'Monopoly and Free Trade', 5–6.

[69] Laspeyres, *Geschichte*, 91–3; Arasaratnam, 'Monopoly and Free Trade', 3–5.

dividends in the mid-1650s. In Ceylon the resumed Dutch–Portuguese struggle reached its climax with the epic siege of Colombo in 1655–6, a seven-month operation in which the VOC employed two thousand Dutch troops supported by Sinhalese auxiliaries.[70] With Colombo in their hands, the Dutch finally enjoyed undisputed control of the main cinnamon-producing area. Even so, the Portuguese were still ensconced at the northern end of the island and around the southern tip of India, and, as long as they remained there, the Dutch grip on the world's cinnamon supply was incomplete, especially as a coarse variety was cultivated across the water on the Malabar coast under the Portuguese. Then, when war broke out officially between Portugal and the United Provinces, in 1657, the VOC launched into the most ambitious war of conquest in Asia that it ever waged. First Dutch troops, crossing from Ceylon, captured the Portuguese fort at Tuticorin at the tip of India commanding the straits between the mainland and Ceylon. Then van Goens conquered the Jaffna peninsula, capturing Mannar and Jaffna, the last two remaining Portuguese strongholds in Ceylon. Next van Goens crossed back to the mainland and reduced the massive Portuguese fortress at Negapatnam, dominating the southern part of the Coromandel coast. Finally, after these successes, he launched into his conquest of the Malabar coast.

For decades the Dutch had been probing the Portuguese hold on the Malabar coast and by the early 1660s the Portuguese had built up a formidable line of fortifications.[71] At first these resisted. But van Goens pressed on. The English both in India and at home became extremely alarmed, realizing that, if the Dutch succeeded, they would be the masters of southern India. It was suddenly grasped in London that blocking the Dutch–Portuguese peace talks in Europe with the intention of preventing the Dutch from acquiring commercial privileges in Portugal as favourable as those enjoyed by the English might well lead to the total collapse of Portuguese power in southern India. Whilst England was obstructing the Dutch–Portuguese settlement in Europe, Charles II's ambassador warned from The Hague that the 'Dutch East Indye

---

[70] Goonewardena, *Foundation of Dutch Power in Ceylon*, 164–74.
[71] Meilink-Roelofsz, *De vestiging*, 54–62.

Company are still making a vast progress in the East Indyes'.[72] Charles II withdrew his objections. The Dutch–Portuguese peace treaty was signed. But van Goens, success within his grasp, had no intention of stopping now. He captured Cranganore in January 1662 after the signing of the peace treaty but before its ratification in Lisbon. Finally, in 1663, at the head of a VOC army of two thousand Dutch troops plus auxiliaries, and in blatant violation of the now ratified treaty, he took the Portuguese forts at Cochin and Cananore.[73]

These final Dutch conquests in southern India soured Dutch–Portuguese relations for decades to come. They also met with the strong disapproval of both England and France. As expected, van Goens's conquest of the Malabar coast had a markedly adverse effect on English interests in India.[74] Since the 1640s the English factories on the north-west coast of India had co-operated increasingly closely with the Portuguese and, as a reward for their help, for example in carrying part of the Portuguese trade in English ships so as to protect it from the Dutch, the English East India Company had gained a considerable slice of the Malabar traffic. By 1660 between one-third and one-half of Malabar's total annual pepper exports, that is around 400 out of 1,000 lasts (some ten ship loads), was being handled by the English.[75] This traffic was now completely lost, confirming English suspicions that all along the VOC had designed to 'ruinate' English commerce in south-west India as well as that of the Portuguese.

Van Goens's trade strategy in south-west India consisted of a judicious mixture of business, diplomacy, and force. The corner-stone of his policy was his agreement with the king of Cochin whereby the latter ceded the Portuguese citadel to the Dutch in perpetuity and recognized the VOC as his 'protector', in return for the Company agreeing to support his claims to supremacy over the lesser rajas of the region.[76] Under the terms of the treaty, signed in March 1663, all the political and trading privileges which the Portuguese had possessed previously were now conferred on the Dutch, the Dutch being assigned exclusive rights to export

---

[72] Lister, *Life and Administration*, iii. 153.
[73] Meilink-Roelofsz, *De vestiging*, 338–40.
[74] Ibid. 368–9.
[75] Ibid. 369.
[76] Heeres and Stapel (eds.), *Corpus-diplomaticum*, ii. 237–9.

Cochin's pepper and cinnamon output. The neighbouring raja of Porca, as the English factors at Surat learnt with dismay, signed the same terms, agreeing to 'turne the English factors out of his countrey' and 'weigh all his pepper to the Dutch'.[77] In another treaty of the same month, the raja of Cananore similarly ceded the local Portuguese fortress to the VOC and signed away his pepper.[78] Finally, in 1665, even the proud raja of Trevancore, at the southern end of the coast, yielded, agreeing to shut the English, Portuguese, and Danes out of his territory and sell his pepper to the VOC exclusively.[79] 'Tis evident', commented an English observer, 'they doe intend to make themselves as much the masters of all the pepper countries as now they are of the other spices.'[80]

To enforce their grip on the Malabar coast the Dutch instituted regular naval patrols along the coast to keep excluded shipping away.[81] By the mid-1660s Dutch dominance of the maritime trade of south-west India was almost total. Portuguese power south of Goa was broken, English involvement in the Malabar trade virtually suppressed. Undeniably much of this outcome was due to military success, large garrisons, and a vigorous diplomacy backed by force. The Dutch also had certain purely commercial advantages which the English and Portuguese lacked. They were in an unrivalled position, for example, to supply the cloves and Japanese copper imported to Malabar and Coromandel. But the English could furnish some of the other items required, including opium from Bengal, a product which was crucially important in the Malabar trade. Accordingly, the Dutch took considerable pains to prevent Gujarati and Bengali merchants acting as intermediaries for the English in the traffic in opium and pepper. 'They have prohibited', explained the president of the English factory at Surat,

as well the natives of the country where the pepper growes as also the merchants and people of this place from dealing in it or transporting it to any other port or place, upon the penalty of confiscation of ship and goods where it shall be found. The like penalty they have laid upon

[77] Foster, *English Factories ... 1661–4*, 254.
[78] Heeres and Stapel (eds.), *Corpus-diplomaticum*, ii. 246–51.
[79] Ibid. ii. 323–36.
[80] Foster, *English Factories ... 1665–7*, 102.
[81] Meilink-Roelofsz, *De vestiging*, 354–6.

opium, cotton and cardamons; and with this restriction the Dutch give their passes to all vessels that trade, who (poor people) are faine to accept them on those terms, not daring to transgresse upon any considerations whatsoever; for the Dutch have already secured all ports and places from whence all such commodities are brought and carried, by making blockhouses on the sea side on convenient distances, with a guard of eight or tenne men in each, which are as watch houses; besides small vessels of theirs, which coast to and fro, that nothing can escape them. This hath already brought the cittadell of Cochin to their beck; for the natives of those parts not being able to live without opium, which now they cannot have but from the Dutch, who have already brought it into such esteeme among them, that they have all the pepper which is the growth of those parts in truck for it.[82]

Convinced that the Dutch 'drive at ingrossing all the trade of India to themselves', the English Company strove to salvage what it could of its former role around the southern tip of the sub-continent. English trade with Trevancore continued until 1665. Sporadic contact with the interior of Ceylon continued for a few years, notably via the English lodge at Kayalpatnam, near Tuticorin, which had been established in 1659.[83] But this residual traffic was liquidated during the Second Anglo-Dutch War when the factory at Kayalpatnam was captured and the English ejected.

With every fresh step in van Goens's expansionist programme, the number of Dutch garrisons and the cost of the Dutch establishment in the Indian sub-continent increased. In 1664, exploiting a revolt against the king of Kandy, van Goens annexed those parts of the cinnamon-producing zone of the interior of Ceylon which had not previously been under the Dutch. By the mid-1660s the cost of the Dutch forces in Ceylon alone had risen in a decade from 700,000 to over 1,000,000 guilders yearly.[84] Yet, for all the cost, the policy paid off. From the end of the 1650s the Dutch exercised an effective monopoly over the world's supply of cinnamon, which was an important export commodity not only to Europe but also to northern India and, via Spain and the Caribbean, to Spanish America. Indeed, according to contemporary estimates, as much as two-thirds of the total supply of cinnamon

---

[82] Foster, *English Factories . . . 1665–7*, 101.
[83] Arasaratnam, *Dutch Power in Ceylon*, 157.
[84] Ibid. 48.

which the Dutch shipped from Asia to Europe was finally consumed in Spain and Spanish America.[85]

If Dutch military expenditure in the Indian sub-continent rose
sharply during these years, the profits extracted by the Dutch rose
faster. In the early 1650s the VOC had been exporting some
250,000 lb. of cinnamon yearly to Europe. Then, in the mid-1650s
the Portuguese share was eliminated. From 1659 onwards the
Dutch exported over 400,000 lb. annually to Europe and another
150,000 lb. to Coromandel, Bengal, and Surat.[86] But more striking
than the rise in Dutch cinnamon exports was the increase in the
profits from those exports.[87] In the early 1650s cinnamon sold at
Amsterdam for around 1.5 guilders per pound. By September 1658
the price was up to nearly 3 guilders, and, by the early 1660s, to
over 3 guilders. Taking both price and quantity into account the
Dutch more than quadrupled the value of their cinnamon traffic
in a decade (see table 6.12). Then, on top of this, they gained
control of the traffic in elephants and areca nuts between Ceylon
and northern India.

TABLE 6.12. *VOC shipments of Ceylon cinnamon to the Dutch entrepôt, 1652–1669*

Year	Quantity (lbs.)	Price (guilders/lb.)	Year	Quantity (lbs.)	Price (guilders/lb.)
1652	232,880	1.45	1660	515,020	—
1653	248,400	—	1662	420,040	—
1654	268,540	1.90	1663	363,520	—
1657	227,680	—	1664	1,516,800	3.60
1658	247,440	—	1665	569,920	—
1659	404,580	—	1667	1,362,000	—
			1669	—	3.08

Sources: *Hollandsche Mercurius*; Posthumus, *Inquiry*, i. 147.

Confident of the success of his strategy of monopolization, van
Goens eventually tried to go even further. Ceylon and Malabar
needed rice, other foodstuffs, and cotton cloth from Coromandel,

[85] Savary des Bruslons, *Dictionnaire universel*, i. 930.
[86] Arasaratnam, *Dutch Power in Ceylon*, 186–7.
[87] See Manuel de Belmonte's comments on the cinnamon trade (Biblioteca Nacional,
Madrid, MS 899, fo. 79ᵛ).

Gujarat, and Bengal. In the 1660s the VOC reserved the traffic in spices and drugs to itself; but traders were allowed to come from northern India to sell rice and cloth, and to purchase elephants, areca nuts, and other goods. Van Goens's ultimate objective, however, was to eliminate the role of the Gujaratis and Bengalis and gather all the trade of the region into the hands of the Company. In the early 1670s the monopolization policy was stretched to its furthest point and efforts were made to stop the trade of northern India merchants at any rate with Ceylon.[88]

Having triumphed in southern India, the Dutch turned eastwards to bolster their slackening stance among the Indonesian sultanates.[89] Here the main European opponents were the English, who possessed trade factories at Macassar, Bantam, Pulo Run, and on Sumatra. The foremost loophole in the Dutch trading system in the Archipelago, and chief thorn in the side of the VOC, was the sultanate of Macassar, which had long been the ally of whoever opposed the VOC. The Company moved into action during the Second Anglo-Dutch War. In December 1665 the Dutch forced the surrender of the English fort on Pulo Run. Next one of the most gifted of the VOC's commanders and diplomats, Cornelis Speelman, carried out the conquest of Macassar. The sultan was reduced to the status of a vassal of the VOC and made to agree to exclude the English (and the Danes) from his territory. Simultaneously, the Dutch extended their power in Java, and, with the withdrawal of the Spaniards, also in the Moluccas. On top of all this, the VOC scored some notable successes in Sumatra, compelling the sultans of Jambi and Palembang to sell their pepper exclusively to the Company. Finally, the seal was put on this catalogue of Dutch success in the Archipelago by the Anglo-Dutch peace treaty at the conclusion of the Third Anglo-Dutch War, in 1674, under which the English Company finally abandoned its claims to Pulo Run and accepted its permanent exclusion from the Banda Islands.

But while the Dutch achieved a string of striking successes during Phase Four in India and in the Archipelago, their very concentration on these areas accelerated the decline of Dutch influence in the China Sea which had been evident since the late

[88] Arasaratnam, *Dutch Power in Ceylon*, 162–3.
[89] De Hullu, 'Mr Johan van Dam's rapport', 1013; de Hullu, 'Algemeene toestand', 824; Heeres and Stapel (eds.), *Corpus-diplomaticum*, ii. 333.

1640s. Here, on top of its other difficulties, the VOC had to deal with an increasingly confused and chaotic situation arising from a series of major internal upheavals in China itself. In 1662 a large Chinese force, taking advantage of the absence of Dutch forces in the area, overran Taiwan and captured Fort Zeelandia. For the VOC this was a deeply humiliating setback, for it had been entrenched on Taiwan for nearly forty years, even if Fort Zeelandia had now lost much of its former significance as a Dutch trade depot. In the years 1664–8 the Company made a determined attempt to restore its influence in the China Sea, resuming a powerful naval presence in the area, reoccupying the fort at Keelung in northern Taiwan for a time, and establishing a sporadic trade with mainland China at Foochow.[90] The Dutch were still the leading European nation trading with China. But the Chinese authorities with great finesse wrapped their trade in a mass of ritual and bureaucratic restrictions, some of which were in effect devices to force down the prices of the commodities the Dutch were selling. This and the Chinese refusal to permit the Dutch to settle permanent factors on the coast cut the VOC's profits to what were considered in Batavia to be paltry levels. In the years 1663–5, for instance, the Company shipped 750,000 guilders' worth of pepper, cloves, and sandalwood to the south China coast but made only a 40 per cent profit on its transactions. Before long, the Chinese court became even more difficult to deal with until finally, at the end of 1666, Peking withdrew the limited trade privileges which had been conceded. The door was once again firmly shut. In China the power of the VOC machine was totally neutralized. By 1668, despairing of establishing a viable trade with China, the VOC cut back its efforts and abandoned the fort at Keelung.

Meanwhile the loss of Taiwan and the disruption of Dutch trade with China further squeezed the Dutch traffic with Japan. Finally, in 1668, the Japanese Shogunate banned the export of silver from Japan altogether.[91] This still left something. After 1668 the Dutch continued to ply a significant trade with Japan, obtaining, among other commodities, large quantities of copper, which sold well in India and Persia. But the Japan trade now no longer functioned as a vital cog in the mechanism of Dutch inter-Asian commerce.

[90] Wills, *Peppers, Guns and Parleys*, 62, 134–6, 139, 144.
[91] Nachod, *Beziehungen*, 360–1; Glamann, *Dutch–Asiatic Trade*, 58; Prakash, *Dutch East India Company*, 20–1.

The investors at home continued to take a sober view of the VOC's prospects through the 1650s. Even the conquest of

TABLE 6.13. *VOC share prices on the Amsterdam Exchange, 1639–1672*

Date	Circumstance	Price fluctuations
Aug. 1639	Van Diemen's offensive	412
March 1641	Portuguese secession from Spain	481
Apr. 1644		453–405
Apr. 1648	Dutch–Spanish Peace Treaty	539
Dec. 1649		410
Spring 1654	The peace agreement with England	400–450
July 1656	Dutch gains in Ceylon	358–380
June 1658	East India return fleet	400
July 1660	East India return fleet	370–480
July 1663	East India return fleet	470
Mar. 1664	Rumours of war with England	498–481
May 1664	War rumours recede	15% rise
Aug. 1664	East India return fleet	447–490
Nov. 1664	Anglo-Dutch conflict in Africa	down to 452
June 1665	English North Sea victories	348–322
Aug. 1665	Safe return of VOC fleet	up to 395
Sept. 1666	Breda peace talks in progress	400
Sept. 1667	Favourable peace with England	462
Aug. 1670	East India return fleet	500
Aug. 1671	East India return fleet	up to 570
June 1672	French invasion of the Republic	down to 250

Source: *Hollandsche Mercurius*; Centen, *Vervolg*, 182, 198, 209, 272; Lister, *Life and Administration*, iii. 300, 316, 318–19, 382, 387; van Dillen, 'Effectenkoersen', 10–12.

Colombo, in 1656, failed to inspire the public. In 1658 VOC shares at Amsterdam stood below the level they had reached twenty years earlier at the time of van Diemen's invasion of Ceylon. It was only with the arrival of the return fleet of 1660, bearing a larger than usual supply of cinnamon and news of the completion of the conquest of Ceylon, that the public's old zest for VOC shares revived. In July 1660, in what was perhaps the sharpest single rise of the century, the VOC share price jumped from 370 to 480. Confidence sagged once more during the Second Anglo-Dutch War only to rise to its peak for the century during the years

1667–71. In August 1671 the share price stood at 570, the highest level we know of for the seventeenth century (see table 6.13).

Outside the zones where the Dutch exercised political as well as commercial hegemony, in northern India and the south-eastern Asian mainland, the VOC did achieve some expansion to set against the setbacks in the Japan, China, and Persia trades. The main success was the Dutch capture, in the 1650s, of the Bengal trade. Here the Dutch had no political leverage and were entirely dependent for their success on the flow of Spanish bullion arriving from Amsterdam. During the 1660s silver accounted for between 80 and 90 per cent of the value of total Dutch exports to Bengal. If spices, Japanese copper, and Ceylon elephants were always a useful supplement to Dutch purchasing power in Bengal, there can be no doubt that the edge that the Dutch enjoyed over the English in this part of India stood or fell by Holland's stocks of Spanish specie.[92]

In Bengal the Dutch purchased raw silk, Dacca muslins, salt-petre, and opium for Malabar. The attraction of Bengali silk in the eyes of the Heren XVII was that it was appreciably cheaper than Persian or Chinese silk yet sold in the Dutch market for only slightly less.[93] At the same time, while Chinese silk continued to dominate the traffic in the Far East, Bengali silk did also sell in Japan, Cambodia, and Siam, so that the rising Bengal trade to some extent mitigated the impact on the VOC of the loss of Taiwan and the reduced role the Company now played in the China trade (see table 6.14).[94] From the outset the Dutch faced stiff competition from the English in the buying up of Bengal textiles. Until the 1670s the VOC consistently had the edge over the English in the scale of their purchases, but in some years theirs was but a narrow lead.[95] Where the Dutch far outstripped the English in Bengal was in their purchases of commodities other than textiles, especially silk and the rice and opium required for southern India, Ceylon, and other Asian markets. In the scale of their inter-Asian trade, the Dutch had no rivals.

The expansion in the VOC's operations and the volume of its trade during Phase Four is reflected in the large increases registered

[92] Prakash, *Dutch East India Company*, 54.
[93] Ibid. 55.
[94] Nachod, *Beziehungen*, 360–1.
[95] Prakash, *Dutch East India Company*, 82.

TABLE 6.14. *VOC shipments of Asian raw silk to the Dutch entrepôt, 1655–1665* (Dutch pounds)

Year	Bengali	Persian	Chinese
1655	55,350	81,600	5,061
1657	144,186	44,864	79,369
1658	21,309	137,322	—
1660	126,265	59,188	—
1662	114,438	57,380	—
1663	74,135	63,728	2,198
1664	49,896	34,500	—
1665	54,394	41,968	—

Source: Hollandsche Mercurius.

in the decades 1650–70 in the volume of shipping out from the Republic to the East Indies. From an average level for the decade of about sixteen ships per year in the 1640s, the outgoing East India fleets grew to an average of nearly twenty-four ships in the 1660s. In the 1650s, at least, there was also an exceptionally rapid growth in the size of the return fleets, though, as we have seen, in terms of the value of the returns, there was a more decisive jump around 1660.

It is true that the size of the return fleets during Phase Four was still only modest, some ten to twelve ships per year (see table 6.15). This was very small even compared to the 'silver fleets' returning from Cadiz, let alone the grain fleets from the Baltic. But such was the value of the cargo, usually between fifteen and twenty million guilders, and very exceptionally, as in 1660, up to as much as thirty millions,[96] that the safe homecoming of the annual East India fleet was regarded as one of the central events of Amsterdam's commercial calendar. The only other comparable events were the return of the Cadiz, Smyrna, and Archangel fleets. During Phase Four the combined value of the returning Cadiz and Smyrna convoys was reckoned to be roughly equivalent to, or somewhat more than, that of the East India fleets.[97] As a rough rule of thumb, the combined value of these two fleets was put at somewhat over

[96] On the other hand, the returning VOC fleet of August 1672 was valued at only 14 millions (*Hollandsche Mercurius* (1672), 3 Aug.).
[97] *Lettres, instructions et mémoires de Colbert*, ii. 659.

TABLE 6.15. *VOC ships sailing out from, and returning to, the Dutch entrepôt from the East Indies, 1640–1795.*

Years	Out	Return	Years	Out	Return
1640–50	165	93	1720–30	382	318
1650–60	205	103	1730–40	375	311
1660–70	238	127	1740–50	314	235
1670–80	232	133	1750–60	291	245
1680–90	204	141	1760–70	292	233
1690–1700	235	156	1770–80	290	245
1700–10	280	193	1780–90	276	195
1710–20	311	244	1790–95	119	75

Source: Gaastra, 'Geld tegen goederen', 250.

twenty millions, the average annual value of the Dutch Levant fleets during Phase Four being estimated at ten to twelve millions.[98] The return of the 'great ships' from the Mediterranean could thus easily be a larger event even than the homecoming of the East India fleet. In October 1654, for example, thirty-six large ships arrived back from Cadiz and Smyrna together, the five 'silver ships' alone carrying ten million guilders' worth of Spanish bullion.[99]

But the four great rich trades fed on and reinforced each other. On less than a hundred ships, the Dutch brought in each year some fifty million guilders' worth of riches from Batavia, Cadiz, Smyrna, and Archangel. After 1647 the four were in a crucial sense a collectivity. The revived Dutch Smyrna and Cadiz trades, as we have seen, nourished each other; but neither could survive without the spices and pepper which figured so largely in Dutch exports to Italy, North Africa, the Levant, Spain, and Spanish America. The ultimate proceeds of Dutch success in Ceylon, for example, came mainly from Spanish America. But the Dutch East India trade, in turn, certainly could not have manifested the dynamism it did without the proceeds of post-1647 Dutch enterprise in the Mediterranean and the Spanish Indies.

[98] See p. 296.
[99] *Hollandsche Mercurius* (1654), 102.

INDUSTRY

The view that Dutch overseas commerce began to contract around 1650 in line with Braudel's *renversement de la tendance séculaire* has become deeply entrenched in historical literature.[1] Even those scholars who show caution on this point agree that 1650 marked the end of the long phase of expansion, the commencement of a 'stationary state' preceding a long period of decline.[2] This has led historians into some difficulty with respect to Holland's export-orientated industries, most of which, on the evidence we have, undeniably expanded during the decades after 1650. Industry has had to be labelled as an exception to the rule that Dutch economic life after 1650 was contracting.[3] Once, however, we accept that most of Dutch overseas commerce—except in the Baltic—was, after all, expanding in the 1650s and 1660s, and that in many key sectors—such as Spain, the Levant, Caribbean, and East Indies— the bulk of the post-1650 gains was retained in the late seventeenth century, the difficulty is removed. There is absolutely no need for historians to contort themselves into maintaining the inherently improbable proposition that Dutch export-orientated industry expanded whilst Dutch overseas trade itself declined.

The decline in the importance of low-value, bulk carrying in the Dutch economy relative to the rich trades in fact reaches back to an early stage, at least to 1620 if not before. It is usual to argue that Dutch bulk carrying continued to expand down to around 1650. But, when we take into account the masking effect of the artificial rise in Dutch customs returns after 1621,[4] this premise is open to doubt. It may well turn out, when all Dutch bulk carriage in European waters is allowed for, including bulk carrying to Portugal which was at a higher level in the early seventeenth century than later, that Dutch bulk carriage reached its peak not around 1650 but earlier, in 1620. What is not in doubt is that Dutch bulk carrying was near its peak by 1620 but that at that point the Republic's development as an industrial power was still at an early stage. Until the 1620s manufactures still accounted for

---

[1] Faber, 'Decline of the Baltic Grain Trade', 119, 130; van der Woude, 'De "Nieuwe Geschiedenis"', 18–19, 23; Schöffer, 'Holland's Golden Age', 100–1.
[2] Klein, 'De zeventiende eeuw', 105, 108–11.
[3] Ibid. 98–99.
[4] See pp. 280–2.

only a small proportion of the value of total Dutch exports to the Baltic (see table 5.8). In 1620 the Dutch Republic hardly counted as a supplier of manufactured goods to France, where Dutch textiles then played an insignificant role compared with those of Flanders or Italy.[5] By the 1640s, however, the picture was changing rapidly. Dutch manufactures now reigned supreme among foreign finished goods selling in France, those of Flanders and Italy now counting for much less. Dutch *lakens* and camlets led the field. This particular *renversement* came about owing to the increasing technical sophistication of Dutch industry and the headway which the Dutch made at that time in capturing control of the trade in key raw materials such as Spanish wool and Turkish mohair yarns. After 1650 Dutch industry geared to overseas trade continued to grow and was both fed by, and increasingly bolstered, the Dutch entrepôt's burgeoning network of rich trades. The output capacity of Holland's industries may have remained modest by French, English, or Indian standards, but, technically and qualitatively, Dutch industry attained a margin of superiority in the production of expensive fabrics, an edge which was to be retained down to the early eighteenth century.

At Leiden, the decisive years of adaptation and reorganization were the late 1630s and 1640s. Once high-value raw materials became available to Dutch industry on advantageous terms via the Dover entrepôt,[6] the Leiden work-force shifted over from low-value 'new draperies' manufactured from Baltic wools, to producing fine cloth from Spanish wool and Venetian-style camlets.[7] This shift was accompanied by a substantial overall increase in the size of the work-force, fine cloth being more labour intensive than 'new draperies'. By the mid-1650s *lakens* and camlets together employed two-thirds of Leiden's textile work-force (see table 6.16). The transition to fine products also vastly increased the value of Leiden's output. By 1654 this had risen to over nine million guilders and by 1665 to over ten. Leiden's textile production, in other words, trebled in value in less than thirty years, an astounding change (see table 6.17). During Phase Four the Dutch cloth industry made not just a larger, but a vastly greater contribution to Holland's overseas commerce than during

---

[5] Montchrétien, *Traicté*, 207–8; Malvezin, *Histoire*, 267–8.
[6] See pp. 194–5.
[7] De La Court, *Welvaren van Leiden*, 95.

TABLE 6.16. *The Leiden work-force as employed in each textile branch, 1654*

Branch	Work-force
Lakens (Spanish wools)	14,000
Camlets (Turkish mohairs)	9,000
Says (Baltic wools)	7,000
Fustians	2,000
Other 'new draperies'	4,650
TOTAL	36,650

Source: Posthumus, *Geschiedenis*, ii. 937.

TABLE 6.17. *Value of annual textile output at Leiden, 1630–1701* (guilders)

Branch	1630	1642	1654	1665	1679	1701
Lakens	110,000	3,000,000	4,000,000	3,000,000	2,720,000	4,200,000
Camlets	110,000	330,000	3,000,000	3,060,000	1,190,000	1,200,000
Says	1,630,000	1,380,000	960,000	770,000	410,000	150,000
Bays	1,000,000	1,170,000	635,000	550,000	250,000	200,000

Source: Posthumus, *Geschiedenis*, ii. 941.

previous phases.[8] In France, Dutch textiles were perceived as a major factor in the home market only from the 1640s onwards.

Lakens, Holland's pre-eminent textile product, sold in many markets, including Germany, Scandinavia, and Russia. The Republic expanded its role as a supplier of textiles to the north as well as to the south. But it is clear that the principal markets for Dutch fine cloth were France, Spain, and the Levant, Ottoman Turkey absorbing some five or six thousand *lakens* yearly during Phase Four, an amount equivalent to almost a third of Leiden's total output.[9] Despite the specialization of the Trip family in Sweden, the Marcellis in Denmark, and several élite Dutch merchant houses in the Russia trade, there had always been a tendency among the Dutch merchant élite as a whole, from 1590 onwards, to concentrate on southern European and colonial markets. The reorganization of the Dutch cloth industry during the 1630s and 1640s could only reinforce that trend.

[8] Malvezin, *Histoire*, 267–8; Israel, 'Phases of the Dutch *straatvaart*', 18.
[9] *BGLH*, ii. 98, 303; Masson, *Histoire*, 126.

Holland's role as the supplier of Europe's most highly esteemed fine cloth after 1647 rested, as we have seen, on a combination of technical and commercial factors. Dominance of the Spanish wool trade was fundamental. As the Dutch economic writer Arend Tollenaer expressed it in 1672, whoever is master of Spanish wool is 'at once master of all'.[10] Spanish wool was priced three times as high as English wool during the 1650s and much more than three times the wools of the Baltic. In terms of shipping space needed, the rise of Dutch wool imports from Spain after 1648 may have merely compensated for the fall in Dutch imports of wool from the Baltic. But in terms of value and impact on the rich trades, the substitution of Spanish for Baltic wool represented an enormous gain for the Republic.

But the technical factor was crucial to both the continuance of Dutch dominance of the Spanish wool trade and the dominance of fine-cloth production itself. This was universally recognized. After the peace with Spain, the Amsterdam council could reassure Leiden that Spanish Brabant was no longer a threat to the Dutch textile industry, as Brabant *lakens* lacked the characteristic smooth finish of the Dutch product and were no longer esteemed.[11] At Venice where, in the years around 1670, the Senate tried to revive that city's once flourishing fine-cloth industry based on Spanish wool, it was decided that the only way of doing this would be to import Dutch methods and machinery so as to reproduce the lightness and smoothness of Leiden fine cloth which was what the Turks now expected.[12] In France, Colbert came to the same conclusion. French observers noted that, with Dutch machines and methods, one-third less wool was needed than was the case in France to produce a given quantity of fine cloth; and also less labour.[13] Also unable to compete was the Spanish fine-cloth industry, based at Segovia, an industry which reached its nadir at this time.[14]

Camlets (*greinen*), produced primarily at Leiden but also at Haarlem, Delft, and Amsterdam, came almost to rival *lakens* in importance (see table 6.18). After 1650, just as Holland each year

---

[10] Tollenaer, *Remonstrantie ofte vertoogh*, 6.
[11] Marperger, *Beschreibung*, 107–8; Pringsheim, *Beiträge*, 86.
[12] ASV CSM new ser. 125, cinque savii to Senate, 17 Dec. 1676; Francesco Alborelli to Senate, Venice, 9 Aug. 1684.
[13] Boissonade, 'Colbert, son système', 11–12; Thomson, *Clermont-de-Lodève*, 94.
[14] García Sanz, *Desarrollo y crisis*, 217.

absorbed about two-thirds of Spain's total wool exports, so the province also consumed the major part of Turkey's mohair yarn. Moreover, as in the case of *lakens*, the main markets, as well as the exclusive source of supply, were in southern Europe: most of Holland's camlet output was exported to France, Spain, and Italy.[15]

Lakens and camlets represented the two most dramatic but by no means the only breakthroughs in the sphere of textiles for export. The silk industry at Amsterdam and Haarlem, of little significance before 1647, first attracted attention in the 1650s, and

TABLE 6.18. *Textile output at Leiden 1647–1672* (pieces)

Year	Lakens	Camlets	Says	Fustians
1647	15,955	—	33,240	13,919
1648	15,872	—	35,645	12,982
1649	16,411	—	34,785	11,935
1650	21,139	—	37,796	11,434
1651	22,069	—	38,779	10,006
1652	17,304	—	34,832	11,298
1653	17,614	—	30,116	8,708
1654	21,547	—	29,874	8,116
1655	18,555	30,465	27,585	9,111
1656	14,647	31,195	29,647	8,734
1657	17,523	33,170	33,157	8,128
1658	19,341	29,811	35,232	8,183
1659	20,361	33,000	35,486	7,722
1660	20,041	38,000	34,230	6,866
1661	16,901	42,780	35,861	6,202
1662	18,832	42,939	39,127	5,697
1663	21,485	42,086	37,775	3,937
1664	21,149	51,198	32,611	4,779
1665	18,342	40,805	27,961	4,192
1666	18,977	39,000	27,107	3,407
1667	16,349	50,956	23,033	3,279
1668	20,918	57,003	27,370	3,273
1669	18,062	67,335	23,588	2,180
1670	16,412	54,979	19,493	2,065
1671	22,740	63,096	29,062	2,936
1672	15,122	45,500	30,369	3,052

Source: Posthumus, *Geschiedenis*, ii. 930–1.

[15] *Bronnen . . . Leidsche textielnijverheid*, v. 259–60.

in the 1660s began to compete with French and Italian silks on the Spanish market.[16] The most flourishing era for the Dutch silk industry came later, with the influx of Huguenots in the 1680s, but the industry already had a certain standing during the 1647–72 period. Another growing textile industry of the post-1650 period was linen weaving. Before 1647 there had existed an incipient linen-weaving industry in the Twenthe region, in the east of Overijssel, and a more developed, but somewhat disrupted, linen-weaving industry around Helmond, in part of North Brabant captured from the Spaniards in 1629. The peace of Münster confirmed the incorporation of the North Brabant textile district within the Republic and brought a new stability to Twenthe. Reviving under the stimulus of peace, and the growing demand for linens to service the burgeoning traffic to Spain and the Caribbean, both areas evolved during the third quarter of the century into major linen-producing districts.[17]

Another success was the sail-canvas industry. Down to the 1660s the leading export-orientated sail-canvas industry in north-west Europe was that of Brittany.[18] Holland and England both imported a large part of their sail-canvas from France. However, during the Second Anglo-Dutch War, at Colbert's prompting, Louis XIV suppressed the export of French canvas with a view to impeding other nations' navigation and promoting that of France. As a result, canvas production in the Republic rapidly increased.[19] The main centres for this industry were Haarlem, Enkhuizen, and the Zaan industrial belt, especially the village of Krommenie, which, by the early eighteenth century, was producing nearly half the Republic's total output. By 1668 North Holland was turning out around 70,000 rolls of sail-canvas yearly and had replaced France as the main supplier for England and Spain, as well as the Dutch market.

Also growing in importance was the finishing of colonial products, especially sugar, dyestuffs, tobacco, and diamonds. Of these, the refining of sugar proved particularly sensitive to the great

[16] Van Dillen (ed.), 'Memorie betreffende den handel met Spanje', 174; Thijs, *Zijdennijverheid te Antwerpen*, 100–1.

[17] Benthem, *Geschiedenis van Enschede*, 523; Frenken, *Helmond in het verleden*, 312–13; Slicher van Bath, *Samenleving onder spanning*, 59, 200–1.

[18] *Humble Representation*, 1–2; Girard, *Commerce français*, 344–5.

[19] GA Amsterdam *vroed.* xxvii, fo. 137, res. 24 Sept. 1671.

politico-economic shifts of the seventeenth century. Blocked in the years 1598–1609 by the Spanish embargoes, the Amsterdam sugar industry had then burgeoned during the Twelve Years' Truce. Stifled by the Spanish embargoes of 1621, the industry recovered with the rise of Dutch Brazil in the 1630s. The devastation of the sugar plantations in Netherlands Brazil in 1645 was a heavy blow; but the Dutch entrepôt filled the gap by stepping up imports of raw sugar from Lisbon and stimulating sugar-cane cultivation in the Caribbean. After 1645 Dutch dominance of the Caribbean carrying trade made up for the débâcle in Brazil. Meanwhile European sugar consumption was rising steadily. The number of sugar-refineries in Holland increased during the 1650s by about half.[20] By 1662 some fifty sugar-refineries were operative at Amsterdam, about half of the total for the whole of Europe.[21] Another dozen or so were located at Rotterdam, Middelburg, Delft, and Gouda. But in the 1660s the Dutch sugar boom broke. Under the impact especially of French, Swedish, and Danish mercantilist measures, the number of sugar-refineries at Amsterdam slumped in a few years from fifty to thirty-four.[22] Nevertheless, despite the loss of the French market, previously the largest market for Dutch refined sugar, the Dutch sugar-refining industry continued to be the largest in Europe and to supply much of the rising sugar consumption of the German and Baltic markets. The major reason for this was again the technical sophistication of the Dutch industry backed by commercial factors. By the late seventeenth century England was the largest importer of raw sugar from the Caribbean but still exported hardly any refined sugar to the continent. Rather, London re-exported raw sugar to Amsterdam for refining.[23] In 1700 there were still around thirty sugar-refineries at Amsterdam.[24]

More consistently successful during Phase Four was the Dutch tobacco industry, again concentrated at Amsterdam. The Dutch dominated the European market for processed tobacco by blending inexpensive, home-grown tobacco with the choicer tobaccos of Brazil, the Caribbean, and Virginia. The Dutch had reigned

[20] *Bronnen ... bedrijfsleven*, iii. 783–4, 798–9.
[21] Aitzema, *Historie*, ix. 240.
[22] Van Dillen, *Bronnen ... bedrijfsleven*, iii. 798–9.
[23] Barbour, *Capitalism in Amsterdam*, 93.
[24] Le Moine de L'Espine, *Négoce d'Amsterdam*, 42.

supreme in the distribution of tobacco in Europe since around 1600. But after 1650 there was a dramatic expansion in both the Dutch tobacco-finishing industry and the trade on which it was based. This is reflected in the vast increase in tobacco cultivation within the Republic in the provinces of Utrecht and Gelderland as well as adjoining parts of Germany.[25] The quantity and cheapness of this home-produced leaf, and the practice of blending it with smaller amounts of quality tobacco from the Americas, yielded a product which was not only cheap, plentiful, and which had some flavour, but which was also extremely difficult for rivals to compete with. In fact, there was no competing with seventeenth-century Holland as a producer of blended tobacco. Until the early eighteenth century a high proportion of the Virginia tobacco shipped by the English was re-exported from London to Amsterdam in an unprocessed state. For in Holland the leaf could be more profitably spun, blended, and sold. The Amsterdam workshops mixing home-grown and American tobaccos thus ensured that the Dutch entrepôt remained the central reservoir for all tobaccos. Amsterdam was the staple for Brazil, Spanish American, and Virginia tobaccos. By 1670 there were some thirty importers of Brazil and Spanish Caribbean tobacco at Amsterdam, ten of them Jewish. At the end of the century, Dutch supremacy over the European tobacco trade was still intact. In 1700 there were twenty-three tobacco-spinning and blending establishments at Amsterdam, of which about a dozen were in the hands of Jews.[26]

Dutch pre-eminence in diamonds was more specifically due to technical factors. Diamonds are an extreme instance of the role of industrial techniques in bolstering the Dutch world entrepôt in the seventeenth century, for in this case, rather exceptionally, the Dutch lacked control over the traffic in the raw material. Down to the early 1660s the Portuguese, and later the English, handled the lion's share of the trade in rough diamonds. But the rough diamonds shipped to England from India, the major source of supply until the eighteenth century, were generally re-exported unprocessed to Amsterdam for cutting and polishing,[27] for the skills involved were not at all easy to reproduce and Dutch primacy in this sphere was never challenged. As a

[25] Luzac, *Hollands rijkdom*, iv. bijlage A; Herks, *Geschiedenis*, 175, 195.
[26] Ibid.
[27] Yogev, *Diamonds and Coral*, 141-2.

result, the export of finished jewellery, especially high-quality work, to the courts of France, Spain, and Germany, and also to Poland and Russia, remained securely in Dutch hands. As with tobacco, much of the Dutch diamond-processing and export business was handled by Amsterdam Sephardi and later also Ashkenazi Jews.

Many other industries also played a significant part in the expansion of Dutch overseas trade after 1647. The major industry at Delft was Delftware pottery. The rise of Delftware began in the late 1640s following the disruption of the VOC's trade in Chinese products due to political upheaveal in China.[28] Post-1647 access to high-quality potters' clays in the South Netherlands was also a factor. Delftware, an imitation of Chinese 'blue' porcelain, proved enormously popular in Europe from the middle of the seventeenth down to the early eighteenth century. But the data show that the decisive period of growth was during Phase Four (see table 6.19). By 1670 the Delftware industry was at its height, employing some 20 per cent of the Delft work-force. Here, again, most of the output was for export.

TABLE 6.19. *The number of Delft potteries, 1600–1795*

1600	2	1678	29
1620	8	1702	30
1647	11	1721	29
1655	15	1741	27
1661	26	1775	20
1670	32	1795	10

Source: Wijsenbeek-Olthuis, *Achter de gevels van Delft*, 419.

The main industry at Gouda was the manufacture of white clay tobacco pipes, which enjoyed an extraordinary vogue, especially in France, Germany, and Scandinavia, from the middle of the seventeenth century down to the early eighteenth. As with Delftware, the decisive expansion of this industry took place after 1647, though this industry continued to expand for rather longer than the Delft potteries.[29]

[28] Montias, *Artists and Artisans*, 296–7; Wijsenbeek-Olthuis, *Achter de gevels van Delft*, 59, 419.
[29] Goedewaagen, *Geschiedenis*, 2–4.

Another industrial sector which grew prodigiously during these years was that of soap, lighting fuel, and other whale products. This phenomenon was a direct result of the enormous expansion from the 1640s onwards of the Dutch whale fishery. This followed the abandonment of coastal whaling around Spitsbergen, from where the whales were learning to keep away, in favour of deep-sea whaling in the Greenland sea. This switch involved larger ships and more specialized techniques which proved difficult for the rivals of the Dutch to compete with.[30] The result was overwhelming Dutch dominance and an explosive expansion in Dutch whaling. From around forty vessels in 1642, the whaling fleet grew to around seventy ships by the mid-1650s and to 148 by 1670.[31] The whale-blubber refineries, using peat-fired cauldrons, increased in numbers and capacity correspondingly. Dozens of these establishments sprang up along the Zaan and around the Maas estuary.

Also proliferating on the Zaan were the new-style paper mills. The manufacture of paper in the North Netherlands had begun in the late sixteenth century. But, as with most Dutch industries, Dutch paper only achieved real significance in international commerce during Phase Four.[32] Until the third quarter of the seventeenth century, the Dutch paper mills were small establishments, most of them in Gelderland, making low-grade paper.[33] Around 1670, however, technical innovation gave rise to a new type of paper mill using much heavier and more expensive equipment.[34] Concentrated on the Zaan, these mills produced a smooth, white, high-quality paper, which began to compete, with increasing success, with the good quality paper of France and Italy.

The Zaan area remained a major centre of shipbuilding and the world's largest timber depot throughout the second half of the century. Timber-sawing mills continued to be the most common type of industrial plant along the river. But, after 1650, the Zaan emerged as much the most intensive and varied industrial belt that then existed in the world. Besides paper mills, whale-

[30] Brinner, *Die deutsche Grönlandfahrt*, 140–1.
[31] De Jong, 'Walvisvaart', 313.
[32] *Correspondance administrative*, iii. 437.
[33] Roessingh, 'Veluwse inwonertal', 120–1.
[34] Van Braam, *Bloei en verval*, 23.

oil refineries and sail- and rope-making establishments, there were a large number of other refineries processing animal fats and oils. As at Amsterdam, Rotterdam, and, to a lesser extent, Delft and Middelburg, there were also numerous plants producing processed foods—biscuits, spiced cakes, chocolate, mustard, and all sorts of exotic liqueurs made from tropical and sub-tropical fruits.

During Phase Four the role of manufacturing industry in Dutch overseas trade was far greater than had been the case previously. The effect was to enhance Dutch primacy in a wide range of overseas markets. This remarkable industrial advance was due to several factors. Most important perhaps was Dutch commercial control of key raw-material imports such as Spanish wool, Turkish yarns, Swedish iron and copper, and Spanish American dyestuffs. Crucial too was the spur to mechanical innovation inherent in high wage costs and scarcity of labour. Availability of cheap fuel in the shape of peat played a part, as did low interest rates.[35] But, at the same time as we emphasize these economic factors, it should not be forgotten that here too a fundamental role was played by the Dutch state. The States General, provinces, and municipalities tightly regulated many areas of industrial activity, such as product quality, packaging of goods, and patents for inventions. If, as Sir Josiah Child put it, the Dutch acquired a universal reputation for the 'exact making of all their native commodities' and gave 'great encouragement and immunities to the inventors of new manufactures',[36] this was mainly due to the perpetual vigilance and traditional intervention in the industrial sphere of the Dutch public authorities.

ENGLAND. THE DUTCH AND THE CONTEST FOR WORLD-TRADE SUPREMACY, 1654–1667

At first sight it appears rather baffling that the zenith of Dutch world-trade primacy should have been attained in the period 1647–72, which also witnessed the climax of the Anglo-Dutch conflict. How can the Dutch world-trade system have been at its

---

[35] De Zeeuw, 'Peat', 10, 25.
[36] Child, *A New Discourse*, 2–4.

most successful just when the English onslaught on that system was at its height? England was the strongest maritime power on earth and there can be no doubt that, in addition to her greater population and land mass, England enjoyed many strategic advantages over the Republic. In the perceptions of Venetian, Swedish, and other neutral observers and diplomats, Dutch world maritime supremacy had never been more precarious than in the 1650s and 1660s since the Dutch first achieved their global ascendancy in the 1590s. When the Swedish resident at The Hague noted, on the eve of the Second Anglo-Dutch War (1665–7), that it was all too likely that England would shortly be 'maîtresse des mers' and arbiter of world commerce, he was merely echoing the general view.[37]

Yet, contrary to expectation, events proved that England's advantages and superior fire-power were not enough in themselves to overthrow Dutch world-trade primacy. Indeed, remarkably, the overall impact of England's onslaught on the Dutch world-trading system seems, despite her formidable sea power, to have been rather less than that achieved previously by Spain and subsequently by France. There are several reasons for this paradoxical state of affairs. In the first place, there is the question of leverage over European markets. Compared with Spain or France, England in fact possessed relatively little sway over European markets vital to the functioning of the Dutch world-trade system. Whilst the English market itself was sealed against the Dutch with the passing of the Navigation Act of 1651, as a market England was much less important to Dutch overseas trade than Spain or France. Then there was England's relative financial weakness at government level compared with pre-1648 Spain and post-1667 France. Finally, English trade and shipping were much more vulnerable to Dutch counter-pressure than was the case with Spain or France and it was this, perhaps, which proved decisive. Fighting the Dutch meant seeing the Danish Sound closed to English shipping, English Baltic commerce suspended, a stop put on English Mediterranean trade,[38] the paralysing of English commerce in the East Indies, and heavy losses of shipping to Dutch privateers. The fact is that England could not sustain such pressure for long

---

[37] 'Memoriën ... Harald Appelboom', 365.
[38] PRO SP 105/151, p. 183; SP 98/7, Chillingworth to Arlington, Livorno, 23 Aug. 1666, Finch to Arlington, Florence, 26 Oct. 1666.

enough to inflict any really serious damage on the Dutch entrepôt.

The First Anglo-Dutch War, as we saw, grew out of the adverse effects on English trade of the restructuring of the Dutch world-trade system in the years 1646–8. The second and hardest-fought of the three seventeenth-century Anglo-Dutch wars grew out of the unresolved legacy of the first, aggravated by England's accelerating colonial expansion after 1654 and Dutch efforts to obstruct it. After 1654 the Dutch improved their position in the Spanish trade and in the Levant and East Indies.[39] On the other hand, England profited from the Dutch–Portuguese War of 1657–61 to consolidate her trade ascendancy in Portugal and made rapid progress in the Caribbean and, after the setting up of the Royal Africa Company (1660), in West Africa. With the establishment of a line of English forts in the area during the early 1660s, the English became the main threat to Dutch trade primacy along the Guinea coast.[40]

Dutch attempts to impede English progress in Africa and the Indies gave rise to feelings of outrage and bitterness eloquently expressed by the notoriously anti-Dutch English ambassador at The Hague, Sir George Downing, after whom Downing Street is named. The Dutch were accused of every sort of underhand machination, the most widely resented being their practice of intimidating the Asians and Africans into conceding preferential trade terms and often an outright monopoly to the Dutch, at the expense of their rivals. 'This trick of the Hollanders', wrote Downing in one dispatch,

to declare warre with the natives in the East Indies and upon the Coast of Africa, with whom His Majesty's subjects have any trade, and then thereupon to forbid them all trade with them, and to continue the warre till they have brought those natives to an agreement with them, to sell them all their commodities, and then to keep the English from trading, upon the account that the natives have agreed with them, to sell all to them;—this trick, I say, hath not only bin the ruine of numbers of His Majesty's subjects, but beaten them out of many mighty trades, and will certainly in conclusion utterly overthrow the English East Indian and African Companies, if nothing be applied for remedie but wordes.[41]

---

[39] Farnell, 'Navigation Act', 454; Israel, 'Diplomatic Career', 181–5; Chaudhuri, *Trading World of Asia*, 283, 315–16.

[40] Wilson, *Profit and Power*, 111–15.

[41] Lister, *Life and Administration*, iii. 249.

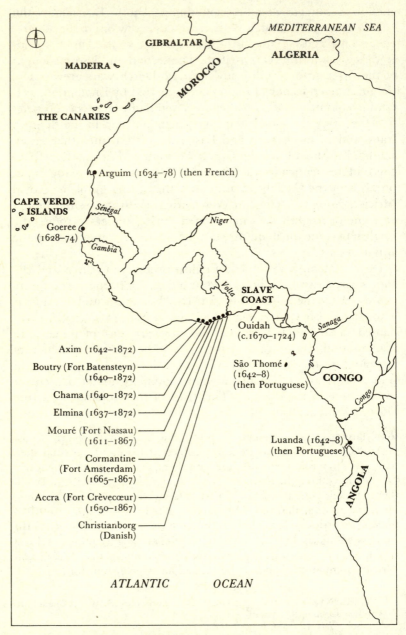

6.3 The Dutch forts in West Africa during the mid-seventeenth century.

When it came to engrossing trade, the Dutch had most of the advantages. The advantage the English possessed was superior naval force and it was inevitable that sooner or later strong-armed tactics would be used to resolve the intensifying rivalry and widening contradictions in the situation. In November 1663 Charles II allowed the sending of an expedition to West Africa to beat the Dutch out of the Guinea trade. This force, under Sir Robert Holmes, attacked and captured the entire cordon of Dutch strongholds in West Africa except for their headquarters at Elmina, and Fort Nassau at Mouré. But English jubilation was short-lived. Orders were sent from The Hague to de Ruyter, who was cruising in the Mediterranean, and he sailed for Guinea. He recaptured all but one of the lost forts and took the main English stronghold, at Cormantine, for good measure.[42] He also seized the Africa Company's stocks of merchandise and stores and five of its ships, putting the finishing touch to his success by having his portrait painted, at Elmina Castle, with an African background and a black figure kneeling at his feet, symbolizing Africa's subjection.[43] The English public was incensed. De Ruyter was accused of all manner of 'barbarityes in Guinea', though in fact, as Samuel Pepys privately acknowledged, he behaved in an impeccably correct manner.

This crushing reply in Africa triggered the Second Anglo-Dutch War. The English, in Pepys's words, were 'beaten to dirt at Guinny by De Ruyter to the utter ruine of our Royal Company and reproach and shame to the whole nation'.[44] It was an affront not to be suffered. Charles replied by sending an expedition to North America to occupy New Netherland. This was accomplished in September 1664, the name of the principal Dutch settlement, New Amsterdam, being changed to 'New York'. Soon afterwards instructions were sent to Jamaica, putting the privateers there 'at liberty to dispossess the Dutch from Curaçao and their other plantations'.[45] For Charles and his ministers one of the main objectives of the war which now ensued was to strip the Dutch completely of their possessions in the Americas.

There was every prospect of sweeping gains, or so it seemed,

[42] *Cal. St. Papers, America and the West Indies, 1661–1668*, 266, 294.
[43] Lawrence, *Trade Castles*, 139.
[44] Wilson, *Profit and Power*, 114.
[45] *Cal. St. Papers, America and the West Indies, 1661–1668*, 252.

and to begin with the English public was in a fiercely anti-Dutch mood. Although the Dutch had considerably strengthened their fleet since 1654, Charles and Parliament had ensured that England's navy had kept its lead, so that the English were still equipped with many more and heavier 'first-rates' than the Dutch, as well as with heavier guns. And then there was the burgeoning fleet of privateers. By the time Charles II finally declared war officially, in March 1665, no less than two hundred Dutch merchantmen had already been brought in.[46] In the Caribbean, St Eustatius and Saba were quickly overrun, as were Essequebo and most of the other Dutch outposts in the Guyanas. The governors of Barbados and Jamaica were instructed to 'proceed with the settling of St Eustatius and Saba, scattering the Dutch inhabitants over other (English) plantations whereby their labour may be of use without danger; and in case Tobago is still held by the Dutch to endeavour to reduce it to the king's obedience'.[47] Delighted by these successes, Charles declared himself

full of hope shortly to hear of the like success against Curaçao . . . desiring him [the governor of Jamaica] to go on to root the Dutch out of all places in the West Indies, and where he shall have success, to transplant the greatest part of them to Jamaica or other plantations which may have the benefit of their industry without hazard of revolt, leaving garrisons in the places reduced, especially Curaçao, if God give success.[48]

The mood in the Republic was correspondingly grim. The main Dutch battle fleet, 103 ships carrying 21,613 men and 4,869 guns, the most powerful the Republic had ever assembled, was shattered off Lowestoft, in June. The Dutch lost seventeen warships. Obdam's flagship, the *Eendracht* (84 guns; 500 men), blew up, killing the admiral and all but five of his men. The blast reportedly shook windows as far away as The Hague. The public was aghast. VOC shares on the Amsterdam Exchange plummeted to 336 and soon to 322 (see table 6.13).

The Dutch leadership knew that they had to repair their fleet quickly and get it out to shield their incoming convoys. In the short term there was little they could do to correct the gap in firepower. There was now an acute shortage of men for the fleet.

---

[46] Jones, *Britain and the World*, 80.
[47] *Cal. St. Papers, America and the West Indies, 1661–1668*, 328.
[48] Ibid. 329.

Many had been killed or maimed at Lowestoft and the country's temporarily redundant fishermen and seamen were less than enthusiastic at the prospect of signing on to face the English guns. Yet, unlike in England, it was not permissible to press men for the navy. Empressment went against the Republic's traditions. The only solution was to raise naval wages to unheard of levels. 'Cost what it will,' remarked Downing, 'they will have their fleet out.'[49]

At the news of the Dutch defeat off the English coast, the convoys returning to the United Provinces 'northabout', around Ireland and Scotland, took refuge in the Norwegian port of Bergen. English naval forces closed in. With Denmark hourly expected to side with England, the English admiral attacked. But, to his amazement, the Danish–Norwegian garrison, instead of joining in against the Dutch, joined them in repulsing the assault. The Danish king, it turned out, had played a double game and now entered the war on the Dutch side. This 'foule tergiversation of the Danes' had an immediate impact on the struggle. The Danish Sound was sealed against England. During 1666 not a single English ship entered or left the Baltic (see table 6.4). But this was not the only indication that England might not after all emerge victorious from the conflict. In Asian waters, English shipping was once again disrupted by the VOC.[50] In the Mediterranean, English commerce almost completely ceased.[51] England had made a triumphant start. But could she long withstand the unremitting economic and strategic pressure building up against her? It was perhaps already clear to the more perceptive that the answer was no.

A major factor in the struggle was the almost universal dread in Europe of an English victory. Not the least ironic feature of Dutch world-trade hegemony in the seventeenth century is that, while, to an extent, it was resented, when it came to the crunch Europe decidedly preferred it to the only feasible alternatives— English hegemony or that of France. This, after all, was logical. In the Dutch Republic, Europe had a dominant entrepôt and financial centre which lacked the manpower and military resources ever to translate that economic primacy into political domination. English diplomacy had tried to persuade the Danes, Swedes, and

---

[49] Lister, *Life and Administration*, iii. 384.
[50] Chaudhuri, *Trading World of Asia*, 283.
[51] Israel, 'Phases of the Dutch *straatvaart*', 27.

Hanseatics that England's triumph would liberate them from Dutch economic tutelage. But this is not at all how the prospect was perceived. Normally Sweden automatically did the opposite to Denmark. But not this time. The Swedish resident at The Hague advised Stockholm that, if the Dutch were presumptuous, the English were worse and that it was not in Sweden's interests that England should win.[52]

In the furious Anglo-Dutch diplomatic contest which raged throughout Europe, the Dutch had matters all their own way—except, owing to the special circumstances, in Portugal. At the moment of its apparently impending overthrow, Dutch world economic dominance proved almost popular, at any rate among Europeans. There was no support for the English cause in Scandinavia.[53] Despite Hamburg's old jealousy of Amsterdam, support there for the Dutch cause was total and was rooted, as the English resident put it, not just in policy but in 'their humeurs and inclinations'.[54] Hamburg helped the Dutch stop the flow of naval stores to England and covered the Dutch Russia trade. Twenty-three Hamburg vessels docked at Archangel in July 1665, Hamburg merchants having never before dispatched more than seven or eight yearly 'for their own account'.[55] Dutch importers of Spanish wools were able to use Hamburg ships to carry the wool from Spain to Hamburg and then use small boats to bring the wool in from Hamburg to Amsterdam.[56] This small-boat traffic between Hamburg and Amsterdam, traversing the shallows behind the Frisian islands, too close in for the English warships to disrupt, employed 'forty or fifty vessels' a week during the summer of 1665.[57]

In Italy, the war of words reached a pitch of frantic intensity following the so-called 'Four Days' Fight' of June 1666 in the North Sea, an indecisive battle which, for once, was marginally a Dutch victory. A wave of conflicting reports, rival claims, and attempts to pack the Italian news-sheets provoked uproar throughout Italy. At Livorno and Florence, the English wagered the

---

[52] 'Memoriën ... Harald Appelboom', 365.
[53] Barbour, *Capitalism in Amsterdam*, 103.
[54] PRO SP 82/10, fo. 248, Swann to Arlington, Hamburg, 25 July 1665; see also Baasch, 'Hamburg und Holland', 55–7.
[55] PRO SP 82/10, fo. 247.
[56] GA Amsterdam NA 2898, p. 415, Padhuysen, 10 Sept. 1668.
[57] PRO SP 82/10, fo. 248.

Dutch, French, and Italians 'who are all against us 500 pistolles that we have got the victory'.[58] The Livorno dock-workers rioted in the streets against the English, shouting 'Long live the Dutch!' When the Dutch merchants at Livorno received permission to light bonfires and 'make publick rejoycings for the victory they have obtained', the English ships in the harbour fired off their guns in protest and ran up the 'Dutch colours reversed under the King's banner in token of victory'. At this, Livorno erupted in Dutch flags, the Dutch 'on shore upon the steeple of the Madonna set his Majesty's Jack reversed, and with the addition of mourning, under the Holland colours'.[59] 'All the Italians' were so hostile to England, according to the English resident at Florence, that he could 'hardly tell whether the Dutch or they expressed the greater satisfaction in His Majesty's supposed losse'.[60] Nor did England's cause fare any better in Spain. 'All the (English) merchants upon the coast', reported the English ambassador in July 1665, 'complaine of the Spaniards' partiality towards the Dutch.'[61] At Corunna, where, it was reported, Dutch privateers were being permitted to sell off captured English prizes, the local populace was said to be nothing less than 'passionate for the Hollanders'.[62]

But if the Dutch triumphed in the psychological war, there was no answering the weight of English fire-power. De Ruyter marginally won the Four Days' Fight, but the verdict was soon reversed with the more decisive English victory in the St James's Day Fight (4 August 1666), which cost the Dutch heavy losses and forced de Ruyter to seek refuge in the Scheldt estuary, leaving North Holland unprotected. Holmes then penetrated between the West Frisian islands and burned the 150 merchant ships which had been waiting for de Ruyter to clear their path. This was one of the greatest disasters of Dutch maritime history. Yet, from September 1666 onwards, nothing went right for King Charles. If, in the First Anglo-Dutch War, the English won the war in the North Sea but lost the peace, in the Second they won the battles but lost the war. How is this paradox to be explained?

At the heart of England's difficulties was the country's complete

---

[58] PRO SP 98/7, Finch to Arlington, Florence, 6 July 1666.

[59] Ibid., Finch to Prince Leopold, Florence, 7 July 1666.

[60] Ibid., Finch to Arlington, Florence, 13 July 1666.

[61] PRO SP 94/49, fo. 43, Fanshawe to Arlington, Madrid, 29 July 1665.

[62] PRO SP 94/47, fo. 213, Travers to Arlington, Pontevedra, 8 May 1665.

loss of appetite for the struggle, despite the resounding victories at
sea. By the summer of 1666 all the anti-Dutch fervour of previous
years had evaporated. There was simply no will to go on with the
fight. Nor is this in the slightest degree surprising. For, besides
the chronic shortages of Baltic stores and Newcastle coal, the
diplomatic reverses, and the suspension of the Levant and East
India trades, there was the growing impact of the Dutch privateering onslaught. During the Second Anglo-Dutch War many
more privateers operated out of Dutch ports than during the first.[63]
England was still inflicting serious damage on Dutch shipping.
Altogether, during the second war the English navy and privateers
captured around 522 Dutch vessels.[64] But nearly half of these were
seized on the high seas before war was officially declared. There
seems little doubt in the light of recent research that, once the war
began in earnest, in March 1665, the Dutch were disposing of
English merchant ships at a faster rate than vice versa. Just the
privateers operating under the Zeeland and Amsterdam admiralty
colleges captured 360 English ships and confiscated some sixty
English cargoes from neutral ships.[65] At least another hundred
prizes would have been brought into the other admiralty colleges.
Then to these totals we must add the twenty-seven ships captured
by de Ruyter off West Africa and in the Caribbean and the
substantial number of English prizes auctioned off by Dutch privateers in Spain, France, and in Denmark–Norway. For example,
twenty-eight English ships, taken in the Atlantic, were sold off at
Corunna alone.[66] These were crushing losses which eradicated for
good the old notion, formerly prevalent in England, that Dutch
merchant shipping was appetizingly vulnerable to English attack.
Although it has taken historians a long time to realize it, by 1666
it was English merchant shipping which was the more exposed to
attack.

   Paralysed by lack of money to go on with the war, by shortage
of stores, and by the loss of will to fight, in 1667 the decision
was made to lay up the most powerful English ships and fight
defensively. The Dutch were handed the initiative on a plate and

   [63] De Bruijn, 'Kaapvaart', 411, 415.
   [64] Davis, *Rise of the English Shipping Industry*, 48–54.
   [65] It is noteworthy that only 20 of these 360 captured vessels were colliers (De Bruijn,
'Kaapvaart', 422).
   [66] PRO SP 94/50, fo. 238.

they used it. The coast of south-east England as far up as Harwich was blockaded. In June 1667, de Ruyter carried out his famous raid up the Medway, penetrating to Upnor Castle, burning five warships, and towing away the English flagship, the *Royal Charles*. Church bells were rung throughout the United Provinces. The country erupted in jubilation, victory bonfires, and the burning of King Charles in effigy.

From late 1666 the tide turned also in the Caribbean. The Dutch recovered Essequebo and Pomeroon. A Zeelandian expedition, of only seven ships and a thousand men, captured the English fort at Paramaribo and, with it, the whole of the potentially rich sugar colony of Surinam. The Dutch also reoccupied Tobago. At the outset, having been almost 'rooted out' of the region, the Dutch ended by consolidating their position in tropical America.

Peace between England and the United Provinces was signed at Breda in July 1667. Under the terms, England kept New York but returned St Eustatius and Saba and ceded Surinam. England also gave up her longstanding claim to Pola Run in the Banda Islands. In addition, Charles conceded the principle of 'free ship, free goods', which meant that in any future war between England and another power in which the United Provinces were neutral the English would no longer be entitled to board Dutch ships on the high seas—as had frequently occurred during the Anglo-Spanish War of 1655–60—to remove cargoes belonging to subjects of England's enemy. Finally, the terms of the Navigation Act were clarified so as to confirm that Germany was part of the Republic's natural hinterland so that German products such as Rhine wine and Silesian linens could be legally shipped to England in Dutch vessels.[67]

THE OVERALL TREND

After a period of prolonged stagnation during the quarter century 1621–47, Dutch overseas trade as a whole expanded during what we have termed Phase Four (1647–72), despite the fact that during this period Anglo-Dutch conflict was at its height. However surprising it may seem, the impact of England's challenge to the

---

[67] Van Winter, 'Acte van Navigatie', 44, 53.

Dutch world-trade system on the vitality and volume of Dutch seaborne commerce was less than that of Spain's challenge in the preceding period. But is there any general statistical evidence which might confirm our view that the overall trend during the period 1647–72 was one of expansion despite the undoubted contraction in the Dutch Baltic trade? Perhaps the most important block of such evidence are the Dutch customs returns, the so-called *convoyen* and *licenten* collected on incoming and outgoing goods by the five admiralty colleges and their staff under the supervision of the States General. Looked at carefully, these do indeed confirm that the real rhythm in Dutch overseas enterprise was not up until 1650 and then down, as Braudel and the Braudelians supposed, but up (1609–21), then down (1621–47), then again up (1647–71), and then only finally down from 1672.

Superficially, it is true, these figures appear to suggest an expansion of trade during the second quarter, followed by a downturn after 1650. However, as Westermann and van Dillen pointed out in 1948, these statistics cannot be used unadjusted without ignoring the very substantial changes in the rates at which Dutch customs were collected. Westermann argued that the figures for the years 1609–25 and for the three and a half decades after 1651 have to be raised by approximately 30 per cent to render them comparable with the figures for the 1625–51 period.[68]

Westermann's adjustments, however, require some further correction. In the first place, he assumed that the higher rates under the Dutch war-list were introduced in 1625, when they were published by the States General, and only removed again in 1651. In fact, as we now know, the 1603 war-list was re-introduced not in 1625 but in April 1621.[69] The rates were then lowered again not in 1651 but on a 'provisional basis' in October 1648.[70] These corrections are important, for they effectively remove any suggestion that Dutch overseas trade increased from 1621 when all the other evidence points to a sharp setback[71]—or that the end of the Spanish war in 1648 failed to stimulate an explosive expansion to which all other evidence points. But still further corrections to

---

[68] Westermann, 'Statistische gegevens', 6–9.

[69] ARH SG 3180, fos. 168ᵛ, 170ᵛ, 201, res. SG 19, 21 Apr. 1621 and 7 May 1621; *Notulen Zeeland* (1621), 89, res. 5 Apr. 1621; Israel, *Dutch Republic and the Hispanic World*, 88–9.

[70] Israel, *Dutch Republic and the Hispanic World*, 428; Res. Holl. 3 and 10 Oct. 1648.

[71] Snapper, *Oorlogsinvloeden*, 71.

Westermann's analysis are needed. For the idea that the Dutch customs statistics for the 1621–47 period are inflated by only around 30 per cent compared with the previous and subsequent periods hardly seems tenable. In the first place, Westermann made no allowance for the very high rates, inflating the returns many times over, imposed in 1621 on all river traffic, not only to the Spanish Netherlands but also to Germany.[72] In the second place, while 30 per cent would seem a reasonable adjustment for returns on imports where increases were, on the whole, rather modest, and where grains, such as rye, were left untouched, the larger part of the returns were collected on exports and re-exports and here the increases, in most cases, were very much more than 30 per cent. Given that we possess no breakdown of actual imports and exports, final proof is impossible. But I believe that it is clear that the inflating effect of the 1621 changes and deflating effect of those of 1648 must have been considerably greater than the 30 per cent postulated by Westermann (see table 6.20). In the South Holland (Rotterdam) admiralty jurisdiction, a maritime zone trading mainly with France and Britain and relatively unaffected by the collapse of Dutch Iberian and Mediterranean trade in 1621, the jump in average annual returns for the four years 1621–4 compared with those for the four exceptionally good trading years 1615–18 (the last Truce years for which we have returns for the Rotterdam area) was no less than 62 per cent. My own view would be that the post-1621 statistics may well be inflated by slightly more than 60 per cent compared with those for the 1609–21 and 1648–71 periods but can hardly be supposed to have been inflated by much less. Average annual returns at Rotterdam during the last three years in which the war-list applied (1646–8) were 78 per cent higher than the comparable average for the first three years after the rates were lowered (1649–51), years which we know to have been bumper years for trade (see table 6.21).

What conclusion can be drawn from these considerations? While our own corrective of 60 per cent remains a hypothesis, it is plain, even on the basis of Westermann's lower corrective of 30 per cent, that Dutch non-Baltic trade must have expanded vigorously after 1647. For we know that there was a drastic cut-back in Dutch Baltic trade in the 1650s, while Westermann's corrected figures

---

[72] *Groot Placaet-Boeck*, i. 2389–486.

TABLE 6.20. *Changes in Dutch tariffs, 1609–1651* (guilders)

Commodity	List 1609	1621	1648	1651
Exports				
wheat (per last)	6.00	8.00	6.00	8.00
rye (per last)	3.50	4.50	3.50	4.50
cheese (100 lb.)	0.75	2.00	0.75	1.00
herring (per last)	2.00	3.50	2.00	3.50
pepper (100 lb.)	1.50	2.25	1.50	1.50
Baltic wool (100 lb.)	0.30	1.10	0.30	0.30
refined salt (per 'hundred')	10.00	15.00	10.00	10.00
Imports				
rye (per last)	1.25	1.25	1.25	1.25
pepper (100 lb.)	1.50	2.00	1.50	2.00
Rhine wine (six 'Amen')	3.00	7.50	3.00	5.00
Baltic wool (100 lb.)	0.30	0.50	0.30	00
indigo (100 lb.)	3.00	6.00	3.00	5.00
gallnuts (100 lb.)	0.50	1.25	0.50	0.75
caviare (per tub)	0.50	1.00	0.50	1.00

Source: *Groot Placaet-Boeck*, i, cols. 2389–544.

for the returns in the Amsterdam jurisdiction show that there was no falling off after 1648 (see table 6.22). This can only be explained in terms of a massive compensating expansion of commerce with regions outside the Baltic. If our higher corrective of 60 per cent, is accepted, then it is clear that the period 1621–47 was a time of relative stagnation for the Dutch entrepôt and that after 1647, the decline in Dutch Baltic trade notwithstanding, there was a vigorous expansion of the Dutch trading system as a whole.

THE FRENCH CHALLENGE, 1667–1672

It was evident by the late 1660s that Dutch hegemony in world trade, having earlier survived Spain's attempts to topple it, had now also surmounted the English challenge. But at this very moment arose a new and ominous menace to the Republic's commerce. It was in 1667 that France took the lead in efforts

TABLE 6.21. *'Convoy and License' returns within the jurisdiction of the Rotterdam admiralty college, 1614–1630 and 1646–1657* (guilders)

1614	284,117	1629	413,671
1615	284,140	1630	369,882
1616	302,435	1646	528,868
1617	271,335	1647	607,137
1618	259,815	1648	540,800
1619	—	1649	392,506
1620	—	1650	181,292
1621	369,039	1651	366,029
1622	425,518	1652	256,474
1623	531,898	1653	235,169
1624	487,716	1654	324,806
1625	303,588	1655	321,457
1626	193,609	1656	388,137
1627	257,823	1657	349,587
1628	328,118		

Source: Becht, *Statistische gegevens*, table 1.

TABLE 6.22. *'Convoy and License' returns within the jurisdiction of the Amsterdam admiralty college, 1640–1671 (as corrected by Westermann)* (guilders)

1640	1,046,468	1656	1,250,000
1641	1,180,809	1657	1,062,000
1642	1,249,028	1658	1,047,000
1643	1,356,663	1659	1,115,000
1644	1,109,035	1660	1,413,000
1645	1,047,482	1661	1,223,000
1646	1,199,969	1662	1,294,000
1647	1,237,066	1663	1,300,000
1648	1,344,292	1664	955,000
1649*	1,786,000	1665	493,000
1650*	1,741,000	1666	653,000
1651	1,508,000	1667	830,000
1652	1,067,000	1668	1,364,000
1653	705,000	1669	1,240,000
1654	1,205,000	1670	1,143,000
1655	1,138,000	1671	1,218,000

Source: Westermann, 'Statistische gegevens', 8–9.

* Westermann in his table of corrected statistics, failed to adjust the figures for 1649–50, not realizing that the States General's war-list was already suspended in October 1648; I have raised the figures for those years using his corrective.

to break Dutch trade primacy. The French court and business community alike were tired of the country's, 'dépendence servile' on the Dutch entrepôt.[73]

Nowhere in mid-seventeenth-century Europe did there arise a more acute resentment at being enmeshed in the tentacles of Dutch economic power than in the France of Louis XIV.[74] Merchants, manufacturers, and court alike exuded hostility towards the Dutch entrepôt and its activities. In France, the Dutch Republic was perceived as 'le magazin général' which, by means of cheap freight-age, low interest, the buying up of commodities ahead, and superi-ority in industrial techniques, had reduced France and all Europe to a humiliating subjection in matters maritime and commercial.[75] England alone, French observers recognized, had, by means of state-power and brute force, cut free from this bondage.

From the 1660s onwards Louis XIV and his minister for finance and commerce, Colbert, were, like the English, determined not only to break free of Dutch trade primacy in so far as it held their own country in subjection, but also to overthrow Dutch trade hegemony generally and replace it with that of France. Braudel insisted, and many have agreed, that the efforts of the French state in this direction were totally futile.[76] It is perfectly true that France simply could not make much impact on bulk freightage. Given the scale of her wine, brandy, and salt exports, and her lack of carrying capacity, it was out of the question for France to attempt to emulate the English Navigation Acts. But this does not mean that France was less well placed than England to challenge Dutch world-trade hegemony. Once again, the Braudelian vision is simply wrong.

England had a stronger navy than France and a much larger merchant fleet. Nevertheless, it was France which was the better placed to damage the Dutch trading system once Louis and Colbert unleashed a full-scale 'guerre de commerce' against the Dutch Republic in 1667. There were several reasons for this state of affairs. Firstly, France was less vulnerable than England to Dutch counter-pressure on trade routes and shipping. Then, the

[73] Arnould, De la balance du commerce, i. 192.
[74] Pomponne, Relation, 43–6; Sée, 'Commerce des Hollandais à Nantes', 247–50; Morineau, 'Balance du commerce franco-néerlandais', 172–3.
[75] Eon, Commerce honorable, 31; Pomponne, Relation, 44.
[76] Braudel, Civilisation matérielle, iii. 217–18.

French market was much more important to the Dutch than was England. Dutch exports to France were several times greater than to England while Dutch imports from France exceeded by five to ten times in value Dutch imports from England (see tables 6.23 and 6.24).[77] France indeed had become, since the 1640s, probably the largest of all overseas markets for Dutch exports and colonial re-exports. France absorbed a high proportion of total Dutch fine cloth and camlet output,[78] a great part of the Dutch East India spices sold in Europe, around one-third of the Republic's herring exports,[79] some 20 per cent of Dutch cheese exports,[80] a vast proportion of Holland's whale-oil exports, and—until 1664—approximately half of Amsterdam's output of refined sugar (see table 6.23).[81]

France was also better placed than England to oust the Dutch from another key market, namely Spain. French linen was already the most sought-after foreign textile product in Spain and Spanish America. If France with her linens, silks, and paper could capture effective control of the Spanish trade, and this was well within the bounds of immediate possibility, French merchants would secure the lion's share of the silver and dyestuffs of the Spanish Indies and the bulk of Spain's wool exports. This, in turn, should enable France to capture the Ottoman market for fine cloth and assume first place in the commerce of the Near East. France, in other words, was well placed not only to dislocate the Dutch world entrepôt but also to capture Europe's rich trades. Owing to her linens, silks, brandy, and paper, France was also basically a more serious threat than England to Dutch dominance of the direct-transit trade to Spanish America via the Caribbean.

The beginnings of the Franco-Dutch struggle for world-trade hegemony go back to the years immediately preceding the Second Anglo-Dutch War, in which the French backed the Dutch as their nominal allies. Amid great fanfares, Louis and Colbert set up the new French West and East India companies in 1664 and took

---

[77] Dutch exports to England in 1663 were valued at only £491,376 and imports from England at a mere £105,216 (Davenant, *An Account*; 4; Morineau, 'Balance du commerce franco-néerlandais', 173–5.

[78] Eon, *Commerce honorable*, 31, 35; Savary, *Le Parfait Négociant*, 63.

[79] PRO SP 84/219, fo. 285; Aitzema, *Historie*, ix. 240.

[80] Morineau, 'Balance du commerce franco-néerlandais', 175.

[81] *Bronnen ... bedrijfsleven*, iii. 742.

TABLE 6.23. *Dutch exports to France, 1645*

Commodity	Value (livres)	% of total
Lakens, camlets, etc.	6,889,960	32.10
Pepper, spices, etc.	3,193,130	14.90
Refined sugar	1,885,150	8.75
Jewellery, luxury goods	1,835,200	8.55
Timber, masts, ropes, pitch	1,700,170	7.90
Copper, iron, lead	1,500,000	7.00
Arms, gunpowder, etc.	1,235,000	5.80
Dyes, glazes, chemicals	1,035,220	4.85
Drugs	842,080	3.90
Furs, leather, etc.	675,300	3.15
Herring, whale oil, etc.	454,300	2.10
Cheese, butter, etc.	200,010	0.95
TOTAL	21,445,520	100.00

Source: Eon, *Commerce honorable*, 31; Morineau, 'Balance du commerce franco-néer-landais', 173–5.

TABLE 6.24. *Dutch imports from France, 1645**

Commodity	Value (livres)	% of total
Wine, brandy, vinegar	6,192,632	39.5
Grain	3,450,450	21.9
Salt	2,488,750	15.8
Linen	1,583,432	10.1
Silks, woollens, paper	915,525	5.8
Olive oil, prunes	715,177	4.5
Other	355,500	2.3
TOTAL	15,701,466	100.00

* The figures for this year show an untypically high level of grain shipments.
Source: Eon, *Commerce honorable*, 35; Morineau, 'Balance du commerce franco-néer-landais', 173–5.

vigorous steps to promote investment in them within France.[82] The longstanding dispute between France and the Dutch over the colony of Cayenne culminated in 1664, when a French expedition was sent to seize the colony and eject the Dutch by force. Then there was Colbert's tariff-list of 1664, which raised the French duties on incoming Dutch products, moderately as yet in most

[82] *Lettres, instructions et mémoires de Colbert*, ii. 428–9, 437.

cases, but more drastically with respect to East India spices (so as to help the New East India company) and refined sugar (see table 6.25). Particularly insidious from the Dutch point of view were Colbert's efforts to invite sugar-refinery workers, and other skilled men, along with their equipment and techniques, to France. In the first decade of Colbert's mercantilism, twenty to thirty sugar-refineries were set up in France at Nantes, Orléans, Rouen, and Bayonne.[83]

By 1665 the Amsterdam city council had become convinced that the cardinal aim of French economic and colonial policy was to 'damage the trade of this state and, wherever possible, divert our commerce there'.[84] Even so, until the closing stages of the Second Anglo-Dutch War Louis took care to restrain France's mercantilist drive. For, in common with other European rulers, he judged England to be the stronger of the two adversaries, at any rate in fire-power, and he had no intention of helping his northern neighbour become mistress of world trade and navigation. Only with England's defeat, in 1667, did he conclude that there was now no further need to curb Colbert's mercantilist programme. Even before the Anglo-Dutch peace was signed a new and altogether more menacing phase in the maritime and commercial rivalry between France and the United Provinces set in. If the French tariff-list of 1664 had worried the Dutch, Colbert's second tariff-list, proclaimed in April 1667, proved a much greater shock. This list was extremely drastic in its effects on Dutch trade with France.[85] At a stroke French imposts on Dutch fine cloth, camlets, linen, *says*, and Delftware entering France were doubled, on whale oil—and France was Holland's biggest customer for this product[86]—quadrupled, and on processed tobacco raised seven times.

The regents and the Dutch business community were aghast. Colbert's second tariff-list amounted to a declaration of economic war. To make matters worse France and the United Provinces were also drifting into antagonism on the political front. Louis's

[83] Boissonade, *Colbert*, 151, 174; Gabory, 'La marine', 39.

[84] Brugmans, 'Notulen', 191, 268.

[85] ARH SH 2498, fo. 74; ARH SH 2904/2, Amsterdam *vroed.* res. 6 Nov. 1676; Elzinga, 'Tarif de Colbert', 221–3; Cole, *French Mercantilism*, 308.

[86] Aitzema, *Historie*, ix. 240; *Hollands Ondergang*, 11.

TABLE 6.25. *French tariffs on imports from the Dutch entrepôt, 1664–1713* (livres)

Commodity	1664 (restored 1678)	1667	1687–92	1699 (restored 1713)
Leiden *lakens*	40.00	80.00	80.00	55.00
Leiden camlets	6.00	12.00	12.00	8.00
Says (20 ells)	6.00	12.00	24.00 (1687)	8.00
Dutch linen (15 ells)	2.00	4.00	8.00 (1692)	2.00
Delftware (100 lb.)	10.00	20.00	20.00 (1689)	10.00
Gouda pipes (gross of 144)	5%	—	1.02 (1692)	0.03
Spun tobacco (100 lb.)	13.00	100.00	—	—
Refined sugar (100 lb.)	15.00	22.05	22.05	22.05
Refined white candle wax (100 lb.)	10.00	10.00	20.00 (1688)	11.00
Whale oil (barrel of 520 lb.)	3.00	12.00	12.00	7.05
Soap (100 lb.)	2.00	5.00	5.00	2.00
Cheese (100 lb.)	0.08	0.08	6.00 (1692)	1.05
Butter (100 lb.)	0.06	0.06	6.00 (1692)	0.06
Herring	—	40.00 (1671)	—	—

Sources: ARH SH 2498, fos. 76–9; ARH SH 2904/2, 'Extract uyt de vroetschap der stadt Amsterdam, 6 Nov. 1676'; Elzinga, 'Tarif de Colbert', 221–3, 266–70; Cole, *French Mercantilism*, 308.

blatant aggression against the Spanish Netherlands in 1667 was only halted owing to an Anglo-Dutch–Swedish alliance, in the formation of which Johan de Witt, as Pensionary the leading figure in the States of Holland, played the principal part. Louis was forced to halt his armies for the moment. But he was also incensed against the Dutch and was never to forgive them for their presumption and 'ingratitude'. Franco-Dutch relations, from 1668, deteriorated with every passing month.

French colonial policy also assumed a more directly challenging character after 1667. Initial efforts to establish lodges and develop French trade with India (Surat), Persia, and Madagascar had made only modest progress.[87] By the late 1660s Louis and Colbert were preparing to adopt an altogether more forceful approach in both the eastern and western Indies. From 1669 the French began regular naval patrols in the Caribbean, especially around the sugar-rich island of Martinique, to break the Dutch carrying

[87] Benoit du Rey, *Recherches*, 156–9.

traffic to the French islands, much as the English had done earlier to cut off the Dutch trade to their colonies.[88] Fanning Portuguese resentment over the Dutch seizure of Cochin and Cananore in 1662–3, Louis urged the Portuguese crown that a Franco-Portuguese condominium in the East Indies would be strong enough to overthrow Dutch hegemony and take control of trade.[89] The Portuguese, however, proved less than enthusiastic to open their Asian ports to the French. Finally, in 1669, Louis sent off an expeditionary force of ten warships and 2,500 men with orders to establish French bases by force in southern India.

The Republic now faced a rising tide of French and also Swedish mercantilist pressure. The question was how best to deal with it. De Witt wished neither to align with France's enemies, Spain and Austria, nor to retaliate against French commerce. As he saw it, confronting French pressure head-on was the most dangerous course the Republic could pursue. He did not believe that the Dutch had any realistic option but to try to mitigate French policy through negotiation.[90] By no means all of the Dutch ruling élite thought like this, however. The dominant factions at Amsterdam and Leiden, encouraged by Coenraad van Beuningen, a leading regent–diplomat with long experience of both France and Sweden, urged that the Republic take a vigorous stand. A States of Holland committee was formed to devise ways of retaliating against France without excessively disrupting Dutch commercial interests in the process. This proved difficult. Zeeland and especially Rotterdam, now the leading Dutch staple for French wine and brandy, opposed retaliation, and one did not ride roughshod over the basic trade interests of particular towns, at any rate not in Holland or Zeeland. But Amsterdam, Leiden, and Haarlem proved adamant.[91] After carefully consulting the merchants and manufacturers, Amsterdam urged the States to suspend imports of brandy, paper, silks, and sail-canvas from France but advised that, until the matter had been given further thought, no action should yet be taken against French wine.[92] After further discussion and

---

[88] Mims, *Colbert's West India Policy*, 195–6.
[89] *Lettres, instructions et mémoires de Colbert*, ii. 456–9.
[90] Rowen, *The Ambassador*, 190.
[91] Franken, *Coenraad van Beuningen's politieke en diplomatieke aktiviteiten*, 92–3.
[92] GA Amsterdam *vroed.* xxvii, fos. 7, 14, 120–1, res. 16 Sept. 1669, 5 Nov. 1669, 27 July 1670, 24 Sept. 1671.

amendments, in January 1671 the States General banned the importing of French brandy and slapped retaliatory tariffs on French silks and sail-canvas, over the vehement objections of Zeeland and Friesland as well as Rotterdam.[93]

Colbert followed all this with avid attention, warning that the only result of Dutch attempts to retaliate against France would be to provoke Louis into taking even more draconian action against Dutch interests. 'L'emportement du sieur Van Beuningen', admonished Colbert, 'causera à son pays le plus grand préjudice qu'il ayt jamais reçu.'[94] Louis was not slow to act. Five days after the States General's measure, the French tariffs on Dutch herring and spices were raised again.

The States General's first package against France was too limited in scope to impress even Dutch opinion, let alone the French. Van Beuningen argued that the measures would damage France and would also stimulate the Dutch silk and sail-canvas industries, as well as the gin distilleries, which could be expected to fill the gap left by the absence of brandy.[95] But many regents were openly sceptical about such half-hearted measures, fearing that the Republic would fall between two stools—inflicting little harm on France while antagonizing Louis to no real purpose. But, despite widespread fears that interfering with the French wine trade would simply divert business to Sweden and Denmark which would then be difficult or impossible to recover,[96] and against the advice of de Witt, Amsterdam and Leiden continued to press for action. Finally, an expedient was found to compensate Rotterdam for its losses, and the States General adopted a second package totally suspending the importing of French wine, vinegar, paper, and sail-canvas. Amongst the regents and foreign diplomats, this bolder step was regarded as quite a legislative feat, proof that the Dutch consultative state was after all capable of tough measures in response to an aggressive challenge. The Dutch prohibition of 1671 on French wine was based on the calculation that France, England, Sweden and Denmark collectively lacked the spare six hundred ships needed to shift France's annual wine exports and

---

[93] Res. Holl. 26 and 30 July, 6 and 11 Dec. 1670.
[94] *Lettres, instructions et mémoires de Colbert*, ii. 500, 506.
[95] Franken, *Coenraad van Beuningen's politieke en diplomatieke aktiviteiten*, 93.
[96] GA Amsterdam *vroed.* xxvii, fo. 137ᵛ. res. 24 Sept. 1671.

the necessary storage facilities to handle such quantities.[97] The gamble was that the Dutch entrepôt was still indispensable. In the expectation of the Holland regents, France's exports would now slump and a severe depression grip France's wine-producing regions, which, in turn, would depress noble and ecclesiastical rents.[98] The German mercantilist writer, Joachim Becher, who was then residing in Holland, estimated that the whole package of Dutch measures against French wine, brandy, vinegar, paper, silks, and sail-canvas would cost France some fourteen million guilders yearly in lost exports.[99] The Franco-Dutch 'guerre de commerce' had begun in earnest.

---

[97] *Lettres, instructions et mémoires de Colbert*, ii. 462–3; van der Kooy, *Hollands stapel-markt*, 13.
[98] *Lettres de Pierre de Groot*, 53.
[99] Becher, *Politischer Discurs*, 696–7.

7
Beyond the Zenith,
1672–1700

THE CRASH OF 1672

During Phase Four (1647–72) the Dutch world trading system reached its fullest point of development. Dutch Baltic commerce, it is true, declined, but this was more than compensated for by expansion elsewhere, especially Spain, the Mediterranean, the Caribbean, and the East Indies. After 1647 the Dutch considerably increased their commerce with these regions and the degree of control that they exerted over a wide range of markets. Dutch industrial capacity and financial power continued to grow. But this was success of a kind that could not long continue. By 1670 the European powers were no longer prepared to tolerate it. English resentment and the abrasiveness of French and Swedish policy after 1667 were evidence enough of the storm clouds gathering above the Republic. Deeply anxious, the Amsterdam city council noted, in October 1671, that

our trade in general, and seaborne commerce in particular, has declined noticeably in recent years and has been diverted from here by other nations; for not only the French but also other kings and states seem more and more to scheme how to ruin what remains of the trade and navigation of these United Provinces and each to take over part of it for themselves.[1]

Although customs returns show that there was in fact no decline in actual levels of trade as yet, immediate prospects for the Dutch entrepôt looked precarious in the extreme. France, its army at a peak of readiness, was drifting towards war with the Republic and there was every likelihood that England or Sweden, or both, would join in the French attack. By early 1672 the Amsterdam Exchange

[1] GA Amsterdam *vroed.* xxvii, fo. 142, res. 8 Oct. 1671; nevertheless, Dutch customs revenues in the years 1668–71 remained at a high level (see table 6.22).

was acutely jittery. Share prices began to slide. The English resumed their harassment of Dutch ships on the high seas. Finally, on 6 April 1672 Louis XIV declared war, mobilizing both his army and his navy and prohibiting all trade between France and the Republic. England followed suit the next day. A new phase, Phase Five in the history of the Dutch world entrepôt, had begun.

Louis, at the head of 120,000 men, together with the armies of Cologne and Münster, advanced on the Republic from the east. The English and French battle fleets joined off the Suffolk coast to attack from the west. The combined Anglo-French armada of 146 warships, 34,000 men, and over 5,000 guns was the most powerful naval force ever assembled. The Dutch were heavily outmatched. Nevertheless, surprising the stronger fleet in South-wold Bay on 6 June, de Ruyter managed to damage just enough of the English 'first-rates' to force the cancellation of the planned crossing to the Dutch coast.

But, even without the landing from the sea, the Republic's situation was disastrous. The main Dutch defences collapsed under the impact of the French onslaught from the east. In three weeks Louis conquered three provinces of the Union—Gelderland, Over-ijssel, and Utrecht—and advanced to the borders of Holland. By late June it looked so bad that many of the Dutch regent élite, and doubtless many others, concluded that the Republic was done for, and that there was nothing left but to capitulate and throw themselves on the mercy of the French monarch. Many merchants and their families fled the country.

Defeat and the partial overrunning of the Republic plunged the maritime zone—Holland, Zeeland, and Friesland—into chaos. Refugees choked the roads and waterways. The river trade east-wards stopped. There was a massive run on the banks.[2] Millions of guilders were transferred abroad.[3] Yet, miraculously, the Amsterdam Wisselbank withstood this prodigious draining of funds, saved by the burgomasters' policy of matching a high proportion of nominal deposits with specie and the flight of cash from the eastern provinces.[4] For weeks the Amsterdam Exchange was in the grip of panic.[5] States of Holland bonds fell to 30 per

---

[2] *Bronnen ... Wisselbanken*, ii. 1025–6, 1340.
[3] Burrish, *Batavia illustrata*, ii. 291–2; Barbour, *Capitalism in Amsterdam*, 57–8.
[4] Van Dillen, 'Banque de Change', 178.
[5] Savary des Bruslons, *Dictionnaire universel*, i. 19; Smith, *Tijd-affaires*, 64, 69.

cent of nominal value. WIC shares collapsed almost to nothing. VOC shares plummeted from over 500 to 250, the nadir for the half-century. Work on public buildings ceased, leaving, among others, the huge new Sephardi synagogue of Amsterdam standing half-finished. The art market collapsed, ruining numerous artist–entrepreneurs, Vermeer and van Ostade among them.

The great crash of 1672 temporarily paralysed the entire Dutch trading system in European waters. Prompted by Holland, the States General suspended all navigation out of Dutch ports.[6] The herring and whaling fleets were kept in and the men made redundant. With the seas infested with enemy warships and privateers, it was simply too risky for Dutch merchant and fishing vessels to venture out. The ban was temporarily lifted over the winter of 1672–3 but re-imposed in March 1673 with effect until the following September.[7]

It was the States General, then, in the face of the combined Anglo-French challenge, which forced the almost total cessation of Dutch seaborne traffic in European waters for nearly two years. It was a drastic step to take. But it was one which gained some important strategic advantages for the Republic.[8] This time, in contrast to the first two Anglo-Dutch Wars, Dutch losses at sea were minimal. Enemy privateers were left with nothing to capture. Soon they began to vanish from the seas. 'And, indeed, if there were any,' remarked the English ambassador at Madrid, with reference to their disappearance from Spanish waters, 'they would find no matter to work upon, for the Dutch since the warre are so lost to navigation in these parts that not one merchantman of theirs appears, but daily either English or French are seen going to or coming from the Straights.'[9]

But the cessation of trade and shipping caused huge losses not only to Dutch merchants and seamen, and to Dutch industry, but also to many other countries suddenly deprived of the services the Dutch trading system provided. Exports of Norwegian timber, Polish grain, and Portuguese as well as French salt all stopped for the most part.

Dismay spread among the Dutch merchant colonies abroad.

[6] *Groot Placaet-Boeck*, iii. 298.
[7] Ibid. iii. 300–1.
[8] Valkenier, *'t Verwerd Europa*, 343–4.
[9] PRO SP 94/62, fo. 51ᵛ, Godolphin to Arlington, Madrid, 27 July 1673.

'Some Dutch merchants here', reported the English consul at
Venice in June 1672, 'on opening this weekes letters were observed
to weep when they understood the progressions the French king
had made by land and how their fleet retyred before His Majesty
at sea: I for my part hope to hear ere long those *Hogen Mogens* will
once more write to His Majesty as they did to his royal progenitors,
"We the poor distressed States, etc...." '[10]

International sympathy, as in the previous Anglo-Dutch War,
was strongly on the side of the Dutch. But it was hard to believe
that the Republic could survive as a major political and economic
force. It seemed that the era of Dutch primacy in world commerce
had come to a sudden and catastrophic end. 'Did your Lordship
but see', Lord Arlington was written to from Venice,

> how pitifully ... all the Italians doe look, especially since they perceive
> His Most Christian Majesty (of France) is so near Amsterdam, your
> Lordship would imagine they were all Dutchmen, and in truth such they
> are at bottome, though to do them right, I must confess their fear of
> France more than their love of Holland makes them such. All here give
> that Republic for dispatched.[11]

At Livorno, the fall of Amsterdam was actually announced, a
report, the English consul noted, which 'makes many a sad face'.
In reply to Italian dismay, the English merchantmen in the
harbour spent the day 'firing their guns for joy'. For a time, all
Dutch–Italian trade ceased, for the overland route to Holland
across Germany was blocked also. By August twenty Dutch Levant
ships were laid up in the inner mole at Livorno, 'landing their
goods here and dismissing their men, not daring to go home'.[12]
The crews returned home overland.

Louis XIV's attack on the Dutch Republic in 1672 was inspired
by political and territorial as well as mercantilist considerations.
This was far from being just a 'guerre de commerce' fought with
guns. But this does not mean that the economic and colonial
objectives which France and England had in mind in launching
their war on the Republic were not far-reaching. Braudel objected
that it was futile to imagine that anything fundamental in the
economic relationship between France and the Republic could be

---

[10] PRO SP 99/51, fo. 218, Doddington to Williamson, Venice, 17 June 1672.
[11] Ibid. fo. 230ᵛ, Doddington to Arlington, Venice, 1 July 1672.
[12] PRO SP 98/14, fos. 177, 191.

changed by force of arms.[13] France, he insisted, lacked the shipping capacity to take over the bulk-carrying trade between France and the Baltic and therefore could not overthrow Dutch trade supremacy through war. But this is to miss the essential logic of the situation. Colbert did not consider the bulk trade to be especially important in the struggle for mastery over world trade. His clear objective was to capture the rich trades. Of the four main Dutch rich trades, he believed, with considerable justification, that three were highly vulnerable to French pressure. His list of these, in order of value, is shown in table 7.1.

TABLE 7.1. *Colbert's estimates of the annual value of the principal Dutch rich trades* (guilders)

Dutch Levant Trade	10–12 m.
East India Trade	10–12 m.
Caribbean and Guinea trade	6 m.

Source: Lettres, instructions et mémoires de Colbert, ii. 658–9; *Recueil des instructions*, xxix. *Turquie*, 71; Tongas, *Relations*, 208–9.

In Colbert's view, should the Republic be overwhelmed, France would easily be able to destroy Dutch trade in the Mediterranean using naval power and political means. The States General would be made to withdraw their ambassador from Turkey and consuls from Italy and the Levant. If France applied such pressure, he wrote, 'il est certain que ce commerce passeroit presque entier entre les mains des sujets de Sa Majesté'.[14] In the East Indies it would suffice if France stripped the VOC of 'une ou deux places sur la coste de Malabar', preferably Cochin and Cannanore, and one of the major Dutch strongholds in the Moluccas. 'Avec ces avantages Sa Majesté partageroit avec eux ce commerce, et ses sujets en pourroient profiter tous les ans de 5 à 6 millions de livres.'[15] In the Caribbean and West Africa, if France took Curaçao, St Eustatius, and Tobago from the Dutch, together with one or two main bases on the Guinea coast, preferably Elmina and Cormantine, Louis 'mettroit ce commerce tout entier entre les mains de ses sujets', an optimistic assumption but perhaps partly true.

[13] Braudel, *Civilisation matérielle*, iii. 217–18.
[14] *Lettres, instructions et mémoires de Colbert*, ii. 658–9.
[15] Ibid. ii. 659.

The suspension of Dutch navigation, bulk trade, and fishing continued until the withdrawal of England from the war, without any gains, in February 1674. There was some revival of Dutch Baltic trade during the winter months of 1673 with 359 Dutch ships recorded as entering the Baltic. But, in the rest of Europe, Dutch commercial navigation remained at a virtual standstill. One solitary Dutch ship is recorded as loading salt at Setúbal in the whole of 1673.[16] No Dutch merchant vessels sailed in the Mediterranean. But the paralysis of navigation, bulk trade, and fishing did not involve more than a short interruption in the Dutch rich trades within Europe, despite the blocking of the overland route. Dutch commerce with Spain, albeit on a reduced basis, soon resumed via Hamburg, and on Hamburg ships, just as during the previous Anglo-Dutch War. The convoy of twenty Hamburg ships which reached Cadiz in March 1674 was reportedly crammed with Dutch merchandise.[17] Similarly, we can be sure that the Hamburg convoy which docked at Livorno in August 1673 carried large quantities of Dutch textiles and spices. But the situation was one in which the English, French, Hamburgers and indeed also the Venetians and Genoese inevitably increased their Mediterranean trade at the expense of the Dutch.[18] The first Dutch convoy to reach Italy since 1672 arrived only in 1675.[19]

Colbert's expectations of aborting Dutch world-trade supremacy through war were in fact perfectly feasible. But, in the end, despite the vast odds against the Dutch, France and England failed. A combination of luck and strategy saved the Republic. The sluices were opened along a defensive line from in front of Amsterdam to the Maas. This was the last line of defence and, for a time, there were gaps in it, but it held. When, in 1673, Spain and Austria entered the war against France, Louis was forced to divert much of his strength from Dutch territory. For England, the war proved wretchedly frustrating and was never popular. De Ruyter fought a brilliant defensive campaign, checking the English in a series of battles despite their superior weight in ships and fire-power. Worse still, England's privateers took few prizes. But worst of all was the terrible havoc the Dutch privateers wrought on

---

[16] ARH SG 7014/i, 'Lijste vande schepen', 3 Feb. 1676.
[17] PRO SP 94/63, fo. 49.
[18] PRO SP 98/7, fo. 377; Pàstine, *Genova e l'Imperio Ottomano*, 129, 168–9, 176.
[19] PRO SP 98/16, fo. 144, Bull to Williamson, Livorno, 5 July 1675.

England's shipping. With thousands of Dutch seamen redundant, it proved possible to build up the Dutch privateering fleet to the point that it became a devastating instrument of pressure against England. The Dutch privateers hunted in packs off the east coast of England, in the Channel, around the coasts of France and Spain, in the Mediterranean, and in Caribbean and North American waters. Everywhere the losses were heavy.

One of the blackspots was the coastline around Spain. It became clear early on the way things were going. 'Their privateers,' the English ambassador reported gloomily from Madrid,

which swarme about the sea coasts of Spain, especially off Cape Finisterre and the Bay of Biscay, have had a rich harvest this summer in all these seas, the Ocean, Bay of Biscay and Mediterranean, having taken at least twenty English vessels and some of them richly laden; I have not heard that we have brought into any of these ports one of theirs which proves exceedingly to the prejudice of our honour as well as profit, especially among the people of this countrie who rejoice at our misfortunes in this warre and judge of the disputed successes in the north by those which are undoubted before their eyes.[20]

Ten more English ships were captured off Spain by Dutch privateers in the next two months, the losses continuing over the winter. A heavily manned Smyrna ship, *The Constantinople*, with cargo worth £80,000, was 'shamefully taken' in February 1673 by a little Zeelander with only twelve guns. The Zeelanders were able to operate out of Spanish ports, their running costs being paid by the Dutch merchant houses at Cadiz. In December 1673 a pack of fourteen privateers took up its cruising station off Cadiz. 'With these came out of Holland . . . thirty-six other privateers, dispersing themselves to several stations, of which eight ply on the coast of Portugal, and four came into Corunna.'[21] This group of packs took fourteen English and French prizes on their way out.

Complete figures for England's shipping losses to Dutch privateers are lacking. But enough data are available to give some idea of the scale of the losses. About six hundred English and French prizes were brought into Dutch ports, roughly four hundred of them English, during the years 1672–4, but without counting those brought into Zeeland in 1672 or at any stage into the West Frisian

[20] PRO SP 94/60, fos. 116ᵛ–17, Godolphin to Arlington, Madrid, 14 Sept. 1672.
[21] PRO SP 94/61, fo. 197, Godolphin to Arlington, Madrid, 6 Dec. 1673.

ports.[22] If we allow another two hundred English prizes for those brought into Zeeland in 1672 and into the West Frisian ports, plus at least another fifty for English prizes brought into Spanish ports and perhaps a similar number brought into the ports of Denmark–Norway, it is clear that the Dutch must have captured at least some seven hundred English ships and the real total was probably higher. In England, the memory of the disaster remained vivid for many years. According to Daniel Defoe, writing in 1712, 'in the last war with the Dutch we lost 2,000 sail of ships great and small in the first year'.[23]

In 1672 the Dutch Republic was attacked in overwhelming force by two great powers, France and England, which were determined to strip it of its commercial hegemony and colonies and to weaken it permanently. By June 1672 it seemed impossible that they should fail or that the Dutch world entrepôt should not be largely wrecked. Yet, remarkably, the Republic survived politically and militarily, and with its entrepôt, shipping, and colonies intact. Spanish and Austrian intervention played an important part in this. But the exploits of the Dutch navy and privateers also contributed in a major way to salvaging and, therefore, to reinstating, Dutch world-trade hegemony after 1674. That England, whose merchants were bitterly resentful that the Dutch had 'miserably lessened us in all trades of the world', should have retired from the struggle early in 1674, after losing over seven hundred ships but without gaining anything, not even recovering Surinam or the lost foothold in the Banda Islands, is perhaps the most dramatic of all demonstrations of how fundamental the role of the Dutch state really was in buttressing the Dutch world entrepôt.

THE BALTIC

Dutch world-trade primacy was restored with England's retirement from the struggle in 1674. The Dutch recovered most of the traffic they had previously had; but not all. Overall, Phase Five was one in which Dutch world-trade hegemony was gradually

---

[22] De Bruijn, 'Kaapvaart', 420.
[23] Defoe, *An Enquiry*, 4.

eroded. In the Baltic, the Dutch share was particularly depressed in the years 1672–8 and 1689–97, whilst the Republic was at war with France. Once Dutch ships reappeared in large numbers, following the signing of the Anglo-Dutch peace of 1674, French privateering, based at Dunkirk, became a crucial factor, inflicting heavy losses on both Dutch merchant shipping in the North Sea and the Dutch herring and whaling fleets.[24] Just as happened during the 1621–47 Spanish war, the Dunkirk privateers, now operating under the French flag, forced up Dutch freight and insurance charges. The result was a sharp drop in the Dutch share of the traffic (see table 7.2).

Dutch naval power was vital to the post-1674 revival of Dutch commerce. Once the peace with England was signed, the balance of power at sea was totally transformed. French shipping, already heavily disrupted by the Dutch privateers, was now completely paralysed. Colbert's Compagnie du Nord collapsed.[25] Dutch sea-borne trade, formed into heavily armed convoys, resumed. The Dutch navy checked the French fleet and, at the same time, blunted Swedish mercantilism in the north. In 1667 the Swedish crown had gone back on its 1660 undertaking not to discriminate against Dutch shipping in Swedish ports and had imposed heavy tolls on salt and wine shipped to Swedish ports in vessels neither Swedish nor belonging to the country of origin of the cargo, normally France or Portugal.[26] To Amsterdam and the West Frisian ports this was intolerable.[27] When the Republic's ally, Denmark, joined the war against France's ally, Sweden, the States General did not hesitate to send a large part of the Dutch navy to tip the balance against the Swedes at sea. The strategy succeeded. A combined Dutch–Danish force defeated the main Swedish fleet in June 1676. Dutch and Danish troops were landed on the southern Swedish mainland.

Once England withdrew from the conflict, the Republic had two major objectives in the politico-economic sphere: to compel France to abrogate the detested 1667 tariff-list and to force Sweden to accept 'absolute equality', or something very near it, for Dutch

---

[24] Zorgdrager, *Bloeyende opkomst*, 268; Malo, *Corsaires dunkerquois et Jean Bart,* ii. 418–20.

[25] Boissonade and Charliat, *Colbert et la Compagnie du Nord,* 110–11, 114.

[26] GA Amsterdam *vroed.* xxxii. 95–8, res. 6 Nov. 1676.

[27] Ibid. 95–6.

TABLE 7.2. *Voyages eastwards through the Danish Sound, 1672–1700*

Year	All shipping	Dutch	English/ Scottish	Swedish	Danish/ Norwegian
1672	862	163	6/7	274	—
1673	992	359	5/3	229	—
1674	1,533	652	120/42	254	—
1675	1,335	434	364/73	73	—
1676	1,144	467	408/103	0	—
1677	1,159	599	350/111	0	—
1678	1,153	637	318/71	0	—
1679	1,522	937	327/86	2	—
1680	1,737	832	213/53	212	—
1681	1,924	934	276/50	221	—
1682	1,990	1,001	289/57	215	—
1683	2,196	1,102	325/61	196	—
1684	2,146	1,101	250/76	241	—
1685	2,033	998	265/50	226	—
1686	2,211	1,033	270/50	276	—
1687	2,130	985	265/54	252	—
1688	1,733	1,016	258/66	268	156/173
1689	1,733	795	157/36	205	164/155
1690	1,583	598	77/19	281	228/147
1691	1,703	444	109/37	328	271/134
1692	2,027	561	103/40	373	302/149
1693	2,333	759	99/18	423	325/151
1694	1,905	564	100/8	367	315/137
1695	1,868	538	90/13	369	319/159
1696	1,379	322	86/22	336	306/130
1697	1,344	359	55/19	327	234/128
1698	2,083	866	175/60	334	217/110
1699	2,085	818	236/62	321	214/143
1700	1,419	589	264/74	106	119/106

Source: Bang and Korst, *Tabeller over skibsfart og varetransport*, i. 2–42.

and Swedish shipping carrying to ports under Swedish control.[28] Remarkably, the Republic succeeded in the end on both counts. Thanks to Brandenburg and Denmark, Sweden was badly beaten

[28] Ibid. 98; ARH SH 2806/i, fos. 38ᵛ–41, Pieter de Groot to de Witt, Stockholm, 5 Sept. 1668.

in the Scanian War and was in no position to resist Dutch demands. The Dutch–Swedish maritime treaty of 1679 cancelled the offending shipping regulations,[29] This marked the end of an era of Dutch–Swedish tension. To salvage her empire and strategic position, Sweden had to modify her mercantilist aims. Under the Dutch–Swedish pact of 1681, Sweden broke with France and entered once again into friendly relations with the Republic. It is this which explains the eventual strength of the Dutch Baltic trade revival of the 1680s.

At the end of the 1670s Dutch grain shipments from the Baltic were still at an extremely low level.[30] But during the 1680s a genuine, if temporary, revival did materialize. During the 1680s Dutch shipping once again accounted for 50–60 per cent of the total traffic passing through the Sound. Over a thousand ships entered the Baltic nearly every year of the decade. But the revival lasted only so long as political conditions permitted. As from 1689 France and the Republic were again at war. The Dunkirkers and French navy resumed their attack on Dutch shipping. Once more Dutch freight and insurance charges soared. It was owing to this that the Dutch share of shipping entering the Baltic dropped below the 40 per cent mark for much of the 1690s and in 1696 fell even below 25 per cent (see table 7.2). In the years 1674–9, when both Dutch shipping and that of the Scandinavian powers had been disrupted by war, the English had been the principal gainers. But this time, with England also at war with France, it was the Scandinavians who picked up what the Dutch lost.[31] The 1690s were a decade of vigorous expansion for all the Scandinavian merchant fleets. In the eight years 1690–7, 6,239 Danish, Norwegian, and Swedish vessels passed eastwards through the Sound compared with only 4,145 Dutch vessels.

Through the last two decades of the century, the Republic based its Baltic policy on better relations with Sweden. This helped the Dutch recovery of the 1680s. But it also soured relations with Denmark, which had never ceased to nurture its own mercantilist ambitions. Denmark–Norway was heavily dependent on the Dutch entrepôt. But, like the Swedes, the Danes and Norwegians also keenly resented the ascendancy of the Dutch over their eco-

---

[29] Diferee, *Geschiedenis*, 367–70.
[30] Van Dillen, 'Eenige stukken', 221.
[31] Bang and Korst, *Tabeller over skibsfart og varetransport*, i. 2–40.

nomic life. The great crash of 1672 in the Republic had temporarily paralysed the economy of Denmark–Norway.[32] The only answer was for Denmark–Norway to emancipate itself from Dutch economic tutelage by whatever means were at hand. Since 1645 Denmark had been bound by treaty not to discriminate against Dutch shipping. Nevertheless, various surreptitious expedients had been found to promote the Danish and Norwegian merchant fleets.[33] Then, from 1679, as Dutch–Swedish relations improved, Dutch–Danish relations deteriorated. Finally, in 1682, Denmark swung round and allied with France. An aggressively anti-Dutch mercantilist tariff-list followed in 1683.[34] The Dutch retaliated by suspending imports of Norwegian timber, fish, and pitch. The Danes held out for a time, but were eventually forced to give in. The country was reduced to a virtual standstill. In June 1688 the Danish crown cancelled the 1683 tariff-list and signed a new treaty with the Dutch.[35] This final Dutch–Danish encounter ended the period of mercantilist struggle in the north until well into the eighteenth century. Not until decades later did either Danes or Swedes try again to squeeze the Dutch out by means of discriminatory tariffs and tolls.

Yet the results of the 1683–8 Dutch–Danish 'guerre de commerce' were not altogether satisfactory from the Dutch point of view. The Dutch ascendancy over the economic life of Denmark–Norway was never again to be quite what it had been. Dutch demand for Norwegian timber and masts was in any case now falling off with the decline of the Dutch shipbuilding industry. The classic era of Norway's role as a supplier of raw materials for the Dutch entrepôt was now over. In 1691 an English observer noted that the overseas traffic of Denmark–Norway 'is now considerably diminished since their late quarrel with the Dutch; who thereupon gave over their traffick with them, and transferred it for some time to Sweden. These differences have indeed been since adjusted but it is a hard matter to reduce trade thoroughly into the former channel when once it has taken another course.'[36]

Denmark–Norway's subordination to the Dutch entrepôt

[32] Valkenier, *'t Verwerd Europa*, 344.
[33] GA Amsterdam *vroed.* xxxii. 161.
[34] Johnsen, *Norwegische Wirtschaftsgeschichte*, 333; Christensen, *Industriens historie i Danmark*, 122–3; Glamann, 'Ældste danske kommercekollegium', 134–6.
[35] Christensen, *Industriens historie i Danmark*, 123.
[36] Molesworth, *An Account*, 115.

persisted into the eighteenth century. Around 1700 the Dutch still plied 'more trade with Norway than all other nations put together'.[37] It was still the case that most of Norway's timber products were shipped to Holland and that Norway imported salt, spices, sugar, and other manufactures from Holland. But a certain loosening of grip was also evident. Denmark and Norway had acquired substantial merchant fleets of their own. A considerable part of Norway's timber was now carried in cheaply built Norwegian vessels to Britain and France.[38] Both in terms of the volume of the Dutch traffic with Denmark–Norway, and the degree of leverage exerted, the Dutch hold was being eroded.

THE HERRING AND WHALE FISHERIES

A marked slackening was also evident in the case of the North Sea herring fishery. Here the erosion was due principally to French pressure. Despite the Anglo-Dutch Wars during Phase Four, the Dutch herring fleets had recovered from the heavy blows sustained during the Spanish offensive of the 1620s and 1630s and regained their full vitality. It was only after 1672 that final decline set in. During the years 1675–7 and 1689–97 the Dunkirkers disposed of considerable numbers of Dutch herring busses. The Delftshaven fleet shrank from forty-three busses in 1685, to only twenty-three a decade later.[39] At Schiedam, too, there was some contraction, though not so serious as during the 1630s, as a result of Spanish action.[40] Meanwhile, the largest of the herring fleets, that of Enkhuizen, declined during the last quarter of the seventeenth century from around 250 to 200 busses.[41]

How vital was the North Sea herring fishery to the functioning of the Dutch world-trade entrepôt in the late seventeenth century? It is traditional to insist on the fundamental importance of the herring fishery to the Dutch entrepôt in general and to the Baltic trade in particular. By 1700 the Dutch North Sea herring fishery was only slightly reduced compared with the 1630s and 1640s.

---

[37] Huet, *Mémoires*, 57.
[38] Tveite, *Engelsk-Norsk trelasthandel*, 571–4.
[39] Wätjen, 'Zur Statistik', 159–61.
[40] Feijst, *Geschiedenis*, 105.
[41] Kranenburg, *Zeevisscherij*, 36–7.

But, if our argument that the Baltic trade had greatly receded in importance as a component of Dutch world-trade hegemony by the late seventeenth century is correct, might this not also be true of the herring fishery? It is certainly possible to argue that it is. Each Dutch herring buss provided roughly thirty lasts of salt herring annually which sold at around 5,000 guilders.[42] The total yearly catch, oscillating at around 15,000 lasts, was thus worth between two and three million guilders (see table 7.3). This means that, while the herring fishery was indeed a significant factor in

TABLE 7.3. *Dutch herring exports, c.1680.*

Market	Quantity (lasts)	Approx. %
Northern France, especially Rouen	5,000	34.4
Danzig, Königsberg, Riga	4,000	27.5
Cologne and the Rhineland	2,200	15.1
Overijssel, Gelderland, Westphalia	1,600	11.0
Denmark, Norway, Sweden	1,000	6.9
Hamburg, Bremen	600	4.1
Russia	150	1.0
TOTAL	14,550	100.0

Source: PRO SP 84/219, fo. 285, 'The Hollanders Carry of Herrings Yearly'.

Dutch prosperity, it is a mistake to suppose that herring played anything like so vital a part in the functioning of the Dutch trade system as it had in the sixteenth century or early seventeenth. In the late seventeenth century, the annual value of the Dutch herring catch was worth less than a quarter of that of Leiden's textile output, for example, or of the Dutch returns from the Levant or Cadiz.

The Dutch whale fishery held up well during the last quarter of the seventeenth century, but the period of sustained growth was now over. It reached a peak in the early 1680s when in some years over two hundred Dutch whalers sailed to the Greenland sea; in the peak year, 1682, 186 Dutch whalers sailed, of which nine were lost in the ice; they caught 1,470 whales. Then there was a marked decline in the yield (see table 7.4). This cannot be entirely

---

[42] Centen, *Vervolg*, 265; Feijst, *Geschiedenis*, 108.

accounted for in terms of French raiding against the Dutch whalers, but there is no doubt that this was a major factor. During the Nine Years' War (1689–97), for example, Dutch whaling was depressed to very low levels.[43] At the same time, the signs are that foreign competitors were gradually acquiring the techniques of deep-sea whaling that the Dutch had developed. There arose a thriving whaling industry at Hamburg during the 1670s, which took full advantage of the suspension of Dutch whaling during the years 1672–4.[44] In the early 1680s the Hamburg fleet of around fifty whalers continued to offer serious competition to the Dutch. In the five years 1680–5, when the Dutch whaling industry was at its peak, yielding 290,000 quarters of whale blubber to the Dutch refineries, the Hamburg fleet supplied 29 per cent of this quantity to Hamburg.[45] While the Hamburg yield fell off even more sharply than that of the Dutch in the late 1680s, the Hamburg whaling fleet remained at around fifty ships. During the 1690s the States General forcibly prevented the Hamburg fleet from sailing so as to prevent Hamburg from taking advantage of the temporary collapse of the Dutch industry. Nor was Hamburg the only serious competitor. Louis XIV was aware of the scale of Dutch profits from whale oil and determined to revive the French Basque whale industry.[46] The Danes and English too began to make progress.

Thus, while the Dutch continued to dominate the herring and whale fisheries during Phase Five, many signs of incipient decline were evident. The three Anglo-Dutch wars of the seventeenth century had little effect; but French raiding from 1674 onwards, when the States General lifted its suspension of Dutch navigation, inflicted serious damage. If the Dutch herring fleet gradually contracted during the last quarter of the century, the whaling fleet held up. In 1699, 151 Dutch whalers sailed out to the Greenland sea, a very similar number to the fleet of 1670. But foreign competition was now an increasing factor in both sectors.

---

[43] Zorgdrager, *Bloeyende opkomst*, 262–3, 269.
[44] Ibid.; Baasch, 'Hamburg und Holland', 64.
[45] Zorgdrager, *Bloeyende opkomst*, 262–3, 269.
[46] ARH SH 2497, fo. 344, Heemskerk to SG, Fontainebleau, 9 Oct. 1698.

TABLE 7.4. *Dutch whaling voyages, 1675–1700*

Year	Ships	Blubber (quarters)
1675	148	—
1676	145	—
1677	149	30,050
1678	110	—
1679	126	39,857
1680	148	52,406
1681	172	30,306
1682	186	62,960
1683	242	43,540
1684	246	44,730
1685	212	55,960
1686	189	29,543
1687	194	23,211
1688	214	14,600
1689	163	10,120
1690	117	34,960
1691	(States General suspends whaling)	
1692	32	2,748
1693	89	8,480
1694	62	7,562
1695	96	9,106
1696	100	14,975
1697	111	42,281
1698	140	55,985
1699	151	30,385
1700	173	36,548

Source: Zorgdrager, *Bloeyende opkomst*, 262–3, 269.

THE MEDITERRANEAN

If French mercantilist policy after 1667, backed by French sea
power, made deep inroads into the Dutch trading system in the
north, the impact in the Mediterranean, as one might expect,
was still greater. The most significant single success of Colbert's
ambitious programme was his eventual overthrow of the Dutch
Levant trade. Arguably, this was the most serious setback suffered
by the Dutch entrepôt at the close of the seventeenth century.

Colbert had been chiselling away at the Dutch Levant trade since the 1660s; but it took many years of effort before real results began to show. In 1670 Colbert admitted that the French Levant trade was still in the same 'languissant estat' in which it had languished for half a century. Nor was it only French mercantilism which recognized that the Dutch position in the Ottoman Near East was vulnerable to a trading power able to match Leiden *lakens* with an equivalent fine cloth. Genoa made strenuous efforts to exploit Dutch distress during the 1665–7 war and in the 1670s, while the Venetian Senate, once the Cretan War ended in 1669, was full of plans to establish a Dutch-style fine-cloth industry at Venice and recover some of its former trade with the Levant.[47] The problem for all these trading powers was that of how to acquire the skills on which the success of the Dutch fine-cloth industry was based and to challenge Dutch control of the Spanish wool trade.[48] Where France had the edge over Italy was that she was better placed, notably during the 1665–7 war, to obtain Dutch workers and machinery.

During the 1665–7 war the Dutch and English had paralysed each other's trade with the Mediterranean.[49] This caused a severe slump in the Dutch textile towns: 'if this warre goes on,' Downing had noted, 'and the Turkey yarne and Spanish woolles be kept from coming,' Leiden will soon 'be but a very thin towne'.[50] It was this slump which enabled French diplomats, on Colbert's instructions, to persuade a considerable number of Dutch fine-cloth workers to move with their equipment and families to France.[51] During these years, fine-cloth factories, heavily subsidized by the crown, were established at Sédan and, especially, in the Languedoc, at Saptes and Villenouvette.[52] It did not take long before France had the techniques and had achieved the necessary fineness of texture. By 1670 the Languedoc was manufacturing from Spanish wool 'draps fins de toutes sortes de couleurs,

---

[47] ASV CSM new ser. 125, advice of the cinque savii, Venice, 17 Dec. 1676; Pàstine, *Genova e l'Imperio Ottomano*, 129, 176; Bulferetti, *Assolutismo e mercantilismo*, 219–22.

[48] *BGLH* ii. 98, 303; Masson, *Histoire*, 126; Tongas, *Relations*, 208–9; Sella, *Commerci e industrie*, 64; van Dillen, *Van rijkdom en regenten*, 357.

[49] PRO SP 98/7, Chillingworth to Arlington, Livorno, 23 Aug. 1666, and Finch to Arlington, Florence, 26 Oct. 1666.

[50] Lister, *Life and Administration*, iii. 361.

[51] Tollenaer, *Remonstrantie ofte Vertoogh*, 4; Savary, *Le Parfait Négociant*, 63, 73.

[52] Boissonade 'Colbert, son système', 11–12; Thomson, *Clermont-de-Lodève*, 144–5.

aussi beaux et aussi fins que ceaux de Hollande'.[53] But the quantity
of French fine-cloth output was still quite inadequate for the
capture of the Ottoman market.[54] In the four years 1667–70 for
example, a mere 859 Languedoc fine cloths were shipped to the
Near East. In the whole of the first seventeen years of Colbert's
initiative in this sector (1666–83), a mere 4,506 Dutch-style 'draps
fins' were shipped from France to the Levant, a quantity equivalent to a single year's Dutch fine-cloth exports to Turkey during
the 1680s.[55]

But, despite its extremely gradual beginnings, Colbert's
ambitious project succeeded in the end. All the money and effort
which was invested, the provision of royal loans, free premises,
and export premiums, and Fench diplomats' 'debauching' of
Dutch fine-cloth workers during the depression of the Second
Anglo-Dutch War, eventually paid off. Slowly, production of
Languedoc fine cloth for the Ottoman market rose, attracting
increased levels of imports of Spanish wool. The crucial breakthrough was achieved during the mid-1680s. Around 1686, sales
of French cloth in the Near East began to accelerate. Reports
reached Paris from Constantinople and Smyrna that French fine
cloth was now seriously undermining sales of Dutch *lakens* in the

TABLE 7.5. *Value of western purchases at Smyrna, 1687* (piastres)

Trading nation	Value
English	1,300,000
Dutch	1,100,000
French	254,450
Venetians	79,860

Sources: Aspetti e cause della decadenza economica veneziana, 59–61; Sella, Commerci e industrie, 500.

Ottoman context.[56] The French still had a long way to go. In 1687
the Dutch Levant trade still rivalled that of England and vastly
outstripped that of France (see table 7.5). But a decisive and
irreversible shift had taken place. The ground was ready for the

[53] Boissonade, 'Colbert, son système', 12.
[54] *Lettres, instructions et mémoires de Colbert*, ii. 640–1.
[55] *BGLH* ii. 98, 303; Boissonade, 'Colbert, son système', 16–17.
[56] *Correspondence administrative*, iii. 650; *Recueil des instructions*, xxix. Turquie, 124.

astoundingly rapid expansion of French commerce and influence which took place in the Ottoman Near East over the next two decades.

It was because the Nine Years' War (1689–97) followed immediately after this decisive breakthrough that this conflict proved more destructive of Dutch interests in the Mediterranean than any other war since 1648. In this war, the Republic's adversary deployed both sea power and the right product to supplant the Dutch in the Ottoman market. The rapid progress which the French made in the Mediterranean from this point on was helped by the failure of the Maritime Powers, England, and the Dutch seriously to challenge French naval superiority in the region. For four whole years (1689–93) the French were left in undisputed command from Gibraltar to Smyrna.

The effect of this on the Dutch Levant trade and on the Dutch textile towns was devastating. Once again, shortage of Turkish yarns and Spanish wools threatened to bring Leiden to its knees.[57] In desperation, the Amsterdam merchant élite and the Leiden cloth buyers—twelve Amsterdam and twelve Leiden firms—petitioned the Venetian Senate for permission to transport Dutch textiles across Germany to Venice overland and then to distribute in the Near East from Venice.[58] But the Venetians, alive to the opportunity for themselves, had no intention of raising their ban on the entry of foreign woollen cloth into Venetian territory.

So intense was the pressure of both Dutch and English merchants on their respective governments that by 1693 they were forced to take drastic action to try to break the French grip on the Mediterranean. It was decided to push a gigantic Anglo-Dutch convoy through to Cadiz, Livorno, and Smyrna. This turned out to be one of the key episodes of the Nine Years' War at sea. The Dutch made ready their 'silver fleet' for Cadiz and 'salt fleet' for Setúbal to sail out with their Smyrna convoy. But from the outset the venture was one immense disaster. The Dutch ships were delayed for four months at the Isle of Wight while they waited for the English who were to supply most of the naval escort. Amsterdam's merchants complained that this setback alone cost them half a million guilders in extra wages and provisions for the crews (see table 7.6). The final total of ships that sailed in the

[57] *BGLH* ii. 98–9.
[58] *Relazioni veneziane*, 321–32.

great convoy of 1693, including the Zeeland, Rotterdam, and Hamburg contingents as well as the English, came to around four hundred sail. This forest of shipping, trailed by the main French war fleet out from Brest, was intercepted a short distance from Cadiz. About ninety merchantmen, mostly Dutch, were lost, inflicting millions of guilders of losses on the Dutch entrepôt.

TABLE 7.6. *Monthly wage and food costs of each category of Dutch ships delayed at the Isle of Wight, 1693* (ships/guilders)

'Great ships' for Livorno and Smyrna*	14	31,500
Cadiz 'silver fleet'	22	30,800
Other ships for Spain and Italy	15	18,000
Salt ships for Setúbal	60	48,000
Ships for Lisbon	12	14,400
TOTAL	123	142,700

* The largest and most heavily armed ships used by the Dutch entrepôt.
Source: ARH Levantse Handel 7, 'Memorie vande schepen', 15 Apr. 1693.

The predicament in which the Dutch Levant merchants and textile towns found themselves at the end of the war was, in some respects, even worse than that which they faced between 1689 and 1697. For it now became clear that the Dutch were not going to recover what they had recently lost to the French. On the contrary, what remained of the Dutch share of the Ottoman market was rapidly crumbling under French pressure.[59] During the short interval of peace preceding the outbreak of the next major European war, in 1702, it became clear that a fundamental shift had taken place in the economic life of the Mediterranean world, a shift very much to the disadvantage of the Dutch entrepôt. The Dutch consul at Smyrna reported in 1701 that sales of Leiden *lakens* in Turkey were now down to 2,500 yearly, under half the level of before 1672.[60] The French, by contrast, were now selling more fine cloth in the Ottoman market than the Dutch. In 1698, for instance, the French sold 3,200 rolls of their fine cloth in Turkey.[61] As a result, Marseilles merchants were now stockpiling more mohair yarn as well as Persian raw silk, gallnuts, and coffee than the

[59] *BGLH* ii. 98–9.
[60] Ibid. 99, 303.
[61] Boissonade, 'Colbert, son système', 27.

merchants of Amsterdam. To make matters worse, Dutch merchants, endeavouring to meet the French challenge, were being forced to cut their profit margin on fine-cloth sales in the Levant to the minimum.

Some of the Turkish yarn procured by Marseilles was for use in France. But, after 1697, most was for re-export, generally to Holland, which remained the major European consumer of this raw material.[62] From the moment the Nine Years' War ended, Turkish commodities began to pour into the Dutch entrepôt (often on Dutch ships) from France. (How Colbert would have smiled to think that within a few years of his death the French would be acting as middlemen for the Dutch!) To this the Amsterdam merchant élite raised angry objections. Holland was losing control of the traffic in a key group of commodities. A lively and typically mercantilist debate ensued, which vividly brought out the dilemmas of the Dutch entrepôt at the close of the seventeenth century. The merchants, backed by the colleges of the Levant directorate at Middelburg and Rotterdam as well as at Amsterdam, and by the Amsterdam city council, urged immediate action in the shape of a States General ban on the importing of Turkish commodities into the United Provinces from any country other than Turkey.[63] But there was strong opposition from the textile towns.[64] The representatives of Leiden and Haarlem argued that their citizens had already suffered severely from shortages of mohair yarn and other raw materials over a period of years and that, if the flow of these commodities from France were blocked, the only result would be still greater scarcity and higher prices. The debate ended in deadlock, leaving the Dutch state unable to make any response to the French breakthrough in the Levant trade. In the Near East, the power of the Dutch world entrepôt was now broken. There were still eighteen Dutch factors based at Smyrna in 1702, only a few less than in 1672, but their influence on the commerce of the region was now drastically reduced, as was that of the smaller Dutch merchant colonies at Constantinople, Aleppo, Larnaca, and Tripoli.[65] Meanwhile, French commercial

[62] *BGLH* ii. 305.

[63] ARH Levantse Handel 323, res. Middelburg college, 17 Feb. 1699; *BGLH* ii. 198, 275–6.

[64] *BGLH* ii. 98–9; Israel, 'Phases of the Dutch *straatvaart*', 29.

[65] Bossch-Erdbrink, *At the Threshold of Felicity*, 195; Israel, 'Dutch Merchant Colonies', 100–1.

influence spread rapidly not only in Asia Minor but also in Syria, Palestine, and Egypt. The French captured control of the traffic in cottons and coffee as well as in mohair yarn. In the sudden upsurge of the coffee trade from the Red Sea, via Egypt, to the west characteristic of this period, the Dutch played little part.[66] By the early eighteenth century the French largely dominated the scene from Egypt to Constantinople.

SPAIN AND SPANISH AMERICA

After 1672 the Dutch position held up much better in the Spanish trade than it did in the Levant. In fact, relative both to France and England, the Dutch strengthened their position in the commerce of Spain and Spanish America during the last quarter of the seventeenth century. There seems little doubt that Phase Five was the period of greatest Dutch sway in the Spanish trade and in the transit trade to the Spanish Indies. But how influential was the Dutch entrepôt in the commerce of the Hispanic world? Were Huet and Savary des Bruslons right in claiming that the late-seventeenth-century wars between Spain and France enabled the Dutch, as allies of Spain, to engross the 'meilleure partie du commerce d'Espagne'?[67]

The answer to this question is necessarily a complex one. But what stands out most is that, while the wars of this period undermined Dutch trade in the Levant, it was the French who lost ground in the Spanish and Spanish America trade. When Spain entered the war against France on the side of the Dutch in 1673, French participation in trade with Spain and Spanish America was officially suspended, and, while the Spanish administration by this period was weaker and more corrupt than it had been during the Olivares period, it is evident that a powerful faction at the Castilian court, in collusion with the Dutch, made it its business to root out French commerce.[68] We know that in the years 1673–7 the Spanish *flotas* returning from the Indies were searched for merchandise belonging to French merchants and that very little

---

[66] *BGLH* ii. 461–4.

[67] Savary des Bruslons, *Dictionnaire universel*, i. 930; Huet, *Mémoires*, 98–104.

[68] Van Dillen (ed.), 'Memorie betreffende den handel met Spanje', 171; Girard, *Commerce français*, 273–5.

Spanish American silver was shipped to France either during the war or in the post-war period at least down to 1680.[69] But it is also clear that French participation in the Spanish trade recovered strongly in the 1680s.[70] Finally, during the Nine Years' War (1689–97), the French role was once again cut back drastically.

Thus, if we are to arrive at a viable judgement as to the respective roles of the Dutch and French in the struggle for mastery of the Spanish trade during the last part of the seventeenth century, close attention must be given to the political context and date of each piece of evidence. Van Dillen argued that the Dutch not the French dominated the Spanish trade in this period, relying partly on the evidence of a French report compiled in 1680 which asserts that

Les Hollandois font a present le plus grand commerce d'Espagne et quoyqu'il ne se fabrique pas dans leurs Estats toutes les sortes de marchandises qui y sont nécessaires tant pour l'usage du pays que pour les Indes de la domination des espagnoles, ils ne laissent pas d'y apporter de tout plus facilement et plus abondamment qu'aucune autre nation de l'Europe.[71]

The memorialist goes on to state that France had no share in the direct transit trade to Spanish America, via the Caribbean, a traffic dominated by the Dutch, and that French commerce with both Spain itself and the Spanish Indies had undoubtedly suffered grave setbacks over the last eight or ten years. As we know that the first Spanish fleet to return from the Indies after the end of the war, in 1679, carried twenty-five million pesos in bullion, less than five million of which was for French merchants, there seems little doubt that the Dutch did in fact dominate the scene through most of the 1670s. Van Dillen's mistake was to assume that this evidence is valid also for the 1680s, which, we now know, is not the case.

Most of the historians who have discussed the question of who dominated the Spanish trade in the late seventeenth century, however, have made the opposite mistake to van Dillen and completely ignored the evidence for Dutch dominance in the 1670s and 1690s, preferring to focus on a report of 1686 compiled by the French intendant, Patoulet, who presented a highly favourable

[69] Girard, *Commerce français*, 273–5; Cole, *Colbert*, i. 407.
[70] Savary, *Le Parfait Négociant*, ii. 67.
[71] Girard, *Commerce français*, 448.

TABLE 7.7. *Goods shipped to Cadiz from elsewhere in Europe, 1670 and 1686*

Country of origin of merchandise	1670		1686 (Patoulet)	
	Livres	%	Livres	%
France	12,000,000	29.9	19,990,000	38.4
Italy (via Genoa)	7,500,000	18.7	8,600,000	16.5
United Provinces	6,000,000	14.9	5,150,000	9.9
England	4,500,000	11.2	9,660,000	18.5
Hamburg	1,500,000	3.7	3,150,000	6.0

Sources: Everaert, *Internationale en koloniale handel*, 278–79, 453; Morineau, *Incroyables gazettes*, 326–43.

view of the French participation in the Cadiz trade.[72] Consequently, the currently accepted view is that the French were much the most preponderant nation in the Spanish trade in the late seventeenth century and that (again following Patoulet) the Dutch share was, in fact, less than that of either England or Genoa (see table 7.7).[73]

But there are major difficulties with Patoulet's *mémoire*, quite apart from its having been compiled at a time when there was no political obstruction to French involvement in the Spanish market. In the first place it analyses the Cadiz trade in terms of origin of merchandise rather than in terms of which merchants dealt in what and to whom the profits accrued. Doubtless French exporters to Spain did furnish French commodities almost exclusively. But the Dutch did not operate in this way. Dutch commerce was an entrepôt traffic and part of what was supplied to Spain from the Dutch entrepôt consisted of Flemish or French products. Even the high-value luxury linens which Patoulet himself terms 'holans', which were bleached at Haarlem and generally shipped from Amsterdam, he assigns under 'commerce des flamands' to Cadiz.[74] Secondly, while Patoulet does acknowledge Dutch supremacy in the spice traffic to Cadiz and Spanish America, his estimate of the value of Dutch spice sales in the Hispanic world is surely far too

[72] Everaert, *Internationale en koloniale handel*, 278–81; Kamen, *Spain*, 116–19; Morineau, *Incroyables gazettes*, 300–2.

[73] Everaert, *Internationale en koloniale handel*, 278–9, 453.

[74] Morineau, *Incroyables gazettes*, 338.

TABLE 7.8. *Dutch exports to Cadiz, according to Intendant Patoulet, 1686* (livres)

Commodity	For Spain	For Spanish South America	For Mexico	Total
Brocades and silks	—	1,000,000		1,000,000
Camlets	—	900,000	—	(900,000?)
Leiden *lakens*	20,000	450,000	400,000	870,000
Indian cotton cloth	55,000	175,000	120,000	350,000
Timber, herring, and dairy produce	350,000	—	—	350,000
Dutch linen				300,000
Cinnamon	20,000	70,000	200,000	290,000
Copper utensils				275,000
Leiden *says*	85,000	95,000	85,000	265,000
Other textiles	—	—	—	200,000
Threads and yarns	—	—	—	200,000
Other spices	—	—	—	150,000
Breda hats	—	—	—	25,000
TOTAL				5,175,000

Source: Morineau, *Incroyables gazettes*, 333–4.

low (see table 7.8). If we accept the evidence that the Hispanic world absorbed up to two-thirds of the total quantity of cinnamon which the VOC imported from Ceylon, then even at cost price in Amsterdam Dutch cinnamon sales alone to Spain and Spanish America must have been worth more than a million livres yearly.[75] Thirdly, in listing camlets, possibly the single most successful product furnished by the Dutch entrepôt to the Hispanic lands, Patoulet states only that 900,000 livres worth of this textile were shipped to the South American mainland yearly, omitting all mention of sales in Spain and Mexico.[76] Finally, while Patoulet fully acknowledges the importance of white candle wax, which was imported in prodigious quantities for the churches of Spain and Spanish America, estimating the value of this traffic at four

[75] Morineau, *Incroyables gazettes*, 338; Biblioteca Nacional, Madrid, MS 899, fo. 79ᵛ; Savary des Bruslons, *Dictionnaire universel*, i. 930.
[76] Morineau, *Incroyables gazettes*, 333–4.

million livres yearly, he assigns the whole of this under England's exports while other sources emphasize that it was not the English but the Dutch who supplied this commodity.[77] All considered, then, Patoulet's analysis would seem drastically to underestimate the Dutch role in the Cadiz traffic.

A better guide as to the extent of Dutch involvement are the estimates for bullion returns from the Spanish New World, through Cadiz, to the main commercial centres of Europe which are available for several years (see table 7.9). These statistics still show the French share as being larger than that of the Dutch in some years. But the gap is always much narrower than would be the case were Patoulet's statistics reflecting the real picture, and in other years it was the Dutch who were well ahead. These figures also tally better with other evidence in that they show the returns for England being always behind those for both France and Holland. Nevertheless, here too there is distortion which leads to underestimation of the Dutch role, for much of the bullion remitted to Genoa and Livorno was in fact for the account of Dutch firms allocated for the settling of Dutch balances in Italy and the Levant.[78]

In any case, given that silver returns from Spanish America to the Dutch entrepôt in some years greatly exceeded the returns for France, it is clearly nonsense to argue that, by comparison with the French traffic, Dutch trade with Cadiz occupied 'un rang beaucoup plus modeste'.[79] On the contrary, all the evidence confirms that for the 1670s and 1690s, the Dutch far outstripped the French, and in the 1680s, when the French were not impeded by political factors, the French had to share dominance of the Spanish trade with the Dutch.[80] The bullion returns of 1698, when more than twice as much silver was shipped from Cadiz to Amsterdam as to France, in no way exaggerates the extent of Dutch primacy during the 1690s. For, as in the war of 1672–8, French participation in the Spanish trade was severely disrupted by the Nine Years' War. No doubt an indirect French trade with Cadiz persisted, principally, we learn, via Lisbon and Genoa.[81] The

[77] Ibid. 336; *Correspondance administrative*, iii. 437; Forbonnais, *Mémoires et considérations*, 227.

[78] Barbour, *Capitalism in Amsterdam*, 51; Attman, *Dutch Enterprise*, 37.

[79] Morineau, *Incroyables gazettes*, 265.

[80] Sée (ed.), 'Documents', 47; Girard, *Commerce français*, 452.

[81] Girard, *Commerce français*, 529–30.

TABLE 7.9. *Silver remittances from Cadiz, 1670–1698* (pesos)

Year	For France	For Holland	For Genoa	For England
1670	4,000,000	2,000,000	2,000,000	1,500,000
1681	3,000,000	2,000,000	3,000,000	1,500,000
1682	3,000,000	3,500,000	4,500,000	2,500,000
1685	670,000	3,000,000	—	(very little)
1686	3,100,000	2,300,000	2,600,000	1,500,000
1698	1,600,000	4,000,000	1,700,000	600,000

Source: Girard, *Commerce français*, 445–52.

Leiden burgomasters were greatly perturbed in 1690 at reports of 'very large amounts of wool' seeping across the Pyrenees, via Spanish Navarre, into France and urged the States of Holland to urge Carlos II to urge his viceroy of Navarre to put a stop to this seepage.[82] In Valencia all pretence at observing an embargo on French goods collapsed when the French Toulon squadron bombarded Alicante in 1693 and the viceroy allowed the resumption of French trade.[83] When the Dutch and English ambassadors at Madrid protested to the king, his ministers replied that the king possessed no greater power in Valencia than did his allies' ambassadors! But all this only goes to prove that the Spanish embargo of 1689–97 against French merchandise was much more than an empty formality and that the French had to go to some lengths to keep their Iberian trade flowing, even in the case of outlying regions such as Valencia and Aragon, where Spanish royal control was admittedly very weak. The presumption has to be, and the evidence of the silver returns points clearly to this, that the embargo had considerably more impact in Castile, including the all-important port of Cadiz.

The rapid progress of the Languedoc fine-cloth industry from the mid-1680s and the French breakthrough in the Ottoman fine-cloth market show that the Dutch hold on the Spanish wool trade must have been weaker by the 1690s than at any time since 1648. The Leiden burgomasters were surely right that a good deal of Castilian wool seeped into France via Navarre in the 1690s. The

[82] Res. Holl. 30 Aug. 1690.
[83] PRO SP 94/73, fos. 151, 161ᵛ.

French breakthrough in the Levant also weakened the Dutch role in the Spanish trade by impeding the flow of mohair yarn to Holland, which, in turn, must have cut back Dutch camlet exports to Spanish America. By the 1690s these traditional intruments of Dutch commercial ascendancy in the Hispanic world counted for less than they had formerly.

However, compensating for these setbacks, the Dutch entrepôt was strengthened as a supplier of manufactures to Spain and Spanish America in several other sectors, notably silks, paper, and linen.[84] The rise in Dutch output of fine linens for Spain, especially linen woven in the Twenthe area of eastern Overijssel, may be regarded as a direct consequence of the obstruction to French linen exports caused by the war.[85] In the case of silks and paper, on the other hand, it was the exodus of Huguenots from France to Holland in the 1680s and the boost this gave to the Dutch silk industry which was the main factor. After 1685 the Dutch captured a large part of what had previously been the Spanish market for French silks.[86] So significant was the impact of the Revocation of the Edict of Nantes that French observers during the 1690s generally considered that it was this rather than the war which was the 'plus essentielle cause de la diminution du commerce de France à Cadix'.[87]

In the direct-transit trade to Spanish America via the Caribbean, the Dutch remained pre-eminent through Phase Five but with increasing signs of erosion by the 1690s. Louis XIV, like Charles II before him, did not succeed in his attempt to wreck the Dutch Caribbean trade system by taking Curaçao. In 1672 the English reoccupied St Eustatius and Saba and the French overran the Dutch half of St Martin. But the French attack on Curaçao in March 1673 failed, and later that year de Ruyter was sent out to shore up the Dutch Caribbean empire. De Ruyter failed in his attack on Martinique. But, under the peace with England, the Dutch recovered St Eustatius and Saba and then, in 1676, recaptured Cayenne and Tobago. In their final offensive, at the end of the war, the French retook Cayenne and after a fierce battle

---

[84] Sée (ed.), 'Documents', 48–9; Huet, *Mémoires,* 98–9; Everaert, *Internationale en koloniale handel,* 457.

[85] Girard, *Commerce français,* 352–7; Slicher van Bath, *Samenleving onder spanning,* 201.

[86] Sée (ed.), 'Documents', 48; Savary des Bruslons, *Dictionnaire universel,* i. 930.

[87] Sée (ed.), 'Documents'.

cleared the Dutch from Tobago. But their second attempt on Curaçao, in 1678, ended in dismal failure with the wrecking of the French fleet on the coral reefs off Bonaire.

Curaçao continued to function as the linchpin of the Dutch direct-transit trade to the Spanish Indies. The bulk of the twenty thousand black slaves which the WIC shipped from West Africa in the years 1676–89 were shipped to Curaçao, from where they were distributed around the Spanish Caribbean.[88] Until 1679 Curaçao's role as the slave depot of the Spanish Indies had been essentially informal. It was the resolution of the Council of the Indies, at Madrid in May 1679, to obtain the next five thousand slaves for Spanish America exclusively from Curaçao, excluding shipments from elsewhere, which conferred official Spanish government recognition of what was in effect a Dutch monopoly of supply.[89] Along with the slaves, Curaçao's fleet of barques delivered much of the cinnamon, linen, and brandy, supplied by the Dutch to the Spanish Indies.

The Spanish *asentista*, Don Juan Barroso, who administered the slave asiento for the Spanish crown from 1679, was a partner of the house of Coymans at Cadiz and was rightly regarded as a tool of Dutch interests.[90] In 1682, however, the Council of the Indies awarded the asiento to Don Nicolas Porcio, who was known to be less subservient to the Dutch than his predecessor. The tension which resulted between Porcio and Balthasar Coymans, the leading Dutch merchant at Cadiz, soon led to an open break. To defeat Porcio's scheme of playing the English off against the Dutch, Coymans, backed by Dutch diplomats at Madrid, instigated a campaign to discredit Porcio and wrest the asiento from him.[91] Spanish ministers knew that, by ending the Dutch monopoly and bringing in the English, they could obtain slaves for their colonies more cheaply; but, as against this, they were susceptible to the self-interested Dutch counter-argument that this would widen the scope for contrabandists to smuggle unregistered goods into Spanish America.[92] Egged on by the Dutch resident at Madrid, the Jewish diplomat Francisco Schonenberg, the Spanish crown

[88] Schneeloch, 'Bewindhebber', 71; Goslinga, *Dutch in the Caribbean* (1985), 610.
[89] Scelle, *Traite négrière*, i. 628–30.
[90] Ibid. i, 631.
[91] Ibid.; Wright, 'The Coymans Asiento', 25–6.
[92] Scelle, *Traite négrière*, i. 628–о

transferred the asiento to the house of Coymans in February 1685.[93] The next few years marked the zenith of Dutch commercial influence in the Spanish Indies. Under the terms of the asiento, the firm of Coymans had the right to post resident factors at Porto Bello and Cartagena and employ three travelling factors to ply back and forth between the Dutch and Spanish colonies.[94] A vast network of commercial links was set up, connecting Amsterdam, Madrid, Cadiz, West Africa, Curaçao, Cartagena, and Porto Bello. The Amsterdam agents of what the Dutch called the 'Generale Asiento der slaven' were Jan Coymans, Balthasar's brother and one of the largest Dutch exporters of linen and spices to the Hispanic world, and the Sephardi 'Agent of Spain in the United Provinces', Baron Manuel de Belmonte, a nephew of Schonenberg.[95] The brothers Coymans, descendants of the élite Calvinist merchant family which had fled Antwerp in 1585, also sent several Catholic priests to Curaçao, as they were obliged to do under the asiento, to indoctrinate the slaves which they procured from the WIC in Catholicism prior to their transfer to the mainland.

But the Dutch failed to consolidate their grip on the asiento. Don Nicolas, who was well connected in ecclesiastical circles, was able to whip up a fervent propaganda campaign against the Dutch and the house of Coymans, castigating the latter as scheming Calvinists, friends of Jews, and apt to infect the entire Indies with heresy. This proved highly effective, especially as the Inquisition Suprema at Madrid came to Porcio's support. The countervailing efforts of Coymans, Schonenberg, and Belmonte, backed by the WIC and the Amsterdam city council, proved insufficient to prevent the Spanish king setting up a committee to reconsider the arrangements for the asiento. At bottom the struggle may have been a politico-commercial one, but religion proved the decisive factor. Would, as the governor of Curaçao expressed it,[96] the 'friends of Amsterdam continue with the asiento' or would the friends of the Inquisition come out on top. The answer was a foregone conclusion.

The fourth and last year in which the Dutch asiento was in

[93] Wright, 'The Coymans Asiento', 29–30; Goslinga, *Dutch in the Caribbean* (1985), 163–5.

[94] BL MS Egerton 341, fo. 273ᵛ.

[95] ARH WIC 658, fo. 27ᵛ; further on Belmonte, see Israel, *European Jewry*, 134 *et seq.*

[96] ARG WIC 658, fos. 152–3.

effect was 1688. In that year Coymans consigned 1,189 slaves in two shiploads to Porto Bello and several hundred more to Cartagena.[97] Bullion worth nearly one million guilders, along with letters for Belmonte, at Amsterdam, was shipped from Cartagena to Curaçao in boxes sealed with the cachet of the Inquisition! In April 1689 the king's ministers cancelled the contract with the house of Coymans and reassigned the asiento to Porcio. There was a storm of protest from Amsterdam and The Hague, but Spanish ministers refused to reconsider. The WIC retaliated by proclaiming a free market in slaves at Curaçao and inviting Spaniards from the mainland to come and make their own purchases irrespective of the asiento.[98]

The virtual monopoly of slave shipments to the Spanish Indies which the Dutch had exercised for some thirty years was now at an end. As expected, Porcio, whilst still buying some slaves from the WIC, also arranged for deliveries of slaves to Porto Bello and Cartagena from Jamaica. From 1689 there was a sudden upsurge of traffic both in slaves and other commodities from Jamaica to the Spanish American mainland.[99] For the rest of the century, Spain maintained a balance, purchasing slaves from both the English and the Dutch. The last asiento contract drawn up in the Habsburg era, in 1696, placed the traffic in the hands of the Portuguese Guinea Company. This concern bought from the English, but also, through its Amsterdam agents—Baron Belmonte and the brothers Simon and Luis Rodrigues da Sousa—from Dutch sources.[1] As far as we can judge from the data for slave shipments to Cartagena, which accounted for about a quarter of the total number of slaves imported to the Spanish colonies, the policy was to buy in roughly equal amounts from the English islands and from Curaçao.[2]

But even after Jamaica became a serious rival, in 1689, Curaçao continued for the time being to be the most important depot for the direct-transit trade to Spanish America. The Dutch were better placed than the English to provide the commodities most in demand—linen, spices, candles, silks, and paper. In addition,

[97] ARH WIC 658, fo. 174.
[98] AGI Indiferente de Indias leg. 2845, Belmonte to Los Vélez, Amsterdam, 19 Dec. 1689.
[99] Ibid.; Zahedieh, 'Trade', 218.
[1] ARH WIC 356, fos. 166ᵛ, 287, 290; ARH SH 2548, fo. 257.
[2] Palacios Preciado, *Trata de negros*, 62.

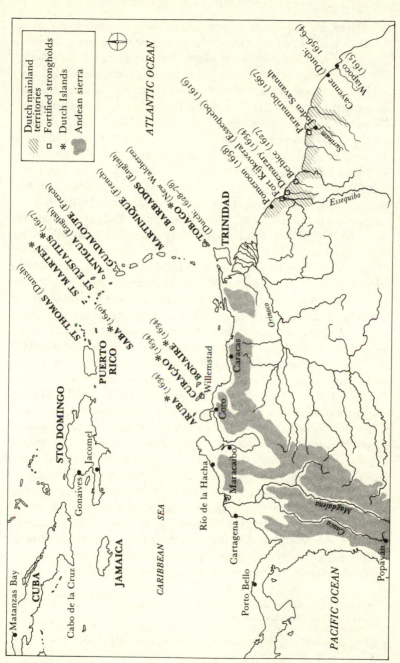

7.1 The Dutch empire in the Caribbean and the Guyanas during the late seventeenth century.

there was an important geographical factor. Curaçao had an excellent harbour located exceptionally close to the Spanish American mainland. But, besides this, the Spanish settlements to which the island lay in close proximity—Coro, Maracaibo, and Río de la Hacha—stood at the entrance to the key passes running south-westwards through the Andes to Popayán, Quito, and Peru.[3] These settlements and passes, it is no exaggeration to say, formed, during the late seventeenth and early eighteenth centuries, one of the most crucial connections in the Dutch world-trading system. This was the channel whereby Dutch manufactures and cinnamon flowed to the heart of Spanish South America. This was well known in Madrid, where there was sporadic talk of establishing a fort at the entrance to the Maracaibo lagune. But no fort was ever built, perhaps due to a realization that it would not be difficult to circumvent it.

How important was the Curaçao traffic by comparison with the regular transatlantic trade with Spanish America via Cadiz? There was much debate about this point in the late seventeenth century, not least in Spain. At Madrid it was rumoured that the Dutch were making vast profits, indeed undermining the official trade, with their contraband business through Curaçao. Opponents of the Coymans asiento alleged that the Dutch, under cover of legal slave shipments, were extracting as much as three million pesos (eight million guilders) yearly from Spanish America.[4] This, it is safe to assume, was a gross exaggeration. Much closer to the mark was a Spanish report which put the value of the contraband trade through Río de la Hacha and Maracaibo at around one million pesos yearly.[5] This fits with Colbert's estimate, in 1672, which was based on advice from Amsterdam, that the value of the Dutch Caribbean and Guinea trades together amounted to about half the value of the Dutch Cadiz trade, that is to around six million guilders yearly,[6] for the Guinea gold traffic brought in a million guilders yearly and so did the Dutch slave trade. After allowing for the sugar trade and other items, this would leave about three million guilders as the yearly value of the transit traffic to the

---

[3] 'Proposiciones del marqués de Variñas', 244–5.

[4] Wright, 'The Coymans Asiento', 36.

[5] Scelle, *Traite négrière*, ii. 66.

[6] Colbert writes 'plus de 6 millions de livres' but he clearly means guilders (*Lettres, instructions et mémoires de Colbert*, ii. 659).

Spanish colonies. As a rough rule of thumb, the Dutch transit trade direct to the Spanish Indies may be reckoned to have been worth about a quarter of the Dutch Cadiz trade.

If Río de la Hacha and the passes to Peru were the main avenue of Dutch commercial penetration of Spanish America in the late seventeenth century, there was still also the old Dutch traffic to Española, Cuba, and Puerto Rico. Here again the main commodities which the Dutch supplied were linens, spices, paper, and candles. The cargo of a WIC barque which sailed to Puerto Rico from Curaçao in 1700, for instance, consisted of a mixture of Flemish, French, and German linens, candles, and pepper.[7] The returns from Peru, Quito, and New Granada to Curaçao consisted largely of silver. From nearby Venezuela, the Dutch imported large quantities of cacao and the high quality tobacco of Variñas.[8] From the Spanish islands the Dutch imported mainly hides and, again, tobacco.[9] Via Cartagena, the Dutch also procured large quantities of Campeche wood and other tropical dyewoods.[10] In addition, there were still some pearls and emeralds from New Granada. At its height, in the 1680s and 1690s, Curaçao boasted a fleet of about eighty barques, each manned by between fifteen and eighty men. A high proportion of these were owned by Sephardi Jews. Curaçao may have been a barren island with few plantations but it was nevertheless the most flourishing and vibrant of all Dutch colonies at the close of the seventeenth century. Few Dutch Protestants lived there and the garrison was small, usually totalling less than two hundred troops. But the port positively swarmed with Dutch seamen, slaves, black freemen, and Jews, as well as crowds of mulatta prostitutes.

The other Dutch islands played only a very minor part in the Dutch Caribbean trade system. Aruba was little more than a cattle ranch. The salt-pan on Bonaire, which had once raised extravagant hopes in the mother country, proved uneconomic to exploit.[11] Bonaire was mainly significant for its maize plantations belonging to the WIC, which were used to feed the slaves housed

[7] ARH WIC 566, fo. 44.
[8] ARH WIC 566 and 567, lists of Dutch cargoes from Curaçao to Amsterdam, 1701–3.
[9] ARH WIC 566, fos. 33–5, 272–4, 401–2.
[10] Ibid., fos. 401–2.
[11] ARH WIC 200, fo. 272ᵛ.

on Curaçao.[12] Tobago, from which the Dutch were driven by the French in 1678, was under Dutch occupation for too brief a time to fulfil its promise as a sugar island and trading base. The remaining three Dutch islands, in the Leewards, were slightly more productive than the Curaçao group but were too small to attain real significance as plantation colonies and, by the 1690s, counted between them only a few dozen sugar plantations.[13] St Eustatius, the most significant, had by this time a modest interloping trade with neighbouring French and Spanish islands but until after 1713 was still only a minor depot compared with Curaçao.

The one major interest of the Dutch in tropical America apart from the transit trade to the Spanish colonies was sugar. The output of the Dutch islands may have been modest, but Curaçao nevertheless played a notable part in supplying Amsterdam with raw sugar. Indeed, almost every ship that sailed from Curaçao to Holland included some sugar in its cargo.[14] Some of this sugar came from the island of St Thomas, which was nominally Danish but where most of the planters were in fact Dutch.[15] Curaçao barques sailed to St Thomas more frequently than to any other Caribbean island. The rest came from a variety of sources including Barbados, where the English authorities never entirely succeeded in stamping out the Dutch interloping trade.

But by the 1680s a large part of the sugar the Dutch obtained in tropical America was coming from their colonies in the Guyanas, especially Surinam. By the 1680s Surinam had turned into an extremely lucrative asset. The number of sugar plantations steadily increased, roughly doubling between 1672 and 1700. By 1700 Surinam was firmly established as one of the most important Dutch colonies, exporting some 10,000 chests of sugar to Holland yearly.[16] This was substantial, far outstripping the output of Essequebo, Berbice, and Demerara, but still rather less than the output of Barbados or Martinique. As Brazil at this time was still exporting about three times as much sugar to Portugal,[17] Amsterdam mer

[12] ARH WIC 200, fo. 67.
[13] Goslinga, *Dutch in the Caribbean* (1985), 128, 131.
[14] ARH WIC 566, fos. 203–5, 405–6, 407–8.
[15] Westergaard, *Danish West Indies*, 209, 121.
[16] *Essai historique sur la colonie de Surinam*, table of exports; Dentz, *Kolonisatie*, 13–16; Bondois, 'Colbert', 54–5.
[17] ARG SG 7017/i, Famars to SG, Lisbon, 29 Oct. 1698.

chants still showed keen interest in buying up raw sugar at Lisbon as well as in London.

THE WEST AFRICA TRADE

One of the areas where the weakening of the Dutch world entrepôt was most evident during Phase Five was West Africa. During the 1670s the French failed to strip the Dutch of the bulk of their Africa trade. But in 1677 a French force, on its way to attack the Dutch in the Caribbean, did capture the Dutch fort at Goeree, which gave the French control of the slave trade in the regions of Joal and Portudal. In 1678 the French also took the fort at Arguim, giving the French Guinea Company control of the Gambia estuary.[18]

Still more serious was the steady increase after 1678 in the number of English, French, Danish, and Brandenburg forts along the Gold Coast, always the main focus of Dutch energy, and the mounting international rivalry for gold, ivory, and slaves. The Dutch were still the foremost European trading power in West Africa down to 1700, but their position was becoming more and more precarious. The Dutch were failing in their efforts to mobilize the Africans against their competitors and, in the circumstances of the post-1678 period, it was no longer politically nor militarily feasible to use force against either the English or the French. The Dutch military apparatus in Africa was in fact very small compared with that of the VOC in Asia. By 1699 the WIC maintained eleven main forts in West Africa plus several subsidiary lodges and two or three patrol vessels (see table 7.10). Altogether the total complement came to under five hundred men. Apart from occasional sorties against the Brandenburgers, scope for strong-arm tactics in these circumstances was very limited. The Dutch therefore concentrated on obstructing other Europeans by means of native proxies. But, despite occasional successes against the English and, in 1687, arranging for the French lodge at Commenda to be burned down, such methods could not check the mounting competition.

---

[18] Chemin-Dupontes, *Compagnies*, 93–4; Ly, *Compagnie du Sénégal*, 141–4.

TABLE 7.10. *The Dutch forts on the Guinea Coast, 1699*

Fort	Year of acquisition	Troops and other employees
Elmina	1637	104
Fort Conradsburg	—	28
Mouré (Fort Nassau)	1612	28
Cormantine (Fort Amsterdam)	1664	28
Appam (Fort Lijtsaemheid)	1697	15
Accra (Fort Crèvecoeur)	1650	32
Axim (Fort St Anthony)	1642	28
Boutry (Fort Batensteyn)	1640	13
Saccondé (Fort Oranje)	1640	13
Chama (Fort St Sebastian)	1640	17
Commenda (Fort Vredenburg)	1687	24
Plus craftsmen with no fixed base		17
TOTAL		347

Source: ARH WIC 573, fos. 35, 55.

Despite the Company's financial difficulties and the fragility of its military establishment in West Africa, the cordon of forts continued to be considered essential. Indeed, as the situation deteriorated, the WIC considered establishing yet more forts.[19] For the directors and their governors on the spot were convinced that forts, and the intricate diplomacy among the Africans that went with them, were decisive in determining share of trade. The disastrous slide in the amount of gold the Dutch were obtaining on the Gold Coast from 1697 (see table 7.11) was considered by the director-general at Elmina to be a direct consequence of new forts established by the English and Brandenburgers.[20]

By the late 1690s the Dutch faced an insoluble dilemma in West Africa. Where they lacked forts, they lacked leverage over the natives. The absence of a fort in a given area meant that the local populace could play the Dutch off against their rivals and push up prices for their gold, ivory, and slaves. But the growing pro-

[19] ARH WIC 97, fo. 56.
[20] ARH WIC 97, fos. 5ᵛ–6, 56–7, director-general to Bewindhebbers, Elmina, 1 Mar. and 8 May 1699.

liferation of forts of all nations was, in any case, proving fatal to the ascendancy the Dutch had previously exercised. The English now had eleven forts on the Guinea Coast, as many as the Dutch, the one erected at Commenda in 1694 being a mere stone's throw from Fort Vredenburg. The Brandenburgisch-Afrikanische Compagnie, which had established its first fort, Gross-Friedrichsburg, on the Guinea Coast near Elmina in 1684, now possessed three forts. According to the WIC's director-general at Elmina, there were stretches of the coast where the intense competition between the European nations had, by 1703, forced up the price of slaves to no less than three times the level of 1685.[21] By 1700 effective

TABLE 7.11. *WIC imports of gold from Guinea, 1676–1702* (guilders)

1676	484,421	1685	515,119	1694	405,798
1677	506,474	1686	619,353	1695	422,470
1678	594,235	1687	669,796	1696	473,561
1679	616,004	1688	587,022	1697	317,232
1680	552,054	1689	513,240	1698	256,163
1681	463,008	1690	707,986	1699	287,970
1682	445,651	1691	682,236	1700	252,503
1683	645,360	1692	552,364	1701	169,573
1684	558,242	1693	451,676	1702	274,238

Source: Schneeloch, 'Bewindhebber', 71.

Dutch primacy in the trade of West Africa was a thing of the past. By that year, according to a well-informed Dutch observer, the Dutch were obtaining at most about half the total amount of gold exported from West Africa, only 20 per cent or so more than the English.[22]

THE EAST INDIES

In Asia, by contrast, the Dutch maintained their supremacy intact until, and beyond, the end of the century. There was, arguably,

---

[21] ARH WIC 98, fos. 38ᵛ–39, director-general to Bewindhebbers, Elmina, 10 Oct. 1703.

[22] Bosman, *Nauwkeurige beschryvinge*, 87–8.

some loss of dynamism evident by the 1690s.[23] The VOC became increasingly passive and static in its operations. In certain sectors, most notably China, there were signs that the English might soon be gaining the upper hand. But overall Dutch trade hegemony in the East was still overwhelming.

By 1675 VOC share prices on the Amsterdam Exchange had recovered to a level not far beneath that of the pre-1672 period. Confidence had returned. And, from then, the level remained fairly static for several decades. There were short-term fluctuations, of course, usually due to brief political scares in Europe such as the crisis of 1683–4 and the likelihood of a new French attack on the Republic in 1688. But, in general, the VOC share price remained stable, even the news of the Dutch defeat at

TABLE 7.12 *VOC share prices on the Amsterdam Exchange, 1671–1690*

Date	Circumstances	Price fluctuations
Aug. 1671	Arrival home of VOC fleet	Rise to 570
June 1672	French invasion of the Republic	250
May 1675	Improving war situation	428/443
Oct. 1682	Rising tension in Europe	394
Feb. 1685	Improving political situation	479
13 Aug. 1688	The peak for the entire 17th century	582
5 Sept. 1688	Market panic owing to fear of war	366
14 Sept. 1688 {	Growing confidence that the Dutch	414
Oct. 1688 {	invasion of England will succeed	420
July 1690	Battle of Fleurus	496/487

Sources: PRO SP 84/199, fo. 5, and SP 84/221, fo. 157ᵛ; BL MS Add. 41815, fo. 258, Add. 41816, fos. 173ᵛ, 236ᵛ, and MS 41821, fos. 254ᵛ, 236ᵛ; Penso de la Vega, *Confusión de Confusiones*, 136, 173; Leti, *Teatro Belgico*, ii. 243.

Fleurus, in Flanders, in July 1690, to the surprise of some observers, wiping only a few per cent off the price (see table 7.12).

The VOC dealt with the major French attack of 1672 convincingly enough. The main French force invaded Ceylon in alliance with the king of Kandy but was blockaded on the east coast and forced to withdraw. The French then attempted the Coromandel coast. There, van Goens, in alliance with the local rajas, encircled the bulk of the enemy at São Thomé, south of

[23] Boxer, *Jan Compagnie*, 59–61; Furber, *Rival Empires of Trade*, 126.

Madras. For the long siege which followed, the VOC brought up reinforcements from Batavia as well as Ceylon. The French finally capitulated in September 1674.[24]

Having learnt that the Dutch in Asia could humiliate France as well as the Portuguese and English, Louis XIV was never to try another large-scale attack on Dutch power in the East. But the French did emerge from the débâcle of 1672–4 with one significant gain: they kept the fort which a subsidiary force had established at Pondichéry. During the 1680s the French were able to consolidate at Pondichéry and, from there, built up a significant trade along the Coromandel coast. As a result, Franco-Dutch tension in the area persisted. With the outbreak of the Nine Years' War, the VOC's headquarters and main military force on the Coromandel coast were moved southwards from Pulicat (Fort Geldria) to the large fortress at Negapatnam, from where the Dutch could more easily squeeze Pondichéry and draw upon reinforcements from Ceylon. This was an advantage in the short run but, as Pieter van Dam noted, a strategic error in the longer term, as it fatally weakened the Dutch position on the northern half of the Coromandel coast.

The Dutch, backed by the local raja, set siege to Pondichéry in August 1693 with seventeen ships, 2,000 seamen, and 1,579 troops. After sixteen days of bombardment, the French capitulated.[25] The Dutch garrisoned Pondichéry; but the VOC's hopes of retaining the stronghold were frustrated at the peace table. At the end of the war, the States General agreed to return Pondichéry to France, though the Dutch held it long enough—until September 1699—to use their occupation as a lever in the arduous Franco-Dutch tariff negotiations of 1697–9.[26]

There was no falling off in the volume of Dutch trade on the Coromandel coast during this period nor in the opening decades of the eighteenth century.[27] Historians rarely make the point, but the Dutch continued to outstrip both the British and the French in the commerce of south-east India right down to the 1740s. Nevertheless, it is possible to speak of a relative Dutch decline in the area due, principally, to the displacement of Dutch power

[24] Heeres and Stapel (eds), *Corpus-diplomaticum*, ii. 505.
[25] Ibid. iv. 58–61; Van Dam, *Beschryvinge* i. pt. 2, pp. 621–2.
[26] See pp. 344–5.
[27] Arasaratnam, 'Dutch East India Company and its Coromandel Trade', 337, 346.

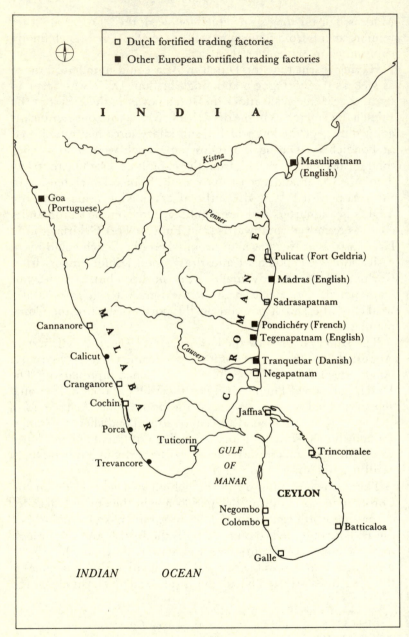

7.2 Dutch power in southern India and Ceylon during the late seventeenth century.

southwards, to Negapatnam. For this, combined with the French retrieval of Pondichéry, led to a crumbling of Dutch influence and trade throughout the central and northern stretches of the coast.[28] North of the Danish factory at Tranquebar, the Dutch ceased to be dominant after 1699. The vacuum was filled by the British and French. A similar process set in at the northern end of the Malabar coast, where the Dutch had been supreme since 1663. There, too, British influence replaced that of the Dutch from around 1700.[29]

Also in Ceylon, the VOC eventually settled for a policy of partial retreat and retrenchment, for the repulse of the French by no means ended the Company's difficulties there. In the 1670s van Goens's grandiose attempt to achieve a total monopoly of trade between the island and India led to an intensifying war of attrition against the king of Kandy, Raja Sinha. Dutch costs in Ceylon began to escalate. Consequently, what had been a healthy balance sheet before turned, by the late 1670s, into one of growing deficits.[30] This in turn undermined faith in van Goens's general political and commercial strategy. At Batavia, the VOC's ruling council split between the adherents of van Goens and those of his great rival, Speelman. Eventually Speelman suceeded van Goens as governor-general in 1681, and ended the war in Ceylon. He ordered the evacuation of some of the territory which van Goens had annexed and modified trade policy, reverting to the pattern of the 1660s whereby the VOC claimed exclusive rights only over exports of cinnamon and elephants. The rest of Ceylon's trade with India, in provisions and cloth, albeit permanently damaged, was again thrown open. Heavy-handed Dutch methods had, by this time, inflicted a degree of impoverishment and deterioration of life comparable with what was to be seen in many parts of the Indonesian Archipelago.[31]

Speelman also reduced the garrisons in Ceylon and southern India and shifted the emphasis of Dutch power in Asia back to the islands. Here the VOC, though broadly dominant, had been some way off from exercising a full monopoly of the spice and pepper trade ever since the English first appeared on the scene during the second decade of the century. Since then there had

---

[28] Ibid. 326.
[29] Das Gupta, *Malabar in Asian Trade*, 18.
[30] Arasaratnam, *Dutch Power in Ceylon*, 96.
[31] Ibid. 176–7.

been many shifts in the relative positions of the Dutch and English in the Archipelago, but, through it all, the English had shown great persistence in retaining enough footholds to procure a meaningful slice of the traffic. After the defeat of the French in southern India in the 1670s, English competition for the spices of the Archipelago was the sharpest thorn in the VOC's side.[32] During the First Anglo-Dutch War, the Dutch had blockaded the English factories. During the Second War the Dutch had captured Pulo Run and Macassar and made considerable progress, where the English were strongest, in Sumatra. As an English factor put it, the ceaseless extension of Dutch influence in the Archipelago was the essential cause of the 'great fermentation between the Dutch and us'.[33]

During the 1670s, when the Dutch had concentrated their forces in Ceylon and southern India, the English had seized the opportunity to recover some of the ground lost in the 1660s. The 1670s marked what has been described as the 'high-tide' of English pepper shipments from Java and Sumatra.[34] The Danes too gained ground, particularly at Bantam, the main point of access for the English in Java. The Muslim sultans of Java and Sumatra, anxious to exploit the displacement of Dutch power away from the Archipelago, were keen to play off the English and Danes against the Dutch. But, after 1678, large reinforcements were shipped out from Holland and Speelman scaled down Dutch strength in Ceylon and India with the design of seizing the initiative in the Archipelago.[35] In 1679 Speelman conquered and put a puppet on the throne of Mataram, compelling the latter to cede the VOC a monopoly of his pepper. Then, in 1682, Speelman sent troops into Bantam, overpowering the sultan, forcing him to shut down the English and Danish factories, and extracting exclusive rights to his spices. After this, Speelman put the squeeze on the sultans of Jambi and Palembang and established Dutch garrisons on Sumatra. With this, the Dutch finally broke the back of English competition in the Indonesian Archipelago. By the mid-1680s all that remained was a trickle of English pepper shipments from West Sumatra.[36]

[32] Van Dam, *Beschryvinge*, ii. pt 2, 276–7, 307.
[33] Chaudhuri, *Trading World of Asia*, 316.
[34] Ibid. 319–20.
[35] Van Dam, *Beschryvinge*, iii. pt. 1, 323; Marperger, *Historischer Kauffmann*, 256–7.
[36] Chaudhuri, *Trading World of Asia*, 319.

By the mid-1680s the VOC was at the peak of its success and prestige as an Asian power. Dutch forces, totalling some eight thousand troops, in sixteen major garrisons, were strung out around the south of the continent from Malabar to Ternate (see table 7.13). Yet, at the very moment when the VOC finally triumphed in its struggle to master the spice and pepper trade of Asia, the underlying shift in Europe's Asian trade, which had

TABLE 7.13. *The Dutch garrisons in the East Indies and South Africa, 1685*

Garrison	Troops
Batavia (Java)	2,043
Ceylon*	1,696
Amboina	667
Banda Islands	564
Macassar	417
Malabar†	411
Ternate	386
Bantam	373
Malacca	303
West Sumatra	256
East Java	220
Coromandel†	205
Cape of Good Hope (and Mauritius)	202
Palembang (Sumatra)	76
Timor	73
Surat	32
In subsidiary lodges	255
TOTAL	8,179

* Dutch troop strength in Ceylon fell from 2,506 in 1678 to 1,654 by 1695.
† Dutch forces in southern India had been roughly halved in the years 1678–82.
Source: Van Dam, *Beschryvinge,* iii, pt. 1, 320–1.

been in evidence for some decades, from spices towards other commodities, became more marked.[37] In the 1650s, when the Dutch completed their conquest of Ceylon, spices fine and coarse had still accounted for something like two-thirds of the total value of Dutch imports from Asia to Europe. By 1672 the share accounted for by spices was down to 40 per cent. Then, in the

---

[37] Glamann, *Dutch–Asiatic Trade,* 13; Prakash, *Dutch East India Company,* 201.

1680s, the shift in favour of other commodities began to accelerate. By 1700 spices and pepper provided only 23 per cent of the total value of the merchandise the VOC shipped to the United Provinces and there was a similar shift of emphasis in the English trade.

This radical restructuring of commerce between Europe and Asia was due in the first place to increasing demand for Asian raw silks, especially those of Bengal, and, in Spanish America as well as Europe, for Indian cotton cloth and calicoes. By the 1690s the rise of the tea and coffee trades and the revival of porcelain shipments from China were also having a significant effect, though Indian textiles remained the decisive factor. The proportion of VOC imports to the United Provinces consisting of silks and cottons rose, from 14 per cent in 1650, to no less than 55 per cent by 1700.[38] By the end of the century, in other words, a preponderant and growing percentage of Dutch imports from the East originated in areas such as Bengal and Gujarat where the Dutch lacked garrisons and which were remote from the centres of Dutch political power. This is another way of saying that, by 1700, the VOC's naval and military establishment in Asia was an inherently less efficient instrument for promoting the Company's trade, and obstructing its rivals, than it had been in the past.

We may be sure that the marked increase in Dutch trade in Indian raw silk from the 1670s onwards was in part a consequence of the Franco-Dutch struggle in Europe and the undermining of the Dutch Levant trade. The slump in Dutch imports of raw silk from the Near East, combined with the convenience of buying raw silk in Bengal rather than Persia, brought Bengal increasingly to the centre of the Company's purchasing strategy. Dutch demand for Asian raw silk was further boosted by the Huguenot influx into Holland after 1685, which lent new impetus to silk weaving at Haarlem and Amsterdam. No doubt the VOC's success in meeting the demand, and dominating the Bengal silk traffic, made life all the harder for Amsterdam's Levant merchants (see table 7.14).

In the case of silk, the shift away from spices posed no particular danger to Dutch trade dominance. The English and French, with their thriving Levant commerce, did not try to compete with the

<hr/>

[38] Glamann, *Dutch–Asiatic Trade*, 13.

TABLE 7.14. *VOC shipments of Bengali raw silk to the Dutch entrepot, 1663–1700* (lbs.)

1663	74,135	1691	121,096
1664	49,896	1692	137,182
1666	74,277	1693	171,326
1669/70	80,563	1694	263,590
1671	120,568	1695	109,260
1679	128,077	1699	170,567
1680	82,703	1700	198,944

Sources: Prakash, *Dutch East India Company*, 218; *Hollandsche Mercurius*.

Dutch in the buying up of Bengal silk.[39] Cottons and calicoes, however, were another matter. Here the competition was intense and increasingly so as these fabrics became fashionable among the middling ranks of society in Europe during the last two decades of the century. Even so, the VOC managed to retain a slight edge over the English, at least in Bengal, down to around 1710. The Dutch were helped by the fact that there was opposition in England from the cloth interest to the importing of finished textiles from India for consumption within Britain. Under an act of 1700, Parliament permitted the English East India Company to ship calicoes for re-export to the continent only. The VOC, on the other hand, while facing opposition from Haarlem to the importing of finished silks,[40] had a free hand in the sphere of cotton cloth and calicoes. The effect of this, according to Charles Davenant, was to give the Dutch more leverage than the English over supply and pricing in Europe, making 'Amsterdam and Rotterdam... the Magazine for the Bengall stuffs and of all calicoes dyed, printed or stained there'.[41]

Bengal, by the 1690s, was playing a pivotal role in the VOC's trade strategy. Of 2.35 million guilders' worth of finished textiles shipped to the United Provinces from Asia in 1697, 55 per cent originated in Bengal, most of the rest coming from Gujarat and Coromandel. As in the past, only a small part of the VOC's purchases in Bengal could be paid for through sales of spices.[42] As

[39] Prakash, *Dutch East India Company*, 217.
[40] GA Amsterdam *vroed.* xxxi. 198, res. 25 Mar. 1677.
[41] Davenant, *An Account*, 36–7.
[42] Prakash, *Dutch East India Company*, 159, 212.

before, the basis of Dutch supremacy in the Bengal trade was the rising flow of Spanish silver from Amsterdam (see table 7.15). One consequence of the changing structure of Europe's trade with Asia in the late seventeenth century, therefore, was to render Dutch Asiatic enterprise even more dependent on the health of Dutch trade with the Spanish imperium than had been the case before.

TABLE 7.15. *Silver shipped from the Dutch entrepôt to the East Indies by the VOC, 1670–1740* (guilders)

1670–80	10,980,000
1680–90	19,720,000
1690–1700	29,005,000
1700–10	39,125,000
1710–20	38,827,000
1720–30	66,027,000
1730–40	42,540,000

Source: Gaastra, 'Geld tegen goederen', 253.

If the rise in European demand for Indian cottons and calicoes contributed to the erosion of Dutch dominance over Asian trade towards the close of the seventeenth century, this trend was reinforced by the rise in Europe's tea and coffee consumption. By 1700 tea and coffee were sufficiently popular in the United Provinces to be exerting a strong adverse effect on beer consumption.[43] The Amsterdam Exchange, where frantic consumption of both beverages had been part of the daily routine for decades, was well aware that these new items represented a significant up-and-coming force in the commodity markets. The VOC and WIC directors knew this too. The VOC re-established its lodge at Mocha in 1696 and, in the same year, introduced coffee cultivation in Java. At the same time, coffee cultivation was introduced to Surinam. But the main supplies continued to come from the Red Sea area, to a large extent via Egypt, where the French had the upper hand. At Mocha, the Dutch, with their cumbersome organization, failed to do as well as the French and English.

The Dutch fared poorly also in the contest for mastery of the burgeoning tea traffic. The tea emanated from China and the

---

[43] GA Haarlem *vroed*. xxi, fo. 63, res. 12 July 1701.

VOC's total failure to re-establish a firm footing in the China trade during the late seventeenth century was perhaps the most significant indication yet that Dutch trade hegemony in Asia was beginning to weaken. It cannot be said that the VOC was insensible to the danger posed by its weak position in China. During the 1680s the directors gave high priority to efforts to break back in. There was talk of doing a deal with Portugal to exchange Cochin, which now seemed less essential to Dutch interests than it had formerly, for Macao.[44] A major VOC embassy, bearing costly gifts, was dispatched to Peking in 1685. But the Chinese emperor remained adamant in offering the Dutch only tightly regulated temporary stays for their factors, refusing permission for permanent trade lodges on the South China coast.[45] Then, in 1689, the VOC directors lost patience with their negotiations with the Chinese court and discontinued these efforts.[46] It was an admission of defeat that was to have major long-term consequences, for the Dutch strategy in the 1690s was to concentrate on attracting tea-carrying junk traffic to Batavia. This left the English and French with the privilege of making temporary stays on the South China coast and buying their tea and Chinese porcelain at source.[47] The English and French rapidly built on their advantage, and by 1701 the English were in permanent residence at Canton. It was perhaps all part of the price which the VOC paid for the ruthless policies of Jan Pietersz. Coen, which had left a lasting legacy of ill will towards the Dutch in China.[48]

THE FRANCO-DUTCH 'GUERRE DE COMMERCE' AFTER
1672

Louis XIV extricated himself from his deadlocked war with the Dutch in 1678 by offering the Dutch maritime towns a major concession: cancellation of the 1667 tariff-list and France's rever-

[44] Israel, 'Diplomatic Career', 188.
[45] Wills, *Embassies*, 162–3.
[46] De Hullu, 'Over den Chinaschen handel', 34–5.
[47] Dermigny, *La Chine et L'Occident*, i. 137–9, 152–4; Jörg, *Porcelain and the Dutch China Trade*, 18–19, 93.
[48] De Hullu, 'Over den Chinaschen handel', 34–5; Wills, *Pepper, Guns and Parleys*, 195.

sion to the list of 1664.[49] After 1678 Franco-Dutch rivalry in the economic sphere eased off for almost a decade. The Dutch had already dropped many of their retaliatory measures against French products in 1674 when they made peace with England, fearful lest otherwise a neutral England should capture too much trade.[50] The rest of the Dutch retaliatory measures were removed in 1678.

An uneasy lull persisted until the late 1680s. Franco-Dutch commercial rivalry remained intense in Spain, the Levant, the East Indies, and many other spheres. There were also periods of acute political tension arising from Louis's insatiable territorial ambitions. But Amsterdam and the Dutch commercial interest were determined not to give up this uneasy peace with France unless, and until, the economic damage inflicted on the Dutch entrepôt by French policy again reached unacceptable levels. Thus, when Louis annexed Luxemburg, sparking off a new European political crisis in 1682–4, but without renewing the economic war against the Dutch, Amsterdam and the commercial interest refused to allow the Dutch state to be drawn into another confrontation with France. The Stadholder, William III, bitterly criticized Amsterdam's attitude. Appearing before the States of Holland, William acknowledged that 'commerce is the pillar of the state' and that Dutch foreign policy must be based on the requirements of Dutch shipping and trade. But, he insisted, if the security of the state was destroyed by French territorial expansion, the ruin of Dutch shipping and trade would assuredly follow.[51]

In essence, the fragile Franco-Dutch peace of the years 1678–88 was based on a deal: Amsterdam and the Dutch commercial interest would not allow the Stadholder to commit the Dutch state to oppose France's creeping expansionism at the expense of Spain and Austria as long as Louis refrained from unleashing a new mercantilist assault on the Dutch trading system. But, despite Louis's own preferences for territory and prestige, it was an understanding unlikely to endure for long. The underlying conflict between French and Dutch mercantile and industrial interests was simply too strong. During the 1680s great resentment against the Dutch built up in the French ports and business circles. Then,

[49] GA Leiden Sec. Arch. 2402, Colbert's cancellation of the 1667 tariff, 30 Aug. 1678; Cole, *French Mercantilism*, 449.
[50] Res. Holl. 15 Sept. and 24 Dec. 1674.
[51] Kurtz, *Willem III en Amsterdam*, 67–8.

in August 1687, on the pretext—which in the opinion of the Amsterdam city council was partly justified[52]—that the Dutch had been shipping some rotting herring to France, Louis banned the importing of any Dutch herring into France except when certified as having been preserved with French salt.[53] Even had the erroneous French notion that their salt was better suited than Portuguese salt to the preservation of herring been correct, this would still have been a stinging blow to the Dutch trading system. For, since the Dutch–Portuguese peace of 1661, the Holland entre-pôt had been geared primarily to the use of Portuguese salt. In fact, this French ban 'dealt such a blow to the trade' that total exports of herring from South Holland had by July 1688 'been reduced by a third'.[54]

Once the fuse of renewed Franco-Dutch economic war was lit, there was no preventing the tremendous consequences which followed.[55] In September 1687 Louis reimposed the 1667 tariffs on Dutch *lakens* and camlets, doubling the duty on both. Outrage swept Amsterdam and Leiden. During the next weeks the agents of the Dutch exporters at Paris, Lyons, Lille, and Metz reported that they could no longer sell any Dutch textiles in France.[56] With great bitterness, Leiden's delegates in the States of Holland complained that this 'heavy impost in effect signifies a complete ban on the sale of our *lakens* in France'.[57]

First the usual diplomatic representations were tried. When these achieved no result, the States of Holland turned their attention, as in 1671, to the question of retaliation. The towns began to consider reintroducing the placard of February 1674, forbidding the importation of French wine, brandy, vinegar, paper, sail-canvas, refined sugar, salt, and glass into the United Provinces, the only French commodities to be left unaffected being certain categories of textiles needed for the Cadiz trade and prunes which were considered indispensable for the navy.[58] The regents of Amsterdam hoped for a time that the mere deliberation of such

---

[52] GA Amsterdam *vroed.* xxxix. 18, res. 13 Jan. 1688.
[53] Cole, *French Mercantilism* 294.
[54] Res. Holl. 31 July 1688.
[55] Arnould, *De la balance du commerce*, i. 188.
[56] GA Leiden Sec. Arch. 2402, 'Extracten uyt brieven raekende belastinge van manufacturen' 1687.
[57] Res. Holl. 18 Mar. 1688.
[58] Res. Holl. 27 July 1688.

measures might suffice to cause Louis to pull back from the brink.[59] But before long came the news of a general embargo of Dutch shipping in French ports. With this even Rotterdam gave up any thought of preserving the peace. Nothing now remained but to fight it out.

Strangely enough, Louis still seems to have imagined that Amsterdam might be induced to help obstruct the Stadholder's bold scheme to land with a large part of the Dutch forces in England. He was counting on what he took to be Amsterdam's deep reluctance to be dragged into war with France and England combined. In the past Amsterdam had opposed William III's anti-French policy. But what the king failed sufficiently to grasp was that for Amsterdam questions of war and peace were essentially matters of maritime and commercial calculation. The French ambassador at The Hague had to explain to his master that, as a consequence of recent French economic measures, 'le commerce de Hollande étoit diminué de plus du quart et que les peuples en estoient extrememement touchés et fort aigris contre la France'.[60] Consequently, Amsterdam was now entirely in accord with the Prince of Orange and the rest of the towns 'qu'ils ne pouvoient rétablir leur commerce qu'en se mettant actuellement en état de faire la guerre'.

The Dutch public may have been indignant at Louis's proceedings but there was also acute anxiety over the prospect of the Stadholder leaving the country with a large part of the Dutch army to invade England just as a general European war was about to break out and a French army, ready for the offensive, was advancing towards the Low Countries. The Amsterdam Exchange became extremely nervous. VOC share prices began to slide but then rose suddenly by 10 per cent on the news that the French forces had veered to the south to engage the Austrians on the Rhine (see table 7.12).

The Dutch ban on French commodities remained in force until the end of the Nine Years' War, in 1697. In the years 1688–97 the Republic waged economic war more systematically than ever before or since. The Stadholder pulled off his English venture and became king of England. England and the Republic could now act hand in hand against France and French products without

[59] GA Amsterdam *vroed.* xxxix. 139–40, res. 21 and 24 Sept. 1688.
[60] *Négociations de Monsieur le Comte d'Avaux*, vi. 176, 180, 198, 211.

fear of diverting business to the other. Together, England and the Republic were also able to put pressure on their allies, Spain and Austria, to join in the blockade of France.[61] The results of Spain's action to cut off trade with France were far from completely satisfactory from the Dutch and English point of view, but nevertheless had a considerable effect. Austria's action was also useful. The Imperial Diet extended the ban on trade with France to the entire Holy Roman Empire, which gave England and the Dutch the excuse to post a joint naval force at the Elbe estuary and prevent Hamburg trading with France.[62] The Nine Years' War was a struggle of armies and navies and, in part, was fought for territory. But it was also the most relentless economic war of the mercantilist era.

But the economic war which England favoured was not quite the same as that desired by the Dutch. The States of Holland had, in fact, never been keen on the idea of a total ban on French commodities and continued to insist on the need for flexibility, which evoked considerable displeasure in London. A few Holland towns, notably Leiden, supported the English concept of a complete prohibition of trade with France.[63] But Amsterdam, Rotterdam, and also Middelburg were firmly opposed to this. Amsterdam was particularly resistant to the proposal for a ban on postal communication to and through France and on the remitting of money to and from that country.[64] Shrugging off accusations that large sums were being remitted to France from Amsterdam, helping to pay for the French war effort, the Amsterdam city council pointed out that a postal ban would seriously compromise Dutch commercial interests in Spain to the advantage of England by forcing Dutch merchants to send their letters for Madrid and Cadiz on the English packet boats to Corunna, instead of by courier through France, which would mean that London merchants would receive news and replies from Spain before their colleagues in Amsterdam.[65] Amsterdam also continued to insist that certain items, such as French wool-cards, silk furnishings for Spain, and prunes, were indispensable.

[61] Res. Holl. 20 Jan. and 20 July 1689, 28 Apr. and 11 May 1690.
[62] Baasch, 'Hamburg und Holland', 68.
[63] Res. Holl. 18 Aug. 1690.
[64] Aglionby, *Quelques considérations*, 6–7; Clark, *The Dutch Alliance*, 80–5.
[65] Res. Holl. 18 Aug. 1690.

The Dutch also refused to ban the consumption of French wine and brandy in the United Provinces as distinct from their importation. The logic of this was that otherwise the Zeeland privateers would not be able to auction off captured French wine and brandy.[66] But it was a notorious fact that this loophole abetted smuggling and some of the lesser provinces, in particular Friesland, became quite incensed about it.[67] That cheating went on on a considerable scale is not to be doubted. Yet this does not mean that the Dutch ban on importing from France did not have an enormous impact. During the 1680s the Dutch entrepôt had been importing some 70,000 vats, or 300,000 oxheads, of wine, worth ten million guilders, from France yearly. From 1689 this total was slashed to a small fraction.[68] The Dutch mercantilist writer Christopher Indise-Raven estimated the quantity of French brandy entering the Republic in 1690 as a result of smuggling and loopholes at only around one-tenth of the 70,000 oxheads which the Dutch entrepôt imported yearly from France during the 1680s.[69]

France suffered severe loss as a result of the allied blockade during the Nine Years' War. Outside the Mediterranean her commerce was largely paralysed. Nevertheless, the French armies held their own on the battle field and the war ended in deadlock. There was no great allied victory. As was to be expected the peace negotiations were arduous. The Dutch had two main war aims: firstly that of securing a 'barrier' of designated towns in the South Netherlands to be garrisoned by Dutch troops indefinitely, which, it was supposed, would reduce Dutch vulnerability to a land attack by France; and, secondly, cancellation of those parts of the French mercantilist programme which were most damaging to Dutch interests. The 'barrier' was conceded. Louis agreed to cancel the discriminatory toll on non-French shipping using French ports known as the '50 sous par tonneau' which had been introduced in the 1660s to help promote French shipping and which had long been a bane to the Dutch business community. However, the French plenipotentiaries refused to concede the 1664 tariff-list outright as they had in 1678. The French argued that cir-

---

[66] ARH Provinciale Resoluties 385, pp. 133–4, 181, 225–6.
[67] Ibid. 237–8, res. States of Friesland, 18 July 1691.
[68] Indise-Raven, *Consideratie*, 3, 12.
[69] Ibid.

cumstances had changed since the 1660s and that a new French tariff-list should be settled through negotiation. The States General nevertheless assumed that they had in essence extracted what was wanted with this clause of the treaty: 'L'on fera un nouveau tarif commun, et suivant la convenance réciproque, dans le temps de trois mois, et cependant le tarif de l'an 1667 sera executé par provision, et en cas qu'on ne convienne pas dans le dit temps du dit tarif nouveau, le tarif de l'an 1664 aura lieu pour l'avenir'.[70] In the Republic this was taken to mean that France acquiesced either in the 1664 list or something approximately as advantageous from the Dutch point of view.

But that is not at all how it turned out. Predictably, the three months of talks settled nothing. When this was over, Louis, bolder now that arms had been laid down, chose to construe the vital clause to mean that the 1664 list should apply only in those instances where the 1667 list had not been superceded by other tariffs imposed subsequently.[71] Since various Dutch products had in act been burdened with still higher duties since 1667—that on Leiden *says* for instance had been raised to twice the 1667 level in 1687 and there had been even more drastic increases on Gouda pipes and cheese—the Dutch were thus cheated of what they thought they had gained. To the consternation of the Gouda pipe manufacturers, a ship which reached France after the expiry of the three-month transition period, its hold bulging with Gouda pipes, finding that its cargo would be charged under the 1687 tariff, sailed home with its cargo still on board.[72] The French attitude aroused immense indignation in the Republic.

However, Louis was willing to negotiate and the Dutch possessed a useful lever in the shape of Pondichéry, the French base in India which the Dutch still retained but which was due to be returned to France under the peace treaty. But the talks made no progress. The plenipotentiaries wrangled at Paris for four hours each session, three times a week, for months on end, but the impasse remained unbroken. Matters were not improved by Louis personally receiving the head of the Dutch delegation, van Heemskerk, at Fontainebleau on 7 October 1698 with no one else

[70] Res. Holl. 5 Oct. 1697.
[71] ARH SH 2497, 'Response au mémoire présenté par les commissaires des États Généraux', Jan. 1698.
[72] ARH SH 2497, fos. 64–5ᵛ, 107–10.

present. 'Le roi soleil' descended to haggling at some length with the Dutchman over the ins and outs of the traffic in whale blubber and Spanish wool.[73]

The most difficult point was the tariff on Leiden *lakens*. Louis insisted that he had to protect his subjects' legitimate interests, refusing to consider a tariff below 60 livres. The Dutch, however, had been instructed by the States of Holland—after consultation with the Leiden city council which, in turn had consulted the cloth manufacturers—not to agree to anything above 50 livres.[74] After months of wrangling 55 livres was proposed. The Dutch side sent word to the States General, which consulted the States of Holland, which referred the matter to the Leiden city council, which again consulted the manufacturers. Finally, the reply worked its way back to Paris. Fifty-five would, after all, be acceptable.[75] But, even with that settled, there was plenty to argue about. It was not until June 1699 that a comprehensive new tariff-list could be drawn up and signed. Pondichéry was returned to the French three months later.

The new French tariff-list, of June 1699, was to remain in force until the outbreak of the next great European war in 1702. The Dutch had little reason to be pleased over how matters had gone. The new tariff on *lakens* was substantially higher than the 40 livres stipulated in 1664, albeit closer to the 1664 than to the 1667 level. Much the same can be said for other items.[76] The French import duty on Dutch camlets was trimmed from 12 to 8 livres, two more than in 1664. But as several tariffs were adjusted from post-1667 levels, the reductions here were quite drastic. Duty on Leiden *says*, for example, was cut from 24 to 8 livres, and on every 100 lbs. of Delftware from 20 livres to 10, the same as in 1664.

INDUSTRY

Phase Five in the evolution of Dutch world-trade primacy was, above all, an era of confrontation with France. In opting for retaliation against French products in 1671, van Beuningen and

[73] ARH SH 2497, van Heemskerk to SG, Fontainebleau, 9 Oct. 1698.
[74] Res. Holl. 23 Dec. 1698; *Bronnen . . . Leidsche textielnijverheid*, v. 102.
[75] *Bronnen . . . Leidsche textielnijverheid*, v. 102.
[76] Arnould, *De la balance du commerce*, i. 188.

his colleagues on the special committee for economic affairs of the Amsterdam city council opened a new era in Dutch economic thought, one characterized by more overtly mercantilist attitudes than had been prevalent in the Dutch context previously.[77] Besides van Beuningen, it was protectionist writers such as Arend Tollenaer and Christopher Indise-Raven who set the tone of Dutch discourse on trade policy in the three closing decades of the seventeenth century.[78]

The central feature in the thought of van Beuningen, Tollenaer, and Indise-Raven is their recognition of the need to make a virtue of necessity and use the economic conflict with France to stimulate industrial development in the Republic.[79] Indeed, Indise-Raven, who goes furthest in this respect, argues that the bulk-carrying trade in French commodities, such as flourished in the 1680s, was not worth having. All those hundreds of shiploads of French wines, he urged, in a memorable passage, had served only to undermine the Dutch brewing and distilling industries: 'let Denmark, Sweden, and other neutral countries collect French wares, wines and brandy in vast and overflowing quantity.'[80] By reducing or interrupting the flow of Franco-Dutch trade, these writers argued, the way would be opened to expand output of silks, paper, canvas, and linen in the Republic as well as Holland's answer to cognac— jenever, or Dutch gin, at the time still known as 'brandy-wine made from corn'. Under van Beuningen's influence the Amsterdam city council's attention focused on means whereby 'foreign industries can be transferred here and those already established developed more and more'.[81] It was assumed, as a matter of course, that it was up to the town councils and States of Holland to show the way, using the machinery of the state, to promote the new silk, paper, and canvas industries and gin distilleries.[82] By 1672 Amsterdam was urging not only retaliation against French products, and measures to stimulate Dutch industries, but a publicity campaign to change public taste, a theme eagerly taken up by Arend

[77] Franken, *Coenraad van Beuningen's politieke en diplomatieke aktiviteiten*, 92–5.
[78] Laspeyres called Indise-Raven the 'Hauptvertreter des aus der Sperre gegen Frankreich enstandenen Schutzsystems' *Geschichte*, 138–9.
[79] Laspeyres, *Geschichte*, 138–9, 141–2; Tollenaer, *Remonstrantie ofte vertoogh*, 3, 14.
[80] Indise-Raven, *Vrankryk verduurt en overwonnen*, 6.
[81] GA Amsterdam *vroed.* xxvii, fo. 23ᵛ, res. 3 Feb. 1670.
[82] GA Amsterdam *vroed.* xxvii, fos. 13ᵛ–15, 23ᵛ–25, res. 5 Nov. 1669 and 3 Feb. 1670; GA Amsterdam *vroed.* xxix. 21–2.

Tollenaer. The regent class, army officers, and the clergy were admonished to eschew French finery and use only textiles manufactured within the Republic.[83] Boards of governors of orphanages, schools, hospitals, and old people's homes were urged to do likewise in respect of those in their charge. The Stadholder was asked to set an example to the public by removing French fabrics from his household and entourage. Tollenaer deplored the love of Dutch women for French fashion, denouncing their taste in dresses and hats as a form of prostitution, and describing shops selling French fabrics as the most pernicious 'whorehouse and foul brothel' in the Republic.[84]

In general, Dutch industries geared to export did expand and grow more competitive internationally during Phase Five, especially those manufacturing items which, down to the 1660s, were obtained from France. Indise-Raven was partly right, though, that the resurgence of the bulk trade with France in the 1680s cancelled out much of the initial progress, particularly in the case of the gin distilleries, with which, it appears, he had special links.[85] The expansion soon extended to North Brabant, the Veluwe, and eastern Overijssel, as well as to Amsterdam, Haarlem, Leiden, Rotterdam, The Hague, and the Zaan.

But was this expansion of export-orientated industrial activity in Holland during the last part of the seventeenth century due primarily to the Republic's recently adopted mercantilist stance or, as was usually assumed by French authors around the turn of the eighteenth century, was it mainly the result of the Huguenot influx into Holland's towns in the 1680s? Le Moine de l'Espine, like Bishop Huet, had no doubt that the Huguenots were the main factor: 'on remarquera que plusieurs manufactures sur tout celle de soye se sont perfectionnées et même fort augmentées depuis que les Protestants françois ont commencé à se retirer en Hollande, et qu'ils y en ont établi plusieurs, qui n'y étoient pas encore connues il y a vingt-cinq ans.'[86] Clearly the impact of the Huguenots on towns such as Amsterdam, Haarlem, Leiden, and The Hague, where they were most heavily concentrated,[87] was considerable.

[83] GA Amsterdam *vroed.* xxix. 21–2, res. 11 Nov. 1672.
[84] Tollenaer, *De Voor-Looper*, 1–4.
[85] Indise-Raven, *Vrankryk verduurt en overwonnen*, 5; Laspeyres, *Geschichte*, 138.
[86] Le Moine de l'Espine, *Négoce d'Amsterdam*, 41; Huet *Mémoires*, 49–50.
[87] Leti assumed that more than a quarter of the immigrants settled in Amsterdam, though he gives a low estimate, 1,200 families out of an estimated total of only 4,000 families (*Teatro Belgico*, ii. 146).

Yet, despite this, the signs are that, with the possible exception of the silk industry, the main stimulus came not from the Huguenot influx but from the economic war between France and the Republic and from Dutch (and paradoxically also French) mercantilist measures. We have seen something of this already in the case of the sail-canvas industry, which first began to flourish in Holland in the 1660s. That the decisive shift from France to Holland occurred before 1685 was later recognized in an English petition of 1720 deploring the supremacy which the Dutch had won in this industry, noting that the

French had in a manner the sole Trade of sail cloath and very little was made in Holland [until the reign of Charles II]. But since then the Dutch have so greatly improved that Manufacture and arrived at such perfection in the making thereof, that at this very day they furnish all their neighbouring nations with canvas for sails, and the French have utterly lost that trade. By which means Holland does now draw from this Kingdom above two hundred thousand pounds a year for this one commodity which might be prevented in giving encouragement to the making of sail cloath in England.[88]

Dutch output of sail-canvas was already up to 60,000–70,000 rolls yearly as early as 1668. Subsequently, production climbed higher and continued to do well down to the 1720s.[89]

Paper is another case where primacy shifted from France to Holland before 1685. In the period before 1672 the Dutch paper industry, still in its infancy, was mainly confined to the Veluwe area of Gelderland and employed at most a few hundred men. France provided the quality paper, including the 8,000 reams (about 4 million sheets) the Dutch shipped each year to Archangel and the 2,000 reams needed for the Swedish market.[90] But, with the States General's 1671 ban on the importing of paper from France, and the inception of new types of paper mill on the Zaan, more expensive and sophisticated than their predecessors, the initiative passed to the Dutch, who now began turning out, in quantity, a paper which in Huet's words 'passe en blancheur celui de France'.[91] By 1700 there were to be thirty-six of the new-style

[88] *Humble Representation*, 1.
[89] *Bronnen ... bedrijfsleven*, iii. 83–4.
[90] Savary, *Le Parfait Négociant*, 88, 105.
[91] Huet, *Mémoires*, 48.

paper mills in the Zaan area, employing some 1,500 men and producing 120,000 reams (60 million sheets) of paper annually.[92] At the same time there was a marked increase in the number of mills in Gelderland, though the latter continued to be smaller, employing only about a third as many men.[93] It is true that the exodus of Huguenots from France imparted fresh impetus to the Dutch paper industry. In the late 1660s the Republic had been importing around 200,000 reams of paper per year from France.[94] After 1678 Dutch paper imports from France resumed and, although the quantity was now smaller, it still acted as a brake on the growth of the Dutch industry. Much of the French industry was in Huguenot hands, notably at Angoulême, one of the principal centres of production. With the Revocation of the Edict of Nantes, in 1685, the industry at Angoulême collapsed, many of the Huguenot work-force emigrating to the United Provinces.[95] This benefited the Dutch industry mainly by reducing the competition. There is little sign that Huguenot *émigrés* in Holland were particularly significant in the evolution of the industry either on the Zaan or in Gelderland.

Another major element in Dutch industrial growth at the end of the seventeenth century was the linen industry, the weaving centred in North Brabant and the Twenthe area of Overijssel and the finishing at Haarlem. Again, there is little sign that the increase in vitality was directly linked with the influx of the Huguenots, who tended not to settle in the Dutch linen-weaving areas. In the third quarter of the seventeenth century, it is true, the Dutch linen-weaving industry had made only modest progress. While Haarlem had retained its primacy in the bleaching of linen to a high standard, the Dutch entrepôt had become increasingly dependent, after 1648, on imports of unfinished linens from Flanders, Westphalia, and Silesia. The main obstacle to Dutch progress in linen weaving, as an English economic writer observed, was that the 'people of Holland eat dear and pay great rents for their houses'.[96] The finishing processes undertaken at Haarlem

[92] Van Braam, *Bloei en verval*, 16; Enschedé, 'Papier en papierhandel', 186–8; van der Woude, *Het Noorderkwartier*, ii. 489–90.

[93] Roessingh, 'Veluwse inwonertal', 120–1.

[94] Ibid.

[95] Enschedé, 'Papier en papierhandel', 186–8; the number of paper mills at Angoulême fell from 60 in 1672 to only 16 by 1700 (Scoville, *Persecution of Huguenots*, 182).

[96] Yarranton, *England's Improvement*, 45.

reportedly accounted for 'not above the tenth part of the labour', though, as the German mercantilist Becher ruefully noted, very much more than a tenth of the profit.[97]

But in its border areas, well away from Holland, the Republic also had zones of low wages and costs where 'victuals are cheap'.[98] What made the difference between the slow progress of the third quarter and the dynamism of the last quarter of the century was the impact of the French wars on the crucial Spanish and Spanish American market (and in the 1690s the English market), these two being much the most important markets for linens.[99] Both in Spain, where French linens gradually lost ground after 1680,[1] and in England, after 1688, the political factor was decisive. It is no accident that the upsurge in Dutch linen weaving, both in eastern Overijssel and in North Brabant, was at its most vigorous in the 1690s, when the United Provinces, England, and Spain were jointly participating in economic war against France.[2] The 1688 Revolution in England inaugurated the golden half-century of the Dutch linen industry.

Another success story which had little connection with the Huguenot influx was the rise of the Dutch gin industry. With the Dutch ban of 1671 on importing French brandy, several Holland town councils took steps to encourage gin distilling and new establishments sprang up at Haarlem, Amsterdam, and especially at Schiedam and Rotterdam, which now emerged as the main centres of this industry. Expansion was interrupted for a time by the lifting of the States General's ban on French brandy imports in 1674, but resumed with the longer prohibition which commenced in 1688. As with linen weaving, the 1690s were a decade of particularly rapid growth. By 1705 there were some forty gin distilleries at Schiedam and almost as many at Rotterdam, besides additional plants manufacturing liqueurs.[3] Having long supplied the copper stills for the French brandy industry, the Dutch had a technological command of distilling techniques which made Dutch

---

[97] Becher, *Politischer Discurs*, 476.
[98] De Vries, 'An Inquiry into the Behaviour of Wages', 85.
[99] Van Bel, *De linnenhandel*, 48–66.
[1] Girard, *Commerce français*, 341–2.
[2] Frenken, *Helmond in het verleden*, 313; Slicher van Bath, *Samenleving onder spanning*, 201.
[3] Hazewinckel, *Geschiedenis*, ii. 300–5; Feijst, *Geschiedenis*, 126–9.

gin cheap, plentiful, and consistent to the point that it began to rival French brandy as a major international export article, becoming popular as far afield as Russia, West Africa, and the Caribbean.[4] Despite a rapid rise in consumption of this drink in the Republic, the great bulk, some 80 per cent of total output, was exported.[5]

The success of the Dutch gin distilleries also had the advantage of bolstering the ailing Dutch Baltic grain trade, for the industry required enormous quantities of grain. Anxious to show that shipping grain for the gin industry benefited the Dutch entrepôt more than did the shipping of French brandy, Indise-Raven demonstrated that, while it needed only eighty-eight ships, of 150 lasts, to shift France's peacetime brandy exports, running at 70,000 oxheads yearly during the 1680s,[6] to transport the 26,250 lasts of grain required to produce the same quantity of gin needed no less than 175 ships of the same size.[7] In addition, he pointed out, the distilleries benefited the home economy by using great quantities of Dutch peat and home-produced copper equipment.

Where the Huguenots did make an impact was in the silk industry. This sector, as we have seen, was already showing signs of vitality before 1685 and was sufficiently important by the 1670s for Haarlem and Leiden to adopt a strongly protective attitude towards the home silk industry.[8] By the time the Huguenots began to arrive in large numbers, in the mid-1680s, Dutch gold and silver brocades already rivalled *lakens* and camlets as a highly lucrative textile export to the Hispanic world.[9] Dutch silks began to undercut French silks in Spain mainly because of their cheapness,[10] and this was due not to the Huguenots but to the VOC's stockpiles of Bengali raw silks. Nevertheless, the stream of silk-workers which arrived in Haarlem and Amsterdam from Tours, Lyons, and Nîmes significantly increased the range, output, and, in some

---

[4] Indise-Raven, *Consideratie*, 12.

[5] Hazewinckel, *Geschiedenis*, ii. 308.

[6] It is worth noting that in the 1660s the Dutch market itself was estimated to consume 30,000 oxheads of French brandy yearly, which suggests that the Dutch entrepôt re-exported 40,000 oxheads to Germany, Russia and the Baltic (GA Amsterdam *vroed.* xxix. 257).

[7] Indise-Raven, *Consideratie*, 12.

[8] GA Amsterdam *vroed.* xxvii, fo. 87, res. 9 Aug. 1674, and xxxi. fo. 198, res. 25 Mar. 1677.

[9] Morineau, *Incroyables gazettes*, 334.

[10] Sée (ed.), 'Documents', 49; Huet, *Mémoires*, 99.

cases, the quality of Holland's silk production.[11] By 1700 the Dutch Republic was one of Europe's leading silk-producing nations.

Not all industries which decayed in France in the late seventeenth century then flourished in Holland. There were certain industries where the Dutch entrepôt offered no particular advantages. A good example is glass. France had long been a centre of the European glass industry, but there was some decline after 1670, especially in north-eastern France.[12] The Dutch towns had long been eager to foment a home glass industry to tap some of the profits being made by the glass-exporters of Liège and France. Like Colbert, the Dutch regents brought in specialist glass-makers from Venice on privileged terms.[13] The ban on the importing of French glass into the Republic in the years 1671–4 led to a mushrooming of new glass-works at Haarlem, The Hague, Rotterdam, Amsterdam, and Muiden.[14] But by 1679, with the return of French glass, most of these had closed down again,[15] for the Dutch entrepôt had no hold over the basic ingredients of glass manufacture. International competition remained intense and the decisive factor in determining competitiveness was wages; and it was precisely here that the Dutch were at a severe disadvantage. A Haarlem glass-manufacturer, lamenting his failure, in 1679, asserted that Dutch glass-workers had to be paid 18 to 20 stuivers, virtually a guilder each day—by no means a high wage in Holland—whereas in Liège, a highly successful glass-manufacturing centre, workers were paid only half as much for the same work.[16] The Huguenot influx and the 1688 ban on French glass produced a new crop of Dutch glass-works. Of seven new establishments in the 1690s, four were located in the east of the country, three at Zwolle and one at Zutphen, where wages were lower than in Holland. But to no avail. The Dutch glass industry never succeeded in becoming viable.[17]

Most Dutch industries which had come up during the middle

---

[11] Van Nierop (ed.), 'Stukken', 180–95; Sée, 'L'Activité commerciale', 19.

[12] Scoville, *Capitalism and French Glassmaking*, 9, 19, 170.

[13] GA Haarlem Gildenarchief 35, Domenico Pallada to Jean Pallada, Murano, 30 May 1687.

[14] GA Haarlem Gildenarchief 35, Anthonie Le Maire,' Propositien wegens glashuys', 1679.

[15] Ibid.

[16] Ibid.

[17] Klein, 'Nederlandse glasmakerijen', 31–4.

decades of the century and contributed to the expansion of the Dutch trade system after 1647 either, as in the cases of Delftware and Gouda pipes, continued to expand after 1672 or else, as in the cases of Leiden *lakens* and the whale-oil refineries, held steady. The one major exception among those industries which buttressed the growth of the Dutch rich trades after 1647 was the camlet industry. Dutch camlet output never fully recovered after 1672 and declined steadily from the 1680s, entering a period of disastrous collapse with the onset of the War of the Spanish Succession in 1702 (see table 7.16). Otherwise, post-1672 contraction in Dutch

TABLE 7.16. *Output of camlets at Leiden, 1667–1702*

1667	50,956	1672	45,500	1697	19,906
1668	57,003	1678	33,894	1699	40,933
1669	67,335	1688	28,162	1700	36,902
1670	54,979	1691	24,474	1701	24,632
1671	63,096	1696	24,795	1702	12,362

Sources: Luzac, *Hollands rijkdom*, ii. 332; Posthumus, *Geschiedenis*, iii. 1181.

industry was mainly evident in traditional sectors which reached back to the sixteenth century and were mainly geared towards the servicing of the bulk trades.

During Phase Five the West Frisian shipping towns—Hoorn, Enkhuizen, and Medemblik—whose prosperity had always depended chiefly on the Baltic bulk traffic, were in full decline.[18] Reduced demand for Baltic freightage was undermining the Dutch shipbuilding industry, at any rate north of the Zaan area. At the same time, the decline in Dutch salt-carrying from western France depressed the salt-refining industry at Dordrecht and Zierikzee. There was, of course, still the Setúbal salt trade, a large part of which continued to be handled by the Hoorn 'salt-fleet'. This traffic recovered in the late 1670s and flourished anew in the 1680s. In 1673 only one, in 1674 thirty-six, and in 1675 forty-five Dutch vessels loaded salt at Setúbal.[19] But during the 1680s Setúbal was, as in the pre-1672 era, visited by over one hundred Dutch ships per year (see table 7.17). In the Portuguese salt trade, the Dutch

[18] Abbing, *Geschiedenis*, 169, 176; van der Woude, *Het Noorderkwartier*.
[19] ARG SG 7014/i, 'Lijste vande schepen en mooijen sout', Feb. 1676; in 1671 the figure was 110, and in 1672, 37.

had an in-built advantage: the treaty of 1661, revised in 1669, guaranteed the United Provinces, or rather the WIC, the bulk of Setúbal's output on special duty-free terms.[20] But possession of

TABLE 7.17. *Voyages to Setúbal to fetch salt, 1680–1689* (ships/year)

Dutch	1,121
English/Scottish	169
Danish/Norwegian	48
Swedish	38
Other	44
TOTAL	1,420

Source: Rau, *Estudos sobre a história do sal português*, 246–7.

Portuguese salt alone was insufficient to guarantee the health of the Dutch salt-refining industry. In the past, the strength of the Dutch salt business had stemmed from its blending of French and Portuguese salt. Shortage of French salt raised prices, reduced output, and led to some jostling between Dordrecht and the Zeeland salt-refining towns. In August 1696, for example, the Dordrecht salt-refiners complained to the States of Holland that their traditional hold on the Rhineland salt market was being threatened by Zierikzee.[21] The Zeelanders were accused of undercutting the Hollanders by illegally admixing banned French salt.

The Dutch Republic was the first European country to have a large urban proletariat and the first in which the urban proletariat formed a large proportion of the total work-force (see table 7.18). As the total population of the Republic amounted to only two million and many women stayed at home or were in domestic service, the adult work-force cannot have been more than about a million, including those at sea or working in agriculture. Well over 100,000 people worked in the main urban industries if we include those employed in construction, and the specialized industries such as food and diamond processing. The full proletariat was of course much larger, as this properly included the seamen, river bargemen, packers, workers in timber mills and yards, and the thousands of prostitutes. Then there were the thousands employed in rural linen weaving in Overijssel and North Brabant.

[20] ARH SG 7014/i, J. Wolfsen to SG, Lisbon, 22 Sept. 1676.
[21] Res. Holl. 16 Aug. 1696.

All considered, it is clear that the proletariat constituted a relatively large proportion of the total work-force.

Given the exceptionally high wage costs that prevailed in the Republic, this proliferation of industrial activity is one of the most impressive features of the Dutch entrepôt during the era of its

TABLE 7.18. *Estimated size of the work-force in the major Dutch industries and fisheries, 1672–1700*

Urban textiles	55,000
Shipbuilding	8,000
Brewing	7,000
Herring fishery	7,000
Whale fishery	7,000
Gouda pipes	4,000
Amsterdam tobacco workshops	3,000
Paper industry (Zaan and Veluwe)	2,000
Delftware and tiles	2,000
Gin distilleries	2,000
Whale-oil refineries	1,000
Salt refineries	1,000
Sugar refineries	1,500
Sail-canvas	1,000
Soap-boiling	1,000
TOTAL	102,500

Sources: Posthumus, *Geschiedenis,* ii. 937; Goedewaagen, *Geschiedenis,* 4; van Braam, *Bloei en verval,* 88; van der Woude, *Het Noorderkwartier,* ii. 488; Wijsenbeek-Olthuis, 'Ondernemen', 71; van Zanden, 'Economie van Holland', 603.

world hegemony. As we have seen, this phenomenon is explained by two key factors: firstly, the control over raw materials and the market leverage that flowed from Dutch hegemony in the rich trades; and, secondly, the incentive to invest in technical innovation occasioned by high wage costs combined with low interest rates.

Visitors to the Republic in the late seventeenth century were greatly struck by the sophistication of Dutch methods and technology. If Paris was Europe's showroom of fashion and furniture, Holland was the display-centre *par excellence* for textile machinery, copper stills, presses, saws, and indeed contraptions and contrivances of every sort. Dutch shipbuilding methods had long been famous, but in the post-1672 period there arose a staggering array of new saleable novelties, ranging from Leeuwenhoek's micro-scopes to grinding machines for processing coffee, chocolate, mustard, and liqueurs. Many of the new Dutch inventions were soon adopted overseas. The new multiple-blade timber saws which Czar Peter the Great inspected whilst staying on the Zaan in 1697, for example, were being adopted in Sweden and Russia before the end of the century.[22]

In the closing decades of the century, the growing reliance of the Dutch entrepôt on the rich trades, and therefore on export industries, was turning Holland into the technical research lab-oratory of the western world. It was a phenomenon manifest in workshops, refineries, and even in the streets. The street-lantern, cased in metal and glass, which burned through the night on a mixture of processed oils, invented by the Amsterdam townscape painter, Jan van der Heyden (1637–1712), who, after his career in art, became one of the outstanding inventors of late-seventeenth-century Holland, was adopted in Amsterdam in the 1670s for the world's first proper system of city street lighting. Within a few years, two thousand street lamps were affixed to wooden posts or the sides of public buildings. By the 1680s the manufacture of street lanterns had become a significant industry, supplying a large number of Dutch and German cities.[23] Van der Heyden also devised water-pumps, which revolutionized Dutch fire-fighting and which were soon also being manufactured for export. The new Amsterdam fire-engines were made 'with long pipes', as an amazed English observer noted, 'as big as a man's thigh which by the assistance of pumps, at which they labour continually for three or four hours, throw up water to the tops of the highest houses and force it three hundred paces over the tiling'.[24]

This was all very impressive. But did the Dutch Republic possess the resources and enough of a technological edge to survive in a hostile world, infused with an increasingly protectionist attitude? So far, a systematic mercantilism which extended also to the industrial sphere had manifested itself only in France under Colbert—and his no less mercantilist-minded and anti-Dutch suc-cessors[25]—and in England. The Dutch had succeeded in coping

---

[22] Åström, 'Technology and Timber Exports', 1–3, 11.
[23] Heikamp-Wagner, *Jan van der Heyden*, 11–14.
[24] *A New Description of Holland*, 43.
[25] Schaeper, *French Council of Commerce*, 63–4.

with this surprisingly well and, in the process, developed an industrial mercantilism of their own as manifested in the thought of van Beuningen, Tollenaer, and Indise-Raven. But, for all that, the Dutch entrepôt was still in essence a world reservoir of commodities which could flourish for only so long as its products enjoyed access to the markets of the world. The Dutch world entrepôt, in other words, was living on borrowed time. It is safe to say that it was bound to decay as soon as protectionist policies were adopted more widely.

8

The Dutch World Entrepôt and the Conflict of the Spanish Succession, 1700–1713

DURING the brief interval of peace between the Nine Years' War (1689–97) and the next great world struggle, which corresponds to Phase Six, prospects for the Dutch trading system were far from reassuring. It was plain to Dutch élite merchants that the Holland entrepôt was entering a period of crisis. In addition to the collapse in the Levant and the loss of grip in West Africa,[1] there were the progress of the English at the Dutch expense in the Caribbean transit trade to Spanish America and the Dutch failure in the new tea and coffee trades. In the Baltic too there was much cause for anxiety. The Dutch conspicuously failed to regain anything like the share of the traffic they had had before 1689. In 1701, for the first time in peacetime, the rivals of the Dutch accounted for well over 50 per cent of the traffic passing through the Danish Sound (see table 8.2).

Yet another disturbing development at the end of the 1690s was the loss of Dutch grip over the economy of the Spanish Netherlands. The southern provinces of the Netherlands had always been crucial to the functioning of the Dutch entrepôt system, and, during the half-century since the peace of Münster (1648), Spain had fully acquiesced in Dutch economic supremacy over the region. The Spanish king, needing Dutch help in his confrontation with France, had adhered to a passive tariff policy in the Low Countries, which had served to facilitate Dutch economic penetration of the southern provinces. Low tariffs had invited a mounting influx of Dutch manufactures, materials, salt, herring, and dairy produce.[2] But, expedient though this was for Spain, and

---

[1] On the dire state of Dutch trade in West Africa, see ARH WIC 97, fos. 267–70, director-general to Bewindhebbers, Elmina, 21 June 1700.

[2] Despretz-Van de Casteele, 'Het protectionisme', 307.

also for Antwerp, which served as the transit point for Dutch goods
entering the South Netherlands,[3] such a situation was bound to
aggravate resentment against Dutch preponderance, especially in
the Flemish textile areas.

Then, in the late 1690s, with Spanish influence at its nadir, the
southern provinces rebelled against their economic subjection. At
the initiative of the pro-French, reforming minister, the Comte de
Bergeyck, representatives from various towns were convened at
Brussels to formulate measures to free the region from economic
tutelage to the Dutch. A package of measures was proclaimed
during 1699 which replaced the existing tariff-list of 1680 (which
was highly favourable to the Dutch) with a list of much higher
tariffs directed against imported refined salt, paper, sugar, and
candles and banned the importation of Dutch *lakens*, camlets, and
other finished textiles.[4] Other measures sought to promote the
bleaching of Flemish unfinished linens within the South Netherlands.
The news aroused fury in the North Netherlands. Zeeland was
particularly incensed by the new impost on imported refined salt,
which was considered an open violation of the terms of the treaty
of Münster of 1648, the basis of the economic relationship between
the two parts of the Netherlands.[5] The States General warned
that retaliation would follow if the offending measures were not
rescinded. When the threat was ignored, the Dutch politico-
commercial machine ground into action: the importing of glass,
paper, woollens, and linen, finished or unfinished, from the
southern provinces into the North Netherlands was suspended.[6]

But most disturbing of all was what was happening in Spain.
On 1 November 1700, Carlos II, sick and childless, finally died.
For decades the statesmen of Europe had been speculating as to
what would happen at his death. The ruling houses of France and
Austria both had claims on the Spanish inheritance. The lapsing
of the Spanish branch of the House of Habsburg seemed likely to
unleash a general conflict for control of the Spanish empire. On
his deathbed, Carlos had chosen the French option. In his last will
he bequeathed his throne and all Spain's vast dominions, in Europe

---

[3] Geyl, 'Een historische legende', 135–7; Craeybeckx, 'Industries d'exportation',
47.
[4] Despretz-Van de Casteele, 'Het protectionisme', 311; de Schryver, *Jan van Brouchoven*, 182–3.
[5] ARH SH 2548, fo. 293, SZ to SG, Middelburg, 29 Aug. 1701.
[6] ARH SH 2547, fos. 291–3, 301; *Groot Placaet-Boeck*, iv. 233.

and the Indies, to Louis XIV's grandson, Philip of Anjou. It seemed that the Spanish crown, the key to the silver of Spanish America and the guarantee of the closure of the Scheldt to seaborne traffic, was about to devolve on a member of the French royal house.

The succession of Philip of Anjou to the Spanish throne implied a radical change in the political and commercial complexion of the entire world. But no part of the world stood to lose more from this change than the Dutch Republic, for the special relationship between the Dutch Republic and Habsburg Spain had, in the international political sphere, been a central pillar of Dutch world-trade hegemony for half a century. That pillar was now gone, and Spain, Spanish America, and the South Netherlands, including the River Scheldt, could all be expected to come within the politico-commercial orbit of France. The Dutch could expect sweeping losses in practically every theatre of world trade.

But what was the alternative to recognizing Philip of Anjou as king of Spain? If war against France alone and with Spain in alliance with the Maritime Powers, had achieved nothing but a gruelling deadlock in the 1690s, what was to be expected if England and the Republic were to try to wage war on France and Spain combined? Either way the outlook seemed disastrous. The Dutch faced a vast, almost terrifying dilemma. The Amsterdam city council, perusing the situation in January 1701, noted all the risks of acquiescing in Philip of Anjou's succession but resolved provisionally that this was better than the dismal alternative: 'it is necessary that war be averted and all the more so in that the burgomasters and council consider that such a war would be utterly ruinous for the commerce and navigation of these provinces.'[7]

It was only gradually, over the course of the next year, that the regents changed their assessment. Over the next months, the position came to seem so dire that it was decided that accepting Philip's succession would be even more ruinous than going to war. First, in February 1701, a French army entered the South Netherlands, forcing the Dutch garrisons stationed there under the terms of the previous peace to withdraw to the Republic. The French now controlled Antwerp and the Scheldt. The anti-Dutch

[7] GA Amsterdam *vroed.* xlv. 103, res. 5 Jan. 1701.

mercantilist measures adopted in the South Netherlands in 1699 were confirmed and extended.[8] In Spain, the atmosphere rapidly turned ominous. The Dutch merchant colonies of Cadiz, Málaga, Alicante, and Bilbao became acutely nervous.[9] In March 1701 the main Amsterdam firms trading with Cadiz instructed their factors to wind down operations and transfer their stock to the warehouses of neutral Genoese and Hamburg merchants for safekeeping.[10] The same menacing atmosphere enveloped the Caribbean. Philip V, the new king of Spain, instructed his colonial governors to permit no more Dutch ships to enter Spanish American ports to deliver slaves or on any other pretext.[11] The governor of Curaçao reported to Amsterdam that the new policy was all too effective and that, with the forcible expulsion of two WIC vessels from Cartagena without receiving payment for slaves they had delivered, and the seizure by the Spaniards of a Dutch ship off Puerto Rico, the Dutch transit trade to the Spanish American colonies had come to a virtual standstill. Finally, an open challenge, Philip V in September 1701 transferred the slave asiento to the French Guinea Company based at St Malo.[12] Spanish America henceforth was to be furnished with slaves by the French.

The Dutch merchant élite was prepared to put up with a lot to avoid war with France and Spain combined but not the loss of the South Netherlands 'barrier' and market, the Republic's hold on the Scheldt, and a large proportion of their commerce with the Hispanic world. Tension rose. There was persistent talk of war. By the autumn of 1701 the Amsterdam Exchange was so jittery that the States of Holland persuaded the States General to intervene and suspend the export of bullion from the Republic except for specially licensed VOC shipments to the East Indies, Danish silver crowns, and *leeuwendaalders* for the Levant trade.[13] By this time, imports of silver as well as cacao, tobacco, hides and Spanish

[8] ARH SH 2548, fos. 19–20, 30–1.
[9] ARH SH 2548, fo. 115, Schonenberg to Fagel, Madrid, 24 Feb. 1701.
[10] ARH SH 2548, fos. 138ᵛ, 155, 173, Dutch consul at Cadiz to SG, 14 and 29 Mar. 1701, and Dutch consul at Alicante to SG, 28 Mar. 1701.
[11] ARH WIC 200, fo. 65, governor of Curaçao to WIC directors, Curaçao, 26 Feb. 1701.
[12] ARH SH 2548, fos. 318ᵛ, 353; Palacios Preciado, *Trata de negros*, 136–8.
[13] Van Dillen, 'Amsterdam als wereldmarkt', 594–6; Jansen, *Koophandel van Amsterdam*, 97.

American dyewoods from Curaçao had slowed to a trickle.[14] Dutch commerce with Spain and the Spanish Netherlands had slackened almost to a halt.

The United Provinces together with England and Austria declared war on both France and Spain in May 1702, unleashing a vast world conflict. The Dutch went to war, subsequently recognizing the Austrian claimant to the Spanish throne, the Archduke Charles, as 'Charles III of Spain', with several aims in view: the Dutch were determined to restore their 'barrier' in the South Netherlands, regain their hold over the Scheldt and the South Netherlands market, and recover their trade with Spain and Spanish America, ensuring that France obtained no special privileges in these key markets. Finally, the Dutch state took it upon itself to compel Louis XIV to concede the 1664 tariff-list in place of the 1699 tariff-list, described in the Dutch declaration of war as 'un tarif beaucoup plus désavantageux'.[15]

The merchants had been expecting war for months. Knowing that prices for French and Spanish goods would soar on the outbreak of war, as they had in 1689, great quantities of commodities from these two countries had been stockpiled at Rotterdam and Middelburg as well as at Amsterdam.[16] To the bafflement of some foreign observers, WIC and VOC share quotations, which had slumped in the years 1700–1, and had fallen on the outbreak of previous wars, now rose.[17] This was because the public expected that war would serve Dutch interests in Spanish America, the Caribbean, and the East Indies better than a 'Bourbon peace'.

Debate as to what 'war commerce' strategy to adopt began at once.[18] Zeeland wanted a comprehensive ban on trade with France. Amsterdam wanted to ban most trade with France but permit most trade with Spain. Rotterdam wanted uninterrupted commerce with France and Spain. England, meanwhile, urged a total prohibition of trade with France and Spain. After more than a year of argument, the States General, in June 1703, finally

---

[14] ARH WIC 200, fo 270, governor of Curaçao to WIC directors, Curaçao, 4 Apr. 1702; ARH WIC 566, fos. 33–505, lists of cargo shipped from Curaçao to Amsterdam in 1701–2.

[15] PRO SP 84/224, fo. 5; Helvetius, 'Mémoire', 191–2.

[16] PRO SP 84/224, fo. 51.

[17] Ibid.

[18] Verhees-van Meer, *De zeeuwse kaapvaart*, 95–7.

banned imports from France except for wool-cards and prunes, from Spain except for wool and Spanish American products, and from the South Netherlands except for Flemish unfinished linen and clays for the Delftware industry.[19] This amounted to a partial ban on trade with France and the South Netherlands but no ban at all worth speaking of on commerce with Spain and Spanish America. But even this partial blockade was found to have such damaging consequences for Dutch trade that the Holland regents refused to go on with it the following year. Even the textile towns now abandoned their old partiality for economic blockades. The Haarlem city council, in May 1704, denounced the 1703 trade ban as of 'not the least use or service but, on the contrary, highly prejudicial and disadvantageous to the state in general and to the people of this city in particular'.[20] In the summer of 1704, except for textiles, the ban on importing French commodities into the Republic was lifted.[21]

The Dutch entrepôt experienced a disastrous slump during the years 1702–3. From the summer of 1704 the gloom lifted slightly. For France, too, was wilting under the strain of the war and readily agreed to reopen commerce with the Republic alone among the allies, retaining only a ban on Dutch manufactures.[22] France was desperate to export her wine, brandy, and salt and eager to import spices, pepper, herring, cheese, and timber from the Dutch. A system of passes was introduced for Dutch vessels sailing to French ports. By 1705 the quantity of French wine and brandy being shipped to the Dutch entrepôt had recovered to peacetime levels (see table 8.1).[23] Rotterdam and Middelburg in particular began to revive.

Nevertheless, in the context of the post-1702 predicament of the Dutch world entrepôt, the return of Dutch shipping and goods to France—in 1705 over four hundred Dutch ships sailed to Bordeaux alone—was a mere palliative. The general outlook remained extremely bleak. Dutch shipping not provided with passes for French ports was still subject to interception, so that Dutch freight and insurance charges for all other destinations remained ruin-

---

[19] Res. Holl. 13 Feb. 1703; Clark, 'War Trade', 271; Verhees-van Meer, De zeeuwse kaapvaart, 95–6.

[20] GA Haarlem vroed. xxxii, fo. 113, res. 26 May 1704.

[21] GA Haarlem vroed xxxii, fos. 145ᵛ–46.

[22] Huetz de Lemps, Géographie, 68–9, 105; Schaeper, French Council of Commerce, 124.

[23] Huetz de Lemps, Géographie, 68–9, 105.

TABLE 8.1. *Dutch wine shipments from Bordeaux, 1699–1705*

Year	Dutch ships	Dutch shipments (tuns)	Neutrals' shipments (tuns)
1699/1700	—	33,217	8,135
1700/1	—	43,733	7,404
1704/5	237	18,098	20,000
1705/6	444	36,035	9,000

Source: Huetz de Lemps, *Géographie*, 68–9, 105.

ously high. It is true that this applied also to British shipping. But the recent burgeoning of the Danish, Norwegian, and Swedish merchant fleets, as well as the continued vitality of Hamburg, meant that the consequences of high Dutch rates were unprecedentedly serious. Each year from 1702, until the entry of Denmark–Norway into the Great Northern War in 1710 prevented Swedish and also most Danish–Norwegian voyages out of and back into the Baltic, the combined total for Scandinavian shipping passing through the Sound far outstripped Dutch shipping. Indeed, in the years 1705–9 the Danish–Norwegian element alone exceeded the Dutch. The War of the Spanish Succession depressed Dutch Baltic commerce to a low point not seen for centuries (see table 8.2).

But the Baltic was just one area of collapse. There were many more. 'Jamais', averred the French agent, Helvetius, in February 1706, 'le commerce des Provinces Unies en Europe n'a été plus endommagé qu'il l'est aujourd'hui.'[24] Dutch exports of manufactures to France ceased. The herring fishery was severely mauled by the Dunkirkers. Between 1702 and 1712 Dutch traffic to the Mediterranean slumped to its lowest point since the 1620s (see table 8.3). The resumption of trade links with France in 1704 expressly included the port of Marseilles. But the assured access of Dutch shipping to that port had the effect of ruining the Dutch position in the rest of the Mediterranean.[25] For now Dutch vessels sailing to Italy and the Levant were subject to interception by the

[24] Helvetius, 'Mémoire', 191–2.
[25] Israel, 'Phases of the Dutch *straatvaart*', 28–9.

TABLE 8.2. *Voyages eastwards through the Danish Sound, 1700–1714*

Year	Dutch	English/ Scottish	Swedish	Danish/ Norwegian	Total including Hamburg
1700	589	264/74	106	119/106	1,419
1701	546	174/54	227	213/96	1,566
1702	422	70/46	248	250/117	1,389
1703	313	71/41	255	213/73	1,177
1704	452	70/43	273	318/105	1,512
1705	334	37/46	291	299/116	1,393
1706	355	33/44	313	289/132	1,441
1707	257	43/63	284	292/132	1,304
1708	315	28/37	327	291/127	1,336
1709	347	23/30	233	221/159	1,175
1710	358	85/36	1	30/35	634
1711	467	81/67	0	76/25	831
1712	471	117/75	0	44/12	839
1713	667	184/92	0	14/23	1,179
1714	569	238/87	0	43/17	1,236

Source: Bang and Korst, *Tabeller over skibsfart og varetransport*, 42–54.

TABLE 8.3. *Dutch voyages to the Mediterranean according to the* lastgeld *returns, 1698–1715*

Year	Ships	Lastgeld (guilders)	Year	Ships	Lastgeld (guilders)
1698	147	16,577	1707	49	4,318
1699	180	17,144	1708	65	5,629
1700	105	9,701	1709	50	3,621
1701	88	6,725	1710	47	3,530
1702	50	4,757	1711	42	2,851
1703	16	2,284	1712	38	2,744
1704	33	3,638	1713	122	7,073
1705	35	3,347	1714	205	13,829
1706	56	5,298	1715	141	8,085

Sources: ARH Levantse Handel vii, res. 26 Oct. 1699; ix, res. 25 Nov. 1700, 30 Nov. 1701, 13 Sept. 1702; *BGLH* ii. 30, 112.

French and Spanish navies, while those sailing to Marseilles for
Italian and Turkish as well as French commodities were guaranteed Louis XIV's protection and, therefore, low freightage and
insurance charges. The consequence of this, as Charles Davenant
noted, was that from 1704 the Dutch not only resumed voyages
to Marseilles for coffee fetched by the French from Egypt, but now
came also for 'all other Turkey goods, which the French can
afford at easier rates than the Dutch can otherwise have 'em, the
insecurity of the Mediterranean and insurance considered, the
same goods being prize when met with by the French coming from
any but their own ports'.[26]

Nor was the vital Dutch trade with Spain, 'le plus considérable
que nous ayons après ceux de la Mer Baltique, des Indes et les
pesches', as a Dutch merchant expressed it,[27] in any better shape.
The Dutch fine-cloth industry was still receiving regular injections
of Castilian wool. But, instead of being shipped, as in the past, by
the Dutch from Spanish ports, much of it was now transported by
mule overland across Navarre and the Pyrenees to the French port
of Bayonne. There the wool was collected by unarmed Dutch ships
provided with French passes.[28] In other respects, too, the Dutch
hold on Spanish trade was being fundamentally weakened. It was
basic to the workings of the Dutch entrepôt that Amsterdam had
always eschewed local commission agents and all forms of indirect
contact and relied on its own network of factors, often members
of the élite Dutch merchant dynasties, sent out from the Republic.[29]
The Dutch merchant colonies, and since 1648 not least in Spain,
had always been integral to the mechanism of Dutch world-
trade primacy. But now the presence of these colonies in Spain,
continuous for over half a century, was abruptly terminated. In
1702, immediately before the outbreak of war, the Dutch factors
at Cadiz, Seville, Málaga, and Alicante had disposed of their
stock, wound up their affairs, and departed. The last dozen Dutch
factors at Cadiz were evacuated on the Hamburg convoy which
left Cadiz in May 1702. By 16 May 1702 there was not a single
Dutch factor, other than the Dutch consuls, to be seen at Cadiz,

[26] Davenant, *New Dialogues*, 225.
[27] Blok (ed), 'Mémoire', 267.
[28] Davenant, *New Dialogues*, 225.
[29] Savary, *Le Parfait Négociant*, 106; *Memorias de Raimundo de Lantéry*, 7.

Seville, Málaga, or Alicante.[30] A vital link in the chain of Dutch world-trade hegemony had been severed. In so far as Dutch firms trading with Spain were able to continue their business during the 1702–13 war, they were compelled to operate through local commission agents, often South Netherlanders who, as subjects of Philip V, could continue unmolested.[31]

In any case, the most crucial strand of the Spanish trade, the bullion traffic through Cadiz, was paralysed by the war. The Anglo-Dutch force which caught the arriving Spanish American galleons at Vigo, in October 1702, missed the silver (some of which belonged to Dutch merchants)[32] but captured much of the other merchandise, burnt the galleons, and convinced Philip V's ministers that Spain's transatlantic trade would have to be suspended for the duration of the war. Very little American silver reached Spain between 1703 and 1713, so that, consequently, hardly any flowed from Spain to Holland.[33]

A little of what was lost in Spain was recouped by expanding the direct-transit traffic with the Spanish colonies via Curaçao and St Thomas. Some major Amsterdam houses specializing in the Cadiz trade, such as those of Jean de Mortier, Louis Victor, and the Sephardi firms of Abraham Semach Ferro and Jean and Luis Mendes da Costa, clearly did switch more business to the Caribbean.[34] But, with the governors on the Spanish American mainland loyal to Philip V and the Franco-Spanish alliance, this was at best a partial and very risky solution. Most of the best-known Amsterdam firms preferred not to hazard their spices, linens, paper, and candles in this way.[35] There was a revival of Dutch commerce at Curaçao in the years 1703–10 but a modest one, and at first even this was seriously impeded by British interference,[36] for the English were openly hostile to Dutch efforts to cultivate trade links with Spanish colonies loyal to Philip V. The Jamaican privateers scoured the sea lanes of the Caribbean, seizing

[30] ARH SG 7099, Dutch consul at Cadiz to SG, 15 May 1702, and Dutch consul at Málaga to SG, 16 May 1702.

[31] Pauw, 'De spaanse lakenfabrieken', 73.

[32] ARH Levantse handel 173/i, 'Inventaire ... Jacques Terond'.

[33] Helvetius, 'Mémoire', 174.

[34] ARH WIC 569, fos. 102, 107ᵛ, 367; ARH WIC 570, fo. 7; on St Thomas, see Westergaard, *Danish West Indies*, 109, 121, 150.

[35] ARH WIC 201, fos. 64, 257, governor to Bewindhebbers, Curaçao, 4 July 1703 and 1 Mar. 1704; Helvetius, 'Mémoire', 174.

[36] ARH WIC 201, fos. 246–53, governor to Bewindhebbers, Curaçao, 1 Mar. 1704.

Dutch barques caught trading with the Spaniards or French. By March 1704 the English had captured twenty-one Curaçao barques and another two, flying Danish flags and ostensibly based at St Thomas.[37] Anglo-Dutch tension in the Caribbean only eased at the end of 1704, when England yielded to Dutch pressure, and that of her own merchants, to throw the Spanish American trade open to both the Dutch and the English.

As the operations of the French Guinea Company were disrupted by the war, both Spaniards and French in the Caribbean showed some interest, after 1703, in buying slaves at Curaçao.[38] The main profits, however, were in shipping spices, linen, paper, and candles to Río de la Hacha, Maracaibo, and Coro, from where mule-trains transported the merchandise southwards through the Andean passes to Popayán and the heartland of Spanish South America. There was also a brisk trade with Española, Puerto Rico, and the Caracas coast. In 1706, when the wartime Curaçao traffic was at its height, 250,000 pesos in silver, some gold, a large quantity of Venezuela cacao, Española hides, Variñas tobacco, and Campeche wood were shipped from Curaçao to Amsterdam.[39] The Curaçao fleet totalled at most about eighty barques; but, as many of these made two or three trips to the Venezuelan coast per year, we need not treat as excessively exaggerated the report which reached Paris in 1706 that 150 Dutch vessels were now unloading merchandise in the Río de la Hacha–Maracaibo area each year, enough to load two thousand mules with spices, linen, and candles 'et inonder les provinces de Popayán, de Sancta Fé et de Quito'.[40] Informed that half of Venezuela's annual output of cacao and most of her tobacco were being shipped via Curaçao to Holland, Louis XIV's minister of commerce lodged some energetic protests at Madrid. But there was little Philip V could do.

Nevertheless, the Curaçao evidence shows that the war weakened the Dutch grip on the Spanish American market as it did on so many others. It is not just that the leading Amsterdam merchants tended to hold back. It seems clear that under wartime conditions the zone of effective Dutch commercial influence in Spanish

---

[37] Ibid., fos. 246–7.
[38] ARH WIC 202, fos. 13, 42–5, 225, 371ᵛ.
[39] See lists of bullion and commodity shipments from Curaçao in ARH WIC 568 and 569.
[40] Scelle, *Traite négrière*, ii. 160, 309–10.

America contracted. After being cut off since 1701, Curaçao did resume a very tentative contact with Porto Bello in 1707.[41] But, in the main, Central America and the western Caribbean were now confirmed as a British sphere of influence, nearly all the transit traffic there emanating from Jamaica. Even more disturbing for the business world of Amsterdam and Curaçao was the progress being made by the French. After some tentative, not very successful, efforts in the 1690s, when Spanish America was still under the Habsburgs, after 1702 the French made much better headway. Sailing from St Malo across the Atlantic and through the Straits of Magellan to the Pacific coast of South America, the French established a highly lucrative traffic in linens, silks, and paper for silver.[42] In 1709 seven French ships returned together from Peru, reportedly carrying 3,396,174 pesos in silver. The collapse of Spain's monopoly trade system with Spanish America during the war, and the accompanying growth of French and British commercial influence, shows to what an extent that system had previously served the interests of the Dutch world entrepôt.

No part of the Dutch economy escaped the impact of the War of the Spanish Succession. Both the bulk and the rich trades were severely disrupted. The Enkhuizen herring fleet lost over a hundred busses in a French attack off the Shetlands in 1703.[43] For the next decade the Dunkirkers kept up a ceaseless pressure on the Dutch fisheries. The Brielle and Delftshaven herring fleets shrank by more than half.[44] After an initial ruinous slump, farm rents recovered somewhat by 1705 when Dutch cheese exports to France revived and prices for dairy products in Holland recovered.[45] But there was no way of affording relief to the textile towns, which found both their supplies of raw materials and their best markets disrupted. According to Helvetius, some three thousand textile workers left Leiden during the opening years of the war and settled abroad.[46]

Yet, despite the vast losses and the prospect of more, criticism of the war among the Dutch public was remarkably muted. There

---

[41] ARH WIC 202, fo. 203ᵛ, governor to Bewindhebbers, Curaçao, 9 Dec. 1707.
[42] Dahlgren, *Commerce de la Mer du Sud*, 102, 439.
[43] Abbing, *Geschiedenis*, 195.
[44] Wätjen, 'Zur Statistik', 144, 159–61, 173; Feijst, *Geschiedenis*, 105, 108.
[45] Davenant, *New Dialogues*, 223.
[46] Helvetius, 'Mémoire', 175.

was little protest or pressure to negotiate.[47] The Dutch public had more say in the nation's affairs than in probably any other European country. In Holland, as Davenant noted, one was dealing with a 'common people long accustomed to be courted, against whose general bent, the respective magistrates cannot easily resolve or put in act any material resolution'.[48] Yet there was no campaign against the war or the regents' handling of it. The situation was extremely grave, yet the public was, and remained, convinced that to acquiesce in the Bourbon Succession in Spain would be even more disastrous. Helvetius exactly grasped the Dutch mood: 'Quant au déperissement de leur commerce, les Hollandois prétendent l'avoir prévu dès le temps mesme qu'ils ont pris les armes et n'avoir pu néanmoins se dispenser de les prendre pour en prévenir la ruine totale.'[49]

Dutch opinion was convinced that, once Louis XIV was permitted to consolidate France's new links with Spain, it would be all over with the Dutch trading system: the trade of the Spanish Indies would be diverted from its old course, which would mean the ruin not only of Dutch manufacturing industry but also of the other Dutch rich trades, for it was common knowledge that the Dutch East India and Levant trades could not survive without the silver of Spanish America. The Dutch view was that the Bourbon Succession in Spain would mean the 'destruction de leur commerce universel, dont toutes les parties liées étroitement ne peuvent se soutenir que par le secours mutuel quelles se prestent les unes aux autres'. The only way out was to fight on and win crucial trade concessions in France, Spain, the Spanish Indies, and the South Netherlands. In its commercial perspectives, participating in the conflict, however vast and costly, was seen as an investment for the future: through making immense sacrifices now, the Dutch world-trade system could perhaps be salvaged.

The notion that war was the only and correct solution was nourished by the early Anglo-Dutch victories in the field. Directed by the genius of Marlborough, the allies inflicted a series of crushing defeats on the French armies. After the victory at Ramillies in May 1706, Anglo-Dutch forces overran most of the South Netherlands and established a joint condominium at Brussels.

[47] PRO SP 84/229, fo. 456ᵛ.
[48] Davenant, *New Dialogues*, 223.
[49] Helvetius, 'Mémoire', 185.

These developments were looked on with keen satisfaction in the United Provinces, especially as the allied regime at Brussels was mainly geared to suit Dutch interests in the economic sphere.[50] Less than three weeks after Ramillies, the States of Holland and Zeeland adopted resolutions directing the new joint administration in Brussels to cancel the Bergeyck restrictions and tariffs and to reimpose the 1680 Spanish tariff-list. This was back in force by July 1706.[51] Not satisfied with this, Holland subsequently arranged for the 1680 imposts on incoming Dutch textiles to be replaced by those of the even more favourable tariff of 1669. Dutch diplomacy also succeeded in obtaining from Britain and Austria formal recognition of the closure of the Scheldt to maritime traffic as specified in the treaty of Münster of 1648, which both Spain and France had, since 1702, repudiated.[52] Britain also agreed that the Dutch should recover their right to maintain a cordon of Dutch garrisons in the South Netherlands as a 'barrier' against French power.

This revived Dutch trade hegemony in the South Netherlands after 1706 was unpopular in Britain and significantly contributed to the growth of Anglo-Dutch tension which overshadowed the later stages of the war. 'We have conquered Flanders for them', complained Jonathan Swift, 'and are in a worse condition as to our trade there, than before the war began.'[53] Yet Dutch gains in the South Netherlands were more than balanced by British gains elsewhere. In Portugal, which was drawn into the allied camp in 1703, the boot was very much on the other foot. There, English cloth, under the Methuen treaty of 1703, was henceforth admitted on more favourable terms than Dutch cloth.[54] The Dutch, forced to concentrate their spending on their army, were deeply uneasy at seeing Britain become more and more dominant in the naval war. Although Gibraltar, the first part of Spain to be captured by the allies, was held in the name of 'Charles III' and jointly garrisoned—for the time being—by the British and Dutch, the Dutch were already suspicious that Britain might try to appropriate Gibraltar for herself.

The underlying rivalry between the two Maritime Powers was

---

[50] Veenendaal, *Het Engels-Nederlands condominium*, 71–3.

[51] Res. Holl. 13 July 1706; Huisman, *La Belgique commerciale*, 69–72.

[52] Huisman, *La Belgique commerciale*, 69–72.

[53] Swift, *Conduct of the Allies*, 32.

[54] ARH SG 7018/i, SG to king of Portugal, The Hague, 3 Mar. 1705, and Schonenberg to SG, Lisbon, 22 Mar. 1706.

never far under the carpet at any stage. 'It is most certain', noted Davenant on the state of affairs in West Africa, 'that without regard to either peace or war at home, the Dutch West Africa Company [*sic*] and the Royal African Company of England have constantly maintained a sort of private war, the one against the other, for the empire of trade on the Coast of Guinea.'[55] In the Caribbean, Anglo-Dutch suspicion was mutual and remained intense.

At the height of their successes, in 1706, it looked briefly as if the allies might, after all, achieve their sweeping aims. Initially, the allied invasion of Spain on two fronts, from Catalonia and Portugal, went well. Aragon and Valencia joined Catalonia in declaring for 'Carlos', as did even a few Castilian towns. Briefly, Madrid itself was occupied. Elated, the Dutch regents turned their thoughts to the pleasing question of how to divide up the Spanish empire and place Dutch trade with the Spanish Indies on secure foundations.[56] The Pensionary of Holland, Heinsius, held secret talks with ministers of 'Charles III' and with the Sephardi leadership. Essentially, what the Dutch wanted was a restoration of Spain's official monopoly of the Spanish American trade on the same basis as before 1700 and a Spanish America freed from the Bourbons and under 'Charles III'. There was talk of joining Britain in sending a powerful expedition to conquer parts of Spanish America. But the Dutch, aware that Britain would be the senior partner in such an enterprise, were afraid that in this way Britain would secure most of the advantages. The best way to obtain the *status quo ante*, it seemed to Heinsius and his colleagues, was to crush Louis XIV in Europe.

In his secret diplomacy, Louis XIV, for his part, continued until 1710 to pursue a policy of trying to detach the United Provinces from the allied coalition ranged against him. In the process, he made more and more extravagant offers to The Hague. By 1710 he was offering to accept 'Charles III' in place of Philip V as king of Spain, provided that Philip were compensated with Spanish territory in Italy, to agree that France should have no special privileges in the trade of the Spanish Indies, and to revert to the French tariff-list of 1664. All this was very tempting; but the Dutch regents, still keenly resenting the way Louis had tricked them in

[55] Davenant, *Political and Commercial Works*, v. 121.
[56] GA Haarlem *vroed.* xxxiii, fos. 84–5, res. 7 June 1706.

1697, realized that, once they laid down arms and broke ranks with their allies, there would be no way of keeping Louis to his promises. It was not trust so much as lack of an alternative that made the Dutch leadership, at this crucial juncture, decide to stick with Britain and Austria.

Louis, enfuriated by his rebuff at The Hague, decided in 1710 to end the special wartime trading relationship between France and the United Provinces established in 1704, and to pile on the economic pressure. French ports were again closed to Dutch ships and goods and, this time, at Louis's request, so were those of Spain.[57] The Dutch, forced to retaliate, could only reimpose their 1703 ban on commerce with France.[58] This imposition of a Franco-Spanish embargo on Dutch trade in Europe was extended also to Spanish America, where a marked hardening in the attitude of Spanish officials took place in the closing years of the war. The Dutch Curaçao traffic declined sharply from 1710, though part of the lost business was re-routed through St Thomas.[59]

Incensed by Dutch presumption, Louis now switched to seeking a deal in London, where, unhappily for Heinsius and his colleagues, the Tories, who were no friends of the Dutch, had taken over the reins of power. The new British government did not hesitate to break ranks with its allies and do a separate deal with the French. At the general peace conference which gathered at Utrecht in 1712, the Dutch and Austrians were appalled by the extent of what they regarded as Britain's treachery. As Britain and France fixed matters between them, Philip V would, after all, remain on the throne of Spain. Instead, there were to be guarantees that the crowns of France and Spain were never to be joined under one king. France was to have no special privileges in the Spanish Indies. The slave asiento for Spanish America was to be assigned to Britain. Britain was to keep Gibraltar and Menorca. In Holland there were riots against British ministers. In their outrage, the Republic and Austria tried to go on with the war without Britain, but soon found that, without Britain, the allies were weaker than France. Anglo-Dutch relations reached such a low point that there

[57] Baasch, 'Hamburg und Holland', 75; Dahlgren, *Commerce de la Mer du Sud*, 620–1.
[58] Res. Holl. 31 July and 1 Aug. 1711.
[59] ARH WIC 203, fos. 9, 68, governor to Bewindhebbers, Curaçao, 17 Mar. 1711, and petition of the Curaçao merchants, 17 Mar. 1711; Westergaard, *Danish West Indies*, 332.

was talk of a new Anglo-Dutch war.[60] The Dutch and Austrians were forced back to the negotiating table. The Dutch tried to obtain the French tariff of 1664, but Louis would now offer only the 1699 list, which the United Provinces had already publicly repudiated in its declaration of war on France in 1702.[61] Efforts were made to secure the Caribbean island of Puerto Rico, with which the Dutch had long had special contacts, or some comparable compensation for the WIC, but again in vain.[62] In the end, the Dutch had no choice but to acquiesce in Franco-British collusion and Britain's gains.

Commenting on the obdurate hostility of the Dutch to Philip V and the Bourbon Succession in Spain after Britain had agreed to it, French negotiators at Utrecht singled out Dutch Sephardi Jewry for special blame. In December 1711 a French diplomat had reported from Holland that 'le parti de la guerre est composé des Juifs, des religionnaires et des marchands'.[63] This and other similar comments exaggerated the role of the Jews. Nevertheless, it is clear that the Dutch Sephardi leadership can to some extent be regarded as a partner in the Dutch enterprise of trying to block the Bourbon Succession and place the Austrian pretender on the throne of Spain. French diplomats ascribed this attitude to fears that, if Philip V were allowed to remain on the throne of Spain, the bullion of the Spanish Indies which returned to Cadiz would be redirected from Holland to France. In this they were right, except that this was precisely the attitude of the Dutch merchant élite as a whole.

The treaty of Utrecht (1713) was a major political defeat for the United Provinces and marked a significant step towards Britain's supplanting of the Dutch as the world's dominant commercial power. But it was not a total defeat and Dutch world-trade hegemony was not overthrown yet. The Dutch had suffered serious setbacks in many spheres, but they did not emerge from the conflict altogether empty-handed. They had their 'barrier' and general recognition of the Scheldt restrictions of 1648, while the South Netherlands was handed over to Austria, which meant

[60] Defoe, *An Enquiry*, 4–5.

[61] GA Leiden Sec. Arch. 464, fos. 345, 405; Res. Holl. 16 Feb. 1713.

[62] GA Leiden Sec. Arch. 464, fos. 291–2; ARH WIC 447, secret res. of the Amsterdam Chamber of the WIC, 12 Jan. 1712.

[63] Blumenkranz (ed.), *Documents modernes*, 389.

that the emperor, some distance away, was likely to need Dutch help in retaining his grip on the region. Under the Austro-Dutch treaty of Antwerp, of November 1715, the emperor confirmed his acceptance of the 1648 Scheldt restrictions and of the 1680 tarriff-list. This agreement provided the foundation for a restored Dutch commercial hegemony in the South Netherlands which was to survive for several decades.[64]

The Dutch also had a major stake in upholding the provisions of the treaty of Utrecht concerning Spain's transatlantic commerce with Spanish America. Under the treaty, the kings of Spain and France agreed that subjects of France should not receive any special privileges in this traffic and were to receive no future concessions from Spain unless the same terms were also granted 'à toute autre nation trafiquante'. Otherwise the treaty stipulated that commercial dealings with Spain and Spanish America 'se feront précisement et en tout de la mesme manière qu'ils se faisoient sous le règne et jusques à la mort du dit Roy Catholique Charles Second'.[65]

With these guarantees in their pockets, the Dutch and English were able to goad Philip V into taking effective action to suppress the direct French commerce through the Straits of Magellan and up to the coast of Peru. Over this issue, the States General made vigorous representations in Madrid in December 1714 and again in April 1715, as well as on subsequent occasions.[66] The post-war French transit trade to Peru reached a peak in the years 1716–17. In 1718, however, an expedition sent out from Spain captured the French ships found on the coast of Peru and suppressed the traffic.[67] It is not the least of the ironies of early modern history that Britain and the Dutch, once the arch-enemies of Spain's imperial pretensions, after 1713 became the guardians of Spain's official monopoly of Europe's trade with Spanish America. The French direct traffic with Peru was never revived.

With the restoration of peace (except in the Baltic) in 1713, we enter the seventh and last of our phases of the evolution of Dutch world-trade primacy (1713–40), the phase in which the basic mechanisms of Dutch world-trade primacy were largely destroyed.

[64] Geyl, 'Een historische legende', 143; Huisman, *La Belgique commerciale*, 69–73, 517–18.
[65] Res. Holl. 28 Apr. 1713; this text was incorporated into article xxxii of the treaty.
[66] Lamberty (ed.), *Mémoires*, ix. 88–92.
[67] Dahlgren, 'L'Expédition de Martinet', 320–3.

9
Decline Relative and Absolute, 1713–1740

THE question of whether and to what extent the Dutch 'empire of trade' declined during the eighteenth century, like questions about the decay of any great empire, political, cultural, or economic, has long intrigued historians. No other aspect of Dutch economic history has been so intensively debated. Yet, despite a growing mass of statistical data on the Dutch economy of the eighteenth century, scholars continue to arrive at strikingly different conclusions.[1] There is general agreement that Dutch bulk carrying, or at least Baltic bulk freightage, did a great deal better than was once supposed and that serious collapse occurred only in the industrial sector, or at any rate parts of it. But that is as far as the consensus goes. One view, and perhaps still the most influential, propounded by Johan de Vries, in a famous book, was that there was no Dutch economic decline in 'absolute terms' before 1780, only a process of 'relative decline' whereby the Dutch, failing to keep place with expansion elsewhere, were left with a shrinking share of trade and shipping.[2] More recently, Jan de Vries has argued that the Dutch economy did in fact suffer serious decline from around 1670 down to the middle of the eighteenth century but recovered strongly after 1750.[3] Still other historians, looking at levels of employment and per capita income, are inclined to the view that the Dutch economy did not decline at any stage.[4]

Given this bewildering variety of views, the reader will no doubt groan with anguish on realizing that we are now about to reject all of these recent approaches and adopt yet another. He might

---

[1] Spooner, *Risks at Sea,* 47; Riley, 'The Dutch Economy after 1650', 522–4; van Zanden, 'Economie van Holland', 562–4.

[2] De Vries, *Economische achteruitgang,* conclusion.

[3] De Vries, 'Decline and Rise', 149–89.

[4] Riley, 'The Dutch Economy after 1650', 521–69.

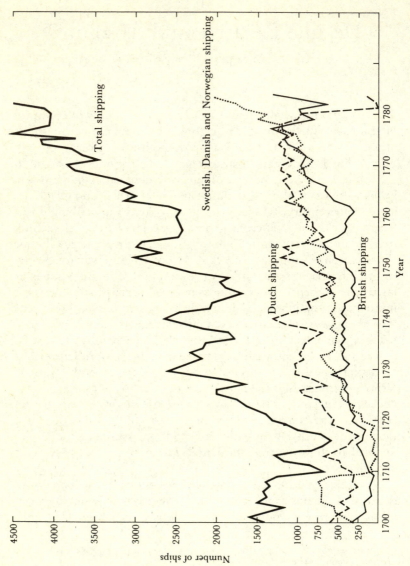

FIG. 9.1 Numbers of ships of each main maritime nation passing eastwards through the Sound, 1700–

well also ask what possible confidence he can have in a fourth view of the fate of the Dutch world-trading system in the eighteenth century when it is wholly at variance with the findings of all the other participants in the debate. It is perhaps therefore worth mentioning before we go further that the analysis about to be set forth is not in fact altogether new in essence and has one immediately obvious advantage over the constructions now being rejected. For the three current views are all conspicuously at odds with the conclusions of eighteenth-century Dutch economic writers such as Elias Luzac and Isaac de Pinto who were convinced that the Dutch economy suffered fundamental decay during the eighteenth century, although Luzac did accept that trade and shipping suffered less severely than Dutch industry.[5] According to de Pinto, most major components of the Dutch world-trade system had crumbled away by the 1760s; all that was left that still showed any vitality was the East India traffic and the fisheries: 'ce sont les deux pivots sur lesquels roule encore le reste de la machine.'[6] Luzac and de Pinto were clear that the essential vitality of the seventeenth-century Dutch entrepôt had, by the middle of the eighteenth century, been largely destroyed. And the fact is that they were right.

But what of modern quantitative techniques? How is it possible that eighteenth-century writers, lacking much of the statistical apparatus now available, can have been closer to the mark than most 'modern' historians? The answer is that there is nothing wrong with the data as such, only with the way that they have been interpreted. The total discrepancy between the views of eighteenth-century Dutch economic writers and 'modern' historians on this matter, in our view, is largely an illusion deriving from misconceptions about the nature of the seventeenth-century Dutch overseas trade empire. The 'modern' perception that the Dutch trading system held up well is only tenable if we accept that 'transfers of bulky commodities lay at the core of Dutch commercial success' during the era of Dutch world-trade primacy, from 1590 down to the beginning of the eighteenth century. But it is precisely here, we have argued throughout, that the basic misapprehension lies. Bulk freightage was not in fact the basis of Dutch world-trade hegemony, though it helped prepare the

[5] Luzac, *Hollands rijkdom*, ii. 324.
[6] De Pinto, *Traité de la circulation*, 242.

ground for it. It was the combination of bulk carrying and the Dutch engrossing of the world's rich trades after 1590 which constituted the basis of Dutch world-trade dominance.

Even if one focuses on bulk carrying, the argument that Dutch overseas commerce recovered strongly after the end of the Great Northern War (1721), and held up well at least down to 1780, is less convincing than is generally claimed. It is true that the Dutch involvement in Baltic commerce, measured in terms of numbers of ships, increased after 1720 almost to the levels attained when the Dutch traffic was at its height in the early seventeenth century and continued at such levels for decade after decade (see fig. 9.1).[7] In terms of ships, the Dutch share of the Baltic traffic after 1720 contracted only in the sense that it failed to keep pace with the rapid growth in Baltic freightage overall.[8] As a result, the Dutch share of the traffic shrank from around 50 per cent of the total in 1720 to less than 30 per cent by the 1770s.[9] Thus far the evidence might seem to support the view that decline was 'relative' but not 'absolute'. But the number of vessels sailing from Holland to the Baltic did decline slightly in absolute terms, the shrinkage being compensated for by an increase in the number of Frisian vessels employed in the traffic.[10] However, the latter were smaller and less likely to be carrying key commodities such as wine, herring, or salt, furnished by other sectors of the Dutch trading system. Thus in reality the trend was one of 'absolute' decline in many of the commodities which had traditionally figured most prominently in the Dutch Baltic bulk trade as well as of a very drastic decline (at any rate after 1740) in relative terms. There is no denying that during the eighteenth century down to 1780 there was a steady increase in the quantities of French wine and brandy, and of colonial goods—Asian, Caribbean, and North American—to the Baltic.[11] In these sectors Dutch decline was purely relative, albeit so steep as to indicate a general loss of leverage over the traffic. But in the case of other key commodities the position was altogether more serious. Around 1740 Dutch exports of Rhine wine to the Baltic began to fall off appreciably in absolute as well as much

---

[7] Knoppers and Snapper, 'Nederlandse scheepvaart op de Oostzee', 144.
[8] De Vries, *Economische achteruitgang*, 19, 29, 83; Unger, 'Publikatie', 149; Faber, 'De achttiende eeuw', 131, 151, 154.
[9] Knoppers, *Dutch Trade with Russia*, i. 259.
[10] Faber, *Drie eeuwen Friesland*, ii. 602.
[11] Unger, 'Publikatie', 191, 194–5.

more steeply than before in relative terms (see Table 9.1). Total Dutch exports of salt, refined and unrefined, to the Baltic, after a

TABLE 9.1. *Dutch shipments of Rhine wine to the Baltic, 1661–1760* (% of total shipments)

1661–70	95.0	1721–30	58.4
1671–80	90.3	1731–40	42.8
1701–10	84.5	1741–50	37.4
1711–20	95.9	1751–60	37.2

Source: Unger, 'Publikatie', 158.

sharp fall in the period 1690–1713, held steady for most of the rest of the eighteenth century at a level only slightly below that of the pre-1690 period; but Dutch exports of refined salt processed in the Republic collapsed in the decades 1740–60 down to only about one-fifth of the level sustained in the period 1660–1700.[12] 'Absolute' decline in Dutch herring exports to the Baltic began in the decade 1701–10. Imports of grain into Holland during the mid- and late-eighteenth century scarcely exceeded the low levels of the 1690s let alone recovered to the heights of the early and mid-seventeenth century.

Had it not been for the vast increase in European demand for colonial products such as raw sugar, tobacco leaves, coffee, and tea during the eighteenth century, and the marked rise in total French wine and brandy exports, there would have been a decisive decline in Dutch Baltic carrying in 'absolute' as well as 'relative' terms. Nor should we forget that the relative decline from around 1740 was itself so pronounced as to erode completely the preponderance the Dutch had once enjoyed.[13] The Dutch share of timber exports from the Baltic fell from over two-thirds of the total in the period 1721–40 to only around one-fifth in the decades 1761–80; in tar the Dutch share collapsed from over half to around one quarter over the same decades; in hemp the Dutch share dwindled from 44 per cent in 1721–40 to 19 per cent in 1761–80.

But Dutch decline after around 1740 was not simply a matter of a drastically reduced share of the total bulk-carrying traffic.

---

[12] Ibid. 188.
[13] Ibid. 170–2; Lindblad, 'Structuur en mededinging', 80–2, 88, 90.

There was a loss of dominance in another sense also. The two growth sectors in the Dutch bulk-carrying trade during the eighteenth century were French wine and colonial goods. But it is striking that in both cases there was a marked fall during the decades 1740–80 in the quantities stored in, and exported from, the Dutch maritime provinces.[14] Dutch ships were carrying more and more produce direct from France to the Baltic, bypassing the Dutch entrepôt and dispensing with its storage, brokerage, financial, and processing services. In the Dutch carrying of French wines this deterioration set in during the 1720s and 1730s. Imports of French wine to Rotterdam fell off between 1720 and 1760 by some 30 per cent.[15]

If the thesis of 'relative rather than absolute decline' is unconvincing even in relation to bulk carrying, it bears hardly any relation to reality in the case of manufactures and processed goods. Here, with the 1720s and 1730s again marking the decisive turning-point, there was a process not just of 'absolute' decline but of catastrophic collapse and loss of market leverage.

As we have seen, the Dutch Levant trade had already collapsed during the War of the Spanish Succession. Since this commerce was beset with special difficulties, observers such as the Dutch consul at Smyrna in the post–1713 period, Daniël Jean de Hochepied, did not expect anything like a full recovery to the flourishing state of this commerce as it had been down to the late 1680s. Even so the results of the peace for the Dutch Levant trade proved a deep disappointment. 'Contrary to all expectations', lamented de Hochepied in 1721, this traffic 'has declined more and more and now seems to be lapsing into total decay'.[16] The root cause of the malaise confronting the Dutch Levant trade, as de Hochepied clearly saw, was that Dutch fine cloth no longer represented a significant factor in the commerce of the Near East. French fine cloth had by the 1720s effectively taken its place. Dutch demand for Turkish mohair yarn was also now at a much lower level than before, due to the decline of the Leiden camlet industry. The decline of the Dutch Levant trade proved irreversible. The number of Dutch merchant houses at Smyrna, the chief

---

[14] Unger, 'Publikatie', 191.
[15] Hazewinckel, *Geschiedenis*, ii. 210.
[16] *BGLH* ii. 98–9, de Hochepied to SG, Smyrna, 10 Jan. 1721.

centre of Dutch activity in the region, fell from about twenty-five in 1688 to eighteen in 1702 and then to only six by 1719.[17]

In the Cadiz trade, the position was somewhat better. Yet here too the Dutch failed to regain all the ground that they had lost since 1700. Dutch linen continued to sell well in Spain down to the middle of the eighteenth century. But most other Dutch manufactures which had in the past figured prominently in the Spanish and Spanish America commerce lost ground steadily after 1720. This was true of *lakens*, silks, and camlets. So alarmed was the Leiden city council by the late 1720s at the drop in demand for Dutch fine cloth in Spain that official inquiries were made to discover the reasons.[18] The conclusions were that there were two main reasons for the decline in Dutch cloth sales in Spain: in the first place, as in the Levant, there was the progress of French fine cloth, which was supplied in colours better suited to Spanish taste than those of the Dutch; secondly, there was a general weakness in Dutch commercial operations in Spain resulting from the disappearance of the Dutch merchant colonies in 1702. After 1713 the former Dutch mercantile presence in Spain was never reconstituted.[19] By 1729 there were 'only two or three' Dutch merchant houses left at Cadiz, two at Seville, and none at all at Málaga, Alicante, or Barcelona.

But the decay of the Dutch rich trades was by no means a phenomenon confined to southern Europe.[20] The basic reason for the decisive decline of the Dutch world-trading system in the 1720s and 1730s was the wave of new-style industrial mercantilism which swept practically the entire continent from around 1720. This was an immensely important change, which has often been stressed in relation to particular countries such as Prussia, Russia, and Sweden–Finland but has never been taken account of sufficiently as a European phenomenon with vast international reverberations, not least for the Dutch world-trading system. During the late seventeenth century the United Provinces had had to cope with French mercantilism. Dutch products had been shut out of France by means of high tariffs or outright prohibition. French

---

[17] Bossch-Erdbrink, *At the Threshold of Felicity*, 195; Israel, 'Dutch Merchant Colonies', 100, 106.

[18] Pauw, 'De Spaanse lakenfabrieken', 74–5.

[19] Ibid.; Sée (ed.), 'Documents', 60–1, 112; Forbonnais, *Mémoires*, 166–7.

[20] Jeannin, 'Hansestädte', 61–2; Van Dillen, *Van rijkdom en regenten*, 501, 508, 514.

ministers had succeeded, by a variety of means, in attracting Dutch skills and personnel to France. Whereas in the 1640s one-third of Dutch exports to France had consisted of textiles, especially *lakens* and camlets, by the early eighteenth century the equivalent figure was under 10 per cent.[21] But elsewhere there had been few obstacles to the flow of Dutch manufactured and semi-manufactured goods. Down to 1720 countries such as Prussia, Russia, Sweden, and Denmark–Norway had lacked the means and, with the Great Northern War in progress, the opportunity, to emulate the aggressive industrial mercantilism of England and France. But in the years around 1720 a heightened sense of competition among the northern powers, combined with the diffusion of new technology and skills, often Dutch or Huguenot in origin, led to a dramatic change. Within the next two decades most of northern Europe was incorporated into a framework of systematic industrial mercantilist policy.

A comprehensive interventionism, encompassing all commercial and industrial activity, in addition to shipping and colonial enterprise, took hold successively in Prussia, Russia, Austria, Denmark–Norway, Sweden–Finland, and in still other states.[22] Everywhere the basic technique was the same. Just as Prussia in 1718 banned the export of raw wool—in the past north-eastern Germany had been one of the main sources of supply of this commodity to the Dutch entrepôt—and, as from 1720, banned the importing of all foreign cloth, fine or otherwise, into Prussian lands,[23] including Cleves and Mark on the very doorstep of the Dutch Republic,[24] so all the major states of northern Europe now set up barriers to stop the outflow of raw materials and prevent the entry of foreign manufactured and semi-manufactured goods. In all these countries vigorous attempts were made to stimulate domestic cloth and silk production, sugar-refineries, tobacco processing, sailcloth weaving, and so on. In many cases, the diffusion of Dutch techniques played a crucial role in this general process of economic renewal. The Russian shipbuilding, sailcloth, and rope-making industries, established by Peter the Great, were all based on the

[21] Eon, *Commerce honorable*, 30–2; Morineau, 'Balance du commerce franco-néerlandais', 174, 180.

[22] Posthumus, *Geschiedenis*, iii. 1114-16; Scheltema, *Rusland en de Nederlanden*, iv. 50–6; Bro Jørgensen, *Industriens historie i Danmark*, 68–9.

[23] Hinrichs, *Wollindustrie in Preussen*, 43, 51, 101.

[24] Ibid. 95-7, 101.

Dutch model. The adoption of Dutch multiple-blade saws in Russia and Scandinavia broke the hegemony of the Zaan timber mills and accelerated the decline of Dutch shipbuilding. Sweden acquired not just Dutch tobacco-processing techniques but whole workshops, transferred lock, stock and barrel, complete with workers, from Amsterdam.[25] Dutch fine-cloth weaving techniques were adopted in Prussia, Savoy, and Spain. By 1719 a colony of three hundred Dutch *laken* workers was resident at Guadalajara, invited by Philip V on favourable terms.[26] Down to 1740 it was generally the declining United Provinces, rather than the rising industrial power of Britain, which set the trends in European industrial and technological innovation.

Britain, cushioned by her burgeoning empire and a belt of subject economies, such as Portugal and Brazil, to which she enjoyed access on special terms, was able to take the changes in her stride. The Dutch, who now lacked the power to intimidate other European regimes and enjoyed privileged terms of trade only in the South Netherlands, could not. The key decades for the spread of systematic interventionism in northern Europe, the 1720s and 1730s, were the same as the decades of decisive decline of the Dutch world-trade system and for a very good reason: the phenomena are two sides of the same coin. In Prussia, the crucial break with the past came in the years 1718–20. In Russia, Peter the Great's programme of mercantilist initiatives goes back well before 1720, but it was in the 1720s that the impact of Russian protectionism began to be felt. In Denmark–Norway, the crown, under the influence of Otto Thott, reverted in 1732 to a systematic mercantilist policy in defiance of the undertakings extracted by the Dutch in 1688. The Danish crown banned the importing of Dutch woollens, silks, refined sugar, and later also processed tobacco and Gouda pipes to its respective territories.[27] In Sweden–Finland, the faction which captured power in 1738 introduced a sweeping package of protectionist measures designed to exclude virtually every category of foreign manufacture from the country.[28] Again the Dutch were hardest hit. It is doubtless true that in all

[25] Westermann (ed.), 'Memorie van 1751', 74; Gerentz, *Kommerskollegium*, 267, 274.
[26] Pauw, 'De Spaanse lakenfabrieken', 37.
[27] Bro Jørgensen, *Industriens historie i Danmark*, 69, 104–5.
[28] Gerentz, *Kommerskollegium*, 242–4; Alanen, *Aussenhandel*, 290, 304; Lindblad, *Sweden's Trade*, 18–20, 161–5.

these countries the advancement of industry was less rapid, and less even, than the architects of these policies hoped. But the shutting out of foreign manufactured goods tended to be the most effective part of the programme and gaps in manufacturing capacity were often filled through carefully calculated political arrangements, again very much to the detriment of the Dutch. If in Russia, for example, the promotion of the domestic cloth industry was not very successful, much of the gap was filled by contracting to buy cloth from Prussia, where the progress of cloth production in the 1720s and 1730s was more impressive.[29]

The onset of systematic industrial mercantilism throughout northern Europe led to immediate and fundamental changes in the structure of those countries' trade with the Dutch entrepôt. Dutch–Prussian commerce was transformed almost overnight in the years 1718–20 from one in which Prussia received large quantities of Dutch manufactured goods to a commercial relationship based on Holland's export of raw materials and spices to Prussia. The restructuring of Dutch–Swedish trade at the end of the 1730s was similarly sudden and complete.[30] The Dutch entrepôt simply ceased exporting cloth, finished silks, refined sugar, paper, and processed tobacco to Sweden–Finland. It may be true that the actual volume of Dutch trade with Sweden held steady, owing to a huge increase in the quantities of raw wool and silk, unprocessed sugar and tobacco leaves, cotton, and dyestuffs being shipped from Holland to Sweden. But this does not alter the fact that the changes of the late 1730s in Sweden–Finland were a shattering blow to the Dutch world entrepôt. Mere volume could not compensate for the loss of a major market for Dutch processed goods. In terms of value, Dutch commerce with Sweden declined not just relatively but also absolutely.[31]

During the 1720s and 1730s the industrial base on which Holland's rich trades rested crumbled away. The woollen and silk industries were especially hard hit.[32] The combined impact of the prohibitions on foreign woollen and silk-cloth imports in Russia (1718), Prussia (1720), Denmark–Norway (1732), and Sweden–

[29] Hinrichs, *Wollindustrie in Preussen*, 325–35.
[30] Lindblad, *Sweden's Trade*, 20, 161–5.
[31] Ibid.
[32] Posthumus, 'De industriële concurrentie', 375–8; de Vries, *Economische achteruitgang*, 102–9; van Dillen, *Van rijkdom en regenten*, 514.

Finland (1739), together with the drop in demand for Dutch cloth in the Spanish and Ottoman markets, had a devastating effect. Output of Leiden *lakens* dropped from over 20,000 pieces yearly in 1717–18 to a mere 7,391 cloths by 1740 (see table 9.2). Output

TABLE 9.2. *Output of* lakens *at Leiden, 1700–1750*

1700	24,782	1726	14,771
1701	25,890	1727	13,466
1702	23,004	1728	12,479
1703	19,975	1729	11,876
1704	18,991	1730	11,552
1705	20,730	1731	11,787
1706	24,178	1732	12,715
1707	25,161	1733	12,250
1708	24,644	1734	11,417
1709	22,170	1735	10,847
1710	23,645	1736	9,390
1711	20,744	1737	8,826
1712	19,324	1738	8,206
1713	18,999	1739	8,101
1714	22,218	1740	7,391
1715	22,264	1741	7,409
1716	19,149	1742	6,793
1717	22,298	1743	6,963
1718	22,104	1744	7,138
1719	18,157	1745	6,627
1720	17,022	1746	6,774
1721	16,576	1747	6,436
1722	18,406	1748	5,934
1723	18,527	1749	6,419
1724	17,223	1750	6,708
1725	16,152		

Sources: Posthumus, *Geschiedenis*, iii. 1185–6; Luzac, *Hollands rijkdom*, ii. 332.

of *says* also fell off sharply. It is true that there was a modest revival in camlet output in the immediate aftermath of the War of the Spanish Succession. But this too proved unsustainable in the harsh mercantilist climate of the 1720s and by 1729 the definitive decline of this industry had set in. Furthermore, it was during the 1720s that the linen industry in Overijssel and North Brabant began to contract,[33] though decline here proceeded slowly at first and Holland continued to export large quantities of finished linen to England and the Hispanic world, the main markets, down to the third quarter of the century.

Before long the collapse extended also to the rest of Dutch industry. The shipbuilding industry rapidly decayed. The Zaan paper industry, one of the prime success stories of the post-1672 era, reached its peak, at 150,000 reams yearly, around 1730 and then began its descent, down to 80,000 reams by 1750 and lower levels subsequently.[34] Tobacco processing was still harder hit, though it is often claimed that the devastation of the Amsterdam tobacco industry in the 1730s and 1740s was compensated by the shift which took place in Dutch tobacco processing, to Rotterdam, Amersfoort, and Nijkerk. There is no doubt that there was such a shift; but it is also clear that the new workshops by no means made good the decline in the number of tobacco workshops at Amsterdam, from around thirty in 1720 (about half being Jewish) to a mere eight by 1751.[35] Indeed, total Dutch output of processed tobacco and snuff by 1750 seems to have shrunk to little more than a quarter of the level for 1720.[36] By 1751 nearly three-quarters of total Dutch tobacco-leaf output was being exported unprocessed, Denmark and Sweden alone receiving around one-third of the total of Dutch output of tobacco leaves. It was in the 1740s that the new tobacco workshops and sugar-refineries of Stockholm took effective control of the Swedish and Finnish markets.[37]

Other Dutch industries which fell victim to the industrial mercantilism of the early and mid-eighteenth century were the sail-canvas, salt-refining, and Delftware industries. The decline of the Delftware industry began in the 1730s, though the main collapse occurred in the 1750s and 1760s. By 1740 the number of potteries at Delft was only slightly down on the peak figure for the early eighteenth century.[38] But the once proud salt-refining industry of Zeeland was in a pitiful condition by the 1730s. From around forty

[33] Frenken, *Helmond in het verleden*, ii. 313–14; Slicher van Bath, *Samenleving onder spanning*, 201–2.

[34] Van Braam, *Bloei en verval*, 23; van der Woude, *Het Noorderkwartier*, ii. 490–2.

[35] Westermann (ed), 'Memorie van 1751', 73; Herks, *Geschiedenis*, 164–6.

[36] Westermann (ed), 'Memorie van 1751', 77; Roessingh, 'Tobacco Growing', 42.

[37] Alanen, *Aussenhandel*, 290, 304.

[38] Wijsenbeek-Olthuis, 'Ondernemen', 71.

salt-boiling kettles in operation at Zierikzee in 1644, the figure was down to only nine by 1750.[39] The Dutch were still shipping great quantities of Iberian salt to northern Europe in the mid-eighteenth century, but Scandinavian mercantilism was compelling the Dutch to deal in unrefined salt. The Zaan sail-canvas industry was hit by a variety of protectionist measures, including the English Act of 1736 compelling every British ship to carry at least one set of sails made in Britain.[40] From its peak of around 60,000 rolls in 1730, output of Dutch sail-canvas was down by a third, to 40,000 rolls, by 1742, and to 28,000 rolls by 1769.[41]

In the 1720s and 1730s the Dutch world emporium lost its capacity to produce and process goods which commanded large shares of overseas markets. The setback was most serious in the industrial sphere, but it was by no means confined to manufacturing activity. There are signs that Dutch dairy exports, notably to France, also fell back sharply in the early eighteenth century.[42] In the case of herring exports, there was a precipitate collapse after 1720, the decisive deterioration occurring in the years 1730–50.[43] It is worth noting how severely this affected Dutch trade in the Baltic. In 1700 the Dutch still supplied around 60 per cent of the total of herring consumed in the Baltic area. After the 1720s there was a dramatic change, as Swedish and Norwegian herring came to dominate the Baltic market. By the 1740s Dutch herring accounted for only about 15 per cent of the herring consumed in the region.[44]

Even those few Dutch industries which survived the 1730s and 1740s intact either declined soon after 1750 or else were sustained in the late eighteenth century owing to heavily increased demand in the home market. The Gouda pipe-making industry reached its peak around 1750 but declined rapidly during the third quarter of the century.[45] The flourishing Dutch gin industry is an apparent exception to the trend towards absolute decline which is often cited to prove that not all Dutch industries collapsed in the eighteenth century. Dutch gin production did hold up throughout the

---

[39] *Tegenwoordige staat van Zeeland*, i. 376–7.
[40] Wilson, 'Economic Decline', 115.
[41] Van der Woude, *Het Noorderkwartier*, ii. 486–7.
[42] Morineau, 'Balance du commerce franco-néerlandais', 174–80.
[43] Kranenburg, 'Haringexport naar het Oostzeegebied', 254–8.
[44] Ibid.; Unger, 'Publikatie', 156.
[45] Goedewaagen, *Geschiedenis*, 5–6.

century. But it is not at all the case that gin continued to contribute to the Dutch Republic's exports in the way that it did before 1720. On the contrary, Dutch gin exports fell off substantially under the pressure of protectionist measures in Prussia, Sweden, and elsewhere. The Dutch gin industry held up after 1720 only because of a spectacular rise in home consumption. Dutch gin output survived because Dutch brewing collapsed, the number of breweries plunging both in rural areas such as Friesland and Overijssel and at Amsterdam.[46] The number of breweries at Leeuwarden, the capital of Friesland, fell between 1700 and 1760 from around forty to eighteen. A symptom of the changing orientation of the Dutch gin industry, was the fall in the number of distilleries in the Schiedam–Rotterdam area, balanced by the rise of new distilleries in inland and rural areas.

Sugar-refining is another apparent exception, being an industry which actually grew. During the first half of the eighteenth century there was a steady increase in the number of sugar-refineries, despite the exclusion of Dutch refined sugar from Sweden–Finland, Denmark–Norway, and other northern markets after 1730.[47] By 1751 there were around ninety sugar-refineries at Amsterdam alone, another thirty at Rotterdam, and more at Middelburg and Dordrecht.[48] But this growth occurred only because of the immense increase in sugar consumption in eighteenth-century Europe, owing to the new habits of drinking tea and coffee and the rise of processed foods, chocolate, and other confectionery. In the United Provinces, sugar consumption increased spectacularly. But the change in consumer habits extended even to the remotest corners of the continent. In Finland, for example, sugar consumption increased by five times in the century 1650–1750.[49] Thus, Dutch output of refined sugar increased, even though it was excluded from more and more markets. By the mid-eighteenth century the Dutch sugar-refineries were serving a relatively narrow range of markets, largely confined to the Low Countries themselves, the Rhineland, and some other areas of Germany.

The Dutch rich trades within Europe, with Sweden, Denmark, Germany, Spain, and the Levant, were all devastated during the

---

[46] Faber, *Drie eeuwen Friesland*, i. 245; Faber, 'De achttiende eeuw', 146.
[47] Johnsen, *Norwegische Wirtschaftsgeschichte*, 364; Alanen, *Aussenhandel*, 290.
[48] Faber, 'De achttiende eeuw', 146.
[49] Alanen, *Aussenhandel*, 290.

1720s and 1730s by the blighting of the Dutch entrepôt's capacity to produce and finish the necessary commodities. Outside Europe the Dutch did much better, for here they had forts, colonies, and political backing to buttress their position. At first glance, Dutch supremacy in Asian trade might seem to have remained intact down to around the middle of the century. There was no significant falling off in the volume of Dutch shipping sailing to and from Asia until the 1760s.[50] VOC silver exports to its Asian depots continued to increase until around 1760 (see table 5.17). But Dutch decline in Asian trade during the eighteenth century was not so much a matter of falling volume of commerce, for in wide regions the Dutch possessed exclusive rights; it was more a question of marked deterioration in the Dutch competitive position, for outside the areas which they controlled politically they had to confront growing British, French, Danish, and other competition. Here again the post–1713 period, down to the middle of the century, represents the decisive phase of erosion. By 1720 the British had caught up with the VOC in the shipping of Bengal cottons and silks to Europe.[51] By 1740 the English East India Company had decisively overtaken the Dutch not only in Bengal and the rest of northern India but also along the northern stretches of the Coromandel coast and Malabar coasts.[52] In India, the Dutch had lost the contest for the areas they did not dominate politically, and the areas they did dominate were contracting.

Even more complete was the VOC's failure during the early eighteenth century in China. Since the 1690s it had been the English who had led the way in the tea trade. After 1713 the British established a secure foothold at Canton, whilst the Dutch continued to cling to their indirect China trade based on Batavia. For a short period, in the years 1729–34, the VOC tried to emulate the British and French by trading direct with Canton, but soon gave up the experiment, reverting to the indirect traffic.[53] Nor was the VOC's striking loss of grip confined to areas which they did not dominate politically. During the period of the decisive weakening of the Dutch world entrepôt, Phase Seven, the VOC's

---

[50] The number of men sailing out to Asia on VOC ships reached its peak in the 1760s (see de Bruijn, 'Personeelsbehoefte', 220).
[51] Prakash, *Dutch East India Company*, 82.
[52] Arasaratnam, 'Dutch East India Company and its Coromandel Trade', 326, 346.
[53] De Hullu, 'Over den Chinaschen handel', 115–18.

grip loosened even at the southern tip of India, in Ceylon, and in the Archipelago. In the immediate post-1713 years the Dutch were still unquestionably an Asian great power. When, in 1715, the prince of Calicut seized the Dutch fort at Chetwai, on the Malabar coast, the VOC sent in three thousand troops to restore Dutch supremacy, the largest display of European military muscle in India until the onset of the Anglo–French struggle in the 1740s. But, between the subjugation of Calicut, in 1715–16, and the end of the 1730s, there was a marked and definitive decline in Dutch power at the tip of India. The crushing defeat the Dutch suffered at the hands of the raja of Trevancore, in 1741, marked the end of that predominance.[54] In the same period there was a waning of Dutch strength in Ceylon, while Dutch primacy on Java was shaken by the revolt of the Chinese in and round Batavia in the years 1740–3.

The decline of the VOC as a political and military power, even where its position was strongest, was inevitably accompanied by a loss of control over trade.[55] After 1713 there was a notable resurgence of British penetration of the pepper trade of Sumatra and Celebes as well as Malabar. British activity at Canton prompted a diversion of part of the Japanese copper traffic out of VOC hands.[56] The Dutch defeat at Trevancore, in 1741, ended the era of almost total Dutch dominance of the commerce of the southern Malabar coast.[57] In addition, the weakening of Dutch control in regions such as Malabar, Coromandel, and Ceylon undermined Dutch efforts to bolster their crumbling position in key northern Indian markets such as Bengal and Gujarat.[58] The VOC simply had progressively less leverage to apply. By the 1740s the British and French were the dominant European powers in India.

All the main sectors of Dutch commerce declined in both relative and absolute terms during the eighteenth century except possibly for Baltic bulk carriage (the significance of which has, in general, been overrated) and certainly for Dutch commerce with the Caribbean and North America. Of course, all transatlantic commerce

---

[54] Das Gupta, *Malabar in Asian Trade*, 19–23.
[55] Arasaratnam, 'Dutch Commercial Policy', 111, 124–5, 128.
[56] Arasaratnam, 'Dutch East India Company and its Coromandel Trade', 343.
[57] Das Gupta, *Malabar in Asian Trade*, 19–23.
[58] Prakash, 'European Trade and South Asian Economies', 201.

expanded vigorously during the eighteenth century, so this in itself is not saying a great deal and especially not when we take account of the almost total failure of the Dutch entrepôt to make any impact on the prolific new traffic which grew up from the end of the seventeenth century with Brazil.[59] For, with the discovery of major gold deposits in Brazil in the 1690s, and later also of diamonds, Brazil took on a quite new significance in the world economy. By the 1720s Brazil had become one of the most important sources of bullion fuelling world trade and one of the most crucial colonial markets for European manufactures. But it was overwhelmingly Britain and British manufactures which dominated the triangular traffic between north-western Europe, Portugal, and Brazil which burgeoned to its peak in the middle decades of the new century.[60] This, in fact, was one of the most striking indications of the Dutch entrepôt's loss of grip over the essential mechanisms of international trade.

In trade to the Caribbean area and North America the Dutch did somewhat better, but only because of the tremendous escalation in demand for sugar, tobacco, and other Caribbean products in Europe during the eighteenth century, and the rapid growth of England's North American colonies, as well as the increasing reluctance of businessmen along North America's Atlantic seaboard to submit to total economic subordination to England.

In part the expansion of Dutch activity in the Caribbean area during the eighteenth century was based on the Republic's own colonies. Dutch plantation agriculture in tropical America was especially successful in Surinam. The blockade of the French Caribbean colonies during the War of the Spanish Succession had encouraged a rapid spurt of output. By 1712 there were around two hundred sugar plantations in what was now one of the most flourishing of all the Dutch colonies, a figure which, by 1730, had risen to nearly four hundred. Of these, 115, concentrated in what was virtually a Jewish autonomous region along the Surinam River, belonged to Sephardi Jews.[61] Total annual sugar shipments from Surinam to the Dutch entrepôt more than doubled during the first quarter of the new century (see table 9.3).

[59] Van Dillen, 'Amsterdam als wereldmarkt', 718; Attman, *American Bullion*, 28–9.
[60] Attman, *American Bullion*, 28–9; Fisher, *The Portugal Trade*, 33–5; Morineau, *Incroyables gazettes*, 136–7.
[61] Dentz, *Kolonisatie*, 17.

TABLE 9.3. *Shipments of raw sugar from Surinam to the Dutch entrepôt, 1700–1724* (chests)

1700	10,500	1713	14,568
1701	10,550	1714	22,068
1702	10,572	1715	19,532
1703	10,700	1716	17,639
1704	12,100	1717	14,552
1705	12,850	1718	12,435
1706	14,683	1719	17,316
1707	18,500	1720	19,480
1708	12,125	1721	25,848
1709	18,401	1722	29,866
1710	15,661	1723	20,734
1711	21,546	1724	25,816
1712	22,695		

Source: Essai historique sur la colonie de Surinam, appendix, 'L'Etat des exportations'.

An expansion of Dutch plantation agriculture occurred on a smaller scale also in some of the other Dutch colonies, especially those of western Guyana. During the seventeenth century the Dutch colonies in this region had been little more than minor Dutch trading posts. In the early eighteenth century, however, they were transformed into plantation colonies. By 1730 there were some thirty sugar plantations in Essequebo and smaller numbers in the other enclaves, Demerara, Berbice, and Pomeroon.[62]

But the primary role of the Dutch trade network in the Caribbean area during the eighteenth century was as an intermediary carrying the products of others. This was not expected in 1713. Initially the gloomy reports emanating from Curaçao during the closing years of the War of the Spanish Succession, and the first years of the subsequent peace, seemed amply justified. Dutch Caribbean trade slackened to very low levels.[63] In February 1714 the governor of Curaçao reported to Amsterdam that Dutch enterprise with both the 'upper and lower coasts' of the Spanish Amer-

[62] Goslinga, *Dutch in the Caribbean* (1985), 438–40, 446.
[63] ARH WIC 571, fos. 733, 749–50, governor of Curaçao to WIC directors, 27 Sept. and 27 Nov. 1714.

ican mainland had shrivelled virtually 'to nothing'.[64] Amid the
dismay which ensued from the assigning of the slave asiento to
Britain, WIC share prices on the Amsterdam Exchange, having
held up well until 1712 on the expectation of the liquidation of
the Bourbon regime in Spanish America, entered on a disastrous
slide which brought the price down from around par to a mere 40
per cent by 1719.[65] But the pessimistic prognostications of 1713,
based on the apparently drastically reduced circumstances of the
Dutch in the Americas, proved premature. From around 1720 a
vigorous expansion set in and continued through the middle
decades of the eighteenth century. It was not that the com-
mentators of 1713 were wrong in asserting that the basic mechanisms of Dutch trade control in the Caribbean had now been
weakened. The Dutch were never again to enjoy anything like the
ascendancy they had had relative to the other European powers
in Caribbean trade during the second half of the seventeenth
century. It was simply that no one had had any inkling of the vast
escalation in Europe's transatlantic trade which was about to take
place.

Even at the nadir, in 1714, the Dutch West Indies retained some
residual trade with the Venezuela coast, Española, and Puerto
Rico, and a wide assortment of connections with the British colonies both in the West Indies and North America as well as the
French Caribbean islands (see table 9.4). After 1720 all this traffic
steadily expanded. By the 1730s some fifty Dutch vessels yearly
were returning from the Guyanas, Curaçao and St Eustatius to
Amsterdam alone, with a substantial additional number based on
Zeeland.[66]

Both the Dutch sugar shipments from the Guyanas and the
intermediary traffic based on the Dutch West Indies reached their
peak during the great wars between Britain and France of the
mid-eighteenth century and in the opening years of the American
War of Independence. In an age in which Britannia ruled the seas
but other powers also had a large stake in a growing transatlantic
trade, the French, Spaniards, and Americans all avidly needed a
trading power, with a large stock of shipping, whose vessels, even

---

[64] ARH WIC 571, fo. 517, governor of Curaçao to WIC directors, 10 Feb. 1714.
[65] Goslinga, *Dutch in the Caribbean* (1985), 568.
[66] Oldewelt, 'Scheepvaartsstatistiek', 131; van Dillen (ed.), 'Memorie betreffende
de kolonie Suriname', 166.

TABLE 9.4. *Ships entering and leaving the harbour of Willemstad, Curaçao, July–December 1714 (six months)*

	Arriving from	Departing for
St Thomas (Danish)	14	1
New York	9	5
Barbados	6	2
Española		
French	4	2
Spanish	3	1
La Guaira (Caracas)	5	2
Jamaica	3	1
Antigua	2	2
Maracaibo	2	1
St Eustatius	2	1
Nevis	2	0
Rhode Island	1	1
Virginia	2	0
Puerto Rico	1	0
Bermudas	0	1
Italy	0	2
United Provinces	1	0
Tobago	1	0
Boston	1	0
TOTAL	59	22

Source: ARH WIC 206, fos. 8–16.

when carrying the goods of enemies of Britain, were protected by treaty against British interference. Meanwhile British re-exports of colonial products to the Dutch entrepôt, a large proportion of which consisted of American tobacco and sugar, also expanded during the early eighteenth century, reaching a peak in the 1720s and 1730s.[67] These did decline slightly after 1740 but remained at a high level for several decades more.

This burgeoning of Dutch trade with the Americas after 1720 was an immensely important feature of Dutch economic life in the eighteenth century. If Leiden, Delft, and Gouda, and other inland manufacturing centres, had become dead towns by the middle of

---

[67] Ormrod, 'English Re-exports and the Dutch Staplemarket', 97–8.

the eighteenth century, the growth in transatlantic commerce went some way towards compensating for the setbacks suffered by the Dutch entrepôt in almost every other sector, helping to sustain the general vitality of the maritime towns of Holland and Zeeland as well as the Amsterdam bullion market and the entire Dutch financial system. The growth in transatlantic trade, in other words, exerted a masking effect which mitigated and partly concealed the impact of Holland's industrial collapse and the decline of her Old World rich trades.

But at the same time it is important to recognize that this steadily rising influx of American commodities, paradoxical though this may seem at first glance, in no sense helped to shore up Holland's declining industries or to perpetuate Dutch control over the distribution of key items. For the expansion in Dutch transatlantic commerce went on simultaneously with an even more impressive expansion in British, French, and Spanish commerce with the Americas, with the result that Dutch leverage over distribution in Europe was progressively eroded. The Republic by the 1740s had become a mere transit point for unprocessed tobacco leaves *en route* to Germany, Flanders, and Scandinavia and was beginning to re-export raw sugar in substantial quantities to markets such as Denmark and Sweden, to which, until the 1730s, she had supplied only refined sugar.[68]

The crumbling of Holland's industries, the decline of the fisheries, and the waning of the Dutch rich trades in Europe and Asia had the effect of transforming the Dutch world entrepôt from an active controlling force in world trade to a passive staple or storehouse. It was in the post-1740 period, with the Dutch intermediary trade with the Caribbean and North America flourishing, that the Dutch entrepôt reverted in essence to its pre-1590 role, except that grain, timber, salt and wine, the key items furnished by the old pre-1590 entrepôt, had now largely been displaced by colonial commodities frequently re-exported unprocessed. Now that Holland and Zeeland exported few domestically produced woollen, linen, or silk products, fewer ships and copper goods, less refined sugar, tobacco, herring, soap, and lighting fuel, and little salt, sail-canvas, paper, or Delftware, the Republic was fast descending to the level of a mere storage and transit depot and

[68] Lindblad, *Sweden's Trade*, 165–6.

one that rarely controlled the terms of distribution at that. Daniel Defoe's comment that the 'Dutch must be understood to be as they really are, the carryers of the world, the middle persons of trade, the factors and brokers of Europe',[69] would have been wildly misleading if intended to capture the essence of the seventeenth-century Dutch entrepôt, but, by the time it was written, in 1728, was rapidly becoming an apt enough characterization of what the Dutch emporium now was.

[69] Defoe, *A Plan of the English Commerce*, 144.

Afterglow and Final Collapse

THERE are several reasons for selecting the year 1740 as marking the key dividing-line between what we have termed the seventh and last phase of Dutch world-trade primacy (1713-40) and the remaining decades (1740-1806) during which the Dutch entrepôt continued to play a major intermediary role in world trade. In the first place, by 1740 most of the powerful states of northern, central, and eastern Europe had adopted aggressively mercantilist industrial strategies shutting out most manufactures and processed goods produced in the Dutch Republic. By 1740 the decisive period of industrial collapse in Holland was already over. Secondly, down to 1740 the Republic continued to dominate the carrying of a large number of bulky products within Europe, including grain, timber, wine, tar, and hemp. As from 1740 began a period of rapid loss of share in the carrying of these commodities, so that by the 1770s and 1780s the share of the Dutch in total bulk freightage had been drastically reduced. Thirdly, the year 1740 marks the commencement of the era of Franco-British global wars and rivalry for world political dominance, a development which reinforced the tendency of the Dutch trading system in these years to evolve into a mere intermediary service, carrying goods on behalf of others. Finally, even though the year 1740 has not figured as a decisive turning-point in most recent discussion of eighteenth-century Dutch economic development, several earlier authorities did regard the years 'around 1740' as a time of rapid and definitive weakening of the Dutch world entrepôt.[1]

In our view, the character of the Dutch world entrepôt changed fundamentally in the years around 1740. During the era of Dutch world-trade primacy proper, from 1590 to 1740, the Dutch entrepôt with its immense array of shipping and commercial, financial, and industrial facilities was an active controlling emporium, able

---

[1] Van Dillen, *Van rijkdom en regenten*, 501, 508, 514; Wilson, 'Economic Decline', 111-13; one recent authority who has called attention to the significance of 1740 as a crucial dividing-line is J. Th. Lindblad; see 'Structuur en mededinging', 80, 88.

not only to bring force and political pressure to bear in pursuit of its objectives but also to regulate the production and processing of many commodities which figured prominently in international high-value commerce and to manipulate their distribution. After 1740 the picture changed radically. The United Provinces no longer produced commodities which figured prominently in international high-value commerce or even, to nearly the same extent as before, refined salt, herring, and dairy products. Consequently, the Dutch entrepôt ceased to be a controlling force in the processes of production and lost its leverage over distribution. Down to the 1790s Amsterdam was still Europe's 'trade emporium par excellence', providing an unrivalled stock of shipping and of commercial and financial services; but, after 1740, its essential function was that of a passive staple, or depot, not unlike Antwerp during the early stages of its rise to world prominence, during the early sixteenth century.

Of course, for many observers, now as in the eighteenth century, the carrying function was the very essence of the Dutch trading system. Dutch world-trade ascendancy had always been chiefly a matter of carrying and stockpiling. If one discounts, or disregards, both the political and the industrial factors which reinforced and, in many cases, made possible Dutch international market control before 1740, preferring to measure the rise and fall of the Dutch emporium in terms of volume of trade and shipping, then one is unlikely to be much impressed by the choice of 1740 as marking the beginning of a new stage in the process of Dutch trade decline. For several of the main Dutch carrying trades of the time, notably to the Baltic and the Caribbean, held level or expanded in absolute terms during the period 1740–80. One late-eighteenth-century economic writer who believed that the middle decades of the century brought little substantial change to the Dutch entrepôt was Adam Smith. 'The trade of Holland,' asserted the great Scots economist, 'it has been presented by some people, is decaying, and it may perhaps be true that some particular branches of it are so. But these symptoms seem to indicate sufficiently that there is no general decay.'[2]

But Adam Smith, the liberal economist and free trader *par excellence*, was oblivious to just those political, politico-commercial,

[2] Adam Smith, *The Wealth of Nations*, ii. 81.

and trade-engrossing factors—treaties, alliances, blockades, enforced restrictions, and monopolistic devices—which, we have argued, underpinned Dutch supremacy in world trade down to 1740. For Adam Smith, writing in the 1770s, the Dutch had long been 'and still are the great carriers of Europe' and this sufficiently explained their success.[3] In this respect, Isaac de Pinto, who was convinced that a ruinous deterioration had set in at the Dutch entrepôt during the middle decades of the century, may be said to have had a sharper eye for the realities of the Dutch trading system. According to de Pinto, the Dutch entrepôt by the 1760s was no longer capable, as it had been down to the recent past, of effectively regulating the distribution of commodities in Europe and the wider world.[4] He illustrated his point with the example of industrial dyestuffs. Down to the early eighteenth century, not only had the Dutch carried vast quantities of indigo, cochineal, Brazil wood, Campeche wood, and gallnuts, but Amsterdam had been in a position to dictate prices and regulate distribution. By the middle of the century, however, this leverage had gone. The Dutch still carried and stockpiled large quantities of dyestuffs. But so did the British, French, Danes, Swedes, and North Germans. A new era had dawned.

The more Holland's industrial base crumbled, the more the Dutch role in high-value, low-volume trade disintegrated. After 1740 the contraction of Dutch industrial activity slowed down, but it continued. Output of woollen textiles sank to dismally low levels. The year 1750 was the last in which production of *lakens* at Leiden exceeded 6,000; the year 1753 was the last in which it topped 5,000, a mere quarter of the quantity turned out a century before.[5] By 1760 camlet output at Leiden had drifted down to a mere 5,350, less than one-tenth of the figure attained in the 1660s.[6] Paper, processed tobacco, and sail-canvas all continued their downward descent. At the same time, it was now the turn of several industries which had survived the collapse of the 1720s and 1730s intact to disintegrate. The linen industry was hard hit by British protectionist measures—designed to foster the growth of the Irish and Scottish linen industries—which curtailed imports

[3] Ibid. i. 407.
[4] De Pinto, *Traité de la circulation*, 251.
[5] Posthumus, *Geschiedenis*, iii. 1185–6.
[6] Ibid. iii. 1181–2; Luzac, *Hollands rijkdom*, ii. 332–4.

from the Republic.[7] The Gouda pipe industry, having survived
the mercantilist onslaught of the second quarter of the century,
fell victim to the banning of imports of Gouda pipes introduced
in Prussia, Denmark–Norway, and other states during the third
quarter.[8] By the 1770s Gouda was ruined. Delftware was swept
from the drawing rooms of Europe. 'La ville de Delft', remarked
Accarias de Sérionne, in the 1770s, 'est pour ainsi dire une ville
morte.'[9]

The last great period of the Dutch carrying trade extended from
1740 until the outbreak of the fourth Anglo-Dutch War (1780–
4). Though the Dutch entrepôt now exported fewer and fewer
manufactured and processed goods, Dutch carrying of unrefined
salt and sugar, of grain and raw materials, positively throve. Until
1780 British warships mostly respected the seventeenth-century
principle of 'free ship, free goods' which the Dutch Republic
had extracted from Charles II and Parliament in 1667 and had
confirmed in the Anglo-Dutch peace of 1674, and this was now
the basis of the Dutch entrepôt's success as an intermediary,
carrying especially French and Spanish colonial produce during
the wars of the mid-eighteenth century and the trade of the rebels
during the American War of Independence. But it was by no
means only the Dutch traffic to the Caribbean and North America
which benefited from the new Dutch carrying role, even though
this was the area of most conspicuous success. British disruption
of French shipping made France itself more dependent on Dutch
shipping services in various sectors, including the Mediterranean,
where there was a late, marginal, but nevertheless noticeable
revival of Dutch carrying activity (see table 10.1). But Dutch
success in becoming the general intermediary of trade during the
mid-eighteenth century took place on borrowed time and on the
basis of political concessions wrung from Britain in an age when
the Republic had possessed the means to exert pressure on her
rivals. That was not the case in the mid-eighteenth century and
after, and it was only a matter of time before Great Britain lost
patience with a state of affairs—the carrying of the trade of her
enemies and rebels—which was not just highly irritating but was
seriously hampering Britain's efforts. By 1780 Britain was doing

[7] Wilson, *Anglo-Dutch Commerce*, 59–61; Veluwenkamp, *Ondernemersgedrag*, 110.
[8] Goedewaagen, *Geschiedenis*, 5–6.
[9] Accarias de Sérionne, *Richesse de la Hollande*, i. 265.

TABLE 10.1. *Ships sailing to Amsterdam from key Atlantic and Mediterranean ports, 1734–1786*

Port	1734	1739	1741	1743	1750	1758	1761	1783	1786
Cadiz	53	43	43	27	53	31	37	35	34
Bordeaux	88	83	210	78	78	142	145	113	112
Marseilles	5	15	16	5	5	5	8	13	8
Smyrna/ Constantinople	8	6	—	11	9	16	18	11	10
Surinam	29	28	44	40	37	34	54	59	50
Curaçao/ St Eustatius	24	20	16	16	36	71	128	82*	43

* All but two from Curaçao.
Sources: Oldewelt, 'Scheepvaartsstatistiek', 131; Snapper, 'Generale listen', 28–39.

rather badly, not only in her war with her American rebels but in the struggle with the French. But this only added to the temptation to launch a war of aggression against the Dutch Republic.[10] For, by attacking the Dutch, not only could Britain put the squeeze on the Americans and French economically, but she could expect to capture Dutch colonies, as well as large quantities of Dutch shipping, with which to offset, at the eventual peace table, the humiliation of failure at American and French hands. War against the enfeebled Dutch Republic promised handsome dividends to the embattled Britain of those days. The war was launched. Dutch shipping and the Dutch colonies were heavily disrupted. In 1781 Admiral Rodney occupied St Eustatius, the main depot from which munitions were shipped to the American rebels, together with Saba and St Martin, capturing 150 Dutch and American vessels in the process. The British also took Essequebo, Demerara, and Berbice. Yet, despite these blows, British sea power could not suppress the Dutch carrying traffic. Organizing their commerce from Curaçao, the Dutch continued to handle large, albeit reduced, quantities of French Caribbean, Spanish American, and North American produce. Dutch Baltic commerce persisted almost undisturbed.

During the last fifteen years of the existence of the Dutch Republic (1780–95), and the first ten years of the French occupation

[10] On this point, I have adopted the views of Hamish Scott, who is preparing several publications on the subject of the Fourth Anglo-Dutch War.

of the Dutch provinces (1795–1805), the Dutch carrying traffic functioned at reduced levels compared with previous decades but was still a major factor in world commerce. The setting up of a Dutch revolutionary republic, the Batavian Republic, in alliance with France, in 1795, precipitated a massive new British onslaught on Dutch shipping and commerce throughout the globe. One by one nearly all the Dutch colonies were captured, this time including Curaçao, South Africa, and many of the Dutch possessions in Asia. But it was not until the imposition of Napoleon's continental blockade in the years 1805–7 that the Dutch carrying traffic was finally swept from the seas, collapsing in the years 1807–12 to wretchedly low levels.[11] But by the time this happened the last period in which Dutch world-trade primacy can be said to have had some reality was no more than a distant memory.

[11] Oddy, *European Commerce*, 369; Knoppers, *Dutch Trade with Russia*, ii. 429–32; Faber, 'Scheepvaart op Nederland', 75–6.

11

Conclusion

THE European world economy which emerged at the end of
the fifteenth century and during the sixteenth was a strikingly
different phenomenon from the collectivity of regional and local-
ized economies, lacking any real centre, which characterized the
world in ancient and medieval times.[1] Medieval Christian Europe
displayed considerable cultural cohesion but, down to the fifteenth
century, the economic ties between the Mediterranean basin, on
the one hand, and the commercial zone of the north, dominated
by the Hanseatic League, were extremely tenuous, limited to the
transfer of spices, silks, and a few other low-volume, high-value,
commodities.[2] It was only with the rise of large fleets of full-rigged
ships, the penetration of the Baltic by French and Iberian bulky
goods such as wine and salt, and the oceanic discoveries, all in the
fifteenth century, that there arose a world economy in the sense
of a network of closely and regularly interacting markets spanning
most of the globe. In this respect, Antwerp—and not Venice,
Bruges, Lübeck, or any great medieval trade emporium—was the
first true general entrepôt whose operations affected, and were
affected by, every part of the world economy. The series Antwerp–
Amsterdam–London, the centres of the world economy from the
sixteenth to the late-nineteenth century, the age when world economic power was concentrated at a single point, surely makes
better sense than the longer sequence Venice–Antwerp–Genoa–
Amsterdam–London, embracing medieval and modern times.

Antwerp, then, was the first general entrepôt of the modern
world. But the process of concentration of economic power at the
north-western tip of Europe which occasioned this phenomenon
did not cease with the rise of Antwerp, nor with its fall after
1585. Antwerp possessed some of the general staple characteristics
regarded by Van der Kooy as the essential attributes of an early
modern world central reservoir of commodities, but not all of

---

[1] Wallerstein, *The Modern World System*, i. 15–16, 36–41.
[2] Jeannin, 'Interdépendances économiques', 155–7.

them.[3] In particular, Antwerp and its immediate hinterland did not dispose of a large merchant fleet of its own, or any major means of transportation of goods, though it did have access to major shipping resources close by. Nor can the world economy of the early and mid-sixteenth century be said to have involved anything like as great a degree of interdependency of markets as developed subsequent to Antwerp's fall from primacy. During the sixteenth century the Baltic grain and other bulk traffic vastly increased and acquired a steadily growing significance for western and southern Europe. From 1590 Baltic grain became a significant factor in the Mediterranean, though by no means so decisive a factor as some historians have claimed.[4] Indeed, there are grounds for arguing that the escalation of the rich trades in the sixteenth and early seventeenth centuries was more crucial as a lever of growing interdependency of markets. The flow of spices swelled, sources of bullion supply proliferated, sugar imports to Europe multiplied many times over, input of dyestuffs, drugs, and jewels from the New World and Asia immeasurably increased, valuable products from Russia, Sweden, and the Arctic Circle came to figure much more prominently.

But how great was the impact of the seventeenth-century, Dutch-dominated, world trading system on European and non-European economic and social life? It is often said that the vast majority of the world's population in early modern times consisted of peasants too poor to spend what little they had on anything other than the most basic foodstuffs and roughest, locally produced textiles. Also, in cases where production of goods for export clearly did exert a fundamental influence on local society, such production may have done so, to just as great an extent, for centuries past. Approximately 40 per cent of the wine produced in the Bordeaux area was for export in early modern times and clearly the production of wine for export profoundly influenced rents, wages, and all economic life throughout the Atlantic seaboard of France from the Loire valley to the Pyrenees. But, as with Italian silk weaving, this had been the case for centuries.[5] But during the sixteenth and early seventeenth centuries, the number of such examples greatly

---

[3] Van der Kooy, 'Holland als centrale stapelmarkt', 10–12; Klein, *De Trippen*, 3–7.

[4] Braudel, *La Méditerranée*, i. 572–4; Israel, 'Phases of the Dutch *straatvaart*', 1–5.

[5] Jeannin, 'Interdépendances économiques', 152–3.

increased as a result of escalating foreign demand for both bulky and high-value commodities. The economies of Poland and the Ukraine were transformed, at every level, by the escalation in demand for their grain and timber in the west. The life of the population of Norway came to be profoundly influenced by the growth of timber exports and the growing use of Iberian salt to preserve fish. In the seventeenth century the economies of Sweden and Finland were highly dependent on copper, iron, timber, and tar exports. Peasant life in western Anatolia came to be deeply influenced by the production and weaving of mohair yarn for export, two-thirds of it by the mid-seventeenth-century being shipped to Holland.

Nor was the growing impact of the world economy on everyday life and peasant society in any way limited to Europe and the Near East. Brazilian society became geared to the production of sugar for export, Venezuela to cacao, Guatemala and Honduras to indigo, and large areas of Mexico and Peru to the production of bullion, most of which was for export either to Europe or to the Far East. In many parts of Indonesia whole societies became geared to the cultivation of spices and pepper and in much of Ceylon to that of cinnamon. Outside Europe, there were numerous societies which came to depend on the Dutch entrepôt traffic for commodities which, in some cases, figured prominently in everyday life. The black slaves of the Caribbean were clothed with rough linen from Westphalia transported via Holland. European copper goods and linen became basic to black life-style in West Africa. A large part of inter-Asian trade came into Dutch hands, including the supply of Indian textiles to Indonesia, of Indonesian spices and Japanese copper and silver to India and Persia, of Ceylonese cinnamon and elephants to northern India.

As a world emporium, the Dutch entrepôt of the 1590-1740 period differed from its precursor, Antwerp, in several fundamental respects. In the first place, the Dutch emporium, with its unrivalled shipping resources, was in a position, as Antwerp never was, to buy commodities at source, wherever they were produced in the world, and to organize the transfer of those goods from one part of the globe to another. The Dutch staple was never dependent, as was Antwerp, on intermediaries such as Lisbon, Seville, Lübeck, and London. From the outset, in the 1590s, Dutch world-trade primacy was characterized by direct access to the markets of Africa, Asia, Russia, and the Americas. Even where their ships could not go, the merchant élite which presided over the Dutch entrepôt, relying on their ability to pay higher prices than local merchants could, sent their factors to buy up products at source. From the 1590s onwards, Dutch factors appeared at Moscow, to engross supplies of caviare, sable furs, and Russian leather, and in Silesia, where they outbid German merchants and Jews for supplies of linen;[6] from the 1630s onwards, they went to the Rhineland to buy up locally produced tobacco. Whereas Antwerp acquired a powerful merchant élite only towards the end of its era of primacy, and never fully completed the transition from passive staple to active, controlling entrepôt, the Dutch Republic functioned as an active, controlling force for the whole of the century and a half from 1590 down to 1740. It was only in its last phase, from 1740 down to 1795, that the Dutch emporium lapsed into the powerless, passive condition of a mere central storehouse.

One aspect of the uniquenness of the Dutch entrepôt as a hub of the world economy in early modern times is that its hegemony extended to both bulk and rich trades, Holland having started out, in the fifteenth and sixteenth centuries, as the depot *par excellence* for Baltic grain, timber, and shipping stores. It is therefore understandable that there should have been a tendency to explain Dutch world-trade primacy in the seventeenth century in terms of this traditional Dutch ascendancy over bulk carriage.[7] It has also been suggested that the 'originality of the Dutch trading system that arose in the seventeenth century derived from the long specialization of Dutch shipowners in bulk trade'.[8] According to this view, it was possibly less the control over distribution of bulky products as such which led to Dutch supremacy over the rich trades than the methods and techniques of Dutch primacy in bulk carrying, such as the building of specialized ships, unprecedentedly low shipping costs, and new ways of financing shipownership: 'when the Dutch expanded their horizons to deal in the rich trades of woollen cloth, silks, spices and colonial goods, they competed with seafaring traditions that had been accustomed to transporting high-value, low-volume goods.'[9] But closer scrutiny suggests that

---

[6] Marperger, *Schlesischer Kauffman*, 195, 230; Zimmermann, 'Schlesischer Garn- und Leinenhandel', 204, 208.
[7] Braudel, *La Méditerranée*, i. 572–4; Verlinden, 'Amsterdam', 330.
[8] De Vries, *Economy of Europe*, 117.   [9] Ibid.

Dutch predominance in bulk trade did not of itself lead to hegemony in the rich trades, not even in the Baltic, and, indeed, could not have done so. For primacy in the rich trades presupposed circumstances and assets which dominance of bulk trade of itself could not provide. In particular, penetration of the rich trades required a highly developed industrial base, a powerful merchant élite with the expertise and resources to undertake 'grandes enter-prises commerciales', and, last but not least, powerful political backing. While there can be no doubt that Dutch methods of shipbuilding and shipowning were key features of the Dutch world entrepôt in the seventeenth century, our findings in this study suggest that the essential originality of the Dutch entrepôt extended far beyond shipping factors and methods of cheap carriage.

While there has perhaps been a certain tendency to overlook the crucial contribution of industries to the making of Dutch world-trade primacy in the seventeenth century, a few scholars have been at pains to point it out.[10] But great care must be taken in defining the nature of the contribution of Dutch industry. One historian who has particularly emphasized the significance of 'Dutch productive efficiency' in the making of Dutch trade hegemony is Immanuel Wallerstein. He, indeed, ascribed what he called 'Dutch hegemony in the seventeenth-century world-economy' less to Dutch dominance of bulk carriage than to 'Dutch productive efficiency', by which he meant Dutch superiority in certain areas of agriculture and a number of fisheries, notably the herring and whale fisheries, as well as in industry. Certainly in these two fisheries and possibly some more specialized sectors of agriculture Dutch supremacy was overwhelming, both quan-titatively and qualitatively. But, in the industrial sphere proper, what precisely did Dutch superiority amount to? To speak of the Dutch Republic as the 'leading producer of industrial products' of its time is surely not exact. The Dutch enjoyed an overwhelming quantitative as well as qualitative advantage over their rivals, comparable with their supremacy in the herring and whale fish-eries, in only one or two industries such as timber-sawing and shipbuilding. Otherwise, there was nothing very exceptional about the volume of Dutch output. Collectively, textiles were the most

---

[10] Wilson, 'Cloth Production', 209–14; Wallerstein, 'Dutch Hegemony', 98–100.

important branch both of industry and of the rich trades in early modern times and in textiles Dutch output lagged well behind that of England, France, India, or China. Dutch industrial superiority in the seventeenth century and at the beginning of the eighteenth was essentially a matter of quality, technical sophistication, and innovation. It is quite clear, for instance, that the astounding success of Dutch fine cloth after 1635 in markets ranging from Russia to France and the Levant was principally due to its smoothness, reputation for consistency, and its competitive price due to economy in the use of wool in its manufacture, resulting from technical advances which other countries were soon eager to emulate.[11] A great part of the dependency of neighbouring countries on Dutch skills in the seventeenth century was due to the technical superiority of the Dutch as dyers of cloth, bleachers of linen, spinners of tobacco, distillers of spirits, grinders of lenses, and makers of all kinds of new presses, rolling and stamping mills, peat-fired furnaces, mechanical saws, stills, minting equipment, and all sorts of other machines.

Yet Dutch productive efficiency was by no means solely the result of technical specialization and innovation. For the rich trades, and for the finishing industries on which the rich trades depended, the stockpiling of the world's commodities in a central storehouse—van der Kooy's world staple—was a factor of decisive importance. Dutch superiority in dyeing, bleaching, grinding, and refining was hard to challenge when it was the Dutch who had the stockpiles of dyestuffs, chemicals, drugs, and rare raw materials on which all these processes depended. Thus, there was a high degree of interdependency between the Dutch commerce in high-value commodities and Dutch industry, each continually reinforcing the other.

Yet productive efficiency, and a powerful merchant élite, even combined with unrivalled shipping resources and financial facilities, still did not suffice to shape and sustain the complex edifice of Dutch world-trade primacy for a whole century and a half. There was yet another vital ingredient to the mix and one that has been ignored more than the contributions of Dutch industry— namely the crucial role of the Dutch state in the advancement of the country's commerce. The erroneous notion that the Dutch

---

[11] Marperger, *Beschreibung*, 107; Pringsheim, *Beiträge*, 86.

were saddled with an exceptionally weak and inefficient state which did not intervene to any great extent in economic activity has got so out of hand in recent decades that it has completely distorted our vision of the Dutch economic miracle of early modern times. For a variety of reasons, the Dutch state apparatus of the seventeenth century has generally been held in much too low esteem by historians, even being dismissed by one authority as an 'absurdly medieval and decentralized federal state'.

In this study we have come to a very different appraisal of the Dutch state and have argued that its trade promoting and protective functions formed one of the three principal pillars of Dutch world-trade primacy, the others being shipping capacity and productive efficiency. Despite all that has been said to disparage the Dutch Republic as cumbersome and slow-moving, the fact is that it was an exceptionally strong and efficient state compared with seventeenth-century France or Sweden, or for that matter pre-1688 England. It was the Dutch state, with its complex federal apparatus, which blocked the Scheldt estuary after 1585, paralysing Antwerp, and which, in 1648, compelled Spain to accept permanent trade restrictions on both the Scheldt and the Flemish coast, as well as to grant the Dutch favourable trade terms in Spain itself. It was the federal Dutch state which forced Denmark to keep the Sound open and the Sound tolls low. Had Denmark not been forcibly restrained by Dutch power, the lowest freight charges in the world would not have sufficed to ensure the continuation of Dutch primacy in the Baltic. By 1651 England was resorting to the deliberate use of force to disrupt Dutch commerce; only the efforts of the Dutch state prevented Dutch shipping from being swept from the seas, until, in the end, this is precisely what happened in the 1780s and 1790s. Furthermore, the Dutch could not have imposed their trade supremacy in Asia, West Africa, and, more sporadically, in the Caribbean and Brazil had the States General not set up and armed politico-commercial organizations of unprecedented scope and resources not just with regard to the scale of their business operations but also in respect of their military and naval power.

But the unique suitability and aptitude of the Dutch federal state for the advancement and protection of trade in the seventeenth century was by no means confined to its external functions. The specific form of the Dutch state also powerfully buttressed Dutch maritime and commercial expansion internally, through its impact on public and private conduct. The United Provinces, as a republic, enjoyed all the advantages of commercial and financial stability which early modern princely and absolutist regimes generally lacked. Dutch merchants, like those of Venice, Genoa, Lübeck, or Hamburg, could rely on their government to adhere to its undertakings, to pay its debts on schedule, and not to tamper disreputably with savings or with the currency. Elsewhere, including in pre-1688 England, businessmen could have no such confidence. But in some areas of public regulation of business practice the United Provinces went well beyond what was achieved even in the other republics. If, for instance, pre-1688 England was considered a less reliable place than Holland for arranging marine insurance and obtaining settlement of claims, Genoa too was considered less reliable.[12]

The Dutch public authorities supervised a broad range of economic activity, extending from banking and insurance to manufacturing processes and the packing of herring, with a rigour not known elsewhere. Dutch fishermen were permitted to unload their herring only in the Dutch entrepôt and every stage of its curing, packaging, storing, and marketing was scrupulously controlled. Sir Josiah Child was struck by the difference between England and the Republic in this respect, asserting that, where Dutch fish products enjoyed universal repute, England's fish exports 'often prove false and deceitfully made and our pilchards from the West-Country false packed'.[13] It was the same with the Dutch textile industries. Regulation of cloth manufacture in the United Provinces, through the provincial states, town councils, and guilds, was as stringent as anywhere in Europe, far too much so, according to Pieter de La Court.[14] But, whilst we may accept that this stringency did have some negative effects, it must also be recognized that it was largely owing to this constant supervision that Dutch textiles enjoyed such high repute in a European market plagued by shoddiness and poor quality. It is striking that Benjamin Worsley, in his pamphlet *The Advocate*, singled out the high level of public intervention in cloth manufacture in the United Provinces as the

[12] Barbour, 'Marine Risks', 581–4.
[13] Child, *A New Discourse*, 3.
[14] De La Court, *Welvaren Van Leiden*, 92–105; van Tijn, 'Pieter de La Court', 344–5.

principal reason why the Dutch made rapid strides at English expense in this sphere during the middle decades of the seventeenth century. Worsley held the chief 'cause of the so great thriving of our [Dutch] Neighbour's cloathing, and of the so great ruine and decaie (on the contrary) of our own woollen manufactures, and of the people depending on them' was the 'singular and prudent care they took in preserving the credit of those commodities which are their own proper manufactures; by which they keep up the repute and sale of them abroad; taking hereby a very great advantage of the contrarie neglect in us; and by this means, likewise, very much damnifying and spoiling us'. Dutch success in textiles, according to Worsley, was built above all on their 'settling a regulation, government, and superspection over them'.[15]

Finally there were the perenially and uniquely low interest rates which pertained in the Dutch Republic. These were much lower than in England or France, around 1670 for example, Dutch rates being as low as 3 per cent and English rates twice that figure.[16] This was a factor of decisive importance for a trade entrepôt where the merchant élite specialized in buying up vast stocks of commodities well ahead, so much so that Josiah Child was of the opinion that 'Dutch low interest hath miserably lessened us in all trades of the world not secured us by laws, or by some natural advantage which over-ballanceth the disproportion of our interest of money'.[17] But why were Dutch interest rates so low? This too can in part be ascribed to the efficiency and meticulousness of the Dutch federal state and the provincial and civic administrations of which it was composed. For low interest rates are not just an expression of abundance of money but also of absence of risk in lending.

The federal state and its extensions, the East and West India Companies, were ever on the alert for challenges to Dutch trade supremacy and prompt to suppress them. The English attempt to wrest control of the dyeing and finishing of English cloth out of Dutch hands, in 1614, met with a prompt and devastating response

---

[15] Worsely, *The Advocate*, 7–9.

[16] Child, *A New Discourse*, B3–4, 8–10; French interest rates were put by Child at 1% higher than the English; Schröder confirms that German and Austrian interest rates in the 1680s were twice as high, at 5 and 6%, as those of the Dutch (*Schatz und Rent-Kammer*, 277–8).

[17] Child, *A New Discourse*, preface.

for the States of Holland and States General. When Genoa set up the Compagnia genovese delle Indie Orientali, in 1647, hired Dutch ships and seamen, and sent them out to the East Indies, the VOC replied by seizing the ships, arresting the Dutchmen, and sending the Genoese back home.[18] Colbert's Compagnie du Nord was first weakened by Dutch dumping of cut-price Baltic goods in western France and then, finally, in the years 1672–5, broken by Dutch seapower. Time and again the joint kingdom of Denmark–Norway sought to free itself from dependency on the Dutch entrepôt only to be slapped down by the Dutch state.

Yet, at least in Europe, resentment of the Dutch and their trade supremacy, though sporadically acute in countries such as Spain, Portugal, England, France, Denmark, and Sweden, was never as universal or as intense as one might suppose. Dutch world-trade primacy involved a good deal of arm-twisting, exploitation, and commodity manipulation. But, to offset this, it also gained a reputation for fair dealing in many spheres where the reputation of others stood less high, and for the consistently high quality of its products. Resentment of the Dutch, at any rate in Europe and the Americas, was further muted by fear of England and France, whose supremacy, it was universally suspected, from Spain to Russia, and from Norway to Italy, would, if achieved, be considerably more unpleasant than that of the Dutch. For these reasons, Dutch trade primacy in the seventeenth century, when under pressure from England or France, or both, could count in the rest of Europe not just on political support but on something approaching actual popularity.

To sum up, we may say that the originality of Dutch world-trade primacy in the 1590–1740 period was wide-ranging and multi-faceted. Historians are gradually coming round to the view that the Dutch trading system of the seventeenth century did in fact display much more originality than used to be thought. The Dutch entrepôt was the first to be a true world entrepôt, sustaining a direct and dominant commerce from the 1590s onwards with all of Europe and much of the rest of the world. The Dutch entrepôt was the first to combine dominance of the bulk with primacy in the rich trades. But the originality the Dutch displayed in bulk carriage, their specialized shipbuilding, and methods of shipown-

---

[18] Haitsma Mulier, 'Genova e l'Olanda nel seicento', 436–7.

ing was not the source of their dominance in the rich trades. Here Dutch originality lay in new forms of productive efficiency and technological innovations in manufacturing, combined with new techniques of stockpiling commodities, buying ahead, and speculative trading. Above all, the Dutch system displayed originality in its large trading and fishing corporations, designed to tap and consolidate investment from a much wider catchment area than any one city, however thriving and dominant, could provide. The notion that the United Provinces was, in any sense, political or economic, the city-state of Amsterdam, implying that Amsterdam ruled the rest as Venice and Genoa ruled their subject territories, is a total misconception. Nowhere else in the early modern world was the close economic collaboration of a network of maritime towns, inland manufacturing towns, fishing ports, and inland specialized agriculture anything like so intricately organized and federated as in the Dutch Republic during the seventeenth century.

BIBLIOGRAPHY

PUBLISHED PRIMARY SOURCES

Abreu y Bertodano, J. A., *Colección de los tratados de paz, alianza, neutralidad,* etc. (12 vols.; Madrid, 1740–52).

Accarias de Sérionne, Jacques, *La Richesse de la Hollande* (2 vols., London, 1778).

Actas de la Cortes de Castilla (vols. 1–60 thus far; Madrid, from 1861).

Aenwysinge datmen van de Oost en West-Indische Compagnien een Compagnie dient te maecken (The Hague, 1644) (Knuttel 5177).

Aglionby, Dr, *Quelques considérations sur la nécessité d'interdire le commerce des lettres avec la France* (The Hague, 1690).

Aitzema, Lieuwe van, *Verhael van de Nederlantsche Vreedehandeling* (2 vols.; The Hague, 1650).

—— *Historie of verhael van saken van staet en oorlogh in, ende ontrent de Vereenigde Nederlanden* (14 vols.; 1667–71).

A New Description of Holland and the rest of the United Provinces in General (London, 1701).

Arnould, M., *De la balance du commerce et des relations commerciales extérieures de la France dans toutes les parties du globe* (2 vols.; Paris, 1791).

Becher, Johann Joachim, *Politische Discurs von den eigentlichen Ursachen des Auff- und Abnehmens der Städte, Länder und Republicken* (Frankfurt, 1673).

Berchet, G. (ed.), *Relazioni dei consoli veneti nella Siria* (Turin, 1866).

Blok, P. J. (ed.), 'Koopmansadviezen aangaande het plan tot oprichting eener compagnie van assurantie (1629–1635)', *BMHG* 21 (1900), 1–60.

—— (ed.), 'Mémoire touchant le négoce et la navigation des Hollandois' (1699), *BMHG* 24 (1903), 221–342.

Blommaert, Samuel, 'Brieven van Samuel Blommaert aan den zweedschen rijkskanselier Axel Oxenstierna, 1635–1641', *BMHG* 28 (1908), 3–16.

Blumenkranz, B. (ed.), *Documents modernes sur les Juifs (XVIe–XXe siècles)* (Toulouse, 1979).

Bosman, Willem, *Nauwkeurige beschryvinge van de Guinese goud-, tand- en slavenkust* (Utrecht, 1704).

Brief Narration of the Present State of the Bilbao Trade, A (n.p., n.d.) (London?, 1650?).

Briefwisseling tusschen de Gebroeders Van der Goes (1659–1673), ed. C. J. Gonnet (2 vols.; Amsterdam, 1899–1909).

Bronnen tot de geschiedenis van het bedrijfsleven en het gildewezen van Amsterdam, ed. J. G. van Dillen (3 vols.; The Hague, 1929–74).

Bronnen tot de geschiedenis van de Leidsche textielnijverheid, ed. N. W. Posthumus (6 vols.; The Hague, 1910–22).

Bronnen tot de geschiedenis van den Levantschen handel, ed. K. Heeringa (2 vols. in 3 parts; The Hague, 1910–17).

Bronnen tot de geschiedenis der Oostindische Compagnie in Perzië (1611–38), ed. H. Dunlop (The Hague, 1930).

Bronnen tot de geschiedenis der wisselbanken (Amsterdam, Middelburg, Delft, Rotterdam), ed. J. G. van Dillen (2 vols.; The Hague, 1925).

Bronnen voor de geschiedenis van de Nederlandse Oostzeehandel in de zeventiende eeuw, ed. P. H. Winkelman (4 vols. thus far; The Hague, 1971–).

Burrish, Onslow, *Batavia illustrata. Or a view of the Policy and Commerce of the United Provinces* (2 vols.; London, 1728).

Calendar of State Papers, Colonial Series, America and the West Indies, 1661–1668 (London, 1880).

Calendar of State Papers, Domestic, 1649–50 (London, 1875).

Calendar of State Papers and Manuscripts Relating to English Affairs existing in Venice (40 vols.; London, 1864–1947).

Child, Sir Josiah, *A New Discourse of Trade* (1672) (London, 1693).

Correspondence administrative sous le règne de Louis XIV, ed. G. B. Depping (4 vols.; Paris, 1850–5).

Correspondência diplomática de Francisco de Sousa Coutinho durante a sua embaixada em Holanda (3 vols.; Coimbra, 1920–55).

Correspondencia diplomática de los plenipotenciarios españoles en el Congreso de Munster (1643–1648), 3 vols. in *Colección de documentos inéditos para la historia de España* (113 vols.; Madrid, 1842–95), nos. lxxxii–lxxxiv.

Dam, Pieter van, *Beschryvinge van de Oostindische Compagnie,* ed. F. W. Stapel (4 vols. in 7 parts; The Hague, 1927–54).

—— 'Concept en consideratiën . . . op 't stuk van den handel van Indiën', *BTLVNI* 74 (1918), 270–98.

Davenant, Charles, *New Dialogues upon the Present Posture of Affairs, the Species of Mony . . . and the Trade now carried on between France and Holland* (London, 1710).

—— *An Account of the Trade between Great Britain, France, Holland, Spain, Portugal, Italy, Africa, Newfoundland, etc.* (London, 1715).

—— *The Political and Commercial Works* (5 vols.; London, 1771).

Defoe, Daniel, *An Enquiry into the Danger and Consequences of a War with the Dutch* (London, 1712).

—— *A Plan of the English Commerce* (1728) (Oxford, 1928).

Dillen, J. G. van (ed.), 'Memorie betreffende den handel met Spanje omstreeks 1680', *Economisch-Historisch Jaarboek,* 24 (1950), 168–74.

—— (ed.), 'Memorie betreffende de kolonie Suriname' (*c.*1730), *Economisch-Historisch Jaarboek,* 24 (1950), 162–7.

Discours op den swermenden Treves (Middelburg, 1609) (Knuttel 1576).

Edmundson, G. (ed.), 'Verhaal van de inneming van Paramaribo (1665) door Generaal William Byam', *BMHG* 19 (1898), 231–62.

Eon, Jean, *Le Commerce honorable ou considérations politiques* (Nantes, 1646).

Essai historique sur la colonie de Surinam, sa fondation, ses révolutions, ses progrès, depuis son origine jusqu'à nos jours (Paramaribo, 1788).

Forbonnais, Veron de, *Mémoires et considérations sur le commerce et les finances d'Espagne* (2 vols.; Amsterdam, 1761).

Foster, W. (ed.), *The English Factories in India, 1618–1669* (13 vols.; Oxford, 1906–27).

Franco Mendes, David, *Memórias do estabelicimento e progresso dos judeus portuguezes e espanhões nesta famosa citade de Amsterdam* in *Studia Rosenthaliana*, ix (1975).

Gardiner, S. R., and Atkinson, C. T. (eds.), *Letters and Papers Relating to the First Dutch War, 1652–1654* (6 vols.; London, 1898–1930).

Gedenkstukken van Johan van Oldenbarnevelt en zijn tijd, ed. M. L. van Deventer (3 vols.; The Hague, 1860–5).

Gentil da Silva, José, *Stratégie des affaires à Lisbonne entre 1595 et 1607: Lettres marchandes des Rodrigues d'Evora et Veiga* (Paris, 1956).

Gerritsz, Hessel, *Histoire du pays nommé Spitsberghe* (Amsterdam, 1613); repr. in vol. xxiii of the publications of the Linschoten-Vereeniging).

Godolphin, Sir William, *Hispania illustrata, or The Maxims of the Spanish Court from the Year 1667 to the Year 1678* (London, 1703).

Goens, Rijkloff van, 'Vertooch wegens den presenten staet van de generale Nederlantse geoctroijeerde Oost-Indische Compe.' (1655), *BTLVNI* 4 (1856), 141–80.

Gomes Solis, Duarte, *Discursos sobre los comercios de las dos Indias* (1622), ed. M. Bensbat Amzalak (Lisbon, 1943).

Groot Placaet-Boeck, inhoudende de placaten ende ordonnantiën vande Hoogh Mog: Heeren Staten Generael der Vereenighde Nederlanden (The Hague, 1658–83), i–ii.

Häpke, Rudolph (ed.), *Niederländische Akten und Urkunden zur Geschichte der Hanse und zur deutschen Seegeschichte* (2 vols.; Munich, 1913–23).

Heeres, J. E., and F. W. Stapel (eds.), *Corpus-diplomaticum Neerlando-Indicum* (4 vols; The Hague, 1907–53).

Helvetius, Adrianus Engelhard, 'Mémoire sur l'état présent du gouvernement des Provinces Unies' (1706), ed. M. van der Bijl, *BMHG* 80 (1966), 152–94.

Hollands Ondergang by Vranckrijck vastgestelt en door desselfs Koningh Lodewyck de XIV door alle bedeckelike middelen sedert veertig jaren herwaarts bevordert (Warmond, 1689) (Knuttel 13,121).

Hollandsche Mercurius (41 vols.; Haarlem, 1650–91).

Huet, Pierre Daniel, *Mémoires sur le commerce des Hollandois dans tous les états et empires du monde* (Amsterdam, 1718).

Humble Representation to the Commons of England . . . in Relation to the Importation of Sail Cloth from Holland (London, *c.*1720).

Indise-Raven, Christopher, *Vrankryk verduurt en overwonnen door de band van de Unie deser Staten* (Amsterdam, 1690).

——— Consideratie op de Middelen tot voordeel van den staat ende afbreuk van den vyand aengewesen en bewaerheyt (Amsterdam, 1691).

IJzerman, J. W. (ed.), 'Deductie vervatende den oorspronck ende progres van de vaert ende handel op Brasil', in *Journael van de reis naar Zuid-Amerika (1598–1601) door Hendrik Ottsen* (The Hague, 1918).

Journalen van de gedenckwaerdige reijsen van Willem Ijsbrantsz. Bontekoe, ed. G. J. Hoogewerff (The Hague, 1952).

Kroniek van het Historisch Genootschap gevestigd te Utrecht (31 vols; Utrecht, 1846–75).

La Court, Pieter de, *Interest van Holland ofte Gronden van Hollands welvaren* (Amsterdam, 1662).

——— *Het welvaren van Leiden: Handschrift uit her jaar 1659,* ed. F. Driessen (The Hague, 1911).

Laet, Johannes de, *Iaerlyck verhael van de verrichtinghen der Geoctroyeerde West-Indische Compagnie* (1644), ed. S. P. L'Honoré Naber (4 vols; The Hague, 1931–7).

Lamberty, M. de (ed.), *Mémoires pour servir à l'histoire du XVIII* siècle (14 vols.; Amsterdam, 1735–40).

Laursen, L., *Danmark-Norges traktater, 1523–1750,* iv. *1626–49* (Copenhagen, 1917).

Le Moine de L'Espine, Jacques, *Le Négoce d'Amsterdam* (Amsterdam, 1694).

Leti, Gregorio, *Il ceremoniale historico e politico* (6 vols.; Amsterdam, 1685).

——— *Teatro Belgico, o vero ritratti historici, chronologici, politici e geografici, delle sette Provincie Unite* (2 vols.; Amsterdam, 1690).

Letters from and to Sir Dudley Carleton, Knt. During his Embassy in Holland, from January 1616 to Dec. 1620 (2nd edn.; London 1775).

Lettres de Pierre de Groot à Abraham Wicquefort (1668–1674), ed. F. J. L. Krämer (The Hague, 1894).

Lettres, instructions et mémoires de Colbert, ed. Pierre Clément (8 vols; Paris, 1861–1882).

Lister, T. H., *Life and Administration of Edward, First Earl of Clarendon,* iii (documentary appendix) (London, 1838).

Luzac, Elias, *Hollands rijkdom, behelzende den oorsprong van den koophandel en van de magt van dezen Staat* (4 vols.; Leiden, 1780–3).

Luzzatto, Simone, *Discurso circa il stato de gl'hebrei et in particular dimoranti nell'inclita città di Venetia* (Venice, 1638).

Malynes, Gerard de, *Lex mercatoria or The Ancient Law-Merchant* (London, 1629).

Marperger, Paul Jacob, *Historischer Kauffmann* (Lübeck–Leipzig, 1708).

——*Schlesischer Kauffmann oder ausführliche Beschreibung der schlesischen Commercien und deren ietzigen Zustandes* (Breslau–Leipzig, 1714).

——*Beschreibung des Tuchmacher-Handwercks und der aus grob und fein sortirter Wolle verfertigten Tücher* (Dresden–Leipzig, 1723).

McCulloch, J. R. (ed.), *Early English Tracts on Commerce* (Cambridge, 1954).

Mémoires de François Martin, fondateur de Pondichéry (1665–1696) (3 vols.; Paris, 1931–4).

Memorias de Raimundo de Lantéry, mercader de Indias en Cádiz, 1673–1700 (Cadiz, 1949).

'Memoriën van den zweedschen resident Harald Appelboom', ed. G. W. Kernkamp, *BMHG* 26 (1905), 290–375.

Molesworth, Robert, *An Account of Denmark as it was in the Year 1692* (London, 1694).

Montchrétien, Antoine de, *Traicté de l'œconomie politique* (1615) (Paris, 1899).

Négociations de Monsieur le Comte d'Avaux en Hollande depuis 1679 jusqu'en 1688 (6 vols.; Paris, 1752–3).

Nicrop, Leonie van (ed.), 'Stukken betreffende de nijverheid der *refugiés* te Amsterdam', *EHJ* 7 (1921), 147–49.

Notulen der Staten van Zeeland (Middelburg, 1595–1713).

Nykerke, Joost, *Klaer-Bericht ofte Aenwysinge hoe ende op wat wijse de tegenwoordige dierte der Granen sal konnen geremedieert werden ende de schipvaart deser landen vergroot* (The Hague, 1630).

Oddy, J. T., *European Commerce, Shewing New and Secure Channels of Trade with the Continent of Europe* (London, 1805).

Penso de la Vega, Joseph, *Confusión de confusiones* (1688), ed. M. F. J. Smith (The Hague, 1939).

Pinto, Isaac de, *Traité de la circulation et du crédit* (Amsterdam, 1771).

Pomponne, Simon-Nicolas Arnauld de, *La Relation de mon ambassade en Hollande*, ed. H. H. Rowen (Utrecht, 1955).

Pontanus, Johannes Isacius, *Historische beschrijvinghe der seer wijt beroemde coop-stadt Amsterdam* (Amsterdam, 1614).

Posthumus, N. W. (ed.), *De nationale organisatie der lakenkoopers tijdens de Republiek* (Utrecht, 1927).

'Proposiciones del marqués de Variñas' in the *Colección de documentos inéditos relativos al descubrimiento, conquista y organización de las antiguas posesiones españolas de América y Oceanía*, xix (1873), 239–75.

Ratelband, K. (ed.), *Reizen naar West-Afrika van Pieter van den Broeke, 1605–1614* (The Hague, 1950).

Reael, Laurens, 'Verslag over de toestand in Oost-Indië' (1620), in *Nederlandse Historische Bronnen*, i (The Hague, 1979), 175–210.

Recueil des instructions données aux ambassadeurs et ministres de France depuis les traités de Westphalie jusqu'à la Révolution Française, xxix. *Turquie* ed. P. Duparc (Paris, 1969).

Reden van dat de West-Indische Compagnie oft Handelinge niet alleen profitelijck maar oock noodtsaeckelijck is tot behoudenisse van onsen staet (n.p., 1636).

Relaciones de Pedro Teixeira (Antwerp, 1610).

Relazioni veneziane. Venetiaanse berichten over de Vereenigde Nederlanden van 1600–1795, ed. P. J. Blok (The Hague, 1909).

Resolutiën der Staten-Generaal, new ser. 1610–1670, ii. *1613–1616*, ed. A. Th. van Deursen (The Hague, 1984).

Resolutiën van de Staten van Holland (289 vols.; Amsterdam, 1789–1814).

Roberts, Lewes, *The Marchants Mapp of Commerce* (London, 1638).

Ruyters, Dierick, *Toortse der zeevaert*, ed. S. P. L'Honoré-Naber (The Hague, 1913).

Savary, Jacques, *Le Parfait Négociant* (2 vols.; Paris, 1675).

Savary des Bruslons, Jacques, *Dictionnaire universel de commerce* (3 vols.; Paris, 1723).

Schröder, Freiherr Wilhelm von, *Schatz und Rent-Kammer* (Leipzig-Königsberg, 1744).

Sée, Henri (ed.), 'Documents sur le commerce de Cadix', *Revue de l'histoire des colonies françaises*, 19 (1926), 465–520; 20 (1927), 259–76.

—— 'Un document sur le commerce des Hollandais à Nantes en 1645', *Economisch-Historisch Jaarboek*, 12 (1926), 125–34.

—— and Vignols, L. (eds.), 'Quelques documents sur les relations commerciales entre la France et la Hollande au début du 18e siècle', *EHJ* 15 (1929), 287–306.

Smith, Adam, *The Wealth of Nations*, ed. E. R. A. Seligman (2 vols.; London–New York, 1910).

Swift, Jonathan, *The Conduct of the Allies* (Oxford, 1916).

Tegenwoordige staat van Zeeland, ed. Pieter Boddaert *et al.* (2 vols.; Amsterdam, 1751–3).

Tertre, R. P. du, *Histoire générale des Antilles habitées par les françois* (4 vols.; Paris, 1667).

Thurloe, John, *A Collection of State Papers* (7 vols.; London, 1742).

Tollenaer, Arend, *Remonstrantie ofte vertoogh inhoudende verscheyden schatten van groote consideratie* (The Hague, 1672).

—— *Stucken, bewysen ende berichtingen dienende voor verdere Bylagen ende als een tweede deel van de Remonstrantie ofte vertoogh* (The Hague, 1672).

—— *De Voor-Looper, wegens de ontdeckinge van diverse seer schadelicke en schandelicke In ende Uytheemsche Landtverraders–Landtverraderessen in Hollandt en West-Vrieslandt* (The Hague, 1674).

Usselinx, Willem, *Grondich discours over desen aen-staenden vredehandel* (n.p., 1608).

—— *Naerder bedenckingen over de zee-vaerdt, coophandel ende nerringhe als mede de versekeringhe vanden staet deser landen inde tegenwoordighe vrede handeling met den Coninck van Spaengien* (n.p. 1608).

—— *Waerschouwinghe over den Treves met den Coninck van Spaengien aen alle goede patriotten ghedaen met ghewichtige redenen* (Flushing, 1630).

Valkenier, Petrus, *'t Verwerd Europa, ofte politijke en historische beschryvinge der waare fundamenten en oorsaken van de oorlogen en revolutiën in Europa* (Amsterdam, 1742).

Velius, Theodorus, *Chronyk van Hoorn* (4th edn.; Hoorn, 1740).

Wagenaar, Jan, *Vaderlandsche historie, vervattende de geschiedenissen der nu Vereenigde Nederlanden* (21 vols.; Amsterdam, 1752–9).

Westermann, J. C. (ed.), 'Een memorie van 1751 over de tabaksindustrie en den tabakshandel in de republiek', *EHJ* 22 (1943), 68–81.

Witsen, Nicolaas, *Moscovische Reyse, 1664–1665: Journaal en aentekeningen,* ed. Th. J. G. Locher and P. de Buck (3 vols.; The Hague, 1966).

Worsley, Benjamin, *The Advocate, or a Narrative of the State and Condition of Things between the English and Dutch Nation, in Relation to Trade* (London, 1652).

Yarranton, Andrew, *England's Improvement by Sea and Land to out-do the Dutch without Fighting* (London, 1677).

Zorgdrager, C. G., *Bloeyende opkomst der aloude en hedendaagsche Groenlandsche Visscherij* (Amsterdam, 1720).

SECONDARY LITERATURE

Aalbers, A. J., *Rycklof van Goens, commissaris en veldoverste der Oost-Indische Compagnie* (Groningen, 1916).

Abbing, C. A., *Geschiedenis der stad Hoorn hoofdstad van West-Vriesland gedurende het grootste gedeelte der XVIIe en XVIIIe eeuw* (Hoorn, 1841).

Alanen, A. J., *Der Aussenhandel und die Schiffahrt Finnlands im 18. Jahrhundert* (Helsinki, 1957).

Alcalá-Zamora, José, *España, Flandes y el Mar del Norte (1618–1639)* (Barcelona, 1975).

Arasaratnam, Sinnapah, *Dutch Power in Ceylon, 1658–1687* (Djambatan–The Hague, 1958).

—— 'Dutch Commercial Policy in Ceylon and its Effects on the Indo-Ceylon Trade (1690–1750)', *Indian Economic and Social History Review,* iv (1967), 109–30.

—— 'The Dutch East India Company and its Coromandel Trade, 1700–1740', *BTLVNI* 123 (1967), 325–46.

—— 'Some Notes on the Dutch in Malacca and the Indo-Malayan Trade, 1641–1670', *Journal of Southeast Asian History,* 10 (1969), 480–90.

Arasaratnam, Sinnapah, 'Monopoly and Free Trade in Dutch–Asian Commercial Policy: Debate and Controversy within the VOC', *Journal of Southeast Asian Studies*, 4 (1973), 1–15.

Aspetti e cause della decadenza economica veneziana nel secolo XVII, conference proceedings published by the Istituto per la Collaborazione Culturale (Venice–Rome, 1961).

Åström, Sven-Erik, 'Technology and Timber Exports from the Gulf of Finland, 1661–1740', *Scandinavian Economic History Review*, 23 (1975), 1–14.

——'Commercial and Industrial Development in the Baltic Region in Relation to the Other Areas of Europe', ISEPA 10 (1983), 435–54.

Attman, Artur, *Dutch Enterprise in the World Bullion Trade, 1550–1800* (Göteborg, 1983).

——*Swedish Aspirations and the Russian Market during the 17th Century (Göteborg, 1985)*.

——*American Bullion in the European World Trade, 1600–1800* (Göteborg, 1986).

Aymard, Maurice (ed.), *Dutch Capitalism and World Capitalism* (Cambridge–Paris, 1982).

Baasch, Ernst, 'Hamburgs Seeschiffahrt und Warenhandel vom Ende des 16. bis zur Mitte des 17. Jahrhunderts', *Zeitschrift für Hamburgische Geschichte*, 9 (1894), 295–420.

——'Zur Geschichte des hamburgischen Heringshandels', *Hansische Geschichtsblätter*, 12 (1906), 61–100.

——'Hamburg und Holland im 17. und 18. Jahrhundert', *Hansische Geschichtsblätter*, 16 (1910), 45–102.

——*Holländische Wirtschaftsgeschichte* (Jena, 1927).

Baetens, R. *De nazomer van Antwerpens welvaart: De diaspora en het handelshuis De Groote tijdens de erste helft der 17e eeuw* (2 vols.; Brussels, 1976).

——'The Organisation and Effects of Flemish Privateering in the Seventeenth Century', *Acta Historiae Neerlandicae*, 9 (1976), 48–75.

Bang, Nina Ellinger, *Tabeller over Skibsfart og Varetransport gennem Øresund, 1497–1660* (3 vols.; Copenhagen, 1906–33).

——and Korst, K., *Tabeller over Skibsfart og Varetransport gennem Øresund, 1661–1783 og gennem Store Bælt 1701–1748* (3 vols.; Copenhagen, 1930–53).

Bangs, C. O., 'Regents and Remonstrants in Amsterdam', in *In het spoor van Arminius* (Nieuwkoop, 1975), 15–29.

Barbour, Violet, *Capitalism in Amsterdam in the 17th Century* (1950; 3rd printing, Ann Arbor, 1976).

——'Marine Risks and Insurance in the Seventeenth Century', *Journal of Economic and Business History*, 1 (1929), 561–96.

Bastin, J., 'De Gentse lijnwaadmarkt en linnenhandel in de XVIIe eeuw', *Handelingen der Maatschappij voor Geschiedenis en Oudheidkunde te Gent*, ser. XXI (1967), 131–62.

Becht, H. E., *Statistische gegevens betreffende de handelsomzet van de Republiek der Vereenigde Nederlanden gedurende de 17de eeuw* (The Hague, 1923).

Bel, J. G. van, *De linnenhandel van Amsterdam in de XVIIIe eeuw* (Amsterdam, 1940).

Benedict, Ph., 'Rouen's Trade during the Era of the Religious Wars (1560–1600)', *Journal of European Economic History*, 13 (1984), 29–74.

Benoit du Rey, E., *Recherches sur la politique coloniale de Colbert* (Paris, 1902).

Bentham, A., *Geschiedenis van Enschede en zijne naaste omgeving* (Enschede, 1920).

Bentley Duncan, T., *Atlantic Islands: Madeira, The Azores and the Cape Verdes in Seventeenth-century Commerce and Navigation* (Chicago, 1972).

—— 'Niels Steensgaard and the Europe–Asia Trade of the Early Seventeenth Century', *Journal of Modern History*, 47 (1975), 512–18.

Berchet, Guglielmo, *Cromwell e la Repubblica di Venezia* (Venice, 1864).

—— *La Repubblica di Venezia e la Persia* (Turin, 1865).

Bering Liisberg, H. C., *Danmarks søfart of søhandel* (2 vols.; Copenhagen, 1919).

Beutin, Ludwig, *Der deutsche Seehandel im Mittelmeergebiet bis zu den Napoleonischen Kriegen* (Neumünster, 1933).

—— 'Nordwestdeutschland und die Niederlande seit dem Dreissigjährigen Kriege', *Vierteljahrschrift fur Sozial- und Wirtschaftsgeschichte*, 32 (1939), 104–47.

—— 'Der wirtschaftliche Niedergang Venedigs im 16. und 17. Jahrhundert', *Hansische Geschichtsblätter*, 76 (1958).

—— and Entholt, H., *Bremen und die Niederlande* (Weimar, 1939).

Bicci, Antonella, 'Gli olandesi nel Mediterraneo: Amsterdam e l'Italia (sec. XVII°)', *Centre de recherches neohelleniques: actes du IIᵉ colloque international d'histoire* (Athens, 1985), 39–76.

Bijlsma, R., 'Rotterdams Amerika-vaart in de eerste helft der zeventiende eeuw', *BVGO* 5th ser. 3 (1916), 97–142.

Binder, Franz, 'Die Zeeländische Kaperfahrt, 1654–1662', *Archief uitgegeven door het Koninklijk Zeeuwsch Genootschap der Wetenschappen* (Middelburg, 1976).

—— 'Die Goldeinfuhr von der Goldküste in die Vereinigten Provinzen, 1655–1675', in Hermann Kellenbenz (ed.), *Precious Metals in the Age of Expansion* (Stuttgart, 1981), 131–49.

Blendinger, Friedrich, 'Augsburger Handel im Dreissigjährigen Kriege' in J. Schneider (ed.), *Wirtschaftskräfte und Wirtschaftswege: Festschrift für Hermann Kellenbenz* (5 vols.; Nuremberg, 1978–81), ii. 287–323.

Blok, P. J., *Michiel Adriaanszoon de Ruyter* (The Hague, 1930).

Bloom, H. I., *The Economic Activities of the Jews of Amsterdam in the Seventeenth and Eighteenth Centuries* (1937; reissued Port Washington, New York, 1969).

Bogucka, M. 'Amsterdam and the Baltic in the First Half of the Seventeenth Century', *Economic History Review*, 2nd ser. 26 (1973), 433–47.

—— 'Danzig an der Wende zur Neuzeit: Von der Aktiven Handelstadt zum Stapel und Produktionszentrum', *Hansische Geschichtsblätter*, 102 (1984), 91–103.

Boissonade, P., 'Colbert, son système et les entreprises industrielles d'Etat en Languedoc (1661–1683)', *Annales du Midi*, 14 (1902), 5–49.

—— *Colbert: Le Triomphe de l'étatisme: La Fondation de la suprématie industrielle de la France (1661–1683)* (Paris, 1932).

—— and Charliat, P., *Colbert et la Compagnie du Nord (1661–89)* (Paris, 1930).

Bondois, P. M., 'Colbert et la question du sucre: La Rivalité franco-hollandaise', *Revue d'histoire économique et sociale*, 11 (1923), 12–61.

Boogaart, E. van den, 'De Nederlandse expansie in het Atlantisch gebied 1590–1674', in the (New) *Algemene geschiedenis der Nederlanden*, vii. 220–54.

Bos Radwan, A., *The Dutch in Western India, 1601–1632* (Calcutta, 1978).

Bossch-Erdbrink, G. R., *At the Threshold of Felicity: Ottoman–Dutch Relations during the Embassy of Cornelius Calkoen at the Sublime Porte, 1726–1744* (Ankara, 1975).

Boumans, R., 'Le Dépeuplement d'Anvers dans dernier quart du XVIe siècle', *Revue du nord*, 29 (1947), 181–94.

Bowman, F. J. 'Dutch Diplomacy and the Baltic Grain Trade, 1600–1660', *The Pacific Historical Review*, 5 (1936), 337–48.

Boxer, C. R., *The Dutch Seaborne Empire, 1600–1800* (London, 1965).

—— *The Dutch in Brazil, 1624–54* (1957; reissued Hamden, Conn., 1973).

—— *Jan Compagnie in War and Peace, 1602–1799* (London–Hong Kong, 1979).

Braam, Aris van, *Bloei en verval van het economisch-sociale leven aan de Zaan in de 17de en 18de eeuw* (Wormerveer, 1944).

Brakel, S. van, *De hollandsche handelscompagniën der zeventiende eeuw* (The Hague, 1908).

—— 'Statistische en andere gegevens betreffende onzen handel en scheepvaart op Rusland gedurende de 18de eeuw', *BMHG* 34 (1913), 350–404.

—— 'Bescheiden over den slavenhandel der West-Indische Compagnie', *EHJ* 4 (1918), 47–83.

Braudel, Fernand, *La Méditerranée et la monde méditerranéen à l'époque de Philippe II* (2 vols.; Paris, 1966).

—— *The Mediterranean and the Mediterranean World in the Age of Philip II*, trans. Sian Reynolds (2 vols.; London, 1973).

—— *Afterthoughts on Material Civilization and Capitalism* (Baltimore, 1977).

—— *Civilisation matérielle, économie et capitalisme, XVe–XVIIIe siècle* (3 vols.; Paris, 1979).

—— and Romano, Ruggiero, *Navires et marchandises à l'entrée du Port de Livourne (1547–1611)* (Paris, 1951).

Briels, J. G. C. A., *De Zuidnederlandse immigratie 1572–1630* (Bussum, 1978).

Brinner, Ludwig, *Die deutsche Grönlandfahrt* (Berlin, 1913).

Bro Jørgensen, J. O., *Industriens historie i Danmark tiden 1730–1820* (Copenhagen, 1943).

Bromley, J. S., *Corsairs and Navies, 1660–1760* (London, 1987).

Brugmans, H., 'De notulen en monumenten van het College van Commercie te Amsterdam, 1663–1665', *BMHG* 18 (1897), 181–330.

—— 'Statistiek van den in- en uitvoer van Amsterdam, 1 Oct. 1667–30, Sept. 1668', *BMHG* 19 (1898), 125–83.

Bruijn, J. R. de, 'Scheepvaart in de Noordelijke Nederlanden, 1580–1650', in the (New) *Algemene geschiedenis der Nederlanden*, vii. 137–55.

—— 'Kaapvaart in de tweede en derde Engelse oorlog', *BMGN* 90 (1975), 408–29.

—— 'De personeelsbehoefte van de VOC overzee en aan boord', *BMGN* 91 (1976), 218–48.

Bruijn, J. R. de, and Davids, C. A., 'Jonas vrij: De Nederlandse walvisvaart in het bijzonder de Amsterdamse, in de jaren 1640–1664', *EHJ* 38 (1975), 141–78.

Brulez, Wilfrid, 'De zoutinvoer in de Nederlanden in de 16de eeuw', *TvG* 68 (1955), 181–92.

—— 'La Navigation flamande vers la Méditerranée à la fin du XVIe siècle', *Revue belge de philologie et d'histoire*, 36 (1958), 1210–42.

—— *De Firma Della Faille en de internationale handel van Vlaamse firma's in de 16de eeuw* (Brussels, 1959).

—— 'De diaspora der Vlaamse kooplui op het einde der XVIe eeuw', *Bijdragen voor de Geschiedenis der Nederlanden*, 15 (1960), 279–306.

—— 'Les Routes commerciales d'Angleterre en Italie au XVIe siècle', *Studi in onore di Amintore Fanfani*, 4 (Milan, 1962), 123–84.

—— 'Anvers de 1585 à 1650', *Vierteljahrschrift für Sozial- und Wirtschaftsgeschichte*, 54 (1967), 75–99.

—— 'Scheepvaart in de Zuidelijke Nederlanden' in the (New) *Algemene geschiedenis der Nederlanden*', vi. 123–8.

Brünner, E. C. G., 'Een excerpt uit Finsche tolregisters over de jaren 1559–1595', *EHJ* 15 (1929), 185–217.

Buck, P. de, 'Rusland en Polen als markten voor het Westen omstreeks 1600', *TvG* 90 (1977), 211–30.

—— and Lindblad, J. Th., 'De scheepvaart en handel uit de Oostzee op Amsterdam en de Republiek, 1722–1780', *TvG* 96 (1983), 536–62.

Bulferetti, Luigi, *Assolutismo e mercantilismo nel Piemonte di Carlo Emmanuele II* (Turin, 1953).

Bushkovitch, Paul, *The Merchants of Moscow, 1580–1650* (Cambridge, 1980).

Cabral de Mello, E., *Olinda restaurada. Guerra e açúcar no Nordeste, 1630–1654* (São Paulo, 1975).

Castillo Pintado, Alvaró, *Tráfico marítimo y comercio de importación en Valencia a comienzos del siglo XVII* (Madrid, 1967).

Chaudhuri, K. N., *The Trading World of Asia and the English East India Company, 1660–1760* (Cambridge, 1978).

Chaunu, H., and P., *Séville et l'Atlantique* (1504–1650) (8 parts; Paris, 1955–9).

Chaunu, P., 'Seville et la Belgique (1555–1648)', *Revue du nord*, 42 (1960), 259–92.

Chemin-Dupontes, Paul, *Les Compagnies de colonisation en Afrique occidentale sous Colbert* (Paris, 1903).

Christensen, Axel E., *Dutch Trade to the Baltic around 1600* (Copenhagen–The Hague, 1941).

—— *Industriens historie i Danmark indtil c.1730* (Copenhagen, 1943).

Clark, G. N., *The Dutch Alliance and the War against French Trade (1688–97)* (Manchester, 1923).

—— 'War Trade and Trade War, 1701–1713', *Economic History Review*, 1 (1927–8), 262–80.

Cole, Charles W., *Colbert and a Century of French Mercantilism* (2 vols.; New York, 1939).

—— *French Mercantilism, 1683–1700* (New York, 1943).

Colenbrander, H. T., *Koloniale geschiedenis* (3 vols.; The Hague, 1925–6).

Collins, J. B., 'The Role of Atlantic France in Baltic Trade: Dutch Traders and Polish Grain at Nantes, 1625–1675', *Journal of European Economic History*, 13 (1984), 239–89.

Colmeiro, Manuel, *Historia de la economía política en Espanã* (2 vols.; Madrid, 1863).

Coniglio, Giusseppe, *Il viceregno di Napoli nel secolo XVII* (Rome, 1955).

Coornaert, E., *Un centre industriel d'autrefois: La draperie-sayetterie d'Hondschoote* (Paris, 1930).

Craeybeckx, Jean, *Un grand commerce d'importation: Les vins de France aux anciens Pays-Bas (XIIIe–XVIe siècles)* (Paris, 1958).

—— 'Les Industries d'exportation dans les villes flamandes au XVIIe siècle, particulièrement à Gand et Bruges', in *Studi in onore di Amintore Fanfani* (6 vols.; Milan, 1962), iv. 411–68.

Dahlgren, E. W., *Le Commerce de la Mer du Sud jusqu'à la Paix d'Utrecht* (Paris, 1909).

—— 'L'Expédition de Martinet et la fin du commerce français dans la Mer du Sud', *Revue de l'histoire des colonies françaises*, 1 (1913), 257–332.

Das Gupta, A., *Malabar in Asian Trade* (1967).

Davies, D. W., *A Primer of Dutch Seventeenth Century Overseas Trade* (The Hague, 1961).

Davis, Ralph, 'Influences de l'Angleterre sur le déclin de Venise au XVIIième siècle' in *Aspetti e cause della decadenza veneziana*, 210–29.

—— *The rise of the English Shipping Industry* (London, 1962).

—— 'English Imports from the Middle East, 1580–1780', in M. A. Cook (ed.), *Studies in the Economic History of the Middle East* (London, 1970), 193–206.

—— *The Rise of the Atlantic Economies* (Ithaca—New York, 1973).

—— 'English Merchant Shipping and Anglo-Dutch Rivalry in the Seventeenth Century (National Maritime Museum pamphlet) (London, 1975).

Deerr, Noël, *The History of Sugar* (2 vols.; London, 1949).

Dentz, F. O., *De kolonisatie van de Portugeesch-Joodsche natie in Suriname* (Amsterdam, 1927).

Denucé, J., 'De beurs van Antwerpen: Oorsprong en eerste ontwikkeling (15e en 16e eeuwen)', *Antwerpsch Archievenblad*, 2nd ser. 6 (1931), 81–145.

Dermigny, Louis, *Le Chine et l'Occident: Le Commerce à Canton au XVIIIe siècle, 1719–1833* (3 vols.; Paris, 1964).

Despretz-Van de Casteele, S., 'Het protectionisme in de zuidelijke Nederlanden gedurende de tweede helft der 17de eeuw', *TvG* 78 (1965), 294–317.

Diferee, H. C., *De geschiedenis van den Nederlandschen handel tot den val der Republiek* (Amsterdam, 1908).

Dillen, J. G. van, 'Amsterdam als wereldmarkt der edele metalen in de 17de en 18de eeuw', *De Economist* (1923), 538–50, 583–98, 717–30.

—— 'Eenige stukken aangaande den Amsterdamschen graanhandel in de tweede helft der zeventiende eeuw', *EHJ* 9 (1923), 221–30.

—— 'Isaac le Maire en de handel in actiën der Oost-Indische Compagnie', *EHJ* 16 (1930), 1–105.

—— 'Nieuwe gegevens omtrent de Amsterdamsche Compagniëen van Verre', *TvG* 45 (1930), 350–9.

—— 'Effectenkoersen aan de Amsterdamsche beurs', *EHJ* 17 (1931), 1–46.

—— 'Summiere staat van de in 1622 in de provincie Holland gehouden volkstelling', *EHJ* 21 (1940), 167–89.

—— 'Leiden als industriestad tijdens de Republiek', *TvG* 59 (1946), 25–51.

—— *Het oudste aandeelhoudersregister van de kamer Amsterdam der Oost-Indische Compagnie* (The Hague, 1958).

—— 'De Opstand en het Amerikaanse zilver', *TvG* 73 (1960), 25–38.

—— 'De West-Indische Compagnie, het calvinisme en de politiek', *TvG* 74 (1961), 145–71.

Dillen, J. G. van, 'La Banque de Change et les banquiers privés à Amsterdam aux XVIIe et XVIIIe siècles', *Troisième conférence internationale d'histoire économique* (Munich, 1965), 177–85.
—— *Van rijkdom en regenten: Handboek tot de economische en sociale geschiedenis van Nederland tijdens de Republiek* (The Hague, 1970).
Disney, A. R., *Twilight of the Pepper Empire: Portuguese Trade in Southwest India in the Early Seventeenth Century* (Harvard, 1978).
Domínguez Ortiz, Antonio, 'Guerra económica y comercio extranjero en el reinado de Felipe IV', *Hispania*, 23 (1963), 71–113.
Driesch, Wilhelm von den, *Die ausländischen Kaufleute während des 18. Jahrhunderts in Spanien und ihre Beteiligung am Kolonialhandel* (Cologne–Vienna, 1972).
Edmundson, G., 'The Dutch in Western Guiana', *English Historical Review*, 16 (1901), 640–75.
—— 'The Dutch on the Amazon and Negro in the Seventeenth Century', *English Historical Review*, 18 (1903), 642–63; 19 (1904), 1–25.
Eggen, J. L. M., *De invloed door Zuid-Nederland op Noord-Nederland uitgeoefend op het einde der XVIe en het begin der XVIIe eeuw* (Ghent, 1908).
Elias, J. E., *De vroedschap van Amsterdam* (2 vols.; Haarlem, 1903–8).

—— *Het voorspel van den eersten Engelschen Oorlog* (2 vols.; The Hague, 1920).
Elzinga, Simon, *Het voorspel van den oorlog van 1672: De economisch-politieke betrekkingen tusschen Frankrijk en Nederland in de jaren 1666–1672* (Haarlem, 1926).
—— 'Le Tarif de Colbert de 1664 et celui de 1667 et leur signification', *EHJ* 15 (1929), 221–73.
Emmanuel, I. S., 'Les Juifs de la Martinique et leurs coreligionnaires d'Amsterdam au XVIIe siècle', *Revue des études juives*, 123 (1964), 511–16.
—— and Emmanuel, S. A., *History of the Jews of the Netherlands Antilles* (2 vols.; Cincinnati, 1970).
Enschedé, J. W., 'Papier en papierhandel in Noord-Nederland gedurende de zeventiende eeuw', *Tijdschrift voor boek- en bibliotheekwezen*, 7 (1909), 97–188, 205–31.
Everaert, J., *De internationale en koloniale handel der Vlaamse firma's te Cadiz, 1670–1700* (Bruges, 1973).
Faber, J. A., 'The Decline of the Baltic Grain Trade in the Second Half of the Seventeenth Century', *Acta Historiae Neerlandica*, 1, (1966), 108–31.
—— *Drie eeuwen Friesland: Economische en sociale ontwikkelingen van 1500 tot 1800* (2 vols.; Leeuwarden, 1973).
—— 'De achttiende eeuw', in J. H. van Stuijvenberg (ed.), *De economische geschiedenis van Nederland* (Groningen, 1977), 119–56.

—— 'Scheepvaart op Nederland in een woelige periode: 1784–1810', *EHJ* 47 (1984), 67–78.

Farnell, J. E., 'The Navigation Act of 1651: The First Dutch War and the London Merchant Community', *Economic History Review*, 2nd ser. 16 (1964), 439–54.

Federowicz, J. K., 'Anglo-Polish Commercial Relations in the First Half of the Seventeenth Century', *Journal of European Economic History*, 5 (1976), 359–78.

—— *England's Baltic Trade in the Early Seventeenth Century* (Cambridge, 1980).

Feijst, G. van der, *Geschiedenis van Schiedam* (Schiedam, 1975).

Fisher, H. E. S., *The Portugal Trade: A Study of Anglo-Portuguese Commerce, 1700–1770* (London, 1971).

Franken, M. A. M., *Coenraad van Beuningen's politieke en diplomatieke aktiviteiten in de jaren 1667–1684* (Groningen, 1966).

Frenken, A. M., *Helmond in het verleden* (2 vols.; Helmond, 1928–9).

Fridericia, J. A., *Danmarks ydre politiske historie i tiden fra Freden i Prag til Freden i Bromsebrö (1635–1645)* (Copenhagen, 1881).

Friis, Astrid, *Alderman Cockayne's Project and the Cloth Trade* (Copenhagen–London, 1927).

Fruin, Robert, *Tien jaren uit den tachtigjarigen oorlog, 1588–1598* (The Hague, 1924).

Furber, Holden, *Rival Empires of Trade in the Orient, 1600–1800* (Minneapolis, 1976).

Gaastra, F. S., 'Geld tegen goederen: Een structurele verandering in het Nederlands–Aziatisch handelsverkeer', *BMGN* 89 (1976), 249–72.

—— 'The Shifting Balance of Trade of the Dutch East India Company', in L. Blussé and F. S. Gaastra (eds.), *Companies and Trade* (Leiden, 1981), 47–70.

—— *De geschiedenis van de VOC* (Bussum, 1982).

Gabory, E., 'La Marine et le commerce de Nantes au XVIIe siècle et au commencement du XVIIIe (1661–1715), *Annales de Bretagne*, 17 (1901/2), 1–44, 235–90.

García Fuentes, Lutgardo, *El comercio español con América (1650–1700)* (Seville, 1980).

García Sanz, Angel, *Desarrollo y crisis del Antiguo Régimen en Castilla la Vieja: Economía y sociedad en tierras de Segovia de 1500 a 1814* (Madrid, 1977).

Gentil da Silva, J., 'Trafics du Nord, marchés du 'Mezzogiorno', *Revue du Nord*, 41 (1959), 129–52.

Gerentz, Sven, *Kommerskollegium och Näringslivet* (Stockholm, 1951).

Geyl, Pieter, 'Een historische legende: Het Zuid-Nederlands tarief van 21 Dec. 1680', in his *Kernproblemen van onze geschiedenis: Opstellen en voordrachten, 1925–1936* (Utrecht, 1937).

Gezelschap, E., 'De lakennijverheid, 1331–1778', in *Gouda: Zeven eeuwen stad* (Gouda, 1972).

Gielens, A., 'Onderhandelingen met Zeeland over de opening van der Schelde (1612–1613)', *Antwerpsch Archievenblad*, 2nd ser. 6 (1931), 194–221.

Girard, A. *Le Commerce français à Seville et Cadix au temps des Habsbourg* (Bordeaux–Paris, 1932).

Glamann, Kirsten, 'Det ældste danske kommercekollegium', in S. Ellehøj (ed.), *Festskrift til Astrid Friis* (Copenhagen, 1963).

Glamann, Kristof, *Dutch-Asiatic Trade, 1620–1740* (Copenhagen–The Hague, 1958).

Goedewaagen, D. A., *De geschiedenis van de pijpmakerij te Gouda* (Gouda, 1942).

Gómez-Centurión Jiménez, Carlos, 'Las relaciones hispano-hanseáticas durante el reinado de Felipe II', *Revista de historia naval*, 15 (1986), 65–83.

——*Felipe II, la empresa de Inglaterra y el comercio septentrional (1566–1609)* (Madrid, 1988).

Goodman, G. K., *The Dutch Impact on Japan (1640–1853)* (Leiden, 1967).

Goonewardena, K. W., *The Foundation of Dutch Power in Ceylon* (Djambatan–Amsterdam, 1958).

Goslinga, C. Ch., *The Dutch in the Caribbean and on the Wild Coast, 1580–1680* (Assen, 1971).

——*The Dutch in the Caribbean and in the Guianas, 1680–1791* (Assen, 1985).

Graaf, H. J. de, *De regering van Sultan Agung van Mataram, 1613–1645* (The Hague, 1958).

Gramulla, G. S., *Handelsbeziehungen Kölner Kaufleute zwischen 1500 und 1650* (Cologne, 1972).

Grayson, J. C., 'From Protectorate to Partnership: Anglo-Dutch Relations, 1598–1625' (unpublished University of London Ph. D. thesis, 1978).

Grendi, Edoardo, 'I nordici e il traffico del porto di Genova, 1590–1666', *Rivista storica italiana*, 83 (1971), 28–55.

Groenevelt, W. P., *De Nederlanders in China* (The Hague, 1898).

Groenveld, Simon, *Verlopend getij: De Nederlandse Republiek en de Engelse Burgeroorlog, 1640–1646* (Dieren, 1984).

——'The English Civil Wars as a Cause of the First Anglo-Dutch War, 1640–1652', *Historical Journal*, 30 (1987), 541–66.

Grol, H. G. van, *Het beheer van het zeeuwsche zeewezen, 1577–1587* (The Hague, 1936).

Groot, A. H. de, *The Ottoman Empire and the Dutch Republic* (Leiden–Istanbul, 1978).

——'The Organization of Western European Trade in the Levant, 1500–

Bibliography 433

1800', in L. Blussé and F. S. Gaastra (eds.), *Companies and Trade* (Leiden, 1981), 231–41.

Grossmann, J., *Die Amsterdamer Börse vor zwei Hundert Jahren* (The Hague, 1876).

Guarnieri, G. G., *Il movimento delle navi di guerra e mercantili nel porto di Livorno al tempo del terzo granduca di Toscano (1587–1609)* (Livorno, 1911).

Günter, H., *Die Habsburger-Liga, 1625–1635: Briefe und Akten aus dem General-Archiv zu Simancas* (Berlin, 1908).

Haan, H. den, *Moedernegotie en grote vaart* (Amsterdam, 1977).

Hagedorn, B., *Ostfrieslands Handel und Schiffahrt vom Ausgang des 16. Jahrhunderts bis zum Westfälischen Frieden (1580–1648)* (Berlin, 1912).

Haitsma Mulier, E. O. G., 'Genova e l'Olanda nel seicento, contatti mercantili e ispirazione politica', in R. Belveder (ed.), *Atti del Congresso Internazionale di Studi Storici: Rapporti Genova–Mediterraneo–Atlantico nell'età moderna*, v (Genoa, 1983), 429–44.

Hallema, A., 'Friesland en de voormalige compagnieën voor den handel op oost en west', *West Indische Gids*, 15 (1933), 81–96.

Hanson, C. A., *Economy and Society in Baroque Portugal, 1668–1703* (Minnesota, 1981).

Harlow, V. T., *A History of Barbados, 1625–1685* (Oxford, 1926).

Harper, L. A., *The English Navigation Laws* (New York, 1939).

Hart, Simon, *Prehistory of the New Netherland Company* (Amsterdam, 1959).

——*Geschrift en getal* (Dordrecht, 1976).

——'Rederij' in *MGN* ii. 106–25.

——'Die Amsterdamer Italienfahrt, 1590–1620', in J. Schneider (ed.), *Wirtschaftskräfte und Wirtschaftswege. Festschrift für Hermann Kellenbenz* (5 vols.; Nuremberg, 1978–81) ii. 145–70.

Hartog, Johannes, *Geschiedenis van de Nederlandse Antillen* (5 vols.; Oranjestad, 1956–64).

Hazewinckel, H. C., *Geschiedenis van Rotterdam* (3 vols.; Amsterdam, 1940–2).

Heckscher, E. F., *Mercantilism* (2 vols.; London, 1935).

——and Boëthius, B., *Svensk handelsstatistik, 1637–1737* (Stockholm, 1938).

Heikamp-Wagner, Helga, *Jan van der Heyden, 1637–1712* (Amsterdam, 1971).

Herks, J. J., *De geschiedenis van de Amersfoortse tabak* (The Hague, 1967).

Hill, Charles E., *The Danish Sound Dues and the Command of the Baltic* (Durham, North Carolina, 1926).

Hinrichs, Carl, *Die Wollindustrie in Preussen unter Friedrich Wilhelm I* (Berlin, 1933).

Hinton, R. W. K., *The Eastland Trade and the Common Weal* (Cambridge, 1959).

Hoboken, W. J. van, 'De West-Indische Compagnie en de Vrede van Munster', *TvG* 57 (1957), 359–68.

—— 'The Dutch West India Company: The Political Background of its Rise and Fall', in J. S. Bromley and E. H. Kossmann (eds.), *Britain and the Netherlands I* (London, 1960), 41–61.

Hoeven, F. P. van der, *Bijdrage tot de geschiedenis van den Sonttol* (Leiden, 1855).

Houtte, J. A. van, 'Anvers aux xvᵉ et xviᵉ siècles: Expansion et apogée', *Annales économies, sociétés, civilisations*, 16 (1961), 248–78.

—— 'Bruges et Anvers marchés "nationaux" ou "internationaux" du XIVᵉ au XVIᵉ siècle, *Revue du nord*, 36 (1952), 89–108.

—— *Economische en sociale geschiedenis van de Lage Landen* (Zeist, 1964).

Huetz de Lemps, Ch., *Géographie du commerce de Bordeaux à la fin du régime de Louis XIV* (Paris–The Hague, 1975).

Huisman, M., *La Belgique commerciale sous l'empereur Charles VI: La Compagnie d'Ostende* (Brussels, 1902).

Hullu, J. de, 'De algemeene toestand van de Compagnie's bedrijf in Indië in 1663', *De Indische Gids*, 36 (1914), 819–36.

—— 'Over den Chinaschen handel der Oost-Indische Compagnie in de eerste dertig jaar van de 18ᵉ eeuw', *BTLVNI* 73 (1917), 32–151.

—— 'Mr Johan van Dam's rapport over den staat van zaken in Oost-Indië in 1666', *De Indische Gids*, 42 (1920), 1010–24, 1093–111.

Hussey, R. D., *The Caracas Company, 1728–1784* (Harvard, 1934).

IJzerman, J. W., 'Amsterdamsche bevrachtingscontracten 1591–1602, i. De vaart op Spanje en Portugal', *EHJ* 17 (1931), 163–291.

Irwin, G. W., 'The Dutch and the Tin Trade of Malaya in the Seventeenth Century', in J. Ch'en and N. Tarling (eds.), *Studies in the Social History of China and Southeast Asia* (Cambridge, 1970).

Israel, Jonathan I., *Race, Class and Politics in Colonial Mexico, 1610–1670* (Oxford, 1975).

—— 'Spanish Wool Exports and the European Economy, 1610–1640', *Economic History Review*, 2nd ser. 33 (1980), 193–211.

—— 'The States General and the Strategic Regulation of the Dutch River Trade, 1621–1636', *BMGN* 95 (1980), 461–91.

—— *The Dutch Republic and the Hispanic World, 1606–1661* (Oxford, 1982).

—— 'The Economic Contributions of Dutch Sephardi Jewry to Holland's Golden Age, 1595–1713', *TvG* 96 (1983), 505–35.

—— 'The Diplomatic Career of Jeronimo Nunes da Costa: An Episode in Dutch–Portuguese Relations of the Seventeenth Century', *BMGN* 98 (1983), 167–90.

—— *European Jewry in the Age of Mercantilism, 1550–1750* (Oxford, 1985).

—— 'The Phases of the Dutch *straatvaart* (1590–1713); A Chapter in the Economic History of the Mediterranean', *TvG* 99 (1986), 1–30.

—— 'The Dutch Merchant Colonies in the Mediterranean during the Seventeenth Century, *Renaissance and Modern Studies*, 30 (1986), 87–108.

—— 'The Politics of International Trade Rivalry during the Thirty Years' War: Gabriel de Roy and Olivares' Mercantilist Projects, 1621–1645', *International History Review*, 8 (1986), 517–49.

Jameson, J. F., *Willem Usselinx: Founder of the Dutch and Swedish West India Companies* (New York, 1887).

Jansen, L., *De koophandel van Amsterdam* (Amsterdam, 1946).

Jeannin, Pierre, 'Anvers et la Baltique au xvie siècle', *Revue du Nord*, 37 (1955), 93–114.

—— 'Le Commerce du Lübeck aux environs de 1580', *Annales ESC*, xvi (1961), 36–65.

—— 'Les Comptes du Sund comme source pour la construction d'indices généraux de l'activité économique en Europe (xvie–xviiie siècle)', *Revue historique*, 231 (1964), 55–102, 307–40.

—— 'Die Hansestädte im Europäischen Handel des 18. Jahrhunderts', *Hansische Geschichtsblätter*, 89 (1971), 41–73.

—— 'Entreprises hanséates et commerce méditerranean à la fin du xvie siècle', *Mélanges en l'honneur de Fernand Braudel* (Toulouse, 1973).

—— 'Entre La Russie et l'Occident au début du xviiie siècle', in *Etudes Européennes: Mélanges offerts à Victor-Lucien Tapié* (Paris, 1973), 503–24.

—— 'Les Interdépendences économiques dans le champ d'action européen des Hollandais (xvie–xviiie siècle)', in M. Aymard (ed.), *Dutch Capitalism and World Capitalism*, 147–70.

—— 'The Sea-borne and the Overland Trade Routes of Northern Europe in the XVIth and XVIIth Centuries', *Journal of European Economic History*, 11 (1982), 5–59.

Johnsen, O. A., 'Les Relations commerciales entre la Norvège et l'Espagne dans les temps modernes', *Revue Historique*, 55 (1930), 77–82.

—— *Norwegische Wirtschaftsgeschichte* (Jena, 1939).

Jones, J. R., *Britain and the World, 1649–1815* (London, 1980).

Jong, C. de, 'De Walvisvaart', in *MGN* ii. 309–14.

Jonge, J. K. L. de, *De oorsprong van Nederland's bezittingen op de kust van Guinea* (The Hague, 1871).

Jörg, C. J. A., *Porcelain and the Dutch China Trade* (The Hague, 1982).

Jürgens, Adolf, *Zur schleswig-holsteinischen Handelsgeschichte des 16. und 17. Jahrhunderts* (Berlin, 1914).

Kamen, H., 'The Decline of Spain: A Historical Myth?', *Past and Present*, 8 (1978), 24–50.

—— *Spain in the Later Seventeenth Century, 1665–1700* (London, 1980).

Kaper, R., *Pamfletten over oorlog of vrede* (Amsterdam, 1980).

Kato, E., 'Unification and Adaptation, the Early Shogunate and Dutch Trade Policies', in L. Blussé and F. S. Gaastra (eds.), *Companies and Trade* (Leiden, 1981), 207–30.

Kellenbenz, Hermann, 'Spanien, die nördlichen Niederlande und der skandinavisch-baltische Raum in der Weltwirtschaft und Politik', *Vierteljahrschrift für Sozial- und Wirtschaftsgeschichte*, 41 (1954), 289–332.

—— *Unternehmerkräfte im Hamburger Portugal- und Spanienhandel, 1590–1625* (Hamburg, 1956).

—— 'Der Pfeffermarkt um 1600 und die Hansestädte', *Hansische Geschichtsblätter*, 74 (1956), 28–49.

—— *As relações econômicas entre o Brasil e a Alemanha na época colonial* (Recife, 1961).

—— 'Der russische Transithandel mit dem Orient im 17. und zu Beginn des 18. Jahrhunderts', *Jahrbücher für Geschichte Osteuropas*, 12 (1964), 481–98.

—— 'The Economic Significance of the Archangel Route (from the Late 16th to the Late 18th Century)', *Journal of European Economic History*, 2 (1973), 541–81.

—— 'Dänische Pässe für fremde Russlandfahrer', in *Społeczénstwo gospodarka kultura: Studia ofiarowane Marianowi Małowistowi* (Warsaw, 1974).

Kepler, J. S., *The Exchange of Christendom: The International Entrepôt at Dover, 1622–1641* (Leicester, 1976).

Kernkamp, G. W., *De sleutels van de Sont* (The Hague, 1890).

—— 'De Nederlanders op de Oostzee', *Vragen des tijds* (1909), ii. 65–96.

Kernkamp, J. H., *De handel op den vijand, 1572–1609* (2 vols; Utrecht, 1931–4).

—— 'Scheepvaart en handelsbetrekkingen met Italië tijdens de opkomst der Republiek', *Mededelingen van het Nederlandsch Historisch Instituut te Rome*, 2nd ser. 6 (1936), 53–85.

—— *De economische artikelen inzake Europa van het Munsterse vredesverdrag* (Amsterdam, 1951).

Klein, P. W., *De Trippen in de 17e eeuw: Een studie over het ondernemersgedrag op de Hollandse stapelmarkt* (Assen, 1965).

—— 'Dutch Capitalism and the European World-economy', in M. Aymard, (ed.), *Dutch Capitalism and World Capitalism*, 75–92.

—— 'De zeventiende eeuw (1585–1700)', in J. H. van Stuijvenberg (ed.), *De economische geschiedenis van Nederland* (Groningen, 1977), 79–118.

—— 'Nederlandse glasmakerijen in de zeventiende en achttiende eeuw', *EHJ* 44 (1982), 31–43.

—— 'De wereldhandel in edele metalen 1500–1800: Centraliteit of polycentrisme?', *TvG* 100 (1987), 185–97.

Knight, W. S. M., *The Life and Works of Hugo Grotius* (London, 1925).

Knoppers, J. V. T., *Dutch Trade with Russia from the Time of Peter I to Alexander I* (3 vols.; Montreal, 1976).

—— and Snapper, F., 'De Nederlandse scheepvaart op de Oostzee vanaf het eind van de 17e eeuw tot het begin van de 19e eeuw', *EHJ* 41 (1978), 115–53.

Köhn, G., 'Ostfriesen und Niederländer in der Neugründung Glückstadt von 1620 bis 1652', *Hansische Geschichtsblätter*, 90 (1972), 81.

Kolkert, W., *Nederland en het zweedsche imperialisme* (Deventer, 1908).

Kooy, T. P. van der, *Hollands stapelmarkt en haar verval* (Amsterdam, 1931).

—— 'Holland als centrale stapelmarkt in de zeventiende en achttiende eeuw', in P. W. Klein (ed.), *Van stapelmarkt tot welvaartsstaat* (Rotterdam, 1970), 9–20.

Kranenburg, H. A. H., *De zeevisscherij van Holland in den tijd der Republiek* (Amsterdam, 1946).

—— 'De Haringexport naar het Oostzeegebied', *TvG* 72 (1959), 251–8.

Kurtz, G. H., *Willem III en Amsterdam, 1683–85* (Utrecht, 1928).

Lane, Frederic, C., 'Venetian Shipping during the Commercial Revolution', in Brian Pullan (ed.), *Crisis and Change in the Venetian Economy* (London, 1968), 47–58.

Larraz López, José, *La época del mercantilismo en Castilla, 1500–1700* (Madrid, 1943).

Laspeyres, Étienne, *Geschichte der volkswirtschaftlichen Anschauungen der Niederländer und ihrer Litteratur zur Zeit der Republik* (Leipzig, 1863).

Lawrence, A. W., *Trade Castles and Forts of West Africa* (London, 1963).

L'Honoré-Naber, S. P., *Reizen van Jan Huighen van Linschoten naar het Noorden (1594–1595)* (The Hague, 1914).

Lind, I., *Göteborgs handel och sjöfart, 1637–1920* (Göteborg, 1923).

Lindblad, J. Th., *Sweden's Trade with the Dutch Republic, 1738–1795* (Assen, 1982).

—— 'Structuur en mededinging in de handel van de Republiek op de Oostzee in de achttiende eeuw', *EHJ* 47 (1984), 79–90.

Logan, Anne-Marie, *The 'Cabinet' of the Brothers Gerard and Jan Reynst* (Amsterdam, 1979).

Lombard, Denys, *Le Sultanat d'Atjeh au temps d'Iskander Muda, 1607–1636* (Paris, 1967).

Lootsma, J., *Bijdrage tot de geschiedenis der Nederlandsche walvischvaart* (Amsterdam, 1937).

Lubimenko, I., 'The Struggle of the Dutch with the English for the Russian Market in the Seventeenth Century', *Transactions of the Royal Historical Society*, 4th ser. 7 (1924), 27–51.

Lúcio de Azevedo, J., *Epocas de Portugal económico: Esboços de história* (Lisbon, 1929).

Ly, Abdoulaye, *La Compagnie du Sénégal* (Paris, 1958).

Maanen, R. C. J. van, 'De vermogensopbouw van de Leidse bevolking in het laatste kwart van de zestiende eeuw', *BMHG* 93 (1978), 1–42.

MacLeod, N., *De Oost-Indische Compagnie als zeemogendheid in Azië* (2 vols.; Rijswijk, 1927).

438 *Bibliography*

Malo, Henri, *Les Corsaires dunquerquois et Jean Bart* (2 vols.; Paris, 1913– 14).

Malvezin, Théophile, *Histoire du commerce de Bordeaux depuis les origines jusqu'à nos jours* (4 vols.; Bordeaux, 1892).

Masson, Paul, *Histoire du commerce français dans le Levant au XVIIᵉ siècle* (The Hague, 1943).

Mauro, F., *Le Portugal et l'Atlantique au XVIIe siècle, 1570–1670* (Paris, 1964).

Meilink-Roelofsz, M. A. P., *De vestiging der Nederlanders ter kuste Malabar* (The Hague, 1943).

Menkman, W. R., 'Van de verovering van Curaçao tot de vrede van Munster', *West Indische Gids*, 18 (1935), 65–115.

——*De Nederlanders in het Caraïbische zeegebied waarin vervat de geschiedenis der Nederlandsche antillen* (Amsterdam, 1942).

Mims, S. L., *Colbert's West India Policy* (Yale, 1912).

Montias, J. M., *Artists and Artisans in Delft* (Princeton, 1982).

Morineau, Michel, 'La Balance du commerce franco-néerlandais et le resserrement économique des Provinces-Unies au xviiie siècle', *EHJ* 30 (1965), 170–235.

——'Hommage aux historiens hollandais et contribution à l'histoire économique des Provinces-Unies', in M. Aymard (ed.), *Dutch Capitalism and World Capitalism*, 285–304.

——*Incroyables gazettes et fabuleux métaux* (Cambridge–Paris, 1985).

Nachod, Oskar, *Die Beziehungen der Niederländischen Ostindischen Kompagnie zu Japan im siebzehnten Jahrhundert* (Leipzig, 1897).

Netscher, P. M., *Geschiedenis van de koloniën Essequibo, Demerary en Berbice van de vestiging der Nederlanders aldaar tot op onzen tijd* (The Hague, 1888).

Nierop, Leonie van, 'De zijdennijverheid van Amsterdam historisch geschetst', *TvG* 45 (1930), 18–40, 151–72.

Öhberg, Arne, 'Russia and the World Market in the Seventeenth Century', *Scandinavian Economic History Review*, 3 (1955), 123–62.

Oldewelt, W. F. H., 'De scheepvaartsstatistiek van Amsterdam in de 17de en 18de eeuw', *Jaarboek van het Genootschap Amstelodamum*, 45 (1953), 114–51.

Olechnowitz, K. F., *Der Schiffbau der Hansischen Spätzeit* (Weimar, 1960).

——*Handel und Seeschiffahrt der späten Hanse* (Weimar, 1965).

Ormrod, D., 'English Re-exports and the Dutch Staplemarket in the Eighteenth Century', in D. C. Coleman and P. Mathias (eds.), *Enterprise and History: Essays in Honour of Charles Wilson* (Cambridge, 1984), 89–115.

Paci, Renzo, *La 'Scala' di Spalato e il comercio veneziano nei Balcani fra cinque e seicento* (Venice, 1971).

Pagano de Divitiis, Gigliola, 'Il Mediterraneo nel XVII secolo: L'espansione commerciale inglese e l'Italia', *Studi storici*, 1 (1986), 109–48.

Palacios Preciado, Jorge, *La trata de negros por Cartagena de Indias* (Tunja, 1973).

Pares, Richard, *War and Trade in the West Indies, 1739–1763* (Oxford, 1936).

Parker, Geoffrey, 'War and Economic Change: The Economic Costs of the Dutch Revolt', in J. M. Winter (ed.), *War and Economic Development* (Cambridge, 1975), 49–71.

Pàstine, Onerato, *Genova e l'Imperio Ottomano nel secolo XVII* (Genoa, 1952).

Pauw, C., 'De Spaanse lakenfabrieken te Guadalajara en de Leidse lakenindustrie in het begin der achttiende eeuw', *EHJ* 24 (1950), 34–79.

Pigeaud, Th. G. Th., and de Graaf, H. J., *Islamic States in Java, 1500–1700* (The Hague, 1976).

Pirenne, Henri, 'The Place of the Netherlands in the Economic History of Medieval Europe', *Economic History Review*, 2 (1920), 20–40.

Pohl, Hans, *Die Portugiesen in Antwerpen (1567–1648): Zur Geschichte einer Minderheit* (Wiesbaden, 1977).

Pollentier, F, *De admiraliteit en de oorlog ter zee onder de Aartshertogen (1596–1609)* (Brussels, 1972).

Posthumus, N. W., *De geschiedenis van de Leidsche lakenindustrie* (3 vols.; The Hague, 1908–39).

—— 'De industriële concurrentie tusschen Noord en Zuid Nederlandsche nijverheidscentra in de XVIIe en XVIIIe eeuw', in *Mélanges d'histoire offerts à Henri Pirenne* (Brussels, 1926), 369–78.

—— *Nederlandsche prijsgeschiedenis* (2 vols.; Leiden, 1943–64).

—— *Inquiry into the History of Prices in Holland* (2 vols.; Leiden, 1946–64).

Postma, Johannes, 'The Dimension of the Dutch Slave Trade from Western Africa', *Journal of African History*, 13 (1972), 237–48.

—— 'West African Exports and the Dutch West India Company, 1675–1731', *EHJ* 36 (1973), 53–74.

Prakash, Om, 'European Trade and South Asian Economies: Some Regional Contrasts 1600–1800', in L. Blussé and F. S. Gaastra (eds.), *Companies and Trade*, (Leiden, 1981), 189–205.

—— *The Dutch Factories in India, 1617–1623* (Delhi, 1984).

—— *The Dutch East India Company and the Economy of Bengal, 1630–1720* (Princeton, 1985).

Pringsheim, Otto, *Beiträge zur wirtschaftlichen Entwickelungsgeschichte der Vereinigten Niederlande im 17. und 18. Jahrhundert* (Leipzig, 1890).

Prins, J. H., 'Prince William of Orange and the Jews' (Hebrew), *Zion*, 15 (1950), 93–106.

Rapp, R. T., 'The Unmaking of Mediterranean Trade Hegemony: International Trade Rivalry and the Commercial Revolution', *Journal of Economic History*, 35 (1975), 499–525.

—— *Industry and Economic Decline in Seventeenth-century Venice* (Harvard, 1976).

Raptschinsky, B., 'Uit de geschiedenis van den Amsterdamschen handel op Rusland in de XVIIᵉ eeuw. Georg Everhard Klenck', *Jaarboek van het Genootschap Amstelodamum*, 34 (1937), 57–83.

Rau, Virginia, 'Subsídios para o estudo do movimento dos portos de Faro e Lisboa durante o século XVII', *Academia Portuguesa de História. Anais*, 2nd ser. 5 (1954).

—— 'A embaixada de Tristão de Mendonça Furtado e os arquivos notariais holandeses', *Academia Portuguesa de História. Anais*, 2nd ser. 8 (1958), 95–151.

—— *Estudos sobre a história do sal português* (Lisbon, 1984).

Raychaudhuri, T., *Jan Company in Coromandel, 1605–1690* (The Hague, 1962).

Regtdoorzee Greup-Roldanus, R. C., *Geschiedenis der Haarlemmer bleekerijen* (The Hague, 1936).

Riley, J. C., 'The Dutch Economy after 1650: Decline or Growth?', *Journal of European Economic History*, 13 (1984), 521–69.

Ringrose, David, *Madrid and the Spanish Economy, 1560–1850* (Berkeley and Los Angeles, 1983).

Roberts, Michael, *Gustavus Adolphus: A History of Sweden, 1611–1632* (2 vols.; London, 1953).

Ródenas Vilar, Rafael, 'Un gran proyecto anti-holandés en tiempo de Felipe IV: La destrucción del comercio rebelde en Europa', *Hispania*, 22 (1962), 542–58.

Rodríguez Villa, Antonio, *Ambrosio Spínola: Primer marqués de los Balbases* (Madrid, 1905).

Roessingh, H. K., 'Het Veluwse inwonertal, 1526–1947', *AAG Bijdragen*, 11 (1964), 126–150.

—— 'Tobacco Growing in Holland in the Seventeenth and Eighteenth Centuries: A Case Study of the Innovative Spirit of Dutch Peasants', *Acta Historiae Neerlandicae*, 11 (1978), 18–54.

Romano, Ruggiero, 'Tra XVI e XVII secolo: Una crisi economica: 1619–1622', *Rivista storica italiana*, 74 (1962), 480–531.

Roosbroeck, R. van, *Emigranten: Nederlandse vluchtelingen in Duitsland (1550–1600)* (Louvain, n.d.).

Rowen, H. H., *The Ambassador Prepares for War: The Dutch Embassy of Arnauld de Pomponne, 1669–1671* (The Hague, 1957).

Sabbe, E., *De Belgische vlasnijverheid; 1. De Zuidnederlandse vlasnijverheid tot het verdrag van Utrecht (1713)* (Bruges, 1943).

Samberg, J. W., *De hollandsche gereformeerde gemeente te Smirna* (Leiden, 1928).

Samuel, W. S., 'Review of the Jewish Colonists in Barbados, 1680', *Transactions of the Jewish Historical Society of England*, 13 (1936), 1–111.

Santen, H. W. van, *De Verenigde Oost-Indische Compagnie in Gujarat en Hindustan, 1620–1660* (Meppel, 1982).

Sayous, André E., 'Le Rôle d'Amsterdam dans l'histoire du capitalisme commercial et financier', *Revue historique*, 183 (1938), 242–80.

—— 'Die grössen Handler und Kapitalisten im Amsterdam gegen Ende des sechszehnten und während des siebzehnten Jahrhunderts', *Weltwirtschaftliches Archiv*, 47 (1938), 115–44.

Scelle, Georges, *La Traite négrière aux Indes de Castille: Contrats et traités d'Assiento* (2 vols.; Paris, 1906).

Schaeper, Thomas T., *The French Council of Commerce, 1700–1715: A Study of Mercantilism after Colbert* (Columbus, Ohio, 1983).

Scheltema, Jacobus, *Rusland en de Nederlanden beschouwd in derzelver wederkeerige betrekkingen* (4 vols.; Amsterdam, 1817).

Schmoller, Gustav, *The Mercantile System and its Historical Significance* (New York–London, 1896).

Schneeloch, N. H., 'Die Bewindhebber der Westindischen Compagnie in der Kammer Amsterdam, 1674–1700', *EHJ* 36 (1973), 1–74.

—— 'Das Kapitalengagement der Amsterdamer Familie Bartolotti in der Westindischen Compagnie', in J. Schneider (ed.), *Wirtschaftskräfte und Wirtschaftswege: Festschrift für Hermann Kellenbenz* (5 vols.; Nuremberg, 1978–81), ii. 171–92.

—— *Aktionäre der Westindischen Compagnie von 1674* (Stuttgart, 1982).

Schöffer, I., 'Did Holland's Golden Age Co-incide with a Period of Crisis?', *Acta Historiae Neerlandica*, 1 (1966), 82–107.

Schreiner, J., *Nederland og Norge, 1625–1650: Trelastutførsel og handelspolitik* (Oslo, 1933).

—— 'Die Niederländer und die norwegische Holzausfuhr im 17. Jahrhundert', *TvG* 49 (1934), 303–28.

Schryver, Reginald de, *Jan van Brouchoven, Graaf van Bergeyck, 1644–1725* (Brussels, 1965).

Scoville, W. C., *Capitalism and French Glassmaking, 1640–1789* (Berkeley and Los Angeles, 1950).

—— *The Persecution of Huguenots and French Economic Development 1680–1720* (Berkeley and Los Angeles, 1960).

Sée, Henri, 'L'Activité commerciale de la Hollande à la fin du XVIIᵉ siècle', *Revue d'histoire économique et sociale* (1926), 10–30.

—— 'Le Commerce des Hollandais à Nantes pendant la minorité de Louis XIV', *TvG* 41 (1926), 246–60.

Sella, Domencio, *Commerci e industrie a Venezia nel secolo XVII* (Venice, 1961).

Sideri, S., *Trade and Power: Informal Colonialism in Anglo-Portuguese Relations* (Rotterdam, 1970).

Slicher van Bath, B. H., *Een samenleving onder spanning: Geschiedenis van het platteland van Overijssel* (Assen, 1957).

—— 'The Economic Situation in the Dutch Republic during the

Seventeenth Century' in M. Aymard (ed.), *Dutch Capitalism and World Capitalism*.

Sluiter, E., 'Dutch–Spanish Rivalry in the Caribbean Area, 1594–1609', *Hispanic American Historical Review*, 28 (1948), 165–96.

Smith, George L., *Religion and Trade in New Netherland* (Ithaca, New York, 1973).

Smith, M. F. J., *Tijd-affaires in effecten aan de Amsterdamsche beurs* (The Hague, 1919).

Smith, Woodruff, 'The European–Asian Trade of the Seventeenth Century and the Modernization of Commercial Capitalism', *Itinerario*, 6 (1982), 68–90.

Snapper, F., *Oorlogsinvloeden op de overzeese handel van Holland, 1551–1719* (Amsterdam, 1959).

——— 'De generale listen van de schepen die in de perioden 1758–1761 en 1783–1786 in Holland zijn binnengelopen', *EHJ* 42 (1979), 26–44.

Sneller, Z. W., 'De stapel der Westfaalsche linnens te Rotterdam, 1669–1672', *BVGO* ser. VII, 2 (1932), 179–218.

Spooner, F. C., *Risks at Sea: Amsterdam Insurance and Maritime Europe, 1766–1780* (Cambridge, 1983).

Srbik, Heinrich Ritter von, *Der staatliche Exporthandel Österreichs von Leopold I. bis Maria Theresa* (Vienna, 1907).

Steensgaard, Niels, *The Asian Trade Revolution of the Seventeenth Century* (Chicago 1974; originally issued under the title *Carracks, Caravans Companies*, Copenhagen, 1973).

——— 'The Dutch East India Company as an Institutional Innovation', in M. Aymard (ed.), *Dutch Capitalism and World Capitalism*, 235–58.

Stols, Eddy, *De Spaanse Brabanders of de handelsbetrekkingen der Zuidelijke Nederlanden met de Iberische Wereld, 1598–1648* (Brussels, 1971).

Stoppelaer, J. H. de, *Balthasar de Moucheron: Een bladzijde uit de Nederlandsche handelsgeschiedenis tijdens den tachtigjarigen oorlog* (The Hague, 1901).

Supple, B. E., *Commercial Crisis and Change in England, 1600–1642* (Cambridge, 1964).

Swetschinski, Daniel, 'The Spanish Consul and the Jews of Amsterdam', in M. A. Fishbane and P. R. Flohr (eds.), *Texts and Responses: Studies Presented to Nahum N. Glatzer* (Leiden, 1975), 158–72.

Taylor, H., 'Trade, Neutrality and the "English Road", 1630–1648', *Economic History Review*, 2nd ser. 25 (1972), 236–60.

Tenenti, Albert, *Naufrages, corsaires et assurances maritimes à Venise, 1592–1609* (Paris, 1959).

Terpstra, H., 'Nederland's gouden tijd aan de Goud Kust', *TvG* 73 (1960).

Thijs, A. K. L., *De zijdennijverheid te Antwerpen in de zeventiende eeuw* (Brussels, 1969).

Thinne, H., 'Der Handel Kölns am Ende des 16. Jahrhunderts und die internationale Zusammensetzung der Kölner Kaufmannschaft', *Westdeutsche Zeitschrift für Geschichte und Kunst*, 31 (1912), 389–473.

Thomson, J. K. L., *Clermont-de-Lodève, 1633–1789: Fluctuations in the Prosperity of a Languedocian Cloth-making Town* (Cambridge, 1982).

Tijn, Th. van, 'Pieter de La Court: zijn leven en zijn economische denkbeelden', *TvG* 69 (1956), 304–70.

Tongas, Gérard, *Les Relations de la France avec l'empire Ottoman durant la première moitié du XVIIᵉ siècle* (Toulouse, 1942).

Tracy, J. D., *A Financial Revolution in the Habsburg Netherlands* (Berkeley and Los Angeles, 1985).

Tveite, Stein, *Engelsk-Norsk trelasthandel 1640–1710* (Bergen–Oslo, 1961).

Unger, R. W., *Dutch Shipbuilding before 1800* (Assen, 1978).

—— 'Scheepvaart in de Noordelijke Nederlanden', in the (New) *Algemene geschiedenis der Nederlanden*, vi. 109–22.

—— 'Dutch Herring Technology and International Trade in the Seventeenth Century', *Journal of Economic History*, 40 (1980), 253–79.

Unger, W. S., 'Nieuwe gegevens betreffende het begin der vaart op Guinea', *EHJ* 21 (1940), 194–217.

—— *De oudste reizen van de Zeeuwen naar Oost-Indië* (The Hague, 1948).

—— 'Bijdragen tot de geschiedenis van de Nederlandse slavenhandel', *EHJ* 26 (1956), 133–74.

—— 'De publikatie der Sonttabellen voltooid', *TvG* 71 (1958), 147–205.

Uytven, R. van, 'La Draperie brabançonne et malinoise du XIIᵉ au XVIIᵉ siècle: Grandeur éphemère et décadence', *ISEPA* 2. 85–97.

Vandenbroeke, Chr., 'Mutations économiques et sociales en Flandre au cours de la phase proto-industrielle, 1650–1850', *Revue du Nord*, 63 (1981), 73–94.

Veenendaal, A. J., *Het Engels-Nederlands condominium in de Zuidelijke Nederlanden tijdens de Spaanse Successie-oorlog, 1706–1716* (Utrecht, 1945).

Veluwenkamp, J. W., *Ondernemersgedrag op de Hollandse stapelmarkt in de tijd van de Republiek: De Amsterdamse handelsfirma Jan Isaac de Neufville & Comp., 1730–1764* (Meppel, 1981).

Verhees-van Meer, J. Th. H., *De zeeuwse kaapvaart tijdens de Spaanse Successieoorlog, 1702–1713* (Middelburg, 1986).

Verkade, M. A., *De opkomst van de Zaanstreek* (Utrecht, 1952).

Verlinden, Ch., 'Amsterdam', in A. Fanfani (ed.), *Città mercanti dottrine nell'economia europea dal IV al XVIII secolo* (Milan, 1964).

Voet, L., *Antwerp: The Golden Age* (Antwerp, 1973).

Voeten, P., 'Antwerpens handel over Duinkerken tijdens het Twaalfjarig Bestand', *Bijdragen tot de geschiedenis inzonderheid van het oud hertogdom Brabant*, 39 (1956), 67–78.

—— 'Antwerpse reacties op het Twaalfjarig Bestand', *Bijdragen tot de geschiedenis ... Brabant*, 41 (1958), 202–39.

Vogel, W., 'Beiträge zum Statistik der deutschen Seeschiffahrt im 17. und 18. Jahrhundert', *Hansische Geschichtsblätter*, 53 (1928), 110–52.

Voorthuijsen, W. D., *De Republiek der Verenigde Nederlanden en het mercantilisme* (The Hague, 1965).

Vries, Jan de, *The Dutch Rural Economy in the Golden Age, 1500–1700* (Yale, 1974).

—— *The Economy of Europe in an Age of Crisis, 1600–1750* (Cambridge, 1976).

—— 'An Inquiry into the Behaviour of Wages in the Dutch Republic and the Southern Netherlands', *Acta historiae neerlandicae*, 10 (1978), 79–97.

—— 'The Strengths and Limitations of Dutch Capitalism', ISEPA 10 (1983), 153–74.

—— *European Urbanization, 1500–1800* (London, 1984).

—— 'The Decline and Rise of the Dutch Economy, 1675–1900', in G. Saxonhouse and G. Wright (eds.), *Technique, Spirit and Form in Making of Modern Economies: Essays in Honor of William N. Parket* (Greenwich, 1984).

Vries, Johan de, *De economische achteruitgang der Republiek in de achttiende eeuw* (Leiden, 1968).

Wallerstein, Immanuel, *The Modern World System* (3 vols.; New York, 1974–80).

—— 'Dutch Hegemony in the Seventeenth-century World-economy', in M. Aymard (ed.), *Dutch Capitalism and World Capitalism*, 93–145.

Wätjen, Hermann, *Die Niederländer im Mittelmeergebiet zur Zeit ihrer höchsten Machstellung* (Berlin, 1909).

—— 'Zur Statistik der holländischen Heringfischerei im 17. und 18. Jahrhundert', *Hansische Geschichtsblätter* 16 (1910), 129–85.

—— *Das holländische Kolonialreich in Brasilien* (Gotha, 1921).

Wee, H. van der, *The Growth of the Antwerp Market and the European Economy (Fourteenth–Sixteenth Century)* (3 vols.; The Hague, 1963).

—— 'De handelsbetrekkingen tusschen Antwerpen en de Noordelijke Nederlanden tijdens de 14e–15e en 16e eeuw', *Bijdragen voor de geschiedenis der Nederlanden*, 20 (1965–6), 267–85.

—— 'Antwoord op een industriële uitdaging: De Nederlandse steden tijdens de late middeleeuwen en nieuwe tijd', *TvG* 100 (1987), 169–84.

—— and Peeters, Th., 'Un modèle économique de croissance interséculaire du commerce mondial (xiie–xviiie siècles)', *Annales ESC* 25 (1970), 100–26.

Westergaard, Waldemar, *The Danish West Indies under Company Rule (1671–1754)* (New York, 1917).

Westermann, J. C., 'Statistishe gegevens over den handel van Amsterdam in de zeventiende eeuw', *TvG* 61 (1948), 3–30.

Wiese, Ernst, *Die Politik der Niederländer wahrend des Kalmar Kriegs (1611–1613)* (Heidelberg, 1903).

Wijsenbeek-Olthuis, Th. F., 'Ondernemen in moeilijke tijden: Delftse bierbrouwers en plateelbakkers in de achttiende eeuw', *EHJ* 44 (1981) 65–78.

—— *Achter de gevels van Delft: Bezit en bestaan van rijk en arm in een periode van achteruitgang* (Hilversum, 1987).

Willan, T. S., 'Trade between England and Russia in the second half of the Sixteenth Century', *Economic History Review*, 63 (1948), 307–21.

—— *The Early History of the Russia Company, 1553–1603* (Manchester, 1956).

Williamson, J. A., *English Colonies in Guiana and on the Amazon, 1604–1668* (Oxford, 1923).

Wills, J. E., *Pepper, Guns and Parleys: The Dutch East India Company and China, 1622–1681* (Cambridge, Mass., 1974).

—— *Embassies and Illusions: Dutch and Portuguese Envoys to K'ang-hsi, 1666–1687* (Harvard, 1984).

Wilson, Charles, 'The Economic Decline of the Netherlands', *Economic History Review*, 9 (1939) 111–27.

—— *Anglo-Dutch Commerce and Finance in the Eighteenth Century* (Cambridge, 1941).

—— 'Cloth Production and International Competition in the Seventeenth Century', *Economic History Review*, 2nd ser. 13 (1960), 209–21.

—— *Profit and Power: A Study of England and the Dutch Wars* (2nd printing, The Hague–London, 1978).

Winter, P. J. van, 'De Acte van Navigatie en de Vrede van Breda', *Bijdragen voor de geschiedenis der Nederlanden*, 4 (1949), 27–65.

—— *De Westindische Compagnie ter kamer Stad en Lande* (The Hague, 1978).

Wiznitzer, A., *Jews in Colonial Brazil* (New York, 1960).

Wolbers, J., *Geschiedenis van Suriname* (Amsterdam, 1861).

Woude, A. M. van der, *Het Noorderkwartier* (3 vols.; Wageningen, 1972).

—— 'De "Nieuwe Geschiedenis" in een nieuwe gedaante', in the (New) *Algemene geschiedenis der Nederlanden*, v. 9–35.

Wright, I. A., 'The Coymans Asiento (1685–1689)', *BVGO* 6th ser. 1 (1924), 23–62.

—— *Nederlandsche Zeevaarders op de eilanden in de Caraïbische zee en aan de kust van Colombia en Venezuela (1621–1648)* (2 vols.; Utrecht, 1934–5).

Wurm, Ch. F., *Über den Lebensschicksale des Foppius van Aitzema, ersten niederländischen Residenten bei den Hansestädten* (Hamburg, 1854).

Yogev, G., *Diamonds and Coral: Anglo-Dutch Jews and Eighteenth-century Trade* (Leicester, 1978).

Zahedieh, N., 'Trade, Plunder and Economic Development in early English Jamaica, 1655–1689', *Economic History Review*, 2nd ser. 32 (1986), 205–22.

Zanden, J. L. van, 'De economie van Holland in de periode 1650–1805; Groei of achteruitgang?' *BMGN* 102 (1987), 562–609.

Zeeuw, J. W. de, 'Peat and the Dutch Golden Age: The Historical Meaning of Energy-attainability', *AAG Bijdragen* 21 (1978), 3–31.

Zimmermann, E., 'Der schlesische Garn- und Leinenhandel mit Holland im 16. und 17. Jahrhundert', *EHJ* 26 (1956), 193–254; 27 (1957), 154–74.

Index

Moor, Jan de, Flushing burgomaster and
merchant trading with Amazonia
and the Caribbean 64, 157–8, 161
Moscow, Dutch trade at 43, 46, 152, 154,
408
Moucheron, Balthasar de (b. Antwerp
1552; d. Middelburg c. 1610),
Antwerp emigré merchant at
Middelburg 47–8, 60, 62, 64, 67
Mouré, Fort Nassau (West Africa) 163,
273, 328
Mun, Thomas, author of *England's
Treasure by Forraign Trade* 12–13
Münster, treaty of (1648), 197–8, 263,
359–60, 372
Munter, Jan (b. Harlingen 1570;
d. Amsterdam 1617), Anabaptist
merchant at Amsterdam trading
with Italy and the Levant 52, 60

Nagasaki 172
Nantes 224, 287
Napoleon's 'Continental Blockade' 404
Narva 43–4, 49–50
naval expeditions, Dutch
to Danzig 219, 411
to Denmark 148–9, 219–21, 411
to England (1667 and 1688) 279, 342,
411
against Portugal (1657) 218–19
against Sweden (1676) 300
to West Africa (1664) 273
Navarre 131–2, 319, 367
Navigation Act (1651) 208, 226, 279, 284
Negapatnam (Coromandel) 248, 331–3
New Amsterdam (New York) 109–10,
160, 273, 396
New Christians, Portuguese 42, 62, 131–2
New Granada 165, 325
New Netherland 109–10, 160, 273, 396
New Netherland Company (1614–18)
109–10
Nijmegen 17, 40
Nine Years' War (1689–97), effects of on
international trade 310–12, 314,
317–19, 331, 342, 344, 351, 359
North Africa 150, 227, 229, 258
North America 298, 380, 392–4, 397,
402–3; *see also* New Netherland
North Brabant 198–9, 263, 350–1, 355,
387–8
Northern Company (1614–42), 109, 112,
161; *see also* whale fishery

Norway
Dutch trade with 136, 146, 198, 222–
3, 275, 294, 305, 407, 414
shipping of 57–8, 129, 301–2, 365–6
Nova Zemblaya 47, 111–12
Nunes da Costa, Jeronimo, agent of the
crown of Portugal at Amsterdam
(1645–97), 235, 242
Nuremberg 5–6
nutmeg 73, 104

Oldenbarnevelt, Johan van, Advocate of
Holland (1586–1618) 38, 68–72,
82–5, 93, 101–2, 108, 119–20
Olivares, Don Gaspar de Guzmán,
Conde-Duque de, chief minister of
Spain (1621–43) 132, 313
olive oil 202, 226–7, 286
opium 250–1, 256
Os, Dirk van (b. Antwerp c.1557; d.
Amsterdam 1615), Antwerp emigré
merchant at Amsterdam and VOC
director 45–6, 54, 67, 71
Ostend 85, 113, 134
Ottoman Empire *see* Levant trade
Overijssel 263, 293, 305, 319, 348, 350–
1, 355, 387–8, 390

Palembang (Sumatra) 253, 334–5
Palestine 97, 151–2, 313
Pamplona 131, 319
paper
in the Russia trade 44, 349
in the Spanish America trade 369–70
in Swedish trade 349, 386
paper industry
Dutch 268, 319, 347, 356, 389, 397,
401
French 268, 285–6, 290, 341
Paraíba 63; *see also* Brazil, Dutch
Paris 341, 345, 356, 369
Pauw, Adriaan, 158
Pauw, Renier (1564–1636), Amsterdam
burgomaster and merchant trading
with Brazil, the Caribbean, and the
East Indies 67, 71, 82–3, 158
Penso de la Vega, Joseph Felix, (late-
seventeenth-century Sephardi
writer on the Amsterdam stock
exchange 75, 421
pepper
in European markets 44, 50, 97, 100,
174, 227, 364